Lecture Notes in Computer Science

Lecture Notes in Bioinformatics

7

The series Lecture Notes in Bioinformatics (LNBI) was established in 2003 as a topical subseries of LNCS devoted to bioinformatics and computational biology.

The series publishes state-of-the-art research results at a high level. As with the LNCS mother series, the mission of the series is to serve the international R & D community by providing an invaluable service, mainly focused on the publication of conference and workshop proceedings and postproceedings.

Jing Tang · Xin Lai · Zhipeng Cai · Wei Peng ·
Yanjie Wei

Editors

Bioinformatics Research and Applications

21st International Symposium, ISBRA 2025
Helsinki, Finland, August 3–5, 2025
Proceedings, Part II

 Springer

Editors
Jing Tang
University of Helsinki
Helsinki, Finland

Zhipeng Cai
Georgia State University
Atlanta, GA, USA

Yanjie Wei
Shenzhen Institutes of Advanced Technology
Shenzhen, China

Xin Lai
Tampere University
Tampere, Finland

Wei Peng
Kunming University of Science
and Technology
Kunming, China

ISSN 0302-9743　　　　　　　ISSN 1611-3349　(electronic)
Lecture Notes in Bioinformatics
ISBN 978-981-95-0694-1　　　ISBN 978-981-95-0695-8　(eBook)
https://doi.org/10.1007/978-981-95-0695-8

LNCS Sublibrary: SL8 – Bioinformatics

Preface

On behalf of the Program Committee, it is our great pleasure to welcome you to the 21st International Symposium on Bioinformatics Research and Applications (ISBRA 2025), held in the beautiful city of Helsinki, Finland, August 3–5, 2025. This year's symposium brought together leading researchers, scientists, and industry professionals from around the world to share cutting-edge advancements, foster collaboration, and explore the future of bioinformatics and computational biology.

We received 167 submissions presenting original research articles across all areas of bioinformatics and computational biology. Each submission was single-blindly reviewed by at least three independent reviewers. The Program Committee selected 66 papers for full publication in the symposium proceedings.

The scientific program further featured four keynote talks delivered by distinguished speakers, namely:

- Walter Kolch from University College Dublin,
- Ritambhara Singh from Brown University,
- Kwang-Hyun Cho from the Korea Advanced Institute of Science and Technology,
- Serghei Mangul from the University of Southern California.

We would like to express our sincere gratitude to all the Program Committee members and reviewers for their contributions. We also extend out special thanks to the steering committee and general chairs for their leadership and guidance throughout the organization of ISBRA 2025. Our appreciation also goes to the Academy of Finland and the University of Helsinki for their financial support, as well as to the publicity and publication chairs for their dedication. We hope you enjoyed an exciting and inspiring symposium.

June 2025

Jing Tang
Xin Lai
Zhipeng Cai
Wei Peng
Yanjie Wei

Organization

Steering Committee

Dan Gusfield	University of California, Davis, USA
Ion Mandoiu	University of Connecticut, USA
Yi Pan (Chair)	Shenzhen Institutes of Advanced Technology, China
Marie-France Sagot	Inria, France
Zhirong Sun	Tsinghua University, China
Ying Xu	University of Georgia, USA
Aidong Zhang	University of Virginia, USA
Zhipeng Cai	Georgia State University, USA

General Chairs

Sampsa Hautaniemi	University of Helsinki, Finland
Matti Nykter	Tampere University, Finland
Alexander Zelikovsky	Georgia State University, USA
Jianxin Wang	Central South University, China

Program Chairs

Jing Tang	University of Helsinki, Finland
Xin Lai	Tampere University, Finland
Zhipeng Cai	Georgia State University, USA
Wei Peng	Kunming University of Science and Technology, China
Yanjie Wei	Shenzhen Institutes of Advanced Technology, China

Publicity Chairs

Julio Vera	University of Erlangen-Nuremberg, Germany
Pavel Skums	University of Connecticut, USA
Yulian Ding	Shenzhen University of Advanced Technology, China

Publication Chairs

Xiaoqing Peng   Central South University, China
Xiujuan Lei   Shaanxi Normal University, China

Program Committee

Hisham Al-Mubaid	University of Houston - Clear Lake, USA
Ying An	Central South University, China
Mukul Bansal	University of Connecticut, USA
Mahua Bhattacharya	IIIT Gwalior, India
Xia-an Bi	Hunan Normal University, China
Dan Brown	University of Waterloo, Canada
Yunpeng Cai	Shenzhen Institutes of Advanced Technology, China
Bolin Chen	Northwestern Polytechnical University, China
Xiang Chen	Hunan University of Science and Technology, China
Hebing Chen	Institute of Health Service and Transfusion Medicine, China
Jianhong Cheng	Institute of Guizhou Aerospace Measuring and Testing Technology, China
Young-Rae Cho	Yonsei University, South Korea
Xuefeng Cui	Shandong University, China
Xiaojun Ding	Yulin Normal University, China
Lei Du	Northwestern Polytechnical University, China
Oliver Eulenstein	Iowa State University, USA
Lívia Gama	Universidade de São Paulo, Brazil
Jin Gu	Tsinghua University, China
Fei Guo	Central South University, China
Guosheng Han	Xiangtan University, China
Zengyou He	Dalian University of Technology, China
Steffen Heber	North Carolina State University, USA
Kai Hu	Xiangtan University, China
Bruno Iha	Universidade de São Paulo, Brazil
Rita Casadio	University of Bologna, Italy
Jicai Jiang	North Carolina State University, USA
Wooyoung Kim	University of Washington Bothell, USA
Xiangyong Kong	University of Shanghai for Science and Technology, China
Danny Krizanc	Wesleyan University, USA

Hulin Kuang	Central South University, China
Pavel Kuksa	University of Pennsylvania, USA
Kiril Kuzmin	Georgia State University, USA
Manuel Lafond	Université de Sherbrooke, Canada
Wei Lan	Guangxi University, China
Zhang Le	Sichuan University, China
Xiujuan Lei	Shaanxi Normal University, China
Hong-Dong Li	Central South University, China
Min Li	Central South University, China
Xiaobo Li	Lishui University, China
Xingyi Li	Northwestern Polytechnical University, China
Yaohang Li	Old Dominion University, USA
Xingyu Liao	Northwestern Polytechnical University, China
Zhendong Liu	University of Shanghai for Science and Technology, China
Zhi-Ping Liu	Shandong University, China
Xiaowen Liu	Tulane University, USA
Weiguo Liu	Shandong University, China
Liangliang Liu	Henan Agricultural University, China
Juan Liu	Wuhan University, China
Jin Liu	Central South University, China
Chengqian Lu	Xiangtan University, China
Huimin Luo	Henan University, China
Junwei Luo	Henan Polytechnic University, China
Ion Mandoiu	University of Connecticut, USA
Xiangmao Meng	Xiangtan University, China
Wenwen Min	Yunnan University, China
Wancen Mu	University of North Carolina at Chapel Hill, USA
Rafael Nascimento	Universidade de São Paulo, Brazil
Beifang Niu	Computer Network Information Center, CAS, China
Le Ou-Yang	Shenzhen University, China
Murray Patterson	Georgia State University, USA
Wei Peng	Kunming University of Science and Technology, China
Xiaoqing Peng	Central South University, China
Wu Qiu	Huazhong University of Science and Technology, China
Bikram Sahoo	Georgia State University, USA
Joao Setubal	Universidade de São Paulo, Brazil
Junliang Shang	Qufu Normal University, China
Jian-yu Shi	Northwestern Polytechnical University, China

Xinghua Shi	Temple University, USA
Gianluca Silva	Universidade de São Paulo, Brazil
Arthur Solano	Universidade de São Paulo, Brazil
Mingzhou Song	New Mexico State University, USA
Jiarui Sun	Southeast University, China
Shiwei Sun	Institute of Computing & Technology, CAS, China
Huiyan Sun	Jilin University, China
Weitian Tong	Georgia Southern University, USA
Tomas Vinar	Comenius University in Bratislava, Slovakia
Han Wang	Northeast Normal University, China
Hong-Qiang Wang	University of Science and Technology of China, China
Jianxin Wang	Central South University, China
Jiayin Wang	Xi'an Jiaotong University, China
Juan Wang	Inner Mongolia University, China
Kaili Wang	Donghua University, China
Shunfang Wang	Yunnan University, China
Xinyue Wang	Rutgers University, USA
Ying Wang	Xiamen University, China
Yanjie Wei	Shenzhen Institute of Advanced Technology, China
Ka-Chun Wong	City University of Hong Kong, China
Fang-Xiang Wu	University of Saskatchewan, Canada
Jingli Wu	Guangxi Normal University, China
Hongyan Wu	Shenzhen Institutes of Advanced Technology, China
Ju Xiang	Changsha University of Science and Technology, China
Yuying Xie	Michigan State University, USA
Juanying Xie	Shaanxi Normal University, China
Minzhu Xie	Hunan Normal University, China
Guangzhi Xiong	University of Virginia, USA
Cheng Yan	Hunan University of Chinese Medicine, China
Yang Yang	Shanghai Jiao Tong University, China
Yuedong Yang	Sun Yat-sen University, China
Yusen Ye	Xidian University, China
Liang Yu	Xidian University, China
Min Zeng	Central South University, China
Feng Zeng	Xiamen University, China
Wen Zhang	Huazhong Agricultural University, China
Houwang Zhang	City University of Hong Kong, China

Han Zhang	Nankai University, China
Cheng Zhang	Peking University, China
Fa Zhang	Beijing Institute of Technology, China
Eric Lu Zhang	Hong Kong Baptist University, China
Yiming Zhang	University of Connecticut, USA
Fuhao Zhang	Northwest A&F University, China
Yongqing Zhang	Chengdu University of Information Technology, China
Ruiqing Zheng	Central South University, China
Jiancheng Zhong	Hunan Normal University, China

Contents – Part II

Contents – Part I

Prediction of High-Altitude Pulmonary Edema Based on Resampling and Ensemble Learning

Saisai Ma[1], Xuehua Bi[2], Linlin Zhang[3,4], Haifeng Xu[5(✉)], and Kai Zhao[1(✉)]

[1] School of Computer Science and Technology (School of Cyberspace Security), Xinjiang University, Urumqi 830046, China
zhawkk@xju.edu.cn
[2] College of Medical Engineering and Technology, Xinjiang Medical University, Urumqi 830017, China
[3] School of Software, Xinjiang University, Urumqi 830046, China
[4] Center of Network and Information Technology, Xinjiang University, Urumqi 830046, China
[5] Information Department, General Hospital of Xinjiang Military Command, Urumqi 830000, China
xuhf1321@foxmail.com

Abstract. Objective: Since High Altitude Pulmonary Edema (HAPE) has a rapid onset and fast progression-posing serious health risks-and research on HAPE prediction remains limited, this study employs an ensemble learning and resampling approach to develop a HAPE risk prediction model, aiming to enhance predictive efficiency.

Methods: The HAPE dataset was constructed based on 674 subjects, covering demographic data, vital signs and biochemical indicators. Under-sampling, Synthetic Minority Over-sampling Technique (SMOTE), Adaptive Synthetic Sampling (ADASYN), and a combination of SMOTE and Edited Nearest Neighbors (SMOTE+ENN), were applied to address data imbalance. Stacking generalization was employed to develop an ensemble prediction model (MLP+GB+RF-Logistic), using Multilayer Perceptron (MLP), Gradient Boosting (GB), and Random Forest (RF) as base learners, with Logistic Regression serving as the meta-learner, for predicting the risk of HAPE.

Results: 46 clinical features associated with HAPE, such as neutrophils, leukocytes, and monocyte percentage, were identified. Among the resampling methods, SMOTE+ENN showed the most improvement. For the ensemble models, the MLP+GB+RF-Logistic model achieved the highest AUC and Recall, with an AUC value of 0.926 ± 0.015. Furthermore, model interpretability was analyzed using the SHapley Additive exPlanations (SHAP) algorithm, identifying the top influential clinical features contributing to the prediction.

Conclusions: This study developed an efficient ensemble learning model for HAPE risk prediction and identified key clinical features that markedly influence model performance. These findings provide a robust and interpretable basis for improving clinical decision-making related to HAPE.

J. Tang et al. (Eds.): ISBRA 2025, LNBI 15757, pp. 1–13, 2026.
https://doi.org/10.1007/978-981-95-0695-8_1

Keywords: High Altitude Pulmonary Edema · Ensemble Learning · Data Imbalance · SHAP Algorithm

1   Introduction

High Altitude Pulmonary Edema (HAPE) is an acute pulmonary condition induced by exposure to high altitudes, primarily characterized by the accumulation of fluid in the lungs and subsequent dyspnea. It is commonly observed among travellers and residents of areas exceeding 2,500 m in elevation [1]. If not addressed promptly, HAPE can result in severe complications and, potentially, fatality. The development of HAPE involves multiple complex factors, such as physiological conditions, genetic predispositions, and the duration and rate of altitude exposure. Therefore, early prediction and timely intervention have become pivotal areas of focus in medical research [2].

According to guidelines from the Wilderness Medical Society (WMS) [3] and the American College of Sports Medicine (ACSM), traditional prediction of HAPE risk in clinical practice relies on a variety of indicators. These indicators include clinical symptoms such as cough, dyspnea, chest tightness, and hemoptysis; personal medical history of altitude illness; physiological responses like oxygen saturation (SpO2), heart rate, and respiratory rate; and the individual's adaptation to high altitudes which encompasses tolerance to hypoxia and the ability to adapt rapid ascent. Recent studies highlight that the rapid Sepsis-Related Organ Failure Assessment (qSOFA) score [4] and the National Early Warning Score (NEWS) [5] can serve as supportive tools in clinical settings. Furthermore, a novel model [6] that integrates clinical symptoms with qSOFA and NEWS scores has been developed to assist physicians in assessing disease severity and predicting adverse outcomes. However, these traditional methods have limitations in the early identification of patients at high risk of HAPE. First, they depend significantly on the subjective judgment of physicians, who base decisions on reported symptoms and patient history, potentially overlooking individuals at high risk. Second, the early symptoms of HAPE often mimic those of Acute Mountain Sickness (AMS), which can lead to delayed or inaccurate diagnoses [7]. Furthermore, the scarcity of medical resources and equipment at high altitudes can compromise the effectiveness of traditional diagnostic tools, rendering HAPE scoring systems less reliable under such conditions. Consequently, developing more accurate and feasible methods for early HAPE prediction has emerged as a critical area of current research.

In recent years, Electronic Medical Records (EMR) have introduced new opportunities for the early prediction and risk assessment of HAPE. These records offer a rich repository of both structured and unstructured medical information, which can be leveraged to identify key disease characteristics [8]. For instance, by analyzing variables such as the patient's age, gender, and laboratory test results, valuable features can be extracted to predict the risk of HAPE. Recently, the rapid advancements in big data technologies and machine learning algorithms have led to the widespread adoption of machine learning-based disease prediction models in the medical field [9]. These models can autonomously identify patterns and associations within vast amounts of clinical data, thereby offering substantial support for the early diagnosis and personalized treatment of diseases. However, in the clinical prediction of HAPE, the imbalance in the proportion of positive cases (patients with HAPE) to negative cases (patients without HAPE) presents a significant challenge to traditional machine learning models. When dealing with unbalanced data, traditional machine learning algorithms tend to favor the prediction of samples representing the majority class, leading to lower prediction accuracies for patients at high risk of HAPE [10]. Consequently, addressing the challenge of imbalanced data has become a critical issue in research on HAPE risk prediction.

To address the issue, this study proposes a multi-model framework that integrates various machine learning algorithms to predict the risk of HAPE. The main contributions are as follows:

1. This study presents a newly derived HAPE dataset from EMR analysis, enhancing data diversity and representativeness for improved model training.
2. This study employs MLP, GB, and RF as base learners, with Logistic Regression serving as the meta-learner, integrating them into an ensemble model to capture latent features in HAPE data.
3. To enhance the interpretability of machine learning models in HAPE diagnosis, this study utilizes SHapley Additive exPlanations (SHAP) to visualize feature importance and identify key biomarkers associated with HAPE risk.
4. The proposed model achieves state-of-the-art results, with an ACC of 0.913 ± 0.032 and an AUC of 0.926 ± 0.015.

2   Materials and Methods

2.1   Datasets

This study collected data from 732 subjects at partner hospitals between March 2022 and June 2024, including 118 confirmed cases of HAPE. The dataset includes demographics, coagulation and biochemical tests, routine and pentameric blood tests, and COVID-19 nucleic acid tests. All data were anonymized. **Inclusion criteria:** (1) age $\geq$ 18 years; (2) complete medical record data. **Exclusion criteria:** (1) non-survivor samples; (2) samples with abnormal or missing values.

The EMR dataset comprised 118 variables, covering demographics, clinical measurements, and laboratory test results: **Demographics:** Sex (SEX), Age (AGE). **Liver function:** Indirect bilirubin (IBIL), total bilirubin (TBIL), albumin/globulin ratio (A/G), albumin (ALB), total protein (TP). **Renal function:** Uric acid (UA), creatinine (Cr), blood urea nitrogen (UN). **Routine tests:** Hemoglobin (HGB), mean platelet volume (MPV), basophil count (Bas), monocyte percentage (MON), lymphocyte count (Lymph), red blood cell count (RBC), plateletcrit (PCT), eosinophil percentage (EOS), platelet distribution width (PDW), platelet count (PLT). Variables with more than 30% missing values were excluded for missing data handling. For discrete data, missing values were imputed with zero. For continuous data, mean imputation was used for normally or nearly normally distributed data to maintain distribution characteristics and minimize bias [11]. For skewed data or variables with significant outliers, median imputation was employed to better reflect central tendency and reduce distortion in the overall distribution [12]. The data processing flow is shown in Fig. 1. To ensure accuracy and consistency of the study results, the raw data underwent strict screening and cleaning. Following strict adherence to inclusion and exclusion criteria, 674 eligible subjects were ultimately included in the study. The patients were divided into two groups: a control group comprising 560 patients (approximately 83.0%) and an experimental group with 114 patients (approximately 17.0%) diagnosed with HAPE. Due to the relatively small number of patients in the HAPE group, the dataset exhibited significant imbalance, necessitating further processing. Figure 2 illustrates the flow chart of this data processing.

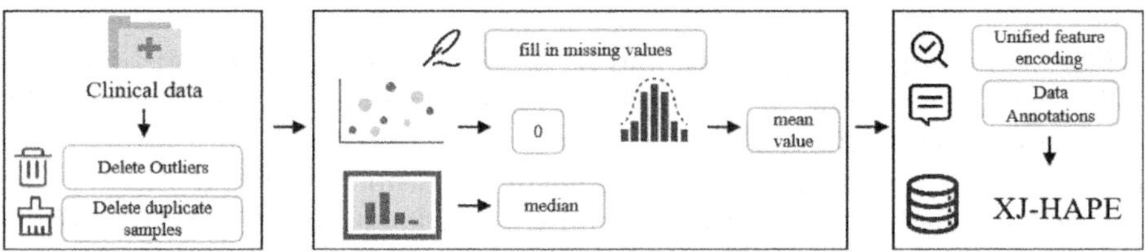

Fig. 1. Flow of clinical data preprocessing

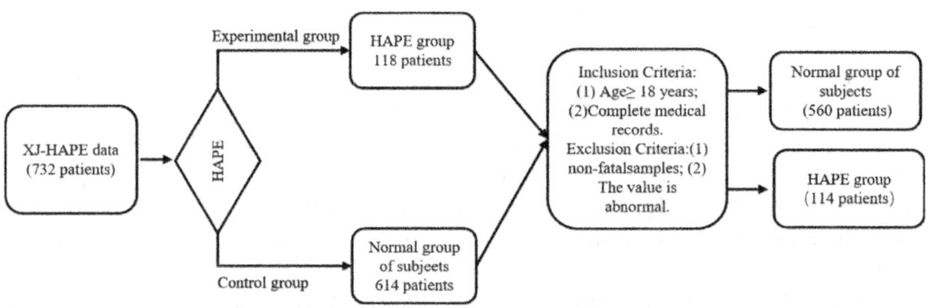

Fig. 2. Subject screening and grouping flow

To further assess the quality of the dataset, the Student's t-test was applied to normally distributed features, while the Mann-Whitney U test was used for non-normally distributed features. The chi-square test was employed to assess differences in categorical variables. All tests were two-sided, with a significance threshold of $p < 0.05$, and were conducted using Python 3.10.6.

Statistical analysis revealed significant differences ($p < 0.001$) between groups for AGE, IBIL, TBIL, A/G, ALB, alkaline phosphatase (ALP), aspartate aminotransferase (AST), TP, and direct bilirubin (DBIL), suggesting their potential relevance to HAPE risk. Similarly, hematological indices such as platelet large cell ratio (PLCR), hematocrit (HCT), HGB, RBC, Mon, and Bas showed significant differences ($p < 0.001$). These findings highlight key features linked to HAPE pathogenesis, forming the basis for subsequent machine learning modeling. Detailed results of the statistical analyses are presented in Table 1.

Table 1. Statistical analysis of characteristics

Feature	Label = 0 (n = 560)	Label = 1 (n = 114)	p-value
AGE	30.000 [25.000,35.000]	25.000 [23.000,28.750]	<0.001
IBIL	13.240 [10.037,15.260]	11.360 [7.863,13.240]	<0.001
TBIL	20.660 [16.155,23.512]	17.725 [11.922,20.660]	<0.001
AG	1.700 [1.610,1.800]	1.635 [1.520,1.715]	<0.001
Alb	45.930 [45.500,47.725]	43.400 [40.200,45.930]	<0.001
ALP	75.890 [66.000,83.000]	72.500 [59.000,75.890]	<0.001
AST	21.190 [17.575,22.500]	19.050 [15.225,21.190]	<0.001
TP	73.350 [72.100,76.225]	70.850 [66.000,73.350]	<0.001
DBIL	7.420 [5.758,8.600]	6.135 [4.287,7.420]	<0.001
PLCR	60.000 [50.000,69.000]	62.000 [58.000,76.750]	<0.001
HCT	53.150 [50.193,57.000]	49.000 [44.365,52.970]	<0.001
HGB	188.000 [178.000,199.000]	170.000 [159.000,186.090]	<0.001
RBC	5.730 [5.380,6.183]	5.285 [4.912,5.710]	<0.001
Mon	0.380 [0.300,0.470]	0.410 [0.400,0.558]	<0.001
Bas	0.300 [0.100,0.400]	0.330 [0.300,0.475]	<0.001

2.2   The Overall Flow of the Model

This study aims to develop an ensemble learning-based model for HAPE risk assessment. The framework, illustrated in Fig. 3, consists of four key modules: (1) Dataset Construction: A HAPE dataset was developed, including demographics, vital signs, and biochemical indicators. HAPE inpatients were labeled as positive samples, while health checkup individuals during the same period served as negative samples. (2) Data Preprocessing: This step involves outlier removal, missing value imputation, variable encoding and standardization, and duplicate sample elimination to ensure data integrity. (3) Feature Optimization: To address data imbalance, multiple sampling techniques (Under-sampling, SMOTE, ADASYN, SMOTE+ENN) were applied. Grid search was used for hyperparameter optimization to enhance model performance. (4) Classifier Construction and Evaluation: Stacking generalization was employed to develop an ensemble model

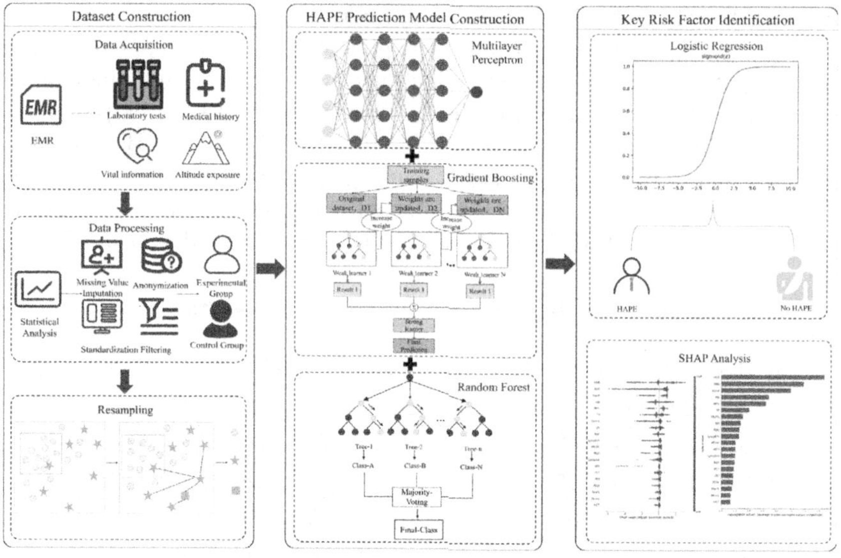

Fig. 3. Overall flow of the framework

based on MLP, GB, and RF-based learners (MLP+GB+RF-Logistic). The optimal model was selected based on a comprehensive evaluation of each classifier's performance in predicting HAPE risk.

2.3 Sampling Method Analysis

This study evaluates four sampling techniques: Under-sampling, SMOTE, ADASYN, and SMOTE+ENN to address data imbalance and improve model performance.

Under-sampling [13] reduces the size of the majority class, lowering computational complexity and storage costs. However, it may discard valuable data, potentially affecting model performance. The process is formulated as:

$$X'_m = \{x \in X_m \mid |X'_m| = |X_s|\} \tag{1}$$

where X_m represents the majority class, and X_s denotes the minority class. The majority class is randomly reduced to match the size of the minority class.

SMOTE [14] synthesizes minority class samples, thereby preserving data distribution and improving the model's ability to recognize minority class features. Yet, its linear interpolation may produce unrealistic boundary samples.

$$x_{new} = x_i + \lambda \cdot (x_j - x_i), \quad \lambda \sim U(0,1) \tag{2}$$

where x_i and x_j are neighboring minority class samples, and λ is a random value drawn from a uniform distribution.

ADASYN [15] refines SMOTE by focusing on sparse boundary regions, improving generalization across distributions. However, excessive synthesis in these regions may introduce noise.

$$G_i = d_i \cdot G, \quad d_i = \frac{\Delta_i}{\sum \Delta_j} \tag{3}$$

where G_i is the number of synthetic samples for instance i, G is the total required samples, and Δ_i represents the class imbalance ratio in the local neighborhood.

ENN [16] removes majority class samples that overlap with the minority class, particularly those near anomalies, thereby enhancing dataset purity.

$$X_n' = \{x \in X_m \mid f_k(x) = y\} \tag{4}$$

where $f_k(x)$ denotes the majority vote of the k-nearest neighbors, and y is the true class label.

The **SMOTE+ENN** method balances oversampling and noise reduction by first generating synthetic samples using SMOTE. Then, ENN is applied to remove misclassified majority class samples, resulting in a cleaner and more balanced dataset.

2.4   Constructing Ensemble Learning Model

Machine learning models are widely used for classification, regression, clustering, and dimensionality reduction [17]. This study developed eight predictive models for **HAPE** risk assessment using **SVM**, Logistic Regression, **RF**, **GB**, **MLP**, and **XGBoost**. In addition, a hybrid model combining **MLP** and **GB** and an ensemble model (**MLP+GB+RF-Logistic**) were constructed. To further enhance prediction performance, **Voting Classifier** and **Stacking Generalization** were implemented for model integration. Voting is denoted as "V-" and Stacking Generalization as "S-" in model names. **Grid search** was applied for hyperparameter optimization to ensure optimal performance [18]. The **Voting Classifier** employed soft voting, generating final predictions based on a weighted average of base learner outputs.

To evaluate model performance in handling data imbalance, the dataset was randomly split into training and test sets (4:1 ratio). Five-fold cross-validation was conducted to ensure robustness and reliability of performance metrics. Finally, all models were tested on the independent test set, and the mean evaluation metrics were calculated to assess model generalization.

3   Experiments and Results

3.1   Predictive Performance Analysis

This study selected 46 out of 118 clinical features based on specific criteria to construct eight machine learning models. The same features were applied across models to ensure a fair performance comparison. Model effectiveness in predicting HAPE was evaluated using four resampling methods on the test dataset.

Performance was assessed using four key metrics: Recall, Accuracy, Area Under the Curve (AUC), and Area Under the Precision-Recall Curve (AUPR). These metrics comprehensively evaluate model performance, particularly in the context of imbalanced data, providing robust support for clinical decision-making.

Under-sampling. Table 2 presents results of the **under-sampling** method, showing that the **S-MLP+GB+RF-Logistic** model achieved optimal performance (**Accuracy**: 0.844 ± 0.031, **AUC**: 0.908 ± 0.023), indicating a moderate improvement in predictive capability for imbalanced datasets. In contrast, the **MLP** model showed poor performance (**AUPR**: 0.534 ± 0.120).

Table 2. Results of Under-Sampling Methods

Model	AUC	Accuracy	Recall	AUPR
SVM	0.883 ± 0.027	0.819 ± 0.041	0.737 ± 0.086	0.729 ± 0.059
Logistic	0.869 ± 0.026	0.792 ± 0.025	0.755 ± 0.070	0.665 ± 0.075
RF	0.906 ± 0.023	0.838 ± 0.024	0.842 ± 0.020	0.749 ± 0.040
XGBoost	0.901 ± 0.018	0.810 ± 0.015	$\mathbf{0.860 \pm 0.032}$	0.736 ± 0.074
GB	0.890 ± 0.013	0.819 ± 0.028	0.815 ± 0.035	0.741 ± 0.059
MLP	0.789 ± 0.092	0.711 ± 0.063	0.747 ± 0.163	0.534 ± 0.120
V-MLP+GB	0.898 ± 0.023	0.837 ± 0.025	0.833 ± 0.036	0.735 ± 0.044
V-MLP+GB+RF	0.904 ± 0.017	0.832 ± 0.033	0.825 ± 0.054	$\mathbf{0.799 \pm 0.030}$
S-MLP+GB	0.896 ± 0.023	0.838 ± 0.030	0.816 ± 0.032	0.726 ± 0.040
S-MLP+GB+RF-Logistic	$\mathbf{0.908 \pm 0.023}$	$\mathbf{0.844 \pm 0.031}$	0.825 ± 0.028	0.776 ± 0.031

SMOTE Table 3 shows that SMOTE significantly enhances prediction performance across all models. The S-MLP+GB+RF-Logistic model achieved the best performance (**Recall: 0.728 ± 0.074, AUC: 0.922 ± 0.015**), highlighting SMOTE's advantage in detecting minority classes. Compared with under-sampling, SMOTE notably improved MLP's **AUPR from 0.534 ± 0.120 to 0.746 ± 0.072**, reflecting greater effectiveness.

ADASYN The results utilizing the ADASYN method are detailed in Table 4, where the integrated S-MLP+GB+RF-Logistic model excels, achieving an AUC of 0.925 ± 0.014 and a Recall of 0.730 ± 0.074. These findings indicate that, compared to SMOTE, the ADASYN method markedly enhances the model's ability to identify smaller classes and boosts overall predictive performance, particularly in datasets characterized by high complexity and severe imbalance.

SMOTE+ENN Table 5 presents the results of the **SMOTE+ENN** method, which enhances model generalization by simultaneously augmenting minority class samples and removing noisy data. The **SMOTE+ENN**-based

Table 3. Results of the SMOTE Method

Model	AUC	Accuracy	Recall	AUPR
SVM	0.887 ± 0.048	0.887 ± 0.015	0.563 ± 0.113	0.736 ± 0.066
Logistic	0.876 ± 0.033	0.831 ± 0.012	0.745 ± 0.075	0.706 ± 0.082
RF	0.921 ± 0.017	0.901 ± 0.012	0.702 ± 0.074	0.804 ± 0.056
XGBoost	0.913 ± 0.022	0.914 ± 0.012	$\mathbf{0.781 \pm 0.062}$	0.816 ± 0.049
GB	0.922 ± 0.014	0.907 ± 0.014	0.772 ± 0.030	0.809 ± 0.046
MLP	0.882 ± 0.046	0.880 ± 0.020	0.703 ± 0.106	0.746 ± 0.072
V-MLP+GB	0.915 ± 0.017	0.910 ± 0.015	0.725 ± 0.077	0.813 ± 0.027
V-MLP+GB+RF	0.919 ± 0.013	0.912 ± 0.014	0.725 ± 0.049	0.803 ± 0.053
S-MLP+GB	0.911 ± 0.032	0.913 ± 0.013	0.711 ± 0.079	0.800 ± 0.053
S-MLP+GB+RF-Logistic	$\mathbf{0.922 \pm 0.015}$	$\mathbf{0.915 \pm 0.019}$	0.728 ± 0.074	$\mathbf{0.817 \pm 0.050}$

Table 4. Results of the ADASYN Method

Model	AUC	Accuracy	Recall	AUPR
SVM	0.888 ± 0.042	0.892 ± 0.012	0.554 ± 0.111	0.739 ± 0.063
Logistic	0.875 ± 0.036	0.816 ± 0.033	$\mathbf{0.755 \pm 0.084}$	0.702 ± 0.080
RF	0.918 ± 0.017	0.921 ± 0.015	0.693 ± 0.081	0.788 ± 0.070
XGBoost	0.888 ± 0.042	0.892 ± 0.012	0.554 ± 0.111	0.739 ± 0.063
GB	0.915 ± 0.009	0.901 ± 0.024	0.728 ± 0.029	0.783 ± 0.053
MLP	0.876 ± 0.058	0.867 ± 0.031	0.676 ± 0.083	0.730 ± 0.083
V-MLP+GB	0.923 ± 0.014	0.917 ± 0.013	0.720 ± 0.063	$\mathbf{0.821 \pm 0.036}$
V-MLP+GB+RF	0.918 ± 0.019	0.918 ± 0.015	0.755 ± 0.043	0.799 ± 0.056
S-MLP+GB	0.896 ± 0.032	0.912 ± 0.016	0.668 ± 0.091	0.781 ± 0.061
S-MLP+GB+RF-Logistic	$\mathbf{0.925 \pm 0.014}$	$\mathbf{0.918 \pm 0.017}$	0.730 ± 0.074	0.814 ± 0.052

S-MLP+GB+RF-Logistic model achieved optimal classification performance on complex and imbalanced datasets. It attains the highest **Accuracy** (0.913 ± 0.032) and **AUC** (0.926 ± 0.015), demonstrating that integrating **SMOTE+ENN** with S-MLP+GB+RF-Logistic significantly enhances stability and accuracy in **HAPE** risk prediction.

Ablation Experiment. This study evaluates the effectiveness of the SMOTE+ENN hybrid sampling method compared to a no-sampling approach in addressing data imbalance. Experimental results across multiple classification models-including SVM, Logistic Regression, RF, XGBoost, GB, MLP, MLP+GB, and MLP+GB+RF-Logistic-demonstrate that SMOTE+ENN significantly enhances minority class recognition, particularly by improving Recall performance.

Table 6 demonstrates that **SMOTE+ENN** significantly improves Recall across all models. For instance, the RF model's Recall increased from 0.465 ± 0.089 to 0.781 ± 0.055, MLP from 0.475 ± 0.179 to 0.825 ± 0.047, and S-MLP+GB+RF-Logistic from 0.614 ± 0.056 to 0.859 ± 0.046. **SMOTE+ENN** enhances the identification of minority classes while maintaining stable Accuracy, improving classification balance.

Table 5. Results of the SMOTE+ENN Method

Model	AUC	Accuracy	Recall	AUPR
SVM	0.865 ± 0.059	0.866 ± 0.028	0.650 ± 0.093	0.676 ± 0.066
Logistic	0.869 ± 0.026	0.746 ± 0.051	0.825 ± 0.039	0.668 ± 0.057
RF	0.905 ± 0.025	0.850 ± 0.028	0.781 ± 0.055	0.749 ± 0.047
XGBoost	0.917 ± 0.017	0.813 ± 0.027	0.849 ± 0.047	0.765 ± 0.065
GB	0.917 ± 0.017	0.847 ± 0.012	0.858 ± 0.048	0.779 ± 0.057
MLP	0.883 ± 0.029	0.788 ± 0.058	0.825 ± 0.047	0.733 ± 0.093
V-MLP+GB	0.916 ± 0.018	0.855 ± 0.026	0.836 ± 0.035	$\mathbf{0.807 \pm 0.035}$
V-MLP+GB+RF	0.910 ± 0.028	0.850 ± 0.036	0.847 ± 0.045	0.784 ± 0.080
S-MLP+GB	0.915 ± 0.026	0.880 ± 0.057	0.825 ± 0.054	0.759 ± 0.078
S-MLP+GB+RF-Logistic	$\mathbf{0.926 \pm 0.015}$	$\mathbf{0.913 \pm 0.032}$	$\mathbf{0.859 \pm 0.046}$	0.798 ± 0.033

Table 6. Results of the No Sampling Method

Model	AUC	Accuracy	Recall	AUPR
SVM	0.902 ± 0.027	0.905 ± 0.013	0.553 ± 0.106	0.777 ± 0.048
Logistic	0.884 ± 0.042	0.896 ± 0.017	0.588 ± 0.078	0.721 ± 0.095
RF	0.924 ± 0.014	0.902 ± 0.020	0.465 ± 0.089	0.789 ± 0.042
XGBoost	0.926 ± 0.019	0.918 ± 0.014	0.614 ± 0.070	0.813 ± 0.063
GB	0.920 ± 0.015	0.912 ± 0.013	0.632 ± 0.087	0.812 ± 0.029
MLP	0.862 ± 0.067	0.892 ± 0.024	0.475 ± 0.179	0.735 ± 0.085
V-MLP+GB	0.925 ± 0.015	0.921 ± 0.011	0.658 ± 0.058	0.824 ± 0.039
V-MLP+GB+RF	0.923 ± 0.019	0.911 ± 0.013	0.526 ± 0.090	0.821 ± 0.036
S-MLP+GB	0.908 ± 0.030	0.917 ± 0.017	$\mathbf{0.693 \pm 0.077}$	0.795 ± 0.052
S-MLP+GB+RF-Logistic	$\mathbf{0.930 \pm 0.012}$	$\mathbf{0.920 \pm 0.006}$	0.614 ± 0.056	$\mathbf{0.825 \pm 0.042}$

3.2 Model Interpretability Analysis

To improve the interpretability of the HAPE prediction model, this study employs the SHAP algorithm to quantify feature contributions. SHAP assigns explanatory values to each feature, assessing its influence on model output. Using SHAP, we analyzed the S-MLP+GB+RF-Logistic integrated model and generated summary plots to visualize feature importance. Figure 4A presents the SHAP value distribution for the top 20 clinical features, with each row representing a feature. The position of each dot indicates the SHAP value, where higher values reflect a greater contribution to the model's predictions. Figure 4B displays a bar chart ranking features by their mean absolute SHAP values, with higher values indicating greater predictive influence. The SHAP analysis identified ten key clinical features that significantly influenced model performance in distinguishing between HAPE and non-HAPE patients. The top features include HGB, AGE, Bas, Alb, MPV, TP, MON, UN, RBC, and Lymph.

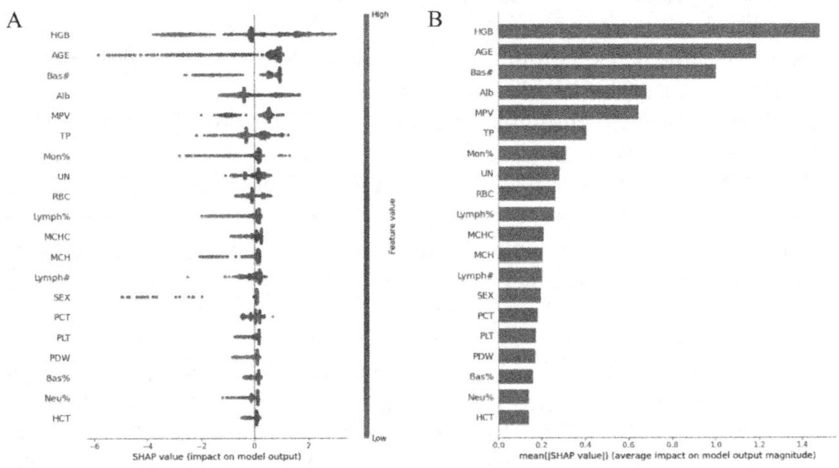

Fig. 4. SHAP analysis and feature importance ranking

4   Discussion and Conclusion

HAPE is a severe altitude illness where early intervention significantly improves outcomes. In high-altitude environments, hemoglobin concentration increases to counteract hypoxia. Research has explored the physiological, genetic, and environmental mechanisms of HAPE, such as gene expression kinetics [19], clinical translation [20], and gene chip analysis in rat models [21]. However, most studies rely on traditional statistical methods, emphasizing correlation analysis while lacking robust predictive models. Existing approaches struggle with high-dimensional, imbalanced data, limiting their ability to elucidate HAPE mechanisms. Thus, developing advanced machine learning models for HAPE risk prediction is of significant clinical value.

The clinical indicators identified in this study are consistent with findings reported in previous research. For example, Bhagi S et al. [22] observed significantly higher HGB levels in patients with HAPE. Taylor A.T. [23] and Hackett P.H. [24] analyzed age-related differences in HAPE risk in high-altitude environments. Gulliksson M et al. [25] investigated the response of Bas and mast cells to hypoxic environments, while Karinen H et al. [26] explored the predictive role of Alb in HAPE. The proposed machine learning model provides a quantitative assessment of early HAPE risk, facilitating timely interventions and mitigating health risks in high-altitude populations.

The SMOTE+ENN method significantly improves recall for minority class samples, thereby enhancing clinical disease prediction by reducing missed diagnoses. A higher recall indicates greater sensitivity in detecting HAPE, thereby strengthening clinical decision-making and early diagnosis reliability. Future research will integrate multimodal clinical data, including time-series measurements and real-time sensor inputs, to enhance model generalization and predictive performance in high-altitude environments.

This study employs ensemble learning and data resampling to develop a HAPE risk prediction model. Under-sampling, SMOTE, ADASYN, and SMOTE+ENN were applied to address data imbalance, while grid search refines feature optimization, improving predictive performance. Additionally, stacked generalization of MLP, GB, and Random Forest optimizes final predictions, strengthening health management in high-altitude environments and reducing HAPE incidence.

Acknowledgments. This work was supported by the Natural Science Foundation of China (No. 62366052), the Natural Science Foundation of Xinjiang Uygur Autonomous Region (No.2024D01C126, 2022D01C427), the Key R&D Program of Xinjiang Uygur Autonomous Region (No. 2022B01046), the Tianshan Talent Training Program, and the Sichuan Province Joint Fund of China (No. 25QYCX0103).

References

1. Yunhong, L.: Research advances in pathogenesis and prophylactic measures of acute high altitude illness. Respir. Med. **145**, 145–152 (2018)
2. Bärtsch, P.: Acute high-altitude illnesses. N. Engl. J. Med. **368**(24), 2294–2302 (2013)
3. Luks, A.M.: Wilderness medical society clinical practice guidelines for the prevention, diagnosis, and treatment of acute altitude illness: 2024 update. Wild. Environ. Med. **35**(1_suppl), 2S–19S (2024)
4. Singer, M.: The third international consensus definitions for sepsis and septic shock (Sepsis-3). JAMA **315**(8), 801–810 (2016)
5. Pimentel, M.: A comparison of the ability of the national early warning score and the national early warning score 2 to identify patients at risk of in-hospital mortality: a multi-centre database study. Resuscitation **134**, 147–156 (2019)
6. Junpeng, R.: qSOFA, NEWS The value of scores and clinical symptoms in the early diagnosis of acute plateau pulmonary oedema. Int. Clin. Med. **5**(2), 34–37 (2024)

7. Kaur, G.: High Altitude Sickness-Solutions from Genomics. Proteomics and Antioxidant Interventions. Springer, Singapore (2022)

8. Ford, E.: Extracting information from the text of electronic medical records to improve case detection: a systematic review. J. Am. Med. Inform. Assoc. **23**(5), 1007–1015 (2016)

9. Topol, E.J.: High-performance medicine: the convergence of human and artificial intelligence. Nat. Med. **25**(1), 44–56 (2019)

10. Liu, L.: Solving the class imbalance problem using ensemble algorithm: application of screening for aortic dissection. BMC Med. Inform. Decis. Mak. **22**(1), 82–97 (2022)

11. Little, R.: Statistical analysis with missing data. Wiley, Hoboken (2019)

12. Horton, N.J.: Much ado about nothing: a comparison of missing data methods and software to fit incomplete data regression models. Am. Stat. **61**(1), 79–90 (2007)

13. Haixiang, G.: Learning from class-imbalanced data: review of methods and applications. Expert Syst. Appl. **73**, 220–239 (2017)

14. Chawla, N.V.: SMOTE: synthetic minority over-sampling technique. J. Artif. Intell. Res. **16**, 321–357 (2002)

15. He, H.: ADASYN: adaptive synthetic sampling approach for imbalanced learning. In: 19th IEEE international joint conference on neural networks (IEEE world congress on computational intelligence, pp. 1322–1328. IEEE, Hong Kong (2008)

16. Tang, B.: ENN: extended nearest neighbor method for pattern recognition [research frontier]. IEEE Comput. Intell. Mag. **10**(3), 52–60 (2015)

17. Murphy, K.P.: Machine Learning: a Probabilistic Perspective. MIT press, Cambridge (2012)

18. Hutter, F.: An efficient approach for assessing hyperparameter importance. In: Proceedings of the 31st International Conference on Machine Learning (ICML), pp. 754–762. PMLR, Beijing (2014)

19. Yuhong, L.: Transcriptomic profiling reveals gene expression kinetics in patients with hypoxia and high altitude pulmonary edema. Gene **651**, 200–205 (2018)

20. Wenxiang, G.: Current status and perspectives on the mechanisms of highland pulmonary oedema and clinical translation. Biomed. Transform. **2**(2), 1–7 (2021)

21. Gang, X.: Gene expression profile of lung tissues in rats with high altitude pulmonary edema. J. Army Med. Univ. **46**(11), 1235–1243 (2024)

22. Bhagi, S.: High-altitude pulmonary edema. J. Occup. Health **56**(4), 235–243 (2014)

23. Taylor, A.T.: High-altitude illnesses: physiology, risk factors, prevention, and treatment. Rambam Maimonides Med. J. **2**(1), e0022 (2011)

24. Hackett, P.: High-altitude illness. N. Engl. J. Med. **345**(2), 107–114 (2001)

25. Gulliksson, M.: Mast cell survival and mediator secretion in response to hypoxia. PLoS ONE **5**(8), e12360 (2010)

26. Karinen, H.: Prevalence of acute mountain sickness among Finnish trekkers on Mount Kilimanjaro, Tanzania: an observational study. High Altitude Med. Biol. **9**(4), 301–306 (2008)

LGFMDA: miRNA-Disease Association Prediction with Local and Global Feature Representation Learning

Chunyang Jiang[1], Yuanbo Guo[2], Linlin Zhang[2,3], Xuehua Bi[4,5(✉)], and Kai Zhao[1(✉)]

[1] School of Computer Science and Technology (School of Cyberspace Security), Xinjiang University, Urumqi 830046, China
zhawkk@xju.edu.cn
[2] School of Software, Xinjiang University, Urumqi 830046, China
[3] Center of Network and Information Technology, Xinjiang University, Urumqi 830046, China
[4] College of Medical Engineering and Technology, Xinjiang Medical University, Urumqi 830017, China
bxh0327@foxmail.com
[5] Institute of Medical Engineering Interdisciplinary Research, Xinjiang Medical University, Urumqi 830017, China

Abstract. As one of biomarkers of diseases, dysregulation of miRNAs is closely related to the occurrence and development of various human diseases. Identifying disease-related miRNAs can contribute to a deeper understanding of the pathological mechanisms of diseases and promote their treatment. Thus, there is an urgent need to develop effective computational methods for predicting potential miRNA-disease associations, which can serve as supplements to time-consuming and labor-intensive biological experimental methods. Although existing Graph Neural Network based methods have achieved good performance, the learning of comprehensive and high-quality miRNAs and diseases feature representations is still a challenge for these methods, as they typically extract information from only one of the local or global perspective. In this study, we propose a new graph representation learning method named LGFMDA for miRNA-disease association prediction. We first construct an attributed bipartite graph by the associations between miRNAs and diseases as well as their similarities. Then, we learn node feature representations from both local and global perspectives, and fuse the two types of features to obtain deep and representative feature embeddings of miRNA and disease nodes. Specifically, we compute an adaptive feature propagation depth for each node in the graph to fully aggregate local neighbourhood information, while global features are captured using the improved graph transformer framework. Finally, the feature representations of miRNA and disease pairs are fed into a MLP classifier to calculate association probabilities. In the five-fold cross-validation, LGFMDA achieves the AUC of 0.9561 and AUPR of 0.9546, outperforming seven state-of-the-art methods. The case study also further validate the performance of LGFMDA in practical applications. The source codes are available at https://github.com/LabBioMedCoder/LGFMDA..

Keywords: MiRNA-disease Association Prediction · Local and Global Feature Representation · Graph Neural Network

1   Introduction

As single-stranded non-coding RNA, microRNAs (miRNAs) play a pivotal role in post-transcriptional gene regulation [1]. The dysregulation of miRNA expression is intricately connected to the initiation and progression of numerous human diseases. Consequently, understanding the association between miRNAs and complex diseases can aid in comprehending pathological mechanisms and developing new therapeutic strategies. Although traditional bio-experimental methods can provide accurate information on miRNA-disease associations (MDAs), they often suffer from long durations, high costs, and are limited to small-scale identification. As the number of confirmed MDAs increases [2] and multi-omics data accumulates [3], many computational approaches have been proposed to predict potential MDAs [4]. These methods assist biological experiments by providing candidate miRNAs relevant to diseases.

The more functionally similar two miRNAs are, the more likely their associated diseases are to exhibit similar phenotypes. Based on this assumption, many approaches designed different scoring functions utilizing the multi-source similarity information of miRNAs/diseases. They then ranked the correlation of miRNA-disease pairs according to the result of these scoring functions to predict potential MDAs [5,6]. Machine learning-based methods for predicting miRNA-disease associations have been widely proposed. These methods focus on the feature representation of miRNAs and diseases, and then use machine learning techniques, such as SVM, XGBoost, and RF, to predict the associations between miRNAs and diseases [7]. However, above methods only use shallow features of miRNAs and diseases, which limits the predictive performance of these models.

Deep learning, which can automatically extract deep and high-quality node feature representations, has proven effective in predicting MDAs. To achieve this, MDA-CF [8] and MLRDFM [9] utilized autoencoders and deep neural networks, respectively, to extract expressive feature representations of miRNAs and disease nodes. Graph Neural Networks (GNNs), a class of deep learning methods, have attracted considerable attention for effectively extracting topological features from graph-structured data. For example, Zhong et al. [10] combined the random dropout mechanism with graph propagation algorithm to derive node embeddings from the miRNA-disease graph, effectively avoiding feature over-smoothing. Dong et al. [11] initially utilized multiple similarities and association information to construct a miRNA-disease heterogeneous graph. They then extracted global feature representations of nodes from the heterogeneous graph using a Transformer encoder, integrating rich semantic information into the representations via four meta-paths.

Despite the promising predictive performance of miRNA-disease association prediction methods based on GNNs, they still face challenges that need to be addressed. On the one hand, in the graph constructed with known miRNA and disease associations, the degrees of nodes are significantly imbalanced. However, current GNNs-based methods do not consider the differences in receptive fields between central nodes and peripheral nodes when aggregating neighborhood information [12]. On the other hand, existing GNNs-based MDAs prediction methods typically set the number of GNN layers to 2–3 to achieve optimal predictive performance [13]. However, this limited stacking of layers fails to capture the global information in the graph structure.

To address the above issues, in this paper, we propose a novel method called LGFMDA, which extracts node features from both local and global perspectives for the MDAs prediction. First, we construct an attributed miRNA-disease bipartite graph. Specifically, known miRNA-disease associations are used as edges in the graph. We calculate various similarities, including disease semantic similarity, miRNA sequence, functional, and Gaussian interaction profile kernel similarity. Autoencoders are used to fuse these similarities into an integrated similarity matrix, which served as the features of the nodes in the graph. Secondly, we utilize an adaptive Simplified Graph Convolutional Network (SGC) to extract local features of nodes from the attributed bipartite graph, where the number of feature iterations is adaptively computed based on the degree of each node. Third, we employ Graph Transformer network to extract node features from a global perspective. Finally, the local and global features of both miRNA and disease nodes are fused and fed into the MLP classifier for predicting potential MDAs. The benchmarking results demonstrate that LGFMDA achieves superior performance compared to existing baseline methods, while the ablation studies further confirm the effectiveness of extracting local and global features.

2 Materials and Methods

2.1 Datasets

The primary dataset used in this study is obtained from the work of Bi et al. [14], where they collected 14,550 associations between 917 miRNAs and 792 diseases from HMDD [2]. We employ a binary matrix $A \in \mathbb{R}^{N_m \times N_d}$ to store the miRNA-disease association data, where N_m and N_d denote the number of miRNAs and diseases, respectively. The value $A(i,j)$ is set to 1 if there is experimentally verified association information between miRNA i and disease j, and 0 otherwise.

2.2 The Overall Flow of the Model

In this section, we present the method LGFMDA for MDAs prediction. As illustrated in Fig. 1, the overall flow of LGFMDA comprises four fundamental components: (a) constructing miRNA-disease bipartite attributed graph by utilizing known MDAs and multiple similarities; (b) applying node adaptive feature encoder to obtain local features of miRNA and disease nodes; (c) extracting global features by employing graph transformer feature extractor; (d) fusing local and global features and predicting potential associations using MLP classifier.

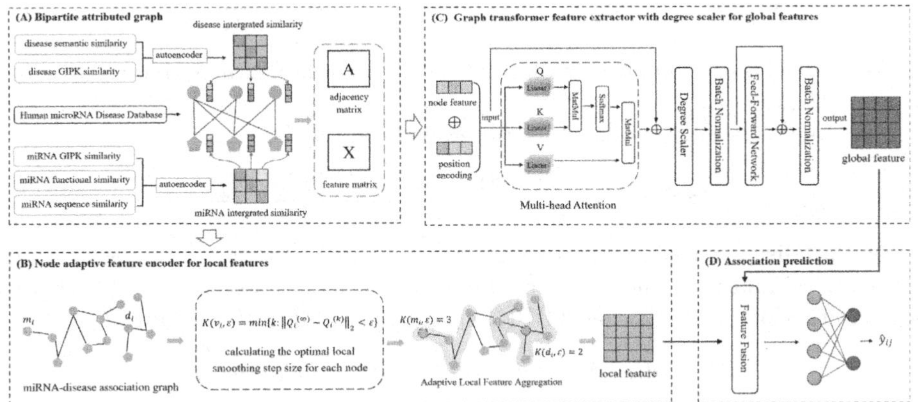

Fig. 1. The overall flow of LGFMDA.

2.3   Disease Similarity

We utilize Medical Subject Headings (MeSH) descriptors to compute the disease semantic similarity. Each disease d_i expresses its hierarchical relationship with other diseases through a directed acyclic graph $DAG(d_i) = (N(d_i), E(d_i))$, $N(d_i)$ denotes the set of all ancestor nodes including d_i, and $E(d_i)$ is the set of all edges describing the 'is-a' relationship in the DAG. Using this structure, we can compute the semantic contribution value $C_{d_i}(d_v)$ of disease d_v to d_i, where d_v is any disease in d_i's DAG except for itself.

$$
\begin{cases}
C_{d_i}(d_v) = 1 & \text{if } d_v = d_i \\
C_{d_i}(d_v) = max\left\{\mu * C_{d_i}(d'_v) | d'_v \in children\ of\ d_v\right\} & \text{otherwise}
\end{cases} , \tag{1}
$$

where μ is the semantic attenuation factor, which is set to 0.5 according to [14].

Based on the prior knowledge that the larger the proportion of the DAG shared by two diseases, the more semantically similar the two diseases are, we calculate the disease semantic similarity matrix $DSS1$.

$$
DSS1(d_i, d_j) = \frac{\sum_{v \in (N_{d_i} \cap N_{d_j})}(C_{d_i}(v) + C_{d_j}(v))}{\sum_{v \in N_{d_i}} C_{d_i}(v) + \sum_{v \in N_{d_j}} C_{d_j}(v)}, \tag{2}
$$

where N_{d_i} and N_{d_j} are the set of nodes of d_i's and d_j's $DAGs$, respectively.

In the aforementioned calculation method, the semantic contribution values are identical for two different diseases within the same layer of the DAG. However, the occurrence frequency of each disease in all $DAGs$ is not the same.

Specific disease with lower occurrence frequencies may have greater semantic contribution. Following [15], we adopt an another approach to compute the contribution of d_v to d_i that takes full account of the frequency of occurrence.

$$C'_{d_i}(d_v) = -log(\frac{the\ number\ of\ DAGs\ including\ d_v}{the\ number\ of\ all\ DAGs}). \tag{3}$$

We obtain the second disease semantic similarity $DSS2(d_i, d_j)$ in the manner of formula (1).

The final semantic similarity of diseases d_i and d_j is:

$$DSS(d_i, d_j) = \frac{DSS1(d_i, d_j) + DSS2(d_i, d_j)}{2}. \tag{4}$$

Not all diseases have explicit semantic associations or similarity data, resulting in zero similarity values for some disease pairs. Therefore, we introduce Gaussian interaction profile kernel (GIPK) similarity to fill in these values.

$$DGS(d_i, d_j) = exp(-\alpha_d \|IP(d_i) - IP(d_j)\|^2), \tag{5}$$

where $IP(d_i)$ is column i in A and α_d regulates the kernel bandwidth, calculated as follows:

$$\alpha_d = 1/(\frac{1}{N_d}\sum_{i=1}^{N_d} \|IP(d_i)\|^2), \tag{6}$$

where N_d is the number of diseases. Similarly, we can obtain the $GIPK$ similarity value $MGS(m_i, m_j)$ between miRNA m_i and m_j.

2.4 MiRNA Similarity

Sequence information of miRNAs is obtained from miRbase [3]. Using the Needleman-Wunsch algorithm, we calculate the sequence similarity score matrix $SSM \in \mathbb{R}^{N_m \times N_m}$ for miRNAs, where N_m is the number of miRNAs. Subsequently, we normalize the SSM to eliminate global inconsistencies. The miRNA sequence similarity matrix MSS is calculated as follows:

$$MSS(m_i, m_j) = \begin{cases} 1 & \text{if } m_i = m_j \\ \frac{SSM(m_i, m_j) - SSM_{min}}{SSM_{max} - SSM_{min}} & \text{otherwise} \end{cases}, \tag{7}$$

where SSM_{max} and SSM_{min} denote the maximum and minimum values in the SSM matrix, respectively.

The functional similarity between two miRNAs is calculated based on the semantic similarity of the diseases associated with these two miRNAs:

$$MFS(m_i, m_j) = \frac{\sum_{d \in D(m_i)} DSS(d, d_j^*) + \sum_{d \in D(m_j)} DSS(d, d_i^*)}{|D(m_i)| + |D(m_j)|}, \tag{8}$$

where $D(m_i)$ is the set of diseases associated with m_i recorded in A and $|D(m_i)|$ represents the number of diseases in $D(m_i)$. d_i^* is the disease with the greatest semantic similarity to d in $D(m_i)$, which is calculated as follows:

$$d_i^* = argmax_{d_i \in D(m_i)} DSS(d, d_i). \tag{9}$$

2.5   Integrated Similarity

To obtain more comprehensive feature representations of miRNAs and diseases, we integrate the aforementioned similarities. For diseases, integrated similarity matrix $ID \in \mathbb{R}^{N_d \times N_d}$ consists of semantic similarity and $GIPK$ similarity. If the semantic similarity value of disease pairs (d_i, d_j) is not 0, the integrated similarity is semantic similarity, otherwise it is $GIPK$ similarity.

$$ID(d_i, d_j) = \begin{cases} DGS(d_i, d_j) & \text{if } DSS(d_i, d_j) = 0 \\ DSS(d_i, d_j) & \text{otherwise} \end{cases}. \tag{10}$$

For miRNAs, we splice the three miRNA similarity matrices. The integrated similarity matrix of miRNAs $IM \in \mathbb{R}^{N_m \times 3N_m}$ is as follows:

$$IM = MSS\|MFS\|MGS, \tag{11}$$

where MSS, MFS, and MGS denote sequence similarity, functional similarity, and $GIPK$ similarity of miRNAs, respectively.

Furthermore, two autoencoders are employed for feature dimensionality reduction and noise mitigation in order to enhance the quality of feature representation. The final feature matrices of disease and miRNA are denoted as $SD \in \mathbb{R}^{N_d \times 64}$ and $SM \in \mathbb{R}^{N_m \times 64}$, respectively.

2.6   Constructing MiRNA-Disease Attributed Bipartite Graph

Using known associations and similarities related to miRNAs and diseases, we construct the miRNA-disease bipartite attributed graph $\mathcal{G} = \{X, V, E\}$ for subsequent node feature extraction, where $X = \{SD, SM\}$ represents the node feature matrix, V is the node set, and E is the edge set.

2.7   Node Adaptive Feature Encoder for Local Features

Existing computational methods based on GNNs typically employ the same number of network layers for each miRNA/disease node in the graph to aggregate and update features. This seemingly fair handling approach is not fair to a certain extent. For those miRNA or disease nodes with lots of association information, the use of shallow networks (e.g., 2–3 layers) to aggregate features from lower-order neighbours is sufficient, while using deeper networks may introduce unnecessary noise. However, shallow networks may not adequately meet the needs of nodes on the periphery of the graph that have less associated information. Therefore, we introduce a node-adaptive feature aggregation approach, which appropriately aggregates the local feature information of nodes by computing independent number of feature aggregations for each node. To facilitate the derivation of formulas, we adopt the feature propagation process in SGC [16]. The output of k-th layer network is: $X^{(k)} = \hat{A}^k X^{(0)}$, $\hat{A} = \tilde{D}^{-\frac{1}{2}} \tilde{A} \tilde{D}^{-\frac{1}{2}} = \tilde{D}^{-\frac{1}{2}} (A + I) \tilde{D}^{-\frac{1}{2}}$, where A is the adjacency matrix of graph G, I is an identity matrix, and $\tilde{D}$ denotes the diagonal matrix of $\tilde{A}$.

After an infinite number of aggregations ($k \rightarrow \infty$), the final feature representation of the node is $X^{(\infty)} = \hat{A}^{\infty} X^{(0)}$, where

$$\hat{A}_{ij}^{\infty} = \frac{(deg_i + 1)^{\frac{1}{2}} (deg_j + 1)^{\frac{1}{2}}}{|V| + 2|E|} \tag{12}$$

denotes the weight relations between node v_i and node v_j after infinite iterations, deg_i and deg_j are the node degrees for v_i and v_j.

Following Zhang et al. [17] and Zhao et al. [18], we calculate the interaction matrix $Q^{(k)} = \left[\hat{A}_{ij}^{k} \right]$ between nodes by measuring the influence of the change of input feature $X_j^{(0)}$ of v_j on the feature $X_i^{(k)}$ of v_i after k aggregations.

The adaptive feature aggregation times of node v_i can be determined using the interaction matrix.

$$K(v_i, \varepsilon) = min \left\{ k : \left\| Q_i^{(\infty)} - Q_i^{(k)} \right\|_2 < \varepsilon \right\}, \tag{13}$$

where $Q_i^{(k)}$ denotes the ith row of $Q^{(k)}$, ε is an arbitrarily constant greater than 0. After that, the averaging operation is used to obtain the local features of v_i:

$$X_i^{local} = \frac{1}{K(v_i, \varepsilon) + 1} \sum_{k=0}^{K(v_i, \varepsilon)} X_i^{(k)}. \tag{14}$$

2.8 Graph Transformer Feature Extractor for Global Features

In addition, we utilize the graph transforemr network [19] to efficiently extract global features of miRNA and disease nodes in the heterogeneous graph G. We employ Laplace position encoding to replace trigonometric form position encoding in traditional transformer, which is obtained by selecting the k smallest non-trivial eigenvectors of $\hat{A}$. Here, $\hat{A}$ represents the Laplacian matrix of the adjacency matrix after normalization. The computation of multi-head attention in graph transformer is as follows:

$$\begin{cases} X_Q = (X + Z_{lpe}) \times W_q \\ X_K = (X + Z_{lpe}) \times W_k \, , \\ X_V = (X + Z_{lpe}) \times W_v \end{cases} \tag{15}$$

$$Attention(X_Q, X_K, X_V) = softmax(\frac{X_Q X_K^T}{\sqrt{d_k}}) X_V, \tag{16}$$

where X denotes the feature matrix of nodes, Z_{lpe} is the Laplace positional encoding, W_q, W_k and W_v are the learnable parameter matrices, and d_k is the dimensionality of the matrix X_K.

We concatenate the outputs of multiple heads and apply a linear transformation to obtain the output X^{mha} of the multi-head attention module.

$$X^{mha} = concat(head_1, head_2 \ldots head_n) W_O, \tag{17}$$

$$head_i = Attention[(X_Q)_i, (X_K)_i, (X_V)_i], \tag{18}$$

where W_O is also a learnable parameter matrix.

The attention mechanism is inherently insensitive to node degree, which is a critical characteristic of graph data. To address this, an adaptive degree scaler is introduced to maintain degree information of the graph.

$$\hat{X}_i^{mha} = X_i^{mha} \odot \theta_1 + (log(1 + deg_i) \cdot X_i^{mha} \odot \theta_2), \tag{19}$$

where deg_i is the degree of node v_i and θ_1, θ_2 are learnable parameters.

Batch normalization is used to replace the original layer normalization to ensure that degree information is retained efficiently. The computational process for the global feature representation of miRNAs and diseases is as follows:

$$X^{'} = BN(\hat{X}^{mha}) + X, \tag{20}$$

$$X^{global} = BN(FFN(X^{'}) + X^{'}), \tag{21}$$

where BN is Batch normalization and FFN denotes a feedforward neural network consisting of two linear layers.

2.9 Feature Fusion and Association Prediction

After obtaining the local and global features of miRNA and disease nodes respectively, we concatenate these two features and obtain the fused feature representation through a linear layer.

$$H = W_l(concat(X^{local}, X^{global})) + b_l, \tag{22}$$

where W_l is the weight matrix and b_l is the bias vector.

We combine feature representations of miRNAs and diseases and input them into the MLP classifier for association prediction:

$$\hat{Y} = sigmoid(MLP(H_{miRNA} \oplus H_{disease})). \tag{23}$$

Binary cross entropy is employed as the loss function:

$$\mathcal{L}(A, \hat{Y}) = -\sum_{i,j \in (Y^+ \cup Y^-)} A_{ij} log(\hat{Y}_{i,j}) + (1 - A_{i,j}) log(1 - \hat{Y}_{i,j}), \tag{24}$$

where $A_{i,j}$ is the true label of the association between miRNA i and disease j and $\hat{Y}_{i,j}$ denotes the label predicted by LGFMDA. Y^+ and Y^- are positive and negative samples.

3   Experiments and Results

3.1   Experiment Settings

LGFMDA is implemented using the PyTorch framework. Adam optimizer is utilized to update the neural network parameters within the model. To comprehensively evaluate the prediction performance of LGFMDA, we conduct 5-fold cross validation experiments, in which the sample set consisting of known associations and an equal number of unknown associations is randomly divided into five equally sized groups. One group serves as testing data, while the remaining groups constitute training data. Consistent with previous studies, we adopt accuracy (Acc), precision (Pre), recall, F1-score (F1), AUC, and AUPR as evaluation metrics to quantify the model's performance.

3.2 Comparison with Baseline Methods

In this section, seven state-of-the-art (SOTA) methods are selected to compare with LGFMDA. These comparison methods include deep learning-based methods (MDA-CF [8], SMALF [20]) and GNNs-based methods (MDformer [11], ADPMDA [21], GRPAMDA [10], JKNMDA [13], ESGC-MDA [14]). Comparison results are shown in Table 1, where the optimal and sub-optimal results are highlighted using bolding and underlining, respectively. From these results, several observations can be made: (1) LGFMDA achieves the highest AUC, AUPR, and F1 values, and other evaluation metrics also achieve competitive performance. These results demonstrate the excellent performance of LGFMDA in predicting potential MDAs. (2) Among all the compared models, MDformer and ESGC-MDA achieve suboptimal results overall. For MDformer, this may benefit from the use of the Transformer architecture similar to LGFMDA. However, due to the difficulty of designing suitable meta-paths and the limitations of its own feature propagation, the local features of the nodes may not be fully taken into account, resulting in a gap between the performance of MDformer and LGFMDA. For ESGC-MDA, the random dropout during message propagation and the adaptive aggregation of features from different network layers enable ESGC-MDA to obtain high-quality local feature representations. Nevertheless, the limited network depth makes it lack in extracting global features. (3) For the deep learning-based methods, the powerful cascading forest classifier makes MDA-CF perform better than SMALF which uses the XGBoost classifier.

Table 1. Comparison results with baseline methods.

	AUC	AUPR	Acc	Pre	Recall	F1
LGFMDA	**0.9561**	**0.9546**	**0.8830**	0.8660	**0.9063**	**0.8856**
MDformer	0.9485	0.9465	0.8787	<u>0.8928</u>	0.8611	0.8765
ESGC-MDA	<u>0.9500</u>	<u>0.9487</u>	<u>0.8805</u>	0.8784	0.8834	<u>0.8808</u>
MDA-CF	0.9460	0.9459	0.8758	0.8814	0.8684	0.8749
ADPMDA	0.9450	0.9423	0.8663	**0.8941**	0.8337	0.8612
GRPAMDA	0.9443	0.9440	0.8753	0.8794	0.8705	0.8746
JKNMDA	0.9325	0.9284	0.8513	0.8193	<u>0.9023</u>	0.8585
SMALF	0.9264	0.9280	0.8515	0.8494	0.8545	0.8519

3.3   Ablation Experiments

To validate the effectiveness of each module in LGFMDA, we propose four variants: LGFMDA_NAFE (using only the node adaptive feature encoder to extract local feature representations of miRNA and disease nodes), LGFMDA_GTE (employing only the graph transformer encoder to extract global feature representations of nodes), LGFMDA_Transformer (utilizing only the traditional transformer encoder) and LGFMDA_GCN (using only a 3-layer GCN to extract local features of nodes). The experimental results are presented in Fig. 2. From the results, we can find that when extracting global features of nodes, the addition of unique attributes of graph data, such as node degree information, is conducive to extracting high-quality features, making the performance of graph transformer better than that of traditional transformer. Node adaptive feature encoder also benefits from a more detailed local feature propagation pattern, surpassing GCN encoders in performance. Furthermore, integrating both local and global features enables the model to capture more comprehensive and expressive representations of node features, so LGFMDA achieves the highest results among the several variant models.

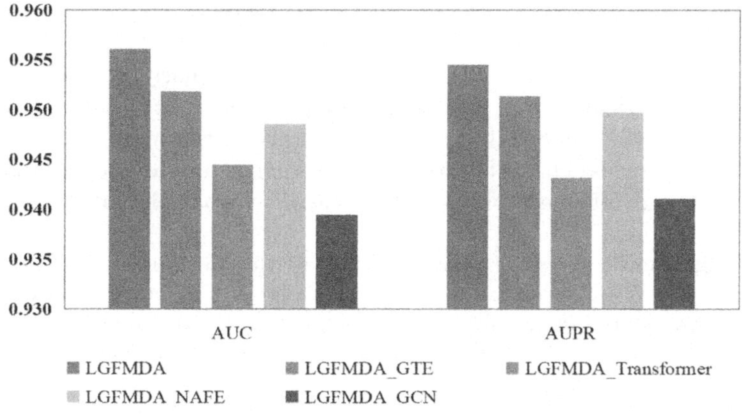

Fig. 2. Comparison results of different components.

3.4   Case Study

In this section, Breast Neoplasms are selected as the subject of case study to evaluate the utility of LGFMDA in practical applications. Breast cancer is a prevalent disease among women, which seriously threatens their health. In recent years, with the accelerated pace of life and increased pressure, its incidence has shown a consistent upward trend, establishing it as the leading malignant tumor in women and raising considerable societal concern. After removing all association records related to Breast Neoplasms from the dataset, we train the model on the remaining data and predict miRNAs potentially associated with Breast Neoplasms. As depicted in Table 2, all predicted associations are validated by documented evidence in PubMed.

Table 2. The results of the case study.

num	miRNA	evidence (PMID)	num	miRNA	evidence (PMID)
1	hsa-mir-150	36340453, 35683791	6	hsa-mir-99a	33177704, 33050096
2	hsa-mir-142	36443711, 35014077	7	hsa-mir-378a	26255816, 25268374
3	hsa-mir-15b	33519190, 32175269	8	hsa-mir-130a	35797350, 35409043
4	hsa-mir-106a	34837907, 33686957	9	hsa-mir-212	33187481, 30594253
5	hsa-mir-192	31485620, 30844143	10	hsa-mir-196b	30416655, 25451164

4   Conclusion and Future Work

In this paper, we propose a new miRNA-disease association prediction model LGFMDA, which utilizes the graph transformer feature extractor with degree scaler and node adaptive feature encoder to learn the global and local feature of miRNA and disease nodes for calculating the association probabilities. The comparison experiments with baseline methods and ablation experiments have demonstrated the superiority of LGFMDA. Case study also validate the practical application value of our model.

There are two interesting directions to continue exploring. Firstly, the addition of other biological entities (e.g. lncRNAs, proteins) associated with miRNAs, diseases, can provide more information. In addition, the meta-paths which are set based on biological characteristics contain rich semantic information. So the application of multiple meta-paths will be one of the goals of our future research.

Acknowledgements. This work was supported by the Natural Science Foundation of China (No. 62366052), the Natural Science Foundation of Xinjiang Uygur Autonomous Region (No. 2024D01C126, 2022D01C427), the Key R&D Program of Xinjiang Uygur Autonomous Region (No. 2022B03023, 2022B01046) and the Sichuan Province Joint Fund of China (No. 25QYCX0103).

References

1. Quah, S., Subramanian, G., Tan, J.S., Utami, K.H., Sampath, P.: Micrornas: a symphony orchestrating evolution and disease dynamics. Trends Mol. Med. (2024)
2. Huang, Z., et al.: Hmdd v3. 0: a database for experimentally supported human microrna–disease associations. Nucleic Acids Res. **47**(D1), D1013–D1017 (2019)
3. Kozomara, A., Birgaoanu, M., Griffiths-Jones, S.: mirbase: from microrna sequences to function. Nucleic Acids Res. **47**(D1), D155–D162 (2019)
4. Chen, X., Xie, D., Zhao, Q., You, Z.-H.: Micrornas and complex diseases: from experimental results to computational models. Brief. Bioinform. **20**(2), 515–539 (2019)
5. Jiang, Q., et al.: Prioritization of disease micrornas through a human phenome-micrornaome network. BMC Syst. Biol. **4**, 1–9 (2010)

6. Chen, X., et al.: Wbsmda: within and between score for mirna-disease association prediction. Sci. Rep. **6**(1), 21106 (2016)

7. Chen, X., Qiao-Feng, W., Yan, G.-Y.: Rknnmda: ranking-based knn for mirna-disease association prediction. RNA Biol. **14**(7), 952–962 (2017)

8. Dai, Q., et al.: Mda-cf: predicting mirna-disease associations based on a cascade forest model by fusing multi-source information. Comput. Biol. Med. **136**, 104706 (2021)

9. Ding, Y., Lei, X., Liao, B., Wu, F.X.: Mlrdfm: a multi-view laplacian regularized deepfm model for predicting mirna-disease associations. Briefings Bioinf. **23**(3), bbac079 (2022)

10. Zhong, T., Li, Z., You, Z.H., Nie, R., Zhao, H.: Predicting mirna–disease associations based on graph random propagation network and attention network. Briefings Bioinf. **23**(2), bbab589 (2022)

11. Dong, B., Sun, W., Dali, X., Wang, G., Zhang, T.: Mdformer: a transformer-based method for predicting mirna-disease associations using multi-source feature fusion and maximal meta-path instances encoding. Comput. Biol. Med. **167**, 107585 (2023)

12. Sheng, N., Xie, X., Wang, Y., Huang, L., Zhang, S., Gao, L., Wang, H.: A survey of deep learning for detecting mirna-disease associations: databases, computational methods, challenges, and future directions. IEEE/ACM Trans. Comput. Biol. Bioinf. (2024)

13. Li, Z.W., Wang, Q.K., Yuan, C.A., Han, P.Y., You, Z.H., Wang, L.: Predicting mirna-disease associations by graph representation learning based on jumping knowledge networks. IEEE/ACM Trans. Comput. Biol. Bioinf. (2022)

14. Bi, X., Jiang, C., Yan, C., Zhao, K., Zhang, L., Wang, J.: Esgc-mda: Identifying mirna-disease associations using enhanced simple graph convolutional networks. IEEE/ACM Trans. Comput. Biol. Bioinf. (2024)

15. Zhao, H., Li, Z., You, Z.H., Nie, R., Zhong, T.: Predicting mirna-disease associations based on neighbor selection graph attention networks. IEEE/ACM Trans. Comput. Biol. Bioinf. **20**(2), 1298–1307 (2022)

16. Wu, F., Souza, A., Zhang, T., Fifty, C., Yu, T., Weinberger, K.: Simplifying graph convolutional networks. In: International Conference on Machine Learning, pp. 6861–6871. PMLR (2019)

17. Zhang, W., et al.: Node dependent local smoothing for scalable graph learning. Adv. Neural. Inf. Process. Syst. **34**, 20321–20332 (2021)

18. Zhao, B.W., Su, X.R., Hu, P.W., Huang, Y.A., You, Z.H., Hu, L.: igrldti: an improved graph representation learning method for predicting drug–target interactions over heterogeneous biological information network. Bioinformatics **39**(8), btad451 (2023)

19. Ma, L., et al.: Graph inductive biases in transformers without message passing. In: International Conference on Machine Learning, pp. 23321–23337. PMLR (2023)

20. Liu, D., Huang, Y., Nie, W., Zhang, J., Deng, L.: Smalf: mirna-disease associations prediction based on stacked autoencoder and xgboost. BMC Bioinf. **22**(1), 219 (2021)

21. Hua, H., et al.: Adaptive deep propagation graph neural network for predicting mirna-disease associations. Brief. Funct. Genomics **22**(5), 453–462 (2023)

TSCF-Net: A Temporal-Spectral Cross-Fusion Network for Low-Channel EEG Motor Imagery Classification

Yang Jiao[2,3], Mingzhe Cui[1], Tao Chen[1(✉)], Ruibin Bai[3], and Yi Pan[2]

[1] State Key Laboratory of Industrial Control Technology, Zhejiang University, Hangzhou, China
chentao227722@163.com
[2] Faculty of Computer Science and Control Engineering, Shenzhen University of Advanced Technology, Shenzhen, China
[3] Ningbo Digital Port Technologies Key Lab, University of Nottingham Ningbo China, Ningbo, China

Abstract. The miniaturization of EEG devices is essential for the development of consumer-grade brain-computer interface technology. However, low-channel EEG signals exacerbate the inherent disadvantages of low signal-to-noise ratio and low spatial resolution, making the decoding of neural activity even more challenging. To overcome these limitations, we propose an advanced multi-model fusion network that combines temporal-spatial and spectral-spatial features, referred to as the temporal-spectral cross-fusion network (TSCF-Net). This novel architecture consists of two parallel models, i.e., the spectral-spatial model and the temporal-spatial model. In the spectral-spatial model, the one-dimensional EEG time series is first transformed into a two-dimensional time-frequency representation to reveal its intrinsic time-varying characteristics. The time-frequency representation is then extended into the depth dimension to capture the spatial characteristics. On the other hand, the temporal-spatial model directly applies the one-dimensional EEG time series as input, and similarly extends it into the depth dimension to extract spatiotemporal features. To constrain the distribution of these features, a maximum mean discrepancy loss is introduced for feature fusion during the training. Finally, a weighted fusion method is employed to integrate these features. Experimental results based on the BCI Competition IV 2a and IV 2b datasets demonstrate that the TSCF-Net outperforms other baseline methods in low-channel EEG decoding tasks, achieving the highest average accuracy and kappa across all datasets. Additionally, a series of ablation experiments further confirm the effectiveness of the multimodal fusion structure.

Keywords: Motor image · Time-frequency analysis · low-channel EEG · Attention Mechanism

---

Y. Jiao and M. Cui—The first two authors contribute equally to this work.

1   Introduction

Electroencephalogram (EEG) is a non-invasive neuroimaging technique that can capture the electrophysiological activity of cortical neurons with millisecond temporal resolution [3] [23]. Compared with other neuroimaging techniques, EEG has higher temporal resolution and relatively lower cost [11]. This makes it one of the core technologies in clinical Brain-Computer Interfaces (BCI) systems [24] [19]. In recent years, motor imagery (MI) tasks based on EEG, as a common experimental paradigm, have attracted increasing attention [15]. Motor imagery tasks refer to the process in which subjects activate the sensorimotor cortex by mentally simulating specific movements without actual limb movement. Studies have shown that motor imagery can induce neural activity patterns similar to those of real movements, mainly manifested as event-related desynchronization or event-related synchronization (ERS) of the sensorimotor rhythm. This endogenous neural marker provides a physiological basis for decoding movement intentions.

Although EEG technology has significant advantages, its signal quality is susceptible to interference from a variety of factors. To achieve high-precision EEG signal acquisition, multi-channel EEG devices are applied for excellent signal fidelity through high-density electrode arrays (such as more than 64 channels). However, the device's large size and the discomfort of long-term wearing severely restrict their continuous application in healthy populations [4]. Thus, the miniaturization of EEG devices is essential for the development of consumer-grade brain-computer interface technology [12].

MI decoding, as a core technology for brain-computer interaction, is still mainly focused on feature optimization strategies under the full-channel configuration in current mainstream research, which is obviously in essential conflict with the realization of portable devices. However, low-channel EEG signals exacerbate the inherent disadvantages of low signal-to-noise ratio and low spatial resolution, making the decoding of motor imagery even more challenging. Thus, it is necessary to develop robust decoding models for low-channel EEG signals [10, 27].

2   Related Work

In recent years, researchers have proposed a variety of feature extraction and classification paradigms for EEG signal decoding. Early studies mainly focused on manually designed time-domain, frequency-domain, or time-frequency (TF) domain features, combined with shallow classifiers to achieve decoding. Common Spatial Pattern (CSP) [25] and its variants, e.g., Filter Bank CSP [1,2], extract spatial features related to brain activity by maximizing the variance ratio of different tasks. However, traditional methods rely on prior knowledge to design features, are sensitive to noise, and have limited generalization ability across subjects. Moreover, the feature extraction capability of CSP-based methods is limited, thereby the CSP-based methods are greatly limited in low-channel EEG signal decoding.

With the development of deep learning technology, its powerful feature extraction ability can automatically extract effective features from EEG signals and then decode them directly [5,9]. These deep learning-based methods mainly fall into the following two categories:

(1) End-to-end network architecture with one-dimensional (1D) EEG time series signals as input. This framework involves directly inputting the time series EEG signals into the neural network for feature extraction and decoding. Schirrmeister et al. [21] presented a variety of architectures such as Shallow ConvNet, Deep ConvNet, and Hybrid ConvNet, all of which achieved high accuracy in MI classification tasks. Similarly, EEGNet [14] is a concise convolutional architecture that is specifically tailored for EEG recognition tasks. Recently, Miao et al. [18] constructed a lightweight multi-dimensional attention network (LMDA-Net) that incorporates channel attention modules and deep attention modules, thereby augmenting the robustness of the model's performance. Besides, a novel architecture called parallel multi-scale attention network (PMSA-net) is proposed by Cui et al. [6]. PMSA-net introduces the parallel structure and channel attention mechanism to enhance the accuracy and robustness of EEG signal classification.
(2) "Signal-to-Image" transformation strategy: In this strategy, 1D EEG time series are converted into two-dimensional (2D) TF representations before being input into neural networks. Khare et al. [13] achieved great progress in emotion recognition tasks by combining pseudo Wigner-Ville distribution with pre-trained CNN models; Similarly, Madhavan et al. [16] introduced the synchrosqueezing transform technique to obtain 2D TF representations with high energy concentration from 1D EEG signals. With these energy-centralized TF representations, the subsequent deep CNN showed great performance in epilepsy focus detection.

However, almost all of these methods only consider full-channel EEG signals and will have a significant decrease in performance with low-channel EEG signals. Inspired by the time-space-frequency feature fusion framework (TSFF-Net) proposed by Miao et al. [17], we developed an advanced multi-model fusion network that combines temporal-spatial and spectral-spatial features, referred to as the temporal-spectral cross-fusion network (TSCF-Net). The major contributions of this paper can be summarized as follows:

(1) This multi-model fusion architecture consists of two parallel models, i.e., the spectral-spatial model and the temporal-spatial model. The introduction of the spectral-spatial model enhances the feature extraction capability of the network for low-channel EEG signals
(2) To address the lack of spatial information in spectral features, we introduce a depth dimension through 2D transpose convolution when decoding TF representations, thereby extracting spectral-spatial features effectively.
(3) To constrain the distribution of the spectral-spatial and temporal-spatial features, a maximum mean discrepancy loss [8] is introduced for feature fusion during the training.

3 The Architecture of TSCF-Net

3.1 Overall Architecture of TSCF-Net

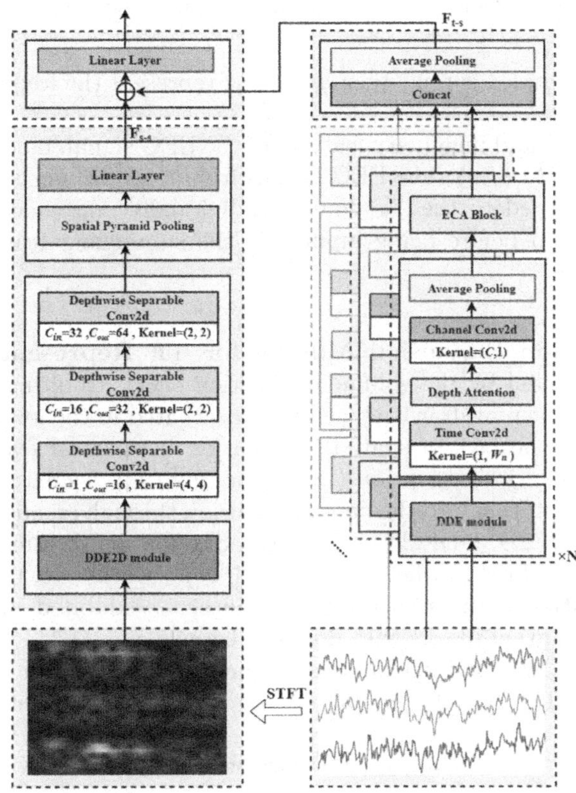

Fig. 1. Architecture of TSCF-Net.

As illustrated in Fig. 1, the proposed TSCF-Net is a multi-model fusion architecture consisting of two parallel models, i.e., the spectral-spatial model (left side) and the temporal-spatial model (right side). These two parallel models extract the spectral-spatial and the temporal-spatial features from 1D EEG time series and 2D TFRs, respectively. Finally, the outputs of multiple models are fused using a simple linear layer to obtain the decoding results. Note that only three channels C3, Cz, and C4, which highly correlated with motor imagery, are considered in this article.

3.2 Spectral-Spatial Model

Time-Frequency Representation. Each channel 1D EEG time series is transformed into the corresponding 2D TF representations by the short-time Fourier transform (STFT). Denote by $L_1(\mathbb{R})$ the space of integrable functions. Let x_i be the ith channel 1D EEG time series in $L_1(\mathbb{R})$. Giving a window g, the STFT of x_i is defined by:

$$STFT^g_{x_i}(f,t) = \int_{\mathbb{R}} x_i(\tau)g^*(\tau - t)e^{-i2\pi\xi(\tau-t)}d\tau \tag{1}$$

where g^* is the complex conjugate of g, f and t represent the frequency and time index.

To fuse the real and imaginary features of the EEG signal, modulus operation is applied to $STFT^g_{x_i}(f,t)$. The EEG signals from three channels, i.e., x_{C3}, x_{C4}, and x_{Cz}, are mapped to the TF domain individually and concatenated along the width direction before being input into the subsequent feature extraction module.

Depth Dimension Expansion Module for TF Representations. EEG acquisition is affected by the volume conduction effect, resulting in low spatial resolution. This inherent drawback will be exacerbated in the low-channel cases. Thus, to address the lack of spatial information in spectral features, inspired by the depth dimension expansion (DDE) module in [], we extended the time-frequency representation into the depth dimension through an advanced module, referred to as DDE2D. DDE2D module introduces a depth dimension through 2D transpose convolutions when decoding TF representations, thereby extracting spectral-spatial features effectively. Besides, as exhibited in Fig. 2, three transposed convolution blocks with different kernels, i.e., (1,1), (3,3), and (5,5), are integrated in the DDE2D module to further enhance the spectral-spatial characteristics. The DDE2D module can be represented by the following formula:

$$\mathbf{F}_{\text{DDE2D}} = \text{TransCov}\,2\text{D}_k(\mathbf{F}) \tag{2}$$

where k is the convolution kernel, while $\mathbf{F}_{\text{DDE2D}}$ refers to the output of DDE2D module.

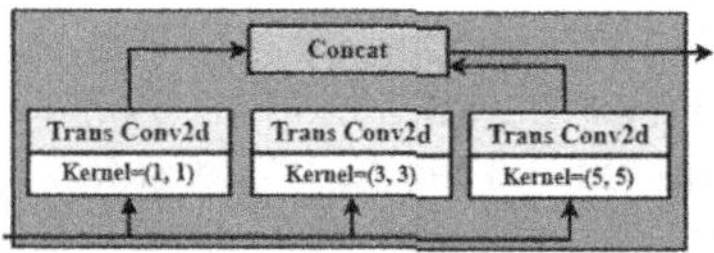

Fig. 2. Diagram of DDE2D module

Spectral-Spatial Feature Extraction. As displayed in the left side of Fig. 1, three cascaded 2D convolution blocks with different kernel sizes are applied after the DDE2D module to extract the spectral-spatial features. To reduce the number of parameters in the spectral-spatial model, these three 2D convolution blocks all adopt depthwise separable convolution. Besides, spatial pyramid pooling is also embedded subsequently to pool the spectral-spatial feature at different scales. The spatial pyramid pooling technique further enhances the spectral-spatial features and achieves the information integration of muti-scales. Finally, a linear layer is applied before the spectral-spatial features output the spectral-spatial model, ensuring that the dimensionality of the features output from the spectral-spatial and temporal-spatial models are matched for subsequent feature fusion (Fig. 3).

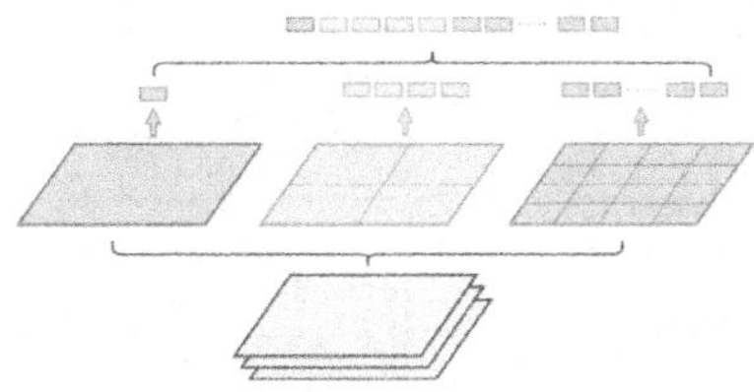

Fig. 3. Diagram of spatial pyramid pooling

3.3   Temporal-Spatial Model

The temporal-spatial model in this paper, as exhibited in the right side of Fig. 1, is the same as the structure in PMSA-net [6]. PMSA-net adopts the parallel architecture while combining the channel attention mechanism and multi-scale technique to enhance the accuracy and robustness of EEG signal classification. The temporal-spatial model consists of three branches that share an identical structure. The features extracted by these three branches are then concated and input into the average pooling.

The detailed structure of the temporal-spatial model is displayed in Fig. 4, consisting of three parts: DDE module, enhanced multi-scale (EMS) module, and efficient channel attention (ECA) block. Firstly, the DDE module expands the 1D EEG time series into depth dimensional space to capture the spatial information from EEG comprehensively. The subsequent EMS Module consists of four components, i.e., the time convolution block, depth attention block, channel convolution block, and average pooling. To capture more temporal and spatial features, the kernel size of the time convolution block was adjusted in each branch, i.e., 75, 125, and 250. The depth attention block aggregated and filtered the dimensional data to enhance the interaction of high-dimensional features across different dimensions. The spatial convolutional block primarily focused on learning the interactions between different channels. Finally, an ECA block was integrated into the model to rescale the temporal-spatial features selectively.

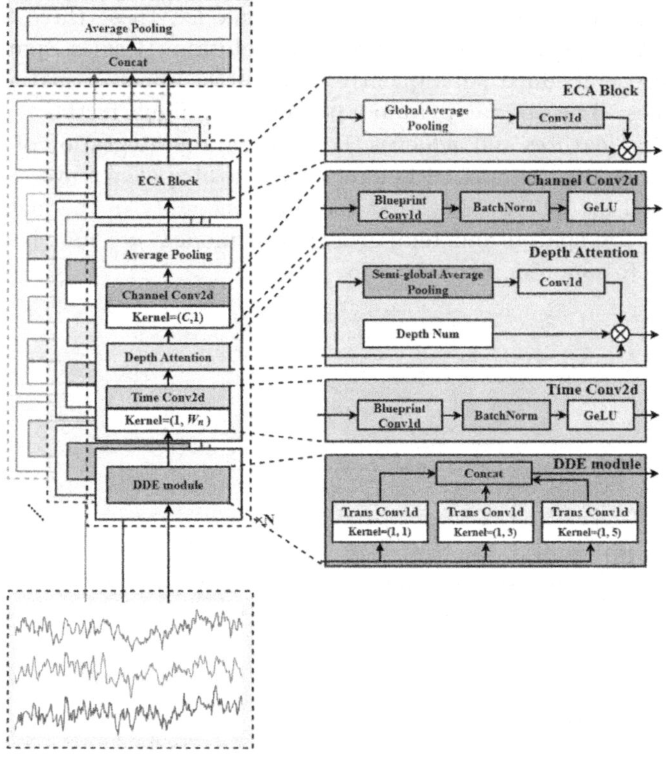

Fig. 4. The detail structure of the temporal-spatial model

3.4 Feature Fusion and Classification

To constrain the distribution of the spectral-spatial and temporal-spatial features, an MMD loss [8] is introduced for feature fusion during the training. The combination of MMD loss and feature-weighted fusion ensures that multi-modal features are integrated effectively, thereby eliminating the limitations of single-modal architecture.

As shown in Fig. 1, Denote $\mathbf{F}_{s-s}$ and $\mathbf{F}_{t-s}$ to be the output from spectral-spatial and temporal-spatial models, respectively. To match the range of $\mathbf{F}_{s-s}$ and $\mathbf{F}_{t-s}$, these two outputs are normalized by the softmax function. With the normalized $\mathbf{F}_{s-s}$ and $\mathbf{F}_{t-s}$, MMD loss can be defined as:

$$Loss_{MMD} \triangleq \|\mathbf{E}_p[\phi(\mathbf{F}_{s-s})] - \mathbf{E}_q[\phi(\mathbf{F}_{t-s})]\|_{\mathcal{H}_k}^2 \tag{3}$$

where, p and q represent the probability distributions of $\mathbf{F}_{s-s}$ and $\mathbf{F}_{t-s}$, respectively. $\mathbf{E}_p$ and $\mathbf{E}_q$ refer to the mean embeddings of probability distributions p and q. $\phi(\cdot)$ denotes the kernel function, while $\mathcal{H}_k$ indicates that the mean difference between the two feature distributions should be constrained within a unit ball in the Reproducing Kernel Hilbert Space [20].

On the other hand, as exhibited in Fig. 1, the output of two models, i.e., $\mathbf{F}_{s-s}$ and $\mathbf{F}_{t-s}$, are performed weighted averaging before input the linear layer. Then the output of the linear layer is classified using cross entropy Loss [22]. Finally, combining the cross entropy loss $Loss_{CE}$ with the MMD loss $Loss_{MMD}$, the total loss function during training is defined as:

$$Loss_{total} = Loss_{CE} + \lambda Loss_{MMD} \tag{4}$$

where λ represents the weight of MMD loss.

4   Experiments

4.1   Datasets

BCI Competition IV Dataset IIA (BCI4-2A). The BCI4-2A dataset encompasses EEG recordings derived from nine healthy subjects (labeled A01-A09) across two experimental sessions, utilizing a 10âĂŞ20 system with 22 channels and a sampling rate of 250 Hz. These subjects engaged in four distinct motor imagery tasks, which involved envisioning the movement of the left hand, right hand, both feet and tongue. The data from the initial session were harnessed for training purposes, whereas the data from the subsequent session were employed for testing. Note that only three channels C3, Cz, and C4, which are highly correlated with motor imagery, are selected for analysis in this paper.

BCI Competition IV Dataset IIB (BCI4-2B). The BCI4-2B dataset comprises EEG data obtained from three electrode channels (C3, Cz, and C4) at a sampling rate of 250 Hz from nine healthy subjects (labeled B01âĂŞB09) across five separate acquisition sessions. Each subject executed two motor imagery tasks, which entailed imagining the movement of the left and right hands. Data from the first three sessions were utilized for training, while data from the final two sessions were used for testing.

4.2   Data Pre-processing

Without introducing additional prior knowledge, we preprocess the raw EEG signals using only a few steps. Firstly, a bandpass filter is applied to the raw EEG signals, constraining the signal frequency range to 4–38 Hz. Then, trial normalization is applied to the raw data, calculated as follows: Without additional prior knowledge, the preprocessing of raw EEG signals is carried out through a few steps. Initially, a bandpass filter is applied to the raw EEG signals, effectively limiting the signal frequency range to 4–38 Hz. Subsequently, trial normalization is performed on the raw data. The acquisition of EEG data is fraught with inherent challenges, such as limited availability and high variability. As a result, EEG datasets often suffer from limited sample sizes, which can lead to overfitting and poor generalization of models. To address this issue, the augmentation of EEG signals is essential. According to [29], we have implemented a time-domain segmentation and reconstruction technique to generate new data. This method entails segmenting the training data of the same class into n parts and then randomly recombining them while preserving the original temporal data structure to produce augmented data.

4.3   Experiment Details

To optimize our model, the Adam algorithm was utilized, coupled with a learning rate that diminishes over time. To avoid experimental errors, all models underwent 300 epochs of training, with each batch comprising 32 samples. To augment model regularization, the dropout methodology [7] was implemented, with the dropout rate set to 0.5. The overall performance was evaluated by classification accuracy, i.e., $\frac{TP+TN}{TP+FN+FP+TN}$, and kappa, i.e. $\frac{P_o-P_e}{1-P_e}$.

4.4   Experiment Results

As mentioned in 4.1, two public datasets, i.e., BCI4-2A and BCI4-2B, are considered to demonstrate the effectiveness and superiority of the proposed TSCF-Net. Several advanced MI classification models, i.e., EEGNet [14], ConvNet [21], Conformer [26], TMSA-Net [28], LMDA-Net [18], and TSFF-Net [17], are introduced as comparisons.

The 4-class classification accuracy and kappa on BCI4-2A are exhibited in Table 1. The displayed results include the model's performance on each subject and the average. Although TSCF-Net did not achieve optimal performance on all subjects, its superiority and robustness can be demonstrated by the highest average accuracy and kappa. We further demonstrate the superior performance of TSCF-Net on BCI4-2B. With this 3-channel binary classification task, the proposed TSCF-Net achieves definite superiority in most subjects. Similar to BCI4-2A, TSCF-Net still maintains the highest average accuracy and kappa, implying its superior performance and robustness (Table 2).

Table 1. Classification accuracy (%) and kappa of different methods on BCI4-2A.

Model	A01	A02	A03	A04	A05	A06	A07	A08	A09	Mean	Kappa
EEGNet	**74.3**	52.1	86.4	48.2	60.7	45.4	65.9	60.4	66.6	62.2	0.496
ConvNet	71.1	47.9	81.2	**52.7**	58.3	47.5	75.0	68.0	66.3	63.1	0.508
Conformer	72.5	49.3	**86.8**	48.2	**64.5**	46.5	68.7	65.9	64.2	63.0	0.506
TMSA-Net	73.2	**53.1**	83.6	54.8	49.6	49.6	**77.0**	66.6	66.6	63.8	0.517
LMDA-Net	71.2	51.0	85.7	53.1	53.1	53.4	68.0	64.9	68.0	63.2	0.509
TSFF-Net	73.6	50.3	84.0	51.0	52.1	52	72.9	63.8	71.1	63.4	0.512
Our model	**74.3**	49.3	86.1	47.2	56.6	**55.9**	70.8	**71.8**	**74.6**	**65.2**	**0.536**

Table 2. Classification accuracy (%) and kappa of different methods on BCI4-2B.

Model	A01	A02	A03	A04	A05	A06	A07	A08	A09	Mean	Kappa
EEGNet	79.1	57.9	**69.6**	98.1	94.7	87.5	84.4	92.8	91.9	83.9	0.680
ConvNet	80.6	54.6	55.3	97.8	92.2	87.5	81.8	90.3	86.9	80.8	0.616
Conformer	80.9	58.6	57.2	97.2	94.1	89.4	85.3	93.1	90.6	82.9	0.659
TMSA-Net	80.6	56.1	55.3	**98.1**	92.8	87.5	81.8	90.3	86.9	81.1	0.621
LMDA-Net	80.6	**61.4**	68.4	**98.1**	94.6	85.6	84.0	92.8	91.5	84.1	0.682
TSFF-Net	81.2	**61.4**	68.7	98.0	**95.3**	87.5	83.4	**93.7**	90.9	84.5	0.689
Our model	**83.1**	60.3	67.1	**98.1**	**95.3**	**90.9**	**85.3**	92.8	**92.2**	**85.0**	**0.700**

4.5   Ablation Study

In this section, ablation experiments have been conducted on BCI4-2A to validate the effectiveness of the three significant improvements in this paper, i.e., the strategy of combining the temporal-spectral model with the spectral-spatial model, the DDE2D module, and the spatial pyramid pooling. The results of the ablation experiments are shown in Fig. 5. Note that 'w/o spp' and 'w/o DDE2D' correspond to the models without the spatial pyramid pooling and the DDE2D module, respectively, while 'w/o time' denotes the spectral-spatial model only. In the vast majority of cases, TSCF-Net has an advantage in performance compared to other ablation models. Thus, these three modification in this paper exactly improve the classification accuracy and robustness of the model.

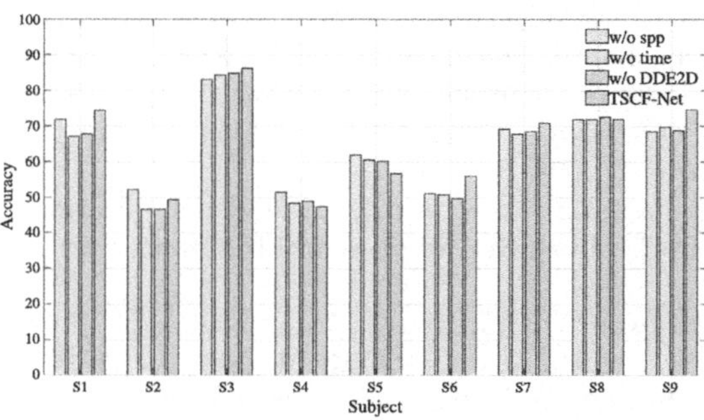

Fig. 5. Ablation study on the spatial pyramid pooling, DDE2D module and temporal-spatial model only

5   Conclusion

In this paper, we propose an advanced multi-model fusion network that combines temporal-spatial and spectral-spatial features, referred to as the temporal-spectral cross-fusion network (TSCF-Net). This multi-model fusion architecture combines the spectral-spatial model and the temporal-spatial model. In the spectral-spatial model, the EEG time series is first mapped into the TF domain to reveal its intrinsic TF characteristics. The TF representation is then extended into the depth dimension to capture the spatial characteristics. On the other hand, the temporal-spatial model directly applies the 1D EEG time series as input, and similarly extends it into the depth dimension to extract spatiotemporal features. Finally, a weighted fusion method is employed to integrate these features, thereby deriving effective multi-modal fused representations. A series of comparison and ablation experiments have been conducted to demonstrate the effectiveness of the proposed structure. Overall, TSCF-Net offers a promising performance for decoding low-channel EEG signals in MI tasks.

References

1. Ang, K.K., Chin, Z.Y., Wang, C., Guan, C., Zhang, H.: Filter bank common spatial pattern algorithm on bci competition iv datasets 2a and 2b. Front. Neurosci. **6**, 39 (2012)
2. Ang, K.K., Chin, Z.Y., Zhang, H., Guan, C.: Filter bank common spatial pattern (fbcsp) in brain-computer interface. In: 2008 IEEE International Joint Conference on Neural Networks (IEEE World Congress on Computational Intelligence), pp. 2390–2397. IEEE (2008)
3. Blinowska, K., Durka, P.: Electroencephalography (EEG). Wiley encyclopedia Biomed. Eng. **10**, 9780471740360 (2006)
4. Casson, A.J., Yates, D.C., Smith, S.J., Duncan, J.S., Rodriguez-Villegas, E.: Wearable electroencephalography. IEEE Eng. Med. Biol. Mag. **29**(3), 44–56 (2010)
5. Craik, A., He, Y., Contreras-Vidal, J.L.: Deep learning for electroencephalogram (EEG) classification tasks: a review. J. Neural Eng. **16**(3), 031001 (2019)
6. Cui, M., Chen, T., Jiao, Y., Zheng, Q., Pan, Y., Xie, L.: Pmsa-net: a parallel multi-scale attention network for mi-bci classification. In: Proceedings of the 15th ACM International Conference on Bioinformatics, Computational Biology and Health Informatics, pp. 1–6 (2024)
7. Gal, Y., Ghahramani, Z.: A theoretically grounded application of dropout in recurrent neural networks. In: Advances in Neural Information Processing Systems, vol. 29 (2016)
8. Gretton, A., Borgwardt, K.M., Rasch, M.J., Schölkopf, B., Smola, A.: A kernel two-sample test. J. Mach. Learn. Res. **13**(1), 723–773 (2012)
9. Hosseini, M.P., Hosseini, A., Ahi, K.: A review on machine learning for EEG signal processing in bioengineering. IEEE Rev. Biomed. Eng. **14**, 204–218 (2020)
10. Hu, X., Chen, J., Wang, F., Zhang, D.: Ten challenges for EEG-based affective computing. Brain Sci. Adv. **5**(1), 1–20 (2019)
11. Kannathal, N., Acharya, U.R., Lim, C.M., Sadasivan, P.: Characterization of EEGg–a comparative study. Comput. Methods Programs Biomed. **80**(1), 17–23 (2005)
12. Kaongoen, N., et al.: The future of wearable EEG: a review of ear-EEG technology and its applications. J. Neural Eng. **20**(5), 051002 (2023)
13. Khare, S.K., Bajaj, V.: Time-frequency representation and convolutional neural network-based emotion recognition. IEEE Trans. Neural Netw. Learn. Syst. **32**(7), 2901–2909 (2020)

14. Lawhern, V.J., Solon, A.J., Waytowich, N.R., Gordon, S.M., Hung, C.P., Lance, B.J.: Eegnet: a compact convolutional neural network for EEG-based brain-computer interfaces. J. Neural Eng. **15**(5), 056013 (2018)

15. Lotze, M., Halsband, U.: Motor imagery. J. Physiol.-Paris **99**(4–6), 386–395 (2006)

16. Madhavan, S., Tripathy, R.K., Pachori, R.B.: Time-frequency domain deep convolutional neural network for the classification of focal and non-focal eeg signals. IEEE Sens. J. **20**(6), 3078–3086 (2019)

17. Miao, Z., Zhao, M.: Time-space-frequency feature fusion for 3-channel motor imagery classification. Biomed. Signal Process. Control **90**, 105867 (2024)

18. Miao, Z., Zhao, M., Zhang, X., Ming, D.: Lmda-net: A lightweight multi-dimensional attention network for general EEG-based brain-computer interfaces and interpretability. Neuroimage **276**, 120209 (2023)

19. Nicolas-Alonso, L.F., Gomez-Gil, J.: Brain computer interfaces, a review. Sensors **12**(2), 1211–1279 (2012)

20. Rosipal, R., Trejo, L.J.: Kernel partial least squares regression in reproducing kernel hilbert space. J. Mach. Learn. Res. **2**(Dec), 97–123 (2001)

21. Schirrmeister, R.T., Springenberg, J.T., Fiederer, L., Glasstetter, M., Eggensperger, K., Tangermann, M., Hutter, F., Burgard, W., Ball, T.: Deep learning with convolutional neural networks for EEG decoding and visualization. Hum. Brain Mapp. **38**(11), 5391–5420 (2017)

22. Shannon, C.E.: A mathematical theory of communication. ACM SIGMOBILE Mobile Comput. Commun. Rev. **5**(1), 3–55 (2001)

23. Teplan, M., et al.: Fundamentals of EEG measurement. Measure. Sci. Rev. **2**(2), 1–11 (2002)

24. Vallabhaneni, A., Wang, T., He, B.: Brain—computer interface. In: Neural Engineering, pp. 85–121. Springer (2005)

25. Wang, Y., Gao, S., Gao, X.: Common spatial pattern method for channel selelction in motor imagery based brain-computer interface. In: 2005 IEEE Engineering in Medicine and Biology 27th Annual Conference, pp. 5392–5395. IEEE (2006)

26. Xie, J., Zhang, J., Sun, J., Ma, Z., Qin, L., Li, G., Zhou, H., Zhan, Y.: A transformer-based approach combining deep learning network and spatial-temporal information for raw EEG classification. IEEE Trans. Neural Syst. Rehabil. Eng. **30**, 2126–2136 (2022)

27. Zhang, H., Zhao, X., Wu, Z., Sun, B., Li, T.: Motor imagery recognition with automatic EEG channel selection and deep learning. J. Neural Eng. **18**(1), 016004 (2021)

28. Zhao, Q., Zhu, W.: Tmsa-net: a novel attention mechanism for improved motor imagery EEG signal processing. Biomed. Signal Process. Control **102**, 107189 (2025)

29. Zheng, Q., Zhu, F., Heng, P.A.: Robust support matrix machine for single trial EEG classification. IEEE Trans. Neural Syst. Rehabil. Eng. **26**(3), 551–562 (2018)

HCM-Net: Hybrid CNN and Mamba Network with Multi-scale Awareness Feature Fusion for Lung Cancer Pathological Complete Response Prediction

Jiancun Zhou, Hulin Kuang[✉], and Jianxin Wang

College of Information and Electronic Engineering, Hunan City University, Yiyang, Hunan, China
hulinkuang@csu.edu.cn

Abstract. Accurate prediction of pathological complete response (pCR) is useful for clinical precision treatment of lung cancer. Computed tomograph (CT) imaging is widely used for predicting pCR in lung cancer due to its rapid acquisition and ease of use. However, existing classification methods for pCR prediction are primarily limited to either convolutional neural networks (CNNs) or Transformer architectures, which can not capture effective global information or have relatively low computational efficiency. Therefore, this study proposes a novel CNN and Mamba hybrid network with multi-scale awareness module to achieve accurate pCR prediction on CT scans of lung cancer patients. In each stage of the proposed hybrid CNN-Mamba encoder, we first employ channel splitting to significantly reduce the number of parameters, and utilize the designed CNN branch and Mamba branch to extract effective local and global features. Specifically, in the Mamba branch, we propose a novel intra-slice and inter-slice scanning mechanism to implement 8-way 3D scanning to replace the original 2D scanning mechanism, thereby substantially enhancing the model's ability to capture global information in 3D images. Furthermore, to better fuse CNN and Mamba features, we design a novel multiscale awareness feature fusion module with channel-level and multi-scale spatial level fusion. The proposed method is evaluated on a private dataset that includes CT scans of 108 lung cancer patients who undergone neoadjuvant chemoimmunotherapy. Experimental results demonstrate that our proposed HCM-Net achieves the best accuracy of 83.33% and AUC of 84.08%, outperforming other state-of-the-art methods.

Keywords: Pathological complete response prediction · Lung Cancer · Hybrid CNN and Mamba · Multi-scale Awareness Feature Fusion

J. Tang et al. (Eds.): ISBRA 2025, LNBI 15757, pp. 38–48, 2026.
https://doi.org/10.1007/978-981-95-0695-8_4

1   Introduction

Lung cancer is one of the most common and deadly cancers worldwide. Neoadjuvant therapies, such as chemoimmunotherapy, can shrink tumors, improve surgical outcomes, and prolong survival [1]. Pathological complete response (pCR) is defined as the absence of viable cancer cells in resected tumor tissue. It is an important marker for assessing the effectiveness of neoadjuvant therapy and predicting prognosis [2]. Compared to non-pCR patients, pCR patients exhibit greater sensitivity to treatment and have higher survival rates. However, traditional pCR assessment depends largely on postoperative pathological analysis and imaging evaluations, which are invasive, time-consuming, and unsuitable for guiding personalized treatment decisions prior to surgery [2]. Computed tomography (CT) imaging offers valuable morphological, textural, and functional features that are useful for pCR prediction [3]. Therefore, designing a non-invasive and accurate pCR prediction of lung cancer patients based on CT scans before treatments is promising and is crucial for optimizing treatment strategies for lung cancer patients.

At present, there are many methods [3–5] based on Convolutional Neural Networks (CNN) to achieve accuracy pCR prediction. Although CNNs can efficiently capture local texture information in CT scans through local receptive fields and weight-sharing mechanisms, they are limited by their architectures and cannot effectively model the global dependencies required for pCR prediction. The Transformer architecture can effectively model global dependencies for pCR prediction but has a quadratic computational complexity, which significantly increases the demand for computational resources [1].

Recently, Mamba based on the Selective State Space Model (SSM) has been developed and it can achieve linear computational complexity while maintain the ability to capture global interactions [6]. Although Mamba exhibits notable advantages, its native 1D sequential scanning mechanism fails to effectively capture spatial information in medical images. To address this limitation, existing studies [7,8] divided images into patches and employed row- and column-prior scanning to model 2D spatial relationships. However, directly applying such 2D methods to 3D CT volumes overlooks inter-slice dependencies. To mitigate this, [9,10] introduced inter-slice scanning mechanisms based on 2D approaches. However, these methods yield incomplete feature representation [9], or may introduce unnecessary computational overhead [10]. Therefore, it is necessary to explore appropriate 3D CT image scanning methods to model spatial information.

Solely using CNN or Mamba cannot effectively capture local and global features, which may negatively impact pCR prediction performance. Therefore, integrating CNN and Mamba is necessary. However, there are few studies on how to fusion the features of CNN and Mamba. To tackle the aforementioned challenges, this study proposes an innovative hybrid CNN-Mamba network augmented with a multi-scale awareness feature fusion module, to achieve precise lung cancer pathological complete response predictions using CT scans before treatments. The key contributions of this study can be summarized as follows:

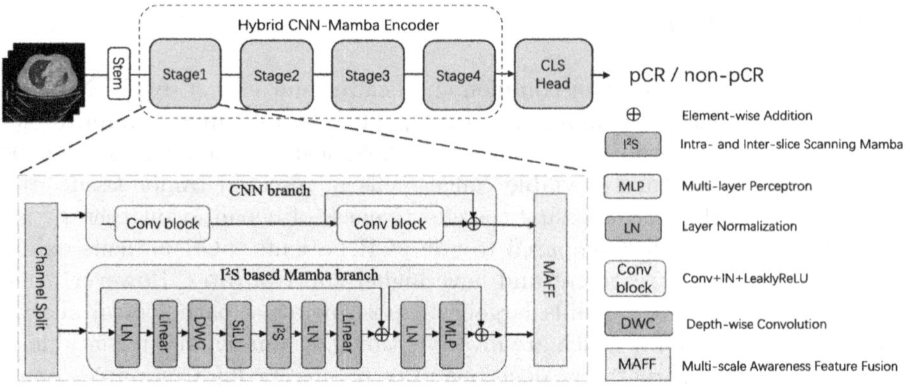

Fig. 1. Overview of our proposed HCM network.

- We develop a novel hybrid CNN-Mamba network with multi-scale awareness feature fusion, specifically tailored for lung cancer pathological complete response prediction. To our knowledge, this study is the first attempt to effectively combine CNN and Mamba for this prognostic task.
- We propose an intra-slice and inter-slice scanning mechanism that effectively models the 3D spatial information in medical images while retaining the powerful global modeling capabilities of the Mamba architecture.
- We design a multi-scale awareness feature fusion module that facilitates the effective integration of CNN and Mamba features, thereby enhancing the model's predictive performance.

2   Methodology

2.1   Overview Architecture of the Proposed Method

The architecture of the proposed parallel CNN and Mamba hybrid network is depicted in Fig. 1. It consists of a convolutional stem, a hybrid CNN-Mamba encoder including four hybrid stages, and a classification head. The convolutional stem consists of two $3 \times 3 \times 3$ CNN layers, which are designed to extract low-level features from the input images. The hybrid CNN-Mamba encoder consists of the channel split operation for computational complexity reduction, the parallel CNN and intra-slice and inter-slice scanning mechanism (I^2S) based Mamba branches, and a multi-scale awareness feature fusion (MAFF) module. The CNN branch captures local features, while the I^2S Mamba branch is responsible for modeling global features. the Mamba model is based on our proposed novel intra-slice and inter-slice 3D scanning mechanism to better capture global 3D CT scan features. The MAFF module is placed between adjacent stages to effectively fuse the features from the CNN and Mamba branches. The classification head is used to obtain the final pCR prediction.

2.2   CNN Branch

As shown in Fig. 1, at the beginning of each stage, the input features are split into two parts (each part has a half of the channel numbers) at the channel level and fed into the CNN and Mamba branches, respectively, to reduce the model's parameter count.

In the CNN branch, we use two stacked convolutional blocks. Each convolutional block consists of a convolutional layer, instance normalization, and a nonlinear activation function LeakyRelu. The first block performs initial convolution on the input features, while the second block reuses the features from the previous block through a residual structure to enhance the model's robustness.

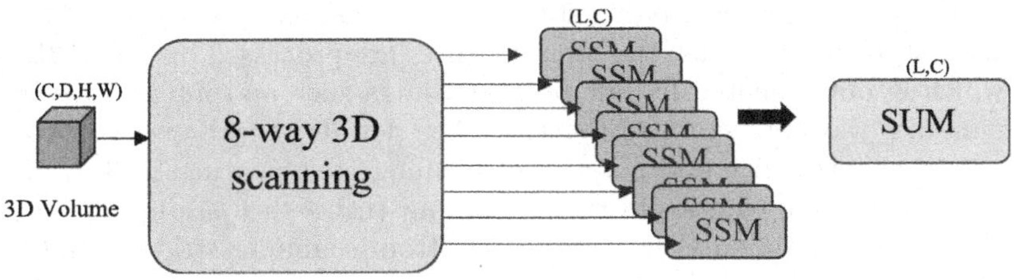

Fig. 2. The overall structure of the I^2S based state space model. The 8-way 3D scanning is implemented by the proposed intra-slice and inter-slice scanning (I^2S).

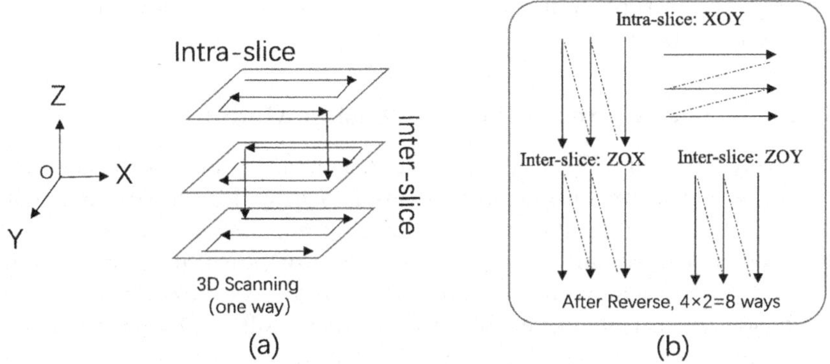

Fig. 3. The details of the 8-way 3D scanning.

2.3 I^2S Based Mamba Branch

Overall Structure of the Mamba Branch. The I^2S based Mamba branch comprising a token mixer and a channel mixer, as shown in Fig. 1. In the token mixer, the input features are first processed by LayerNorm, a Linear layer, Depth-wise convolution, and the SiLU activation function. Subsequently, the features undergo spatial information extraction through the state space model based on I^2S. The Channel mixer is the same as the Transformer, comprising a LayerNorm layer and a Linear layer.

I^2S **Based State Space Model.** Since Mamba was originally designed for sequence modeling, directly using its native scanning approach may lead to the loss of spatial structural information in CT images. To address this challenge, we propose the I^2S mechanism-based state space model, as shown in Fig. 2). In the I^2S based state space model, the input features are processed by 8-way 3D scanning which is implemented by our proposed intra-slice and inter-slice scanning and then all 8 ways are summed together. The details of each one-way 3D scanning based on intra-slice and inter-slice scanning is shown in Fig. 3(a). Within each slice, a top-left to bottom-right scanning (intra-slice scanning) approach is applied, while between slices, a top-to-bottom scanning strategy (inter-slice scanning) is used. Each 3D scan has 3 planes (i.e., axial, sagittal, and coronal planes, named X, Y, and Z axis, respectively). According to Fig. 3(b), we first perform 2 intra-slice scanning and 2 inter-slice scanning and after reversing the scanning direction, we finally achieve 8-way 3D scanning. Specifically, within a slice, scanning from the top-left corner to the bottom-right corner can follow either the Scan row-by-row or column-by-column approach. Between the slices, scanning from the top to the bottom, we can scan through the sagittal or coronal plane. Additionally, by reversing the scanning order(bottom-right to top-left, bottom to top), four more methods are derived, resulting in a total of eight scanning approaches.

2.4 Multi-scale Awareness Feature Fusion Module

To effectively integrate CNN and Mamba features, we propose a novel Multi-scale Awareness feature Fusion Module. As shown in Fig. 4, MAFF includes 4 key steps: 1) CNN and Mamba features are first concatenated and then preliminarily fused at the channel level using depth-wise convolution and point-wise convolution. 2) To achieve more comprehensive feature integration, we design a multi-head hybrid convolution block to extract multi-scale fused information from the spatial level. The preliminary fused features are first processed by a linear layer and then evenly divided into four subsets along the channel dimension. These subsets are subsequently convolved using kernels of sizes 3, 5, 7, and 9 to capture multi-scale information. 3)The multi-scale information is concatenated along the channel dimension and element-wisely multiplied with the preliminary fused features from another linear layer branch to emphasize critical features. 4) After passing through the multi-head hybrid convolution block, batch normalization, point-wise convolution, and channel-wise convolution are applied to extract more diverse features. Ultimately, element-wise addition and a final point-wise convolution are used to complete the fusion of CNN and Mamba features. The above process can be expressed using the following equations:

$$
\begin{aligned}
F_{ch} &= PW(DW(Concat(F_{CNN}, F_{Mamba})), \\
F_{sp_k} &= Conv_k(ChannelSplit(W_A \cdot F_{ch})), \\
F_{MHMC} &= PW((W_B \cdot F_{ch}) \otimes Concat(F_{sp_k})), \\
F_{fusion} &= PW(BN(F_{MHMC}) + DW(F_{MHMC}) + PW(F_{MHMC})),
\end{aligned}
\tag{1}
$$

where F_{CNN} and F_{Mamba} denote the features from the CNN and Mamba branches, respectively. $Conv_k$ represents a convolution with a kernel size of k, where k takes values of 3, 5, 7, and 9, and $\otimes$ denotes element-wise multiplication. W_A and W_B both represent the parameters of linear layers.

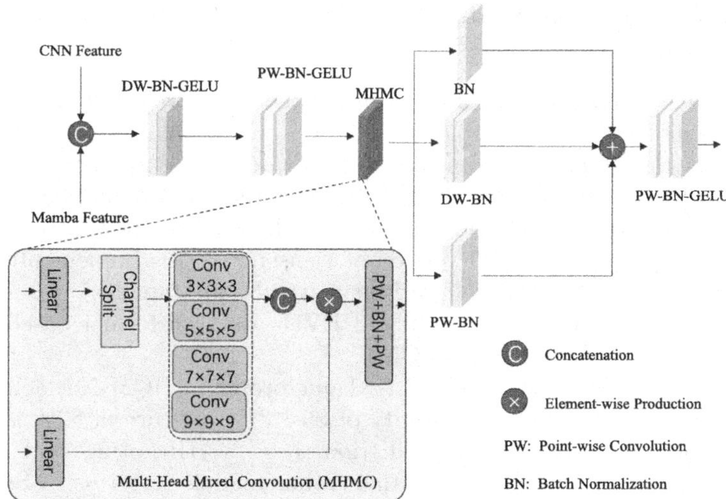

Fig. 4. Overview of our proposed Multi-scale awareness feature fusion module.

3   Experiments

3.1   Dataset

We collected a private dataset including 108 lung cancer patients from Hunan Cancer Hospital. Each patient has a CT scan obtained before eoadjuvant chemoimmunotherapy. The pCR labels were determined by two pathologists via checking pathological images.

3.2 Implementation Details and Evaluation Metrics

All experiments in this study are conducted using PyTorch on an NVIDIA RTX 3090 GPU with 24 GB of memory, running on an Ubuntu system. The proposed method and the comparison methods were trained using the Adam optimizer, with a batch size of 2 and 200 epochs. The initial learning rates were set to 0.0001 and adjusted using a polynomial learning rate schedule with a decay factor of 0.9. The data augmentation methods we performed included randomly flipping and rotating the images, brightness enhancement, and adding Gaussian noise.

The experiments employed five-fold cross-validation across the entire dataset. To quantitatively assess the pCR prediction performance, we utilized multiple metrics, including accuracy, sensitivity, specificity, F1-score, and the area under the curve (AUC).

4 Results

4.1 Comparison with State-of-the-Art Methods for Lung Cancer pCR Prediction

Table 1 shows a quantitative comparison between our proposed HCM-Net and 8 SOTA methods in the collected dataset. Given the limited code availability of 3D medical image classification methods, we adapt the 2D networks MedVit [11], RepVit [12], EVit [13], StartNet [14], UnirepLKNet [15], and FasterNet [16] into 3D versions strictly following the methodologies described in their original papers for comparison. The 3D version of Densenet [17] is implemented by the Monai Library[1]. Among the comparison methods, nnMamba [18] is the CNN and Mamba hybrid model, MediVit and EViT are transformer-based models, and the rest methods are based on CNN.

As shown in Table 1, we can find that our proposed HCM-Net achieves the highest Accuracy of 83.33%, Sensitivity of 89.13%, F1 Score of 82%, and AUC of 84.08% for lung cancer pCR prediction. It is worth noting that although our method performs slightly worse than other models in terms of Specificity, the Sensitivity metric is more critical for pCR prediction, as it helps prevent missed diagnoses of true pCR patients, ensuring they do not miss treatment opportunities. Besides, our model makes a trade-off between the Sensitivity and Specificity metrics (the highest AUC) and is it is promising for lung cancer pCR prediction.

4.2 Ablation Studies

Effectiveness of the CNN Branch. To verify the effectiveness of the CNN branch, we conduct an ablation study by removing the CNN branch. As shown in Table 2, the results indicate that removing the CNN branch leads to a 9.26% drop in Accuracy. Notably, the removal of the CNN branch led to a substantial

---

[1] https://monai.io/.

Table 1. Comparison to SOTA methods on the collected lung cancer dataset. The best metrics are in bold.

Methods	Accuracy(%)	Sensitivity(%)	Specificity(%)	F1 Score(%)	AUC(%)
nnMamba 2024 [18]	74.07	76.09	72.58	71.43	74.33
MedViT 2023 [11]	78.70	80.43	77.42	76.29	78.93
RepViT 2024 [12]	80.56	78.26	82.26	77.42	80.26
EViT 2025 [13]	79.63	67.39	<u>88.71</u>	73.81	78.05
StarNet 2024 [14]	80.56	<u>84.78</u>	77.42	<u>78.79</u>	<u>81.10</u>
Densenet 2017 [17]	70.37	69.57	70.97	66.67	70.27
UnirepLKNet 2024 [15]	79.63	80.43	79.03	77.08	79.73
FasterNet 2023 [16]	<u>81.48</u>	69.57	**90.32**	76.19	79.94
HCM-Net(Ours)	**83.33**	**89.13**	79.03	**82.00**	**84.08**

19.56% decrease in sensitivity, significantly decreasing the predictive accuracy of the model for patients with pCR. This finding demonstrates that the local features extracted by the CNN branch provide critical discriminative information for pCR prediction.

Effectiveness of the I^2S Based Mamba Branch. To validate the effectiveness of the proposed I^2S based Mamba branch, we conduct the following three experiments: (1) removing the proposed Mamba model, (2) replacing the Mamba model with a Transformer, and (3) substituting our designed I^2S scanning method with the original Mamba scanning method. As shown in Table 2, removing the Mamba model resulted in a 16.66% decrease in Accuracy, confirming that the proposed Mamba model effectively models CT image features. Replacing the Mamba model with a Transformer led to a 4.63% drop in Accuracy, indicating that our proposed Mamba model has a significant advantage over traditional Transformers in extracting CT image features. Lastly, substituting our proposed scanning method with the original Mamba scanning method caused a 4.63% decrease in Accuracy. This demonstrates the effectiveness of our proposed I^2S.

Effectiveness of Multi-scale Awareness Feature Fusion Module. To assess the effectiveness of the proposed MAFF module, we conduct two additional experiments: one by replacing the MAFF module with a simple concatenation operation and another by replacing it with cross-attention. As shown in Table 2, replacing the MAFF module with cross attention results in a 9.26% decrease in Accuracy, while replacing it with concat results in a 12.96% decrease in Accuracy. These results demonstrate that the proposed MAFF module obviously enhances pCR prediction performance, confirming its effectiveness.

Effectiveness of the Hybrid Network. To verify the effectiveness of the hybrid CNN and Mamba architecture, we conducted two ablation experiments: one using only the CNN branch and the other using only the Mamba branch. As

Table 2. Ablation studies on the lung cancer dataset. $\leftrightarrow$ stands for replacing one component with another. CA denotes cross-attention.

Methods	Accuracy(%)	Sensitivity(%)	Specificity(%)	F1 Score(%)	AUC(%)
w/o CNN	74.07	69.57	77.42	69.57	73.49
w/o Mamba	66.67	78.26	58.06	71.11	75.10
Mamba$\leftrightarrow$Transformer	78.70	80.43	77.42	76.28	78.92
$I^2S \leftrightarrow$ Mamba Original Scanning	78.70	88.24	69.35	78.50	80.33
MAFF$\leftrightarrow$CA	74.07	76.09	72.58	71.43	74.33
MAFF$\leftrightarrow$Concat	70.37	76.09	66.13	68.63	71.11
All Mamba Branches	71.30	80.43	64.52	70.48	72.48
All CNN Branches	75.93	88.24	64.52	76.36	77.91
HCM-Net(Ours)	**83.33**	**89.13**	**79.03**	**82.00**	**84.08**

shown in Table 2, using only Mamba resulted in a 12.03% decrease in accuracy, indicating that relying solely on Mamba to extract global dependencies is insufficient for effective pCR prediction. On the other hand, using only CNN led to a 7.4% decrease in accuracy. These results confirm the effectiveness of combining CNN and Mamba architectures.

5   Conclusion

This study introduces a novel hybrid network combining CNN and Mamba for predicting pCR in lung cancer using CT images. In each stage, we utilize both CNN blocks and the proposed I^2S-based Mamba blocks to process the local and global features of the images, aiming to extract more effective and comprehensive features. This parallel combination of CNN and Mamba allows us to leverage their respective strengths in modeling different aspects of the data, leading to improved feature representations. Furthermore, we propose a multi-scale awareness feature fusion module to effectively integrate the features from both CNN and Mamba branches. Experimental results show that the proposed HCM-Net delivers superior prediction performance, highlighting its potential for lung cancer prognosis.

Acknowledgments. This work was supported in part by the National Natural Science Foundation of China (No. U24A20256), the Science and Technology Major Project of Changsha (No. kh2402004), the Natural Science Foundation of Hunan Province (No. 2025JJ50374) and the Science and Technology Innovation Program of Hunan Province (No. 2022RC1031). This work was carried out in part using computing resources at the High-Performance Computing Center of Central South University.

References

1. Ye, G., et al.: Non-invasive multimodal ct deep learning biomarker to predict pathological complete response of non-small cell lung cancer following neoadjuvant immunochemotherapy: a multicenter study. J. Immunother. Cancer **12**(9), e009348 (2024)
2. Travis, W.D., et al. Iaslc multidisciplinary recommendations for pathologic assessment of lung cancer resection specimens after neoadjuvant therapy. J. Thoracic Oncol. **15**(5), 709–740 (2020)
3. Wendong, Q., et al.: Non-invasive prediction for pathologic complete response to neoadjuvant chemoimmunotherapy in lung cancer using ct-based deep learning: a multicenter study. Front. Immunol. **15**, 1327779 (2024)
4. She, Y., et al.: Deep learning for predicting major pathological response to neoadjuvant chemoimmunotherapy in non-small cell lung cancer: a multicentre study. EBioMedicine **86** (2022)
5. Caragliano, A.N., et al.: Doctor-in-the-loop: an explainable, multi-view deep learning framework for predicting pathological response in non-small cell lung cancer. *arXiv preprint* arXiv:2502.17503 (2025)
6. Gu, A., Dao, T.: Mamba: linear-time sequence modeling with selective state spaces. *arXiv preprint* arXiv:2312.00752 (2023)
7. Li, G., Huang, Q., Wang, W., Liu, L.: Selective and multi-scale fusion mamba for medical image segmentation. Expert Syst. Appl. **261**, 125518 (2025)
8. Liu, J., et al.: Adapting mamba-based vision foundation models for medical image segmentation. IEEE Trans. Med. Imaging (2024)
9. Xing, Z., Ye, T., Yang, Y., Liu, G., Zhu, L.: Segmamba: long-range sequential modeling mamba for 3d medical image segmentation. In: International Conference on Medical Image Computing and Computer-Assisted Intervention, pp. 578–588. Springer (2024)
10. Cao, A., Li, Z., Jomsky, J., Laine, A.F., Guo, J.: Medsegmamba: 3d cnn-mamba hybrid architecture for brain segmentation. *arXiv preprint* arXiv:2409.08307 (2024)
11. Manzari, O.N., Ahmadabadi, H., Kashiani, H., Shokouhi, S.B., Ayatollahi, A., et al.: Medvit: a robust vision transformer for generalized medical image classification. Comput. Biol. Med. **157**, 106791 (2023)
12. AWang, A., Chen, H., Lin, Z., Han, J., Ding, G.: Repvit: revisiting mobile cnn from vit perspective. In: Proceedings of the IEEE/CVF Conference on Computer Vision and Pattern Recognition, pp. 15909–15920 (2024)
13. Shi, Y., Sun, M., Wang, Y., Ma, J., Chen, Z.: An eagle vision transformer with bi-fovea self-attention. IEEE Trans. Cybern. Evit (2025)
14. Ma, X., Dai, X., Bai, Y., Wang, Y., Fu, Y.: Rewrite the stars. In; Proceedings of the IEEE/CVF Conference on Computer Vision and Pattern Recognition (2024)
15. Ding, X., Zhang, Y., Ge, Y., Zhao, S., Song, L., Yue, X., Shan, Y.: Unireplknet: a universal perception large-kernel convnet for audio video point cloud time-series and image recognition. In: Proceedings of the IEEE/CVF Conference on Computer Vision and Pattern Recognition, pp. 5513–5524 (2024)
16. Chen, J., et al.: Run, don't walk: chasing higher flops for faster neural networks. In: Proceedings of the IEEE/CVF Conference on Computer Vision and Pattern Recognition, pp. 12021–12031 (2023)

17. Huang, G., Liu, Z., Van Der Maaten, L., Weinberger, K.Q.: Densely connected convolutional networks. In: Proceedings of the IEEE Conference on Computer Vision and Pattern Recognition, pp. 4700–4708 (2017)
18. Gong, H., Kang, L., Wang, Y., Wan, X., Li, H.: nnmamba: 3d biomedical image segmentation, classification and landmark detection with state space model. *arXiv preprint* arXiv:2402.03526 (2024)

PrePSL: A Pre-training Method for Protein Subcellular Localization Using Graph Auto-encoder and Protein Language Model

Shicheng Ma[1], Weiyang Liang[2], Kai Zhao[2], Xuehua Bi[3,4(✉)], and Linlin Zhang[1,5(✉)]

[1] College of Software, Xinjiang University, Urumqi 830046, China
zllnadasha@xju.edu.cn

[2] College of Computer Science and Technology, Xinjiang University, Urumqi 830046, China

[3] College of Medical Engineering and Technology, Xinjiang Medical University, Urumqi 830017, China
xuehua@xjmu.edu.cn

[4] Institute of Medical Engineering Interdisciplinary Research, Xinjiang Medical University, Urumqi 830017, China

[5] Center of Network and Information Technology, Xinjiang University, Urumqi 830046, China

Abstract. The subcellular location of proteins is closely associated with their functions. Understanding the subcellular localization of proteins contributes to the comprehension of disease onset and progression. Although existing computational methods have demonstrated advantages over traditional approaches, the scarcity of labeled data remains a hindrance, especially for proteins with multiple locations. To address this issue, we propose a pre-training method for protein subcellular localization, named PrePSL, by using graph auto-encoder and protein language model. Firstly, we construct a network based on protein-protein interactions, employing a graph auto-encoder to capture intricate relationships among proteins. Next, a protein language model is adopted to extract feature from amino acid sequences, which provide important information about the subcellular localization of the protein. Finally, the fusion feature, an integration of two features acquired from both networks and sequences, is fed into a deep neural network (DNN) to predict subcellular locations of the proteins. In the five-fold cross-validation, PrePSL achieves optimal performance with RL, CV, and AP values of 0.0471, 0.9057, and 0.8537, respectively. Various ablation experiments further validate the model's rationality, and case studies demonstrate the practical utility of the model. The source codes of PrePSL are available at: https://github.com/LabBioMedCoder/PrePSL.

Keywords: Protein · Subcellular localization · Graph auto-encoder · Protein language model · Pre-training

J. Tang et al. (Eds.): ISBRA 2025, LNBI 15757, pp. 49–60, 2026.
https://doi.org/10.1007/978-981-95-0695-8_5

1   Introduction

Protein function is tightly linked to their subcellular localization. Protein subcellular localization (PSL) is essential for understanding protein functions [1]. Traditional methods for predicting protein locations are often costly and inefficient, making it impractical to rely solely on them to resolve this issue. In recent years, the advancements in biology and computer technology provide a robust foundation for the development of efficient computational methods [2,3]. These methods, mostly machine learning-based, provide an in-depth comprehension of data and identify key features, enabling precise prediction of PSL. However, a majority of methods only focus on single-site proteins, disregarding the fact that an increasing number of proteins can exist in multiple locations simultaneously [4]. Therefore, studying the subcellular localization of multi-label proteins is the current focus of bioinformatics.

Researchers often use a variety of data sources to obtain feature representations of proteins, enhancing the performance of models. A prevalent method involves sequence-based [5,6], which utilizes the amino acid sequence of proteins. Amino acid sequences cannot be directly used for computation, so they need to be transformed into digital features through specific methods. These methods include both handcrafted features and deep learning techniques.

Handcrafted features, designed and selected manually by domain experts, are typically based on a profound understanding and experience within the field. Nevertheless, these meticulously crafted descriptors often necessitate domain-specific knowledge and may face challenges in processing a sea of intricate protein patterns. To tackle this challenge, deep learning is employed to capture profound features, owing to its robust capability for automatic feature extraction. Zhang et al. [1] utilized bidirectional long short-term memory (BiLSTM) to capture the complex temporal dependencies within amino acid sequences. Furthermore, Liao et al. [6], utilizing one-hot encoding sequences, combined BiLSTM and convolutional neural network (CNN) to analyze the distribution of proteins. Pan et al. [3] designed a model for predicting protein locations in cell that utilized Node2vec [7] to extract node features from PPI networks. Liu et al. [8] employed the Mashup algorithm to simultaneously extract protein node features from multiple PPIs, achieving experimental results of PSL superior to those obtained using a single network.

Although the various methods mentioned above provide valuable insights into PSL, challenges still remain in this issue. The primary challenge is how to obtain high-quality features from various proteomics data for protein location prediction. Furthermore, improving the model's predictive performance for proteins with sparse labels is also a key focus of attention in addressing this issue. Recentlly, pre-trained models have achieved a superior performance in many fields, such as computer vision and natural language processing [9]. It automatically learns useful feature representations from large-scale data without the need to manually design features.

Pre-trained language models can learn universal language representations on the large corpus, which are beneficial for downstream tasks and can avoid training a new model from scratch. Several protein language models (PLM), such as ProtBert [10] and ESM-2 [11], have been introduced to capture long-distance dependencies within sequences. They have been applied in diverse studies, encompassing structural prediction [12] and functional prediction [13] of proteins. Pre-training on graph has demonstrated powerful capabilities in graph representation learning. These approaches have proven effective in drug-target [14] and gene-phenotype [15] predictions through diverse pre-training tasks. Graph auto-encoder (GAE) [16] is a pre-training method that operates with the collaboration of an encoder and a decoder. It has demonstrated advantages in predicting protein function [17] and protein phenotype associations [18].

Inspired by these methods, we propose a novel model, named PrePSL, for predicting subcellular localization of multi-label proteins based on pre-training. PrePSL incorporates two pre-training modules, one based on graph pre-training and the other on sequence pre-training. Initially, we construct an attributed network by integrating protein-protein interactions and gene ontology, and employ GAE to derive the embedding representation for each protein node in the graph. Specifically, we employ the graph attention network as encoder, and train the module by reconstructing node attributes rather than the topology of the network. Subsequently, ProtBert is used to extract protein features from amino acid sequences, and concatenating the network features with the sequence features. Finally, the integrated features are fed into a DNN to predict protein subcellular localizations. Our experiments show that PrePSL achieves satisfactory performance in the prediction of protein subcellular localizations.

2 Materials and Methods

2.1 Datasets

This work utilizes the dataset sourced from a prior study [6], encompassing human proteins along with their corresponding subcellular locations. This dataset comprises a total of 3,106 proteins distributed across one or more of the 14 subcellular locations. Specifically, 2,580 proteins are associated with a single subcellular location, 480 with two locations, 43 with three locations, and 3 with four locations.

2.2 Proposed Methods

The framework of PrePSL consists of three steps. As shown in Fig. 1. Firstly, we design a pre-training task using a graph auto-encoder to extract network features from the constructed attributed network. Secondly, ProtBert [10], a protein language model, is employed to generate sequence embeddings of proteins. Finally, we use a DNN to predict the multi-label subcellular locations of proteins.

Extracting Features from Network. Proteins with close interactions tend to have similar subcellular locations. We construct an attributed network by using

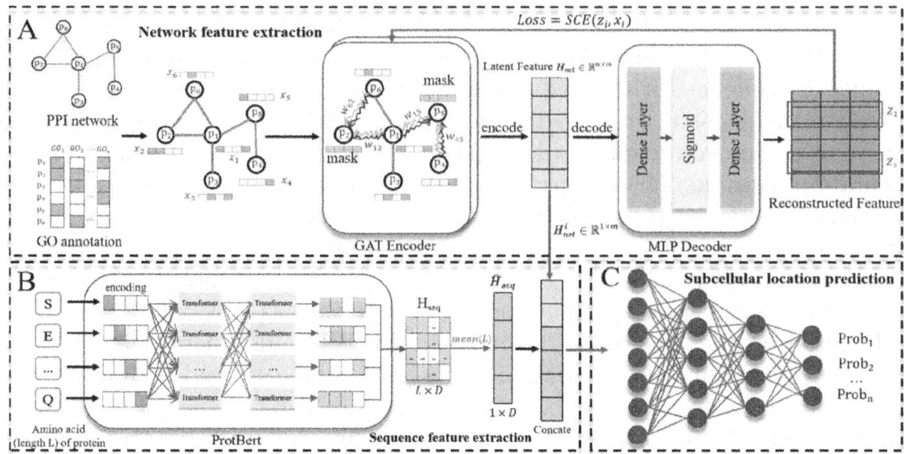

Fig. 1. The framework of PrePSL. This model composes of three components, which are network feature extraction, sequence feature extraction, and subcellular location prediction. (A) Network feature extraction. The encoder is a two-layer GAT, and outputs a low-dimensional representation of each node. The decoder is a MLP that aims to restore the original features of the node. (B) Sequence feature extraction. Each amino acid sequence is converted to a feature matrix using ProtBert. Subsequently, this matrix is distilled into a singular, one-dimensional representation through the utilization of maximum pooling. (C) Subcellular location prediction. We use a DNN to integrate the two features and compute the corresponding possibility at each location.

PPIs from STRING [19]. The 'combined score' provided by STRING is scaled to [0,1] to indicate the interaction of two proteins. To further elucidate the impact of protein function on its subcellular location, PrePSL utilizes gene ontology (GO) to represent the attributes of proteins in the network. The 11,605 GO annotations are obtained from Uniport/Swissport. Following the previou work [20], these GO terms are encoded as a 11,605 dimensional binarized vector, where the i-th bit being 1 indicates having the i-th GO annotation. Finally, the constructed PPI network can be defined as: $G = (V, E, X)$, where $V = \{v_1, v_2, ..., v_n\}$ is nodes set, v_i denotes protein i and n is the number of nodes in the graph. E is the edge set, each edge indicates the interaction of two proteins. $X = [x_1, x_2, ..., x_n]^T$ is the attribute matrix, where $x_i \in \mathbb{R}^{11,605}$ denotes the GO annotation of node v_i. The topology structure of G is represented by an adjacency matrix $A = [a_{ij}] \in \mathbb{R}^{n \times n}$, where $a_{ij} = 1$ if nodes v_i and v_j are connected, otherwise $a_{ij} = 0$.

For the constructed network, we design appropriate encoder and decoder to map the graph-structured data into a low-dimensional vector space. We adopt a graph attention network (GAT) as the encoder. Given a node v and its neighboring node u, GAT computes the attentional weights e_{vu} by using the following formula:

$$e_{vu} = LeakyReLU(a^T[Wx_v||Wx_u]), \tag{1}$$

where x_v and x_u are the raw attribute of nodes v and u, W is a weight matrix that is applied to every node, and a is a learnable parameter vector. Then, α_{vu} is calculated by normalizing the attention weights of all neighboring nodes

$$\alpha_{vu} = \frac{\exp(e_{vu})}{\sum_{k \in \mathcal{N}_v} \exp(e_{vk})}, \tag{2}$$

where $\mathcal{N}(v)$ is the first-order neighbors of node v.

In the training process of GAE, graph reconstruction is a common strategy [17]. However, this approach may not always be optimal for specific tasks, such as node classification [21]. Here, we adopt feature reconstruction for the training objective. During the encoding, by considering node features as initial representations, the kth encoder layer generates the representation of node v as follows:

$$h_v^k = \sigma(\sum_{u \in \mathcal{N}_v} \alpha_{vu} W h_u^{(k-1)}), \tag{3}$$

where $\sigma(\cdot)$ is a nonlinearity transformation, α_{vu} is the attention coefficient between node v and u. After applying 2 encoder layers, the output of the last layer is regarded as the final latent representation $H_{net} \in \mathbb{R}^{n \times m}$. After encoding, the attribute original dimension m is reduced from 11,605 to 512.

Given that the latent feature representation already incorporates node attributes and network structure, we use the multi-layer perceptron (MLP) as the decoder. For the latent features H_{net} obtained by encoder, the decoder employs feature reconstruction as the objective for training, manifested in the following:

$$Z_{decoder}^l = PReLU(f(Z^{l-1})), \tag{4}$$

where $f(\cdot)$ is a layer fully connect neural network (FCNN), FCNN is followed by a Dropout layer to prevent overfitting. The output of the decoder Z is the approximation of attribute matrix X, and we optimize the model so that they are as similar as possible.

A subset of node $\tilde{V} \subset V$ is selected with a random sampling strategy and set all their features to zero. To minimize the reconstruction loss of node features, PrePSL employs the scaled cosine error (SCE) as the loss function rather than the mean square error (MSE), since MSE may have problems with sensitivity and low selectivity [22]. Given the original feature X and reconstructed output Z, SCE is defined as:

$$\mathcal{L}_{sce} = \frac{1}{|\tilde{V}|} \sum_{v_i \in \tilde{V}} (1 - \frac{x_i z_i}{\|x_i\| \|z_i\|})^\gamma, \qquad \gamma \geq 1 \tag{5}$$

which is averaged over all masked nodes. $|\tilde{V}|$ denotes the number of selected nodes and γ is the scaling factor, which is set to 3.

Extracting Features from Amino Acid Sequences. The amino acid sequence is conceptualized as a language, where the alphabet consists of 20 characters representing the 20 amino acids. The amino acid sequence is similar to a sentence composed of words. It is expressed by different combinations of amino acids to express specific biological meanings. Protein language models (PLM) have been demonstrated to allow for a powerful numeric representation of amino acid sequences [12,13]. Our work utilizes ProtBert [10] to obtain the protein feature from sequences. ProtBert takes the protein sequence as input and proceeds to generate its corresponding embeddings. To standardize the input length of proteins, we follow the procedure described in [23] to truncate or padding the sequence to establish a maximum length of 1,000.

A amino acid sequence is denoted S. The embedding matrix of sequence is expressed as $S \xrightarrow{f(\cdot)} H_{seq} \in \mathbb{R}^{1000 \times D}$. The $f(\cdot)$ is ProtBert. The hyperparameter D is embedding dimension of each amino acid, which is set to 1,024. Each row represents the embedding of one residue within the sequence. We calculate the average for each column of H_{seq} to capture the overall properties of the entire protein. Consequently, sequence feature $\bar{H}_{seq} \in \mathbb{R}^{1 \times D}$ is constructed as:

$$\bar{H}_{seq} = [\bar{h}_1, \bar{h}_2, \cdots, \bar{h}_D], \tag{6}$$

where $\bar{h}_i = \frac{\sum_{r=1}^{1000} h_{r,j}}{1000}$, $h_{r,j}$ is the element of row r and column j of the matrix.

Predicting Subcellular Location by DNN. In this paper, a protein P can be denote as $F \in \mathbb{R}^{1 \times 1,536}$, which is formulated by $F = [\bar{H}_{seq} \| H_{net}^i]$. Here, $H_{net}^i \in \mathbb{R}^{1 \times 512}$ denotes $i\text{-}th$ row in the H_{net}. Finally, we use a DNN module to identify the subcellular locations of proteins.

The DNN module consists of multi-layer fully connect neural networks. The input layer receives fusion features and the output layer consists of 14 subcellular classes. Two hidden layers are stacked between the input and output layer. The loss function of DNN is Binary CrossEntropy (BCE). In binary classification tasks, BCE loss is defined as:

$$\mathcal{L}_{dnn} = \frac{1}{N} \sum_{n=1}^{N} y_n \times log(p_n) + (1 - y_n) \times log(1 - p_n), \tag{7}$$

where N denotes the number of samples, p_n is dicted probability value, and y_n is the ground truth label. In multi-lanel task, BCE loss will calculate the loss on each label and then average it.

3   Experiments and Results

3.1   Experiment Settings

In this study, we investigate the performance of PrePSL under varying experiment settings to identify optimal parameter configurations. The 5-fold cross-validation is used for evaluation our model.

We use three metrics to evaluate the accuracy of prediction, including ranking loss (RL), coverage (CV), and average precision (AP). These metrics provide a comprehensive evaluation for multi-label task. The smaller RL and CV indicate the better performance of the model, and the larger AP indicates the better performance of the model.

3.2   Comparison with Baseline Methods

We compare our method with five state-of-the-art methods for PSL employing the same dataset. These methods comprise handcrafted features-based methods, such as IMMMLGP [24], MKSVM [5], and FSVM-KNR [25], a deep learning-based method presented in Liao's work [6], and a PPI network-based method named Node2loc [3]. In order to fairly compare PrePSL and the baseline methods, we preprocess the dataset according to the description of the baseline methods. Table 1 shows the 5-fold cross-validation results on different metrics. The PrePSL, adopting pre-training strategy, achieves optimal performance with RL, CV, and AP values of 0.0471, 0.9057, and 0.8537, respectively. Our model exhibits significant advantages compared to Liao's work using end-to-end training. It indicates that the pre-training strategy can obtain more features related to subcellular locations. Additionally, our method adopts GO as attribute of node and achieves better results than the Node2loc that focuses only on the network structure. Among all methods, IMMMLGP obtains the poorest performance. This may be attributed to IMMMLGP solely relying on one sequence information to represent proteins. It demonstrates that our approach, extracting protein features from multiple perspectives, is a competitive methodology.

Table 1. Performance comparison with baseline methods.

	RL ↓	CV ↓	AP ↑
IMMMLGP	0.4190	4.3030	0.5810
MKSVM	0.1085	1.7193	0.7065
FSVM-KNR	0.1071	1.7025	0.7108
Liao's work	0.0758	1.2848	0.7901
Node2loc	0.0661	1.1317	0.7897
PrePSL	**0.0471**	**0.9057**	**0.8537**

3.3   Analysis of Different Embedding Dimensions

The influence of feature dimensions on the model is very important. Excessive feature dimensions lead to the 'dimension disaster', while too low dimensions may hinder the model's representation of underlying data patterns due to insufficient information. In order to identify the appropriate parameters, we vary the dimension from 256 to 2,048 to analyze the prediction performances. The results over different metrics are illustrated in Fig. 2. As can be seen, the model has the best performance when the dimension of the network features is set to 512, with values of 0.0568, 1.0490, and 0.8335 for the three metrics respectively. For sequence features, the most appropriate dimension is 1,024. The values of RL, CV and AP are 0.0886, 1.4444, and 0.7608 respectively.

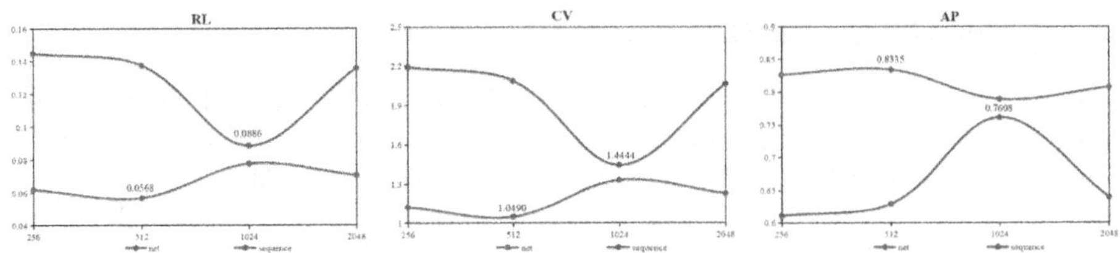

Fig. 2. Comparison of different feature dimensions.

3.4   Ablation Study

Comparison of Different Network Feature Extraction Methods. To explore the impact of different network feature extraction methods on PrePSL. We employ three graph embedding methods that exclusively focus on network topology: Node2vec [7], DeepWalk [26], and Line [27]. Additionally, two graph neural network methods, GCN and GAT, are utilized, integrating both topological information and node attributes during embedding. The prediction results are presented in Table 2. GAT achieves the best results, with 0.0568, 1.0490 and 0.8335 on RL, CV and AP, respectively, outperforming the performance of the other four methods. These results indicate that GAT is better suited for the pre-training task of feature reconstruction.

Table 2. Comparison of different network feature extraction methods.

	RL $\downarrow$	CV $\downarrow$	AP $\uparrow$
Node2vec	0.0720	1.2180	0.7863
Deepwalk	0.0867	1.4128	0.7373
Line	0.0942	1.5200	0.7434
GCN	0.0689	1.2118	0.8003
GAT	**0.0568**	**1.0490**	**0.8335**

Comparison of Different Sequence Feature Extraction Methods. To choose appropriate methods for sequence feature extraction, we use iFeature [28] to extract three handcrafted features, including conjoint triad (CT), dipeptide composition (DC), and moran correlation (Moran). Each amino acid sequence is transformed into a 400-D, 343-D and 240-D feature vector, respectively. Beyond that, One-dimensional convolutional neural network (1D-CNN) is also utilized to extract sequence features. Table 3 shows the performance for different sequence features. The protein language model outperforms the other four methods significantly, achieving impressive scores of 0.0886, 1.4444, and 0.7608 for RL, CV, and AP, respectively. The reason for this is that it can be pre-trained using a large corpus of unlabeled data, which proves pre-training to be a better way to represent proteins.

Table 3. Comparison of different sequence feature extraction methods.

	RL ↓	CV ↓	AP ↑
CT	0.1493	2.2473	0.6080
DC	0.1886	2.7579	0.5250
Moran	0.1687	2.4988	0.5690
CNN	0.1231	1.9050	0.6655
PLM	**0.0886**	**1.4444**	**0.7608**

3.5 Visualization of Different Features

We conduct the task of visualization on the dataset. Linear Discriminant Analysis (LDA) [29] is employed to reduce the dimensionality of these three features to a two-dimensional space. LDA can help visualize and analyze the data in a lower-dimensional space. This visualization can help identify clusters between proteins based on the selected features. The essence lies in the fact that intra-cluster proteins exhibit significant functional similarity in feature space, while there are significant differences between different clusters. For ease of observation, we chose the top five categories with the largest number of samples ('Nucleus', 'Cytoplasm', 'Extracell', 'Mitochondrion', 'Plasma membrane'). As shown in Fig. 3. This confirms that integrating multiple features can yield a more comprehensive and enriched description of protein attributes, thereby enhancing the predictive model's ability to understand protein subcellular localization.

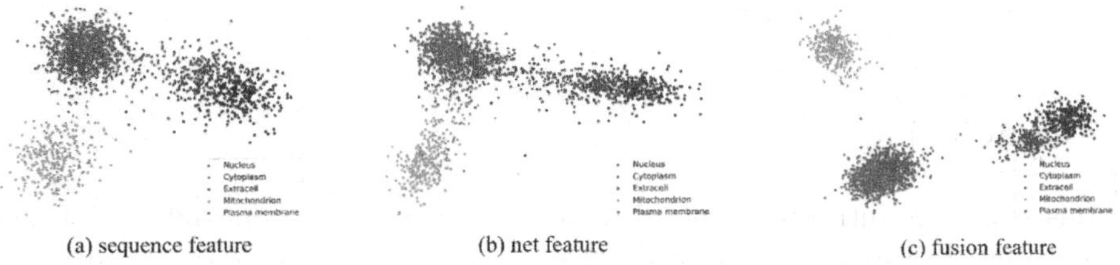

(a) sequence feature   (b) net feature   (c) fusion feature

Fig. 3. Visualization using protein embeddings generated by different features.

3.6   Case Study

Due to certain protein positions being omitted from the dataset, it is plausible that certain of the anticipated false-positive outcomes are indeed accurate. We chose the nucleus for our case study, which has the largest sample size. The nucleus is a crucial component of cell growth and division as well as the control center of cellular metabolism and genetics. In detail, the results from the five test sets are retained, marking positions with probability scores exceeding 0.5 as positive. The top 10 protein predicted false positive of nucleus is checked. We investigate whether the prediction results are reported in the UniProt or Pubmed. There is evidence that 8 of them are found in the nucleus. Six of them can be found in the Pubmed literature, and the other two are demonstrated in the Uniprot database in the entry 'subcellular location'. Table 4 lists the details content.

Table 4. The top 10 predicted false positive proteins of Nucleus with supporting literature.

Rank	Protein name	Evidence
1	Q9NRC8	PMID: 31075303 (Sobuz et al., 2019)
2	Q12778	PMID: 31063815 (Xie et al., 2019)
3	Q9UGK8	PMID: 10571079 (Uhlmann et al., 1999)
4	P51858	PMID: 26845719 (Nüße et al., 2016)
5	Q9UKD1	UniProt
6	Q9NY27	UniProt
7	Q6IMN6	–
8	Q5EBM0	–
9	Q9Y6F1	PMID: 16924674 (Rouleau et al., 2007)
10	Q9UER7	PMID: 25275136 (Tsai et al., 2014)

4   Conclusion

In this study, we introduce a novel approach to predict the subcellular location of multi-label proteins. To alleviate the issue of sparse label data, pre-training is employed to extract protein features from two perspectives. A graph auto-encoder extracts network features from PPIs, and a protein language model, ProtBert, derives sequence features. Extensive experiments demonstrate the effectiveness and rationality of our model.

Determining the exact location of proteins requires consideration of the complex structures and dynamic changes within the cell. The lack of experimentally validated location information poses challenges for computational biology methods. Pre-training methods, leveraging intrinsic information from proteins such as amino acid sequences, protein-protein interactions, and protein functions, provide feature representations for downstream tasks even in the absence of labeled data. Large language models have brought unprecedented novelty to many domains, and protein language models are no exception. Nevertheless, Encoding proteins lacking gene functional descriptions and PPIs still presents obstacles. In forthcoming endeavors, we intend to explore novel computational approaches dedicated to improving the precision of protein subcellular localization solely through the utilization of amino acid sequences.

Acknowledgements. This work was supported by the Natural Science Foundation of China (No. 62366052), the Natural Science Foundation of Xinjiang Uygur Autonomous Region (No. 2024D01C126, 2022D01C427), the Key R&D Program of Xinjiang Uygur Autonomous Region (No. 2022B03023, 2022B01046), and the Sichuan Province Joint Fund of China (No. 25QYCX0103).

Disclosure of Interests. The authors have no competing interests to declare that are relevant to the content of this article.

References

1. Zhang, Y., Zheng, L., Nanxin, Y., Wei, H., Jiang, W., Mingkun, L., et al.: Locpro: a deep learning-based prediction of protein subcellular localization for promoting multi-directional pharmaceutical research. J. Pharm. Anal. 101255 (2025)
2. Xiao, H., Zou, Y., Wang, J., Wan, S.: A review for artificial intelligence based protein subcellular localization. Biomolecules **14**(4), 409 (2024)
3. Pan, X., Chen, L., Liu, M., Niu, Z., Huang, T., Cai, Y.D.: Identifying protein subcellular locations with embeddings-based node2loc. IEEE/ACM Trans. Comput. Biol. Bioinf. **19**(2), 666–675 (2021)
4. Shen, Y., Ding, Y., Tang, J., Zou, Q., Guo, F.: Critical evaluation of web-based prediction tools for human protein subcellular localization. Brief. Bioinform. **21**(5), 1628–1640 (2020)
5. Shen, Y., Tang, J., Guo, F.: Identification of protein subcellular localization via integrating evolutionary and physicochemical information into chou's general pseaac. J. Theor. Biol. **462**, 230–239 (2019)
6. Liao, Z., Pan, G., Sun, C., Tang, J.: Predicting subcellular location of protein with evolution information and sequence-based deep learning. BMC Bioinformatics **22**, 1–23 (2021)
7. Grover, A., Leskovec, J.: node2vec: scalable feature learning for networks. In: Proceedings of the 22nd ACM SIGKDD International Conference on Knowledge Discovery and Data Mining, pp. 855–864 (2016)
8. Liu, H., Hu, B., Chen, L., Lu, L.: Identifying protein subcellular location with embedding features learned from networks. Curr. Proteomics **18**(5), 646–660 (2021)
9. Chen, F.L., et al.: Vlp: a survey on vision-language pre-training. Mach. Intell. Res. **20**(1), 38–56 (2023)
10. Elnaggar, A., et al.: Prottrans: toward understanding the language of life through self-supervised learning. IEEE Trans. Pattern Anal. Mach. Intell. **44**(10), 7112–7127 (2021)

11. Cordoves-Delgado, G., García-Jacas, C.R.: Predicting antimicrobial peptides using esmfold-predicted structures and esm-2-based amino acid features with graph deep learning. J. Chem. Inf. Model. **64**(10), 4310–4321 (2024)
12. Lin, Z., et al.: Evolutionary-scale prediction of atomic-level protein structure with a language model. Science **379**(6637), 1123–1130 (2023)
13. Rives, A., et al.: Biological structure and function emerge from scaling unsupervised learning to 250 million protein sequences. Proc. Natl. Acad. Sci. **118**(15), e2016239118 (2021)
14. Yu, L., Qiu, W., Lin, W., Cheng, X., Xiao, X., Dai, J.: Hgdti: predicting drug-target interaction by using information aggregation based on heterogeneous graph neural network. BMC Bioinformatics **23**(1), 126 (2022)
15. Bi, X., Liang, W., Zhao, Q., Wang, J.: Sslpheno: a self-supervised learning approach for gene–phenotype association prediction using protein–protein interactions and gene ontology data. Bioinformatics **39**(11), btad662 (2023)
16. Goyal, P., Ferrara, E.: Graph embedding techniques, applications, and performance: a survey. Knowl.-Based Syst. **151**, 78–94 (2018)
17. Fan, K., Guan, Y., Zhang, Y.: Graph2go: a multi-modal attributed network embedding method for inferring protein functions. GigaScience **9**(8), giaa081 (2020)
18. Liu, Y., et al.: Integration of human protein sequence and protein-protein interaction data by graph autoencoder to identify novel protein-abnormal phenotype associations. Cells **11**(16), 2485 (2022)
19. Szklarczyk, D., et al.: The string database in 2023: protein-protein association networks and functional enrichment analyses for any sequenced genome of interest. Nucleic Acids Res. **51**(D1), D638–D646 (2023)
20. Pan, X., et al.: Identification of protein subcellular localization with network and functional embeddings. Front. Genet. **11**, 626500 (2021)
21. Li, J., et al.: What's behind the mask: Understanding masked graph modeling for graph autoencoders (2023), https://arxiv.org/abs/2205.10053
22. Hou, Z., et al.: Graphmae: self-supervised masked graph autoencoders. In: Proceedings of the 28th ACM SIGKDD Conference on Knowledge Discovery and Data Mining, pp. 594–604 (2022)
23. Wang, Z., Lin, T., Yang, X., Liang, Y., Shi, X.: Protein subcellular localization prediction by combining protbert and bigru. In: 2022 IEEE International Conference on Bioinformatics and Biomedicine (BIBM), pp. 86–89. IEEE (2022)
24. He, J., Gu, H., Liu, W.: Imbalanced multi-modal multi-label learning for subcellular localization prediction of human proteins with both single and multiple sites. PLoS ONE **7**(6), e37155 (2012)
25. Ding, Y., Tang, J., Guo, F.: Human protein subcellular localization identification via fuzzy model on kernelized neighborhood representation. Appl. Soft Comput. **96**, 106596 (2020)
26. Perozzi, B., Al-Rfou, R., Skiena, S.: Deepwalk: online learning of social representations. In: Proceedings of the 20th ACM SIGKDD International Conference on Knowledge Discovery and Data Mining, pp. 701–710 (2014)
27. Tang, J., Qu, M., Wang, M., Zhang, M., Yan, J., Mei, Q.: Line: large-scale information network embedding. In: Proceedings of the 24th International Conference on World Wide Web, pp. 1067–1077 (2015)
28. Chen, Z., et al.: ifeature: a python package and web server for features extraction and selection from protein and peptide sequences. Bioinformatics **34**(14), 2499–2502 (2018)
29. Zhao, S., Zhang, B., Yang, J., Zhou, J., Xu, Y.: Linear discriminant analysis. Nat. Rev. Methods Primers **4**(1), 70 (2024)

MOGATFF: An Explainable Multi-Omics Prediction Model with Feature Enhancement for Genotype-Phenotype Association Analysis

Zhipeng Gao[1], Kai Zhao[2], Guanglei Yu[3,4], Xuehua Bi[3,4(✉)], and Linlin Zhang[1,5(✉)]

[1] School of Software, Xinjiang University, Urumqi 830046, China
zllnadasha@xju.edu.cn
[2] School of Computer Science and Technology (School of Cyberspace Security), Xinjiang University, Urumqi 830046, China
[3] College of Medical Engineering and Technology, Xinjiang Medical University, Urumqi 830017, China
xuehua@xjmu.edu.cn
[4] Institute of Medical Engineering Interdisciplinary Research, Xinjiang Medical University, Urumqi 830017, China
[5] Center of Network and Information Technology, Xinjiang University, Urumqi 830046, China

Abstract. Investigating genotype-phenotype associations is essential for elucidating disease mechanisms, as it enables the identification of molecular pathways underlying pathological processes and facilitates the development of personalized therapeutic strategies. Therefore, it is urgent to develop efficient computational methods for predicting potential genotype-phenotype associations in order to reduce the cost of biological experiments. Although current prediction methods demonstrate satisfactory performance, their capacity to effectively capture feature-feature and sample-sample relationships remains limited. Additionally, models relying exclusively on single-omics data fail to achieve holistic sample profiling. To fully utilize the advances in omics and achieve a more comprehensive understanding of human diseases, we propose a novel interpretable framework, termed **M**ulti-**O**mics **G**raph **AT**tention network with **F**eature **F**usion (MOGATFF), for phenotype classification and biomarker discovery. Specifically, we first leverage biological networks to reduce the dimensionality of genotypic data. Then we compute associations between features to enable feature fusion and achieve optimization. To better capture complex sample relationships, a feature enhancement module based on graph attention network is employed to aggregate features for phenotype classification. Finally, we utilize the Permutation Method to identify important feature, thereby enhancing interpretability. In the five-fold cross-validation, MOGATFF achieves a mean ACC of 0.9281 on Braak, 0.8613 on Cerad and 0.8716 on Cogdx, outperforming eight baseline approaches. Furthermore, case study provides validation of its efficacy in detecting disease-associated biomarker.

© The Author(s), under exclusive license to Springer Nature Singapore Pte Ltd. 2026
J. Tang et al. (Eds.): ISBRA 2025, LNBI 15757, pp. 61–72, 2026.
https://doi.org/10.1007/978-981-95-0695-8_6

Keywords: genotype-phenotype association · feature enhancing · phenotype prediction · biomarker identification · graph attention network

1   Introduction

The genotypeâĂŞphenotype association has been found in many diseases, such as neurodegenerative disorders and cancer [1]. Exploring this association helps us understand underlying cellular and molecular mechanisms like genes and pathways that causally affect the phenotypes [2]. Considering the high cost of biological experiments, the known genotype-phenotype associations remain limited, and numerous unknown associations are yet to be uncovered [3]. Genome-wide association studies (GWAS) have enabled the search for genetic variants associated with diseases [4,5]. However, single nucleotide polymorphism (SNP) obtained through GWAS may be due to linkage disequilibrium (LD), so it may not have a true causal relationship between SNP and phenotype [5]. In addition, GWAS attempts to find associations between individual variants and diseases, and SNPs that do not pass significance thresholds are eliminated, which may miss some weak but important SNPs [6,7]. Polygenic Risk Scores (PRS) are calculated based on SNPs identified through GWAS, using regression methods to estimate the probability of developing a specific disease [8,9]. With the advancement of machine learning, it has been shown that replacing the PRS with machine learning models can improve the accuracy of disease phenotype prediction [10]. Sigala et al. [11] cite the application of machine learning methods in the identification of SNPs and phenotype prediction. Wang et al. [12] propose a new temporal structure machine learning model to automatically identify longitudinal genotype-phenotype associations. However, although machine learning methods have better performance than complex models in specific tasks [13], they still struggle to capture complex associations effectively.

Deep learning has a wide application in genotype-phenotype association prediction [14,15]. With the advancement of high-throughput sequencing technologies, multi-omics data are utilized to interpret comprehensive biological processes [16]. Samples with similar features often have close manifestations, so many studies apply Graph Neural Networks (GNNs) to aggregate features from neighbor nodes to improve prediction ability. For example, Wang et al. [17] use GNN on different omics level and fuse data for cancer phenotype prediction. It is not easy to construct the appropriate graph in advance, Zheng et al. [18] propose MMGL, which uses an adaptive method to learn the graph structure. On this basis, Dong et al. [19] design the MOGLAM for disease classification by optimizing the association learning between omics. Different from the aforementioned methods, which construct graphs separately based on different omics, MoGCN [20] uses Similarity Network Fusion (SNF) [21] to construct a comprehensive Patient Similarity Network (PSN), achieving the phenotype classification. In addition, Variational Autoencoder (VAE) is also widely employed in predicting genotype-phenotype associations. AVBAE-MODFR [22] uses a VAE to classify and screen of important genes, and XomicVAE model [23] learns the latent features and obtains the contribution score of gene to the phenotype. In order to enrich the research in neurodegenerative diseases, DeepGAMI [24] utilizes biological prior networks to predict Alzheimer's Disease (AD) phenotype and identify related biomarkers. It is well-established that correlations exist between mutation sites. To the best of our knowledge, however, none of the existing studies have addressed how learning the relationships between features affects the prediction results. Moreover, equally weighting neighboring nodes in GNN-based methods may not be appropriate for all scenarios, because the connection in the graph may be affected by various factors and cause noise, which reduces the prediction performance [25].

To address the limitations of the aforementioned studies, we propose a novel interpretable genotype-phenotype associations prediction model named MOGATFF based on Graph Attention Networks (GAT) with feature fusion and Permutation method [26]. Firstly, we use eQTL to filter out SNPs associated with gene expression in genotype data and employ the GRN to retain key regulatory genes in the gene expression data, reducing data dimensionality and simplifying subsequent analysis. Secondly, based on the feature matrix, we calculate the associations between features using cosine similarity on both omics separately, and perform feature fusion based on the association scores. Then, by constructing sample similarity networks, we use GAT to capture complex relationships between samples and optimize features by integrating information. The final feature representations obtained from the above steps are concatenated and fed into a classification network for phenotype classification. Finally, we employ the interpretability method Permutation on our method to determine the importance of features by randomly shuffling the original features and observing the changes in model performance. Outstanding performance results demonstrate that MOGATFF achieves precise classification of AD phenotypes. Furthermore, case study verifies the practical utility of our model in identifying important SNP loci and genes of AD.

2   Materials and Methods

2.1   Datasets

ROSMAP [27] is created to study the genetic factors, pathological mechanisms and cognitive function changes in AD. It provides multi-omics data for Alzheimer's disease research, including whole-genome sequencing, transcriptomics, epigenomics, proteomics, and matched clinical data from brain tissue samples. We use SNP dosage and gene-expression data from ROSMAP. Phenotypes in the ROSMAP included the Diagnostic cognitive (COGDX) score, the neuroplaque measure (CERAD), and the neurofibrillary tangle pathology (BRAAK) score. The score ranges are: COGDX [0–6], CERAD [0–4], and BRAAK [0–6]. For categorical analysis: COGDX is grouped as no CI (0–1), mild CI (2–3), or AD/dementia (4–6); CERAD as no AD (3–4), possible AD (2), or definite AD (0–1); and BRAAK as early (0–3) or late stage (4–6) AD. Further, We extract eQTL from the GTEx consortium [28] and use the GRN network from the PsychENCODE consortium [29] to identify putative regulatory relationships between SNP loci and genes.

2.2 Data Pre-processing

We consider that feature with zero or low variance does not substantially contribute to the prediction results. More specifically, the thresholds are set at 0.1 for SNP dosage and gene expression data. We further preselect the features and compute the ANOVA F-value for each omic in turn, retaining the features with significant differences between different variance categories.

2.3 The Overall Flow of Proposed Method

We propose a novel interpretable prediction model MOGATFF, combining GAT with feature fusion and Permutation for genotype-phenotype association prediction, which consists of four components: (A) biological screening layer, (B) feature fusion module, (C) sample association learning module, (D) phenotype classifier. The flowchart of MOGATFF is shown in Fig. 1.

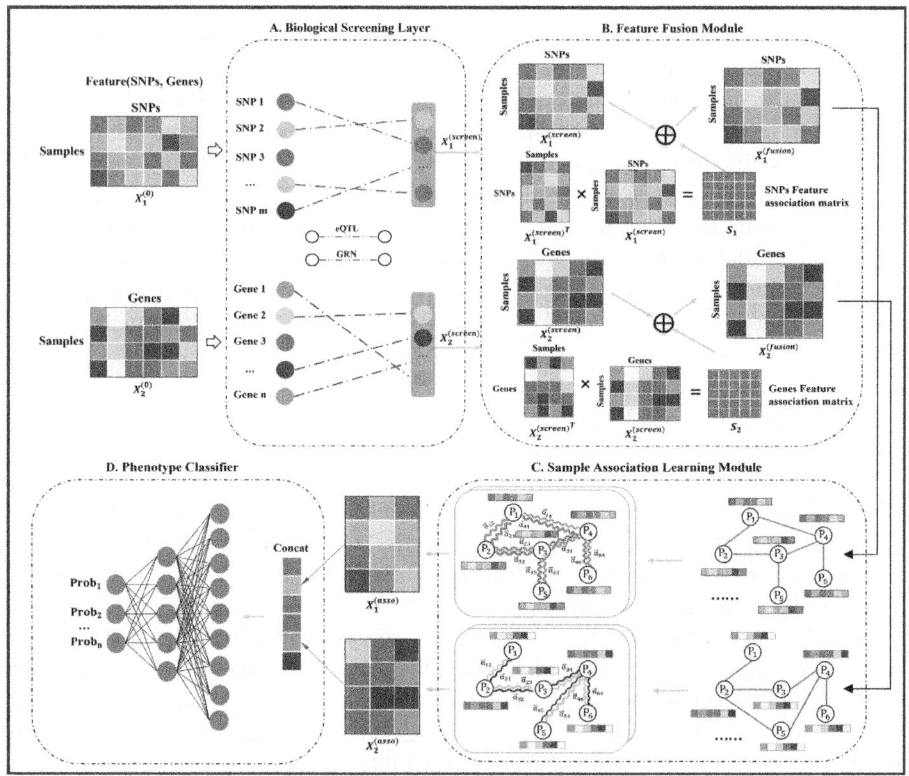

Fig. 1. MOGATFF model architecture.

2.4 Biological Screening Layer

The items in eQTL can be expressed as a mapping $f : G \rightarrow E$, where G and E represent the SNPs and genes sets respectively. GRN can be represented as a directed Graph $\mathcal{G} = (V, A)$, where V is the set of nodes (including genes and regulatory elements) and A is the set of edges, representing regulatory relationships.

For the original SNP dosage $X_1^{(0)}$ and gene expression data $X_2^{(0)}$, as shown in Fig. 1.A, we use G and V to perform feature selection, respectively. Only the features existing in the sets are selected to obtain low-dimensional feature matrix:

$$X_1^{(screen)} = \{All\ Samples,\ SNPs \mid SNPs \in G\}, \tag{1}$$

$$X_2^{(screen)} = \{All\ Samples,\ genes \mid genes \in V\}, \tag{2}$$

where $X_1^{(screen)}$ and $X_2^{(screen)}$ are SNP dosage and gene expression data after screening respectively.

2.5 Feature Fusion Module

Within a single omic, the relationships between features are rich and complex. In our study, we calculate the association between features and aggregate features to achieve feature enhancement. For $X_i^{(screen)} \in R^{N \times d_i}$, $i = \{1, 2\}$, N represents the number of samples, d_i represents the feature dimension of $X_i^{(screen)}$, and we get the feature association matrix $S_i \in R^{d_i \times d_i}$ using inner product:

$$S_i = softmax(\frac{\left(X_i^{(screen)}\right)^T \cdot X_i^{(screen)}}{\sqrt{d_i}}), \tag{3}$$

where S_i is normalized using d_i to eliminate the influence of dimension on the similarity calculation. Association scores are mapped to $[0,1]$ using $softmax(\cdot)$, which helps to highlight significant associations while suppressing noisy or weak associations. Based on the S_i to fuse the features, the process of feature fusion is as follows:

$$O_i = X_i^{(screen)} \cdot S_i, \tag{4}$$

where $O_i \in R^{N \times d_i}$, and output of this module $X_i^{(fusion)}$ is computed as:

$$X_i^{(fusion)} = X_i^{(screen)} + O_i. \tag{5}$$

2.6 Sample Association Learning Module

We introduce GAT to dynamically adjust the importance of neighbor nodes to sample, which improves the ability of the model to capture graph structure information. We use cosine similarity to calculate the adjacency matrix A of samples, and the formula is as follows:

$$A_{ij} = \begin{cases} 1 & i \neq j \text{ and } \cos(x_i, x_j) \geq \varepsilon \\ 0 & otherwise \end{cases}, \tag{6}$$

where x_i and x_j represent the feature representation of sample i and sample j in $X_i^{(fusion)}$, ε is the manually set threshold, and $cos(\cdot)$ is the cosine similarity, which can be calculated as follows:

$$\cos(\mathbf{x_i}, \mathbf{x_j}) = \frac{\mathbf{x_i} \cdot \mathbf{x_j}}{\|\mathbf{x_i}\|\|\mathbf{x_j}\|}. \tag{7}$$

We control the sparsity of the graph through the hyperparameter k, by which we determine the threshold ε:

$$k = \sum_{i,j} I(\cos(x_i, x_j) \geq \varepsilon)/n, \tag{8}$$

where $I(\cdot)$ is the indicator function, n represents the number of patients, and the k specifically refers to the average number of neighbors of each sample in the graph. Then $X_i^{(fusion)}$ is mapped to $H_i \in R^{N \times d_{out}}$ by a learnable weight matrix $W \in R^{d_i \times d_{out}}$:

$$H_i = X_i^{(2)} W. \tag{9}$$

The attention coefficient e_{ij} of sample i and j is calculated as follows:

$$e_{ij} = LeakyRelu(a^T[h_i\|h_j]), \tag{10}$$

where h_i and h_j are the feature representations of sample i and sample j in H_i, $\|$ represents the concatenation of vectors, and $a \in R^{2d_{out}}$ is a learnable vector. We calculate attention weights by masking attention from pairs of nodes that are not connected, then $softmax(\cdot)$ is used to normalize the attention coefficient and obtain the final attention weight α_{ij} between sample i and sample j:

$$\alpha_{ij} = softmax(e_{ij}) = \frac{exp(e_{ij})}{\sum_k exp(e_{ik})}, \quad e_{ij} = \begin{cases} e_{ij}, & if A_{ij} = 1 \\ 0, & if A_{ij} = 0 \end{cases}, \tag{11}$$

where $k \in \mathcal{N}(i)$, $\mathcal{N}(i)$ denotes the neighbors of sample i. In order to prevent overfitting during training, the attention weight α_{ij} is subjected to dropout, that is, some connections are discarded to avoid excessive dependence between nodes. For sample i, We aggregate the features of neighbor $j \in \mathcal{N}(i)$ and output the final feature matrix $X_i^{(asso)}$ using the $ELU()$ function:

$$X_i^{(asso)} = ELU(\sum_j \alpha_{ij} H_i). \tag{12}$$

2.7   Phenotype Classifier

We concatenate the feature representations of SNP dosage and gene expression, and the MLP classifier is used to predict the phenotype. During the training process, we use the dropout to prevent model overfitting, and use the following cross-entropy loss function as the objective function to train our model:

$$Loss = -\frac{1}{N}\sum_{i=1}^{N}\sum_{c=1}^{C} y_{i,c}log(p_{i,c}), \tag{13}$$

where N is the number of samples, C is the number of categories, $y_{i,c}$ is the true label of the sample i, and $p_{i,c}$ is the predicted probability that the sample i belongs to category c.

2.8   Identification of Important Feature

We use Permutation method to calculate feature importance, which evaluates the influence of each feature on the prediction result. Specifically, if the performance is substantially decreased after the feature permutation, we consider the feature can meaningfully affect the classification result, that is, the feature is significantly related to the disease phenotype. First, we divide the data into a training set X_{train} and a test set X_{test}. Train the model according to our method on the X_{train}, and calculated the benchmark performance on the X_{test}:

$$base\_score = accuracy\ (y_{test}, \hat{y}_{test}), \tag{14}$$

where $\hat{y}_{test}$ is the prediction result of the model on the X_{test}. For each feature X_i, the data after permutation is $X_{*,i}$:

$$X_{*,i} = [X_1\ ...\ X_{i-1}\ shuffle(X_i)\ X_{i+1}\ ...\ X_{d_i}]. \tag{15}$$

Then using the $X_{*,i}$ obtain the prediction result $\hat{y}_{*,i}$, and get the acc_i, which is calculated based on the shuffled features:

$$acc_i = accuracy\ (y_{test}, \hat{y}_{*,i}), \tag{16}$$

and the importance of feature i is calculated by comparing the decline in accuracy relative to the baseline accuracy before and after replacement:

$$importance_i = base\_score - acc_i, \tag{17}$$

where larger value of $importance_i$ indicates that feature i has a greater impact on the model prediction and is also more relevant to the phenotype.

3   Experiments and Results

3.1   Experiment Settings

Our model is implemented based on the PyTorch Package and Adam algorithm is applied to optimize the model. We determine the optimal combination of parameters through a grid search. After the search, we set the learning rate to 0.001, dropout rate to 0.2, and GAT layer number 1 to 6 to obtain the best results. In addition, we employ four similarity calculation methods to measure feature associations and compare them with the approach of not calculating feature associations to determine the optimal method. We select 432 samples with complete genomic and phenotypic data. The 5-fold cross-validation method is used to evaluate the model's performance. In each fold, we use 20% of the samples as the test set and the rest as the training set. To quantify the average performance of the model, we employ Accuracy, Precision, Recall, F1-score and AUC as the primary evaluation metrics on binary classification task. In addition, we also use three evaluation metrics Accuracy, F1-weighted, F1-micro to comprehensively evaluate the model performance on multi-class classification task.

3.2   Comparison with Baseline Methods

To evaluate the performance of the MOGATFF model, we compare it with eight models based on multi-omics data: six deep learning methods (MOGONET [17], DeepGAMI [25], MMGL [18], MOGLAM [19], AVBAE-MODFR [23], and MoGCN [20]) and two machine learning methods (XGBoost and SVM). Omics data are directly concatenated as input to SVM and XGBoost. We validate the proposed method using five-fold cross-validation. As shown in Fig. 2, our model significantly outperforms other baseline methods on Braak classification. The poor performance of some baseline models (MOGCN and MOGONET) may be due to overfitting. Similarly, as shown in Fig. 1, our model achieves optimal or suboptimal results on Cerad and Cogdx classification, demonstrating its effectiveness. Notably, some machine learning models outperform certain deep learning models in classification tasks. Overall, our model consistently achieves the best prediction performance.

3.3   Comparison of Different Association Calculation Methods

We compare the prediction performance of models under different association calculation methods. We use inner product similarity, cosine similarity, Pearson similarity and Chebyshev inequality to test on ROSMAP's Braak (binary-classification) as shown in the Fig. 3. By comparing with not calculating feature association, all four methods could improve the prediction performance of the models to varying degrees, and the model performance reaches the best Acc of 0.927 and AUC of 0.981 when using the inner product similarity. This indicates that aggregating associated features can achieve feature enhancement, leading to better prediction results. The improvement may be attributed to the linear additivity of AD-related features, where integrating expression information from multiple features enables superior prediction performance.

3.4   Case Study

In order to illustrate that MOGATFF can help identify biological markers that are significantly associated with phenotypes, we conducted a case study. According to the importance calculation method proposed in this paper, we select the TOP-10 features on data in Braak task and search for relevant literature in Pubmed to verify our conclusions. As shown in Fig. 2, most of the important genes we searched for related to AD could be supported by corresponding literature, and no corresponding cases are found for TM2D2 and ZNF853. Few studies have directly validated our conclusions regarding SNP. We seek to verify our conclusions by determining the association of the gene in which the SNP is located with AD, and finally we identified five SNP loci associated with AD and five were not found. In summary, the proposed method is effective in identifying important biomarker, and we believe biomarkers that are not supported by studies may be undiscovered, so our method also provides research targets for clinical trials in AD.

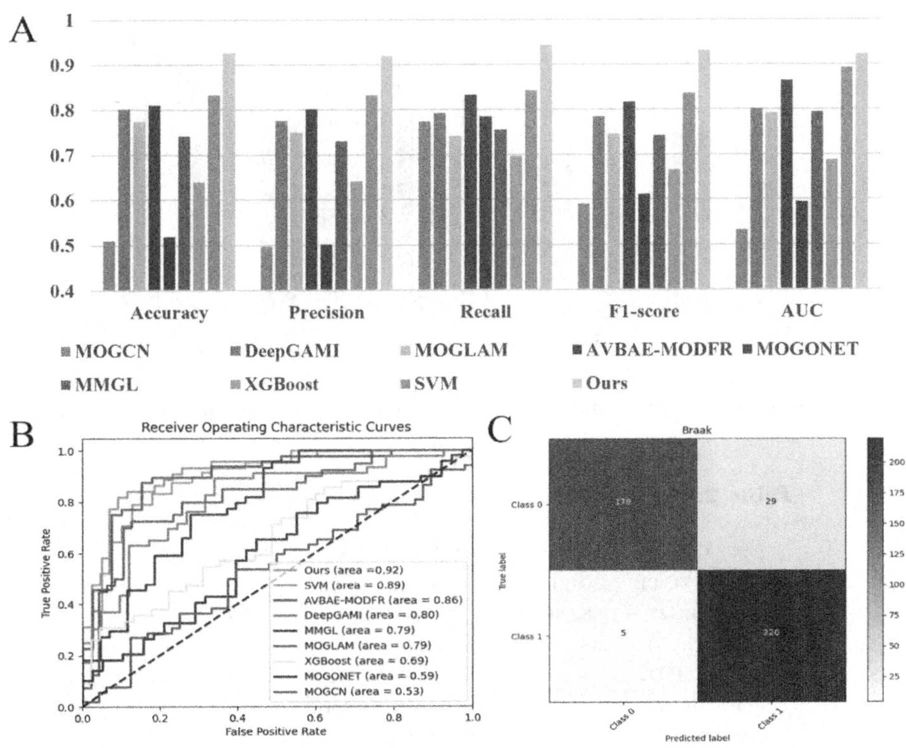

Fig. 2. Performance comparison of methods based on 5-fold cross validation on Braak. **A** Balanced metrics from 5-fold cross-validation. **B** Receiver Operating Characteristic (ROC) curves of Braak. **C** The confusion matrix of Braak task.

Table 1. Performance comparison on Cerad and Cogdx.

Methods	Cerad (Multi-class)			Cogdx (Multi-class)		
	Accuracy	F1-weighted	F1-micro	Accuracy	F1-weighted	F1-micro
SVM	0.849 ± 0.04	0.821 ± 0.04	0.849 ± 0.04	0.824 ± 0.04	0.822 ± 0.04	0.824 ± 0.04
XGBoost	0.555 ± 0.06	0.550 ± 0.06	0.555 ± 0.06	0.555 ± 0.02	0.532 ± 0.02	0.555 ± 0.02
MOGCN	0.784 ± 0.03	0.785 ± 0.04	0.781 ± 0.04	0.798 ± 0.06	0.798 ± 0.06	0.797 ± 0.06
MOGLAM	0.814 ± 0.03	0.813 ± 0.02	0.793 ± 0.03	0.820 ± 0.03	0.821 ± 0.03	0.819 ± 0.02
MOGONET	0.726 ± 0.03	0.725 ± 0.03	0.720 ± 0.03	0.701 ± 0.06	0.700 ± 0.06	0.693 ± 0.06
MMGL	0.794 ± 0.05	0.774 ± 0.04	0.783 ± 0.03	0.752 ± 0.07	0.742 ± 0.03	0.763 ± 0.09
DeepGAMI	0.701 ± 0.04	0.710 ± 0.05	0.699 ± 0.15	0.682 ± 0.02	0.699 ± 0.06	0.681 ± 0.14
AVBAE	0.834 ± 0.03	0.825 ± 0.03	0.841 ± 0.03	0.830 ± 0.11	0.857 ± 0.15	0.840 ± 0.08
Ours	**0.861 ± 0.02**	**0.856 ± 0.01**	**0.860 ± 0.02**	**0.872 ± 0.08**	**0.867 ± 0.09**	**0.871 ± 0.09**

Result: mean ± deviation.

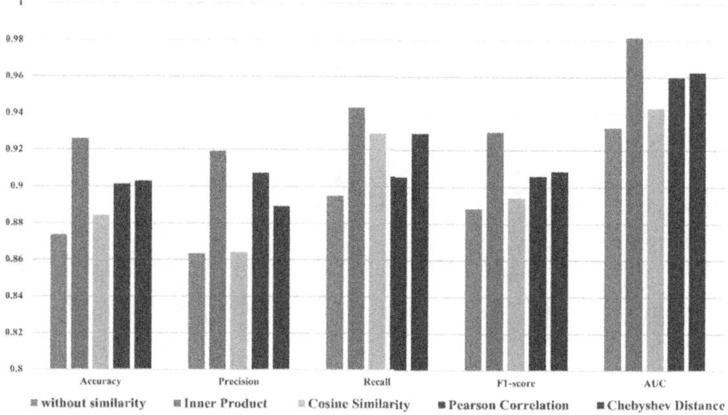

Fig. 3. Comparison of performance under different association calculation methods.

Table 2. Table of important SNPs and Genes with Evidence.

No.	Gene	Evidence	No.	SNP	Gene	Evidence
1	OXCT1	36921750	1	rs7169401	HOMER2	33522999
2	SLC25A11	38099467	2	rs35945684	NIT2	39875978
3	CIAO1	38411040	3	rs2431184	—	—
4	TM2D2	—	4	rs72836215	CD207	28847997
5	MCM7	56985583	5	rs62305644	C4orf36	—
6	NAGLU	36648562	6	rs7218642	RHBDL3	23177596
7	ZNF853	—	7	rs12327751	MYBPC2	—
8	SRD5A1	28552457	8	rs7806980	MUC17	—
9	ARHGEF9	34984308	9	rs3845949	ITGA9	24067533
10	PLXNB1	38802590	10	rs6830478	LINC02505	—

Note: Evidence in the table refers to the PMID in PubMed.

4   Conclusion and Future Work

Elucidating genotype-phenotype associations reveals how specific genetic variations influence physiological or morphological traits, offering insights for disease diagnosis, prevention, and treatment. This study proposes MOGATFF, an interpretable prediction model integrating associated feature fusion and multi-omics graph attention mechanisms, to predict phenotypes and identify disease-related variation sites. Utilizing multiple biological networks, features are screened from genomic data. By calculating feature associations within omic data to aggregate interacting variations and aggregating neighbor information on sample similarity networks to enhance features, precise classification of sample phenotypes is achieved. Permutation methods identify SNPs and gene sites significantly associated with AD, improving model interpretability. Experimental results validate the model's effectiveness in phenotype prediction, and case study confirm its utility in identifying critical genetic variations.

However, missing values in omics data necessitated the exclusion of samples, reducing the dataset size. Future work will focus on utilizing samples with missing data effectively to enhance prediction accuracy and explore associations at more loci.

Acknowledgements. This work was supported by the Natural Science Foundation of China (No. 62366052), the Natural Science Foundation of Xinjiang Uygur Autonomous Region (No. 2024D01C126, 2022D01C427), the Key R&D Program of Xinjiang Uygur Autonomous Region (No. 2022B03023, 2022B01046), and the Sichuan Province Joint Fund of China (No. 25QYCX0103).

Disclosure of Interests. The authors have no competing interests to declare that are relevant to the content of this article.

References

1. Scheltens, P.: Alzheimer's disease. Lancet **397**(10284), 1577–1590 (2021)
2. Bi, J.: Targeting cancer's metabolic co-dependencies: a landscape shaped by genotype and tissue context. Biochim. Biophys. Acta Rev. Cancer **1870**(1), 76–87 (2018)
3. Mountjoy, E.: An open approach to systematically prioritize causal variants and genes at all published human GWAS trait-associated loci. Nat. Genet. **53**(11), 1527–1533 (2021)
4. Lehner, B.: Genotype to phenotype: lessons from model organisms for human genetics. Nat. Rev. Genet. **14**(3), 168–178 (2013)
5. Finucane, H.K.: Heritability enrichment of specifically expressed genes identifies disease-relevant tissues and cell types. Nat. Genet. **50**(4), 621–629 (2018)
6. Tam, V.: Benefits and limitations of genome-wide association studies. Nat. Rev. Genet. **20**(8), 467–484 (2019)
7. Ishigaki, K.: Beyond GWAS: from simple associations to functional insights. Semin Immunopathol. **44**(1), 3–14 (2022)
8. Baker, E.: Polygenic risk scores in Alzheimer's disease: current applications and future directions. Front. Digit. Health **2**, 14 (2020)

9. He, W.: Genome-wide meta-analysis identifies risk loci and improves disease prediction of age-related macular degeneration. Ophthalmology **131**(1), 16–29 (2024)
10. Klau, J.H.: AI-based multi-PRS models outperform classical single-PRS models. Front. Genet. **14**, 1217860 (2023)
11. Sigala, R.E.: Machine learning to advance human genome-wide association studies. Genes **15**(1), 34 (2023)
12. Wang, X.: Longitudinal genotype-phenotype association study through temporal structure auto-learning predictive model. J. Comput. Biol. **25**(7), 809–824 (2018)
13. Gill, M.: Machine learning models outperform deep learning models, provide interpretation and facilitate feature selection for soybean trait prediction. BMC Plant Biol. **22**(1), 180 (2022)
14. Abbas, S.A.: Transfer learning for classification of Alzheimer's disease based on genome wide data. IEEE/ACM Trans. Comput. Biol. and Bioinform. **20**(5), 2700–2711 (2023)
15. Muneeb, M.: Transfer learning for genotype-phenotype prediction using deep learning models. BMC Bioinform. **23**(1), 511 (2022)
16. Huang, Z.: Salmon: survival analysis learning with multi-omics neural networks on breast cancer. Front. Genet. **10**, 166 (2019)
17. Wang, T.: MOGONET integrates multi-omics data using graph convolutional networks allowing patient classification and biomarker identification. Nat. Commun. **12**(1), 3445 (2021)
18. Zheng, S.: Multi-modal graph learning for disease prediction. IEEE Trans. Med. Imaging **41**(9), 2207–2216 (2022)
19. Ouyang, D.: Integration of multi-omics data using adaptive graph learning and attention mechanism for patient classification and biomarker identification. Comput. Biol. Med. **164**, 107303 (2023)
20. Li, X.: MoGCN: a multi-omics integration method based on graph convolutional network for cancer subtype analysis. Front. Genet. **13**, 806842 (2022)
21. Wang, B.: Similarity network fusion for aggregating data types on a genomic scale. Nat. Methods **11**(3), 333–337 (2014)
22. Li, M.: AVBAE-MODFR: a novel deep learning framework of embedding and feature selection on multi-omics data for pan-cancer classification. Comput. Biol. Med. **177**, 108614 (2024)
23. Withnell, E.: XOmiVAE: An interpretable deep learning model for cancer classification using high-dimensional omics data. Brief. Bioinform. **22**(6), bbab315 (2021)
24. Chandrashekar, P.B.: DeepGAMI: deep biologically guided auxiliary learning for multimodal integration and imputation to improve genotype-phenotype prediction. Genome Med. **15**(1), 88 (2023)
25. Wang, X., Zhu, M.: AM-GCN: adaptive multi-channel graph convolutional networks. In: Proceedings of the 26th ACM SIGKDD International Conference on Knowledge Discovery and Data Mining, pp. 1243–1253. ACM, New York (2020). https://doi.org/10.1145/3394486.3403177
26. Breiman, L.: Random forests. Mach. Learn. **45**(1), 5–32 (2001)
27. De, J.P.: A multi-omic atlas of the human frontal cortex for aging and Alzheimer's disease research. Sci. Data. **5**, 180142 (2018)
28. Genetic effects on gene expression across human tissues: GTEx consortium. Nature **550**, 204–213 (2017)
29. Wang D.: Comprehensive functional genomic resource and integrative model for the human brain. Science **362**, eaat8464 (2018)

Accurate and Interpretable Wound Healing Progress Detection Based on a Task-Related Knowledge Refinement Learning Method

Juan He[1,2], Xiaoyan Wang[1], Yi Pan[2,3], Zhengshan Wang[1], Bokai Yang[2,5], Zhiming Zhang[1], Tzu-Ming Liu[1], Yunpeng Cai[2(✉)], Long Chen[1(✉)], and Ruitao Xie[2,3,4(✉)]

[1] University of Macau, Macau 999078, China
longchen@um.edu.mo
[2] Shenzhen Institute of Advanced Technology, Chinese Academy of Sciences, Shenzhen 518055, China
{yp.cai,rt.xie}@siat.ac.cn
[3] Shenzhen Universityof Advanced Technology, Shenzhen 518107, China
[4] University of Chinese Academy of Sciences, Beijing 100049, China
[5] Institute of Intelligence Science and Engineering, Shenzhen Polytechnic University, Shenzhen 518055, China

Abstract. Automatic detection of wound healing progress is essential for assisting clinicians in evaluating wound conditions, guiding clinical treatment, and preventing infections and complications. However, current methods for detecting wound healing progress are often susceptible to interference from irrelevant information, leading to low detection accuracy, and the existing techniques generally lack interpretability. In this study, we construct a new wound healing dataset, the first to provide continuous temporal observations of skin wound healing status. Based on this dataset, we employ a task-related knowledge learning framework for extracting wound-related features of the skin wound images. Utilizing these features, we design several simple and highly interpretable machine learning models for classification study of the wound healing progress. In comparison to existing deep learning models, which lack interpretability, our simple models achieve superior accuracies in predicting wound healing progress. Furthermore, we analyze the learned wound-related features and find that their spatial distribution aligns with established medical principles, further confirming the features we learn are both interpretable and reliable.

Keywords: wound healing progress detection · interpretability · task-related knowledge learning · wound-related feature

---

J. He and X. Wang—contributed equally to this work.

J. Tang et al. (Eds.): ISBRA 2025, LNBI 15757, pp. 73–85, 2026.
https://doi.org/10.1007/978-981-95-0695-8_7

1 Introduction

Wound healing is a complex physiological process that involves multiple cells, cytokines and enzymes and follows specific rules and times [1]. However, when this process is disturbed, the wound is prone to develop into a chronic wound [2]. Studies have shown that chronic wound conditions impair the life quality for about 2.5% of the US population [3] and contribute to a rapid increase in global healthcare spending [2]. Abnormal wound healing status may be also accompanied by the occurrence of other diseases, posing potential health risks to the patients. Using machines to accurately monitor the wound healing progress can help doctors assess the patients' injury recovery status, provide effective guidance for rehabilitation treatment, and at the same time reduce medical costs.

Collagen fibers are the primary structural proteins in skin and other connective tissues, playing a crucial role in providing strength and stability [4]. During wound healing, the synthesis and recombination of collagen fibers is an important step in repairing and regenerating damaged tissues [5]. At different stages of wound healing, the number, type and arrangement of collagen fibers change significantly. Therefore, we predict the healing stage of the wound according to the images of collagen fibers, detect whether there are unexpected situations such as delayed healing, and provide timely guidance for clinicians.

Due to the importance of the wound healing progress detection, related studies have been developed in recent years, which can be divided into two main types: traditional methods and deep learning based methods. Traditional methods rely mainly on designing handcrafted features to assess wound healing progress by quantifying the spatial characteristics of collagen in wound tissue, such as density and growth direction [6,7]. However, these methods often only reflect the one-sidedness of collagen characteristics and the subjective interpretation of the observer, making it difficult to fully capture the complexity of the healing progress, and easily leading to the variability and bias of the results, which affects the consistency of the evaluation and brings challenges for accurate classification of wound healing.

Recently, deep learning is attracting widespread attention for its powerful ability to capture intricate patterns and has shown practical effectiveness across various applications, including image classification [8,9], segmentation [10,11] and enhancement [12], video understanding [13] and enhancement [14], language question answering [15] tasks, etc. In medical scenarios, there are also many deep learning-based methods for disease detection, including myocarditis [16], multiple sclerosis [17], and wound healing status detection [18]- [20], etc. However, many deep learning models in wound healing research used surface images of wound rather than collagen fiber images collected within the internal wound tissue [18], which is susceptible to interference from irrelevant external factors and thus performed poorly at most scenes. Even though the previous works have performed wound healing status detection using collagen fiber images [19,20], the binary collagen datasets they constructed typically include only normal skin and scars (i.e., healed wounds), which is unsuitable for continuous tracking of the wound healing progress. Moreover, existing deep learning methods take the original images as inputs, making it difficult to improve the performance due to the interference from the task-unrelated information within the original images. More importantly, deep learning based methods work like "black boxes" due to a large amount of parameters, which lacks interpretability and hinders their application in clinical practice.

In this paper, we construct a new wound healing dataset. This dataset comprises internal tissue collagen images collected from the normal skin (control group) and skin with wound healing at various continuous stages (0, 3, 7, 10 days) of the mouse. Additionally, to investigate the issue of delayed healing caused by diabetes, collagen images from diabetic mouse skin with wound healing at 10 days have been also collected. To reduce the interference from the irrelevant information, we design a task-related knowledge refinement learning framework using the previous class association embedding method [21], where a generative adversarial network is designed for separating the class/task-related information from the class/task-unrelated information. The network consists of two encoders, a decoder and a multi-class discriminator. One encoder is designed to extract task-related knowledge, i.e., information that is related to the wound healing progress detection (represented by one wound-related code, marked as C_{wr}) of the images, while the other encoder is used to learn task-unrelated knowledge, i.e., information unrelated to the wound healing progress detection (represented by one wound-unrelated code, marked as C_{wu}). Feeding the C_{wr} and the C_{wu} codes into the decoder could generate new samples, and the multi-class discriminator is designed for guiding the generated images to be real and with correct class. A random-pairing and code-swapping training method is used to separate the task-related (wound-related) information from the task-unrelated (wound-unrelated) information. Then we use trained encoder to extract C_{wr} codes from the images in the training set and the test set, and conduct classification study based on these codes. Specifically, Support Vector Machine (SVM) [22], Random Forest [23], XGBoost [24], and LightGBM [25] models (simple and with strong interpretability) are designed for classification task. We compare our algorithm with other complex and non-interpretable models, and the experimental results demonstrates that our algorithm outperforms others. Besides, we perform analysis on our learned C_{wr} codes and further demonstrate the wound-related features we extract are with strong interpretability.

2 Related Work

2.1 The Traditional Methods for Collagen Analysis

There are many methods proposed based on the handcrafted features for collagen image analysis for evaluating the status of wound healing, which are all classified as the traditional methods. For example, Ayres et al. proposed a method based on two-dimensional fast Fourier transform (2D FFT) for measuring the alignment of fibers [26]. Considering that existing techniques are not effective in identifying areas of high fiber alignment, such as hypertrophic scars, Kyle et al. proposed a weighted direction vector summation algorithm, which can simultaneously detect the fiber direction of every pixel in a medical image with 2 to 3° of accuracy within a few seconds, and is used to evaluate changes in collagen fiber arrangement and density during scar formation [6,7]. Clemons et al. proposed a new quantitative method for analyzing the coherency of collagen orientation and demonstrated its superiority in normal and scar skin and tendon tissue [27]. Woessner et al. used quantitative polarized light imaging system to characterize the orientation and thickness of collagen fibers in wound sections, and found that the thickness of collagen fibers increased significantly and the reorganization showed nonlinear changes during wound healing [28].

2.2   Collagen Analysis Methods Based on Deep Learning

Traditional collagen analysis methods primarily rely on handcrafted feature extraction and subjective interpretation by observers to quantify the spatial structure of collagen. However, these approaches face significant challenges in achieving automation and comprehensive analysis. Deep learning methods have gradually gained popularity in recent years. Pham et al. developed deep learning models to classify scar and normal skin tissue using collagen images [19,20]. Jiang et al. designed a collagen classification model using a residual network architecture, which demonstrated remarkable accuracy in predicting the survival rates of colorectal cancer patients [29]. In addition, the deep learning-based collagen classification model has been used to elucidate the relationship between collagen and the development of breast cancer [30]. Alexandra et al. utilized a convolutional neural network to reveal a significant correlation between the overall and local stiffness of breast tissue and the proportion of linear collagen [31]. Park et al. employed deep neural networks to extract the centerlines of collagen fibers from microscopic images of pathological samples, facilitating comprehensive quantitative analyses [32].

3   Method

3.1   Overall Framework of Our Work

Figure 1 illustrates the overall framework of our work. We first construct a continuous-time wound healing dataset (A). Then, using this dataset, we employ a random pairing and code swapping based generative adversarial training approach to train a model capable of extracting task-related information, i.e. features associated with the wound healing progress (B). Finally, using the trained model, we obtain wound-related feature (represented by an 8-dimensional code) for each image, and perform a classification study on these codes using simple machine learning models (C).

3.2   Construction of the Histological Wound Healing Dataset

In order to predict the progress of wound healing based on collagen, we collected histological images reflecting the morphological changes of collagen at

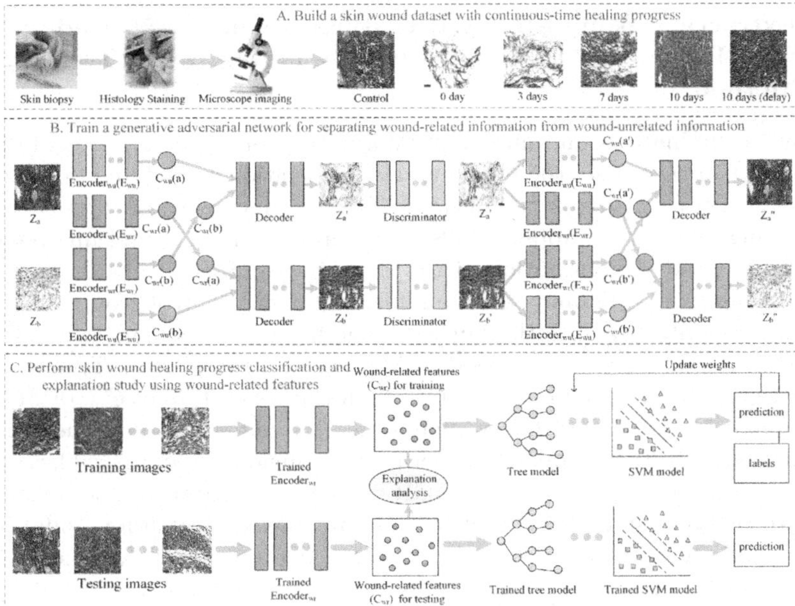

Fig. 1. Overall framework of our work.

different time points of wound healing. Wound healing images are collected from male nude mice, aged between 6–8 weeks and weighing between 20–23 grams. Data collection involved three main steps: skin biopsy, histological staining, and microscope imaging. In skin biopsy, we utilized the wound splint model introduced by X. Wang (2019) [33]. Histological staining was performed using Masson's trichrome staining method, which colors collagen fibers blue, while hair follicles and sweat glands are stained red or purple. Finally, imaging was conducted using a 40× magnification microscope (Hamamatsu NanoZoomer S60, with a resolution of 0.26 μm/pixel) equipped with a digital camera. We acquired histological images of the mouse skin wounds with healing at 0, 3, 7, and 10 days (number of images: 12, 15, 31 and 82 respectively). As the wound healing process progresses, there is a significant trend towards increased number and density of collagen fibers. Therefore, during the early stages of wound healing (0 day, 3 days), due to limited collagen fiber production, we can only obtain relatively few images of healing. Besides, we also collected 33 histological images of skin wounds with healing at 10 days from mouse with diabetes and experiencing delayed healing, which were classified into the 10 days (delay) group. Together with 51 images from normal mouse skin (Control group), our dataset contains images with six classes in total.

3.3 Extracting Wound-Related Features Using GAN Model with Random Pairing and Code Swapping Based Training Method

In order to eliminate wound-unrelated information for better assessment of healing states, as presented in the previous class association embedding work [21], we employ a generative adversarial network (GAN), which is trained based on random pairing and code swapping skills for separating class/wound-unrelated and class/wound-related information of the skin images. Specifically, in each iteration of training, we randomly select an image from the control group, denoted as Z_a, and randomly pair it with another image from other groups (with wound), denoted as Z_b. Then, we use encoders (E_{wu} and E_{wr}) to process Z_a and Z_b separately (with shared weights). This results in the generation of $C_{wu}(a)$, $C_{wr}(a)$, $C_{wu}(b)$, and $C_{wr}(b)$ codes. By swapping the C_{wr} codes, we input the new code combinations into the decoder to generate new images Z'_a and Z'_b. These generated images are then passed into a multi-class discriminator, and loss functions, as shown in Eq. 1 and 2, are used to calculate the loss value for updating the weights of the encoders and decoder. If the generated images are not realistic and fail to deceive the discriminator, it would be penalized based on Eq. 1. If Z'_a is not classified as the same category as Z_b, Z'_b is not classified as the same category as Z_a, by the multi-class discriminator, it would be penalized based on Eq. 2. As a result, the C_{wr} code needs to contain sufficient class-related information, while C_{wu} code should not carry class-related information, otherwise, it will be difficult for achieving successful class transfer on generated samples. We perform the second-round encoding of the generated images and again exchange the class-related codes to form new code combinations, which are fed into the decoder to generate new images Z''_a and Z''_b. A reconstruction loss function, as shown in Eq. 3, is set to guide the generation of Z''_a to resemble Z_a and Z''_b to resemble Z_b, which ensures that the code combinations contain class-unrelated information from the samples. Since the dimension of C_{wr} is low (8), containing sufficient class-related information means that the class-unrelated information would be squeezed out and injected into the C_{wu} code. During each iteration of training, we update the parameters of the encoders and the decoder based on Eqs. 1 to 3, and adjust the discriminator weights using Eqs. 4 and 5. Through numerous rounds of random pairing and exchange training, the class-unrelated (i.e., wound-unrelated) and the class-related (i.e., wound-related) information could be well separated and refined into the C_{wu} and C_{wr} codes as expected.

$$\mathcal{L}_{real} = -log\frac{exp(f_{Dr}(Z'_a)[1])}{exp(f_{Dr}(Z'_a)[0]) + exp(f_{Dr}(Z'_a)[1])}$$
$$-log\frac{exp(f_{Dr}(Z'_b)[1])}{exp(f_{Dr}(Z'_b)[0]) + exp(f_{Dr}(Z'_b)[1])} \tag{1}$$

$$\mathcal{L}_{class} = -log\frac{exp(f_{Dc}(Z'_a)[c_b])}{\sum_{i=0}^{i=C-1}(exp(f_{Dc}(Z'_a)[i]))} - log\frac{exp(f_{Dc}(Z'_b)[c_a])}{\sum_{i=0}^{i=C-1}(exp(f_{Dc}(Z'_b)[i]))} \tag{2}$$

$$\mathcal{L}_{recon} = 1/MN \sum_{i=0}^{i=M-1} \sum_{j=0}^{j=N-1} (|Z_a''(i,j) - Z_a(i,j)|)$$

$$+1/MN \sum_{i=0}^{i=M-1} \sum_{j=0}^{j=N-1} (|Z_b''(i,j) - Z_b(i,j)|) \tag{3}$$

$$\mathcal{L}_{real2} = -log \frac{exp(f_{Dr}(Z_a')[0])}{exp(f_{Dr}(Z_a')[0]) + exp(f_{Dr}(Z_a')[1])}$$

$$-log \frac{exp(f_{Dr}(Z_b')[0])}{exp(f_{Dr}(Z_b')[0]) + exp(f_{Dr}(Z_b')[1])}$$

$$-log \frac{exp(f_{Dr}(Z_a)[1])}{exp(f_{Dr}(Z_a)[0]) + exp(f_{Dr}(Z_a)[1])}$$

$$-log \frac{exp(f_{Dr}(Z_b)[1])}{exp(f_{Dr}(Z_b)[0]) + exp(f_{Dr}(Z_b)[1])} \tag{4}$$

$$\mathcal{L}_{class2} = -log \frac{exp(f_{Dc}(Z_a)[c_a])}{\sum_{i=0}^{i=C-1}(exp(f_{Dc}(Z_a)[i]))} - log \frac{exp(f_{Dc}(Z_b)[c_b])}{\sum_{i=0}^{i=C-1}(exp(f_{Dc}(Z_b)[i]))} \tag{5}$$

3.4 Detecting Wound Healing Status via Would-Related Features

We train a generative network using the method described in Sect. 3.3. Using the trained encoders from this network, we extract the wound-related features C_{wr} from each image in both training and test sets. Then we design several simple models to perform classification study on these wound-related codes. We train these models using the C_{wr} codes from the training set and evaluate the performance of the trained models on the prediction of wound healing status using the C_{wr} codes from the test set. Specifically, we design SVM, Random Forest, LightGBM, and XGBoost models for classification task. Compared with black-box deep learning models, these models have simpler structures and with stronger interpretability, making them more suitable for medical scenarios. In addition, Stripping away class-unrelated (wound-unrelated) information makes the input to the model simpler and cleaner, reducing interference from unnecessary information, which can improve the models' detection efficiency and accuracy.

4 Experiments

4.1 Dataset Split and Implementation Details

To comprehensively evaluate the model's performance and ensure the repeatability of the results, we applied five-fold cross-validation to divide the data into five subsets. In each division, we keep 80% of the data as the training set and 20% as the test set, and ensure that there are no cross-duplications between the five test sets, thus ensuring that all the data has been used as the test set.

During the training of the wound-related feature extraction module, we scaled all images to 256×256 size. We applied data augmentation to the training data by performing random horizontal flips with a probability of 0.5. The network was trained using the Adam optimizer with learning rate of 0.0001. For the classification study of the wound healing status, all models were implemented using publicly available Python libraries (LGBMClassifier, XGBClassifier, and sklearn), and the parameters were set to their default values.

4.2   Evaluation Metrics

We used Accuracy, Precision, Recall and F1 Score, to evaluate the classification performance. Their definitions were presented as Eqs. 6 to 9. Among them, TP refers to true positive instances, TN refers to true negative instances, FP refers to false positive instances, and FN refers to false negative instances.

$$Accuracy = (TP + TN)/(TP + TN + FP + FN) \tag{6}$$

$$Precision = TP/(TP + FP) \tag{7}$$

$$Recall = TP/(TP + FN) \tag{8}$$

$$F1 = 2 \times (Precision \times Recall)/(Precision + Recall) \tag{9}$$

4.3   Experimental Results

As baselines, we employed deep learning models ResNet [34], DeiT [35], Swin-ViT [36], ConvNeXt [37], and Qformer [38] for comparison, where original collagen images are used as input(trained for 300 epochs). We used simple models, XGBoost, LightGBM, SVM and Random Forests for classification study, which took the wound-related features we learned as inputs, and were marked as $XGB+wrf$, $LGBM+wrf$, $SVM+wrf$, $RF+wrf$ respectively. The results of all models on the five dataset partitions are presented in Table 1. Almost all simple machine learning models outperformed the deep learning ones.

Table 1. Results of wound healing status classification.

Methods	Accuracy	Precision	Recall	F1 score
Resnet	0.80 ± 0.04	0.81± 0.02	0.81 ± 0.04	0.79 ± 0.03
Deit	0.72 ± 0.03	0.73 ± 0.04	0.71± 0.02	0.70 ± 0.03
Swin-vit	0.73 ± 0.06	0.72 ± 0.08	0.73± 0.06	0.70 ± 0.07
ConvNeXt	0.75 ± 0.03	0.76 ± 0.02	0.75 ± 0.02	0.73 ± 0.03
Qformer	0.78 ± 0.07	0.77 ± 0.12	0.77 ± 0.07	0.75 ± 0.09
XGB+wrf	0.77 ± 0.02	0.86 ± 0.05	0.79 ± 0.03	0.81 ± 0.04
LGBM+wrf	0.84 ± 0.01	0.85 ± 0.02	0.83 ± 0.01	0.84 ± 0.01
SVM+wrf	0.85 ± 0.02	0.87 ± 0.02	0.86 ± 0.01	0.85 ± 0.02
RF+wrf	**0.88 ± 0.05**	**0.88 ± 0.04**	**0.88 ± 0.04**	**0.87 ± 0.04**

4.4   Ablation Study for Evaluating the Effectiveness of the Wound-Related Features for Healing Progress Classification

Using the task-related knowledge refinement learning method, we can extract the features of the images that are related to the wound healing progress detection (our task), which means that we can eliminate the information that is unrelated to the wound healing progress detection, thus reducing the data interference and achieving higher accuracy even though the simple models are employed. To demonstrate the effectiveness of using wound-related features for classification, we perform ablation study. We used original images as the inputs of the models XGBoost, LightGBM, SVM and Random Forests for classification study, which are marked as $XGB + img$, $LGBM + img$, $SVM + img$, $RF + img$ respectively. As shown in Table 2, we compared the classification results with the experiments where the same models were employed but the inputs of the models were replaced as the wound-related features extracted from the images. We can see that the performance could be well improved when using the wound-related features as model inputs, which demonstrates the effectiveness of task-related knowledge learning for extracting wound-related features for classification.

Table 2. Results of ablation study for wound-related features.

Methods	Accuracy	Precision	Recall	F1 score
XGB+img	0.59 ± 0.03	0.62 ± 0.03	0.59 ± 0.04	0.59 ± 0.03
XGB+wrf	**0.77 ± 0.02**	**0.86 ± 0.05**	**0.79 ± 0.03**	**0.81 ± 0.04**
LGBM+img	0.60 ± 0.04	0.62 ± 0.03	0.60 ± 0.05	0.59 ± 0.05
LGBM+wrf	**0.84 ± 0.01**	**0.85 ± 0.02**	**0.83 ± 0.01**	**0.84 ± 0.01**
SVM+img	0.56±0.04	0.49 ± 0.086	0.55 ± 0.04	0.48 ± 0.06
SVM+wrf	**0.85 ± 0.02**	**0.87 ± 0.02**	**0.86 ± 0.01**	**0.85 ± 0.02**
RF+img	0.60 ± 0.04	0.62 ± 0.03	0.60 ± 0.05	0.59 ± 0.05
RF+wrf	**0.88 ± 0.05**	**0.88 ± 0.04**	**0.88 ± 0.04**	**0.87 ± 0.04**

4.5   Explanability Analysis of the Wound-Related Features

To further validate the reliability of the wound-related features, we applied the trained encoder to extract wound-related features from five different partitioned test sets. We then use t-SNE analysis to visualize the features, as shown in Fig. 2. We can see that different classes were well-separated. More importantly, during the training process, we did not introduce any supervision related to the wound healing time and disease, and the model was only tasked with distinguishing between different classes. However, the results demonstrate that, as healing time progresses (denoted by 1–4), the samples gradually approach the control group (denoted by 0). This suggests that the wound is progressively healing and returning to normal, which aligns with medical knowledge. Furthermore, the samples with diabetes disease and wound healing at 10 days (represented by 5) are further from the control group than those samples without disease and with wound healing at 10 days (represented by 4), which is consistent with clinical knowledge that wound healing can be delayed in the presence of underlying diseases. The above results indicate that the feature distribution in the learned class-related space is consistent with medical rules and is interpretable.

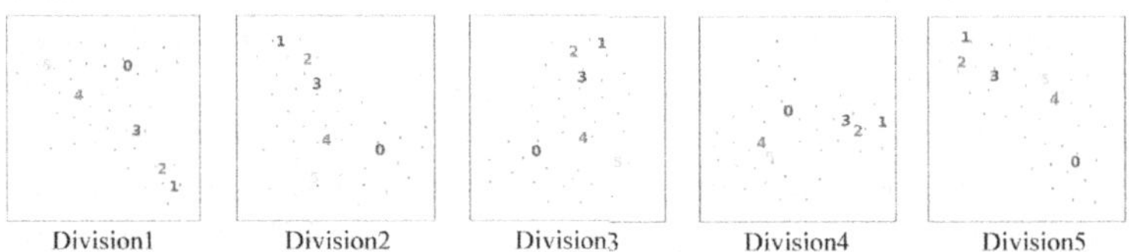

Fig. 2. T-SNE analysis results of the wound-related features extracted from different division test sets, where the numbers 0, 1, 2, 3, 4 represent the control samples, and the samples with wound healing at 0, 3, 7, 10 days respectively (without diabetes), while 5 refers to the samples with diabetes and with wound healing at 10 days. The big numbers in the figures denote the centers of the samples with the same class.

5   Conclusion

Automatic wound healing progress detection holds significant clinical value. However, there is currently no dataset that provides continuous time-series collagen imaging of wound healing, and existing methods typically take the entire images as inputs, which introduces a lot of irrelevant information that hampers performance. To address these issues, we build the first dataset of wound healing collagen images with continuous time observations, filling an important data gap in this field. And based on this dataset, we propose a task-related knowledge refinement learning framework, which employs a generative adversarial network trained by a random-pairing and code-swapping strategy for eliminating task-irrelevant information. Using the trained model, we successfully extract task-related knowledge (i.e., wound-related features) of the images. Based on these wound-related features (where task-unrelated information is removed) that have lower complexity (size of $8 \times 1 \times 1$) and greater specificity, we can apply simple and interpretable machine learning models for classification, achieving superior performance compared to complex black-box models in detecting wound healing progress. Furthermore, the wound-related manifold learned by our approach aligns with established medical principles, demonstrating strong interpretability and reliability of our task-related feature learning method. It is worth noting that our method is also applicable to other complex classification tasks prone to interference from irrelevant information, and in the future, we will conduct further applied study based on our proposed method.

Acknowledgment. This work was supported by the National Natural Science Foundation of China under grant No. U22A2041, in part by the Science and Technology Development Fund, Macao S.A.R under Grant 0046/2023/RIA1, by the University of Macau and the University of Macau Development Foundation under Grant MYRG-GRG2023-00106-FST-UMDF.

References

1. Gonzalez, A., Costa, T.F., et al.: Wound healing - a literature review. An. Bras. Dermatol. **91**(5), 614–620 (2016)
2. Falanga, V., , R.R., Soulika, A.M., et al.: Chronic wounds. Nat. Rev. Dis. Prim. **8**(1), 50[EB/OL] (2022)
3. Sen, C.K.: Human wound and its burden: updated 2020 compendium of estimates. Adv. Wound Care **10**(5), 281–292 (2021)
4. Raeder, K., Jachan, D.E., Müller-Werdan, U., et al.: Prevalence and risk factors of chronic wounds in nursing homes in Germany: a cross-sectional study. Int. Wound J. **17**(5), 1128–1134 (2020)
5. Rodrigues, M., Kosaric, N., Bonham, C.A., et al.: Wound healing: a cellular perspective. Physiol. Rev. (2018)
6. Quinn, K.P., et al.: Rapid quantification of pixel-wise fiber orientation data in micrographs. J. Biomed. Opt. **18**(4) (2013)
7. Quinn, K.P., Golberg, A., Broelsch, G.F., et al.: An automated image processing method to quantify collagen fibre organization within cutaneous scar tissue. Exp. Dermatol. **24**(1), 78–80 (2015)
8. Zhang, F., Chen, G., Wang, H., et al.: CF-DAN: facial-expression recognition based on cross-fusion dual-attention network. Comput. Vis. Media **10**(3), 593–608 (2024)
9. Xie, R., Qiu, C., Qiu, G.: Finding beautiful and happy images for mental health and well-being applications. In: Chinese Conference on Pattern Recognition and Computer Vision (PRCV), pp. 704–717. Springer, Cham (2022)
10. Wu, W., Dai, T., Chen, Z., et al.: Generative prompt controlled diffusion for weakly supervised semantic segmentation. Neurocomputing **638**, 130103 (2025)
11. Wu, W., Qiu, X., Song, S., et al.: Prompt categories cluster for weakly supervised semantic segmentation. arXiv preprint arXiv:2412.13823 (2024)
12. Xiao, H., Liu, S., Zuo, K., et al.: Multiple adverse weather image restoration: a review. Neurocomputing, 129044 (2024)
13. Li, S., Li, B., Sun, B., et al.: Towards visual-prompt temporal answer grounding in instructional video. IEEE Trans. Pattern Anal. Mach. Intell. (2024)
14. Zhang, F., Chen, G., Wang, H., et al.: Multi-scale video super-resolution transformer with polynomial approximation. IEEE Trans. Circuits Syst. Video Technol. **33**(9), 4496–4506 (2023)
15. Weng, Y., Li, B., et al.: Large language models with holistically thought could be better doctors. In: CCF International Conference on Natural Language Processing and Chinese Computing, pp. 319–332. Springer, Singapore (2024)
16. Yang, J., Sadiq, T., Xiong, J., et al.: A novel myocarditis detection combining deep reinforcement learning and an improved differential evolution algorithm. CAAI Trans. Intell. Technol. **9**(6), 1347–1360 (2024)
17. Yang, J., Yang, J., Wu, C., et al.: Multiple sclerosis detection with reinforcement learning and differential evolution. In: ICASSP 2025–2025 IEEE International Conference on Acoustics, Speech and Signal Processing (ICASSP), pp. 1–5. IEEE (2025)

18. Carrión, H., Jafari, M., Yang, H.Y., et al.: Healnet-self-supervised acute wound heal-stage classification. In: International Workshop on Machine Learning in Medical Imaging, pp. 446–455. Springer, Cham (2022)
19. Pham, T., Kim, H., et al.: Deep learning for analysis of collagen fiber organization in scar tissue. IEEE Access **9**, 101755–101764 (2021)
20. Pham, T., Kim, H., Lee, Y., et al.: Universal convolutional neural network for histology-independent analysis of collagen fiber organization in scar tissue. IEEE Access **10**, 34379–34392 (2022)
21. Xie, R., Chen, J., Jiang, L., et al.: Accurate explanation model for image classifiers using class association embedding. In: 2024 IEEE 40th International Conference on Data Engineering (ICDE), pp. 2271–2284. IEEE (2024)
22. Cortes, C.: Support-vector networks. Mach. Learn (1995)
23. Liaw, A.: Classification and regression by Random Forest. R News (2002)
24. Chen, T., Guestrin, C.: XBoost: a scalable tree boosting system. In: Proceedings of the 22nd ACM SIGKDD International Conference on Knowledge Discovery and Data Mining, pp. 785–794 (2016)
25. Ke, G., Meng, Q., Finley, T., et al.: LightGBM: a highly efficient gradient boosting decision tree. In: Advances in Neural Information Processing Systems, vol. 30 (2017)
26. Ayres, C.E., Jha, B.S., Meredith, H., et al.: Measuring fiber alignment in electrospun scaffolds: a user's guide to the 2D fast Fourier transform approach. J. Biomater. Sci. Polym. Ed. **19**(5), 603–621 (2008)
27. Clemons, T.D., Bradshaw, M., Toshniwal, P., et al.: Coherency image analysis to quantify collagen architecture: implications in scar assessment. RSC Adv. **8**(18), 9661–9669 (2018)
28. Woessner, A.E., McGee, J.D., et al.: Characterizing differences in the collagen fiber organization of skin wounds using quantitative polarized light imaging. Wound Repair Regener. **27**(6), 711–714 (2019)
29. Jiang, W., Wang, H., Chen, W., et al.: Association of collagen deep learning classifier with prognosis and chemotherapy benefits in stage II-III colon cancer. Bioeng. Transl. Med. **8**(3), e10526 (2023)
30. Paredes, D., et al.: Automated assessment of the curliness of collagen fiber in breast cancer. In: Bartoli, A., Fusiello, A. (eds.) ECCV 2020. LNCS, vol. 12535, pp. 267–279. Springer, Cham (2020). https://doi.org/10.1007/978-3-030-66415-2_17
31. Sneider, A., Kiemen, A., Kim, J.H., et al.: Deep learning identification of stiffness markers in breast cancer. Biomaterials **285**, 121540 (2022)
32. Park, H., Li, B., et al.: Collagen fiber centerline tracking in fibrotic tissue via deep neural networks with variational autoencoder-based synthetic training data generation. Med. Image Anal. **90**, 102961 (2023)
33. Wang, X., Jiang, B., Sun, H., et al.: Noninvasive application of mesenchymal stem cell spheres derived from hESC accelerates wound healing in a CXCL12-CXCR4 axis-dependent manner. Theranostics **9**(21), 6112 (2019)
34. He, K., Zhang, X., Ren, S., et al.: Deep residual learning for image recognition. In: Proceedings of the IEEE Conference on Computer Vision and Pattern Recognition, pp. 770–778 (2016)
35. Touvron, H., Cord, M., Douze, M., et al.: Training data-efficient image transformers & distillation through attention. In: International Conference on Machine Learning, pp. 10347–10357. PMLR (2021)
36. Liu, Z., Lin, Y., Cao, Y., et al.: Swin transformer: hierarchical vision transformer using shifted windows. In: Proceedings of the IEEE/CVF International Conference on Computer Vision, pp. 10012–10022 (2021)

37. Liu, Z., Mao, H., et al.: A convnet for the 2020s. In: Proceedings of the IEEE/CVF Conference on Computer Vision and Pattern Recognition, pp. 11976–11986 (2022)
38. Zhang, Q., Zhang, J., Xu, Y., et al.: Vision transformer with quadrangle attention. IEEE Trans. Pattern Anal. Mach. Intell. (2024)

A Novel Weighted Network Control Model for Identifying Coding and Non-coding Drivers in Cancer

Bolin Chen[1], Jianjun Zhang[1], Weihua Meng[1], Youpeng Hu[1], Yuhang Li[1], Xinyue Hu[1], Zhouning Xu[2], Zhengyu Wang[1], Xingyu Liao[1], and Xingyi Li[1(✉)]

[1] School of Computer Science, Northwestern Polytechnical University, Xi'an, China
xingyili@nwpu.edu.cn
[2] National Elite Institute of Engineering, Northwestern Polytechnical University, Xi'an, China

Abstract. A key task in cancer genomics research is the identification of cancer driver genes. In recent years, control methods have been applied to identify cancer drivers with notable success. However, these methods primarily focus on exploring the biological network topology, potentially overlooking the critical influence of node and edge weights derived from genomic data. Moreover, many methods have overly simplistic evaluation metrics and do not perform well on large networks. In our previous work, we have proposed a novel control theory-based method, along with a comprehensive evaluation metric to handle those problems. Building upon this foundation, this work further proposes an enhanced approach that incorporates a local optimal control set selection method based on the greedy algorithm to refine the identification of key drivers. Numerical experiments have been conducted to identify both coding and miRNA drivers, as well as drivers across different cancer subtypes. The experimental results demonstrate the effectiveness and robustness of the weighted network control method, highlighting its superior performance in detecting cancer driver genes.

Keywords: biological network · driver gene · control theory

1 Introduction

Cancer is widely recognized as a complex genomic disease, characterized by the accumulation of numerous genetic alterations during its initiation and progression. However, only a subset of these driver mutations contribute directly to cancer development by conferring a selective growth advantage to cancer cells [1]. In contrast, the remaining alterations are referred to as passenger mutations, which

Supported by the National Key R&D Program of China under Grant No. 2021YFA1000402, and the National Natural Science Foundation of China under Grant No. 61972320.

arise incidentally during cell division and do not influence tumor growth. Traditional mutation-based methods for identifying cancer driver genes typically focus on distinguishing driver from passenger mutations based on their recurrence or functional impact. For instance, OncodriveFM [2] identifies cancer driver genes by assessing the functional impact of their mutations. ActiveDriver [3] focuses on detecting driver genes that are significantly enriched in mutations occurring at post-translational modification (PTM) sites. However, these approaches are limited to mutation dependent mechanisms and often fail to identify drivers without observable mutations, such as genes that promote cancer through overexpression (e.g., MYC), or non-coding RNA drivers, such as microRNAs (miRNAs), which are often undetectable through mutation frequency or functional impact alone. while has been validated play diverse roles in tumor progression [4,5].

The network-based approach offers a promising alternative to identify the non-mutated driver genes and non-coding miRNA drivers. These methods typically construct networks that integrate gene expression profiles, regulatory interactions, mutation data, and epigenetic features to comprehensively analyze the functional roles of gene nodes within the network. For example, NIBNA [6] identifies both coding and non-coding drivers by evaluating the impact of removing each node on a centrality-based metric within a conditional gene regulatory network. However, network-based methods often lack a system-level perspective when evaluating node importance. Most of these approaches evaluate individual nodes in an isolation way, ignoring their informative interactions.

Recently, control theory has achieved remarkable success in the analysis of complex networks, offering a system-level framework for understanding and regulating network dynamics. In the context of cancer biology, this approach enables the identification of key control nodes capable of driving the transition of gene regulatory networks from a healthy state to a diseased state. By focusing on the controllability of the entire system, control theory provides a powerful means to uncover critical regulators, such as driver genes or miRNA, that may not exhibit strong individual signals but play essential roles in tumor initiation and progression. For example, CBNA [7] constructs a directed conditional network and identifies driver genes based on Kalman's controllability condition [8,9]. Similarly, PNC [10] utilizes a control-based approach leveraging Feedback Vertex Sets to identify personalized cancer drivers. These methods are primarily grounded in structural controllability theory, where control is largely determined by network topology and node and edge weights as well [11]. However, most existing control-based approaches place heavy emphasis on network topology while neglecting the biological significance encoded in node and edge weights, which may limit their effectiveness in identifying functionally relevant cancer drivers. In addition, current control methods do not guarantee the uniqueness of the identified control set, potentially reducing the robustness and reproducibility of the results. Furthermore, there is a lack of a unified and systematic ranking metric for prioritizing nodes within the control set, which hinders the biological interpretability of the selected drivers.

To address the limitations of existing methods, our previous work proposed the Multi-Criteria Weighted Control Model (MCWCM) [12], which integrates genomic data to generate node embeddings that serve as weights in the control set selection process. Building upon this framework, this study introduces another novel weighted network control approach the Locally Optimal Control Set Selection method (LOCSS). In contrast to the global optimization strategy employed in MCWCM, this method adopts a greedy and iterative procedure to efficiently approximate the optimal control set. At each iteration, the node with the highest marginal contribution to the overall control objective is selected, resulting in a compact yet effective control set. This enhancement not only significantly improves computational efficiency, but also enhances the robustness and stability of the identified driver genes, making the method more suitable for large-scale biological networks.

The proposed weighted control-based method was evaluated for partial control set selection on the breast invasive carcinoma (BRCA) dataset from The Cancer Genome Atlas (TCGA) [13] to identify breast cancer driver genes. The predicted drivers include mutated coding drivers, non-mutated coding drivers, and non-coding miRNA drivers. The Cancer Gene Census (CGC) [14] is used as the gold standard for validation. Experimental results demonstrate that the proposed LOCSS method outperforms the MCWCM method in terms of predictive accuracy. To further assess the biological relevance of the predicted non-mutated coding drivers, we performed Gene Ontology (GO) enrichment analysis [15], which indicates that these genes are functionally meaningful. In addition, the proposed LOCSS method was also applied on subtype-specific networks to identify subtype-specific cancer drivers, and the results were validated using expert domain knowledge. These findings highlight the effectiveness and flexibility of the weighted network control model in uncovering key cancer drivers from multiple perspectives.

2   Materials and Method

The LOCSS method follow the same framework as MCWCM [12], where three steps are conducted as follows. Firstly, a comprehensive gene interaction network is built by integrating multiple gene interaction databases with gene expression data, followed by network propagation to generate informative node attributes for each gene node. Secondly, a weighted network control model is employed to determine a control set composed of candidate driver genes. Thirdly, a multi-criteria ranking strategy is applied by integrating five biological and topological features to compute a comprehensive score for each node. Nodes with higher scores are considered more likely to be critical drivers.

The two methods are different in how the node weights are utilized in the control selection process. MCWCM formulates the problem as a global optimization task, aiming to identify a minimum weighted control set that governs the entire network. In contrast, the LOCSS method employs a greedy strategy based on marginal contribution, iteratively selecting nodes that offer the greatest improvement to the control objective. It can result in a more targeted and compact control set, offering improved computational efficiency while maintaining or even enhancing the accuracy and robustness of driver identification.

2.1 Locally Optimal Control Set Selection Method

Integer Linear Programming (ILP) provides a globally optimal solution to the weighted control problem. However, its application to large-scale networks faces two major challenges. First, ILP has an exponential time complexity, making it computationally expensive and impractical for biological networks with a large number of nodes and edges. Second, as the number of selected nodes increases, the additional contribution of newly selected nodes to target coverage gradually decreases. In some cases, covering a single node $u \in V_\perp$ may require adding multiple control nodes. This diminishing marginal contribution phenomenon suggests that nodes selected in later stages may be less critical within the network.

To address the computational complexity of the weighted control problem and mitigate the impact of diminishing marginal contribution on driver gene identification, a locally optimal control set selection method was proposed here. This method is based on the assumption that driver genes generally exhibit higher connectivity and biological significance, allowing them to be preferentially selected in early iterations. By employing a greedy strategy, the method iteratively selects the node that maximizes both coverage and node weight, efficiently constructing a locally optimal control set. This approach not only facilitates efficient control set selection in large-scale biological networks but also offers a flexible mechanism to dynamically balance coverage and node weight.

Based on the bipartite graph $G(V_\top, V_\perp, E', W_\top)$, the locally optimal control set selection method was employed to identify candidate driver gene nodes. In each iteration, this method selects an optimal node based on its marginal contribution, adhering to the following three core principles:

- **Maximum coverage principle:** Prioritizing nodes that contribute the most to covering previously uncovered target nodes (i.e., $V_\perp$).
- **Weight priority principle:** Incorporating node weight ω_v to prioritize nodes with higher biological significance.
- **Dynamic balance:** Adjusting parameter γ to flexibly balance the importance of coverage and node weight. When γ is small, the algorithm focuses more on coverage; when γ is large, it prioritizes the nodes with high weights.

To be more specific, the control set S and the set of covered nodes C were first initialized, while the set of target nodes to be covered was defined and denoted as $V_\perp$. In each iteration, the algorithm calculates the marginal contribution for each unselected node v:

$$\text{Gain}(v) = |\{u \in V_\perp \mid (v, u) \in E', u \notin C\}| + \gamma \cdot \omega_v \qquad (1)$$

where $\text{Gain}(v)$ represents the marginal contribution of node v, C is the set of already covered nodes, and γ is the parameter balancing the trade-off between the number of covered nodes and node weight. The node with the highest marginal contribution is then selected:

$$v^* = \arg \max_{v \in V_\mathsf{T} \setminus S} \mathrm{Gain}(v) \tag{2}$$

Node v^* is added to the control set S, and the target nodes it covers are updated in C. This process continues until either the maximum allowable number of selected nodes k is reached or the desired coverage ratio is achieved. The coverage ratio is computed as follows:

$$\text{Coverage Ratio} = \frac{|C|}{|V_\perp|} \tag{3}$$

The locally optimal control set selection method ensures that in each iteration, the node with the highest marginal contribution is selected. This design enables the control set to achieve a high coverage ratio with a minimal number of selected nodes while efficiently capturing key nodes in the network. We evaluated the method under different values of k (ranging from 100 to 3000) and various settings of γ, recording the changes in coverage and weight distribution. By employing this locally optimal control set selection method, biologically meaningful control sets were efficiently constructed within the network, which significantly enhancing the identification of cancer driver genes.

2.2   The Identification Metric

Cancer is a highly complex and heterogeneous disease. Relying solely on a single evaluation metric, such as mutation frequency used in CBNA or centrality-based measures employed in NIBNA, is often inadequate for accurately identifying cancer driver genes. Previous studies have demonstrated that genes often cooperate through functional interactions to promote tumorigenesis and that key regulatory nodes in biological networks frequently mediate the transition between healthy and disease states [16]. These findings suggest that the functional impact of genes may arise not solely from individual mutations or positions, but from their coordinated behavior within regulatory modules. Based on this insight, this study hypothesize that many latent driver genes function not in isolation, but as part of co-regulatory modules, collaborating with other genes to regulate specific biological processes. To more effectively capture these cooperative effects, a set of network module-based metrics was introduced that characterize the functional roles of genes within the broader network context. These metrics leverage network topology to uncover complex gene interactions and provide a more comprehensive evaluation of gene importance, thereby improving the accuracy of driver gene identification.

To more effectively capture the complex interactions within gene regulatory networks, a metric was introduced that integrates both genomic and network-based information to evaluate the importance of each gene. In MCWCM, four classical centrality measures were incorporated, including Degree Centrality

(DC), which reflects a node's direct connectivity and potential influence on its immediate neighbors; Betweenness Centrality (BC), which quantifies how often a node acts as a bridge along the shortest paths in the network; Closeness Centrality (CC), which measures how efficiently a node can reach all other nodes; and Eigenvector Centrality (EC), which considers not only a node's connections but also the importance of its neighbors. This study further extends the network characterization by incorporating Subgraph Centrality (SC), which captures a node's participation in all closed walks of different lengths and reflects its influence in local substructures. Together with mutation frequency, these six features collectively quantify each gene's topological role and genomic relevance in the network. The comprehensive metric is defined as:

$$Cm = (\lambda_1 DC + \lambda_2 BC + \lambda_3 CC + \lambda_4 EC + \lambda_5 SC) \cdot \mathrm{MF}^\theta \tag{4}$$

where λ_1 to λ_5 are tunable weights assigned to each centrality measure, and θ is a scaling factor designed to attenuate the dominance of highly mutated genes while amplifying signals from low-frequency or unmutated genes. For genes without recorded mutations, including certain coding genes and miRNAs, a small pseudo mutation frequency was assigned, allowing their topological importance to be considered during prioritization. This integrated strategy enables the identification of both prominent and hidden driver candidates through a balanced assessment of network structure and mutational signals.

3   Results

In MCWCM, a global control set comprising 5,508 nodes was identified. Among them, 1,729 coding genes and 68 non-coding miRNAs were deemed significant based on a Cm score threshold set above the average value (0.06). In this study, a LOCSS strategy was proposed to identify a more compact and targeted control set. To ensure a fair comparison with MCWCM, the same multi-criteria ranking scheme was adopted with parameter settings $\lambda_1 = 0.4$, $\lambda_2 = 0.05$, $\lambda_3 = 0.2$, $\lambda_4 = 0.2$ and $\lambda_5 = 0.15$. The performance of each method is evaluated against a gold-standard list of known cancer driver genes from the Cancer Gene Census (CGC) in the COSMIC database [14], where a higher overlap with CGC indicates better predictive accuracy. Under this evaluation framework, the proposed method identifies only 1,000 nodes in the locally optimal control set, yet achieves superior identification accuracy compared to MCWCM. This demonstrates the effectiveness of our approach in identifying biologically relevant driver genes with a significantly smaller number of selected nodes. Furthermore, the Gene Ontology (GO) enrichment analyses were conducted on the identified non-mutated driver genes and literature validations for the predicted miRNAs were performed, providing additional support for the biological significance and robustness of the identified control sets.

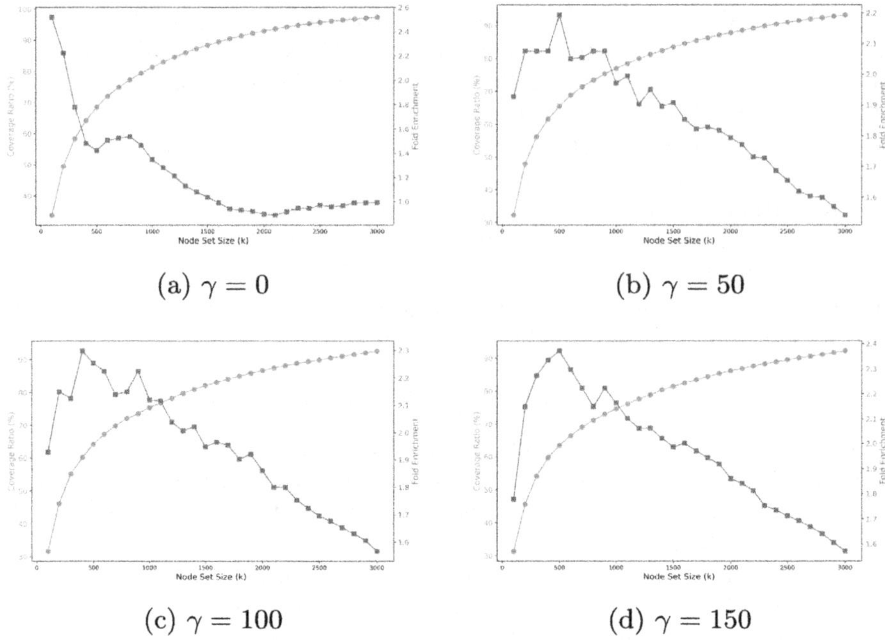

(a) $\gamma = 0$ (b) $\gamma = 50$

(c) $\gamma = 100$ (d) $\gamma = 150$

Fig. 1. Variation of coverage ratio and fold enrichment with node set size under different γ values ($\gamma = 0, 50, 100, 150$). The x-axis represents the node set size (k), i.e., the number of selected nodes in the control set. The left y-axis (in red) indicates the coverage ratio (%), reflecting the proportion of the network covered by the selected nodes. The right y-axis (in blue) shows the fold enrichment, which reflects how strongly known driver genes are enriched within the control set. (Color figure online)

3.1   Locally Optimal Control Set

The impact of different parameter values of γ on network coverage and CGC driver gene enrichment when selecting k nodes ranging from 100 to 3000 were first evaluated. As shown in Fig. 1, when $\gamma = 0$, i.e., node weights ω_v are not considered, nodes are selected greedily based solely on their contribution to covering the uncovered target nodes in $V_\perp$. In this case, the network coverage reaches 81.30% when the top 1000 nodes are selected, increases to 90.48% with 1700 nodes, and further rises to 97.40% with 3000 nodes. At smaller values of k, the method quickly covers a large proportion of target nodes, resulting in a substantial increase in total weight. However, as k increases, the coverage growth rate slows down, and the marginal contribution of newly added nodes decreases, indicating that the subsequently selected nodes tend to be less important. Without considering node weights, the enrichment of CGC driver genes gradually declines, suggesting that the greedy strategy is effective for maximizing coverage, but it lacks the ability to prioritize biologically significant nodes.

When $\gamma \neq 0$, i.e., biologically relevant node weights are incorporated, the overall network coverage does not change significantly, but the enrichment of

CGC driver genes among the selected nodes improves considerably. For example, when selecting the top 1000 nodes, the enrichment ratio increases by 2.1 times compared to the case of $\gamma = 0$; when selecting the top 3000 nodes, the enrichment ratio remains above 1.5. In contrast, with $\gamma = 0$, the enrichment ratio for the top 3000 nodes is only 1. These results indicate that incorporating node weights has limited impact on network coverage but significantly enhances the prioritization of biologically meaningful driver genes.

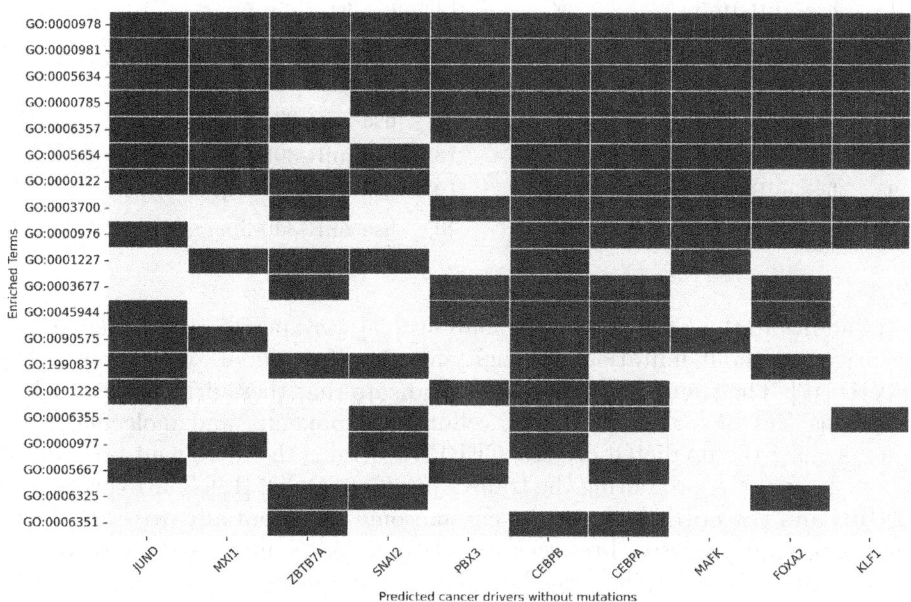

Fig. 2. GO enrichment analysis. The terms shown in the figure represent the ranking of the top 20 most enriched terms in GO biological processes, GO cell components, and GO molecular functions.

3.2 Discovering Coding Cancer Drivers Without Mutations and MiRNA Cancer Drivers

Most current methods focus solely on identifying coding drivers. In contrast, our approach leverages natural advantageous properties, enabling drivers without mutations to achieve high Cm scores. Consequently, by setting Mf^{θ} to a slightly higher value, we can simultaneously identify both coding drivers with mutations and those without mutations. Specifically, we set $Mf^{\theta} = 0.2$ for coding drivers without mutations, while the average Mf^{θ} for coding drivers with mutations is approximately 0.37. This allows us to identify 10 coding drivers without mutations, with CEBPA being one of those listed in the CGC.

Table 1. Top 20 miRNA drivers discovered by the weighted control method. A ✓ in the 'Validated' column indicates whether the miRNA is linked to the formation of BRCA validated by OncomiR.

Rank	Predicted miRNA driver	Validated	Rank	Predicted miRNA driver	Validated
1	hsa-miR-34a-5p	✓	11	hsa-miR-26b-5p	-
2	hsa-miR-15a-5p	✓	12	hsa-miR-320a	✓
3	hsa-miR-93-5p	✓	13	hsa-miR-106b-5p	✓
4	hsa-miR-16-5p	✓	14	hsa-let-7f-5p	-
5	hsa-miR-20a-5p	-	15	hsa-let-7e-5p	✓
6	hsa-miR-17-5p	✓	16	hsa-miR-181b-5p	✓
7	hsa-miR-107	✓	17	hsa-miR-30d-5p	✓
8	hsa-miR-15b-5p	✓	18	hsa-miR-30b-5p	✓
9	hsa-miR-181a-5p	✓	19	hsa-miR-181c-5p	-
10	hsa-miR-103a-3p	✓	20	hsa-miR-340-5p	✓

In addition, the GO enrichment analyses [15] were performed on the 10 coding drivers without mutations through an online functional annotation tool of DAVID [17]. The results, shown in Fig 2, indicate that these drivers are involved in various GO biological processes, cellular components, and molecular functions. Among the predicted drivers, CEBPA restrains the malignant progression of breast cancer by promoting the transcription of SOCS2 [18]. The expression of CEBPB and the miRNA cluster on chromosome 19 potentially drive the development of triple negative breast cancers [19]. SNAI2 enhances the invasiveness of malignant breast cancer cells when its expression is upregulated as a result of the epigenetic silencing of miR-203 [20].

There were 68 non-coding miRNAs identifying as potential cancer drivers that may be associated with breast cancer. To assess the significance of these identified miRNA drivers in tumor formation, the database of OncomiR [21] was utilized, applying a *p-value* threshold of 0.05 for evaluation. This evaluation validated 51 miRNAs(75%) as playing a potential role in breast cancer, demonstrating a higher accuracy compared to other methods.

The top-20 miRNA driver list is documented in Table 1. Among these, 16 miRNAs are involved in tumor formation according to OncomiR. Although some miRNAs in the table, such as hsa-miR-20a-5p, are not validated by OncomiR, recent research has shown that miR-20a-5p promotes or inhibits breast cancer by targeting downstream signaling pathways [22]. Thus, the remaining miRNAs in the list serve as valuable references for further breast cancer research.

3.3   Identifying Drivers for Different Subtypes

Breast cancer is a highly heterogeneous disease comprising various subtypes, each characterized by distinct morphologies, molecular profiles, and clinical manifestations. The heterogeneity of breast cancer subtypes necessitates a tailored approach to subtype driver gene analysis. Each subtypen's unique molecular profile guides the identification of driver genes and offers targeted therapeutic strategies.

The weighted control method was applied for each subtype of BRCA. There are 747 samples in BRCA dataset divided for each subtype according to the Pam50 method [23,24]. As a result, it produces 108 samples of Her2 subtype, 221 samples of Luminal A subtype, 165 samples of Luminal B subtype, 158 samples of the Basal subtype, and 95 samples in Normal-like subtype. We focus exclusively on drivers that are uniquely present in a specific subtype and absent in all other subtypes. The discovered coding drivers and miRNA drivers are listed in Table 2 and Table 3, respectively.

The predicted drivers was validated in each cancer subtype by checking the existing literature. The BIRC6 gene is frequently found to have a higher frequency of amplifications and copy number gains specifically in the HER2-positive subtype of breast cancer [25]. Similarly, OTUD7B is discovered highly expressed especially in the luminal A subtype breast cancer and it stabilizes estrogen receptor α, promoting breast cancer cell proliferation [26]. Additionally, SOX2, is an embryonic transcription factor located at chromosome 3q, a region frequently gained in sporadic basal-like breast cancer, plays a critical role in the development of this aggressive subtype [27].

Table 2. Predicted unique subtype-specific coding drivers for each subtype.

Subtype	Predicted coding drivers
Her2	MGA, UBC, LCOR, BIRC6, SHOC2, THBS1, CHD7, NFE2L1
Luminal A	ELF3, OTUD7B, CDKN1B, WEE1, CNNM2, KLF5, IRF4
Luminal B	ANKFY1, PLXNA2, AAK1, ZBTB16, LUZP1, SCN2A, PRPF8, FN1, WNK3, HNRNPU
Basal	VCL, GLI2, YWHAZ, SOX2, DYRK2, PDE3A, CCND2, AHR, MITF, ATP2B1, ATF1, SCN1A, TP63
Normal-like	BACH2, POU2F1, SPRED1, TNRC6C

Table 3. Predicted unique subtype-specific non-coding drivers for each subtype.

Subtype	Predicted miRNAs drivers
Her2	hsa-miR-3666, hsa-miR-4500, hsa-miR-302e
Luminal A	hsa-miR-320c
Luminal B	hsa-miR-195-5p
Basal	hsa-miR-125b-5p, hsa-miR-374b-5p, hsa-miR-129-5p, hsa-let-7c-5p
Normal-like	hsa-miR-142-5p, hsa-miR-196a-5p, hsa-miR-33a-5p, hsa-miR-520b, hsa-miR-301b-3p, hsa-miR-192-5p

4   Conclusion

While existing control methods primarily focus on network topology, they often overlook the role of node and edge weights in guiding the selection of effective control nodes. Additionally, there is a lack of a unified ranking metric for evaluating the importance of selected gene nodes. To address these limitations, a Locally Optimal Control Set Selection strategy was proposed, which integrates both topological structure and node-level biological information, and employs a greedy algorithm based on marginal contribution to iteratively construct a compact yet effective control set.

Compared to the global optimization approach in MCWCM, the proposed method significantly improves computational efficiency, enhances robustness, and maintains high predictive accuracy with a substantially smaller number of selected nodes. In addition to mutated coding genes, the weighted control framework is capable of identifying non-mutated coding drivers and non-coding miRNA drivers. It was also extended to identify cancer drivers in subtype-specific networks.

Overall, the proposed approach demonstrates excellent performance across diverse scenarios for identifying key cancer drivers and offers a promising framework for studying the molecular mechanisms underlying cancer initiation and progression.

References

1. Vogelstein, B., Papadopoulos, N., Velculescu, V.E., et al.: Cancer genome landscapes. Science **339**(6127), 1546–1558 (2013)
2. Gonzalez-Perez, A., Lopez-Bigas, N.: Functional impact bias reveals cancer drivers. Nucleic Acids Res. **40**(21), e169 (2012)
3. Reimand, J., Bader, G.D.: Systematic analysis of somatic mutations in phosphorylation signaling predicts novel cancer drivers. Mol. Syst. Biol. **9**, 637 (2013)
4. Puente, X.S., Beà, S., Valdés-Mas, R., et al.: Non-coding recurrent mutations in chronic lymphocytic leukaemia. Nature **526**(7574), 519–524 (2015)
5. Weinhold, N., Jacobsen, A., Schultz, N., et al.: Genome-wide analysis of noncoding regulatory mutations in cancer. Nat. Genet. **46**(11), 1160–1165 (2014)
6. Chaudhary, M.S., Pham, V., Le, T.D.: NIBNA: a network-based node importance approach for identifying breast cancer drivers. Bioinformatics **37**(17), 2521–2528 (2021)
7. Pham, V., Liu, L., Bracken, C.P., et al.: CBNA: a control theory based method for identifying coding and non-coding cancer drivers. PLoS Comput. Biol. **15**(12), e1007538 (2019)
8. Liu, Y.Y., Slotine, J.J., Barabási, A.L.: Controllability of complex networks. Nature **473**(7346), 167–173 (2011)
9. Kalman, R.E.: Mathematical description of linear dynamical systems. J. Soc. Ind. Appl. Math. Ser. A: Control **1**(2), 152–192 (1963)
10. Guo, W.F., Zhang, S.W., Zeng, T., et al.: A novel network control model for identifying personalized driver genes in cancer. PLoS Comput. Biol. **15**(11), e1007520 (2019)

11. D'Souza, R.M., di Bernardo, M., Liu, Y.Y.: Controlling complex networks with complex nodes. Nat. Rev. Phys. **5**(4), 250–262 (2023)

12. Chen, B., Wang, Z., Li, Z.: MCWCM: multi-criteria ranking and weighted control model for identifying key drivers in cancer. In: Proceedings of the 15th ACM International Conference on Bioinformatics, Computational Biology and Health Informatics, pp. 1–6 (2024)

13. Weinstein, J.N., Collisson, E.A., Mills, G.B.: The Cancer Genome Atlas Pan-Cancer analysis project. Nat. Genet. **45**(10), 1113–1120 (2013)

14. Futreal, P.A., Coin, L., Marshall, M.: A census of human cancer genes. Nat. Rev. Cancer **4**(3), 177–183 (2004)

15. Harris, M.A., Clark, J., Ireland, A.: The Gene Ontology (GO) database and informatics resource. Nucleic Acids Res. **32**(suppl_1), D258–D261 (2004)

16. Vinayagam, A., Gibson, T.E., Lee, H.J., et al.: Controllability analysis of the directed human protein interaction network identifies disease genes and drug targets. Proc. Natl. Acad. Sci. U.S.A. **113**(18), 4976–4981 (2016)

17. Dennis, G., Jr., Sherman, B.T., Hosack, D.A., et al.: DAVID: database for annotation, visualization, and integrated discovery. Genome Biol. **4**(5), P3 (2003)

18. Wang, J.L., Ji, W.W., Huang, A.L., et al.: CEBPA restrains the malignant progression of breast cancer by prompting the transcription of SOCS2. Mol. Biotechnol. **67**(5), 2127–2137 (2025)

19. Jinesh, G.G., Flores, E.R., Brohl, A.S.: Chromosome 19 miRNA cluster and CEBPB expression specifically mark and potentially drive triple negative breast cancers. PLoS ONE **13**(10), e0206008 (2018)

20. Zhang, Z., Zhang, B., Li, W., et al.: Epigenetic silencing of miR-203 upregulates SNAI2 and contributes to the invasiveness of malignant breast cancer cells. Genes Cancer **2**(8), 782–791 (2011)

21. Wong, N.W., Chen, Y., Chen, S., et al.: OncomiR: an online resource for exploring pan-cancer microRNA dysregulation. Bioinformatics **34**(4), 713–715 (2018)

22. Huang, W., Wu, X., Xiang, S., et al.: Regulatory mechanism of miR-20a-5p expression in Cancer. Cell Death Discov. **8**(1), 262 (2022)

23. Liu, M.C., Pitcher, B.N., Mardis, E.R., et al.: PAM50 gene signatures and breast cancer prognosis with adjuvant anthracycline- and taxane-based chemotherapy: correlative analysis of C9741 (Alliance). NPJ Breast Cancer. **2**, 15023 (2016)

24. Parker, J.S., Mullins, M., Cheang, M.C., et al.: Supervised risk predictor of breast cancer based on intrinsic subtypes. J. Clin. Oncol. **27**(8), 1160–1167 (2009)

25. Gómez, Bergna, S.M., Marchesini, A., Amor'os, Morales, L.C., et al.: Exploring the role of the inhibitor of apoptosis BIRC6 in breast cancer: a database analysis. JCO Clin. Cancer Inform. **6**, e2200093 (2022)

26. Tang, J., Wu, Z., Tian, Z., et al.: OTUD7B stabilizes estrogen receptor and promotes breast cancer cell proliferation. Cell Death Dis. **12**(6), 534 (2021)

27. Rodriguez-Pinilla, S.M., Sarrio, D., Moreno-Bueno, G., et al.: Sox2: a possible driver of the basal-like phenotype in sporadic breast cancer. Mod. Pathol. **20**(4), 474–481 (2007)

A Survival Prediction Model Integrating Hierarchical Pathological Image and Pathway Features

Xinyue Xu[1], Wei Peng[1,2(✉)], Wei Dai[1,2], Xiaodong Fu[1], Li Liu[1], and Lijun Liu[1]

[1] Faculty of Information Engineering and Automation, Kunming University of Science and Technology, Kunming 650050, China
{weipeng,daiwei}@kust.edu.cn

[2] Computer Technology Application Key Lab of Yunnan Province, Kunming University of Science and Technology, Kunming 650050, China

Abstract. Accurate cancer survival prediction is crucial for personalized treatment. Current methods often rely on single-magnification patch features from Whole Slide Images (WSIs), overlooking multi-level image information and facing limitations in patch labeling and feature aggregation. To overcome these challenges, we introduce HiMulti, a novel multi-instance model that integrates pathological images and pathway features for improved survival prediction. HiMulti first processes WSIs into patches and creates a multi-level pyramid through downsampling. It then utilizes an improved mamba-inspired linear attention model and a linear attention transformer for intra- and inter-level feature fusion. Simultaneously, pathway features are constructed from RNA-Seq data. A dual-branch attention mechanism selects key image regions by generating multimodal and single-modal attention weights. Finally, patient-level features are aggregated from these key images for cancer survival prediction. Compared with the existing weakly supervised methods, the average C-Index of HiMulti on the TCGA-LUAD, BRCA, and BLCA datasets increases by 1.39% compared with the sub-optimal value, and the visualization results confirm its superior performance. Implementation is available at: https://github.com/weiba/HiMulti.

Keywords: Cancer Survival Prediction · Whole Slide Image · Pathway Feature · MILA · Transformer · Attention Mechanism

1 Introduction

Cancer remains a significant global health challenge, contributing to nearly 10 million deaths [1]. Accurate prediction of patient survival is vital for personalized treatment strategies. In recent years, survival analysis using pathological images has gained prominence as a research area, as these images reveal crucial tumor microstructural features and potential prognostic biomarkers [2, 3]. Deep learning and related methods applied to pathological images can effectively capture tumor heterogeneity and enhance survival prediction accuracy. The advent of digital pathology and Whole Slide Images (WSIs)

© The Author(s), under exclusive license to Springer Nature Singapore Pte Ltd. 2026
J. Tang et al. (Eds.): ISBRA 2025, LNBI 15757, pp. 98–109, 2026.
https://doi.org/10.1007/978-981-95-0695-8_9

provides rich, high-resolution imaging data for cancer diagnosis, grading, and survival prediction. However, the vast size of these datasets presents significant challenges for efficient image processing and analysis.

WSI-based survival prediction methods generally fall into two categories. The first category utilizes intermediate computer vision tasks, often relying on pathologist-labeled regions of interest (ROIs) to extract morphological features. For example, Peng et al. [4] segmented global and nuclear regions to extract texture features, while Chen et al. [5] partitioned WSIs into patches to encode nuclear locations. While these methods leverage expert annotations, they can potentially overlook overall WSI information due to the focus on specific ROIs.

The second category directly extracts global features from WSIs without relying on intermediate tasks. These methods typically divide WSIs into patches of the same size or selectively sample representative patches. They extract features using pre-trained or custom convolutional neural networks, and then aggregate these patch features for patient-level survival prediction. Examples include methods using pre-trained models like ResNet50 [7, 11] and ViT [12] for feature extraction, or specialized techniques like spectral convolution and adaptive graphs to capture spatial details [8]. For feature aggregation, attention pooling [9, 14], transformer model [13], dual-stream architectures [10], and graph convolutional networks [24] are used to integrate patch-level features into patient-level features. While these methods avoids the need for extensive annotations and captures overall WSI structure, a common limitation is the use of fixed-size patches at a single magnification, which neglects the hierarchical and cross-layer interactions of the same tissue region across different magnifications. Furthermore, existing survival prediction methods face two major challenges: insufficient labeling of image patches and the generation of patient features using simplistic feature aggregation methods. Given the complex nature of cancer prognosis, relying solely on single-magnification image analysis is often insufficient to determine the patient's survival situation. Pathologists evaluate WSIs by considering the overall tissue architecture and fine-grained details, often in conjunction with genomic data for a comprehensive assessment. Hence, effective survival prediction requires the integration of pathological images at various magnifications with genomic data to comprehensively understand the complex information of cancer. Moreover, pathway analysis plays a crucial role in bridging genomic data with tumor function, providing essential biological context to gene expression data and elucidating key molecular mechanisms that drive tumor progression and prognosis.

Addressing the limitations, we introduce HiMulti, a novel survival prediction model that integrates hierarchical WSI features and pathway information. HiMulti comprises three core modules: multi-level image feature extraction and fusion module, pathway feature building module, and image region screening with patient survival prediction module. In the first module, we first divide the WSI into 2048 $\times$ 2048 pixels patches at 20x magnification (callled Regions of Interests (ROIs)). Generate $10\times$ and $5\times$ magnification ROIs through multiple downsampling in order to construct a three-layer pyramid structure ($5\times, 10\times, 20\times$). Next, we extract initial features from the patches at each level using ResNet50 [21]. The improved Mamba-Inspired Linear Attention (MILA) model is then employed to capture intra-layer features. Inter-layer feature fusion is achieved using a linear attention Transformer. Finally, the class token features from the three levels are combined to obtain the final ROI feature. For the pathway feature building module, we analyze patient RNA-Seq data with DESeq2 [22] and perform Gene Set Enrichment Analysis (GSEA) [23] on the human pathway datasets from the KEGG database. Based on the analysis results, we construct pathway feature vectors of each patient. In the image region screening with patient survival prediction modules, we design a dual-branch attention module. The cross-modal branch takes image and pathway features as input to calculate a multimodal attention weight. Simultaneously, the image branch generates an image attention weight through a gated attention mechanism. Utilizing these attention weights, we select key image patches, and pooling them to derive patient-level features for survival prediction. Evaluated on three public datasets from The Cancer Genome Atlas (TCGA) [20], our method significantly outperforms current state-of-the-art approaches, with 2.79% to 19.16% C-Index increase. Furthermore, Kaplan-Meier curves and Log-rank tests provide additional verification of HiMulti's advantages. Summary, the contributions of this paper are as follows:

(1) We propose a multi-level feature extraction framework using a three-level pyramid to integrate image features across magnifications. For the first time, we the MILA structure for intra-level aggregation in WSI-based survival prediction.
(2) We integrate pathway features, enabling joint image and pathway feature screening via a dual-branch attention mechanism.
(3) We achieve state-of-the-art performance on TCGA datasets, surpassing existing methods in average C-Index.

2 Methods

The HiMulti model integrates multi-magnification pathological image features and pathway features to predict patients' survival. The model framework consists of three core modules, as shown in Fig. 1. The multi-level image feature extraction and fusion module breaks the WSIs into ROIs at multiple magnification levels (forming a pyramid). It then extracts patches features using pre-trained ResNet50, and fuses these features through intra-level and inter-level feature extraction modules. Pathway feature building module employs DESeq2 and GSEA to construct patient-level pathway feature vectors. Image region screening with patient survival prediction module utilizes a dual-branch attention mechanism to fuse image and pathway features and aggregates patient-level features via mask-guided weighted.

2.1 Problem Formulation

Given a patient dataset $U = \{U_1, U_2, ..., U_N\}$, each patient has number W of WSIs, denoted as $B = \{b_1, b_2, ..., b_W\}$. Each patient has one pathway vector and is assigned a follow-up label (T_p, C_p), where T_p represents the length of observation and C_p represents survival status. When $C_p = 0$, T_p is the actual survival time of the patient. When $C_p = 1$, T_p indicates the patient's right censoring time (i.e., lost to follow-up or alive at study cut-off). Since this model aims to integrate the patient's WSI and pathway data to predict the survival probability, the discrete-time survival model [15] is used to process the survival data. For analysis, the survival duration is binned into n equal intervals

$[t_0, t_1), ..., [t_{n-1}, t_n)$. Then the patient's observation time is mapped to the corresponding interval. When $t_k \leq T_p \leq t_{k+1}$, the patient's observation time can be located in the corresponding interval k. To design the loss function associated with survival prediction, two core probability functions are defined. Conditional risk probability $h(k|U_p)$ (Eq. (1)): the probability of death within the interval after the patient survives to the k-th time interval. Survival probability $S(k|U_p)$ (Eq. (2)): the probability that the patient will survive to the k-th time interval and still survive.

$$h(k|U_p) = P(T_p = k|T_p \geq k, U_p) \tag{1}$$

$$S(k|U_p) = P(T_p \geq k|U_p) = \prod_{u=1}^{k}(1 - h(u|U_p)) \tag{2}$$

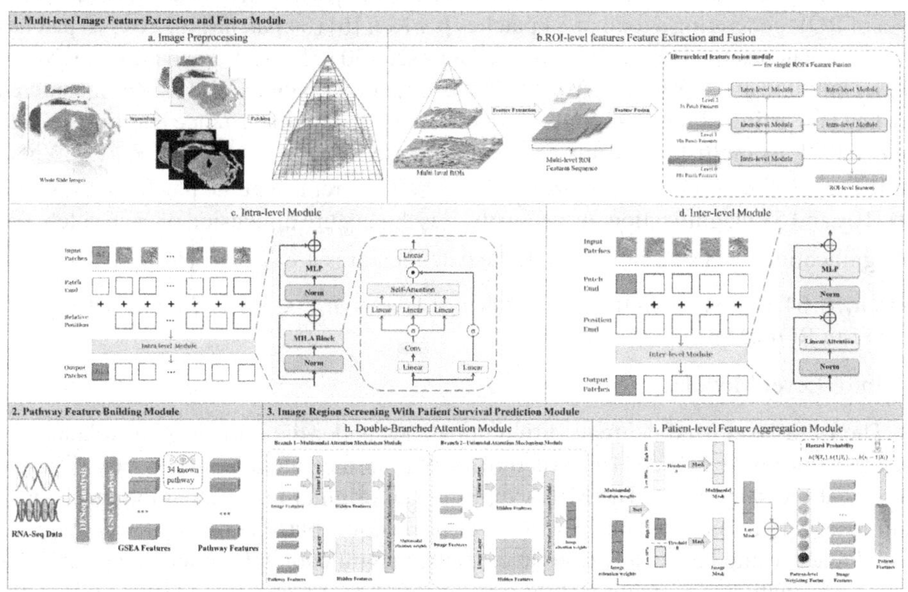

Fig. 1. The framework of the HiMulti model.

We employ the log-likelihood function as our loss function(see Eq. (3)). For uncensored patients ($C_p = 0$) experience failure events within the k-th time interval, the likelihood value is calculated as the product of the survival probability of these patients up to the $(k-1)$-th interval and their risk probability within the k-th time interval. For patients ($C_p = 1$) experiencing censored events within the k-th time interval, the likelihood value is computed based on the survival probability at the end of the k-th interval. Finally, the log-likelihood values of all patients are summed to derive the loss function, which is minimized to optimize the model parameters.

$$L_{surv} = -C_p log(h(k|U_p)S(k-1|U_p)) - (1 - C_p)log(S(k|U_p)) \tag{3}$$

2.2   Multi-level Image Feature Extraction and Fusion Module

To address the limitations of single-magnification analysis and align with pathologists' global-to-local observation patterns, we propose a multi-level image feature extraction and fusion module. This module, consisting of three intra-level and two inter-level components, comprehensively explores fine-grained pathological features across different magnifications, effectively simulating multi-level interactions and accurately extracting features at each level.

For data preprocessing, we used CLAM [14] to segment tissue regions from WSIs and removed handwriting artifacts using a color threshold filter. We then tiled non-overlapping ROIs of 2048×2048 pixels at 20x magnification and stored in HDF5 format after stained and normalized according to Vahadane [25]. During the feature extraction, each ROI is subjected to downsampling operations to simulate 10x and 5x magnifications image. Than we extracted 256×256 non-overlapping patches from each magnification level of ROI, generating a total of 84 patches per ROI [6] (64 patches for 20x, 16 patches for 10x, 4 patches for 5x). Finally, we used a ResNet50 [21] pre-trained on ImageNet to extract initial features from each patch. Hence, after processing, a WSI can be considered as a bag consisting of multiple ROIs (called instances in multi-instance learning). Given the i-th ROI, its multi-level features can be expressed as: $H^i = \{H^{i,s}\} \in \mathbb{R}^{84 \times d}$. Where $s \in 0,1,2$, $H^{i,0} \in \mathbb{R}^{64 \times d}$, $H^{i,1} \in \mathbb{R}^{16 \times d}$, $H^{i,2} \in \mathbb{R}^{4 \times d}$ represent the patch features with 20x, 10x and 5x magnification, respectively. d is the feature dimension of each patch. For a magnification level s of the i-th ROI, the patch features are $H^{i,s} = \left\{ h_1^{i,s}, h_2^{i,s}, ..., h_{n_s}^{i,s} \right\}$. Here $n_s \in 64,16,4$ is the number of patches at level s. $h_j^{i,s} \in \mathbb{R}^d$ is the j-th patch token in the i-th ROI of level s.

(1) Intra-Level Module

The Intra-level Module treats different patches under the same level as tokens, and uses the improved MILA [16] structure to realize the interaction between different patches at the same level. The MILA replaces the original linear attention mechanism with a self-attention mechanism with relative position bias [16] to better capture the spatial relationship between patches at the same magnification. In order to aggregate the global information of a magnification, we create a class token $C_0^{i,s}$ and splice it with the input patch tokens sequence as the Eq. (4):

$$Z_0^{i,s} = \left[C_0^{i,s}; f(h_1^{i,s}), f(h_2^{i,s}), \ldots, f(h_{n_s}^{i,s}) \right] \tag{4}$$

where $f(\cdot)$ is a linear layer, $Z_0^{i,s}$ is the 0-th layer token sequence at the i-th ROI of level s. The Intra-level Module utilizes a multi-layered improved MILA structure (see Eq. (5)–(9)) to capture microscopic pathological image features at the same level. Meanwhile, we computes the index between two tokens' coordinates $((x_m, y_m), (x_n, y_n))$ under window size w and generate the relative position encoding through shared embedding PE (see Eq. (5)).

$$\begin{cases} b_{m,n}^{i,s} = PE\left[(x_m - x_n + w - 1) \cdot (2w - 1) + (y_m - y_n + w - 1) \right], w = n_s \\ SA = Attention(Q, K, V) = Softmax\left(\frac{QK^T}{\sqrt{d}} + B \right)V, B = \left[b_{m,n}^{i,s} \right] \in R^{\sqrt{w} \times \sqrt{w}} \end{cases} \tag{5}$$

$$MILA = SiLU\left(Linear(x_{in})\right) + SA(SiLU\left(Linear(h(x_{in}))\right)) \tag{6}$$

$$MLP = Linear(GELU\left(Linear(x_{in})\right)) \tag{7}$$

$$Z_l^{i,s\prime} = MILA\left(LayerNorm\left(Z_{l-1}^{i,s}\right)\right) + Z_{l-1}^{i,s}, l = 1,2,\dots,L_1 \tag{8}$$

$$Z_l^{i,s} = MLP\left(LayerNorm\left(Z_l^{i,s\prime}\right)\right) + Z_l^{i,s\prime}, l = 1,2,\dots,L_1 \tag{9}$$

where, x_{in} is the inputs of the MILA and MLP structure, which is initialized with $Z_0^{i,s}$. SA represents the self-supervised attention mechanism that incorporates relative position bias. $SiLU$ and $GELU$ are active functions. Finally, the first token $C_{L_1}^{i,s}$ of the last layer output sequence $Z_{L_1}^{i,s}$ is the global feature of the ROI at the current magnification. L_1 is the number of MILA layers. Here, $L_1 = 1$.

(2) Inter-Level Module

Images at different magnification levels of ROIs show a clear correspondence; for instance, one 10x patch aligns with four 20x patches. The inter-level module facilitates information transmission across these magnifications by stitching the features of the low-magnification image (level $s + 1$) with the corresponding features of the four high-magnification images (level s). Therefore, the cross-level token sequence (see Eq. (10)) of the r-th patch in the ROI of level $s+1$ is defined as $Z_{0,i}^{i,s\uparrow} \in \mathbb{R}^{(1+4) \times d_h}$, d_h is the hidden dimension of feature.

$$Z_{0,r}^{i,s\uparrow} = \left[f(h_r^{i,s+1}); Z_{L_1,r_0}^{i,s}, Z_{L_1,r_1}^{i,s}, Z_{L_1,r_2}^{i,s}, Z_{L_1,r_3}^{i,s}\right] \tag{10}$$

where $Z_{L_1,r_0}^{i,s}, Z_{L_1,r_1}^{i,s}, Z_{L_1,r_2}^{i,s}, Z_{L_1,r_3}^{i,s}$ represents the four patch features generated by intra-level module at level s. These features are aligned with the r-th patch at level $s + 1, f(\cdot)$ is a linear layer, and $r \in n_{s+1}$.

The inter-level module (see Eq. (11)–(12)) consists of a multi-layered Transformer structure [17], in which each layer contains a linear attention layer and a multi-layer perceptron module MLP. The linear attention reduces the computational complexity and memory to capture the relationship between cross-level images.

$$Z_{n,r}^{i,s\uparrow\prime} = LA\left(LayerNorm\left(Z_{n-1,r}^{i,s\uparrow}\right)\right) + Z_{n-1,r}^{i,s\uparrow}, n = 1,2,\dots,L_2 \tag{11}$$

$$Z_{n,r}^{i,s\uparrow} = MLP\left(LayerNorm\left(Z_{n-1,r}^{i,s\uparrow\prime}\right)\right) + Z_{n-1,r}^{i,s\uparrow\prime}, n = 1,2,\dots,L_2 \tag{12}$$

where, LA represents the linear attention mechanism. L_2 is the number of Transformer layers (L_2 is 2 in this work). The first token $C_r^{i,s\uparrow}$ from the last layer's output sequence $Z_{L2,r}^{i,s\uparrow}$ is taken as the feature of the r-th patch at level $s + 1$. Then, the output $\left[C_1^{i,s\uparrow}, C_2^{i,s\uparrow}, \dots, C_{n_{s+1}}^{i,s\uparrow}\right]$ from the inter-level module is passed to the next intra-level module to further learn the image features of the ROI at level $s + 1$.

(3) Multi-Level Feature Fusion Module

This iterative process continues until features are obtained for ROI at all magnifications, defined as: $[C_{L_1,0}^{i,0}, C_{L_1,0}^{i,1}, C_{L_1,0}^{i,2}]$. Here $C_{L_1,0}^{i,2}$ is the class token output from the last layer of the intra-level module in the i-th ROI at the 5x magnification. The final feature F_{img}^i of the i-th ROI is calculated with weight coefficient w_s as 0.333.

$$F_{img}^i = \sum_{s=0}^{2} w_s C_{L_1,0}^{i,s} \tag{13}$$

2.3 Pathway Feature Building Module

We selected normalized RNA sequencing gene expression data from cancer and normal tissue samples across three TCGA cancer types. Next, differential expression analysis was performed using DESeq2, comparing each patient's tumor sample to normal samples, which resulted in the generation of molecular features for each patient. Subsequently, pathway enrichment analysis was conducted with GSEA on the differentially expressed genes, obtaining multi-corrected p-values (p.adjust) and normalized enrichment scores (NES) for 347 pathways. We focused on 34 cancer-related pathways [18] to construct patient's pathway feature vector $F_{Path} \in \mathbb{R}^{34} = [v_1, v_2, ..., v_{34}]$, whose value is defined as the follows.

$$v_i = \begin{cases} -lg(\text{p.adjust}_i) \times |\text{NES}_i|, & D_i = 1 \\ 0, & D_i = 0 \end{cases} \tag{14}$$

where D_i is indicator. If the 34 cancer-related pathway was successful matched with one of the 347 pathways, D_i is set to 1. Otherwise, it is set to 0.

2.4 Image Region Screening with Patient Survival Prediction Module

(1) Dual-Branch Attention Mechanism Module

A dual-branch attention mechanism, comprising cross-modal and single-modal branches, was designed to identify key images. The cross-modal branch aims to capture the association between image features and pathway features. This branch utilizes a dual-branch network to compute attention weights: the first branch processes ROI-level features F_{img} to generate $F_{img}^+ \in \mathbb{R}^{M \times d_h}$, and the second branch processes patient-level pathway features $F_{Path} \in \mathbb{R}^{1 \times d_h}$ to generate $F_{Path}^+ \in \mathbb{R}^{M \times d_h}$. Finally, these two sets of processed features are multiplied to obtain the cross-modal attention weight A_c, as shown in Eq. (15)–(17).

$$F_{img}^+ = tanh\left(V_{img} f_{img}\left(F_{img}\right)^T\right) \tag{15}$$

$$F_{Path}^+ = sigmoid\left(V_{Path} f_{Path}(F_{Path})^T\right) \tag{16}$$

$$A_c = \frac{exp\left\{W_c\left(F_{img}^+ \odot F_{Path}^+\right)\right\}}{\sum_{m=1}^{M} exp\left\{W_c\left(F_{img}^+ \odot F_{Path}^+\right)\right\}} \tag{17}$$

Here, M is the number of ROIs of a patient. $f_{img}(\cdot), f_{Path}(\cdot)$ are fully connected layer, $W_c \in \mathbb{R}^{1 \times 256}$, $V_{img} \in \mathbb{R}^{256 \times 256}$, $V_{Path} \in \mathbb{R}^{256 \times 34}$ are learnable weights.

The single-modal branch employs a gating attention mechanism [9] to learn the image modality attention weights A_{img}, as shown in Eq. (18).

$$A_{img} = \frac{exp\left\{W_{img}\left(tanh\left(V_{img}F_{img}^T\right) \odot sigmoid\left(U_{img}F_{img}^T\right)\right)\right\}}{\sum_{m=1}^{M} exp\left\{W_{img}\left(tanh\left(V_{img}F_{img}^T\right) \odot sigmoid\left(U_{img}F_{img}^T\right)\right)\right\}} \tag{18}$$

Here, $U_{img}, V_{img} \in \mathbb{R}^{128 \times 256}$, $W_{img} \in \mathbb{R}^{1 \times 128}$ represent the weights of the fully connected layer, and F_{img} denotes the original ROI-level image features.

(2) Patient-Level Feature Aggregation Module

Let $A_c = \left[a_c^1, \ldots, a_c^M\right]$ be the cross-modal attention weights, $A_{img} = \left[a_{img}^1, \ldots, a_{img}^M\right]$ be the single-modal attention weights. First, sort A_c and A_{img}. Since only the top 50% of key images are preserved, we segment the sorted weights and use the segmentation point weights (denoted as θ_c and θ_{img}) as thresholds for mask matrices M_c and M_{img}. Next, mask matrices M_c and M_{img} is constructed for A_c and A_{img}, respectively, and the final Mask matrix M_f is generated by element-wise multiplication (see Eq. (19–21)).

$$M_c = \begin{cases} 1 \times 10^{-9}, & \text{if } a_c^k < \theta_c \\ 1, & \text{if } a_c^i \geq \theta_c \end{cases}, \quad k = \{1,2,\ldots,M\} \tag{19}$$

$$M_{img} = \begin{cases} 1 \times 10^{-9}, & \text{if } a_{img}^k < \theta_{img} \\ 1, & \text{if } a_{img}^k \geq \theta_{img} \end{cases}, \quad k = \{1,2,\ldots,M\} \tag{20}$$

$$A = A_{img} \odot M_f = (M_{img} \odot M_c) \odot M_f \tag{21}$$

where $\odot$ as the element-wise multiplication. Then, M_f is multiplied with A_{img} to obtain the attention score $A \in \mathbb{R}^M$ of patient-level features. Finally, all ROIs' features are aggregated into patient-level feature $h_{patient}$ through attention pooling (see Eq. (22)).

$$h_{patient} = Attnpool\left(A, F_{img}\right) = \sum_{i=1}^{M} a_i F_{img}^i \tag{22}$$

where $a_i \in A$ and F_{img}^i are the weighting factor and image features for the i-th ROI. $h_{patient}$ is then passed to the classifier f_{cls} to obtain a logits value, which is used to calculate the survival probability $S(k|U_p)$ for survival prediction (see Eq. (23)). The model was subsequently trained using the loss function in Eq. (3)

$$\begin{cases} h(k|U_p) = hazards = sigmoid\left(f_{cls}\left(h_{patient}\right)\right) \\ S(k|U_p) = \prod_{o=1}^{k}(1 - hazards) \end{cases} \tag{23}$$

3 Experiments and Results

3.1 Dataset and Experimental Setup

We utilized TCGA datasets, Lung Adenocarcinoma (LUAD), Breast Cancer (BRCA), and Bladder Urothelial Carcinoma (BLCA) to evaluation the performance of our model. Due to the difference in the number of patients corresponding to the two types of data, the number of patients in the WSI dataset was taken as standard, ultimately including 1780 patients and 1970 whole slide images. The performances of our method and baselines were evaluated via 4-fold cross-validation (60:15:25 train:validation:test) using the Concordance Index (C-index) [7]. Additionally, we plotted the Kaplan-Meier curves and calculated the corresponding p-value using a log-rank test to evaluate different methods. WSIs and labels were processed following PatchGCN [24]. Our HiMulti model featured 3 intra-layer (1 self-attention MILA) and 2 inter-layer (2 linear-attention Transformer) modules, with a batch size of 1. Comparative analysis involved nine baselines, which include AMIL [9], DeepGraphConv [8], DeepSet [11], HIPTNoneFC(a simplified version of HIPT [12]), HVTSurv [7], PatchGCN [24], TransMIL [13], CLAM-SB/CLAM-MB [14], and DSMIL [10], ensuring fair comparisons using identical survival loss, ResNet-50 embeddings, and recommended hyperparameters. These baselines represent diverse approaches (multi-instance learning, graph convolution, Transformer, attention mechanisms, etc.), capturing multi-level WSI features using both single and dual-stream architectures.

3.2 Analysis of Survival Prediction Results

Table 1. Comparison of C-Index Performance in the TCGA Dataset.

	LUAD	BLCA	BRCA	Mean
AMIL	$0.5812 \pm 0.0684^{0.0158}$	$0.4783 \pm 0.0241^{0.1780}$	$0.5435 \pm 0.0668^{0.4700}$	0.5343 ± 0.0531
DeepGraphConv	$0.4928 \pm 0.0647^{0.4030}$	$0.5272 \pm 0.0653^{0.6360}$	$0.5364 \pm 0.0588^{0.0105}$	0.5188 ± 0.0629
DeepSet	$0.4917 \pm 0.0587^{0.8020}$	$0.4962 \pm 0.0068^{0.0016}$	0.5062 ± 0.0144^{nan}	0.4980 ± 0.0266
HIPTNoneFC	$0.5778 \pm 0.0399^{0.0009}$	$0.5371 \pm 0.0381^{0.8550}$	$0.5426 \pm 0.0521^{0.6770}$	0.5525 ± 0.0434
HVTSurv	$0.5596 \pm 0.0315^{0.0009}$	$\mathbf{0.5991 \pm 0.0212^{0.2050}}$	$\underline{0.5731 \pm 0.0962^{0.1040}}$	$\underline{0.5773 \pm 0.0496}$
PatchGCN	$\underline{0.5887 \pm 0.0474^{0.0067}}$	$0.5655 \pm 0.0308^{0.2470}$	$0.5389 \pm 0.0764^{0.4180}$	0.5644 ± 0.0515
TransMIL	$0.5608 \pm 0.0875^{0.0319}$	$0.5496 \pm 0.0579^{0.2190}$	$0.5218 \pm 0.0943^{0.2780}$	0.5441 ± 0.0799
CLAM-SB	$0.5725 \pm 0.0479^{0.0359}$	$0.4553 \pm 0.0418^{0.0001}$	$0.5573 \pm 0.0765^{0.4300}$	0.5284 ± 0.0554
CLAM-MB	$0.5470 \pm 0.0623^{0.2890}$	$0.5124 \pm 0.0539^{0.3220}$	$0.5488 \pm 0.0694^{0.1420}$	0.5361 ± 0.0619
DSMIL	$0.5613 \pm 0.0261^{0.0110}$	$0.5501 \pm 0.0278^{0.4260}$	$0.5348 \pm 0.0667^{0.2140}$	0.5487 ± 0.0402
Ours	$\mathbf{0.6045 \pm 0.0318^{0.0002}}$	$\underline{0.5801 \pm 0.0199^{0.1720}}$	$\mathbf{0.5927 \pm 0.0814^{0.0196}}$	$\mathbf{0.5924 \pm 0.0444}$

Table 1 presents survival prediction performance (C-Index, mean $\pm$ std$^{p-value}$) across LUAD, BLCA, and BRCA datasets compared with baselines. Our model achieved C-Indexes of 0.6045 ± 0.0318, 0.5801 ± 0.0199, and 0.5927 ± 0.0814, respectively, achieving the best in LUAD and BLCA, second best performance in BRCA dataset. Overall, the proposed model has an average C-index value that is 2.79% to 19.16% higher than those of other comparative methods across all datasets. Notably, our hierarchical attention approach outperformed multi-instance learning (AMIL, DeepSet) by 11.06–19.16%, highlighting the efficacy of deep local-global feature integration. Compared to graph convolution methods (DeepGraphConv, PatchGCN), we improved accuracy via hierarchical attention. Our model also surpassed Transformer-based methods (HVTSurv, TransMIL) on complex datasets like BRCA, demonstrating the benefits of cross-level feature fusion and pathway integration. While multi-magnification methods (DSMIL, HIPTNoneFC) showed stable performance, our model achieved superior results across all datasets, validating the synergistic effect of our multi-magnification feature extraction, pathway integration for key region selection. This strategy enhances generalization, balances efficiency and accuracy, and leverages both multi-level image morphology and biological pathway knowledge for robust survival prediction.

3.3 Ablation Study

We evaluated five ablation settings—removing the inter-level module ("w/o Inter-level"), removing the intra-level module ("w/o Intra-level"), ignoring pathway data ("w/o pathway"), replacing MILA with a standard Transformer("w/o MILA") and ignoring multi-level image features("only 20x"). Notably, in the "w/o intra-level" setting, the intra-level module's class token (the level feature) are replaced by the average values of the initial image features. The results in Table 2 indicate that the survival prediction results of the three-level image features are more stable. The average C-index when pathway data is either ignored or absent is significantly lower than that of the full model. Although some ablation settings achieved the best results, they did so only one dataset and performed poorly on others. In contrast, our complete model achieves the highest mean C-Index, with excellent and stable results on all three datasets.

Table 2. Ablation Study.

	LUAD	BLCA	BRCA	Mean
w/o Inter-level	$0.5952 \pm 0.0303^{0.0107}$	$0.5785 \pm 0.0401^{0.0394}$	$0.5860 \pm 0.0841^{0.0758}$	0.5866 ± 0.0515
w/o Intra-level	$0.5908 \pm 0.0484^{0.0002}$	$0.5723 \pm 0.0251^{0.0022}$	$0.5572 \pm 0.0927^{0.0055}$	0.5734 ± 0.0554
w/o MILA	$0.5684 \pm 0.0444^{0.0318}$	$0.5602 \pm 0.0314^{0.2470}$	$0.5625 \pm 0.0771^{0.0453}$	0.5637 ± 0.0510
w/o pathway	$0.5986 \pm 0.0329^{0.0016}$	$0.5408 \pm 0.0401^{0.1900}$	$\mathbf{0.5929 \pm 0.0673^{0.0067}}$	0.5774 ± 0.0468
only 20x	$0.5706 \pm 0.0265^{0.0325}$	$0.5661 \pm 0.0234^{0.0088}$	$0.5892 \pm 0.1147^{0.0133}$	0.5753 ± 0.0549
Ours	$\mathbf{0.6045 \pm 0.0318^{0.0002}}$	$\mathbf{0.5801 \pm 0.0199^{0.1720}}$	$0.5927 \pm 0.0814^{0.0196}$	$\mathbf{0.5924 \pm 0.0444}$

4 Conclusion and Discussion

HiMulti integrates multi-level image and pathway features, improving survival prediction across some cancer datasets over the baselines. Our method has two advantages: on one hand, it employs an improved MILA module and linear attention Transformer to efficiently capture pathological features at different magnifications. On the other hand, it incorporates biological prior knowledge into the image patch selection and feature aggregation processes. Future improvements in generalization and prediction accuracy may be achieved by incorporating self-supervised contrastive learning, hierarchical hypergraph modeling, and integrating diverse omics data.

Acknowledgement. This work is supported in part by the National Natural Science Foundation of China (No. 62472202, No.61972185). Yunnan Ten Thousand Talents Plan young.

References

1. Mostavi, M., et al.: Convolutional neural network models for cancer type prediction based on gene expression. BMC Med. Genom. **13**, 1–13 (2020)
2. Kent, D.M., et al.: Risk and treatment effect heterogeneity: re-analysis of individual participant data from 32 large clinical trials. Int. J. Epidemiol. **45**(6), 2075–2088 (2016)
3. Fisher, R., Pusztai, L., Swanton, C.: Cancer heterogeneity: implications for targeted therapeutics. Br. J. Cancer **108**(3), 479–485 (2013)
4. Peng, Y., et al.: Combining texture features of whole slide images improves prognostic prediction of recurrence-free survival for cutaneous melanoma patients. World J. Surg. Oncol. **18**, 1–8 (2020)
5. Chen, P., et al.: Cellular architecture on whole slide images allows the prediction of survival in lung adenocarcinoma. In: International Workshop on Computational Mathematics Modeling in Cancer Analysis, pp. 1–10. Springer, Cham (2022)
6. Jiang, R., et al.: A transformer-based weakly supervised computational pathology method for clinical-grade diagnosis and molecular marker discovery of gliomas. Nat. Mach. Intell. **6**(8), 876–891 (2024)
7. Shao, Z., et al.: Hvtsurv: hierarchical vision transformer for patient-level survival prediction from whole slide image. In: Proceedings of the AAAI Conference on Artificial Intelligence, vol. 37, no. 2 (2023)
8. Chen, R.J., et al.: Multimodal co-attention transformer for survival prediction in gigapixel whole slide images. In: Proceedings of the IEEE/CVF International Conference on Computer Vision, pp. 4015–4025 (2021)
9. Chen, R.J., et al.: Pan-cancer integrative histology-genomic analysis via multimodal deep learning. Cancer Cell **40**(8), 865–878 (2022)
10. Li, B., Li, Y., Eliceiri, K.W.: Dual-stream multiple instance learning network for whole slide image classification with self-supervised contrastive learning. In: The IEEE/CVF Conference on Computer Vision and Pattern Recognition, pp. 14318–14328 (2021)
11. Zaheer, M., et al.: Deep sets. In: Advances in Neural Information Processing Systems, vol. 30 (2017)
12. Chen, R.J., et al.: Scaling vision transformers to gigapixel images via hierarchical self-supervised learning. In: Proceedings of the IEEE/CVF Conference on Computer Vision and Pattern Recognition, 16144–16155 (2022)
13. Shao, Z., et al.: Transmil: transformer based correlated multiple instance learning for whole slide image classification. In: Advances in Neural Information Processing Systems, vol. 34, pp. 2136–2147 (2021)
14. Lu, M.Y., et al.: Data-efficient and weakly supervised computational pathology on whole-slide images. Nat. Biomedical Eng. **5**(6), 555–570 (2021)

15. Shen, Y., et al.: Explainable survival analysis with convolution-involved vision transformer. Proceedings of the AAAI Conference on Artificial Intelligence, vol. 36, no. 2, pp. 2207–2215 (2022)

16. Zadeh, S.G., Schmid, M.: Bias in cross-entropy-based training of deep survival networks. IEEE Trans. Pattern Anal. Mach. Intell. **43**(9), 3126–3137 (2020)

17. Liu, Z., et al.: Swin transformer: hierarchical vision transformer using shifted windows. In: Proceedings of the IEEE/CVF International Conference on Computer Vision, pp. 10012–10022 (2021)

18. Shin, J., et al.: DRPreter: interpretable anticancer drug response prediction using knowledge-guided graph neural networks and transformer. Int. J. Mol. Sci. **23**(22), 13919 (2022)

19. Han, D., et al.: Demystify mamba in vision: A linear attention perspective. arXiv preprint arXiv:2405.16605 (2024)

20. Weinstein, J.N., et al.: The cancer genome atlas pan-cancer analysis project. Nat. Genet. **45**(10), 1113–1120 (2013)

21. Wang, J., Zucker, J.-D.: Solving multiple-instance problem: a lazy learning approach, pp. 1119–1125 (2000)

22. Anders, S., Huber, W.: Differential expression analysis for sequence count data. Nat. Precedings, pp. 1–1 (2010)

23. Subramanian, A., et al.: Gene set enrichment analysis: a knowledge-based approach for interpreting genome-wide expression profiles. Proc. Natl. Acad. Sci. **102**(43), 15545–15550 (2005)

24. Chen, R.J., et al.: Whole slide images are 2d point clouds: context-aware survival prediction using patch-based graph convolutional networks. In: Medical Image Computing and Computer Assisted Intervention – MICCAI, vol. 24, pp. 339–349 (2021)

25. Vahadane, A., et al.: Structure-preserving color normalization and sparse stain separation for histological images. IEEE Trans. Med. Imaging **35**(8), 1962–1971 (2016)

Identification of piRNA-Disease Association Based on Contrastive Learning

Yajun Liu[1](✉), Fan Zhang[1], Yulian Ding[2], Aimin Li[1], and Rong Fei[1]

[1] Shaanxi Key Laboratory for Network Computing and Security Technology, School of Computer Science and Engineering, Xi'an University of Technology, Xi'an, China
liuyajun@xaut.edu.cn
[2] Center for High Performance Computing, Shenzhen Institutes of Advanced Technology, Chinese Academy of Sciences, Shenzhen, China

Abstract. Increasing studies have shown that piRNA is closely related to the occurrence and development of a variety of complex diseases. Effective identification of disease-related piRNAs is of great significance for early diagnosis, treatment, and prevention of these diseases. However, computational methods to identify piRNA-disease association (PDA) still faces challenges such as sparse data. This paper proposed a PDA identification method based on contrastive learning, demonstrating enhanced capability in capturing latent PDA patterns. First, a multi-source feature matrix is constructed based on the representation of piRNA and disease in four feature spaces. Second, Singular Value Decomposition (SVD) view is generated to enhance node representation, and sample pairs are prepared by the original and SVD view. Finally, lightGCN model serves as encoder to aggregate neighbor information, Kolmogorov-Arnold (KAN) network performs feature mapping, and a temperature cross entropy loss function is employed to maximize the consistency of the two views to predict the PDA score. Five-fold cross-validation demonstrated that CLPDA achieved AUC and AUPR values of 98.58% and 86.25% on the piRheno dataset. Comparison experiments further confirmed the effectiveness of CLPDA has high accuracy and robustness, which helps the future application of piRNA in disease diagnosis and treatment.

Keyword: piRNA · disease · association identification · contrastive learning

1 Overview

piRNA is an important class of small non-coding RNAs (sncRNAs), typically ranging from 26 to 32 nucleotides in length [1]. It primarily exerts its biological effects by binding with PIWI family. piRNAs play a crucial role in various biological processes, including transposon silencing, genome stability maintenance, gene silencing and regulation, germ cell development, transgenerational inheritance, and viral defense [1, 2]. Increasing evidence suggests that piRNAs are aberrantly expressed in a wide range of complex diseases, underscoring their potential as both diagnostic biomarkers and therapeutic targets [3, 4]. For example, piR-hsa-130912 has been found to promote the proliferation, invasion, and

© The Author(s), under exclusive license to Springer Nature Singapore Pte Ltd. 2026
J. Tang et al. (Eds.): ISBRA 2025, LNBI 15757, pp. 110–122, 2026.
https://doi.org/10.1007/978-981-95-0695-8_10

migration of epithelial ovarian cancer cells, potentially through the regulation of cancer-associated signaling pathways such as lipid metabolism and mitogen-activated protein kinase [5]. Additionally, piR-36712 inhibits the proliferation of breast cancer cells by downregulating SEPW1 protein expression [6], while piR-39980 has been implicated in tumor progression and chemotherapy resistance across multiple cancers [7]. Understanding the relationship between piRNAs and disease can provide valuable insights into disease pathogenesis, and drives innovation in clinical treatment and medical research.

Since 2020, increasing studies have focused on applying computational methods to identify piRNA-disease association (PDA). To date, computational identification approaches can be broadly categorized into three main types: methods based on traditional machine learning, methods based on graph neural networks, and methods based on other deep learning.

The first category predominantly utilizes classical machine learning approaches, such as random forest (RF), support vector machines (SVM) and so on. PiDi-PUL [8] is the first computational PDA method, which is based on positive unlabeled learning and multiple RFs. iPiDA-LTR [9] is a Learning-to-Rank-based algorithm that effectively predicts piRNA-disease associations (PDA) by integrating component methods.Although these early PDA identification methods are easy to understand, the recognition performance of complex PDA pattern still needs to be improved.

With the advancement of machine learning technology, an increasing researchers are exploring PDA method based on deep learning models. DFL-PiDA [10] applied the convolutional denoising auto-encoder for PDA identification. piRDA [11] employed dense network and a two-stage positive-unlearning strategy for association recognition. MRDPDA [12] is a PDA prediction method based on deepFM model, which integrated a similarity matrix derived from multi-source data into the optimization objective through Laplace regularization. Although these deep learning models provided automatic feature representation, the capability for capture PDA patterns still requires further enhancement.

Meanwhile, due to the outstanding performance of graph neural networks (GNNs) in processing graph structured data, researchers increasingly employ GNN models to address PDA identification problems. iPiDA-GCN [13] designed two graph convolutional network modules (Asso-GCN and Sim-GCN) to capture PDA patterns from association network and similarity network respectively. iPiDA-SWGCN [14] proposed a complementary weighted GCN model that introduces correlation confidence to learn node representations, enabling more accurate prediction of novel associations. PDA-PRGCN [15] enhanced initial node representations via a residual scaling-based feature enhancement algorithm, and identified potential PDAs through GCN. ETGPDA [16] proposed an embedding-based graph convolutional network method to improve prediction accuracy by mapping piRNA and disease features into a shared latent space. PUTransGCN [17] used heterogeneous GCN, in which the weight parameters of aggregated heterogeneous node features were automatically adjusted by attention mechanism. GNNs and other deep learning approaches have enhanced PDA identification accuracy, however two persistent challenges remain to be addressed: scarcity of annotated data and low utilization of unannotated data,, which necessitates the development of advanced computational frameworks.

In recent years, by constructing positive and negative sample pairs and optimizing their representation similarity differences, contrastive learning has been successfully applied in the fields of processing, text analysis, and speech recognition [18, 19]. DGI [20] is the first study about the contrastive learning paradigm of graph representation learning. Refer to the Deep InfoMax model, DGI re-derived the probability model and loss function to adapt to graph data. COLA [21] combined graph contrastive learning with graph meta-learning, which significantly improved performance on classification of small sample node on standard graph datasets, such as Cora and PubMed. GCLMTP [22] proposed a graph contrastive learning model to infer potential associations between lncRNA, miRNA, and disease, which outperforms traditional supervised methods. However, there are still limitations of the existing contrastive learning methods in bioinformatics, such as data enhancement strategies relying on random processes or empiricism, weak robustness and generalization.

In this study, we proposes a contrastive learning model for PDA identification, CLPDA, which can effectively capture the potential PDA. First, a multi-source feature matrix is constructed based on the representation of piRNA and disease in four feature spaces. Second, singular value decomposition (SVD) view is generated to enhance node representation, and sample pairs are generated from the original and SVD views. Finally, lightGCN model [23] serves as the encoder for neighbor information aggregation, Kolmogorov-Arnold (KAN) network performs feature mapping and a temperature-scaled cross-entropy loss maximizes view consistency for PDA score prediction.

2 Materials and Methods

As shown in Fig. 1, the framework of CLPDA consists of 3 main parts. They are construction of multi-source feature matrix, SVD view generation and contrastive learning module.

2.1 Benchmark Dataset

piRheno V2.0 [24] is a manually curated PDA database, which is updated in 2020. It covers 9,057 experimentally verified associations involving 474 piRNAs and 204 diseases. A benchmark dataset is constructed by removing duplicate and redundant association data, which comprises 4,417 experimentally validated PDAs, covering 462 piRNAs and 102 diseases.

Based on this benchmark dataset, we construct a binary matrix R, in which $a_{i,j}$ indicates the association between the i-th piRNA and the j-th disease. A value of '1' indicates an experimentally confirmed association between the corresponding piRNA and disease, while a value of '0' signifies the absence of such an association. The matrix can be represented as follows:

$$R = \begin{bmatrix} a_{1,1} & a_{1,2} & \cdots & a_{1,n} \\ a_{2,1} & a_{2,2} & \cdots & a_{2,n} \\ \vdots & \vdots & \ddots & \vdots \\ a_{m,1} & a_{m,2} & \cdots & a_{m,n} \end{bmatrix} \tag{1}$$

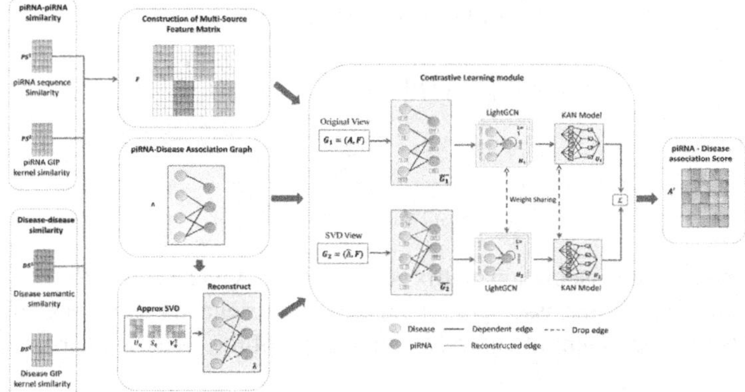

Fig. 1. Framework of CLPDA.

To facilitate subsequent calculations, the PDA matrix A is defined as follows:

$$A = \begin{pmatrix} 0 & R \\ R^T & 0 \end{pmatrix} \tag{2}$$

2.2 Multi-source Feature Matrix

The node similarity is multi-sourced, and a single similarity cannot fully reflect the complex relationship. So piRNA sequence similarity, Gaussian Interaction Profile (GIP) kernel similarity of piRNAs, semantic similarity and GIP kernel similarity of diseases are considered to construct the feature matrix.

2.2.1 piRNA Sequence Similarity

Smith-Waterman (SW) algorithm was used to calculate the piRNA sequence similarity, which is based on local sequence alignment [25]. All piRNA sequence data was downloaded from the piRBase (http://www.regulatoryrna.org/database/piRNA/) database.

The piRNA sequence similarity $PS^1(p_i, p_j)$ between the i-th and the j-th piRNA is calculated as follows:

$$PS^1(p_i, p_j) = \frac{SW(p_i, p_j)}{\sqrt{SW(p_i, p_i) \times SW(p_j, p_j)}} \tag{3}$$

where $SW(p_i, p_j)$ is the sequence alignment value between the i-th and the j-th piRNA calculated by SW algorithm.

2.2.2 piRNA GIP Kernel Similarity

GIP kernel similarity is a similarity calculation method based on Gaussian kernel function, which is successfully used in biological network analysis [26]. In this study, we also use it to calculate piRNA similarity as follows:

$$PS^2(p_i, p_j) = exp\left(-r_p \| R(i,) - R(j,) \|^2\right) \tag{4}$$

$$r_p = \frac{r'_p}{\left(\frac{1}{np} \sum_{i=1}^{np} \| R(i,) \|^2\right)} \tag{5}$$

where R represents the association matrix between piRNA and disease, $R(i,)$ corresponds to the i-th row value of this association matrix, np represents the number of piRNA, and r'_p represents the coefficient of controlling the width of the Gaussian kernel.

2.2.3 Disease Semantic Similarity

Data from MeSH database [27] (https://www.nlm.nih.gov/) was used for calculate disease semantic similarity. Directed Acyclic Graph (DAG) of the i-th disease d_i is represented by $\text{DAG}(d_i) = (d_i, T_{d_i}, E_{d_i})$, where T_{d_i} represents the node set of the i-th disease and its ancestors, and E_{d_i} represents the edge set from the ancestor node to the disease d_i. $D_{d_i}(t)$ denotes the semantic contribution of disease term $t \in T_{d_i}$ related to the i-th disease and can be computed as follows [28]:

$$D_{d_i}(t) = \begin{cases} 1 & t = d_i \\ max\{\Delta * D_{d_i}(t') | t' \in children\ of\ t\} & t \neq d_i \end{cases} \tag{6}$$

where Δ is the semantic contribution factor and is set to 0.5 according to Wang *et al.* [29].

The disease semantic similarity $DS^1(d_i, d_j)$ is calculated as follows:

$$DS^1(d_i, d_j) = \frac{\sum_{t \in T_{d_i} \cap T_{d_j}} \left(D_{d_i}(t) + D_{d_j}(t)\right)}{\sum_{t \in T_{d_i}} D_{d_i}(t) + \sum_{t \in T_{d_j}} D_{d_j}(t)} \tag{7}$$

2.2.4 Disease GIP Nuclear Similarity

Disease GIP nuclear similarity $DS^2(d_i, d_j)$ is calculated by the same method as Sect. 2.2.2:

$$DS^2(d_i, d_j) = exp\left(-r_d \| R(, i) - R(, j) \|^2\right) \tag{8}$$

$$r_d = \frac{r'_d}{\left(\frac{1}{nd} \sum_{i=1}^{nd} \| R(, i) \|^2\right)} \tag{9}$$

where nd represents the number of diseases.

2.2.5 Construction of Multi-source Feature Matrix

To reveal the potential association between piRNAs and diseases from different perspectives, feature matrix F is constructed by the above multi-source similarities and is defined as follows:

$$F = \begin{bmatrix} F_s & F_G \end{bmatrix} \tag{10}$$

$$F_s = \begin{bmatrix} PS^1 & 0 \\ 0 & DS^1 \end{bmatrix}, F_G = \begin{bmatrix} PS^2 & 0 \\ 0 & DS^2 \end{bmatrix} \tag{11}$$

2.3 Multi-view Generation

In contrastive learning, original view and SVD view establish a complementary relationship, providing multi-granular feature representations for graph contrastive learning. The original view, serving as a baseline view, directly reflects the initial topological structure of the graph data. In contrast, the SVD view reduces redundancy by preserving the principal components associated with larger singular values, thereby extracting the global structure and key patterns.

2.3.1 Original View

Original view G_1 is constructed by combining the adjacency matrix A and the feature matrix F, and is defined as follows:

$$G_1 = (A, F) \tag{12}$$

The adjacency matrix represents the connections between nodes in the graph, capturing its structural characteristics. The feature matrix contains node attribute information, providing a detailed description of each node. By combining these two matrices, the original view not only preserves the structural relationships between nodes but also incorporates their attribute features, offering rich contextual information for the learner view.

2.3.2 SVD View

SVD view G_2 use a reconstructed adjacency matrix $\hat{A}$ and is defined as follows:

$$G_2 = \left(\hat{A}, F\right) \tag{13}$$

where $\hat{A}$ is a low-rank approximation of A.

Specifically, SVD is a dimensionality reduction technique, while preserving the key features, and calculated as follows:

$$A = USV^T \tag{14}$$

where U and V are both orthogonal matrices, S is a diagonal matrix that stores singular values.

To retain the most significant components, the singular value list is truncated to preserve the largest q singular values while discarding the smaller ones, thereby obtaining a reconstructed matrix $\hat{A}$. Refer to [30], a low-rank orthogonal matrix is used to approximate the range of the input matrix and SVD is performed on this matrix to efficiently obtain an approximate singular value decomposition result. It is expressed as follows:

$$\hat{A} = U_q S_q V_q^{\top} \tag{15}$$

where U_q and V_q contain the first q columns of U and V, and S_q is a diagonal matrix consisting of the first q singular values.

2.4 Contrastive Learning Module

In contrastive learning module, positive and negative sample pairs are generated based on original view and SVD view, then they are represented by encoder, finally the model is optimized by contrast loss. Specifically, the same piRNA-disease pair from original view and SVD view are treated as positive samples, while randomly-sampled unconnected piRNA-disease pair from two views are considered negative samples.

2.4.1 Embedded Representation

Traditional graph convolutional networks update the embedded representation of a node by aggregating the representations of its neighboring nodes. In contrast, the LightGCN model is employed to obtain the embedded representation of views. Unlike traditional methods, the LightGCN model eliminates the use of feature transformation and nonlinear activation functions, instead updating the node representation through the weighted aggregation of neighbors' embedded representations. It not only simplifies the model structure but also makes model more lightweight and improve efficiency. The embedded representations H_1 and H_2 of the original view G_1 and SVD view G_2 are expressed as follows:

$$H_1 = lg\left(G_1\right), H_2 = lg\left(G_2\right) \tag{16}$$

where $lg\left(\cdot\right)$ represents operation of the lightweight graph convolutional network encoder.

2.4.2 Feature Mapping

To mitigate bias introduced by the initial model state and more effectively capture the nonlinear relationships within the input data, our study utilizes two KAN [31] networks with identical initialization parameters for feature mapping. KAN network offers an effective method for processing and fitting multivariate continuous functions, as demonstrated by the Kolmogorov-Arnold theorem [31]. Its structural flexibility, dynamic adjustment capabilities, and high efficiency provide a significant advantage in graph contrastive learning.

Generally, the activation function $\phi(x)$ of KAN network is expressed as the sum of the basis function $b(x)$ and the spline function $spline(x)$, and the overall amplitude is controlled by the factor w. Considering the difficulty of training the spline function, our study uses one-dimensional Fourier coefficients to replace the spline coefficients. The feature mapping results U_1 and U_2 are expressed as follows:

$$U_1 = kan(H_1), \ U_2 = kan(H_2) \tag{17}$$

where $kan(\cdot)$ represents operation of the KAN network.

2.4.3 Contrastive Loss

Through the above two operations, embedding representations of positive and negative sample pairs based on two perspectives are obtained. To fully considering the cross-view feature representations of positive and negative sample pairs, two optimization goals are set. Specifically, it constrains the embedding vectors of the same pairs in different views to maintain semantic alignment to the maximum extent, and ensures that the embedding representations of different pairs show significantly different distributions in the feature space. The loss function $\mathcal{L}$ is designed as follows:

$$\ell\left(u_{1,i}, u_{2,i}\right) = log \frac{e^{sim(u_{1,i}, u_{2,i})}/\tau}{\sum_{k=1}^{N} e^{sim(u_{1,i}, u_{2,k})}/\tau} \tag{18}$$

$$\mathcal{L} = \frac{1}{2N} \sum_{i=1}^{N} \left[\ell\left(u_{1,i}, u_{2,i}\right) + \ell\left(u_{2,i}, u_{1,i}\right)\right] \tag{19}$$

where $u_{1,i}$ and $u_{2,i}$ represent two special projection representations of pair i under two different views, $sim(\cdot)$ represents the cosine similarity, N is the total number of pairs, τ represents the temperature coefficient, $\ell(u_{1,i}, u_{2,i})$ represents the loss value calculated by pair i through two different views, and k represents an index from 1 to N.

3 Results and Discussion

3.1 Experiment and Hyper-Parameters Selection

Our method is developed based on PyTorch 1.12.0 and implemented by a computer with i7-10700KF CPU, 32 GB memory and GeForce RTX 4070 GPU. Multiple hyper-parameters impact the identification performance. Selection of hyper-parameters rely on experience and comparative experiments. q in SVD view generation step is a key hyper-parameter, which determines reconstructed matrix $\hat{A}$. As shown in Fig. 2, we search the optimal q from {10,15,20,25,30} when all the other hyper-parameters are fixed, which refers to Wall et $al.$ [32]. When q is set to 20, the model demonstrates optimal performance metrics AUC and AUPR.

The model employs a contrastive loss function with a temperature coefficient $\tau = 0.2$. In the LightGCN model, a two-layer graph convolution structure is adopted, the KAN network is configured with a grid size of 5 and a spline function order of 3. The input layer dimension of the model architecture is 128, the hidden layer dimension is 512, and the final output layer dimension is 128. Adam optimizer is used with a learning rate of 0.001, and batch size is 100.

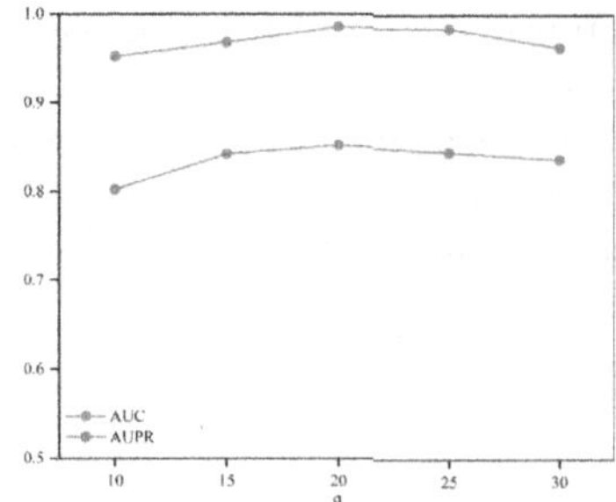

Fig. 2. AUC and AUPR curves with the increasing of q.values

3.2 Performance Evaluation

In our research, 5-fold cross-validation (CV) is used to evaluate the performance of the model. Samples are randomly divided into five subsets, where four of them are used for training and the remaining one is used for testing. AUC and AUPR are still used to evaluate the prediction results.

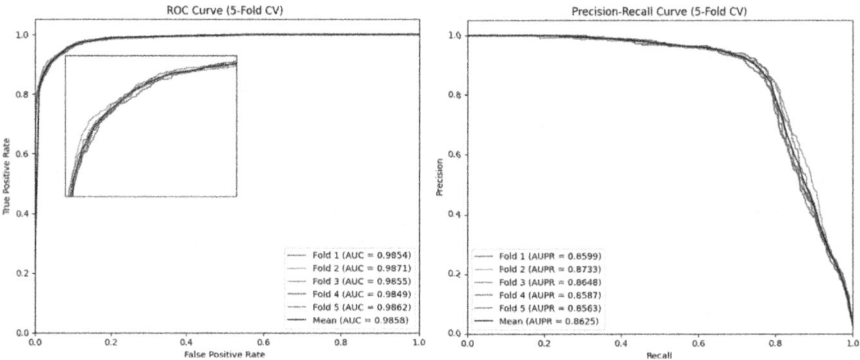

Fig. 3. AUC and AUPR curves of CLPDA in 5-fold CV.

As shown in Fig. 3, CLPDA obtained an average AUC of 0.9858 and an average AUPR of 0.8625 on the piRheno benchmark dataset. This result shows the effectiveness of CLPDA. Due to the limited accumulation of verified PDA data, the AUPR value is not optimal.

3.3 Comparison with Other Methods

To demonstrate the effectiveness of CLPDA, five state-of-the-art PDA methods with public code are used for comparison. They are iPiDA-SWGCN, iPiDA-GCN, piRDA, PUTransGCN and ETGPDA. 5-CV experiment performed based on the piRheno benchmark dataset. AUC and AUPR are still used as performance indicators.

As shown in Table 1, CLPDA achieved the best performance and ETGPDA is the second best method. It shows that contrastive learning can identify complex potential associations, thereby improves PDA identification performance.

Table 1. The comparison between CLPDA and five state-of-the-art methods (bold numbers indicate the best performance)

Method	AUC	AUPR
iPiDA-SWGCN	0.6547	0.4714
iPiDA-GCN	0.7551	0.5963
piRDA	0.8337	0.5754
PUTransGCN	0.8873	0.5327
ETGPDA	0.9502	0.7464
CLPDA	**0.9858**	**0.8625**

3.4 Effectiveness of the Improvements

To illustrate the effectiveness of improvements, we performed three type comparison experiments.

3.4.1 SVD View

In order to evaluate the effectiveness of SVD view, we construct three variant models to compare: 1) Model 1 (ATT + KAN): This model replaces the SVD reconstruction method in CLPDA with a method based on the attention mechanism. 2) Model 2 (FGP + KAN): This model replaces the SVD reconstruction method in CLPDA with the Factorized Graph Pooling (FGP) method. FGP is a method that converts complex graph data into a computable parameter set, which is easy to fall into a local optimum and results in incomplete extracted features. 3) Model 3 (MF+KAN): This model replaces the SVD reconstruction method in CLPDA with the matrix factorization (MF) technology in the literature [32].

Table 2. The comparison between CLPDA and its variant models

Variations	AUC	AUPR
Model 1 (ATT + KAN)	0.9702	0.5390
Model 2 (FGP + KAN)	0.9601	0.4702
Model 3 (MF + KAN)	0.9844	0.8417
CLPDA	**0.9858**	**0.8625**

As shown in Table 2, AUPR significantly dropped, when FGP and Attentive part replace the SVD part. This indicates that the data enhance method based on deterministic strategy is better than empirical rules or heuristic strategies (random) strategies in PDA identification task. In addition, MF method performs well, but is not good at dealing with large-scale datasets. In short, SVD view not only preserves key information, but also effectively suppresses noise information, thereby improving the classification ability of the model.

3.4.2 KAN Model

To illustrate the advantage of KAN network, we construct Model 4 to compare, where MLP is instead of KAN. As shown in Table 3, the KAN network enhances the model adaptability to the complexity of potential PDA data.

Table 3. The comparison between CLPDA and Model 4

Variations	AUC	AUPR
Model 4	0.9825	0.8386
CLPDA	**0.9858**	**0.8625**

3.4.3 Multi-source Similarities

To explore the impact of the number of views on model performance, two models with single similarity are used for comparison. As shown in Table 4, the model using multi-sources similarity performs best, which indicates that combining multi-sources similarities can enhance information.

Table 4. The comparison between CLPDA **and** two models with single similarity

Attributes	AUC	AUPR
Model 5 ($P_{seq} + D_{mesh}$)	0.9838	0.8436
Model 6 ($P_{GIP} + D_{GIP}$)	0.9842	0.8524
CLPDA	**0.9858**	**0.8625**

4 Conclusion

This study proposed a PDA identification method based on contrastive learning, which can effectively capture the potential PDA. Experiment results show that CLPDA has high accuracy and robustness, which helps the future application of piRNA in disease diagnosis and treatment. In the future, we will improve PDA model from multiple directions.

First, transfer learning and meta-learning methods will be introduced to PDA identification, which help to improve performance. In addition, based on the development of contrastive learning algorithms, a graph contrastive learning framework is constructed by multi-modal information, such as piRNA expression and targeting relationships.

Code Availability: https://github.com/zhangfan-source/CLPDA.

Acknowledgments. This work was supported by the National Natural Science Foundation of China (Grant No. 62202374 and 62402489), the Natural Science Basic Research Program of Shaanxi Province of China (Program No. 2024JC-YBMS-484), the China Postdoctoral Science Foundation (2023M743688) ,and the Guangdong Basic and Applied Basic Research Foundations (2023A1515110570) .

References

1. Seto, A.G., Kingston, R.E., Lau, N.C.: The coming of age for Piwi proteins. Mol. Cell **26**(5), 603–609 (2007)
2. Guo, C., Wang, X., Ren, H.: Databases and computational methods for the identification of piRNA-related molecules: a survey. Comput. Struct. Biotechnol. J., 23813–833 (2024)
3. Zhou, J., Zhou, W., Zhang, R.: The potential mechanisms of piRNA to induce hepatocellular carcinoma in human. Med. Hypotheses 146110400 (2021)
4. Halajzadeh, J., Dana, P.M., Asemi, Z., Mansournia, M.A., Yousefi, B.: An insight into the roles of piRNAs and PIWI proteins in the diagnosis and pathogenesis of oral, esophageal, and gastric cancer. J. Cell Mol. Med. **216**(10), 153112 (2020)
5. Chen, X., Zhao, B., Li, Z., Feng, Y., Yang, Z.: The role and mechanism of piR-hsa-130912 in promoting proliferation, invasion and migration ofepithelial ovarian cancer cells. Chinese J. Oncol. Prev. Treat. **15**(3), 263–271 (2023)
6. Liu, Y., et al.: The emerging role of the piRNA/piwi complex in cancer. Mol. Cancer **18**(1), 123 (2019)
7. Das, B., Jain, N., Mallick, B.: PiR-39980 mediates doxorubicin resistance in fibrosarcoma by regulating drug accumulation and DNA repair. Communications Biology **4**(1), 1312 (2021)
8. Wei, H., Xu, Y., Liu, B.: iPiDi-PUL: identifying Piwi-interacting RNA-disease associations based on positive unlabeled learning. Brief. Bioinform. **22**(3), bbaa058 (2021)
9. Zhang, W., Hou, J., Liu, B.: IPiDA-LTR: Identifying piwi-interacting RNA-disease associations based on Learning to Rank. PLoS Comput. Biol. **18**(8), e1010404 (2022)
10. Ji, B., Luo, J., Pan, L., Xie, X., Peng, S., DFL-PiDA: prediction of Piwi-interacting RNA-disease associations based on deep feature learning. In: 2021 IEEE International Conference on Bioinformatics and Biomedicine (BIBM), pp. 406–411. IEEE (2021)
11. Ali, S.D., Tayara, H., Chong, K.T.: Identification of piRNA disease associations using deep learning. Comput. Struct. Biotechnol. J. **20**, 1208–1217 (2022)
12. Liu, Y., Zhang, F., Ding, Y., Fei, R., Li, J., Wu, F.-X.: MRDPDA: a multi-Laplacian regularized deepFM model for predicting piRNA-disease associations. J. Cellular Mol. Med. **28**(17), e70046 (2024)
13. Hou, J., Wei, H., Liu, B.: IPiDA-GCN: identification of piRNA-disease associations based on Graph Convolutional Network. PLoS Comput. Biol. **18**(10), e1010671 (2022)
14. Hou, J., Wei, H., Liu, B.: IPiDA-SWGCN: identification of piRNA-disease associations based on supplementarily weighted graph convolutional network. PLoS Comput. Biol. **19**(6), e101124 (2023)

15. Zhang, P., et al.: PDA-PRGCN: identification of Piwi-interacting RNA-disease associations through subgraph projection and residual scaling-based feature augmentation. BMC Bioinformatics **24**(1), 18 (2023)

16. Meng, X., Shang, J., Ge, D., et al.: ETGPDA: identification of piRNA-disease associations based on embedding transformation graph convolutional network. BMC Genom. **24**(1), 279 (2023)

17. Chen, Q., Zhang, L., Liu, Y., Qin, Z., Zhao, T.: PUTransGCN: identification of piRNA–disease associations based on attention encoding graph convolutional network and positive unlabelled learning. Brief. Bioinform. **25**(3), bbae144 (2024)

18. Züfle, M., Niehues, J.: Contrastive Learning for Task-Independent SpeechLLM-Pretraining. arXiv.org (2024)

19. Le Vuong, T.T., Kwak, J.T.: MoMA: momentum contrastive learning with multi-head attention-based knowledge distillation for histopathology image analysis. Med. Image Anal. **101**, 103421 (2025)

20. Veličković, P., Fedus, W., Hamilton, W.L., Liò, P., Bengio, Y., Hjelm, R.D.: Deep Graph Infomax. arXiv.org (2018)

21. Liu, H., Feng, J., Kong, L., Tao, D., Chen, Y., Zhang, M.: Graph contrastive learning meets graph meta learning: a unified method for few-shot node tasks. In: Proceedings of the ACM on Web Conference 2024, pp. 365–376 (2024)

22. Sheng, N., et al.: Multi-task prediction-based graph contrastive learning for inferring the relationship among lncRNAs, miRNAs and diseases. Brief. Bioinform. **24**(5),bbad276 (2023)

23. He, X.N., Deng, K., Wang, X., Li, Y., Zhang, Y.D., Wang, M.: LightGCN: simplifying and powering graph convolution network for recommendation. arXiv.org ,639–648 (2020)

24. Zhang, W., et al.: piRPheno: a manually curated database to prioritize and analyze human disease related piRNAs. bioRxiv (2020)

25. Smith, T.F., Waterman, M.S.: Identification of common molecular subsequences. J. Mol. Biol. **147**(1), 195–197 (1981)

26. Van Laarhoven, T., Nabuurs, S.B., Marchiori, E.: Gaussian interaction profile kernels for predicting drug–target interaction. Bioinformatics **27**(21), 3036–3043 (2011)

27. Lipscomb, C.E.: Medical subject headings (MeSH). Bull. Med. Libr. Assoc. **88**(3), 265 (2000)

28. Ji, B.-Y., You, Z.-H., Cheng, L., Zhou, J.-R., Alghazzawi, D., Li, L.-P.: Predicting miRNA-disease association from heterogeneous information network with GraRep embedding model. Sci. Rep. **10**(1), 6658 (2020)

29. Wang, D., Wang, J., Lu, M., Song, F., Cui, Q.: Inferring the human microRNA functional similarity and functional network based on microRNA-associated diseases. Bioinformatics **26**(13), 1644–1650 (2010)

30. Halko, N., Martinsson, P.-G., Tropp, J.A.: Finding structure with randomness: probabilistic algorithms for constructing approximate matrix decompositions. SIAM Rev. **53**(2), 217–288 (2011)

31. Liu, Z., et al.: KAN: Kolmogorov-Arnold Networks. arXiv.org (2024)

32. Wall, M.E., Rechtsteiner, A., Rocha, L.M.: Singular value decomposition and principal component analysis. In: Berrar, D.P., et al. (eds.) A Practical Approach to Microarray Data Analysis, pp. 91–109. Springer, US, Boston, MA (2003)

Autonomous Generation of an Autism Knowledge Question-and-Answer Dataset Using Large Language Models

Lei Chu[1,2,3], Hongyan Wu[1(✉)], and Yi Pan[1,2(✉)]

[1] Shenzhen Institute of Advanced Technology, Chinese Academy of Sciences, Shenzhen, China
`{l.chu,hy.wu}@siat.ac.cn, chulei22@mails.ucas.ac.cn`
[2] Shenzhen University of Advanced Technology, Shenzhen, China
`panyi@suat-sz.edu.cn`
[3] University of Chinese Academy of Sciences, Beijing, China

Abstract. Autism Spectrum Disorder (ASD) poses ongoing challenges in diagnosis and intervention due to its complexity and the variability of available information. Large Language Models (LLMs) have demonstrated promising capabilities in general question-answering tasks, but their efficacy in specialized domains such as autism is limited by the scarcity of high-quality, domain-specific training data. In this paper, we introduce a novel methodology for autonomously generating a high-quality autism knowledge question-and-answer (QA) dataset using state-of-the-art LLMs. Our approach addresses the data scarcity issue and enhances the capacity of LLMs to deliver accurate, reliable, and nuanced autism-related information. We describe in detail the domain knowledge integration process, prompt engineering strategies, and dataset generation workflow, followed by a rigorous evaluation framework. The resulting AutismQA dataset and associated generation code are made openly available after careful consideration of safety and ethical implications. Experimental outcomes validate our method, showing notable improvements in the accuracy and reliability of autism-focused QA systems.

Keywords: Autism Spectrum Disorder · Large Language Models · Question Answering · Dataset Generation · Domain Knowledge

1 Introduction

Autism Spectrum Disorder (ASD) is a complex neurodevelopmental condition characterized by persistent challenges in social interaction, communication deficits, repetitive behaviors, and restricted interests. The global prevalence of ASD has been rising, currently estimated at approximately 1% of the population, highlighting an urgent need for accessible and reliable autism-related knowledge resources.

Recent advancements in LLMs, such as GPT-4, have shown extraordinary effectiveness in general natural language understanding and generation tasks,

---

H. Y and Y. Pan—Co-corresponding author

J. Tang et al. (Eds.): ISBRA 2025, LNBI 15757, pp. 123–138, 2026.
https://doi.org/10.1007/978-981-95-0695-8_11

including sophisticated question-answering. However, their applicability within specialized fields—notably medical and health-related domains like autism—is significantly hampered by the lack of substantial domain-specific training resources. General-purpose LLMs often fail to integrate specialized autism knowledge fully, resulting in responses that may be inaccurate, incomplete, or misleading.

To overcome this limitation, we propose an autonomous methodology for generating a comprehensive autism knowledge QA dataset (*AutismQA*). Our approach leverages a powerful LLM guided by structured domain-specific knowledge to produce QA pairs that encapsulate accurate and comprehensive autism information. The generated dataset addresses key topics including diagnostic criteria, symptoms, etiological theories, evidence-based interventions, and available support resources, providing a robust foundation for developing more precise and reliable autism-focused QA systems.

Our contributions can be summarized as follows:

- **Autonomous Dataset Generation:** We develop a systematic methodology for automatic generation of high-quality autism-specific QA datasets, substantially alleviating the reliance on expensive and time-consuming manual annotation.
- **Structured Domain Knowledge Integration:** Instead of a full ontology, we distill autism-specific domain knowledge into an accessible form to guide the LLM, ensuring generated content is contextually accurate and medically informed.
- **Prompt Engineering for Quality Control:** We utilize advanced prompt engineering techniques to carefully guide LLM output, maximizing relevance, factual accuracy, and comprehensive coverage of autism-related topics while minimizing errors.

2   Related Work

2.1   LLMs for Specialized Question-Answering

LLMs have emerged as powerful tools in question-answering due to their ability to understand context, reason effectively, and generate coherent responses. Recent models such as GPT-4 have demonstrated remarkable performance on general knowledge QA benchmarks [1]. However, their effectiveness diminishes in specialized domains where accuracy is paramount, due to inadequate domain-specific training data and inherent tendencies to generate plausible yet incorrect (hallucinated) information [2]. Studies have thus emphasized the necessity of domain adaptation and fine-tuning for specialized applications such as medical QA [3].

2.2   Knowledge Graphs and LLM Integration

Knowledge graphs (KGs) encode factual knowledge as structured triples, providing a reliable semantic framework for knowledge representation and retrieval.

Integrating KGs into QA systems is a common approach to enhance the reliability and accuracy of generated responses, especially in medical and scientific domains [4,5]. Systems like *ChatASD* exemplify the success of combining an autism-specific KG with LLMs to improve answer quality and factual accuracy [6]. However, building and maintaining a comprehensive domain KG can be labor-intensive.

2.3   Autism Knowledge Bases and QA Resources

Several autism-specific knowledge bases and QA resources have been developed, underscoring the need for accurate autism information. Notably, *AsdKB* is a comprehensive Chinese knowledge base that supports early screening and diagnosis of ASD [7]. Additionally, an ASD QA dataset in Russian provided 1,134 QA pairs for evaluating QA models on autism-related questions [8]. These resources, however, are limited in scale, language, or diversity, highlighting the need for scalable, autonomous approaches to dataset creation in the autism domain.

3   Methodology

Our methodology consists of four key phases: (1) distilling domain knowledge, (2) prompt design, (3) autonomous Q&A generation, and (4) quality control and dataset assembly.

3.1   Domain Knowledge Distillation

We began by collecting and distilling authoritative autism knowledge to serve as the foundation for QA generation. Instead of constructing a formal knowledge graph with complex ontology, we opted for a lightweight structured knowledge approach: extracting key facts from trusted sources and organizing them by topic. We gathered information from peer-reviewed autism research (e.g., PubMed articles), established clinical guidelines (DSM-5-TR, ICD-11), and reputable educational and support resources. All content was vetted to ensure it reflects well-established scientific and clinical consensus.

Specifically, we extracted the ASD diagnostic criteria and descriptive text from **DSM-5-TR** and **ICD-11** to cover standardized clinical definitions. We performed targeted literature searches on PubMed (e.g., using queries such as "autism prevalence meta-analysis", "ASD early intervention outcomes") to gather up-to-date research findings on prevalence, risk factors, and interventions. We also consulted authoritative public resources such as the Centers for Disease Control and Prevention (CDC) autism pages and Autism Speaks guides to incorporate widely referenced facts and practical knowledge. The fact compilation was conducted manually by the authors to ensure accuracy and relevance; we excluded any statements not corroborated by multiple sources or that contradicted established consensus, thereby filtering out unsubstantiated claims. Through this process, we aimed to maximize coverage of key autism knowledge areas while minimizing potential bias, though we acknowledge that reliance on primarily English-language academic sources may introduce some Western or research-centric perspective.

From these sources, we compiled roughly 300 concise factual statements covering the essential domains of autism knowledge. These facts were grouped under major categories such as *core characteristics* (definition and primary diagnostic features), *early signs and diagnosis* (early indicators, typical diagnostic age, screening tools), *prevalence and demographics* (e.g., global prevalence $\approx 1\%$, gender ratio $\approx 4{:}1$ male-to-female), *causes and risk factors* (evidence of genetic contributions, debunking myths like vaccines), *interventions and treatments* (recognized therapies like ABA, speech therapy), and *support resources* (education plans, community support). This distilled knowledge base ensured comprehensive coverage of important autism topics while remaining manageable. Each fact was written as a clear, standalone sentence or two, making it easy for an LLM to incorporate. These fact statements serve as the "ground truth" information that will be transformed into QA pairs.

3.2 Prompt Design and LLM Configuration

Designing the right prompt is vital to coax the LLM (GPT-4 in our case) to generate high-quality QA pairs anchored in the provided facts. We crafted a prompt that clearly instructs the model, supplies necessary knowledge, and constrains the output format. The prompt begins with a brief *role and task description*, for example: *"You are an expert autism researcher and educator tasked with creating question-answer pairs for an autism knowledge base."* This sets the tone for authoritative and clear responses. We also include explicit style guidelines: *"The question should be concise and clear. The answer should be factual, comprehensive, and written in an explanatory tone appropriate for parents or students. Do not include any information not supported by the provided fact."* By instructing the model to avoid unsupported content, we aim to reduce hallucinations.

Next, the prompt includes the relevant *domain fact*. We experimented with different ways of providing this information (e.g., as a structured triple vs. natural language). We found that a simple declarative sentence was most effective for the model. Thus, we embed the fact as a sentence (or two) prefaced by a tag like *"Information:"*. For example, the prompt might contain: *"Information: Applied Behavior Analysis (ABA) is a therapy that uses behavioral principles to improve social and communication skills in children with ASD."*

We also employ an *example-based prompting* strategy. At the start of a generation session, we provide a few-shot example to illustrate the desired output format. Specifically, we show one example of a fact turned into a QA pair. For instance, given the fact *"Autism has a global prevalence of about 1%."*, we precede the task with: *Q: What is the global prevalence of autism? A: Approximately 1 in 100 children worldwide are diagnosed with ASD, which is about 1%.* This example demonstrates the transformation of the fact into a question (in this case, asking about prevalence) and an answer that correctly incorporates the fact. We separate the example from the actual task with a clear delimiter (e.g., a line of dashes) to prevent confusion. We found that using one well-chosen example strikes a good balance: it provides a template for the model without over-constraining its creativity or leading it to parrot the format.

Finally, we explicitly instruct the model on the output format: it should produce a question prefixed by "Q:" and an answer prefixed by "A:". These cues, combined with the example, ensured the model almost always followed the Q&A format correctly (we observed about 95% compliance). For generation parameters, we set a moderate creativity level (temperature ≈ 0.4) to allow varied phrasing but not stray from facts. We also imposed a penalty on repeating the input text to encourage the model to rephrase the fact in its own words rather than copying. With these prompt settings, the model is primed to generate a relevant, fact-based question-answer pair for each given piece of information.

3.3 Autonomous Q&A Generation Process

With the prompt template in place, we automated the dataset generation. We wrote a script to feed each fact from our distilled knowledge base into the LLM prompt and record the resulting Q&A. The generation proceeded in batches to handle API rate limits and to allow periodic checks.

For each fact, we aimed to produce at least one QA pair. In most cases, a single fact directly yields a straightforward question. For example, the fact *"Many autistic children have sensory sensitivities (e.g., to loud noises or bright lights)."* naturally leads to a question like *"Why do many autistic children have sensitivities to loud noises or bright lights?"* with an answer explaining sensory processing issues in ASD. In some cases, we created two questions from one fact to capture different angles. For instance, given the fact *"Autism is about four times more common in boys than in girls.",* we generated: (1) *"Is autism more common in boys or girls?"* answered with the direct statistic that autism is four times more common in boys; and (2) *"Why might autism be diagnosed more often in boys than in girls?"* answered by mentioning the 4:1 ratio and discussing possible factors (e.g., diagnostic bias or different symptom presentation). By doing this, we enriched the dataset with both factual and explanatory forms of questions.

Overall, the process ensured that *each fact yielded at least one QA pair,* and often two or more if the fact was broad or multifaceted. We also varied the phrasing and style of questions to improve diversity. The generated questions included a mix of **"What/Which" questions** (definitions or factual queries, e.g. *"What are the common signs of ASD in a young child?"*), **"How" questions** (process or mechanism queries like *"How is autism diagnosed by professionals?"*), **"Why" questions** (explanatory, e.g. *"Why do some autistic individuals engage in repetitive behaviors?"*), **Yes/No questions** (often addressing myths or misconceptions, e.g. *"Can childhood vaccines cause autism?"*), as well as questions about prevalence (*"How common is autism in the population?"*) and definitions of key terms (*"What is an IEP (Individualized Education Program)?"*). This variety was intentionally cultivated to make the dataset comprehensive in both form and content, by prompting the model to produce different types of questions for each fact whenever applicable.

Using this method, we generated approximately 3,000 QA pairs from around 300 facts. This corresponds to roughly 10 questions per fact on average; in practice, many straightforward facts yielded only a single QA pair each, while broader or more multifaceted topics contributed multiple QAs to reach the overall total. The LLM typically produced well-formed QAs without needing further prompting. We logged all outputs, along with the source fact, for the subsequent quality control stage.

3.4   Quality Control and Hallucination Mitigation

Generating a large dataset autonomously is only useful if the results are high quality. We implemented multiple quality control measures to catch errors, remove low-quality outputs, and ensure factual consistency.

Automated Verification (LLM-in-the-loop). We leveraged the LLM itself to verify each generated answer. After producing a QA pair, we fed the model a follow-up prompt such as: *"Information: [fact]. You generated the question: [Q] and answer: [A]. Does the answer directly follow from the information given? Is every claim in the answer supported by that information? Reply with YES or NO and a brief explanation."* This meta-prompt asks the model to reflect on its own answer. In most cases, the model correctly identified whether it had introduced any unsupported content. If it responded with *"NO"* or noted an extra claim not in the fact, we flagged that QA for review (and typically removal or correction). This self-check mechanism helped catch subtle issues where the answer might be plausible but went beyond the provided fact.

Pattern and Content Checks. We performed automatic string checks to ensure that critical keywords from the fact appeared in the question or answer. For instance, if the fact was about *"social communication skills"*, we expected the answer to mention social communication or a related term. If a fact included a statistic (like *"1 in 54"*), we checked that the answer included that number or an equivalent phrasing. These checks helped identify cases where the model produced a very generic answer that missed the key detail (e.g., an answer that said *"Autism is fairly common."* without giving the specific prevalence from the fact). Such answers were either edited to include the missing detail or discarded.

Manual Expert Review. Two domain experts (a developmental pediatrician and an autism researcher) manually reviewed a random sample of approximately 200 QAs (about 7% of the dataset) for correctness and clarity. They found that the vast majority (>95%) of the sampled QAs were accurate and clearly written. They flagged a few instances (around 5%) where wording could be improved or nuanced. For example, one generated answer stated *"Speech therapy cures communication problems in ASD,"* which the expert noted should be rephrased to

"Speech therapy can significantly improve communication skills in ASD" (avoiding the word "cures"). We corrected such issues. The high accuracy in this sample gave us confidence in the overall quality of the dataset, thanks to the earlier automated filtering.

Hallucination Rate Estimation. We define a hallucination as any piece of information in an answer that cannot be traced back to the provided fact or widely accepted general knowledge. Because our generation was tightly grounded in the distilled facts, outright hallucinations were rare. In a few cases, the model added plausible but not provided details (e.g., mentioning a speculative research idea or an additional example that wasn't in the input fact). We identified and removed those during verification. After this cleaning, we estimate that less than 2% of the final answers contained any unsupported content. Importantly, none of the final QA pairs propagate false information; all answers were validated to be consistent with established knowledge.

3.5 Dataset Assembly and Characteristics

After quality control, we compiled the final *AutismQA* dataset. It contains 3,000 QA pairs, each intended to be a self-contained question and answer that a layperson can understand without additional context. We shuffled and split the data into 2,500 training QAs, 250 validation QAs, and 250 test QAs, to facilitate machine learning uses (the training set can be used to fine-tune models, and the held-out test set for evaluation). Each QA is stored as a JSON object with fields: `question`, `answer`, `category`, and `source_fact`. The `category` indicates the topical category (e.g., "Symptom", "Intervention", "Myth") corresponding to the source fact, and `source_fact` retains the original fact text or an ID linking the QA back to its knowledge source. This traceability is important for transparency, allowing users of the dataset to see exactly what knowledge underpins each QA pair.

The questions in AutismQA are generally concise (typically one sentence; mean length ∼7–8 words) and focused on a single idea. The answers are a few sentences long (mean length ∼25 words), providing a complete, factual explanation. We designed answers to be sufficiently detailed to be informative (often providing a brief explanation or context), yet not so long as to overwhelm the reader. The dataset covers a broad range of content: as mentioned, the QAs span categories such as general autism knowledge, symptoms and behaviors, causes/risk factors, interventions and therapies, statistics/prevalence, and common myths. Notably, the largest portions of QAs pertain to interventions and symptoms, reflecting common information needs in the autism community (see Appendix Fig. 1 for a breakdown of topics).

To illustrate the nature of the data, consider two examples. One QA pair asks: *Q: Can childhood vaccines cause autism? A:* **No, vaccines do not cause autism.** *Large-scale studies have shown no link between routine childhood vaccinations and autism; increased autism diagnoses are due to better awareness and* *screening, not vaccines.* This debunks a prevalent myth with a clear answer and supporting explanation. Another example: *Q: How does speech therapy help children with ASD? A: Speech therapy helps improve communication skills in children with ASD. Therapists work with children on language development, social communication (like taking turns in conversation), and articulation. Over time, this intervention can significantly enhance an autistic child's ability to express themselves and understand others.* These examples demonstrate that the QA pairs not only convey factual answers ("no, vaccines do not cause autism") but also provide context or details that make the information useful and self-explanatory. In addition to common questions, about 30% of the QAs address more advanced or nuanced topics (for instance, questions about current research findings or specific clinical terms), which can challenge models and ensure the dataset isn't too trivial. Compared to prior autism QA resources (e.g., the Russian ASD-QA dataset with 1.1k pairs [8]), AutismQA is larger, covers a wider variety of question forms, and provides multi-sentence, explanatory answers. It also complements broader medical QA datasets (many of which are multiple-choice or not specific to autism) by offering open-ended QAs in a focused domain.

4   Experiments and Results

We conducted experiments to evaluate both the quality of the AutismQA dataset and the performance of QA models on this dataset.

Dataset Quality Validation: As part of our validation, three independent ASD experts (not involved in dataset construction) reviewed a random sample of 50 QA pairs from the test set. They rated each QA on a 1–5 scale for *correctness* (factual accuracy and relevance of the answer), *clarity* (clear phrasing of question and answer), and *usefulness* (whether the QA would be useful to someone seeking autism information). The average correctness rating was 4.9/5, clarity 4.7/5, and usefulness 4.8/5, indicating near-universal approval of the content. The experts particularly appreciated the thoroughness and accuracy of the answers. We also verified that all key facts from our knowledge collection were represented in at least one QA pair, confirming 100% coverage of our intended knowledge scope. These checks suggest that the AutismQA dataset is of high quality and suitable as a reliable source of autism information.

QA Model Performance: We next evaluated how well various models can answer the questions in AutismQA. We tested four settings: (1) **GPT-4 (closed-book)**, using GPT-4 directly on the test questions without any additional context (simulating a strong general model with no domain help); (2) **GPT-4 (knowledge-augmented)**, where we provided GPT-4 with the corresponding fact from our dataset as context before asking the question (simulating an ideal retrieval-augmented scenario); (3) **AutismQA-LLaMA**, an open-source 7B parameter model fine-tuned on the 2. The fine-tuning set comprised approximately 2,500 QAs derived from about 90% of the source facts, while the evaluation set contained all QAs originating from the remaining 10% of facts, ensuring no direct overlap of facts between training and testing and eliminating information leakage.5k training QA pairs (we used a LLaMA-based model with instruction tuning as the base, then fine-tuned for 3 epochs on our data); and (4) **ChatGPT (GPT-3.5)**, the baseline of a widely-available large model without fine-tuning, tested in closed-book fashion. We evaluated the models on the 250 test questions using several metrics. The primary metric is accuracy, defined as the percentage of questions for which the model's answer was judged to be correct (meaning it contained essentially the same information as the reference answer). We also computed precision, recall, and F1 of factual points: for each question, we identified key fact elements in the reference answer and checked if the model's answer contained them. Additionally, we measured the hallucination rate, i.e., the fraction of answers that introduced any information not supported by the reference answer or general common knowledge. Two human evaluators reviewed the model outputs to assess correctness and factual alignment for these metrics (with inter-annotator agreement $\kappa = 0.95$ on the accuracy judgment).

Table 1. Performance of different QA models on the AutismQA test set.

Model	Accuracy	Precision	Recall	F1	MRR	Halluc. Rate
GPT-4 (no context)	72.8%	0.74	0.70	0.72	0.785	14.4%
GPT-4 (with context)	92.0%	0.92	0.91	0.915	0.980	1.2%
AutismQA-LLaMA (7B)	81.2%	0.83	0.79	0.81	0.820	10.8%
ChatGPT (GPT-3.5, no context)	60.4%	0.61	0.58	0.59	0.650	18.0%

The results are summarized in Table 1. GPT-4 in the closed-book setting already performs quite well, answering 72.8% of the questions correctly. This indicates that GPT-4's internal knowledge and reasoning cover a good portion of autism information (which is impressive, as many narrower models would struggle to achieve this without training). However, GPT-4's answers without context sometimes included inaccuracies or unsupported details: the hallucination rate was 14.4%, meaning roughly 1 in 7 answers had some content that didn't match our reference truth (for example, on *"What causes autism?"* GPT-4 might mention a speculative cause not in consensus, or on a prevalence question it might recall an outdated statistic). When we augmented GPT-4 with the relevant facts (essentially giving it the exact information needed), its accuracy jumped to 92.0%, and hallucinations dropped to just 1.2%. This highlights that GPT-4's errors were mostly due to knowledge gaps that can be filled with the right information, rather than an inability to reason. In other words, when GPT-4 "knows" the correct answer (because we provided the fact), it almost always produces it and avoids making things up.

Our fine-tuned model, AutismQA-LLaMA, achieved 81.2% accuracy on the test set. Despite having far fewer parameters (7B) and being trained only on our relatively small dataset, it learned the domain knowledge quite well— outperforming the base GPT-3.5 model (which scored 60.4% on accuracy) by a wide margin. The fine-tuned model's precision and recall of key facts were also high (F1 around 0.81), and it hallucinated less than 11% of the time. This demonstrates the value of the AutismQA training data: it allowed a compact model to specialize and even beat a much larger generic model on this domain-specific task. While the fine-tuned model does not reach GPT-4's level of performance, it provides a strong baseline that can be deployed locally and efficiently.

In summary, these experiments confirm that domain-specific data and knowledge integration are key to high performance in autism QA. GPT-4, even without extra context, answered roughly three-quarters of the questions correctly but benefited greatly from being given verified information, which nearly eliminated its errors. The fine-tuned AutismQA-LLaMA model, trained on our dataset, attained strong accuracy and substantially outperformed a general model of similar size in this domain. This demonstrates that our automatically generated data can indeed elevate the capabilities of smaller models. The results also echo findings in prior work on knowledge-enhanced LLMs: when an LLM is provided with accurate supporting knowledge (or trained on it), it can deliver expert-level answers with minimal hallucination. In the next section, we discuss the implications of these findings and potential future steps.

5   Discussion

Our work demonstrates a practical methodology for leveraging a powerful LLM (GPT-4) in conjunction with distilled domain knowledge to automatically construct a specialized QA dataset. A notable outcome is showing that **LLMs can act as *producers* of training data, not just consumers**. By guiding GPT-4 with domain-specific facts, we effectively turned it into a data generator that respects factual accuracy. This approach can be especially valuable for domains where obtaining large annotated datasets is challenging (e.g., rare medical conditions or specialized technical fields). While we used a curated autism knowledge base, the process did not require human annotators to manually write thousands of questions and answers—illustrating a more scalable paradigm for dataset creation.

Another important aspect is the synergy between structured knowledge and LLM generation. Our results highlight that knowledge integration is key for high performance: when GPT-4 had access to the relevant autism facts, it achieved over 90% accuracy with almost no hallucinations, versus about 73% accuracy with notable errors when relying on its pre-training alone. This underscores that even the most advanced general models benefit greatly from domain grounding in specialized applications. Similarly, the fine-tuned 7B model's strong performance shows that with just a few thousand quality examples, a smaller model can approach the correctness of a much larger one in-domain. This has practical implications: organizations can deploy relatively lightweight models fine-tuned on AutismQA (or similar datasets) to get reliable autism QA capabilities without requiring an API call to a giant model. Furthermore, each QA pair in **AutismQA** is derived from a *single* fact. This simplifies verification since every question can be answered directly from one knowledge statement, but it also means the dataset does not evaluate multi-hop or compositional reasoning that requires combining multiple facts. For instance, a question like "How common is autism in females?" would require integrating overall prevalence with the male-to-female ratio and is therefore absent. Future releases of the dataset may introduce such multi-fact questions to assess models' ability to synthesize information across facts.

The approach we used—distilling a knowledge base and using an LLM to generate QAs—could be generalized to other domains. Essentially, we inverted the typical use of a knowledge graph in QA: rather than using the KG only to answer questions, we used it to *generate* questions (and answers) in the first place. This can accelerate dataset creation for any subject matter where a body of knowledge can be identified. For example, one could create a *DiabetesQA* or *ClimateChangeQA* by feeding domain facts to an LLM. The technique harnesses the linguistic and generative prowess of LLMs while anchoring them with factual inputs to ensure accuracy.

That said, there are limitations and considerations. Our method relies on the quality of the initial knowledge distillation—if the source facts are incomplete or biased, the resulting dataset will be as well. We mitigated this by carefully selecting and reviewing autism domain facts. Another consideration is that while our generated answers are factual and have some explanation, they are not personalized or empathetic in the way a human expert might tailor an answer to a specific asker's context. Future work could extend the approach to generate not just factual answers but also variation in tone or detail level for different audiences (e.g., parents vs. clinicians). Additionally, as autism research evolves, new facts will emerge. One advantage of our pipeline is that it can be iteratively updated: if a new finding comes out (say, a revised prevalence figure or a novel therapy), one could add that fact and re-run the generation for that part to obtain updated QAs, keeping the dataset current.

6   Conclusion

We presented a novel approach to autonomously generate a high-quality question-and-answer dataset for a specialized domain (autism spectrum disorder) using an LLM guided by distilled domain knowledge. Our methodology involved distilling key autism knowledge into a structured form, carefully designing prompts to elicit QA pairs from the LLM, and applying rigorous quality control to ensure accuracy. The result was the AutismQA dataset of 3,000 QA pairs, which we have demonstrated to be an effective benchmark and training resource for autism-focused QA systems.

Experiments showed that a state-of-the-art model like GPT-4, when augmented with appropriate domain knowledge, can exceed 90% accuracy on AutismQA and drastically reduce factual errors, compared to using the model alone. Moreover, an open-source 7B model fine-tuned on the generated data achieved over 81% accuracy, substantially outperforming a powerful base model

(ChatGPT/GPT-3.5) on this domain. These findings confirm the value of knowledge-guided data generation and targeted fine-tuning: even smaller models can deliver high accuracy when provided with high-quality domain-specific training data.

Our approach offers a blueprint for other domains with limited QA datasets. By combining knowledge engineering (even in a lightweight form) with the generative strength of LLMs, we can efficiently bootstrap new specialized QA datasets and systems. We hope our work inspires further exploration into LLM-driven dataset generation, and ultimately contributes to more reliable and accessible AI systems for specialized knowledge areas (from medical conditions to technical support and education). In future work, we plan to explore multi-turn dialogues (converting facts into interactive Q&A scenarios), incorporate visual information for multi-modal autism QAs (e.g., interpreting therapy materials), and continuously update the dataset with community feedback to ensure it remains accurate and useful.

Acknowledgments. This work is supported by Shenzhen Science and Technology Program under grant no. KQTD20200820113106007, Shenzhen Key Laboratory of Intelligent Bioinformatics(ZDSYS20220422103800001), the National Natural Science Foundation of China(U22A2041 and 62273322), and Shenzhen Science and Technology Program (CJGJZD20220517142000002).

Ethical Considerations. This study was conducted with careful attention to ethical guidelines. The AutismQA dataset was derived entirely from publicly available knowledge and contains no personal or sensitive individual data, ensuring privacy. The human evaluations (expert reviews) were performed with informed consent and in accordance with our institution's IRB guidelines (our institutional review determined that no formal IRB approval was required for this expert review process, as it did not involve personal data or clinical interventions). We emphasize that while the QA content provides medically relevant information about autism, it is *not* a substitute for professional medical advice. In developing answers, especially for questions that could influence health decisions (e.g., around treatments or vaccine myths), we consulted clinical experts to ensure accuracy and alignment with medical consensus. All content was curated to use respectful and inclusive language (e.g., identity-first language such as "autistic individuals" and discussion of neurodiversity), avoiding stigma or bias. When deploying any system built on AutismQA, we recommend including disclaimers advising users to consult healthcare professionals for personal medical concerns. Finally, we plan to release the AutismQA dataset openly to encourage transparency and community oversight. This will allow other researchers—including autistic individuals and family members—to review and improve the data, helping to maintain accuracy, relevance, and ethical standards over time.

Appendix A: Additional Figures and Examples

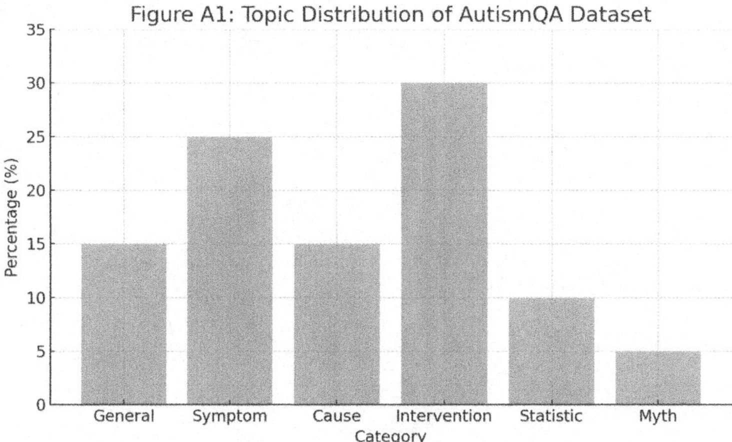

Fig. 1. Topic distribution of questions in the AutismQA dataset (Figure A1). Each bar indicates the percentage of QA pairs pertaining to a given category (General, Symptom, Cause, Intervention, Statistic, Myth, etc.). The dataset covers a broad range of autism-related topics, with Intervention- and Symptom-related QAs being the most frequent.

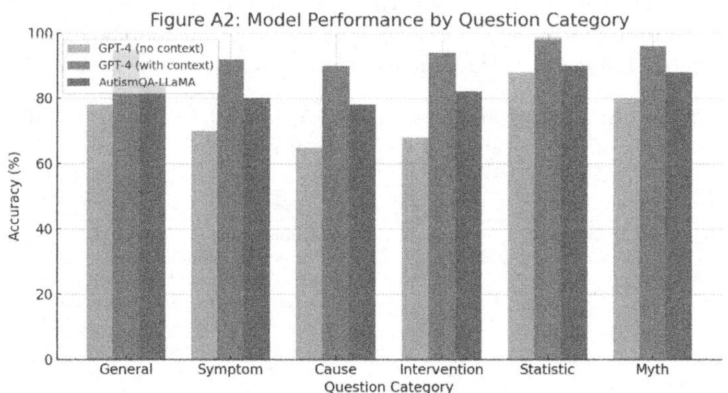

Fig. 2. Model performance by question category (Figure A2). Accuracy of GPT-4 (with and without knowledge) and the fine-tuned AutismQA-LLaMA model is shown for different question categories (e.g., Definition, Symptom, Intervention). This illustrates which topics were easier or harder for the models; for instance, all models perform strongly on straightforward facts (Definitions/Statistics), while GPT-4 without context was weaker on certain Intervention questions until given the relevant knowledge (Table 2).

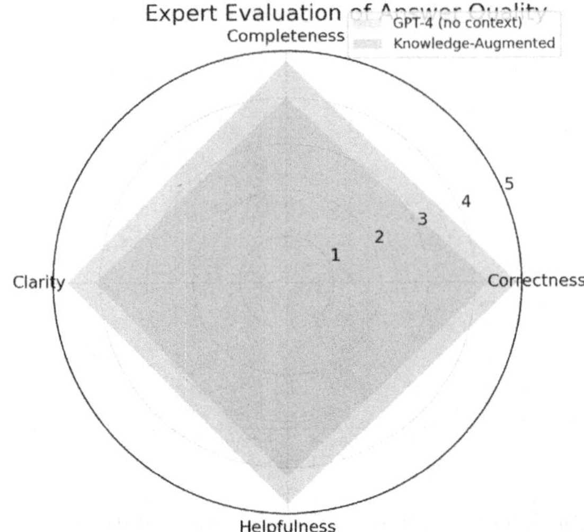

Fig. 3. Expert evaluation of answer quality (Figure A3). A radar chart comparing average ratings (15) by domain experts for answers generated by GPT-4 (no context) versus our knowledge-augmented approach (AutismQA-LLaMA or GPT-4 with knowledge). The criteria include correctness, completeness, clarity, and helpfulness. The knowledge-grounded approach scores higher across all dimensions, reflecting the experts' preference for answers that incorporate domain facts (Fig. 2 and 3).

Table 2. Example QA pairs from the AutismQA dataset (Table A1). These examples illustrate the variety of categories and the style of questions and answers.

ID	Category	Question	Answer
102	Symptom	What are some common signs of autism in a young child?	Young children with autism often show signs such as delayed speech or lack of babbling, limited eye contact, not responding to their name, and repetitive behaviors (like hand flapping). These early indicators typically appear in infancy or toddlerhood.
187	Cause	Do genetics play a role in autism?	Yes. Genetics play a significant role in autism. Research shows that autism can run in families and many different genes have been linked to the condition. For example, having one child with autism increases the chances of another child having autism, indicating a strong genetic contribution.
255	Intervention	How does speech therapy help children with ASD?	Speech therapy helps children with ASD by improving their communication skills. A speech therapist teaches children how to better express themselves and understand language, often by practicing speaking or using alternative communication methods. Over time, this can help autistic children communicate their needs and engage more socially.

continued

Table 2. continued

ID	Category	Question	Answer
333	Myth	Can childhood vaccines cause autism?	**No, vaccines do not cause autism.** Large-scale studies and scientific evidence have shown no link between routine childhood vaccinations (such as the MMR vaccine) and autism. The rise in autism diagnoses over the years is due to improved awareness and broader diagnostic criteria, not vaccines. Health authorities worldwide recommend vaccination to keep children safe from serious diseases.
410	Statistic	How common is autism in the population?	Autism spectrum disorder affects about 1% of the population. In other words, roughly 1 in 100 children worldwide is diagnosed with autism. Some recent studies suggest the number might be slightly higher (e.g., about 1 in 36 in certain countries) due to improved awareness and screening.

References

1. OpenAI: GPT-4 Technical Report. arXiv preprint arXiv:2303.08774 (2023)
2. Ji, Z., Lee, N., Frieske, R., et al.: Survey of hallucination in natural language generation. ACM Comput. Surv. **55**(12), 1–38 (2023)
3. Jin, C., Zhang, M., Ma, W., et al.: RJUA-MedDQA: a multimodal benchmark for medical document question answering and clinical reasoning. In: Proceedings of the 30th ACM SIGKDD Conference on Knowledge Discovery and Data Mining, pp. 5218–5229 (2024)
4. Zhao, X., Liu, S., Yang, S.-Y., et al.: MedRAG: enhancing retrieval-augmented generation with knowledge graph-elicited reasoning for healthcare copilot. arXiv preprint arXiv:2502.04413 (2025)
5. Oduro-Afriyie, J.: Improving Personal Health Question Answering Through Knowledge Graph Enhancement. PhD thesis, University of Idaho (2024)
6. Chu, L., Wu, H., Pan, Y.: ChatASD: A Dialogue Framework for LLMs Enhanced by Autism Knowledge Graph Retrieval. In: Proceedings of the 15th ACM International Conference on Bioinformatics, Computational Biology and Health Informatics, pp. 1–8 (2024)

7. Wu, T., Cao, X., Zhu, Y., et al.: AsdKB: A Chinese knowledge base for the early screening and diagnosis of autism spectrum disorder. In: Proceedings of the International Semantic Web Conference (ISWC), Lecture Notes in Computer Science, vol. 14266, pp. 59–75. Springer, Cham (2023). https://doi.org/10.1007/978-3-031-47243-5_4
8. Firsanova, V.: Transformer models for question answering on autism spectrum disorder Q&A dataset. In: Proceedings of the 6th International Conference on Digital Transformation and Global Society (DTGS 2021), Communications in Computer and Information Science (CCIS), vol. 1503, pp. 122–133. Springer, Cham (2022). https://doi.org/10.1007/978-3-030-93715-7_9

Double Metaphone Blocking: An Innovative Blocking Approach to Record Linkage

Nidhibahen Shah[1], Joyanta Basak[1], Sartaj Sahni[2], Anup Mathur[3], Krista Park[3], Daniel Weinberg[3], and Sanguthevar Rajasekaran[1(✉)]

[1] University of Connecticut, Storrs, CT 06269, USA
sanguthevar.rajasekaran@uconn.edu
[2] University of Florida, Gainesville, FL 32611, USA
[3] US Census Bureau, Washington, USA

Abstract. The task of record linkage aims to link records from diverse datasets into cohesive clusters, where each cluster represents a unique entity. The record linkage process is vital for applications such as healthcare, fraud detection, law enforcement, biology, transportation, and supply chain management. The sheer volume of data involved often poses significant computational challenges. To address these challenges, the blocking technique has emerged as a key strategy to streamline the record linkage process by reducing the number of computations. In this paper, we explore a novel application of Double Metaphone encoding, as a foundation for an innovative blocking method. Traditionally utilized for measuring phonetic similarity, Double Metaphone is here repurposed to enhance the blocking efficiency of the record linkage process. We introduce Double Metaphone as a blocking technique. Our research unveils improvements in record linkage outcomes, leveraging this new approach to achieve greater performance and reduced computational overhead. Through experiments, we demonstrate that our Double Metaphone Blocking approach outperforms the state-of-the-art record linkage algorithms as evidenced by reduced runtime and higher F-1 scores. This approach offers a promising solution for managing large scale data linkage tasks across various domains.

Keywords: Record Linkage · Blocking · Double Metaphone Encoding

1 Introduction

Record linkage seeks to link records from different datasets into distinct clusters, ensuring that each cluster captures all records linked to a single entity and no more. Record linkage sets the stage for effective data integration across diverse applications. From consolidating patient records in healthcare systems to de-duplicating customer data in e-commerce, record linkage enables organizations to build unified and accurate views of their data. The importance of

J. Tang et al. (Eds.): ISBRA 2025, LNBI 15757, pp. 139–150, 2026.
https://doi.org/10.1007/978-981-95-0695-8_12

record linkage is beyond its operational efficiency. Record linkage can uncover familial connections and in fraud detection it can reveal hidden patterns. In addition, it supports evidence-based decision making by linking disparate sources. As datasets grow in size and complexity, the ability to perform record linkage effectively has become a technical necessity. The exponential growth of data in domains such as healthcare, fraud detection, law enforcement, biology, transportation, supply chain management, e-commerce and genealogy has intensified the need for efficient record linkage techniques. At the heart of this challenge lies the problem of identifying records that belong to the same entity.Record linkage faces significant challenges when dealing with large-scale datasets. Real-world data can be messy. Names can be misspelled (e.g."Jon" vs "John"), they may be phonetically similar but distinct (e.g. "Cline" vs "Kline"), and they may be inconsistently formatted (e.g. "Smith, J." vs "J. Smith"). These types of variations complicate the linkage process, while the sheer volume of records exacerbates the problem. Errors or missing data can lead to missed matches, undermining the reliability of the linkage process. Comparing every pair of records in a dataset of size n to identify clusters of records that represent the same entity requires $\Omega(n^2)$ comparisons. This exhaustive matching algorithm is computationally infeasible when there are millions of records.

To address such scalability issues, the blocking technique has emerged as a practical solution. Blocking partitions datasets into smaller groups or manageable chunks that comprise records that are likely to match. These smaller chunks are sufficiently small that it is practical to compare all pairs of records in each chunk. Yet, existing linkage methods often fail to adequately handle phonetic similarities, leaving room for innovation. Phonetic matching algorithms such as double metaphone, offer a promising foundation by encoding names based on their pronunciation. This enables matches despite spelling discrepancies. However, its application as blocking remains unexplored. In this paper, we introduce a novel double metaphone blocking technique that leverages the strengths of phonetic encoding to create accurate and efficient blocks. By adapting double metaphone as a blocking technique, our approach minimizes missed matches while dramatically reducing runtime.

This work addresses a critical gap in the record linkage literature: the need for blocking methods that balance computational efficiency with robustness to phonetic variation. The rest of this paper is organized as follows: we begin with an overview of related work in phonetic matching and blocking, followed by a detailed explanation of our methodology, and experimental results. We conclude with a discussion of the implications of our work and potential extensions.

2   Related Work

Record linkage is a widely explored field, and two strategies, namely, phonetic matching and blocking are key for addressing its challenges. This section reviews prior work and highlights how our approach builds on this prior work. Deterministic and probabilistic algorithms have been proposed for record linkage. The key difference between these two types of algorithms is whether the distance calculation between any pair of records is done deterministically or probabilistically. Phonetic matching focuses on the names or words that sound alike but have different spelling. An early method for phonetic similarity is the Soundex. Soundex was first developed by [1] in 1918 and it was first employed by the United States Census Bureau to categorize names for statistical purposes. According to the National Archives, the soundex index is a method of coding surnames (last names) based on their pronunciation rather than their spelling. Surnames with similar sounds, such as "SMITH" and "SMYTH", are assigned the same code, allowing them to be grouped together [2]. The soundex creates one code for the provided name. The double metaphone algorithm, which was introduced by Philips [3], generates two codes per name: primary and secondary and handles names in a better way for variations like "Kline" and "Cline". The double metaphone is widely adopted as it works well with different languages and catches more phonetic matches than soundex. Previous studies have used double metaphone for matching names in historical records, indicating that it outperforms older methods in accuracy [4]. Another work applied double metaphone to customer data de duplication, proving that it can handle noisy real world data like typographical errors and abbreviations [5].

Double metaphone has also been used beyond simple pairwise matching. In healthcare, the double metaphone is part of systems that link patient records across hospitals, where names might vary due to some transcription errors [6]. It has been used in search systems, tweaking it to rank similar sounding terms for fuzzy queries [7]. However, these studies typically focus on comparing two records at a time and double metaphone is used for measuring similarity only. There is one study that tried to use double metaphone for clustering by pre-computing codes for all records. However, it did not do well for large scale datasets due to memory and time costs [8]. Blocking tackles the problem of speed in record linkage by dividing the dataset into small groups or blocks thereby reducing the number of comparisons required and hence reducing the runtime. Standard blocking uses attributes like first name or zip code to create blocks [9]. Using double metaphone for approximate string matching in databases, but only as a preprocessing step, not as a full blocking strategy was considered in [10]. [11] applied double metaphone to link encrypted records. The codes were used to group data securely. However, the focus was privacy not speed.

In our previous work we have used soundex as a blocking technique to address some of the issues and it worked really well [12]. The previous work highlights the gaps that we are going to address in this research. Double metaphone works well when it is used as phonetic similarity matching. However, its use in blocking is unexplored. Traditional blocking techniques are weak with sound-alike names. Our double metaphone blocking approach combines its phonetic strength with blocking design which improves F-1 scores and reduces run times. The next section explains how we do this.

3   Methodology

This section describes our double metaphone blocking and record linkage processes. Figure 1 illustrates the workflow of the record linkage process using double metaphone blocking. It includes steps for loading data, blocking, matching and clustering. In the following subsections we describe each step in this workflow.

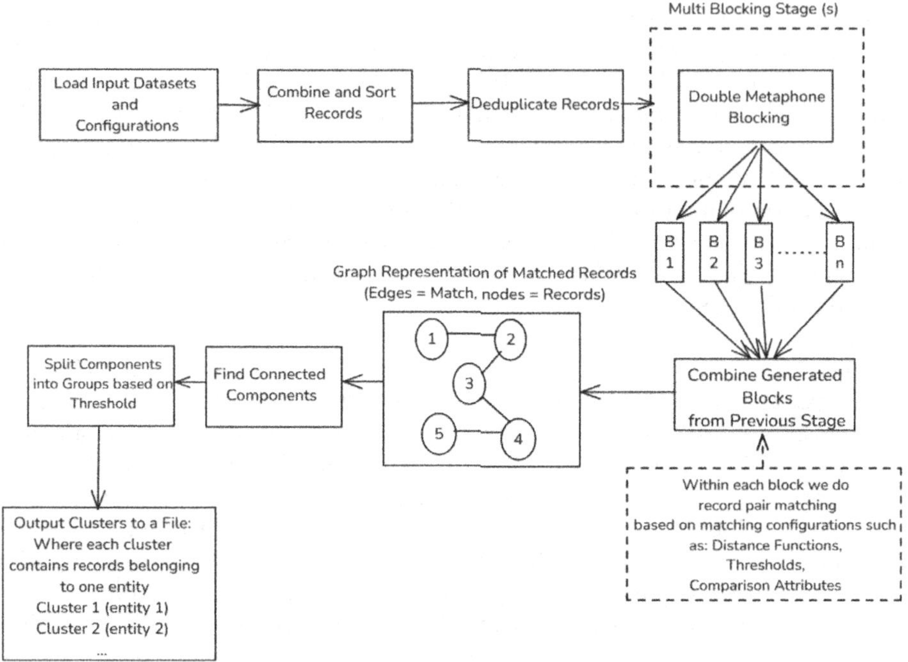

Fig. 1. Record Linkage Workflow

3.1   Loading Input Datasets and Configurations

The first step in the record linkage process is to input datasets from different sources along with configuration settings to guide the linkage process. The configuration settings include blocking fields such as first name and last name, the blocking strategy (e.g., double metaphone, soundex, k-mer) to be employed, the distance metric (e.g., edit distance, q-gram distance, Hausdorff distance, etc.) to be used when comparing two records, and the distance threshold to be used for determining matches. We may also have global and local thresholds and comparison attributes for pair comparison and priority fields. This step ensures that all necessary data and settings are ready before the process begins and it sets the foundation for rest of the workflow.

3.2   Combining and Sorting the Records

Once the datasets and configurations are loaded. We combine all records from different datasets. This allows us to process all records together regardless of their data source. By merging the datasets we ensure that records from different sources can be combined directly. Such process is particularly important for identifying matches across heterogeneous data sources. We sort all the records lexicographically. Sorting makes it easier to identify and remove duplicates (i.e., identical records). It also brings similar records closer to each other.

3.3   Deduplication

After combining and sorting the records, we deduplicate the records to remove the duplicates. This step is crucial in record linkage pipeline as it removes duplicate copies of the records and keeps only one copy for further comparisons. This step identifies identical records across different fields such as two records are listed as "Nidhi Shah" then this step will only keep one copy of this record. This step reduces the data size by avoiding redundant comparisons. This directly reduces number of comparisons required in subsequent steps. This reduction has impact for large scale datasets such as datasets with millions of records where even a small amount of duplicates can lead to unnecessary computations. It also saves time in later steps.

3.4   Double Metaphone Blocking

After deduplication comes the multi-blocking stage in which multiple blocking methods such as k-mer blocking, soundex blocking, and double metaphone blocking may be used together or individually as required. In this work we do not use multi-blocking as we are only working with one blocking technique which is double metaphone blocking. We use the double metaphone blocking technique for encoding the first and last names. The double metaphone algorithm generates two phonetic codes for each name- primary and secondary. For example, for the name "Smith" it generates "SM0" as the primary code and "XMT" as the secondary code. Similar sounding names such as "Smith" and "Smyth" have the same primary code "SM0". All records with the same primary code are grouped into the same block.

The pseudocode for the double metaphone blocking algorithm (DMBA) is presented in Algorithm 1. It takes as input a list of records R, a list of record indices I to process, a field map F to locate fields within records, a list of blocking fields BF and a boolean flag for debugging. The output is a collection of blocks $B_1, B_2, \ldots$. For each record, the algorithm extracts the specified field value and applies double metaphone to obtain its primary phonetic code and uses this code to group together records with the same code. The algorithm also computes the total number of pairwise comparisons required within the blocks. This provides a measure of computational savings achieved through blocking.

Algorithm 1. Double Metaphone Blocking Algorithm (DMBA)

Input: Records R, RecordIndices I, FieldMap F, BlockingFields BF , logBlocks
Output: Blocks B
1: Initialize B as an empty map
2: **for** each record ID $i \in I$ **do**
3:      currentRecord $\leftarrow R[i]$
4:      blockKey $\leftarrow$ ""
5:      **for** each field $f \in BF$ **do**
6:          datasetID $\leftarrow$ currentRecord[last field]
7:          fieldIndex $\leftarrow F[\text{datasetID}][f]$
8:          **if** fieldIndex < 0 then **then**
9:              Continue;
10:         **end if**
11:         fieldValue $\leftarrow$ currentRecord[fieldIndex]
12:         codes $\leftarrow$ DoubleMetaphone(fieldValue)
13:         blockKey $\leftarrow$ blockKey $+$ codes[0]
14:     **end for**
15:     $B[\text{blockKey}].\text{insert}(i)$
16: **end for**
17: **if** logBlocks then **then**
18:     SaveBlocks(I, R, B, "DoubleMetaphoneBlocks")
19: **end if**
20: totalPairs $\leftarrow 0$
21: **for** each key, group $\in B$ **do**
22:     $n \leftarrow$ group.size
23:     totalPairs $\leftarrow$ totalPairs $+ (n \times (n - 1)/2)$
24: **end for**
25: **return** B

3.5 Combining Generated Blocks

In the multi-stage blocking scenario, this step would involve combining blocks obtained using different blocking methods. The outcome of this step is a single set of blocks. Each block contains records that are likely to match.

3.6 Record Pair Matching

Within each block, for each record pair we use the distance functions and thresholds provided in the configurations to determine whether the two records match. In our work, we used edit distance for attributes such as first name, last name, date of birth, and date of death along with thresholds for each attribute and a global threshold for all attributes combined. If the distance between two records is below all specified thresholds then we consider them as a match. For example, in SM0 block we have records "John Smith" and "Jon Smyth". The first names are close as edit distance is 1, so we mark them as a match. Note that only records within the same block are compared.

3.7   Graph Representation

Once the matching record pairs have been determined, we create a graph $G(V, E)$ to represent the matches (Fig. 1). Each record is a node of this graph and there is an edge between two records if they have been matched in at least one of the blocks. For instance, record A matches with record B in one block and records B and C matches in another block. Then the graph connects A, B and C. This indicates that there is a potential that A, B and C belongs to same entity. This graph representation effectively captures the relation between records.

3.8   Finding Connected Components

Using the generated graph $G(V, E)$ we then find the connected components. Each connected component represents records that likely belong to the same entity. This step is essential for reducing the complexity for clustering as it avoids the requirement of exhaustive pairwise comparisons across the entire dataset.

3.9   Splitting Components Into Groups

Some connected components might include records which are not close enough to belong to the same entity. We refine these clusters by splitting each component into smaller groups by ensuring that every pair of records within a group has distance below the threshold. This step ensures that the final clusters contain only matched records.

3.10   Outputting Clusters

Finally, we output the clusters to a file. Each cluster belongs to a single entity.

4   Results

We have performed a series of experiments to evaluate the performance of the Double Metaphone Blocking Algorithm (DMBA).

4.1   Experimental Data

To evaluate our algorithms, we utilized real-world data sourced from the Social Security Death Master File, provided by SSDMF.INFO [13]. Each record includes the following attributes: social security number, last name, first name, date of birth, and date of death. To simulate realistic errors, we employed a modified version of the FEBRL dataset generator program [14] to introduce variations into the data.

4.2   Dataset Generation

In our study, the term "Multiplicity" refers to the number of records in a dataset that correspond to the same entity. To create a dataset of size N with a multiplicity of m, we begin by randomly selecting N/m records from the original dataset. Each of these records is then replicated m times. Subsequently, for each entity, we introduce errors by corrupting exactly one of its m copies, while leaving the remaining $m-1$ copies unchanged. After introducing errors, the dataset consists of $m-1$ original records and one corrupted record per entity. The records in the generated dataset are then randomly shuffled to ensure a realistic distribution. To assess the scalability of our approach, we conducted experiments using 11 datasets of varying size: 50K, 100K, 200K, 400K, 600K, 800K, 1M, 2M, 3M, 4M, and 5M records (the size is the number of records after the replication step).

4.3   Corrupting the Dataset

To introduce errors into the records, we employ a probabilistic model based on an unbiased coin toss, reflecting a realistic scenario where multiple typographical errors in a single record are less common. For 90% of the corrupted records, we insert either two or three new characters into the first name or last name fields, with probabilities of 90% for two characters and 10% for three characters. For the remaining 10% of the corrupted records, we modify the first name or last name fields by altering one, two, or three characters, with probabilities of 80%, 10%, and 10%, respectively. This approach ensures that the introduced errors mimic real-world data inconsistencies while maintaining a controlled level of corruption for experimental purposes.

4.4   Evaluation Metrics

This study employs two primary metrics to evaluate the performance of the proposed method. The first metric is the F-1 score, which is widely used to assess the accuracy of binary classification tasks, such as record linkage. The F-1 score integrates precision and recall into a single measure, offering a balanced evaluation of the model's ability to correctly identify true positive matches while reducing both false positives and false negatives. A higher F-1 score signifies a superior performance. Mathematically, the F-1 score is calculated as:

$$F1 = 2 * (Precison \times Recall)/(Precision + Recall) \tag{1}$$

The second metric used for comparison is runtime. In the domain of record linkage, runtime serves as a crucial evaluation criterion, particularly when processing large datasets, as it directly reflects the computational efficiency of the method.

4.5   F-1 Score Comparison

Table 1 presents the F-1 scores using our DMBA algorithm along with those obtained using three baseline methods: Soundex Blocking, K-mer Blocking, and Super Blocking [15]. DMBA demonstrates superior accuracy, achieving a perfect F-1 score of 100% on smaller datasets (DS1 and DS2) and maintaining near-perfect scores of 99.97% to 99.99% on larger datasets (DS3 to DS11). Soundex Blocking performs comparably, matching DMBA's scores on our datasets of size up to 5M records. In contrast, K-mer Blocking consistently underperforms, with F-1 scores ranging from 99.35% to 99.53%, due to its inability to handle phonetic variations effectively. Super Blocking, while better than K-mer Blocking, achieves scores of 99.96% to 99.98%, falling short of DMBA's performance. These results highlight DMBA's robustness in accurately grouping phonetically similar records, making it a highly effective method for record linkage tasks.

Table 1. F-1 Score Comparison Across Datasets

Datasets	Size	DMBA	Soundex Blocking	K-mer Blocking	Super Blocking
DS1	50k	100%	100%	99.50%	99.98%
DS2	100k	100%	100%	99.53%	99.98%
DS3	200k	99.99%	99.99%	99.50%	99.98%
DS4	400k	99.99%	99.99%	99.45%	99.97%
DS5	600k	99.99%	99.99%	99.41%	99.97%
DS6	800k	99.98%	99.98%	99.41%	99.97%
DS7	1M	99.98%	99.98%	99.35%	99.97%
DS8	2M	99.98%	99.98%	99.37%	99.97%
DS9	3M	99.97%	99.97%	99.37%	99.97%
DS10	4M	99.97%	99.97%	99.35%	99.96%
DS11	5M	99.97%	99.97%	99.35%	99.96%

4.6   Runtime Comparison

Table 2 compares the runtime (in seconds) of DMBA with the baseline methods across the same 11 datasets. DMBA exhibits exceptional efficiency, with runtimes ranging from 0.2 s for DS1 (50k records) to 1660.5 s for DS11 (5M records). Soundex Blocking, while competitive on smaller datasets (e.g., 0.2 s for DS1), scales poorly, requiring 4122.3 s for DS11—over 2.5 times longer than DMBA. K-mer Blocking is the least efficient, with runtimes from 0.6 s (DS1) to 4052.8 s (DS11), due to its high computational overhead. Super Blocking performs better than K-mer Blocking but still lags behind DMBA, with runtimes ranging from 0.34 s to 1342.71 s. Notably, for the largest dataset (DS11), DMBA's runtime is 21% to 60% lower than the baselines, underscoring its scalability and suitability for large-scale record linkage applications. For DS11, Super Blocking has a better runtime than DMBA.

Table 2. Runtime Comparison Across Datasets (in Seconds)

Datasets	Size	DMBA	Soundex Blocking	K-mer Blocking	Super Blocking
DS1	50k	0.2	0.2	0.6	0.34
DS2	100k	0.5	0.8	2.2	1.01
DS3	200k	1.8	3.1	8.3	3.20
DS4	400k	6.3	11.4	30.5	10.55
DS5	600k	13	24.9	63.6	22.19
DS6	800k	23.5	46.6	113.4	37.21
DS7	1M	36	75.1	172.8	56.64
DS8	2M	177.5	435.3	668.4	217.54
DS9	3M	475.2	1225.9	1486.1	502.73
DS10	4M	931.4	2417.3	2592.3	939.96
DS11	5M	1660.5	4122.3	4052.8	1342.71

4.7   Runtime Reduction Analysis

Figure 2 plots the runtime (in seconds) of each blocking method as a function of dataset size, using logarithmic scales for both axes to better visualize the differences between wide range of dataset sizes and runtimes. The graph clearly shows that DMBA consistently outperforms the baseline methods, with a runtime growth rate that is significantly lower than that of the other methods. The logarithmic x-axis spreads out the smaller datasets (50k to 1M records), making it clear that Double Metaphone Blocking (DMBA) consistently outperforms Super Blocking in this range. For example, at 50k records (DS1), DMBA's runtime is 0.2 s compared to Super Blocking's 0.34 s—a 41% reduction. This gap persists at 1M records (DS7), where DMBA completes in 36 s while Super Blocking requires 56.64 s, a 36% improvement. The trend continues up to 4M records (DS10), with DMBA at 931.4 s versus Super Blocking's 939.96 s. Super Blocking shows a lower runtime at 5M records (1342.71 s vs. DMBA's 1660.5 s). DMBA consistently outperforms on all other dataset sizes, combined with its superior F-1 scores (as shown in Table 1), makes it the preferred method for large-scale record linkage. The plot also highlights DMBA's scalability compared to Soundex Blocking (4122.3 s at 5M) and K-mer Blocking (4052.8 s at 5M), which exhibit significantly steeper runtime growth. Furthermore, DMBA effectively reduced computational burden by reducing the number of record pair comparisons.

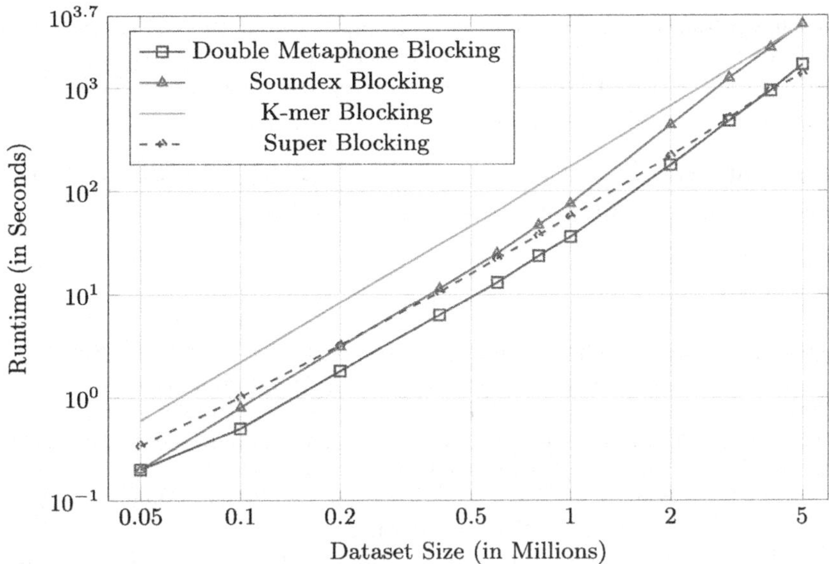

Fig. 2. Runtime Comparison of Blocking Methods Across Dataset Sizes (Logarithmic Scales)

5 Conclusions and Future Work

In this paper, we have proposed the Double Metaphone Blocking Algorithm (DMBA), a novel blocking technique that significantly improves the performance of record linkage process. Our experiments demonstrate that DMBA achieves a superior balance of computational speed and matching quality compared to existing blocking methods like Soundex blocking, K-mer blocking and for the most cases of Super blocking. By using phonetic encoding, DMBA effectively reduces record pair comparisons which enables faster processing for large datasets for record linkage process as evidenced by consistently high F-1 scores across datasets ranging from 50K to 5M records and lower runtimes across all datasets. We also show practical applicability of DMBA in real-world scenarios by using SSDMF files for our experiments. This work contributes to the record linkage field by providing a novel and efficient blocking method that addresses the challenges of datasets where phonetic similarities are difficult to handle.

While DMBA demonstrates promising results, there is a scope for future research that can enhance its performance and applicability. First, the outlier at 5M records, where Super blocking outperforms the DMBA in runtime, has to be explored. This suggests an investigation of DMBA's behavior in extremely large datasets. There is room for optimizing the performance of DMBA. The work can also be extended to handle various types of datasets. These future directions focus on building the strengths of DMBA, and ensure its continued relevance in the evolving field of entity resolution.

Acknowledgments. This work was partially supported by the United States Census Bureau under Award Number CB21RMD0160003. The content is solely the responsibility of the authors and does not necessarily represent the official views of the US Census Bureau.

Disclosure of Interests. The authors have no competing interests to declare that are relevant to the content of this article.

References

1. Odell, M., Russell, R.: The Soundex Coding System, U.S. Patent 1261167 (1918)
2. Russell, R.C.: The Soundex phonetic algorithm. U.S. Patent 1261167 (1918)
3. Philips, L.: The double metaphone search algorithm. Dr. Dobb's Journal (2000)
4. Christen, P.: A comparison of phonetic encoding algorithms for historical name matching. In: Proceedings of ACM CIKM, pp. 123–130 (2006)
5. Talburt, J.R., Zhou, Y.: Entity resolution using double metaphone in commercial datasets. In: Proceedings of IRI, pp. 89–94 (2010)
6. Ong, T.C., Mannino, M.V., Schilling, L.M.: Improving record linkage with phonetic algorithms in healthcare. J. Biomed. Inform. **48**, 45–53 (2014)
7. Behm, A., Ji, S., Li, C., Lu, J.: Fuzzy search with double metaphone for approximate matching. In: Proceedings of ICDE, pp. 456–461 (2009)
8. Hassanzadeh, O., Chiang, F., Miller, R.J.: Clustering records with double metaphone: A scalability study. In: Proceedings of DASFAA, pp. 201–208 (2011)
9. Fellegi, I.P., Sunter, A.B.: A theory for record linkage. J. Am. Stat. Assoc. **64**, 1183–1210 (1969)
10. Gravano, L., Ipeirotis, P.G., Jagadish, H.V., Koudas, N., Muthukrishnan, S., Srivastava, D.: Approximate string joins with double metaphone in databases. VLDB J. **12**(4), 345–364 (2003)
11. Karakasidis, A., Verykios, V.S.: Privacy-preserving record linkage using phonetic codes. In: Proceedings of PCI, pp. 101–106 (2009)
12. N. Shah et al., The soundex blocking: a novel blocking approach for record linkage. In: 2024 IEEE International Conference on Big Data (BigData), Washington, DC, USA, 2024, pp. 4039-4047. https://doi.org/10.1109/BigData62323.2024.10825041
13. SSDMF Homepage. http://ssdmf.info/download.html
14. FEBRL. http://sourceforge.net/projects/febrl/
15. Basak, J., Sahni, S., Rajasekaran, S.: SuperBlocking: an efficient blocking technique for record linkage. In: 2023 IEEE International Conference on Big Data (BigData), pp. 498–503. IEEE Computer Society (2023)
16. Soliman, A., Rajasekaran, S.: A fast incremental record linkage algorithm. J. Biomed. Inform. (2022)
17. Mamun, A., Aseltine, R., Rajasekaran, S.: Efficient record linkage algorithms using complete linkage clustering. PLOS One (2016)

Integrating High-Throughput RNA-RNA Interaction Data Into RNA Secondary Structure Prediction

Denis Skibinski[1,2,6], Thomas Spicher[1,6], Leonhard Sidl[1,2,7],
Paulína Holotová[1,3], Yingjie Pan[1,4,7], Maximilian Faissner[1,7],
Cristian A. Velandia-Huerto[1,5], Ronny Lorenz[3], Maria Waldl[3],
Hua-Ting Yao[1], and Peter F. Stadler[1,3,8,9,10(✉)]

[1] Department of Theoretical Chemistry, University of Vienna, Währinger Straße 17,
1090 Vienna, Austria
{skibinski,tspicher,sidl,paulina,yingjie,maxf,
cavelandiah,htyao}@tbi.univie.ac.at
[2] Research Group Bioinformatics and Computational Biology, University of Vienna,
Währinger Straße 29, 1090 Vienna, Austria
[3] Bioinformatics Group, Department of Computer Science, and Interdisciplinary
Center for Bioinformatics, Universität Leipzig, Härtelstrasse 16-18,
04107 Leipzig, Germany
{ronny,maria,studla}@bioinf.uni-leipzig.de
[4] Department of Mathematics and Computer Science, University of Southern
Denmark, 5230 Odense M, Denmark
[5] Center for Anatomy and Cell Biology, Medical University of Vienna,
Schwarzspanierstraße 17, 1090 Vienna, Austria
[6] UniVie Doctoral School Computer Science (DoCS), University of Vienna,
Währinger Straße 29, 1090 Vienna, Austria
[7] Vienna Doctoral School in Chemistry (DoSChem), University of Vienna,
Währinger Straße 42, 1090 Vienna, Austria
[8] Max Planck Institute for Mathematics in the Sciences, Leipzig, Germany
[9] Facultad de Ciencias, Universidad Nacional de Colombia, Bogotá, Colombia
[10] Santa Fe Institute, Santa Fe, NM, USA

Abstract. In recent years, several methods for detecting RNA-RNA
interactions have become available that use a combination of crosslinking,
ligation, and sequencing of the resulting chimeric reads. In principle,
such data also convey information on intramolecular helices. They are,
however, not accurate enough to identify base pairs directly. Instead, only
regions of direct contacts can be inferred. Here, we show that such data
can be incorporated as pseudo-energies into RNA secondary structure
prediction algorithms by assigning a bonus term to all potential pairs
between crosslinked intervals. Using simulated data, we show that given
sufficient coverage, such data can push the accuracy of the predicted
structure to a base pair-wise MCC of above 90%. Moreover, we observe
that the beneficial effect of such interval-wise pseudo-energies is quite

D. Skibinski, T. Spicher, and L. Sidl—Should be considered as joint first authors.

robust w.r.t. the length of the interval and the value of the bonus term, but depends strongly on the fraction of the sequence that is covered by significant interaction data.

Keywords: RNA folding algorithms · Pseudo-energy · Dynamic programming · RNA crosslinking

1   Introduction

RNA crosslinking methods have been introduced primarily to investigate RNA-RNA interactions in a heterogeneous mixture of RNAs. The same data sets, however, also capture intramolecular helices and thus may contain information about particularly long-range interactions. A wide variety of different experimental protocols have become available that primarily differ in the chemistry of the crosslinking reagent and details of the subsequent steps of library preparation, see [15] for a recent review. Examples include CLASH [5], LIGR-seq [12] SPLASH [1], PARIS [9], COMRADES [19], and RIC-seq [3]. The common result of these methods is a collection of split reads of the form (A, A'), where A and A' are non-overlapping intervals with the same reading directions mapping to a genomic or transcriptomic reference. The exact position (p, q) of the crosslink that gives rise to the split read satisfies $p \in A$ and $q \in A'$ but remains unknown in general. Moreover, the interval pair (A, A') contains a base-pairing region but will in general be larger than the actually interacting region.

These raw sequencing data therefore yield a very noisy signal and thus require extensive further processing [11,12], usually involving at least the following three steps: (1) Overlapping gapped reads are clustered into *Duplex Groups* (DG). These clusters are computed using different measures of overlap between the two arms of mapped split reads (A_1, A'_1) and (A_2, A'_2). Each cluster is represented as a consensus interval pair $(\bar{A}, \bar{A}')$ together with associated coverage values $r_{\bar{A}\bar{A}'}$ for gapped reads and the total coverage $r_{\bar{A}}$ and $r_{\bar{A}'}$ for each arm. (2) Intermolecular and intramolecular contacts are distinguished based on available transcript annotations or, if necessary, genomic proximity and orientation. (3) Finally, a statistical model evaluating the coverage values $r_{\bar{A}\bar{A}'}$, $r_{\bar{A}}$ and $r_{\bar{A}'}$ determines the likelihood that a DG is not the result of random ligation [11,18].

Here, we will only be concerned with *intramolecular* crosslinking signals. The final result of the data analysis pipeline then is a collection Θ of interval pairs (A_k, A'_k) together with the probability p_k that there are base pairs linking A_k with A'_k for a given transcript. We ask whether and how Θ can be used to assist with the prediction of the RNA secondary structure. In Sect. 2 below we show how such data can be converted to pseudo-energies and incorporated directly into well-established dynamic programming RNA folding algorithms [4,20].

An important issue with this type of data is that its usefulness necessarily depends on the size of intervals A and A'. In the extreme case A and A' approach half of the sequence length, and hence the only information we can learn from them is that there is at least one base pair between the first and the second half of the sequence. On the other hand, if A and A' were single nucleotides, the data would specify individual base pairs. We have shown in previous work that such data, available in particular from phylogenetic comparisons, are highly informative and lead to substantial improvements of structure prediction [6]. The aim of this contribution is therefore to determine the resolution at which interval pairs (A, A') are informative in the sense that their inclusion improves the accuracy of secondary structure predictions. Since real-life cross-linking data with known ground-truth secondary structures is not readily accessible, we use synthetic data sets throughout this contribution.

2   Theory

The most commonly used algorithms for RNA structure prediction are based on a carefully measured, sequence-dependent set of thermodynamic parameters for base pair stacking, loop contributions, and additional effects such as dangling ends [14]. Given this energy model and the assumption of non-crossing base pairs and thus pseudoknot-free structures, energy minimization as well as the computation of partition functions can be carried out exactly and efficiently by means of dynamic programming [20]. The ground state energy is obtained as $E_{i,j} = \min\{E_{i,j-1}, \min_{i<k\le j}\left[C_{i,k} + E_{k+1,j}\right]\}$, where $E_{i,j}$ is the ground state energy of the sub sequence from base i to j and $C_{i,k}$ is the minimal energy of a structure enclosed by the base pairs (i, k). The base case of the recursion is $E_{ii} = E_{i,i-1} = 0$ for single nucleotides and the empty string, respectively. In the simplest case, which only accounts for base pairs, $C_{i,k} = \varepsilon(i, k) + E_{i+1,k-1}$, where $\varepsilon(i, k)$ is the energy contribution for a base pair between positions i and k. The recursions implemented e.g. in the `ViennaRNA` package follow this scheme, but use a more elaborate "loop decomposition" for computing $C_{i,j}$, see [7].

External information, such as the probability that a given base is paired or the probability of a specific base pair, can be included as so-called *pseudo-energies* into the standard energy model. In general, given externally derived evidence that a feature μ (such as a paired or unpaired base, a base pair, or a particular stem is present), one can proceed in the following generic way: (1) the experimental signal is converted to a probability $p[\mu]$ and (2) the pseudo-energy is computed as

$$\Gamma[\mu] = \min\left\{-RT\ln\frac{p[\mu]}{1 - p[\mu]}, 0\right\} \tag{1}$$

following [6,17]. This term is in essence a log-odds ratio for the presence versus absence of μ. The truncation at 0 accounts for the fact that the absence of evidence of μ in general does not imply the absence of μ. Chemical probing methods, for instance, only assert that a base is unpaired while phylogenetic methods detect evidence for the presence of base pairs, see [6,13] and the references therein. The truncation is omitted if an experimental procedure such as nextPARS [10] produces direct evidence for both paired and unpaired positions.

In the special case of evidence for specific base pairs, the pseudo-energies can be incorporated by replacing $C_{i,j} \to C_{i,j} + \Gamma[(i, j)]$ in the dynamic programming recursions. Crosslinking data, however, does not specify individual base pairs but instead specifies μ to be a pair of disjoint intervals A and A' such that there is at least one base pair (i, j) with $i \in A$ and $j \in A'$. It is possible in principle to accommodate this situation exactly; however, this requires non-trivial changes in the recursions of the RNA folding algorithms and will be discussed in forthcoming work. Here we take a simpler, approximate approach that is sufficient to investigate the usefulness of crosslinking data for structure prediction empirically.

The basic idea is to replace $\Gamma[(A, A')]$ by a contribution $\tilde{\Gamma}_{ij} = \lambda \Gamma[(A, A')]$ for all base pairs that can be formed between $i \in A$ and $j \in A'$. The pseudo-energies $\tilde{\Gamma}_{ij}$ can be incorporated as above, using the soft-constraint framework of the ViennaRNA package [8]. The parameter λ is a normalization constant that is most naturally set to $1/\ell$, where ℓ is the number of base pairs that can be formed in a co-folding structure between A and A'. In practice there are different choices for computing ℓ, including the maximal number of base pairs, the expected number, or the number of base pairs predicted by computing the minimum energy hybridization structure of A with A' [2]. We set $\tilde{\Gamma}_{ij} = 0$ if there is no predicted interaction between paired intervals. Throughout this work, we report the base pairs predicted by RNAcofold.

3   Methods

Construction of Synthetic Structure Data. At present, real-life datasets to systematically investigate the effect of crosslinking on the accuracy of secondary structure prediction are not available. We therefore work here exclusively with synthetic data. The ViennaRNA package makes it easy to use perturbed energy parameters. In order to produce a perturbed parameter set we multiplied each entry in the standard Turner 2004 tables [14] by a factor uniformly sampled from the interval $[1 - a, 1 + a]$, where $a > 0$ quantifies the amplitude of this superimposed multiplicative noise. Special care was taken to ensure that all symmetries between energy parameters were conserved. To remove trivial instances, we ensured that the structures predicted with the perturbed parameters were sufficiently different from the RNA minimum free energy secondary structure computed with the unperturbed energy parameters by requiring a minimal base pair distance and energy-difference. To add additional variability, the temperature and salt concentration were again uniformly sampled from a user-defined range around the default values. We suggest that these perturbed secondary structures plausibly approximate the differences of RNA secondary structure in the complex environment of the cell compared to the standard conditions used for measuring the energy parameters *in vitro*.

We explored three different settings for the perturbation procedure, corresponding to low, middle, and high differences. The corresponding parameters are listed in Tab. 1. As a measure of accuracy, we use the Matthews Correlation Coefficient (MCC), which captures both missed interactions (false negatives) and incorrect predictions (false positives). An MCC value of 1 indicates perfect agreement with the reference (non-perturbed) structure, while 0 corresponds to random output. For longer sequences, these three datasets yield MCCs of about 0.59, 0.46, and 0.29, respectively. In this work, the MCC value is computed with the `ViennaRNA`-provided function `compare_structure`. A common trend that can be observed across all levels of parameter perturbation is that the MCC is noticeably lower for very short sequences, see Supplement.

Interaction Interval Data and Attribution of Pseudo-Energies. In order to determine the interval pair (A, A'), a base pair (i, j), with $i \in A$ and $j \in A'$, is randomly picked from the full-length reference structure predicted by `RNAfold` with the perturbed energy parameters. The selected base pair is assumed to appear at the center of each arm. The interval pair of length $\delta = 2d + 1$ is then defined as $([i - d, i + d], [j - d, j + d])$, where d is arbitrarily predefined. However, neither the intervals of a single interval pair nor different interval pairs are allowed to overlap; see Supplement for further details. The interval lengths used in this study were chosen to fall into the range observed in popular experimental methods. Again we have to refer to the Supplement for details. For each pair of intervals the minimum energy hybridization structure of A with A' is computed with `RNAcofold`. The total pseudo-energy $\Gamma[(A, A')]$ is arbitrarily set, and a proportional fraction of it is added to each base pair formed according to the RNA folding algorithm, as described in Sect. 2.

Localization of Pairing Regions. Since practical protocols produce crosslinked sequence regions that are much longer than a single stem, tools such as `RNAnue` [11] attempt to identify likely stems. In order to assess the merit of such approaches, we compare the base pairs of the original structure with base pairs predicted between the crosslinked intervals. As a reference, a large randomly generated RNA sequence (15000 nt) was folded using the default parameters of `RNAfold`. From this structure, a maximum of 3000 non-overlapping interval pairs of various lengths centered around randomly selected base pairs were generated as described previously. These local interval pairs were refolded with both `RNAduplex` [7], which does not consider interactions within the individual inter-

Table 1. Parameters used to generate synthetic data with a as the average level of difference to the standard Turner 2004 model. In addition to a, maximal differences ΔT in temperature and Δc in salt concentration are defined. Sequence/structure pairs were only included if a minimum base pair distance min d_{bp} and a minimum energy difference min $|\Delta G|$ were reached. MCC values are averaged over sequences longer than 250 nt (see Supplement).

	a	Δc [mol·L^{-1}]	ΔT [°K]	min d_{bp}	min $|\Delta G|$ [kcal·mol^{-1}]	MCC
low	0.125	0.1	5	5	0.01	0.593
middle	0.250	0.2	10	10	0.02	0.462
high	0.500	0.4	20	20	0.04	0.286

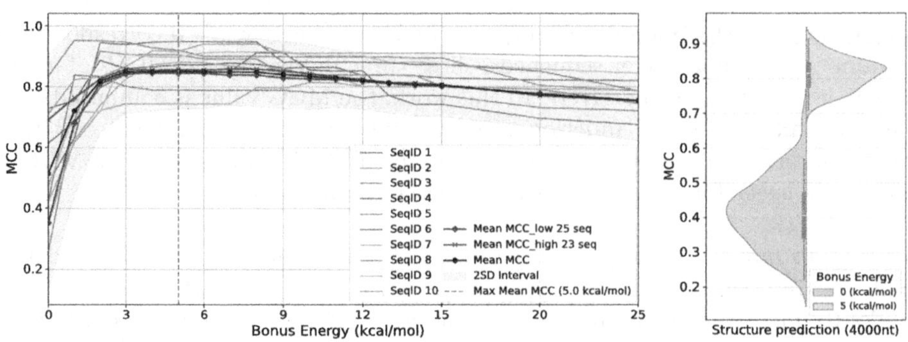

Fig. 1. L.h.s.: Effect of the bonus energy added to intervals on the MCC score compared to the ground truth structure. Interval length was fixed at 23 nucleotides, and intervals were constructed symmetrically around the selected base pairs. A constant sequence length of 1000 nt was selected, while the bonus energy was varied between 0 and 25 kcal/mol. A total of 20 intervals were picked. We observe a rather flat maximum of the MCC at about 5 kcal/mol per interval. R.h.s.: Structure prediction of 4000 nt long with interval bonus energy at 5 kcal/mol and 0 kcal/mol as a baseline. A total of 50 intervals were picked with a length of 23 nucleotides, resulting in a coverage of 0.2875.

vals, and `RNAcofold` [2], which considers the competition between internal structures and base pairs connecting the two intervals.

For each interval pair, the refolded structures were then compared to the base pairs of the reference structure in the same locations. The reference structure in general will contain base pairs with one end within and the other end outside the interval pair. Such base pairs are ignored, i.e. we consider only the difference between the sets of base pairs formed within the interval pair. When comparing to a structure generated by `RNAduplex`, we additionally removed any interactions solely within an individual interval. Those two structures were then compared using both the base pair distance as implemented by the `ViennaRNA` Package and the difference between the free energies. To determine the free energy of the global structure that is contained within the interval pairs, we used `RNAcofold` [8] in conjunction with hard constraints [8] that enforce the base pairs of the global structures that are contained in the paired intervals. A corresponding comparison of the free energies using `RNAduplex` is not possible because hard constraints are at present not implemented in this program.

4   Results

In order to estimate the parameter ranges in which crosslinking data have substantial beneficial effects on the accuracy of secondary structure prediction, we varied (1) the bonus energy, (2) the length of the intervals, and (3) the density of informative interval pairs. We interpret a sequence/structure pair from the synthetic dataset as the ground truth that is to be approximated by the Turner 2004 model together with the pseudo-energies for the interval pairs associated

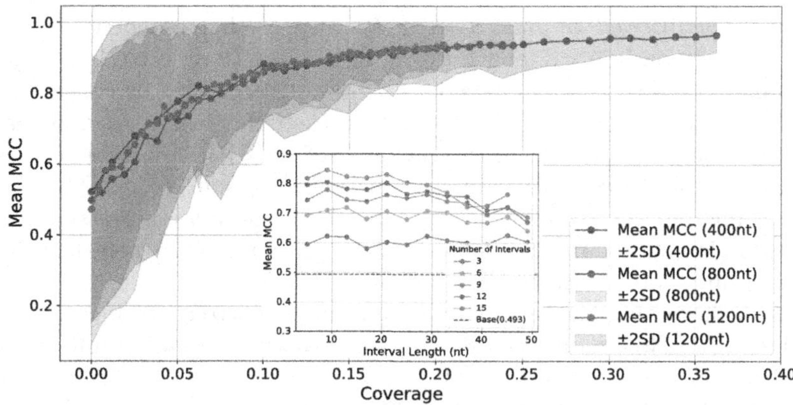

Fig. 2. Effect of the coverage by informative interval pairs on the quality of the secondary structure prediction. Average and distribution for 50 instances for each data point. Interval length 5, bonus energy 3 kcal/mol for each interval. Data are shown for three different sequence lengths [400, 800, 1200 nt]. The inset shows the dependence on the interval length, with an averages over 50 random sequences of length 1000 nt shown. Bonus energies are set to a fixed value of 5 kcal/mol, independent of interval length.

with the perturbed structure. Throughout this contribution, we focus on the set with middle perturbation strength.

Figure 1(left) shows the MCC comparing predicted structures using pseudo-energies with the synthetic ground truth for 10 different sequences. The mean MCC was calculated over 48 sequences. Interestingly, even moderate pseudo-energies of about 2 kcal/mol per interval lead to significantly improved secondary structures, and even smaller bonus energies already have a beneficial effect. Using our best estimate for the interval bonus energy $\Gamma[(A, A')] = 5$ kcal/mol also improves the prediction on longer structure at 4000 nt (Fig. 1(right) suggesting that approach performs robustly. Further computational results show that the chosen bonus energy is also close to optimal for shorter (5 nt) or longer (49 nt) intervals (see Supplement). Not surprisingly, the quality of the structure prediction improves with the number of informative intervals. Figure 2 shows that this dependence is best expressed in terms of coverage of the sequence by intervals. We observe that the MCC reaches close to 90% at about 10% coverage for intervals of length 5.

The inset in Fig. 2 shows that the length of the intervals, i.e. the accuracy of the crosslink position within the paired intervals, has little influence on the accuracy of the predicted secondary structure. This is surprising, since one would have expected that "diluting" the information on the position of the helical region would have significant negative impact. For higher coverage, we observe a shallow maximum at interval length 7. The decrease in MCC for longer intervals is however small and may not be significant for low coverage levels.

Localization of Interaction Base Pairs. We suspect that independence of prediction accuracy on interval length is due to the fact that stable helices formed between paired intervals are in most cases correctly predicted by considering the interaction structure between the two intervals. If this is the case, at least for sufficiently small intervals, then the regional information is indeed sufficient to enforce the correct base pairing in the crosslinked region. To test this hypothesis, we compared the secondary structure of a large reference structure with local interaction structures predicted for interval pairs of different length using `RNAduplex` and `RNAcofold`. See Methods for details.

Figure 3 shows that the base pair distance increases roughly linearly with the interval length. While more than 80% of the structures could be fully recovered using `RNAduplex` for interval lengths of 3, this fraction also drastically decreases as the interval length gets larger. For `RNAcofold`, we also calculated the difference between the energy of the local interaction structure and energy of the original `RNAfold` structure restricted to the individual interval pairs. As expected, the magnitude of this energy difference also increases close to linearly with the interval length. Naturally, the locally refolded and optimized structures are energetically more stable compared to the interactions within the intervals that are part of the reference fold, leading to negative values for the difference.

Overall, the accuracy of base pairs computed directly from the *local* interaction structure between the two paired intervals decreases rapidly with interval length, with few correctly predicted base pairs remaining for interval exceeding about 25 nt in length. This is in stark contrast to the accuracy achieved by incorporating information on the interaction region in a *global* prediction of the structure. While this may be surprising, it is probably explained by the fact that false positive base pairs in the local structure can be prevented by base pairs with other regions in a global structure prediction.

A comparison of pairing energies for interval pairs centered at reference base pairs (true positives) *versus* randomly placed intervals (false positives) shows significantly lower energies when there is no underlying base pair in the reference, see Fig. 4. This effect is likely to reduce the impact of false positive interval

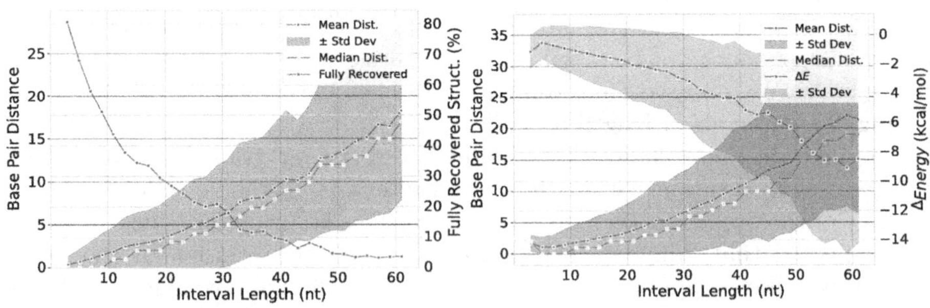

Fig. 3. Comparison between RNA structures in interval pairs of different lengths folded globally with `RNAfold` and regionally with `RNAduplex` (left) and `RNAcofold` (right).

pairs on the guided structure prediction. We also checked how an asymmetric placement of the reference base pair in a paired interval affects the accuracy of the structure prediction. Simulation data that places the reference base pair on one of the interval ends instead of in the middle (see Supplement) indicates that at least for intervals longer than about 15-20 nt there is a noticeable decrease in accuracy. This asymmetry effect, moreover, grows with interval length.

5   Discussion

We have explored here the utilization of RNA crosslinking data as external information for improving RNA secondary structure prediction. We employed synthetic data, since real-life data with known ground-truth structures are scarce.

A surprising discovery is that the MCC of synthetic data is lower for very short sequences, as shown in the Supplement. More interesting, the MCC-distrisbution for short sequences shows two peaks at MMC-values zero and 0.6. This suggests that these sequences are more prone to adopting a completely different structure probably because they are too short to have multiple structural domains of which a subset could be shared. This effect likely explains that we observe a lower average MCC-score. Assigning pseudo-energies to all possible base pairs within crosslinked interval pairs provides a simple approximation algorithm to funnel this information into thermodynamic folding algorithms as soft constraints. Computational results show that such data are informative for secondary structure prediction even if the crosslinked intervals reach a length of about 20nt, thus specifying paired positions only with substantial uncertainty.

Paired intervals in real-life data reach this size range for several protocols, in particular CLASH [5], and PARIS [9]. This suggests that these methods can locate paired areas with sufficient accuracy to improve secondary structure prediction. KARR-Seq [16], on the other hand, produces much longer intervals. In the Supplement, we summarize a literature review on RNA-RNA interactions in

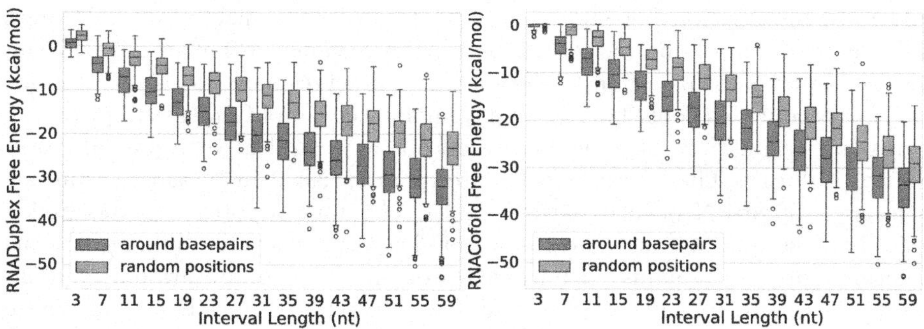

Fig. 4. Energy of structures computed with RNAduplex (left) and RNAcofold (right) for interval pairs centered at base pairs in the global reference structure (blue) and randomly placed positions (orange). The energy returned by RNAduplex for unpaired intervals was set to 0 (instead of an arbitrary large value) to improve readability.

selected datasets. These interval lengths lie well within the range of currently available experimental protocols and surpass the limits of mappability in large genomes. We observed that coverage of the RNA by paired intervals plays a key role. Based on our simulated datasets, MCC values close to 85% are achievable at least if crosslinked intervals cover a sizable portion of the RNA sequence. Interestingly, it seems to be more difficult to localize the relevant base pairs in an interval pair than to use the more diffuse information on paired intervals to improve the global structure directly. This yields a prediction of the relevant base pairs *a posteriori*. In summary, our simulation-based results strongly suggest that integration of RNA crosslinking data produced by currently available experimental protocols will significantly improve secondary structure prediction.

Several open questions remain. We did not systematically investigate the impact of false positive interval pairs, which will be unavoidable in real-life data even with stringent filtering of spurious intervals. The observed energy differences between real and spurious interval pairs, however, can be expected to efficiently suppress this type of noise as long as the bonus energy per interval does not exceed the thermodynamic contribution of one or two stacked pairs. Even though the energy distributions still overlap significantly for longer interval lengths, as shown in Fig. 4, their differences suggest that it may be possible to identify and remove at least a part of the false positive predictions. This may be helpful in particular for data obtained with the more accurate experimental methods mentioned above.

Moreover, we have assumed in most of our simulations that the relevant base pairs are centered in each pair of intervals. If the fragmentation of the crosslinked sequence is not symmetric, the relevant interactions will be off-center. Such an asymmetry has a negative impact on accuracy if the interval lengths exceed about 15-20nt. Since the asymmetry in these simulations was extreme, we expect the observed decrease in prediction quality to be a loose upper bound in comparison to real-life data. It may be possible to improve the accuracy by trimming intervals, i.e., by restricting them to the paired sub-intervals that capture the most stable base pairs. As shown in Fig. 3, recovering part of a global structure using only local information becomes more difficult with increasing interval length. The identification of the individual base pairs responsible for an interval pair, however, appears to be a non-trivial task that deserves more detailed attention.

Throughout this contribution we have made the simplifying assumption that transcription units are disjoint, i.e. we do not have to deal with partially overlapping isoforms. These assumptions are often satisfied in prokaryotes as well as for structured RNAs such as ribosomal RNAs in eukaryotes. It is violated by spliced transcripts in eukaryotes, however. Disentangling crosslinking data and isoform structures remains an unsolved problem. The computational approach taken here readily extends to *intermolecular interactions*. This, however, requires knowledge of the concentrations since the formation of base pairs between two molecules is inherently concentration dependent, see e.g. [2].

Finally, we note that the inclusion of crosslinking data by assigning bonus pseudo-energies to all potential base pairs connecting two paired intervals is an approximation. More precisely, secondary structure with interactions connecting a pair of intervals will in general differ in their number of base pairs, and thus incur different bonus energy contributions. For real-life data we expect that predictions can be improved by accounting for the reliability of RNA crosslinking data. Ideally, pseudo-energies should be assigned according to equ.(1). The probability that a pair of intervals is crosslinked could be derived from the sequencing data as outlined in the introduction. The encouraging results obtained with these methods strongly suggest that developing an exact algorithm for this problem will be worthwhile endeavour.

Acknowledgments. This work was funded by the Deutsche Forschungsgemeinschaft (DFG grant number STA 850/48-1) and by the Austrian Science Fund (FWF grant numbers F-80 and I 6440-N). PFS acknowledges the financial support by the Federal Ministry of Education and Research of Germany (BMBF) through DAAD project 57616814 (SECAI, School of Embedded Composite AI), and jointly with the Sächsische Staatsministerium für Wissenschaft, Kultur und Tourismus in the programme Center of Excellence for AI-research *Center for Scalable Data Analytics and Artificial Intelligence Dresden/Leipzig*, project identification number: SCADS24B.

Disclosure of Interests. The authors have no competing interests.

References

1. Aw, J.G.A., et al.: In Vivo mapping of eukaryotic RNA interactomes reveals principles of higher-order organization and regulation. Mol. Cell **62**, 603–617 (2016). https://doi.org/10.1016/j.molcel.2016.04.028
2. Bernhart, S.H., Tafer, H., Mückstein, U., Flamm, C., Stadler, P.F., Hofacker, I.L.: Partition function and base pairing probabilities of RNA heterodimers. Algorithms Mol. Biol. **1**, 3 (2006). https://doi.org/10.1186/1748-7188-1-3
3. Cai, Z., et al.: RIC-seq for global in situ profiling of RNA-RNA spatial interactions. Nature **582**, 432–437 (2020). https://doi.org/10.1038/s41586-020-2249-1
4. Hofacker, I.L., Fontana, W., Stadler, P.F., Bonhoeffer, L.S., Tacker, M., Schuster, P.: Fast folding and comparison of RNA secondary structures. Monatsh. Chem. **125**, 167–188 (1994). https://doi.org/10.1007/BF00818163
5. Kudla, G., Granneman, S., Hahn, D., Beggs, J.D., Tollervey, D.: Cross-linking, ligation, and sequencing of hybrids reveals RNA-RNA interactions in yeast. Proc. Natl. Acad. Sci. U.S.A. **108**, 10010–10015 (2011). https://doi.org/10.1073/pnas.1017386108
6. von LÖhneysen, S., et al.: Phylogenetic and chemical probing information as soft constraints in RNA secondary structure prediction. J. Comp. Biol. **31**(6), 549–563 (2024). https://doi.org/10.1089/cmb.2024.0519
7. Lorenz, R., Bernhart, S.H., Höner zu Siederdissen, C., Tafer, H., Flamm, C., Stadler, P.F., Hofacker, I.L.: ViennaRNA Package 2.0. Alg. Mol. Biol. **6**, 26 (2011). https://doi.org/10.1186/1748-7188-6-26
8. Lorenz, R., Hofacker, I.L., Stadler, P.F.: RNA folding with hard and soft constraints. Alg. Mol. Biol. **11**, 8 (2016). https://doi.org/10.1186/s13015-016-0070-z
9. Lu, Z., et al.: RNA duplex map in living cells reveals higher-order transcriptome structure. Cell **165**, 1267–1279 (2016). https://doi.org/10.1016/j.cell.2016.04.028

10. Saus, E., Willis, J.R., Pryszcz, L.P., Hafez, A., Llorens, C., Himmelbauer, H., Gabaldón, T.: nextPARS: parallel probing of RNA structures in Illumina. RNA **24**, 609–619 (2018). https://doi.org/10.1261/rna.063073.117

11. Schäfer, R.A., Voß, B.: RNAnue: efficient data analysis for RNA-RNA interactomics. Nucleic Acids Res. **49**(10), 5493–5501 (2021). https://doi.org/10.1093/nar/gkab340

12. Sharma, E., Sterne-Weiler, T., O'Hanlon, D., Blencowe, B.J.: Global mapping of human RNA-RNA interactions. Mol. Cell **62**, 618–626 (2016). https://doi.org/10.1016/j.molcel.2016.04.030

13. Stadler, P.F., von Löhneysen, S., Mörl, M.: Limits of experimental evidence in rna secondary structure prediction. Frontiers Bioinf. **4**, 1346779 (2024). https://doi.org/10.3389/fbinf.2024.1346779

14. Turner, D.H., Mathews, D.H.: NNDB: the nearest neighbor parameter database for predicting stability of nucleic acid secondary structure. Nucl. Acids Res. **38**, D280–D282 (2010). https://doi.org/10.1093/nar/gkp892

15. Velema, W.A., Lu, Z.: Chemical RNA cross-linking: Mechanisms, computational analysis, and biological applications. J. Amer. Chem. Soc. Au **3**, 316–332 (2023). https://doi.org/10.1021/jacsau.2c00625

16. Wu, T., Cheng, A.Y., Zhang, Y., Xu, J., Wu, J., Wen, L., Li, X., Liu, B., Dou, X., Wang, P., Zhang, L., Fei, J., Li, J., Ouyang, Z., He, C.: KARR-seq reveals cellular higher-order RNA structures and RNA-RNA interactions. Nat. Biotechnol. **42**(12), 1909–1920 (2024). https://doi.org/10.1038/s41587-023-02109-8

17. Zarringhalam, K., Meyer, M.M., Dotu, I., Chuang, J.H., Clote, P.: Integrating chemical footprinting data into RNA secondary structure prediction. PLOS ONE **7**(10) (2012). https://doi.org/10.1371/journal.pone.0045160

18. Zhang, M., Hwang, I.T., Li, K., Bai, J., Chen, J.F., Weissman, T., Zou, J.Y., Lu, Z.: Classification and clustering of RNA crosslink-ligation data reveal complex structures and homodimers. Genome Res. **32**, 968–985 (2022). https://doi.org/10.1101/gr.275979.121

19. Ziv, O., et al.: COMRADES determines in vivo RNA structures and interactions. Nat. Methods **15**, 785–788 (2018). https://doi.org/10.1038/s41592-018-0121-0

20. Zuker, M., Stiegler, P.: Optimal computer folding of large RNA sequences using thermodynamics and auxiliary information. Nucleic Acids Res. **9**, 133–148 (1981). https://doi.org/10.1093/nar/9.1.133

GDCA-TransUNet for Dual-Stage Attention Enhanced Multi-organ Segmentation in Abdominal CT Images

Manjir Gurung, Ronald Bbosa, Kafui Efio-Akolly, Feng Liu[✉],
and Ruoshan Kong[✉]

School of Computer Science, Wuhan University, Wuhan, Hubei, China
{fliuwhu,kongruoshan}@whu.edu.cn

Abstract. Medical image segmentation of abdominal organs in CT scans remains challenging due to complex anatomical structures, low contrast, and variable organ boundaries. To address these limitations, we propose GDCA-TransUNet, built upon the TransUNet architecture, which integrates Dual Cross Attention (DCA) and Attention Gates (AGs). The DCA module enhances feature fusion in skip connections by modeling channel-wise and spatial dependencies between encoder and decoder features, while AGs suppress irrelevant background regions, ensuring a sharper focus on relevant organ boundaries. Evaluated on the Synapse multi-organ CT dataset, GDCA-TransUNet achieves a mean Dice score of 79.98%, outperforming TransUNet (77.48%) and SwinUNet (79.13%). Notably, it achieves 61.97% Dice for the pancreas, demonstrating significant improvements for small and complex organs. By enhancing multi-organ segmentation, particularly for intricate structures, our GDCA-TransUNet has the potential to improve the precision of radiotherapy planning and surgical interventions, where accurate organ delineation is crucial for successful outcomes and personalized treatment strategies.

Keywords: Multi-organ Segmentation · Abdominal CT scans · TransUNet · Attention Gate · Dual Cross Attention

1 Introduction

Accurate segmentation of abdominal organs in CT scans is critical for clinical applications such as surgical planning, disease diagnosis, and radiotherapy targeting [1,2]. However, this task remains challenging due to low contrast between adjacent organs, high anatomical variability, and poorly defined boundaries of small structures like the pancreas [3,4]. While deep learning has advanced medical image segmentation, existing methods struggle to balance localized feature extraction and global context modeling, particularly in multi-organ abdominal CT [5,6].

M. Gurung and R. Bbosa—Contributed equally.

J. Tang et al. (Eds.): ISBRA 2025, LNBI 15757, pp. 163–176, 2026.
https://doi.org/10.1007/978-981-95-0695-8_14

1.1 Related Work

CNN-based architectures like U-Net [7] and its variants (e.g., Attention U-Net [8], UNet++ [9]) leverage skip connections to fuse encoder-decoder features. However, their reliance on convolutional operations limits their ability to model long-range spatial dependencies, leading to suboptimal performance in complex abdominal regions [10]. Recent efforts to incorporate attention mechanisms (e.g., channel-spatial attention, gated attention [11]) partially address this by highlighting salient regions, but they often neglect cross-scale feature alignment or introduce computational overhead [12].

Transformer-based models like TransUNet [13] and SwinUNet [14] improve global context capture through self-attention but face two key limitations; Semantic gaps in skip connections, direct concatenation of encoder-decoder features causes misalignment, especially for small organs [15], and Background interference, Transformer's global attention dilutes focus on critical regions, reducing segmentation precision [16].

Recent works attempt to bridge these gaps. For example, UCTransNet [15] uses channel-wise cross-attention to refine skip connections, while DANet [17] employs dual spatial-channel attention. However, these methods either ignore spatial dependencies [15] or fail to suppress irrelevant background [17]. Concurrently, Dual Cross Attention (DCA) [18] and Attention Gates (AGs) [8] have shown promise in other domains: DCA enhances multi-scale fusion by modeling channel-spatial interactions, while AGs dynamically weight feature maps to prioritize target regions. Yet, their integration into transformer-based architectures for abdominal CT remains unexplored.

1.2 Contributions

We propose GDCA-TransUNet, a novel hybrid transformer-CNN model that synergizes DCA [18] and AGs [8] to address the above limitations. Our key contributions are:

1. **Integration of DCA into TransUNet's skip connections** to resolve semantic gaps by jointly modeling channel and spatial dependencies across encoder-decoder layers.
2. **Adaptation of AGs in the decoder** to suppress background noise and enhance focus on small organs, addressing transformer's over-globalization issue.
3. **State-of-the-art performance** in the Synapse multi-organ CT dataset, with a 2.85% Dice improvement over TransUNet [13] and 3.31% gain for the pancreas, a clinically critical organ [19].

2 Method

Given an input image $x \in \mathrm{R}^{H \times W \times C}$, our goal is pixel-wise segmentation map $y \in \mathrm{R}^{H \times W}$. Our proposed model, depicted in Fig. 1, is a hybrid architecture integrating Dual Cross Attention (DCA) [18] and Attention Gates (AG) [8] within a CNN-Transformer framework.

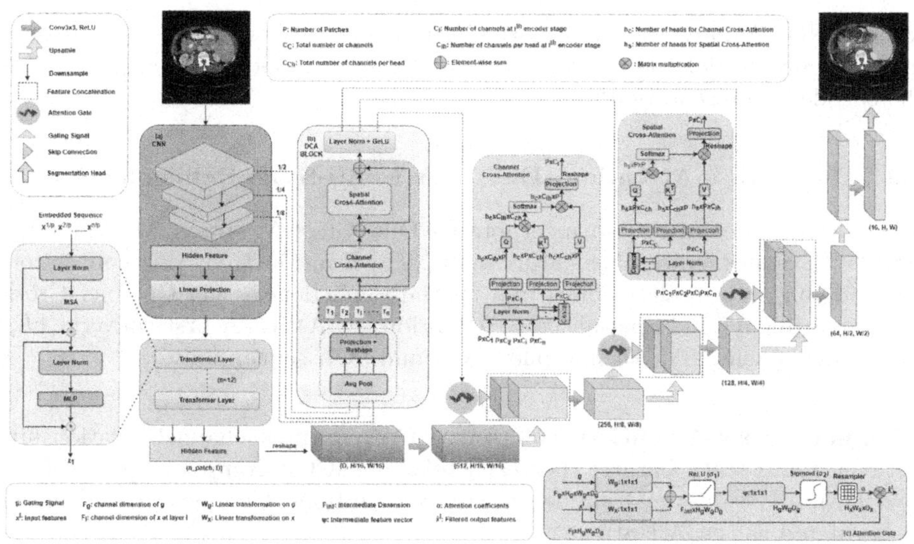

Fig. 1. Overview of the framework. (a) schematic of the CNN-Transformer layer; (b)DCA block; (c) Attention Gate

2.1   Hybrid CNN-Transformer as Encoder

Our encoder, based on TransUNet [13], employs a hybrid CNN-Transformer design to capture both fine-grained spatial details and long-range dependencies for hierarchical feature encoding.

CNN Feature Extraction, A CNN extracts high-resolution feature maps from the input image.

Patch Embedding from CNN Features, CNN-derived feature maps x are converted to 2D patches $\{x_p^i\}$ of size $P \times P$ (where $N = HW/P^2$). These patches are then linearly projected into a D-dimensional embedding space, as in TransUNet [13]:

$$z_0 = [x_p^1 E; x_p^2 E; \cdots ; x_p^N E] + E_{pos} \tag{1}$$

Here, E and E_{pos} are patch embedding and position embedding matrices, respectively.

Transformer Layers, These embeddings are processed by L Transformer encoder layers. Each layer(Eqs. 2 & 3, TransUNet [13]) includes Multi-Head Self-Attention (MSA) and Multi-Layer Perceptron (MLP) blocks with Layer Normalization (LN):

$$z_\ell' = \text{MSA}(\text{LN}(z_{\ell-1})) + z_{\ell-1} \tag{2}$$

$$z_\ell = \text{MLP}(\text{LN}(z_\ell')) + z_\ell' \tag{3}$$

where LN($\cdot$) denotes the layer normalization operator and $\mathbf{z}_\ell$ is the encoded image representation. This Transformer stack learns global context, producing the encoded representation z_L.

2.2 Dual Cross Attention (DCA) for Multi-Scale Refinement

To refine encoder features, we incorporate a Dual Cross Attention (DCA) module [18]. DCA refines multi-scale feature maps $\{E_i\}$ from the CNN skip connections by modeling inter-scale channel and spatial dependencies via Channel Cross-Attention (CCA) and Spatial Cross-Attention (SCA). DCA first converts $\{E_i\}$ to encoder tokens $\{T_i\}$, then applies CCA and SCA sequentially.

Channel Cross-Attention (CCA), CCA captures channel relationships between multi-scale features. For each token T_i, CCA computes queries (Q_i), keys (K), and values (V) via depth-wise convolutions. Channel cross-attention is calculated as (DCA [18]):

$$\text{CCA}(Q_i, K, V) = \text{Softmax}\left(\frac{Q_i^T K}{\sqrt{C_c}}\right) V^T \tag{4}$$

Here, Layer Normalization (LN) is applied to each T_i. Keys (K) and Values (V) are formed by concatenating tokens T_i $(i = 1, ..., n)$ along the channel dimension (T_c). This dynamically weights channel importance across scales.

Spatial Cross-Attention (SCA), SCA models spatial relationships, complementing CCA. Using CCA outputs $\bar{T}_i$, SCA computes queries (Q) and keys (K) from concatenated tokens $\bar{T}_c$, and values (V_i) from individual $\bar{T}_i$ via depth-wise convolutions. Spatial cross-attention is computed as (DCA [18]):

$$\text{SCA}(Q, K, V_i) = \text{Softmax}\left(\frac{QK^T}{\sqrt{d_k}}\right) V_i \tag{5}$$

SCA focuses on spatially relevant regions across scales, enhancing localization.

2.3 Cascaded Decoder with Attention Gates (AG) for Selective Feature Fusion

For segmentation mask reconstruction, we use cascaded decoder with progressive upsampling, employing the Cascaded Upsampler (CUP) from TransUNet [13] and integrating Attention Gates (AGs) from Attention U-Net [7]. This decoder facilitates upsampling, multi-scale feature fusion, and selective skip connection refinement. The Attention Gates (AGs) are integrated at the input of each decoder stage. At each stage, the AG receives skip connection features from DCA and decoder feature from the decdoer, and generates attention coefficients that refines the skip connection features based on the contextual information of

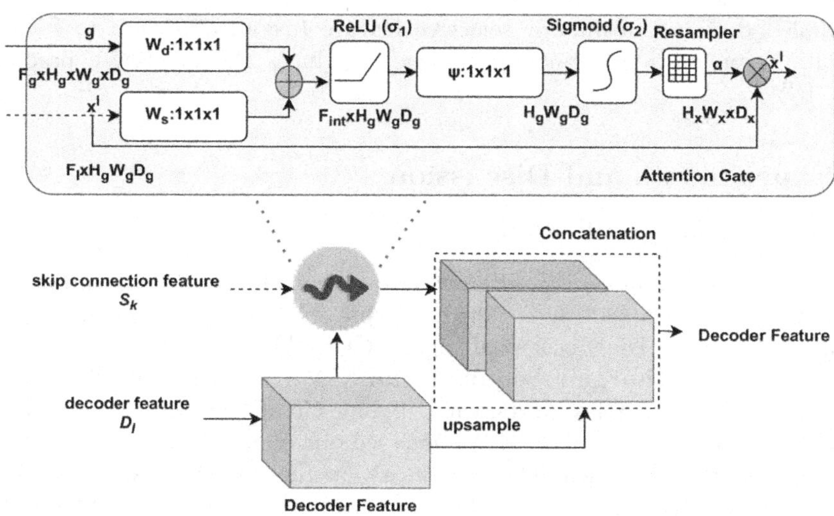

Fig. 2. Cascaded Decoder with Attention Gate

decoder features. This mechanism allows the decoder to focus on relevant organ features while suppressing background noise at multiple resolutions, contributing to more accurate and detailed segmentations. The cascaded nature of the decoder, combined with the AGs at each stage, enables hierarchical attention focusing and progressive boundary refinement.

Cascaded Decoder with Progressive Upsampling, Each decoder block increases spatial resolution, refines features, and integrates skip connections using Attention Gates (AGs), comprising bilinear upsampling, 3×3 convolution with ReLU, and AG-enhanced skip connections.

Attention Gate(AG), Following Attention U-Net [7], we incorporate AG modules in each decoder block. AGs refine skip connections based on decoder context, involving feature transformation, attention coefficient generation, and feature refinement. For a decoder feature map D_l and the corresponding skip connection S_k, both are projected into a shared lower-dimensional attention space using 1×1 convolutions:

$$D_l' = W_d(D_l), \quad S_k' = W_s(S_k) \tag{6}$$

Here, W_d and W_s are 1×1 convolutions. An attention map $\alpha \in [0, 1]$ is generated using additive attention, ReLU, and Sigmoid activations (Attention U-Net [7]):

$$\alpha = \sigma(\mathrm{ReLU}(D_l' + S_k')) \tag{7}$$

This gate scales skip connection features, emphasizing relevant regions and suppressing noise. The refined skip connection $S_{refined}$ is concatenated with the upsampled decoder output for selective feature fusion, as shown in Fig. 2. A final 1×1 convolution segmentation head produces the pixel-wise prediction $\{y\} \in \mathrm{R}^{H \times W}$.

3   Experiments and Discussion

3.1   Dataset and Evaluation

We evaluate our model on 2 different datasets, including BTCV multi-organ segmentation dataset [20], also called Synapse multi-organ Segmentation, and Automated Cardiac Diagnosis Challenge (ACDC) [21] dataset.

Synapse Multi-organ Segmentation[1]**,** We use the publicly available MICCAI 2015 Multi-Atlas Abdomen Labeling Challenge dataset, which comprises 30 abdominal CT volumes. We assessed our model's segmentation performance by reporting the mean Dice Similarity Coefficient (DSC) and mean Hausdorff Distance (HD) across eight abdominal organs: aorta, gallbladder, spleen, left and right kidneys, liver, pancreas, and stomach.

Automated Cardiac Diagnosis Challenge[2]**,** The ACDC dataset is composed of cardiac MRI exams collected from diverse patients using various MRI scanners. These images consist of patient's scan, manual annotations are provided, serving as ground truth for segmenting the left ventricle (LV), right ventricle (RV), and myocardium (MYO). To evaluate performance, we report the mean Dice Similarity Coefficient (DSC).

3.2   Implmentation Details

We implement our model using Pytorch, with training accelerated by an NVIDIA Tesla V100-SXM2 GPU. Data augmentations, including random rotation and flipping, are applied to all experiments. The input resolution is set to 224×224 pixels, with a patch size of 16, requiring four $2\times$ upsampling blocks to reach the full resolution. As our model is a CNN-Transformer hybrid encoder, we combine a pretrained ResNet-50 [22] and a 12-layer Transformer-based Vision Transformer (ViT) [23] model pretrained on ImageNet [24]. The model is trained using the SGD optimizer with a learning rate of 0.01, momentum of 0.9, weight decay of 1e-4 and the batch size 24. We chose the SGD optimizer due to its robustness and efficiency in large-scale training tasks. While alternative optimizers like Adam are often preferred for faster convergence, we opted for SGD to maintain a balance between training stability and performance.

Each 3D volume are inferenced slice by slice and the predicted 2D segmentation maps were stacked to reconstruct the complete 3D volume for evaluation.

---

[1] https://www.synapse.org/#!Synapse:syn3193805/wiki/217789.

[2] https://www.creatis.insa-lyon.fr/Challenge/acdc/.

3.3 Comparison with State-of-the-Arts

We evaluated GDCA-TransUNet against state-of-the-art segmentation models on the Synapse multi-organ CT dataset using Dice Similarity Coefficient (DSC) and Hausdorff Distance (HD). Table 1 shows mean DSC and HD for overall performance, and organ-specific DSC.

GDCA-TransUNet(ours) achieved the highest mean DSC (79.98%, Table 1), outperforming TransUNet (2.5%↑) and SwinUNet (0.85%↑), and notably surpassing recent Mamba-based approaches including VM-UNet [25] (0.89%), Med-Mamba [26] (0.71%↑) and Hc-Mamba [27] (0.40%↑), highlighting DCA's effective multi-scale fusion. While DA-TransUNet [28] approaches our performance (79.80%) through similar dual-attention mechanisms, its lack of dedicated background suppression (Attention Gates) explains our superior performance in noisy anatomical regions like the stomach (80.30% vs 79.73%) and pancreas (61.97% vs 61.62%). Our model maintains a consistent advantage across clinically critical small organs. GDCA-TransUNet also showed competitive boundary precision with a low HD (23.62 mm), though slightly higher than SwinUNet's (21.55 mm). While SwinUNet showed slightly better performance on individual organs like Gallbladder, Kidney (L), Kidney (R), Liver, and Spleen based on DSC, GDCA-TransUNet demonstrated superior DSC for Aorta, Pancreas, and Stomach, ultimately leading to a higher overall mean DSC. SwinUNet excels in larger organs with consistent shapes and homogeneous textures, like liver, kidney, Spleen, and so on, due to its local-window self-attention. Notably, GDCA-TransUNet achieved the highest DSC for pancreas (61.97%, Table 1), surpassing TransUNet (6.09%↑) and SwinUNet (5.39%↑), indicating strong performance on small and intricate organs, as DCA's cross-scale alignment mitigates semantic gaps in fragmented anatomy. Stomach segmentation also improved significantly (80.30% DSC, Table 1), a 4.7%↑ over SwinUNet, likely due to Attention Gates which suppresses fluid-filled luminal backgrounds. Our model achieved better performance on aorta with 87.71%, as spatial cross-attention enhances tubular structure coherence, which is very close to the 89.93% of Hc-Mamba. Overall, GDCA-TransUNet consistently outperformed baselines, with notable gains in gallbladder (+1.86% vs. TransUNet) and spleen (+3.77% vs. UNet). DCA improved performance on small organs and tubular structures. AGs reduced background noise, lowering HD by 8.07 mm compared to TransUNet. Despite SwinUNet's lower HD, GDCA-TransUNet's superior DSC (79.98% vs. 79.13%) highlights a better balance between volumetric overlap and boundary precision, crucial for clinical applications needing accurate organ localization. While VM-UNet excelled in gallbladder segmentation (68.41%) and DA-TransUNet in right kidney (80.45%), our architecture maintains superior balance across all organs.

Table 1. Comparison on the Synapse multi-organ CT dataset (mean dice score in % and mean hausdorff distance in mm). GDCA-TransUNet(Ours), proposed model

Model	mDCS↑	mHD↓	Aorta	Gallb.	Kid (L)	Kid (R)	Liver	Panc.	Spleen	Stom.
U–Net	74.68	36.87	84.18	62.84	79.19	71.29	93.35	48.23	84.41	73.92
AttnUNet	75.57	36.97	55.92	63.91	79.20	72.71	93.56	49.37	87.19	74.95
UNet++	76.09	-	86.93	63.69	77.86	68.29	93.91	59.23	87.81	75.49
SwinUNet	79.13	**21.55**	85.47	66.53	83.28	79.61	94.29	56.58	**90.66**	76.60
TransUNet	77.48	31.69	87.23	63.13	81.87	77.02	94.08	55.86	85.08	75.62
DA-TransUNet	79.80	23.48	86.54	65.27	81.70	80.45	94.57	61.62	88.53	79.73
VM-UNet	79.08	32.21	84.40	**68.41**	83.16	**80.74**	92.07	56.90	87.51	79.42
MedMamba	79.27	28.15	86.23	67.53	81.22	78.49	94.89	58.57	89.29	78.12
Hc-Mamba	79.58	26.34	**89.93**	67.65	**84.57**	78.27	**95.53**	52.08	89.48	79.84
(Ours)	**79.98**	23.62	87.71	64.99	83.12	78.87	94.00	**61.97**	88.85	**80.30**

3.4   Ablation Study

We carried out ablation studies on the Synapse dataset to thoroughly investigate the effects of various factors on model performance. The factors we focused on were different configurations of Dual Cross Attention (DCA) and Attention Gates (AG), and the number of skip connections, which are discussed below.

Effect of Different Configurations: We performed ablation studies, experiment results shown in Table 2, to assess the impact of Dual Cross Attention (DCA) and Attention Gates (AG) in various configurations.

Module Order, DCA+AG yielded the highest DSC (79.98%, Table 2), 3.69%↑ over AG+DCA. Prioritizing DCA for multi-scale fusion before AG-based refinement is crucial. AG+DCA, AG-only configurations were less effective, possibly due to premature attention gating removing context needed for DCA.

Organ-Specific Gains, DCA+AG improved Pancreas DSC by 6.47% over AG-only (61.97% vs 55.50%), highlighting DCA's benefit for small organ segmentation. Stomach DSC increased by 7.59% over AG+DCA (80.30% vs 72.71%), showing AG's refinement in variable regions. Gallbladder DSC improved by 7.29% over DCA-only (64.99% vs 57.70%), confirming AG's background suppression capability.

Results confirm that DCA+AG is the optimal configuration. DCA first ensures robust multi-scale feature aggregation, refined by AG's salient region focus. This order prevents loss of crucial context from premature AG application. While AG+DCA improves HD, its lower DSC makes DCA+AG more suitable for clinical applications needing balanced overlap and precision.

Table 2. Albation study on the impact of different configurations of DCA and AG on the Synapse multi-organ CT dataset.

Model	mDCS↑	mHD↓	Aorta	Gallb.	Kid (L)	Kid (R)	Liver	Panc.	Spleen	Stom.
DCA only	78.04	28.09	**88.23**	57.70	81.32	76.29	**94.73**	61.03	86.51	78.53
AG only	76.55	28.64	87.12	61.16	81.35	72.68	94.43	55.93	84.12	75.61
AG+DCA	76.29	24.47	87.60	59.66	80.66	75.18	94.65	55.50	84.34	72.71
DCA+AG	**79.98**	**23.62**	87.71	**64.99**	**83.12**	**78.87**	94.00	**61.97**	**88.85**	**80.30**

Effect of the Number of Skip Connection: To investigate the effect of skip connections on the segmentation performance of our proposed model, we conducted experiments by varying the number of skip connections. Our model incorporates skip connections at the 1/4, 1/8, and 1/16 resolution scales. We evaluated the model's performance on the Synapse dataset with 0, 1, 2, and 3 skip connections. The results of this ablation study are presented in Table 3. The mean Dice Similarity Coefficient (mDSC) generally improves with an increasing number of skip connections. With zero skip connections, the model achieved an mDSC of 69.51%. Introducing one skip connection significantly boosted the mDSC to 77.10%, accompanied by a notable reduction in mean Hausdorff Distance (mHD) to 21.58 mm. Further increasing the number of skip connections to two resulted in a slight improvement in mDSC to 77.77% and an mHD of 29.37 mm. The best overall performance was achieved with three skip connections, yielding the highest mDSC of 79.98% and a competitive mHD of 23.62 mm. The organ-specific DSC values also reflect this trend. For instance, the DSC for the Gallbladder increased from 52.90% with no skip connections to 64.99% with three skip connections. Similarly, the Pancreas segmentation DSC improved from 45.55% to 61.97% with the addition of skip connections.

These results underscore the importance of skip connections in facilitating the flow of low-level features from the encoder to the decoder, thereby enhancing the model's ability to accurately segment different organs. Based on these findings, we set the number of skip connections to 3 in our final model to ensure robust segmentation performance.

Table 3. Albation study on the impact of the number of skip connection on the Synapse multi-organ CT dataset.

Skip conn.	mDCS↑	mHD↓	Aorta	Gallb.	Kid (L)	Kid (R)	Liver	Panc.	Spleen	Stom.
0	69.51	32.87	71.77	52.90	73.70	66.13	91.61	45.55	81.72	72.69
1	77.10	**21.58**	84.46	61.88	79.09	76.26	94.26	57.06	84.72	79.07
2	77.77	29.37	86.68	57.95	81.09	76.64	**94.28**	57.51	87.32	80.07
3	**79.98**	23.62	**87.71**	**64.99**	**83.12**	**78.87**	94.00	**61.97**	**88.85**	**80.30**

Stability Under Random Initialization: The GDCA-TransUNet model exhibits strong stability across four runs with different initializations on the Synapse dataset, achieving a mean DSC of 79.98% with a standard deviation of 0.26% and a mean HD of 23.62 mm with a standard deviation of 0.31 mm, shown in Table 4. These low standard deviations highlight the model's consistent performance, making it reliable for tasks requiring robust segmentation. This stability reinforces its potential for practical applications.

Table 4. Multiple run on random seed initialization on the Synapse dataset

Run	mDSC↑	mHD↓	Aorta	Gallbladder	Kid(L)	Kid(R)	Liver	Pancreas	Spleen	Stomach
1	80.20	23.20	87.90	65.20	83.30	79.00	94.10	62.10	89.00	80.50
2	79.60	24.00	87.50	64.80	82.90	78.60	93.90	61.80	88.70	80.10
3	80.14	23.66	87.80	65.10	83.20	78.90	94.05	62.05	88.90	80.40
4	79.98	23.62	87.71	64.99	83.12	78.87	94.00	61.97	88.85	80.30

3.5   Visualization

Qualitative results presented in Fig. 3 demonstrate the effectiveness of GDCA-TransUNet's in organ segmentation, particularly for challenging cases like Aorta and Pancreas. Our model delineates organ boundaries more accurately and smoothly compared to SOTA methods, especially in low-contrast regions. For

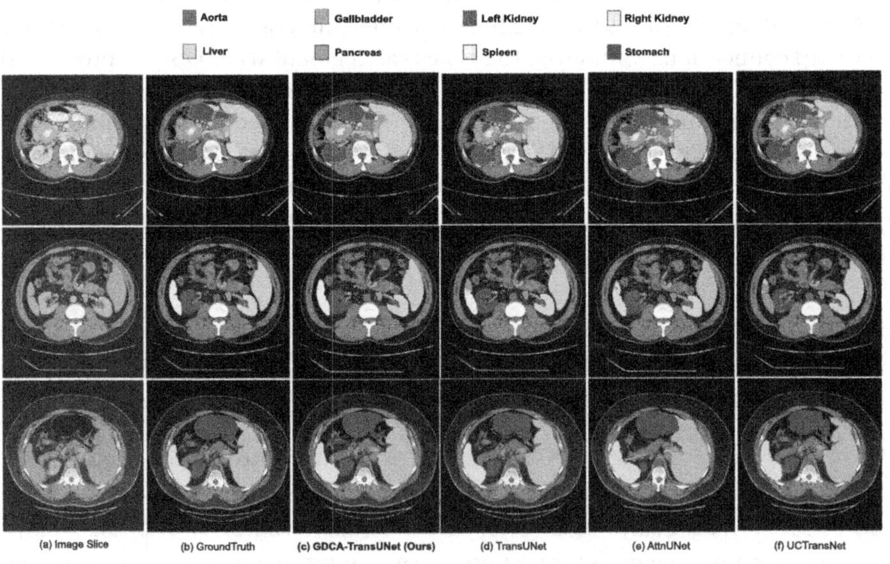

Fig. 3. Qualitative comparison of different approaches by visualization. From left to right: (a) Image Slice, (b) Ground Truth, (c) GDCA-TransUNet (ours), (d) TransUNet, (e) AttnUNet, (f) UCTransNet

small organs, DCA blocks enhance fine-grained feature focus, reducing fragmentation seen in TransUNet [13] and AttnUNet [8]. Attention Gates contribute to sharper boundaries for kidneys, liver, and stomach by suppressing irrelevant activations and boundary leakage, improving spatial accuracy. GDCA-TransUNet generalizes well across organs of varying sizes, showcasing architecture robustness. Overall, qualitative findings visually validate GDCA-TransUNet's superior performance and the effectiveness of DCA and AG components for reliable multi-organ segmentation.

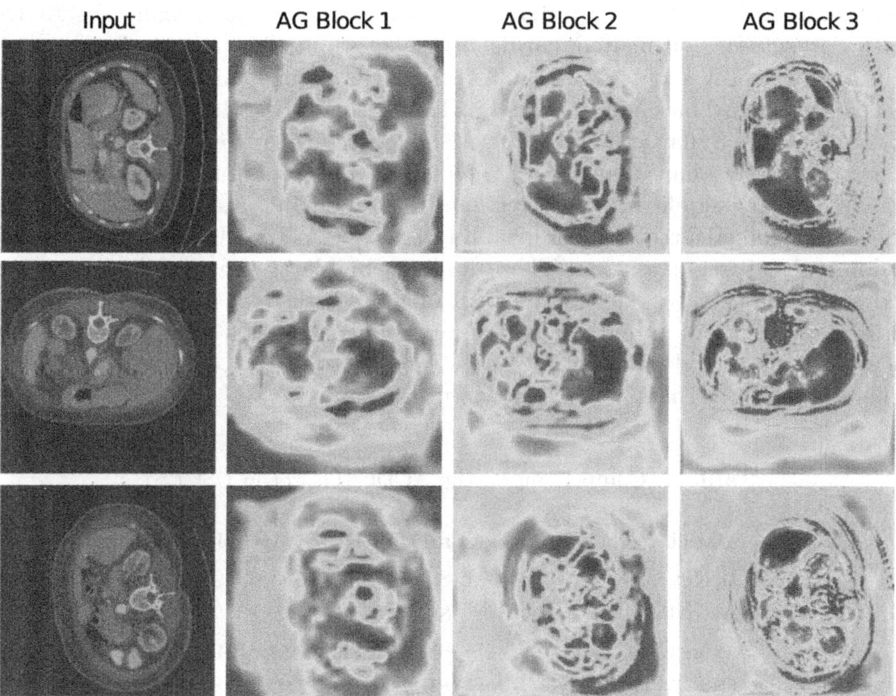

Fig. 4. Attention Heap maps after each attention gate block. From left to right: (a) Input, (b) AG Block 1, (c) AG Block 2, (d) AG Block 3

The heatmaps shown in Fig. 4, derived from the three Attention Gate (AG) blocks at skip connections of 1/8, 1/4, and 1/2 scales and processed through the Dual Cross Attention (DCA) module, demonstrate the model's progressive refinement of attention, particularly on small and intricate organs, a critical yet challenging for segmentation. At the lowest resolution (1/8 scale), the heatmap shows moderate attention on the small organs like pancreas (yellow-green), with broader focus (red areas) on larger organs like the kidneys and spleen, indicating initial detection without prioritization. At the intermediate resolution (1/4 scale), attention sharpens, with increased focus (red areas) on the pancreas alongside the kidneys, while background noise (blue areas) decreases, reflecting the AGs and DCA's noise-filtering capability. At the highest resolution (1/2 scale), the heatmap reveals intense, localized attention (red areas) on the pancreas, highlighting its prioritization, with sustained focus on the kidneys and spleen and a fully suppressed background (blue), showcasing precise targeting. This coarse-to-fine progression, aligned with the model's skip connection architecture, enhances segmentation accuracy for complex organs.

3.6   Generalization

To evaluate the generalization capability of GDCA-TransUNet, we conducted additional experiments on a different imaging modality, specifically the ACDC MRI dataset for automated cardiac segmentation. The results demonstrate consistent improvements of GDCA-TransUNet over TransUNet and other transformer-based baselines reported in Table 5, mirroring the performance gains observed on the Synapse CT dataset. Although the Dice score for the LV class is marginally lower than TransUNet, the overall robust performance across other organs and the significant improvements in challenging cases like the pancreas suggest a strong degree of generalizability for GDCA-TransUNet on multi-organ abdominal CT segmentation. These findings highlight the model's robustness and adaptability across diverse medical imaging tasks and suggests an area for future investigation, potentially involving the incorporation of more specific LV-focused features or data augmentation strategies to further enhance the model's generalizability to this particular structure.

Table 5. Comparison on the ACDC dataset in DSC(%)

Model	mDCS↑	RV	Myo	LV
U-Net	87.50	87.90	81.63	94.92
AttnUNet	86.75	87.58	79.20	93.47
TransUNet	89.71	88.86	84.01	**95.73**
GDCA-TransUNet (Ours)	**89.79**	**89.72**	**92.16**	87.87

4   Conclusion

In this paper, we proposed the GDCA-TransUNet, a novel model that leverages the strengths of transformer-based architectures and attention mechanisms to enhance multi-organ segmentation. Our model introduces key innovations, including the Dual Cross-Attention (DCA) module integrated into the skip connections of TransUNet and attention gates that refine focus on important features, particularly in complex and small organ structures such as the pancreas.

Experimental results demonstrate that GDCA-TransUNet outperforms TransUNet and SwinUNet along with other state-of-the-art models, particularly in terms of Dice Similarity Coefficient (DSC) and Hausdorff Distance (HD).

Acknowledgments. This work is supported by National Natural Science Foundation of China (NSFC No.62172309).

Disclosure of Interests. The authors declare that they have no known competing financial interests or personal relationships that could have appeared to influence the work reported in this paper.

References

1. Litjens, G., et al.: A survey on deep learning in medical image analysis. MedIA (2017)
2. Gibson, E., et al.: Automatic multi-organ segmentation on abdominal CT with dense V-networks. IEEE Trans. Med. Imaging **37**(8), 1822–1834 (2018)
3. Zhou, Y., Xie, L., Shen, W., Wang, Y., Fishman, E.K., Yuille, A.L.: A fixed-point model for pancreas segmentation in abdominal CT scans. In: International Conference on Medical Image Computing and Computer-assisted Intervention, pp. 693–701. Springer (2017)
4. Tajbakhsh, N., et al.: Surrogate supervision for medical image analysis: Effective deep learning from limited quantities of labeled data. In: 2019 IEEE 16th International Symposium on Biomedical Imaging (ISBI 2019), pp. 1251–1255. IEEE (2019)
5. Isensee, F., Jaeger, P.F., Kohl, S., Petersen, J., Maier-Hein, K.H.: nnU-Net: a self-configuring method for deep learning-based biomedical image segmentation. Nat. Methods **18**(2), 203–211 (2021)
6. Ho, T.-Y., et al.: Automated Esophageal Gross Tumor Volume Segmentation in 18F-FDG PET and CT for Radiotherapy using Two-Stream 3D Deep Network Fusion. Society of Nuclear Medicine (2020)
7. Ronneberger, O., Fischer, P., Brox, T.: U-Net: Convolutional Networks for Biomedical Image Segmentation. In: Medical Image Computing and Computer-Assisted Intervention (MICCAI), pp. 234–241. Springer (2015)
8. Oza, P., Litsios, V.: Attention U-Net: hybrid deep learning image segmentation model for medical imaging. J. Med. Imag. **7**(1), 101–108 (2020)
9. Zhou, Z., Rahman Siddiquee, M.M., Tajbakhsh, N., Liang, J.: Unet++: A nested u-net architecture for medical image segmentation. In: Deep Learning in Medical Image Analysis and Multimodal Learning for Clinical Decision Support: 4th International Workshop, DLMIA 2018, and 8th International Workshop, ML-CDS 2018, Held in Conjunction with MICCAI 2018, Granada, Spain, September 20, 2018, Proceedings 4, pp. 3–11. Springer (2018)
10. Hatamizadeh, A., et al.: Unetr: Transformers for 3d medical image segmentation. In: Proceedings of the IEEE/CVF Winter Conference on Applications of Computer Vision, pp. 574–584 (2022)
11. Woo, S., Park, J., Lee, J.-Y., Kweon, I.S.: Cbam: Convolutional block attention module. In: Proceedings of the European Conference on Computer Vision (ECCV), pp. 3–19 (2018)
12. Valanarasu, J.M.J., Oza, P., Hacihaliloglu, I., Patel, V.M.: Medical transformer: gated axial-attention for medical image segmentation. In: Medical image computing and computer assisted intervention–MICCAI 2021: 24th international conference, Strasbourg, France, September 27–October 1, 2021, proceedings, part I 24, pp. 36–46. Springer (2021)

13. Chen, J., Qin, Z., Li, L.: TransUNet: transformers make strong encoders for medical image segmentation. In: Medical Image Computing and Computer-Assisted Intervention (MICCAI) (2021)
14. Cao, H., et al.: Swin-unet: Unet-like pure transformer for medical image segmentation. In: European Conference on Computer Vision, pp. 205–218. Springer (2022)
15. Wang, H., Cao, P., Wang, J., Zaiane, O.R.: Uctransnet: rethinking the skip connections in u-net from a channel-wise perspective with transformer. In: Proceedings of the AAAI Conference on Artificial Intelligence $36(3)$, 2441–2449 (2022)
16. Xie, Y., Zhang, J., Shen, C., Xia, Y.: COTR: efficiently bridging CNN and transformer for 3D medical image segmentation. In: Medical Image Computing and Computer Assisted Intervention–MICCAI 2021: 24th International Conference, Strasbourg, France, September 27–October 1, 2021, Proceedings, Part III 24, pp. 171–180. Springer (2021)
17. Fu, J., et al.: Dual attention network for scene segmentation. In: Proceedings of the IEEE/CVF Conference on Computer Vision and Pattern Recognition, pp. 3146–3154 (2019)
18. Ates, G.C., Demir, E.: Dual cross-attention for medical image segmentation. IEEE Transactions on Medical Imaging (2020)
19. Yu, Q., Xie, L., Wang, Y., Zhou, Y., Fishman, E.K., Yuille, A.L.: Recurrent saliency transformation network: incorporating multi-stage visual cues for small organ segmentation. In: Proceedings of the IEEE Conference on Computer Vision and Pattern Recognition, pp. 8280–8289 (2018)
20. Xu, Z.: Multi-atlas labeling beyond the cranial vault-workshop and challenge (2016) (2017)
21. Bernard, O., et al.: Deep learning techniques for automatic MRI cardiac multi-structures segmentation and diagnosis: is the problem solved? IEEE Trans. Med. Imaging $37(11)$, 2514–2525 (2018)
22. He, K., Zhang, X., Ren, S., Sun, J.: Deep residual learning for image recognition. In: Proceedings of the IEEE Conference on Computer Vision and Pattern Recognition, pp. 770–778 (2016)
23. Alexey, D.: An image is worth 16x16 words: Transformers for image recognition at scale. arXiv preprint arXiv: 2010.11929 (2020)
24. Deng, J., Dong, W., Socher, R., Li, L.-J., Li, K., Fei-Fei, L.: Imagenet: A large-scale hierarchical image database. In: 2009 IEEE Conference on Computer Vision and Pattern Recognition, pp. 248–255. IEEE (2009)
25. Ruan, J., Li, J., Xiang, S.: Vm-unet: Vision mamba unet for medical image segmentation. arXiv preprint arXiv: 2402.02491 (2024)
26. Yue, Y., Li, Z.: Medmamba: Vision mamba for medical image classification. arXiv preprint arXiv: 2403.03849 (2024)
27. Xu, J.: Hc-mamba: Vision mamba with hybrid convolutional techniques for medical image segmentation. arXiv preprint arXiv: 2405.05007 (2024)
28. Sun, G., et al.: DA-TransUNet: integrating spatial and channel dual attention with transformer U-net for medical image segmentation. Front. Bioeng. Biotechnol. **12**, 1398237 (2024)

E(3)-Invariant Diffusion Model for Pocket-Aware Peptide Generation

Po-Yu Liang and Jun Bai[✉]

Department of Computer Science, University of Cincinnati, Ohio, USA
baiju@ucmail.uc.edu

Abstract. Biologists frequently desire protein inhibitors for a variety of reasons, including their use as research tools to understand biological processes and their application to social problems in agriculture, healthcare, etc. Immunotherapy, for instance, relies on immune checkpoint inhibitors to block checkpoint proteins, preventing their binding with partner proteins and boosting immune cell function against abnormal cells. Inhibitor discovery has long been a tedious process, which in recent years has been accelerated by computational approaches. Advances in artificial intelligence now provide an opportunity to make inhibitor discovery smarter than ever before. Although extensive research has been conducted on computer-aided inhibitor discovery, it has mainly focused on either sequence-to-structure mapping, reverse mapping, or bio-activity prediction, making it unrealistic for biologists to utilize such tools. Instead, our work proposes a new method for computer-assisted inhibitor discovery: de novo pocket-aware peptide structure and sequence generation network. Our approach consists of two sequential diffusion models for end-to-end structure generation and sequence prediction. By leveraging geometric relationships between backbone atoms, we ensure an E(3)-invariant representation of peptide structures. In addition, we introduce multiple evaluation metrics that incorporate biological information to more effectively assess model performance. Our results demonstrate that our method outperforms state-of-the-art models at binding success rate and structure generation, highlighting its potential in pocket-aware peptide design. This work offers a new approach to precise drug discovery using receptor-specific peptide generation. The code used for this research is available at Github.[1] https://github.com/LabJunBMI/ E3-invaraint-diffusion-model-for-pocket-aware-peptide-generation.

Keywords: Deep Learning · Diffusion Model · Drug Discovery · Protein Design

1 Introduction

Biologists seek peptides for various applications, from studying biological mechanisms to developing healthcare solutions, such as immunotherapy using checkpoint inhibitors to enhance immune responses against cancer. Traditionally, pep-

J. Tang et al. (Eds.): ISBRA 2025, LNBI 15757, pp. 177–189, 2026.
https://doi.org/10.1007/978-981-95-0695-8_15

tide discovery has been slow and expensive, but computational methods have significantly accelerated the process [4,26]. Techniques such as molecular coupling, virtual screening, and deep learning were utilized to predict peptide-protein interactions, optimize sequences, and identify candidates [5,6,16]. Among computational methods, deep learning stands out as a promising tool for generating peptides with desired properties, advancing research on peptide design [17,18].

Although significant research has been conducted on computer-aided peptide discovery [23], most efforts focus on generating peptide sequences with general properties [10,11] or specific structural features [8,9] make them less practical to biologists. Few studies [28] have explored peptide inhibitor discovery, where the lack of target-specific information hinders the design of peptides for specific receptor pockets. RFdiffusion [30] offers a potential solution by generating peptide structures around target pockets, with inverse folding models [3]. However, it has limitations, such as training on broad datasets that often contain large protein complexes, reducing specificity in the generation of the peptide binder.

Beyond these methodological challenges, the evaluation of the generated peptides presents significant issues. Common evaluation metrics have drawbacks: sequence recovery does not account for amino acid similarity, TM-Score [34] assesses structural similarity but does not measure how well the generated structures reflect natural conformations, and binding energy measures only interactions with the target receptor while overlooking interactions with other receptors.

To address these challenges, we propose a method that generates peptide backbone structures and sequences while incorporating information from the receptor pocket. In addition, we introduce multiple evaluation metrics to provide a more comprehensive assessment of the performance of the model. Finally, we compare our approach with that of state-of-the-art peptide generation methods.

2   Method

Our proposed method (shown in Fig. 1) contains twin modules : a) conditional structure diffusion model and b) conditional sequence diffusion model. The structure diffusion model generates the peptide structures using pocket information as condition. Once the peptide structure is obtained, the sequence diffusion model generates the corresponding amino acid sequence, using pocket information as condition. In this section, we explain the E(3)-invariant representation of proteins and peptides, and our novel twin conditional diffusion models.

2.1   Data Representation

Representation of Protein. Inspired by FoldingDiff [31], the backbone structure of an amino acid is described by bond and dihedral (torsion) angles between the backbone nitrogen, α-carbon, and carbon atoms. This creates an E(3)-invariant representation, ensuring that the structure remains consistent under 3D rotations or translations. Building on their work, we introduce a novel representation of protein structures by explicitly incorporating the oxygen atom

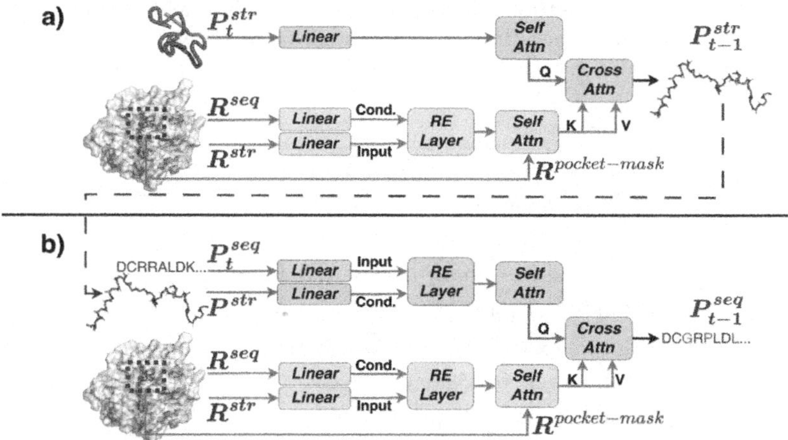

Fig. 1. The figure illustrates the main architecture of our method, including peptide structure prediction model and peptide sequence prediction model. The "Self Attn" and "Cross Attn" blocks represent the self-attention and cross-attention mechanisms. The "RE Layer" blocks refer to the gated adaptive layer normalization [13,19]. "Cond." and "Input" denote the conditioning input and the main input for the RE layer.

into the backbone's bond and dihedral angles. This inclusion of the oxygen atom is a critical advancement, as demonstrated by tools like DSSP [14], which rely on backbone oxygen information to significantly improve secondary structure predictions. To create a comprehensive representation of protein structures, we also introduced bond distances between backbone atoms. This ensures that no information from the backbone structure is lost. We exclude the first and last residues since their internal angles cannot be fully determined. The specific definitions of the angles and dihedrals used are provided in Table 1, where each backbone atom is represented as: AtomType_i, corresponding to the backbone atom of the i-th amino acid residue. We define the representation of a protein as $X = \{X^{\text{str}}, X^{\text{seq}}\}$, where $X^{\text{str}} = \{X^{\text{dih}}, X^{\text{ang}}, X^{\text{dist}}\}$ represents the structure features of the protein backbone; $X^{\text{dih}} \in [-\pi, \pi]^{n \times 4}$ represents the four dihedral angles of the protein backbone; n is the protein length; $X^{\text{ang}} \in [-\pi, \pi]^{n \times 4}$ represents the four bond angles of the protein backbone; $X^{\text{dist}} \in \mathbb{R}^{n \times 4}$ represents the four bond distances between backbone atoms and $X^{\text{seq}} \in \mathbb{R}^{n \times 20}$ represents the one-hot encoding of 20 amino acid types. The data representation of receptor R and peptide P are denoted as $R = \{R^{\text{str}}, R^{\text{seq}}\}$ and $P = \{P^{\text{str}}, P^{\text{seq}}\}$.

2.2   Twin Conditional Diffusion Model

Structure Diffusion Model. We designed a transformer-based [27] diffusion model to generate peptide structures conditioned on the receptor pocket. The diffusion model architecture contains two major processes, the Markov noising process and de-noising process. The Markov noising process corrupts the data by progressively adding noise to it over a series of time steps, which could be

Table 1. Amino acid structure representation. The amino acid backbone structure represented as position of the nitrogen: ψ_i, θ_1, and d_1, followed by the position of the alpha-carbon: ω_i, θ_2 and d_2, the carbon: ϕ_i, θ_3, and d_3, and the oxygen: δ_i, θ_4, and d_4.

	Description
ψ_i	Dihedral torsion of $N_{i-1} - C\alpha_{i-1} - C_{i-1} - N_i$
ω_i	Dihedral torsion of $C\alpha_{i-1} - C_{i-1} - N_i - C\alpha_i$
ϕ_i	Dihedral torsion of $C_{i-1} - N_i - C\alpha_i - C_i$
δ_i	Dihedral torsion of $N_i - C\alpha_i - C_i - O_i$
θ_1	Bond angle of $C\alpha_{i-1} - C_{i-1} - N_i$
θ_2	Bond angle of $C_{i-1} - N_i - C\alpha_i$
θ_3	Bond angle of $N_i - C\alpha_i - C_i$
θ_4	Bond angle of $C\alpha_i - C_i - O_i$
d_1	Bond distance of $C_{i-1} - N_i$
d_2	Bond distance of $N_i - C\alpha_i$
d_3	Bond distance of $C\alpha_i - C_i$
d_4	Bond distance of $C_i - O_i$

represented as $q(P_t^{str}|P_{t-1}^{str})$, where t is the discrete time step in the noising process, indicating the level of noise applied to the data at that particular step. To perform the de-noising process, a model, denoted as $p(P_{t-1}^{str}|P_t^{str}, R)$, is trained to reverse a Markov noising process. To capture the wrapped nature of angle, we utilize the wrapped normal distribution for Markov noising process and the wrapped smooth L_1 loss (Eq. 2)for model training [31].

$$d(\cdot) = ((\epsilon_t - \epsilon_p + \pi) \quad \mathrm{mod}\ 2\pi) - \pi$$

$$L_{str} = \begin{cases} 0.5d(\cdot)/\beta, & \text{if } |d(\cdot)| < \beta \\ |d(\cdot)| - 0.5\beta, & \text{otherwise} \end{cases} \tag{1}$$

where the function $d(\cdot)$ wrap the angle difference about $[-\pi, \pi)$, ϵ_t represent the noise sampled from noising process, ϵ_p represent the noise predicted by our model, and β is a hyper-parameter, which we set to 0.1π.

Sequence Diffusion Model. To inverse fold the peptide structure, we proposed a discrete diffusion model. Inspired by GraDe-IF [32], for the corrupted n-th amino acid type of a sequence—represent as $X_t^{seq}[n] = A_t \in \mathbb{R}^{20}$—the transition probability between amino acid type i and j at step t is described as a matrix $[Q_t]_{ij} = q(A_t = i|A_{t-1} = j)$. The noising process could be defined as $q(A_t|A_{t-1}) = A_{t-1}Q_t$. To reverse the noising process, a model $p(P_0^{seq}|P_t^{seq}, P^{str}, R)$ is trained to estimate $p(P_{t-1}^{seq}|P_t^{seq}, P^{str}, R)$. We adapt the BLOSUM62 transition matrix to better capture the property of transition between amino acid types. For learning the natural distribution of amino acids in peptides, we combine the ELBO loss and cross-entropy loss as shown in Eq. 2.

$$L_{seq} = L_{ELBO} + L_{CE} \tag{2}$$

where the L_{ELBO} loss (shown in Equation 3) is applied measure the distribution divergence between the amino acid from ground truth and prediction, and the L_{CE} (shown in Equation 4) is applied to measure the probability distance between each noised residue amino acid between ground truth and prediction.

$$L_{ELBO} = \mathbb{E}_{q(\hat{A}|A_0)}[\log p(A_0|\hat{A})] - KL(q(\hat{A}|A_0)\|p(\hat{A})) \tag{3}$$

where KL is the Kullback–Leibler divergence, and $\hat{A}$ is the sequence prediction.

$$L_{CE} = -\sum_{i}^{20} p(i) \log q(i) \tag{4}$$

where $p(\cdot)$ is label and $q(\cdot)$ is predicted probability distribution of i amino acid.

2.3 Conditional Layers

Residue Encoding(RE) Layer. To encode the structure and sequence features of residues, we employ gated adaptive layer normalization [13,19]. In the structural diffusion model, sequence is a conditioning variable for structural features, while in the sequence diffusion model, the relationship is reversed. This approach allows us to maintain the essential characteristics of one type of feature while integrating the effects of the other.

$$GatedLN(\cdot) = Gate \odot \left(Scale \odot \frac{h - \mu(h)}{\sigma(h)} + Shift\right) \tag{5}$$

where h is the hidden state; $Gate$, $Scale$, and $Shift$ are the layer normalization from the condition hidden state, and the $\odot$ denote the Hadamard product.

Cross-Attention Layer. After obtaining the embeddings for the pocket and peptide, represented as and respectively, we condition the peptide features using the pocket features through a cross-attention mechanism [27]. In this mechanism, the query Q is calculated as $W_q h^{pep}$, while the key K and value V are derived from the pocket features using $W_k h^{pocket}$ and $W_v h^{pocket}$. The output of this layer can be expressed as $h_{out} = Softmax(QK^T/\sqrt{d_K}) \cdot V$ where d_k denotes the dimension of K. The resulting output represents the conditioned features, effectively integrating information from both the pocket and peptide embeddings.

2.4 Data Source and Evaluation Metrics

Data Source and Preprocessing. We used the BioLip [33] protein-ligand dataset and processed it with Biopython [2], DSSP [14], and PDBFixer from OpenMM [7]. BioLip contains 35,167 protein-peptide interactions. We excluded complexes with resolutions less than 5 Å [22], unknown amino acids, peptides shorter than five residues, duplicate PDB IDs, and those incompatible with

Biopython or DSSP, resulting in 9,261 receptor-peptide complexes. To prevent data leakage, we clustered sequences using MMSeqs2 [25] (70% identity, 80% coverage), forming 1,992 clusters. We selected 199 clusters (10%) for testing, ensuring each contained a single unique sequence. The remaining sequences are randomly split into training and validation set with 80:20 ratio. We also incorporated the PepPC-F dataset from DiffPepBuilder [29], applying the same clustering to prevent leakage. After augmentation, the training set contained 13,227 sequences, and the test set had 199 unique sequences.

Structure Evaluation Metrics. We evaluate the performance of all structure models using *TM-Score* and *structure distribution*.

TM-Score. TM-Score is a length-normalized structural similarity metric. We report the highest scoring structure among the five generated peptides. Note that although TM-Score is widely used to evaluate structural similarity, it does not indicate whether the generated structure is natural.

Natural Structure Distribution We assess the model's ability to capture natural structural properties by measuring the KL divergence between the generated structures and testing set. The Ramachandran plot is used to visualize the model's ability to capture secondary structure. To evaluate structure generation, we generate five peptides per receptor. All generated structures are included to assess whether the model can generate natural structures.

Sequence Evaluation Metrics. Most studies evaluate the performance of the sequence module using the amino acid sequence recovery rate. Note that this metric may underestimate performance due to minor misalignments (e.g., an extra amino acid reduces recovery to zero). To address this, we propose robust alternatives: alignment-based *sequence similarity* and *diversity metrics*.

Sequence similarity. Sequence similarity is defined in Eq. 6, where $N.W.$ denotes the Needleman-Wunsch algorithm [20] with the BLOSUM62 [12] substitution matrix. The numerator measures sequence similarity and the denominator normalizes the score of identical sequence (maximum alignment score possible). We report the highest score among five generated sequences

$$SequenceSimilarity = \frac{N.W.(x_{pred}^{seq}, x_{true}^{seq})}{N.W.(x_{true}^{seq}, x_{true}^{seq})} \tag{6}$$

Diversity. Following a similar concept, we define a diversity metric (Eq. 7), where X_i^{seq} and X_j^{seq} represent the i-th and the j-th sequences in a set X^{seq} contains N sequences. Diversity is calculated as one minus the normalized pairwise alignment score. We used ProteinMPNN and the newer Grade-IF model to generate one sequence per structure for RFdiffusion-based methods for a fair comparison. We reported all five sequences to capture overall variation.

$$SequenceDiversity = 1 - \frac{1}{N}\frac{1}{N}\sum_{i=1}^{N}\sum_{j=1}^{N}\frac{N.W.(X_i^{seq}, X_j^{seq})}{N.W.(X_j^{seq}, X_j^{seq})} \tag{7}$$

Binding Metrics We evaluate the overall performance of our model by estimating the binding energy, selectivity, and success rate.

Binding energy (ΔG). All the models' binding energy estimated between the receptor and the generated peptide using PyRosetta [1,15]. The generated peptide is aligned with the position of the original peptide, followed by side chain packing and a fast relaxation step [21,24]. We then used the Rosetta energy function to compute the energy sums for the individual receptor, peptide structures, and the energy of the combined complex. The difference between these energy terms represents the overall binding energy of the complex, denoted as ΔG.

Selectivity measurement ($\Delta\Delta G$). Beyond the estimated energy terms, we propose a protocol to evaluate the selectivity of the generated peptide. Specifically, we randomly assign the generated peptide to a different receptor, perform fast relaxation, and measure the binding energy differences, denoted as $\Delta\Delta G$. Ideally, the binding energy between a peptide and a random receptor should be lower than that between the peptide and its target receptor.

Success rate. Finally, we calculate the success rate in generating effective peptides. A peptide is considered successful if it has a negative ΔG, indicating strong binding affinity, and a positive $\Delta\Delta G$, meaning it binds more strongly to the target receptor than to the randomly selected non-target receptor. The highest ΔG among the five generated peptides is reported. The peptide with the highest ΔG is then used to calculate $\Delta\Delta G$ and the success rate.

Pocket similarity. We observed that although each model attempts to generate or position the peptide around the pocket area, the contact residues often differ after relaxation. To address this, we evaluated the similarity of residues interacting with the generated peptide before and after relaxation using Jaccard similarity. We defined the interaction as having a distance cutoff of 8 Å. This measure is denoted as Pocket Similarity in the binding analysis (Sect. 3.3).

SOTA Models. We compared the performance of proposed model with RFdiffusion [30] and DiffPepDuilder [29]. Note that RFdiffusion is trained on the entire PDB dataset—which includes the BioLip—its structural similarity results should be treated as a reference rather than a direct performance measure; we thus label it the "Data-Leaked Model" in the results section. For DiffPepBuilder, we ensure no overlap between its training set (PepPC-F) and our testing set.

3   Result

3.1   Structure Prediction

Figure 2 shows the Ramachandran plot of generated structures of all models. The plot visualizes the model's ability to capture the three main secondary structures: right-handed (RH) α-helix, left-handed (LH) α-helix, and β-sheet. The

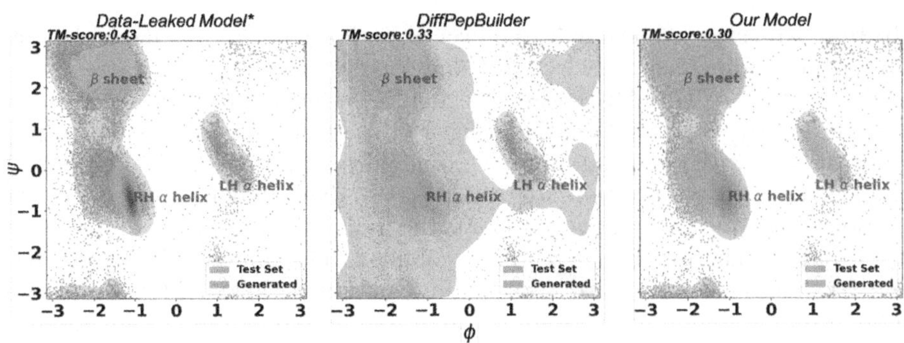

Fig. 2. Ramachandran plot visualizes the distribution of secondary structure by comparing the ϕ and ψ dihedral angles of amino acids. The areas corresponding to three main secondary structures – namely β-sheet, right-handed (RH) α-helix, and left-handed (LH) α-helix – are marked on the plot. Blue represent the data from testing set, and orange represent the generated data. *RFdiffusion, explained at Sect. 2.4 (Color figure online)

TM-Score is also marked on the top-let of each plot. The structures generated by RFdiffusion exhibit a high density in the RH α-helix region, some presence in the β-sheet region and no structures in the LH α-helix region indicates a relatively low diversity in secondary structure generation. For DiffPepBuilder, although the model successfully captures RH α-helix structures, it fails to generate LH α-helices. In addition, it produces some structures that deviate from the distribution observed in the test set. In general, our model demonstrates the best performance in capturing secondary structures. It not only successfully generates RH α-helices and β-sheets but also captures LH α-helices, which are relatively rare and more challenging to model. In terms of TM-Score, our model showed a comparable performance of 0.30, with only 0.03 difference comparing to DiffPepBuilder. RFdiffusion achieves TM-Score of 0.43. However, as discussed in Sect. 2.4, this score should be considered a reference rather than a direct performance measure due to the data leakage issue. The TM-Score distribution is shown in Appendix Figure S10.

Table 2. Structure similarity and KL Divergence

	Dihedrals				Angles				Atom Distances			
	ψ	ω	ϕ	δ	θ_1	θ_2	θ_3	θ_4	d_1	d_2	d_3	d_4
Data-Leaked Model*	0.68	0.71	0.55	1.96	8.46	0.06	6.50	0.25	2.79	2.70	1.35	0.97
DiffPepBuilder	0.38	0.06	0.32	0.20	8.53	2.09	1.48	0.25	2.03	2.72	2.08	3.00
Our Model	**0.17**	**0.05**	**0.18**	**0.16**	**0.05**	**0.04**	**0.04**	**0.02**	**0.13**	**0.09**	**0.04**	**0.08**

*RFdiffusion, explained at Section 2.4.   Best score is in **bold**.

As shown in Table 2, our model outperforms both RFdiffusion and DiffPep-Builder across all structural properties. Notably, for the two main properties, ψ and ϕ, our model shows KL divergences of only 0.17 and 0.05. These results demonstrate that our model generates structures that more closely resemble natural configurations compared to other methods while maintaining comparable structural similarity (distribution plots are shown in Appendix S1~S9).

3.2   Sequence Prediction

In terms of sequence similarity(Table 3), both our model and ProteinMPNN achieve the highest score of 0.37. Additionally, our model exhibits the highest sequence diversity of 0.66 among all models. Interestingly, while DiffPepBuilder generates sequences with a relatively low similarity, it attains a comparable sequence similarity of 0.36 and a higher diversity score of 0.61 than Grade-IF and ProteinMPNN(0.58). The distribution plots of similarity and diversity are shown in Appendix Figure S11 and S12. Note that ProteinMPNN's performance should be interpreted as a reference rather than a direct benchmark due to potential data leakage issues.

Table 3. Peptide Sequence prediction performance comparing to other models.

	Data-Leaked Model*		DiffPepBuilder	OurModel
	ProteinMPNN	Grade-IF		
↑ Sequence Similarity	**0.37**	0.32	0.36	**0.37**
↑ Diversity	0.58	0.58	0.61	**0.66**

*RFdiffusion, explained at Section2.4.   Best score is in **bold**.*

3.3   Binding Analysis

In the two energy-based metrics (Table 4), the Data-Leaked Model combined with ProteinMPNN achieves the best performance, as expected. However, its pocket similarity is lower than both our model and DiffPepBuilder, which achieve the highest similarity at 46.80% and 60.50%, respectively. This may be due to its high helix-structure bias, as discussed in Sect. 3.1, which limits its ability to generalize across different receptors. When comparing DiffPepBuilder to our model, although DiffPepBuilder generates peptides with relatively strong affinity, it exhibits the lowest $\Delta\Delta G$ at 11.48%. In contrast, our model generates peptides that show lower affinity to other receptors, leading to the highest overall success rate of 85.40%. The distribution of binding analysis metrics are shown in Appendix Figure S13 ~ S15.

Table 4. Binding Energy Analysis for all models.

	Ground Truth	Data-Leaked Model*		DiffPepBuilder	Our Model
		ProteinMPNN	Grade-IF		
↑Success Rate(%)	-	<u>83.24</u>	78.49	77.30	**85.40**
↑Pocket Sim.(%)	-	41.28	42.61	**60.50**	<u>46.80</u>
↓ΔG	-45.93	**-47.56**	<u>-41.13</u>	-36.23	-31.54
↑$\Delta\Delta G$	18.94	**19.44**	12.67	11.48	<u>13.72</u>

*Best score is in **bold**. Second best is in <u>underline</u>.*
**RFdiffusion, explained at Section 2.4*

RFdiffusion has been observed to frequently generate helical structures for binder design, often achieving a high success rate. Similarly, DiffPepBuilder tends to generate helical peptides, likely due to a strong bias toward helical structures in its training set. However, helical structures do not always perform well. Figure 3 presents an example of generated peptides for a given receptor (PDB: 2BZ8). Both RFdiffusion (Fig. 3c) and DiffPepBuilder (Fig. 3d) generated helical structures. In contrast, our model (Fig. 3.) successfully generates a strand-like structure, which more closely resembles the ground truth peptide. As a result, our model outperforms the others on this receptor, not only in structural similarity but also in binding energy.

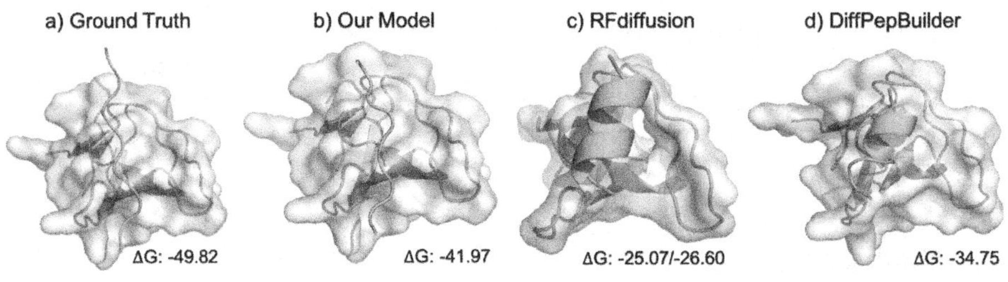

Fig. 3. Demo of generated peptides of all models on receptor PDB:2BZ8. Two ΔG scores in c) RFdiffusion are sequences generated by Grade-IF and ProteinMPNN.

4   Discussion

In this study, we propose a novel method for generating pocket-aware peptides using diffusion models with an E(3)-invariant structure representation. We proposed new metrics to better evaluate structure, sequence, and binding performance. One challenge in peptide generation research is the lack of consistency in evaluation methods, particularly with regard to number peptides are generated. Many studies report the best scoring peptide from multiple generations, but it is unclear how many trials are reasonable. For example, DiffPepBuilder's default settings generate peptides of varying lengths (8–30 residues) with eight samples per length. Meanwhile, Grade-IF combines results from multiple shorter diffusion runs to improve efficiency. These differences make fair comparisons difficult. In this work, we generated exactly five peptides of the same length as the original binder. For structural evaluation, we find that many generated peptides do not adopt natural folds, which causes issues for tools like AutoDock CrankPep [35]. This suggests TM-Score alone may not fully reflect structure quality. Instead, KL divergency-based metric assess geometric properties, ensuring the generated structures follow realistic distributions. Recovery rate is the most common sequence evaluation metric, but undervalue model's performance by ignoring amino acid similarities. Functionally similar substitutions can enable effective binding, but recovery rate fails to capture this. To solve this, we used the Needleman-Wunsch algorithm to measure similarity in a more robust way. Current methods assume that the peptide binds only at the desired hot spot and measure its affinity with the target receptor. However, in reality, peptides can interact with multiple receptors, affecting selectivity. They may also interact with other molecules, such as the cell membrane, which is often overlooked. To overcome this, we compared the binding affinity of a peptide with both the target receptor and a random receptor, providing a wider measure of the binding specificity. Overall, standard evaluation methods for the generation of peptides have several limitations that make comparisons between models difficult. Our study proposes more controlled and informative metrics. However, including experimental validation will be key to advancing this field in the future.

Disclosure of Interests. The authors have no competing interests to declare that are relevant to the content of this article.

References

1. Chaudhury, S., Lyskov, S., Gray, J.J.: Pyrosetta: a script-based interface for implementing molecular modeling algorithms using Rosetta. Bioinformatics **26**(5), 689–691 (2010)
2. Cock, P., et al.: Biopython: freely available python tools for computational molecular biology and bioinformatics. Bioinformatics **25**(11), 1422–1423 (2009)
3. Dauparas, J., et al.: Robust deep learning-based protein sequence design using proteinmpnn. Science **378**(6615), 49–56 (2022)
4. Duran, T., Chaudhuri, B.: Where might artificial intelligence be going in pharmaceutical development? (2024)
5. Duran, T., Minatovicz, B., Bai, J., Shin, D., Mohammadiarani, H., Chaudhuri, B.: Molecular dynamics simulation to uncover the mechanisms of protein instability during freezing. J. Pharm. Sci. **110**(6), 2457–2471 (2021)
6. Duran, T., Minatovicz, B., Bellucci, R., Bai, J., Chaudhuri, B.: Molecular dynamics modeling based investigation of the effect of freezing rate on lysozyme stability. Pharm. Res. **39**(10), 2585–2596 (2022)
7. Eastman, P., Pande, V.: Openmm: a hardware-independent framework for molecular simulations. Comput. Sci. Eng. **12**(4), 34–39 (2010)
8. Goverde, C.A., et al.: Computational design of soluble and functional membrane protein analogues. Nature 1–10 (2024)

9. Goverde, C.A., Wolf, B., Khakzad, H., Rosset, S., Correia, B.E.: De novo protein design by inversion of the alphafold structure prediction network. Protein Sci. **32**(6), e4653 (2023)

10. Greener, J.G., Moffat, L., Jones, D.T.: Design of metalloproteins and novel protein folds using variational autoencoders. Sci. Rep. **8**(1), 16189 (2018)

11. Gupta, A., Zou, J.: Feedback gan for dna optimizes protein functions. Nature Machine Intelligence **1**(2), 105–111 (2019)

12. Henikoff, S., Henikoff, J.G.: Amino acid substitution matrices from protein blocks. Proc. Natl. Acad. Sci. **89**(22), 10915–10919 (1992)

13. Huang, X., Belongie, S.: Arbitrary style transfer in real-time with adaptive instance normalization. In: Proceedings of the IEEE international conference on computer vision. pp. 1501–1510 (2017)

14. Kabsch, W., Sander, C.: Dictionary of protein secondary structure: pattern recognition of hydrogen-bonded and geometrical features. Biopolymers: Original Res. Biomol. **22**(12), 2577–2637 (1983)

15. Leaver-Fay, A., et al.: Scientific benchmarks for guiding macromolecular energy function improvement. In: Methods in enzymology, vol. 523, pp. 109–143. Elsevier (2013)

16. Lei, Y., Li, S., Liu, Z., Wan, F., Tian, T., Li, S., Zhao, D., Zeng, J.: A deep-learning framework for multi-level peptide-protein interaction prediction. Nat. Commun. **12**(1), 5465 (2021)

17. Liang, P.Y., Huang, X., Duran, T., Wiemer, A.J., Bai, J.: Exploring latent space for generating peptide analogs using protein language models. arXiv preprint arXiv:2408.08341 (2024)

18. Lin, E., Lin, C.H., Lane, H.Y.: De novo peptide and protein design using generative adversarial networks: an update. J. Chem. Inf. Model. **62**(4), 761–774 (2022)

19. Liu, G., Xu, J., Luo, T., Jiang, M.: Inverse molecular design with multi-conditional diffusion guidance. arXiv preprint arXiv:2401.13858 (2024)

20. Needleman, S.B., Wunsch, C.D.: A general method applicable to the search for similarities in the amino acid sequence of two proteins. J. Mol. Biol. **48**(3), 443–453 (1970)

21. Renfrew, P.D., Craven, T.W., Butterfoss, G.L., Kirshenbaum, K., Bonneau, R.: A rotamer library to enable modeling and design of peptoid foldamers. J. Am. Chem. Soc. **136**(24), 8772–8782 (2014)

22. Salamanca Viloria, J., Allega, M.F., Lambrughi, M., Papaleo, E.: An optimal distance cutoff for contact-based protein structure networks using side-chain centers of mass. Sci. Rep. **7**(1), 2838 (2017)

23. Sharma, K., Sharma, K.K., Sharma, A., Jain, R.: Peptide-based drug discovery: Current status and recent advances. Drug Discovery Today **28**(2), 103464 (2023)

24. Simons, K.T., Ruczinski, I., Kooperberg, C., Fox, B.A., Bystroff, C., Baker, D.: Improved recognition of native-like protein structures using a combination of sequence-dependent and sequence-independent features of proteins. Proteins: Structure, Funct. Bioinform. **34**(1), 82–95 (1999)

25. Steinegger, M., Söding, J.: Mmseqs2 enables sensitive protein sequence searching for the analysis of massive data sets. Nat. Biotechnol. **35**(11), 1026–1028 (2017)

26. Valentinuzzi, D., Jeraj, R.: Computational modelling of modern cancer immunotherapy. Phys. Med. Biol. **65**(24), 24TR01 (2020)

27. Vaswani, A.: Attention is all you need. Advances in Neural Information Processing Systems (2017)

28. Wan, F., Kontogiorgos-Heintz, D., de la Fuente-Nunez, C.: Deep generative models for peptide design. Digital Discovery **1**(3), 195–208 (2022)

29. Wang, F., Wang, Y., Feng, L., Zhang, C., Lai, L.: Target-specific de novo peptide binder design with diffpepbuilder. J. Chem. Inf. Model. **64**(24), 9135–9149 (2024)
30. Watson, J.L., et al.: Broadly applicable and accurate protein design by integrating structure prediction networks and diffusion generative models. BioRxiv pp. 2022–12 (2022)
31. Wu, K.E., et al.: Protein structure generation via folding diffusion. Nat. Commun. **15**(1), 1059 (2024)
32. Yi, K., Zhou, B., Shen, Y., Liò, P., Wang, Y.: Graph denoising diffusion for inverse protein folding. In: Advances in Neural Information Processing Systems, vol. 36 (2024)
33. Zhang, C., Zhang, X., Freddolino, P.L., Zhang, Y.: Biolip2: an updated structure database for biologically relevant ligand-protein interactions. Nucleic Acids Res. **52**(D1), D404–D412 (2024)
34. Zhang, Y., Skolnick, J.: Scoring function for automated assessment of protein structure template quality. Proteins: Struct., Funct., Bioinform. **57**(4), 702–710 (2004)
35. Zhang, Y., Sanner, M.F.: Autodock crankpep: combining folding and docking to predict protein-peptide complexes. Bioinformatics **35**(24), 5121–5127 (2019)

Simulating Viral Evolution and Immune Escape Reinfection Dynamics Using Agent-Based Modelling

C. Malcolm Todd[1][iD], Yuan Tian[1][iD], Nathaniel Osgood[1,2][iD], Ian McQuillan[1][iD], and Lingling Jin[1(✉)][iD]

[1] University of Saskatchewan, Saskatoon, SK, Canada
`malcolm.todd@usask.ca`, `yut473@mail.usask.ca`,
`{osgood,mcquillan,lingling.jin}@cs.usask.ca`
[2] Centre for Forensic Behavioural Science and Justice Studies,
Saskatoon, SK, Canada

Abstract. Viral mutations and waning immunity play a key role in the spread of infectious diseases. Traditional compartmental models often assume that individuals acquire complete but temporary immunity after their infection, overlooking the complex dynamics of immune escape by emerging variants. To address this oversight, we built an agent-based model using empirical data from COVID-19 to investigate how viral evolution, mutation, and immune escape reinfections shape transmission dynamics. For the pathogen characteristics examined here, simulations with and without immune escape reinfections revealed that immune escape reinfections cause approximately 30% of infections and accelerate the accumulation of viral mutations. Sensitivity analyses using varying infection rates and evolutionary distances revealed that increasing the evolutionary distance required for immune escape reinfections caused a reduction in mutation counts. In addition, restricting agent interactions to localized connections in a ring-lattice network reduced infections by 47% and mutations by 95%. These findings demonstrate the importance of immune escape reinfections and agent-interaction networks in disease transmission, and offer insights to improve future epidemiological modelling, particularly in addressing mutations and their influence on transmission dynamics.

Keywords: reinfection dynamics · viral mutations · interaction networks · agent-based modelling · computer simulation

1 Introduction

The study of pathogen spread and immunity loss in a population has been modelled extensively using Susceptible-Exposed-Infected-Recovered-Susceptible

Supplementary Information The online version contains supplementary material available at https://doi.org/10.1007/978-981-95-0695-8_16.

(SEIRS) compartmental models [3]. Traditionally, these models represent waning immunity with first-order delays, where hosts remain completely immune either permanently or for an average duration before returning to the Susceptible state. However, real-world viral outbreaks can be more complex, limiting the accuracy of these models. For example, sometimes reinfection can occur shortly after recovery when a related strain with sufficient mutations can evade the immune system, termed *viral immune escape* [10]. Viral immune escape is an evolutionary outcome resulting from viral mutation when the right mutations are introduced into a virus' phenotype through mutation. This work addresses this limitation by developing an agent-based mutation-aware model for virus transmissions with immune escape dynamics.

During the COVID-19 pandemic, several prominent SARS-CoV-2 (COVID-19) variants of concern emerged through mutation, including Alpha, Beta, Delta, Gamma [9,18], and Omicron [6]. Several of these variants rose successively to represent the dominant variant at different periods during the pandemic, resulting in multiple waves as of December 2022 [8]. Each of these variants of interest contained several impactful mutations within COVID-19's spike protein, which is involved in the virus' ability to infect host cells [2,12]. For example, the Omicron variants that emerged later contained 30 mutations in the spike protein, increasing their infectiousness and ability to evade the immune system [5]. Given the stochastic nature of genetic mutation and its interplay with transmissibility and viral immune escape during pathogen spread, a virus' mutation rate represents a valuable feature for further study using simulation.

This research builds upon a standard SEIRS modelling architecture by introducing mutational mechanisms during pathogen spread to investigate the differences the mutation creates in the frequencies of a pathogen's infections, mutations, and immune escape reinfections. We developed the model using COVID-19 for context to assess the impact of different agent-interaction networks and to study the relationship between their topologies and outbreak outcomes. The key contributions of this work include:

1. Developing an agent-based and mutation-aware model of pathogen spread with a new limited host immunity mechanism.
2. Integrating evolutionary distances between pathogens to incorporate more transmission dynamics into epidemiological modelling.
3. Incorporating empirical agent-mobility patterns to examine how mobility-related behaviors influence transmission.
4. Quantifying the frequency of immune escape reinfection and the extent to which localized agent connections can lower mutation and reinfection counts.

2 Methodology

2.1 Model Architecture and Formulation

We constructed an agent-based COVID-19 transmission model to investigate the effects of viral immune escape of an initial virus phenotype introduced into a completely susceptible population. There are several reasons to choose agent-based modelling (ABM) over the more commonly used System Dynamics (SD) method in SIRS models. For example, ABM can capture stochasticity, which is essential to model the infrequent and random nature of mutation. Unlike SD models that rely on aggregate population dynamics, ABM provides a more granular view of the host population and their interactions. This view allows for the representation of agent mobility and different agent interaction networks while also enabling the tracking of individual agents' histories to help improve our understanding of transmission pathways [11]. In addition, ABM offers additive scalability when adding more agent features and demographics while avoiding the combinatorial explosion in SD models, which require stratification to add heterogeneity in demographic and population characteristics, leading to increased complexity. This scalability made ABM the preferable choice for studying the virus dynamics this research sought to examine.

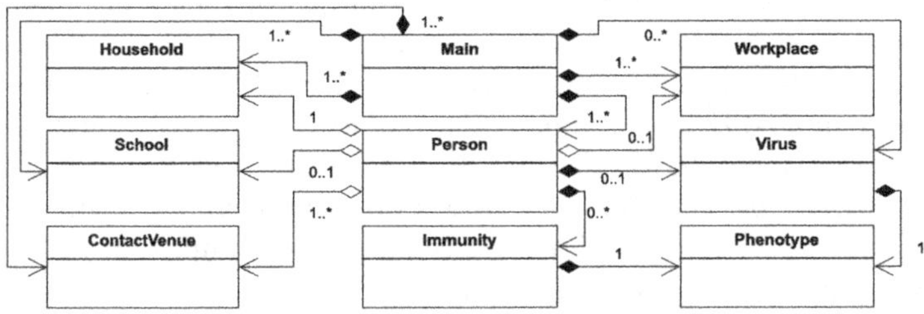

Fig. 1. UML diagram of the agent and class types, including their multiplicity.

Figure 1 provides an overview of the model architecture implemented in Any-Logic [1], illustrating the agent types and their relationships. The *Phenotype*, *Virus*, and *Person* agents capture the core elements of pathogen spread and the evolutionary changes of the virus within the host population. Similarly, the *Household, School, Workplace, ContactVenue*, and *Main* agents create the simulation's environment and experimental conditions.

The *Phenotype* agent abstracts a phenotype using three scalar values, each storing the net modification of its infectiousness, viral load characteristics, and propensity for viral shedding. These scalars quantify trait differences between phenotypes and model the effects of productive and detrimental mutations. We chose this representation to provide a higher-level view of genomic mutations through phenotypic traits while deliberately omitting the specifics of the underlying genotype that the mutations would modify. The key advantage of this abstraction lies in its ability to reduce the complexity of the evolutionary tree generated in the simulation by avoiding the need to assign each mutation with a unique phenotype identifier. By tracking the relative change to virus fitness through this representation, the model incorporates evolutionary dynamics by allowing selection pressure on the virus' infectiousness (transmissibility) to influence the prevalence of the phenotype.

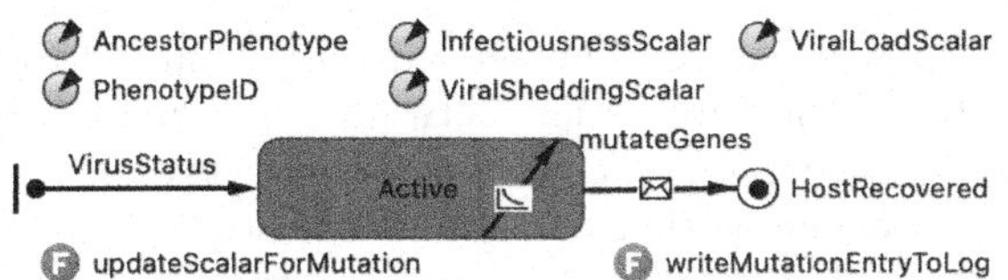

Fig. 2. The *Virus* agent type.

The *Virus* agent, as shown in Fig. 2, represents the pathogen that spreads through the host population. Each *Virus* agent stores several parameters, such as the *ancestorPhenotype*, *phenotypeID*, *infectiousnessScalar*, *viralLoadScalar*, and *viralSheddingScalar*. The *infectiousnessScalar*, *viralLoadScalar*, and *viralSheddingScalar* serve as multipliers for the feature they represent and are utilized to simulate the impact of the selective pressure created by differences between phenotypes in different virus strains. While active, *Virus* agents can mutate their phenotypes with a low probability, determined by the mutation rate. The *phenotypeID* parameter stores the virus' current *Phenotype* agent. When a mutation occurs, the current phenotype (stored in *phenotypeID*) is copied into the *ancestorPhenotype* to preserve its evolutionary history and allow for backtracking mutations. *Virus* agents mutate at a certain hazard rate while active by randomly selecting one of their phenotype's scalars (representing different viral traits) and whether the mutation is productive or detrimental. The selected scalar is then adjusted accordingly. Finally, a *Person* removes their stored *Virus* agent when they recover.

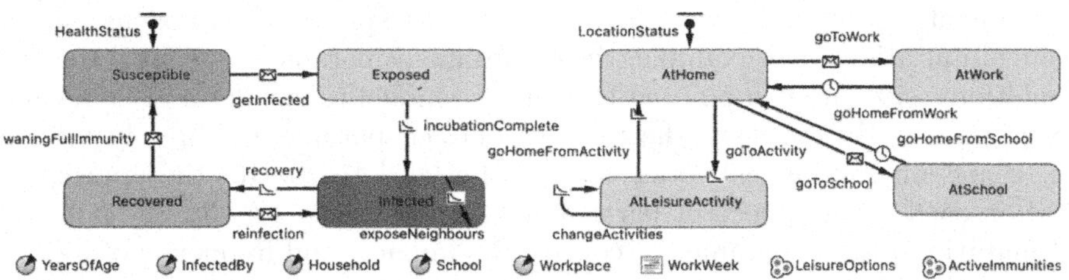

Fig. 3. The *Person* agent type.

The *Person* agent in Fig. 3 represents an individual host for the *Virus* agents. The *Person* agent has two state charts: *HealthStatus* and *LocationStatus*. The *HealthStatus* state chart tracks disease progression with four mutually exclusive states: Susceptible, Exposed, Infected, and Recovered. When a *Person* becomes infected, it stores a *Virus* with the same characteristics as the one from the *Person* who infected them. When a *Person* recovers, it removes the *Virus* and adds a *HostImmunity* instance to its *ActiveImmunities* list. Each *HostImmunity* stores a *Phenotype* and records the time of recovery to help determine when the *Immunity* will expire. The second state chart, *LocationStatus*, governs mobility patterns and interaction networks. The model has four location agents – *Household*, *Workplace*, *School*, and *ContactVenue* – which represent places where *Person* agents gather and interact. Each location agent tracks the individuals present at that location for a given period, forming local networks. These local networks facilitate the spread of infections based on host interactions within shared locations. Each *Person* belongs to a *Household*, which stores their cohabitants. Similarly, each *Person* is assigned either a *Workplace* or a *School*, depending on their age. Furthermore, every *Person* stores a collection of randomly selected *ContactVenues* in its *LeisureActivities* parameter, representing the other locations it can visit during simulation. During mobility, a *Person* removes itself from the list of connections at its origin location and then adds itself to the list at its destination. When another agent attempts to infect a *Person*, the infecting *Virus' Phenotype* is tested against each *HostImmunity* in the *Person*'s *ActiveImmunites*, with the infection or immune escape reinfection only occurring if none of the *Immunity* instances have a *Phenotype* with a distance below the required minimum evolutionary distance.

The *Main* agent is responsible for the setup, configuration, execution, and output of the results of all simulations performed by the model. During execution, the *Main* agent stores several populations, including the *People, Households, Schools, Workplaces, VirusInstances*, and *LeisureActivities* populations. Using these populations, the *Main* agent creates the environment for simulating the rise of viral mutations based on the underlying interactions between *Person* agents that control the dynamics of pathogen spread. The *Main* agent also provides numerous parameters to allow simulation scenarios to configure the model. Such parameters fall into several categories, including the simulation environment, the mobility of *Person* agents, the spread of pathogens, and the effects of mutations. For example, the environment parameters control the agent populations' size and can be used to scale the model to smaller and larger numbers of people. By contrast, the mobility-related parameters directly influence the agents' interaction networks and can be used to control the approximate duration each agent spends at particular locations daily. Finally, the pathogen- and mutation-related parameters control the impacts and frequency of infection and mutation during simulation.

2.2   Simulation Scenario Experiments

We conducted two simulation scenarios to evaluate how viral mutation and immune escape reinfections influence pathogen transmission dynamics:

1. The *Baseline* scenario served as a control condition with immune escape reinfections disabled, with an implied structure resembling that of a standard SEIRS model.
2. The *Immune Escape* scenario introduced structural changes by explicitly enabling viral immune escape reinfections, thereby allowing for assessment of the impact of these additional mechanisms on infection and mutation counts.

Table 1. Summary of model parameter values. Parameters featuring citations represent those configured based on COVID-19 resources and literature.

Category	Field name	Baseline value	Units
Environment	$PopulationSize$	2000	Persons
	$HouseholdSize$	4	Households
	$SchoolSize$	800	Schools
	$WorkplaceSize$	225	Workplaces
	$TotalNumberOfLeisureActivities$	10	ContactVenues
Mobility	$MeanWorkingAgeTimeAtHomeInHours$	15.8	Hours/Day
	$MeanWorkingAgeTimeAtSchoolInHours$	7.14	Hours/Day
	$MeanWorkingAgeTimeAtWorkInHours$	7.14	Hours/Day
	$MeanWorkingAgeTimeAtLeisureActivitiesInHours$	3.1	Hours/Day
	$MeanRetireesTimeAtHomeInHours$	20.1	Hours/Day
	$MeanRetireesTimeAtLeisureActivitiesHours$	3.9	Hours/Day
	$AvgLeisureActivitesVisitedPerDay$	2.0	ContactVenues/Day
Transmission	$InitialInfectionCount$	3	Infected agents
	$InfectionRate$ [17]	11.9%	Dimensionless
	$ContactsPerDay$	10	Contacts/Day
	$LatentPeriodInDays$ [14]	3.7	Days
	$MeanTimeOfInfectionInDays$ [20]	8.8	Days
	$MeanTimeOfImmunityInDays$ [19]	180	Days
Mutation	$TotalOfGeneLengths$	3789	Nucleotides
	$MutationRateModifier$ [17]	1.333%	Dimensionless
	$AnnualPerBaseMutationRate$ [13]	0.112	Nucleotides/Site-Year
	$MinimumMutationsToEvadeImmunity$ [12]	10.0	Mutations
	$NonSynonymousFraction$ [7]	63.6%	Dimensionless

The population initially starts immunologically naive. Both scenarios featured a two-year simulation period using the *mobility* network, and we ran 500 realizations per scenario to account for stochasticity. The *Immune Escape* scenario also served as the basis for sensitivity analyses concerning key model parameters. Table 1 details the parameters and configurations used in the model.

During simulation, the total mutation rate is the product of the *AnnualPerBaseMutationRate*, *NonSynonymousFraction*, and *TotalOfGeneLengths* mutation parameters. We chose a minimum evolutionary distance of 10 mutations as the threshold required for a *Virus' Phenotype* to achieve viral immune escape. This threshold comes from the Delta variant, which contains 10 defining mutations in its spike protein [12] and can evade host immunity [16]. To simulate more realistic daily mobility patterns in the *mobility* network, the model governs *Person* agent movements using transition rates based on empirical data from the 2022 Statistics Canada Table 5-10-0104-01 [4], which reports the average number of hours spent daily on various activities at different locations (e.g., home, work, and school). The model adjusts several transition rates for activities typically applicable to midweek behaviours to better mimic real-world activities, such as work and school hours, by dividing the total weekly hours across five days rather than seven. The model then controls the availability of these midweek transitions using a schedule that suspends them during weekends. Each agent maintains an average of 26 network connections but interacts with only a subset of them by making 10 *ContactsPerDay*, representing the daily interactions that drive transmission.

2.3   Sensitivity Analyses

We conducted sensitivity analyses to evaluate changes to the model's structure and parameter values based on the *Immune Escape* scenario, studying:

1. How changes to the hosts' interaction networks affected model outputs.
2. The impacts of changing the *MinimumMutationsToEvadeImmunity* and *InfectionRate* parameters on the model's results.

We performed a structural sensitivity analysis on the agents' interaction network by changing the network type that connects agents. For each network type, we ran 500 realizations of the model to study the network's impact on total infection, total mutation, and immune escape reinfection counts over the two-year simulation period. The analysed network types included the *ring-lattice, scale-free, small-world, random,* and *mobility* networks. Providing *Person* agents with mobility is treated as one network type and is disabled while simulating the other networks. We calibrated and validated the model to ensure that the average number of connections between *Person* agents in the *mobility* network was consistent with those used for other interaction networks. This calibration was necessary to compare the outcomes across network types fairly. The supplementary materials provide further details on the model's calibrations.

The first parameter sensitivity analysis explored the effects of varying the hazard rate of successful transmission between *Person* agents (the *infection rate*) on outbreak outcomes over a two-year simulation period. The infection rates ranged between 4.7% and 25.7%, with a step size of 1.0%. These rates were chosen based on the lower bound reported by Manski et al. [15], and the household rate reported among all variants by Miyahara et al. [17]. The second parameter sensitivity analysis examined the impact of the minimum number of mutations required for immune escape reinfections. This sensitivity analysis studies how changing the minimum evolutionary distance necessary for immune evasion affects infection and mutation counts. The parameter was varied from 5 to 35 mutations, with a step size of 1. We chose this range to test mutation counts similar to those in Omicron variants, which were greater than 30 [12]. During each analysis, we performed 500 model realizations using each parameter value.

3   Results

3.1   Simulation Results

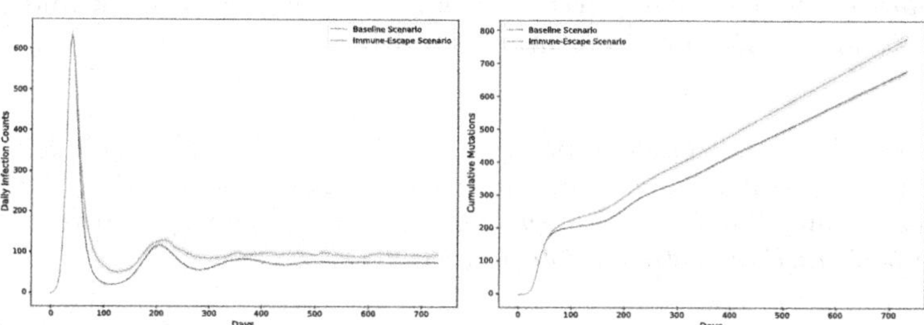

Fig. 4. Average daily infections and cumulative mutations for the *Baseline* (blue) and *Immune Escape* (orange) scenarios with 95% confidence intervals from 500 realizations.

Figure 4 presents the daily infection and cumulative mutation counts produced during the *Baseline* and *Immune Escape* scenario simulations. In the *Baseline* scenario, daily infection counts surged rapidly within the fully susceptible population. Following this initial wave, the level of infection declined due to a decreasing number of Susceptible *Person* agents, eventually stabilizing into an endemic state. Introducing immune escape reinfections in the *Immune Escape* scenario produced a similar initial infection wave; however, the immune escape reinfections also elevated the daily infection counts following the initial surge and produced greater uncertainty in the average daily infection counts compared to the *Baseline* scenario, as indicated by wider confidence intervals in daily infection counts.

The accumulation of mutations over time differed substantially between the *Baseline* and *Immune Escape* scenarios, reflecting the influence of immune escape reinfections. In the *Baseline* scenario, mutation counts surged rapidly during the virus' initial infection wave but increased more gradually once the virus established an endemic presence. The initial surge of infection produced approximately 30% of the total mutations before day 100. Although the *Immune Escape* scenario featured a similar initial surge, higher average infection counts following the initial wave caused mutation counts to diverge between scenarios. These results suggest a positive relationship between infection counts and the rate at which mutations accumulate, as evidenced by differences in their slopes after day 100. In the *Baseline* scenario, mutations accumulated at an average rate of 0.75 per day between days 100 and 730. However, mutations in the *Immune Escape* scenario accumulated at a rate of 0.87 per day over the same period.

Table 2 summarizes the median, mean, and standard deviation of the outcome measures per realization for both the *Baseline* and *Immune Escape* scenarios at the end of the two-year simulation period, based on 500 realizations per scenario.

The *Immune Escape* scenario produced a per-realization average of 2,740.49 immune escape reinfections out of 9,152.68 total infections, representing 29.94% of all infections. The *small-world* network was the most similar to the *mobility* network based on their medians, means, and standard deviations. By contrast, the *ring-lattice* deviated the furthest from the *mobility* network and provided significantly lower infections, mutations, and reinfections.

Table 2. Result of the *Baseline* and *Immune Escape* scenarios. *Differences in the distributions were statistically significant when compared against the *Baseline* using a two-sided Mann-Whitney U Test ($p < 0.05$). [1]Total Reinfection percentages were calculated as $Total Reinfections/Total Infections$.

Scenario	Outcome Measure	Median	Mean	Standard Deviation
Baseline	Total Infections	7,351.5	7,282.15	549.61
	Total Mutations	680.0	677.66	79.64
Immune Escape	Total Infections*	8,505.0	9,152.68	2,531.31
	Total Mutations*	752.5	776.88	180.19
	Total Reinfections	1,664.0 (19.56%)[1]	2,740.49 (29.94%)[1]	3,105.23

3.2 Sensitivity Analysis Results

Table 3 summarizes the structural sensitivity analysis results, which induced substantial variability across different network types. All networks exhibited significant differences in infections, mutations, and reinfections compared to the *mobility* network. The *ring-lattice* network resulted in notably lower infection, mutation and reinfection values, suggesting a more constrained spread and reduced evolutionary potential for the pathogen in this highly localized network structure. Conversely, the *random* network produced the highest median and mean values for infections, mutations, and reinfections, reflecting a higher chance of transmission due to its more randomized connectivity. The *small-world* network provided the most similar totals to the *mobility* network but still provided statistically significant differences from the *mobility* network in its distribution when performing a two-sided Mann-Whitney U test on their results.

Table 3. Structural sensitivity analysis results for different network types. *Differences in the distributions were statistically significant when compared against the *mobility* network using a two-sided Mann-Whitney U Test ($p < 0.05$). [1]Percentages were calculated as $Total Reinfections/Total Infections$.

Network Type	Outcome Measure	Median	Mean	Standard Deviation
Mobility	Total Infections	8,505.0	9,152.68	2,531.23
	Total Mutations	752.5	776.88	180.19
	Total Reinfections	1,664.0 (19.56%)[1]	2,740.49 (29.94%)[1]	3,105.23
Ring-lattice	Total Infections*	4,809.5	4,891.69	1,395.35
	Total Mutations*	433.0	436.11	119.13
	Total Reinfections*	102.5 (2.13%)[1]	517.19 (10.57%)[1]	888.36
Scale-free	Total Infections*	9,290.0	10,152.92	2,638.23
	Total Mutations*	822.5	849.34	167.99
	Total Reinfections*	2,293.0 (24.68%)[1]	3,590.36 (35.36%)[1]	3,590.09
Small-world	Total Infections*	8,878.0	9,568.08	2,535.98
	Total Mutations*	786.5	806.26	179.16
	Total Reinfections*	2,041.0 (22.99%)[1]	3,130.05 (32.71%)[1]	3,244.34
Random	Total Infections*	9,997.5	10,978.39	2,938.31
	Total Mutations*	864.0	902.83	182.39
	Total Reinfections*	2,767.0 (27.68%)[1]	4,309.16 (39.25%)[1]	4,162.02

Parameter sensitivity analysis revealed a positive correlation between infection rates and the infection and mutation counts. Figure 5 presents boxplots that illustrate the distribution of these counts across the range of infection rates explored. These counts also exhibited diminishing returns as infection rates increased, particularly for infection rates greater than 16.7%, where the medians in infection counts mostly plateaued and did not continue their previously upward trend. These diminishing returns were also present in the mutation counts; however, they did not plateau as strongly and continued to increase more slowly.

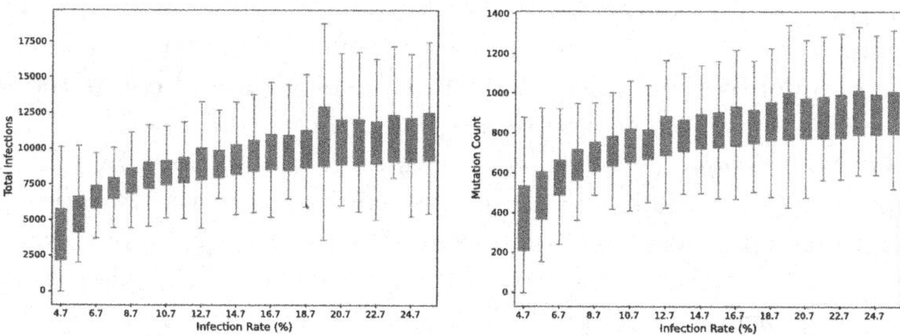

Fig. 5. Boxplots of infection and mutation counts from the parameter sensitivity analysis across varying infection rates.

Sensitivity analysis on the minimum evolutionary distance required to evade the host immunity suggested a negative relationship between the minimum evolutionary distance and the number of infections and mutations (seen in Fig. 6). As the minimum distance increased, both outcomes exhibited a marked decline in medians and overall variability. At lower minimum evolution distance thresholds (e.g., 5 to 12 mutations), the number of infections and mutations remained high, with wide interquartile ranges, indicating substantial variability in epidemic outcomes across realizations. As the minimum evolutionary distance increased beyond approximately 16 mutations, there was considerable narrowing in the distributions, as shown by reduced interquartile ranges and stabilized median values. This plateau suggested that the outcomes became less sensitive to further increases in minimum evolution distance beyond a certain threshold.

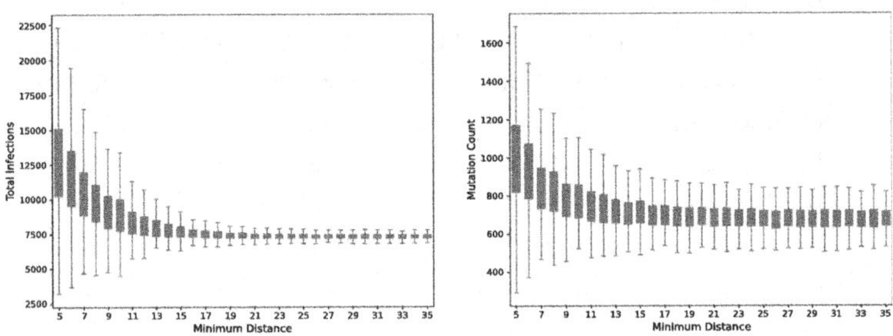

Fig. 6. Boxplots of infection and mutation counts from the parameter sensitivity analysis across varying minimum evolution distances.

4   Discussion and Conclusions

This research extends the traditional SEIRS modelling architecture for pathogen spread by incorporating viral mutation and immune escape mechanisms, parameterized using values from existing literature on COVID-19. This work explored how these mechanisms shape transmission dynamics once sufficient mutations allow immune escape reinfections. To investigate their impact, we constructed an agent-based model to simulate COVID-19 transmission and compared scenarios with and without immune escape reinfections.

The *Immune Escape* scenarios led to more uncertainty in daily infections and substantially increased their average counts compared to the *Baseline* scenario. The simulations also revealed a reinforcing feedback loop: higher average daily infection counts resulted in more mutations, increasing the likelihood of new immune escape variants emerging. These variants, in turn, created additional waves of reinfection, further increasing infection counts. This cycle accelerates viral evolution by enabling the virus to accumulate mutations more rapidly, increasing its ability to reach the evolutionary distances necessary for repeated immune escape reinfections. Across multiple realizations of the *Immune Escape* scenario, approximately 30% of the infections were immune escape reinfections. The proportion of immune escape reinfections highlights the need to reduce infection rates. By curbing transmission through vaccination and public health measures, interventions can help hold back the development of subsequent variants of concern by reducing the number of infections and mitigating the risk of immune escape variants creating future waves of reinfection.

Performing structural sensitivity analyses on different interaction networks revealed that the ring-lattice network led to fewer infections than the other network types. Restricting interactions to only localized network connections reduced median infection and mutation counts by roughly 47% and reinfections by 95%. These findings indicate that limiting the range of contacts to localized connections – such as the ring-lattice network – can slow transmission, mutations, and immune escape reinfection dynamics. Moreover, this highlights the importance of health interventions that promote or enforce more locality in host-to-host interactions, such as quarantines, social distancing, work-from-home advisories, gathering restrictions, and lockdowns. Sensitivity analysis on minimum mutation distance revealed that increasing the minimum evolutionary distances reduced the medians and variability in infection and mutation counts. These outcomes align with our expectation that a broader diversity of virus phenotypes must emerge before the virus can successfully evade host immunity when more considerable evolutionary distances are required. Our findings suggest a possible direction for future vaccine development that considers evolutionary distance to improve the robustness of public health interventions. Designing vaccines that target phenotypes at some evolutionary distance around a dominant strain could help provide hosts with a broader range of protection against immune escape variants by forcing the dominant strains to evolve further before evading a host's immune system. However, translating these distances into practical vaccine targets requires integrating detailed knowledge of antigenic variation and immunodominant epitope evolution – areas that remain under investigation.

Although the present model secured great advantages due to its stylized representation of mutation, future work could improve the model by enriching the representation of mutation to a higher dimensional space. By expanding the representation to several alleles, the model could provide insights into how the representation of diversity and mutation shape results. However, the high complexity and expense may limit the number of alleles that can be included in the near future. Integrating computational biology methods into the model could improve the modelling of selection pressures by evaluating how specific mutations influence viral fitness. For instance, a protein-to-protein assessment between the modified virus genes and the host species' receptor-binding domains could quantify how well they interact and assess the mutated phenotype's fitness.

References

1. AnyLogic Simulation Software @ONLINE. https://www.anylogic.com/ (2025)
2. Alexandridi, M., Mazej, J., Palermo, E., Hiscott, J.: The Coronavirus pandemic-2022: Viruses, variants & vaccines. Cytokine & Growth Factor Rev. **63**, 1–9 (2022)
3. Anderson, R.M., May, R.M.: Infectious Diseases of Humans: Dynamics and Control
4. Statistics Canada. Table 45-10-0104-01 Daily average time spent on various activities, by age group and gender, 2022 @ONLINE. https://doi.org/10.25318/4510010401-eng (June 2024)
5. Cui, Z., et al.: Structural and functional characterizations of infectivity and immune evasion of SARS-CoV-2 Omicron. Cell **185**(5), 860–871 (2022)
6. Fan, Y., Li, X., Zhang, L., Wan, S., Zhang, L., Zhou, F.: SARS-CoV-2 Omicron variant: recent progress and future perspectives. Signal Transduct. Target. Ther. **7**(1), 1–11 (2022)
7. Feng, Y., et al.: COV2Var, a function annotation database of SARS-CoV-2 genetic variation. Nucleic Acids Res. **52**(D1), D701–D713 (2024)
8. Giacomelli, A., et al. Mortality rates among COVID-19 patients hospitalised during the first three waves of the epidemic in Milan, Italy: A prospective observational study. PLOS ONE **17**(4), e0263548 (2022)
9. Ikbel Hadj Hassine: Covid-19 vaccines and variants of concern: a review. Rev. Med. Virol. **32**(4), e2313 (2022)
10. Hie, B., Zhong, E.D., Berger, B., Bryson, B.: Learning the language of viral evolution and escape. Science **371**(6526), 284–288 (2021). https://doi.org/10.1126/science.abd7331
11. Hinch, R., et al.: OpenABM-Covid19—an agent-based model for non-pharmaceutical interventions against COVID-19 including contact tracing. PLOS Comput. Biol. **17**(7), e1009146 (2021). https://doi.org/10.1371/journal.pcbi.1009146
12. Emma Hodcroft. CoVariants @ONLINE. https://covariants.org (Oct 2024)
13. Koyama, T., Platt, D., Parida, L.: Variant analysis of SARS-CoV-2 genomes. Bull. World Health Organ. **98**(7), 495 (2020)
14. Li, R., et al.: Substantial undocumented infection facilitates the rapid dissemination of novel coronavirus (SARS-COV-2). Science **368**(6490), 489–493 (2020)
15. Manski, C.F., Molinari, F.: Estimating the COVID-19 infection rate: Anatomy of an inference problem. J. Econom. **220**(1), 181–192 (2021)
16. McCallum, M., et al.: Molecular basis of immune evasion by the delta and kappa sars-cov-2 variants. Science **374**(6575):1621–1626, 2021
17. Miyahara, R., et al.: Sars-cov-2 variants and age-dependent infection rates among household and nonhousehold contacts. Emerg. Infect. Diseases **29**(8), 1648 (2023)
18. Ong, S.W.X., et al.: Clinical and virological features of severe acute respiratory syndrome coronavirus 2 (SARS-CoV-2) variants of concern: a retrospective cohort study comparing B. 1.1. 7 (Alpha), B. 1.351 (Beta), and B. 1.617. 2 (Delta). Clinical Infectious Diseases **75**(1), e1128–e1136 (2022)
19. Truszkowska, A., Zino, L., Butail, S., Caroppo, E., Jiang, Z.-P., Rizzo, A., Porfiri, M.: Predicting the effects of waning vaccine immunity against COVID-19 through high-resolution agent-based modeling. Adv. Theor. Simul. **5**(6), 2100521 (2022)
20. Walsh, K.A., et al.: The duration of infectiousness of individuals infected with SARS-CoV-2. J. Infect. **81**(6), 847–856 (2020)

Practical Colinear Chaining on Sequences Revisited

Nicola Rizzo[1]([✉]) [iD], Manuel Cáceres[2] [iD], and Veli Mäkinen[1] [iD]

[1] Department of Computer Science, University of Helsinki, Helsinki, Finland
{nicola.rizzo,veli.makinen}@helsinki.fi
[2] Department of Computer Science, Aalto University, Espoo, Finland
manuel.caceres@aalto.fi

Abstract. Colinear chaining is a classical heuristic for sequence alignment and is widely used in modern practical aligners. Jain et al. (J. Comput. Biol. 2022) proposed an $O(n \log^3 n)$ time algorithm to chain a set of n anchors so that the chaining cost matches the edit distance of the input sequences, when anchors are all the maximal exact matches. Moreover, assuming a uniform and sparse distribution of anchors, they provided a practical solution (`ChainX`) working in $O(n \cdot \mathrm{SOL} + n \log n)$ average-case time, where SOL is the cost of the output chain. This practical solution is not guaranteed to be optimal: we study the failing cases, introduce the *anchor diagonal distance*, and find and implement an optimal algorithm working in $O(n \cdot \mathrm{OPT} + n \log n)$ average-case time, where $\mathrm{OPT} \leq \mathrm{SOL}$ is the optimal chaining cost. We validate the results by Jain et al., show that `ChainX` can be suboptimal with a realistic long read dataset, and show minimal computational slowdown for our solution.

Keywords: sequence alignment · seed-chain-extend · sparse dynamic programming

1 Introduction

Colinear chaining is a popular technique to approximate the alignment of two sequences [4,7,10,12,17]. It is used as one critical step in practical aligners like `minimap2` [9] and `nucmer4` [11], and also speeds up exact alignment tools like `A*PA2` [6]. The main idea of the approach is to first identify short common parts between two sequences (seeds) as alignment anchors, and then to select a subset of these anchors that forms a linear ordering of seeds simultaneously on both sequences (colinear chain). A colinear chain can be converted into an alignment, but the approach is heuristic unless anchors, overlaps, and gaps are treated properly: namely, Mäkinen and Sahlin [10], while revisiting the work of Shibuya and Kurochkin [17], proposed a chaining formulation solvable in $O(n \log n)$ time (using sparse dynamic programming) considering both anchor overlaps and gaps between n anchors so that the chaining score equals the longest common subsequence (LCS) length when all maximal exact matches (MEMs) are used as

© The Author(s), under exclusive license to Springer Nature Singapore Pte Ltd. 2026
J. Tang et al. (Eds.): ISBRA 2025, LNBI 15757, pp. 203–216, 2026.
https://doi.org/10.1007/978-981-95-0695-8_17

anchors. This connection requires that the MEMs are not filtered by length, a common optimization used by practical tools: there are a quadratic number of MEM anchors on most pairs of sequences, so this approach does not directly yield an improvement over the classical dynamic programming approach [8] nor violates the conditional lower bound for LCS [3]. However, when a subset of MEMs is selected, for example by imposing uniqueness (see e.g. [11]) or a minimum length threshold, or even when the input is an arbitrary set of exact matches, the chaining formulation yields a non-trivial connection to a so-called *anchored* version of LCS [10].

Recently, Jain et al. [7] extended the colinear chaining framework by considering both overlap and gap costs, obtained analogous results to those of Mäkinen and Sahlin, and connected chaining to the classical Levenshtein distance (unit-cost edit distance), that—similarly to LCS—is also unlikely to be solved exactly in subquadratic time [5]. Jain et al. solved such chaining formulation in $O(n \log^3 n)$ time. Moreover, the authors provided a practical solution working in $O(n \cdot \text{SOL} + n \log n)$ average-case time, assuming a uniform and sparse distribution of anchors, where SOL is the cost of the output chain. Such solution was implemented in tool ChainX [1]. We show that the ChainX solution, although verified experimentally, is not guaranteed to be optimal.

We start by introducing the problem in Sect. 2; we reformulate the ChainX algorithm and show the failing cases in Sect. 3; in Sect. 4 we introduce the *anchor diagonal distance* and complete the strategy of ChainX to find a provably correct solution in the same $O(n \cdot \text{OPT} + n \log n)$ average-case time, where $\text{OPT} \leq \text{SOL}$ is the optimal chaining cost. Finally, in Sect. 5, we verify the experimental results of Jain et al. [7], perform tests on a realistic human dataset, and show that using maximal unique match (MUM) anchors our solution improves the chaining cost of approximately 2000 of 100k sampled long reads against a human reference.

2 Preliminaries

We denote integer interval $\{x, x+1, \ldots, y\}$ as $[x..y]$, or just $[x]$ if $x = y$. Given a finite alphabet Σ ($\Sigma = \{\text{A}, \text{C}, \text{G}, \text{T}\}$ for all examples of this paper), let T, Q be two strings over Σ of length $|T|$ and $|Q|$, respectively. We indicate with $T[x..y]$ the string obtained by concatenating the characters of T from the x-th to the y-th (strings are thus 1-indexed), and we call $T[x..y]$ a *substring* of T. We say that interval pair $a = ([q_s..q_e], [t_s..t_e])$ is an *exact match anchor*, or just anchor, between Q and T if $Q[q_s..q_e] = T[t_s..t_e]$, with $q_s, q_e \in [1..|Q|]$, $t_s, t_e \in [1..|T|]$,

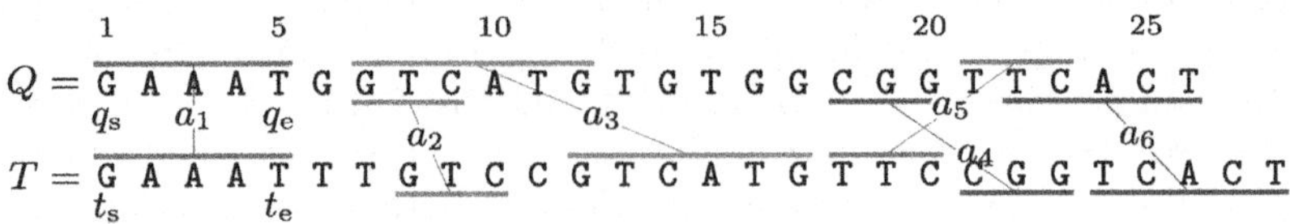

Fig. 1. A set $\mathcal{A} = \{a_1, \ldots, a_6\}$ of exact match anchors between strings T and Q.

$q_s \le q_e$, and $t_s \le t_e$. Moreover, we use a to denote a k-length anchor with $k = q_e - q_s + 1$. See Fig. 1.

Observation 1 (Exact match invariant). *The main invariant of an exact match anchor $a = ([q_s..q_e], [t_s..t_e])$ is that they indicate a substring of both Q and T of the same length, in symbols $q_e - q_s + 1 = t_e - t_s + 1$, which can be rewritten as $q_e - q_s = t_e - t_s$ and also $q_s - t_s = q_e - t_e$.*

A colinear chaining formulation is defined by the concept of *anchor precedence*—which sequences of anchors are coherent with an alignment and thus form a chain—and the concept of *chain cost*, the score of a chain when the gaps and overlaps between the anchors are interpreted as insertions, deletions, and substitutions of the alignment these represent.

Definition 1 (Anchor precedence [7]). *Let a, a' be two exact match anchors between $Q, T \in \Sigma^+$ such that $a = ([q_s..q_e], [t_s..t_e])$ and $a' = ([q'_s..q'_e], [t'_s..t'_e])$. Then we say that:*

- *a strictly precedes a', in symbols $a \prec a'$, if $q_s \le q'_s$, $q_e \le q'_e$, $t_s \le t'_s$, $t_e \le t'_e$, and strict inequality holds for at least one of the four inequalities;*
- *a weakly precedes a', in symbols $a_1 \prec_w a_2$, if $q_s \le q'_s$, $t_s \le t'_s$, and strict inequality holds for at least one of the two inequalities;*
- *a strongly precedes a', in symbols $a_1 \prec_{\text{ChainX}} a_2$, if $q_s < q'_s$, $q_e < q'_e$, $t_s < t'_s$, and $t_e < t'_e$ (the notation $\prec_{\text{ChainX}}$ derives from its use in the **ChainX** implementation).*

Note that $a \prec_{\text{ChainX}} a'$ implies $a \prec_w a'$ and $a \prec a'$. In Fig. 1, we have that $a_2 \prec a_3$, $a_2 \prec_w a_3$, but $a_2 \not\prec_{\text{ChainX}} a_3$. We refer the reader to [7] for insight on the difference between $\prec$ and $\prec_w$ (which will not be needed in this paper).

Problem 1 (Colinear chaining with overlap and gap costs [7]). Given $T, Q \in \Sigma^+$, a sequence of anchors $a_1, \ldots, a_c$ between Q and T is called a *colinear chain* (or just chain) if $a_i \prec a_{i+1}$ for all $i \in [1..c-1]$. The *cost* of a chain $A = a_1, \ldots, a_c$ is $\mathsf{gcost}(A) = \sum_{i=0}^{c} \mathsf{connect}(a_i, a_{i+1})$, where as a convention $a_0 = a_{\text{start}} = ([0..0], [0..0])$, $a_{c+1} = a_{\text{end}} = ([|Q| + 1..|Q| + 1], [|T| + 1..|T| + 1])$, and function connect on $a = ([q_s..q_e], [t_s..t_e])$, $a' = ([q'_s..q'_e], [t'_s..t'_e])$ is defined as $\mathsf{connect}(a, a') = \mathsf{g}(a, a') + \mathsf{o}(a, a')$ with

$$\mathsf{g}(a, a') = \max\big(0, q'_s - q_e - 1, t'_s - t_e - 1\big), \qquad \text{(gap cost)}$$

$$\mathsf{o}(a, a') = \big| \max\big(0, q_e - q'_s + 1\big) - \max\big(0, t_e - t'_s + 1\big)\big|. \qquad \text{(overlap cost)}$$

Given set $\mathcal{A} = \{a_1, \ldots, a_n\}$ of anchors between Q and T, the *colinear chaining problem with overlap and gap costs* consists of finding an ordered subset $A = a_1, \ldots, a_c$ of $\mathcal{A}$ that is a colinear chain and has minimum cost.

See Fig. 2 for an example of a colinear chain A and the computation of $\mathsf{gcost}(A)$. The colinear chaining problem can be also stated using weak precedence $\prec_w$ and strong precedence $\prec_{\text{ChainX}}$: to discriminate between the three versions, we say that the formulation of Problem 1 is *under strict precedence*, while

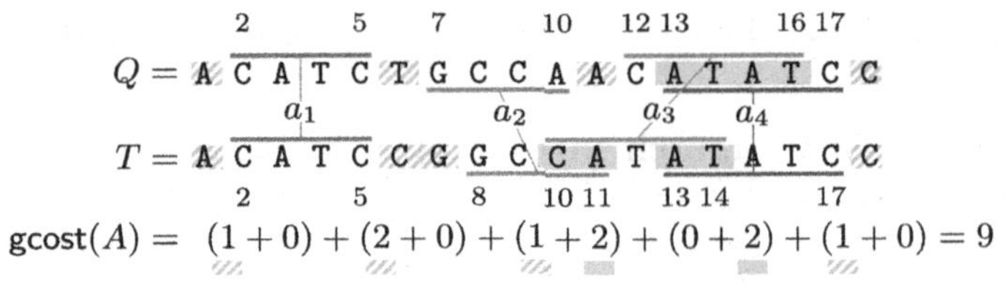

Fig. 2. Example of a chain $A = a_1, a_2, a_3, a_4$ (under all precedence notions introduced) and of cost $\mathsf{gcost}(A) = 9$, where the gaps and overlaps between consecutive anchors are marked with striped and solid background, respectively.

the latter variants are *under weak precedence* or *under* `ChainX` *or* strong *precedence.*

Next, we recall the main theoretical result from [7].

Problem 2 **(Anchored edit distance [7]).** Given $Q, T \in \Sigma^+$ and a set of anchors $\mathcal{A} = \{a_1, \ldots, a_n\}$, we say that for any anchor $a = ([q_s..q_e], [t_s..t_e]) \in \mathcal{A}$ and integer $k \in [0..t_e - t_s]$ the character match $Q[q_s + k] = T[t_s + k]$ is *supported.* Compute the optimal alignment between Q and T subject to the conditions that a match supported by some anchor has edit cost 0, a match that is not supported by any anchor has edit cost 1, and insertions, deletions, and substitutions have cost 1.

Theorem 1 ([7, Theorem 2]). *For a fixed set of anchors $\mathcal{A}$, the following quantities are equal: the anchored edit distance, the optimal colinear chaining cost under strict precedence, and the optimal colinear chaining cost under weak precedence.*

Theorem 1 connects the chaining of (exact) matches to unit-cost edit distance: if the anchors in input are the set of all maximal exact matches (MEMs), then all character matches are supported and thus the cost of the optimal colinear chain is exactly equal to unit-cost edit distance. Note however that Problem 1 and Theorem 1 admit an anchor set chosen arbitrarily. An alternative interpretation of the result is that breaking each anchor into many length-1 anchors, obtaining a setting equivalent to that of anchored edit distance, does not change the cost of the optimal solution to chaining nor anchored edit distance. This holds true even when we break the anchors into matches of different lengths, for example, if we break down a match of length 5 into two matches of length 3 and 2. Conversely, we can merge together anchors obtaining longer exact matches. We formalize this intuition into the following corollary of Theorem 1.

Corollary 1 (Equivalence under perfect chain operations). *For a given set of anchors $\mathcal{A} = \{a_1, \ldots, a_n\}$, consider the new set $\mathcal{A}'$ obtained by breaking down each anchor $a_i = ([q_s..q_e], [t_s..t_e])$ into length-1 anchors $a_{i,k} = ([q_s{+}k], [t_s{+}k])$ for $i \in [1..n]$, $k \in [0..q_e - q_s]$. Conversely, let $a = ([q_s..q_e], [t_s..t_e])$ and $a' = ([q'_s..q'_e], [t'_s..t'_e])$ be two anchors of $\mathcal{A}$ that form a* perfect chain, *that is, $a \prec a'$ and* $\mathrm{connect}(a, a') = 0$*: the overlap difference is 0 and there is no gap in Q nor* *in T. Then we can merge a and a' into a longer anchor $a \cdot a' := ([q_s..q'_e], [t_s..t'_e])$. Let $\mathcal{A}''$ be the set of anchors obtained from $\mathcal{A}$ by arbitrarily splitting anchors and merging those forming perfect chains. Then the anchored edit distance and the optimal colinear chaining cost of $\mathcal{A}$, $\mathcal{A}'$, and $\mathcal{A}''$ are the same value.*

Proof. The operation of breaking down any given anchor a into smaller anchors does not change the character matches of Q and T supported by the anchors. Similarly, the inverse operation of merging two anchors forming a perfect chain, even when they overlap, does not change the matches supported by the anchors. Since the corresponding set of supported character matches is not affected by these operations, Theorem 1 guarantees that the optimal colinear chaining cost stays the same as well. $\square$

3 Pitfalls of Practical Colinear Chaining

Let $\mathcal{A} = \{a_1, \ldots, a_n\}$ be a set of anchors between Q and T. Jain et al. [7] proposed a solution to Problem 1 on input $\mathcal{A}$ based on the following intuitive dynamic programming formulation. Assume the anchors of $\mathcal{A}$ are already sorted by increasing starting position q_s in Q. Then we can compute $C[i]$ for $i \in [0..n+1]$, equal to the cost of the optimal chain ending with anchor a_i, using the following recursion:

$$C[0] = 0$$
$$C[i] = \min_{j < i\,:\,a_j \prec a_i} C[j] + \operatorname{connect}(a_j, a_i) \qquad \text{for } i \in [1..n]. \qquad (1)$$

The formula is well-defined, since by construction $a_0 = a_{\text{start}}$ precedes all other anchors, and the correctness follows (for the most part) from the additivity of the connect function: the cost of adding anchor a' to an optimal chain ending at a, with $a \prec a'$, depends only on the gap and overlap costs between a and a'.

However, in [7] it is not proven explicitly whether all optimal recursive cases under the strict (or even weak) precedence are considered by looking only back in the ordered list of anchors, or in other words, that the correctness in computing $C[i]$ is still valid when skipping some or all anchors $a_j \prec a_i$ with $j > i$ and such that the starting positions q_s in Q of a_i and a_j are equal. Moreover, the actual implementation of `ChainX` [1] uses the strong precedence formulation $\prec_{\text{ChainX}}$ (see Definition 1). We leave the proof of equivalence of the optimal chaining cost under $\prec$ (or $\prec_{\text{w}}$) and $\prec_{\text{ChainX}}$ as future work for the extended version of this paper, and we concentrate on Problem 1 under $\prec_{\text{ChainX}}$.

Jain et al. also develop a practical solution to colinear chaining [7, Algorithm 2]. Intuitively, if we guess that the cost of the optimal chain is at most B, initially set to some fixed parameter B_{start}, then we do not have to consider all recursive cases from Eq. (1) in computing $C[i]$. In particular, we can skip all anchors $a_j \prec a_i$ such that $\operatorname{connect}(a_j, a_i) > B$, since they clearly cannot be used in a chain of cost at most B. If $a_j = ([q_s^j..q_e^j], [t_s^j..t_e^j])$ and $a_i = ([q_s^i..q_e^i], [t_s^i..t_e^i])$, Jain et al. relax the previous constraint to condition

$$q_s^i - q_s^j \leq B \qquad \text{(with } j < i \text{ and } a_j \prec_{\text{ChainX}} a_i\text{)}, \qquad (2)$$

208   N. Rizzo et al.

and argue that if a chain of cost at most B exists, then Eq. (2) holds for all adjacent anchors of an optimal-cost chain. They implement this modified computation of values $C[i]$ as the main loop of ChainX. After its execution, if $C[n+1] > B$, the algorithm updates guess B to $B \cdot \alpha$, with $\alpha > 1$ a constant ramp-up factor.

Assuming that:

- there are less anchors than $|Q|$ and $|T|$, that is, $n \leq \min\left(|Q|, |T|\right)$; and
- the anchors are distributed uniformly, that is, the probability that anchor a_i's interval in Q starts at position x (in symbols $q_s^i = x$) is equal to $1/|Q| \leq 1/n$;

then ChainX yields a $O(\mathrm{SOL}\cdot n + n \log n)$-time solution, where SOL is the chaining cost of the output chain (and $B_{\max}/\alpha < \mathrm{SOL} \leq B_{\max}$ with $B_{\max}$ the last value of B considered).

We note the following error in the main strategy of ChainX.

Observation 2. *Plugging condition $q_s^i - q_s^j \leq B$ (Eq. (2)) into the subscript of the* min *operator in Eq. (1) does not guarantee that all chains of cost at most B are considered, including optimal chains, and ChainX [7, Algorithm 2] is not always correct. Indeed, consider $T, Q \in \Sigma^+$ with $|T| = |Q| = 13$ and anchor set $\mathcal{A} = a_1, a_2, a_3, a_4$ with $a_1 = ([1..7], [1..7])$, $a_2 = ([9..12], [7..10])$, $a_3 = ([7..10], [9..12])$, and $a_4 = ([11..13], [11..13])$ as visualized in Fig. 3. Then* connect$(a_1, a_4) = 3$, *distance $q_s^4 - q_s^1$ is equal to 10, optimal chain a_1, a_4 has cost 3, whereas suboptimal chains a_1, a_2, a_4 and a_1, a_3, a_4 have cost 4. If $B_{\mathrm{start}} = 9$, recursive case* connect(a_1, a_4) *is skipped but the suboptimal chains are considered, and thus $C[n + 1] = 4 \leq 9 = B$ and the termination condition is met.*[1]

$$Q = A\ A\ A\ A\ A\ A\ T\ G\ T\ C\ T\ C\ C$$
$$T = A\ A\ A\ A\ A\ A\ T\ C\ T\ G\ T\ C\ C$$

(a) Anchors $\mathcal{A}$ in input.

$$Q = A\ A\ A\ A\ A\ A\ T\ G\ T\ C\ T\ C\ C$$
$$T = A\ A\ A\ A\ A\ A\ T\ C\ T\ G\ T\ C\ C$$
$$\mathrm{gcost}(A) = 0 + (1 + 1) + (0 + 2) + 0 = 4$$

(b) Suboptimal chain.

$$Q = A\ A\ A\ A\ A\ A\ T\ G\ T\ C\ T\ C\ C$$
$$T = A\ A\ A\ A\ A\ A\ T\ C\ T\ G\ T\ C\ C$$
$$\mathrm{gcost}(A) = 0 + (1 + 1) + (0 + 2) + 0 = 4$$

(c) Suboptimal chain.

$$Q = A\ A\ A\ A\ A\ A\ T\ G\ T\ C\ T\ C\ C$$
$$T = A\ A\ A\ A\ A\ A\ T\ C\ T\ G\ T\ C\ C$$
$$\mathrm{gcost}(A) = 0 + (3 + 0) + 0 = 3$$

(d) Optimal chain.

Fig. 3. Example where ChainX with $B_{\mathrm{start}} = 9$ returns a suboptimal chain.

---

[1] The implementation of ChainX, that uses value $B_{\mathrm{start}} = 100$, returns a suboptimal chain on a similarly crafted example where the initial runs of A in Q and T have length 98 and maximal unique match (MUM) anchors of length at least 3 are computed.

Note that substituting the condition of Eq. (2) with condition $q_s^i - q_e^j - 1 \leq$ B considers correctly all anchors a_j with gap cost in Q of at most B but is harder to compute efficiently, since $\mathcal{A}$ is sorted by q_s and all anchor overlaps in Q are also included: additionally sorting $\mathcal{A}$ by end position in Q (i.e. q_e) would make it simpler to consider all anchor overlaps, but the total number of comparisons[2] could be $O(n^2)$. On the other hand, when anchors of $\mathcal{A}$ are exact match anchors of a fixed constant length $k \in O(1)$ like in the case of minimizer anchors, using the simple condition $q_s^i - q_s^j \leq B +$ k does obtain optimality. In the next section, we show complete the strategy of $\texttt{ChainX}$ to obtain an optimal chain regardless of the anchors in input.

4   Chaining with the Diagonal Distance

In the previous section, we showed that $\texttt{ChainX}$ approximates a correct strategy—guessing an optimal chaining cost of B and considering only anchor pairs (a_j, a_i) of distance at most B in Q—but sacrifices correctness (Observation 2). Consider how function connect (Problem 1) is defined: given $a_j \prec a_i$, if a_j and a_i do not overlap in Q, in symbols $q_s^i - q_e^j > 0$, then we can replace the condition from Eq. (2) with $q_s^i - q_e^j - 1 \leq B$. On the other hand, if a_j and a_i do overlap in Q, then we do not want to consider all of these cases explicitly , as described at the end of the last section. Keeping this in mind, we tentatively rewrite Eq. (1) as

$$C[i] = \min\left(\text{gap}_Q(i), \text{overlap}_Q(i)\right), \qquad \text{with}$$

$$\text{gap}_Q(i) = \min\left\{ C[j] + \text{connect}(a_j, a_i) \;\middle|\; j < i : \begin{smallmatrix} a_j \prec a_i, \\ 0 \leq q_s^i - q_e^j - 1 \leq B, \\ \text{connect}(a_j, a_i) \leq B \end{smallmatrix} \right\},$$

$$\text{overlap}_Q(i) = \min\left\{ C[j] + \text{connect}(a_j, a_i) \;\middle|\; j < i : \begin{smallmatrix} a_j \prec a_i, \\ q_s^j \leq q_s^i \leq q_e^j, \\ \text{connect}(a_j, a_i) \leq B \end{smallmatrix} \right\}, \qquad (3)$$

where $\text{gap}_Q(i)$ considers all anchors a_j with no overlap in Q, and $\text{overlap}_Q(i)$ considers those with an overlap in Q. In the example of Fig. 1, if $B = 11$ then $\text{gap}_Q(6)$ considers a_4 and a_3 and $\text{overlap}_Q(6)$ considers a_5. To compute $\text{gap}_Q(i)$ we use the original strategy of $\texttt{ChainX}$, whereas we devise an efficient way of computing $\text{overlap}_Q(i)$ based on *diagonal distance*. This simple metric has been used in some chaining formulations (see [16]) but has not yet been connected to Problem 1, to the best of our knowledge. See also Fig. 4.

Lemma 1. *Given $Q, T \in \Sigma^+$, if $a = ([q_s..q_e], [t_s..t_e])$ is an exact match anchor between Q and T, we define the diagonal of a as $\text{diag}(a) = q_s - t_s$. Let $a = ([q_s..q_e], [t_s..t_e])$ and $a' = ([q'_s..q'_e], [t'_s..t'_e])$ be anchors between Q and T such that $a \prec a'$ or $a \prec_w a'$. Then:*

---

[2] While we do assume a uniform distribution of anchors, we do not assume anything about their length. Indeed, long MUM and MEM anchors are expected in the comparison of similar strings, intuitively resulting in many anchor overlaps.

- *(gap-gap case) if a and a' do not overlap in Q nor in T, in symbols $q_e < q'_s$ and $t_e < t'_s$, then* $\mathrm{connect}(a, a') = \mathrm{g}(a, a') = \max(q'_s - q_e - 1, t'_s - t_e - 1)$;
- *in all other cases,* $\mathrm{connect}(a, a') = |\mathrm{diag}(a) - \mathrm{diag}(a')|$, *a value that we call diagonal distance.*

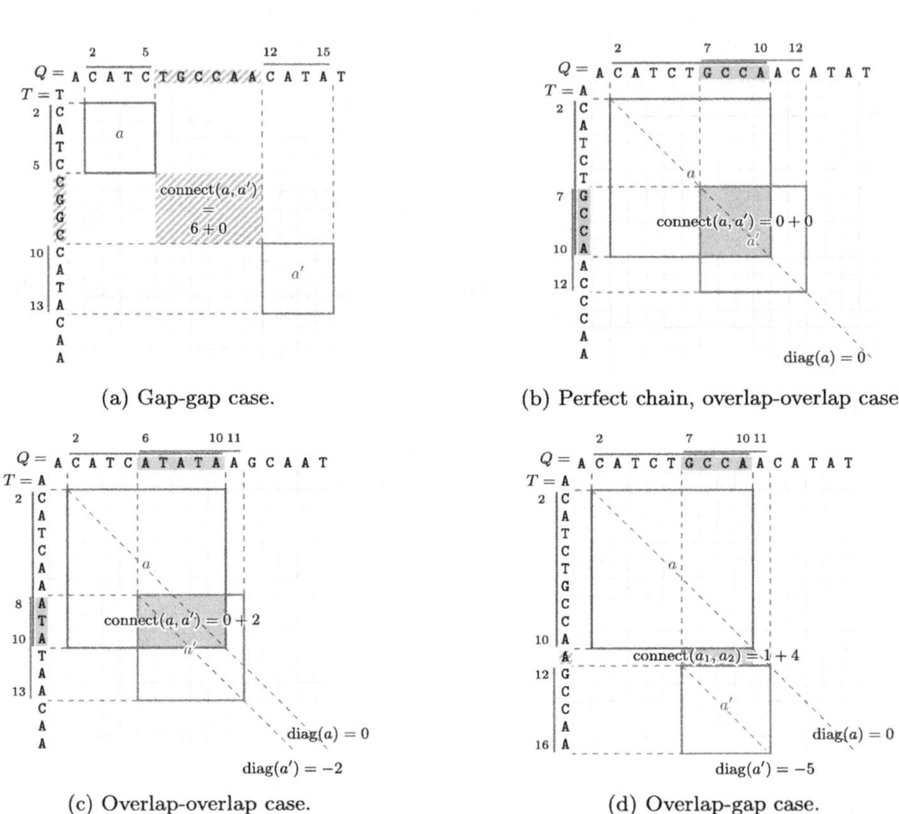

(a) Gap-gap case.

(b) Perfect chain, overlap-overlap case.

(c) Overlap-overlap case.

(d) Overlap-gap case.

Fig. 4. 2D interpretation of exact match anchors and of function $\mathrm{connect}(a, a')$, where a and a' are represented as squares. The gap-gap case is represented with striped background, and the overlap in the other cases is represented with solid background.

Proof. From the exact match anchor definition, it follows that $\mathrm{diag}(a) = q_s - t_s = q_e - t_e$ (Problem 1). We can prove the thesis by considering all possible overlap cases for the connect function, knowing that $a \prec a'$ or $a \prec_{\mathrm{w}} a'$ by hypothesis:

- (gap-gap) $\mathrm{connect}(a, a') = \mathrm{g}(a, a')$ directly from the definition of gap cost (Problem 1);

- (overlap-gap) if a overlaps with a' in Q but not in T, in symbols $q'_s \leq q_e \leq q'_e$ and $t_e < t'_s$, we have that

$$\text{connect}(a, a') = \text{g}(a, a') + \text{o}(a, a')$$
$$= t'_s - t_e - 1 + q_e - q'_s + 1 = (q_e - t_e) - (q'_s - t'_s)$$
$$= \text{diag}(a) - \text{diag}(a') = |\text{diag}(a) - \text{diag}(a')|$$

where the last equality follows due to the connect function being always greater than or equal to 0 (alternatively, note that $\text{diag}(a) = q_e - t_e > q'_s - t'_s = \text{diag}(a')$, since in the overlap-gap case $q'_s \leq q_e$ and $t_e < t'_s$);
- (gap-overlap) symmetrically, if a overlaps with a' in Q but not in T, we have that $\text{connect}(a, a') = \text{diag}(a') - \text{diag}(a) > 0$;
- (overlap-overlap) if a overlaps with a' in both Q and T, in symbols $q'_s \leq q_e \leq q'_e$ and $t'_s \leq t_e \leq t'_e$, we have that $\text{g}(a, a') = 0$ and

$$\text{connect}(a, a') = \text{o}(a, a') = \left| (q_e - q'_s + 1) - (t_e - t'_s + 1) \right|$$
$$= \left| (q_e - t_e) - (q'_s - t'_s) \right| = \left| \text{diag}(a) - \text{diag}(a') \right|.$$

Thus, function connect can be described by only two cases: gap-gap and all other cases. $\square$

Using Lemma 1, we can rewrite $\text{overlap}_Q(i)$ from Eq. (3) as

$$\text{overlap}_Q(i) = \min \left\{ C[j] + \text{connect}(a_j, a_i) \;\middle|\; j < i : \begin{array}{c} a_j \prec a_i, \\ q^j_s \leq q^i_s \leq q^j_e, \\ |\text{diag}(a_j) - \text{diag}(a_i)| \leq B \end{array} \right\} \quad (4)$$

requiring us to consider only anchors $a_j \prec a_i$ such that: (i) $j < i$ (recall that we assume anchors of $\mathcal{A}$ to be sorted by increasing order of q_s); (ii) a_j overlaps with a_i in Q; and (iii) the diagonal distance between a_i and a_j is at most B. This can be obtained by preprocessing in linear time the diagonals of all anchors in $\mathcal{A}$ and putting the anchors in at most n sorted buckets corresponding to their diagonals.

Our final optimization is obtained as follows: after $O(n \log n)$-time preprocessing, we can assume that for each diagonal D, there is at most one anchor a_j such that a_j overlaps a_i in Q and $\text{diag}(a_j) = D$.

Lemma 2. *Given instance* $\mathcal{A} = \{a_1, \ldots, a_n\}$ *of Problem 1 under* ChainX *precedence, we can obtain* $\mathcal{A}'$ *in* $O(n \log n)$ *time such that the anchored edit distance on* $\mathcal{A}$ *and* $\mathcal{A}'$ *coincide and* $\mathcal{A}'$ *is maximal under perfect chains, defined as follows: for any anchors* $a_i = ([q^i_s..q^i_e], [t^i_s..t^i_e]), a_j = ([q^j_s..q^j_e], [t^j_s..t^j_e]) \in \mathcal{A}'$ *such that* $a_i \prec_{\text{ChainX}} a_j$ *and* $\text{connect}(a_i, a_j) = 0$, *we have that* $q^i_e < q^j_s$ *and* $t^i_e < t^j_s$.

Proof. First, note that from Lemma 1 and Observation 1 it follows that $\text{connect}(a_i, a_j) = 0$ ($a_i \prec_{\text{ChainX}} a_j$), that is, a_i and a_j form a perfect chain, if and only if $\text{diag}(a_i) = \text{diag}(a_j)$ and $q_e = q'_s - 1$ (gap-gap case) or $q_e > q'_s - 1$ (other cases, see Fig. 4(b)). We construct $\mathcal{A}'$ by merging all anchors of $\mathcal{A}$ forming perfect chains as in Corollary 1 in $O(n \log n)$ time, by first sorting $\mathcal{A}$ by start position q_s in Q, then by stable sorting $\mathcal{A}$ by diagonal $\mathrm{diag}(a)$, and merging adjacent anchors with connect value equal to 0. The procedure terminates and merging order does not matter, since the binary relation $\mathrm{R} \subseteq \mathcal{A} \times \mathcal{A}$ containing pairs (a, a') such that a, a' are part of a perfect chain of $\mathcal{A}$ is an equivalence. The correctness follows from Corollary 1.

Theorem 2. *Given anchors $\mathcal{A} = a_1, \ldots, a_n$ between $Q \in \Sigma^+$ and $T \in \Sigma^+$ Algorithm 1 solves colinear chaining with overlap and gap costs (Problem 1) under $\prec_{\mathrm{ChainX}}$ on $\mathcal{A}$ in $O(\mathrm{OPT} \cdot n + n \log n)$ average-case time, assuming that $n \leq |Q|$, the anchors are uniformly distributed in Q, and the anchor set is maximal under perfect chains.*

Proof. The correctness follows from Eqs. (3) and (4): the inner loop (lines 8–30) computes $C[i]$ by considering only and all anchors a_j with $\mathrm{connect}(a_j, a_i) \leq B$; in particular, lines 17–23 compute $\mathrm{gap}_Q(i)$ by considering all anchor startpoints and endpoints at distance at most B in Q, and lines 24–26 compute $\mathrm{overlap}_Q(i)$ by considering all diagonals at distance at most B from $\mathrm{diag}(a_i)$ in the sorted sequence of diagonals computed in the form of buckets (line 2). The algorithm maintains at most one active anchor per diagonal (lines 12 and 30) due to the maximality under perfect chains (Lemma 2): for any given startpoint q_s and diagonal, there can be only one active anchor.

The $O(n \log n)$ term comes from sorting and bucketing the anchors in lines 1–2. Each iteration of the main loop (lines 6–33) takes $O(nB)$ time: the handling of diagonals takes $O(n)$ time in total; at most $2B + 2$ diagonals are considered for each $C[i]$ in the computation of $\mathrm{gap}_Q(i)$; and the average-case analysis of [7, Lemma 6] also holds for lines 17–23. Indeed, let $Y_{j,q}$ be the indicator random variable equal to 1 if anchor a_j ends at position q of Q, in symbols $q_e^j = q$, and 0 otherwise. Then, $\mathbb{E}[Y_{j,q}] = 1/|Q|$ for all $j \in [1..n]$ and $q \in [1..|Q|]$ due to the uniform distribution assumption. Similarly, if $X_{j,q}$ is defined as $Y_{j,q}$ but with condition $q_s^j = q$ (anchor a_j starts at position q), $\mathbb{E}[X_{j,q}] = 1/|Q|$.[3] If Z^i is the number of anchor startpoints q_s^j such that $q_s^i - B \leq q_s^j \leq q_s^i$ plus the number of endpoints q_e^j with $q_s^i - B \leq q_e^j \leq q_s^i$, then $Z^i = \sum_{j=1}^{n} \sum_{q=q_s^i - B}^{q_s^i} (X_{j,q} + Y_{j,q})$. Finally, if Z is the total number of anchors processed in lines 17–23, then

$$
\begin{aligned}
\mathbb{E}(Z) &= \mathbb{E}\left(\sum_{i=1}^{n} Z^i \right) \\
&= \sum_{i=1}^{n} \sum_{j=1}^{n} \sum_{q=q_s^i - B}^{q_s^i} \left(\mathbb{E}(X_{j,q}) + \mathbb{E}(Y_{j,q}) \right) && \text{linearity of expectation} \\
&= \frac{n^2 \cdot 2(B+1)}{|Q|} && \mathbb{E}(X_{j,q}), \mathbb{E}(Y_{j,q}) = \frac{1}{|Q|} \\
&\leq 2n(B+1) && n \leq |Q|
\end{aligned}
$$

---

[3] The algorithm can be further engineered to avoid these comparisons and the use of $X_{j,q}$. However the average-case time complexity analysis stays the same.

Algorithm 1: Practical colinear chaining on sequences revisited.

Input: Anchors $\mathcal{A} = \{a_1, \ldots, a_n\}$ between $Q \in \Sigma^+$ and $T \in \Sigma^+$ that are maximal under perfect chains (Lemma 2) and parameters B_{start} (initial guess), $\alpha > 1$ (ramp-up factor).

Output: Maximum cost $\mathbf{gcost}(A)$ of a chain $A = \overline{a}_1, \ldots, \overline{a}_c$ under $\prec_{\text{ChainX}}$.

1   Sort pairs (q_{s}, i) and (q_{e}, i), for $a_i = ([q_{\text{s}}..q_{\text{e}}], [t_{\text{s}}..t_{\text{e}}]) \in \mathcal{A}$, into array $\mathbf{A}[1..2n]$ by first component;

2   Sort pairs $(\text{diag}(a), a)$, for $a = ([q_{\text{s}}..q_{\text{e}}], [t_{\text{s}}..t_{\text{e}}]) \in \mathcal{A}$, into non-empty buckets $\mathcal{D}_1$, $\ldots, \mathcal{D}_d$ by first component, with the buckets ordered by increasing $\text{diag}(a)$, and let $\text{bucket}(a) = f$ if anchor a belongs to the f-th bucket, and $\text{diag}(f) = \text{diag}(a)$ for any anchor a in bucket $\mathcal{D}_f$;

3   $B \leftarrow B_{\text{start}}$;

4   Initialize $\mathbf{C}[1..n+1]$ to values $+\infty$; $\triangleright$ recursive values from Eq. (3)

5   Initialize $\mathbf{D}[1..d]$ to values $\bot$; $\triangleright$ $\mathbf{D}[f] = i$ if anchor $a_i \in \mathcal{D}_f$ is active

6   **repeat**

7      $\mathbf{C}[n+1] \leftarrow +\infty$;

8   **for** $k \leftarrow 1$ **to** $2n$ **do** $\triangleright$ iterate over all startpoint q_{s} and endpoints q_{e}

9         $(q, i) \leftarrow \mathbf{A}[k]$;

10        $([q_{\text{s}}..q_{\text{e}}], [t_{\text{s}}..t_{\text{e}}]) \leftarrow a_i$;

11   **if** $q = q_s$ **then** $\triangleright$ if startpoint, update active anchor and compute $C[i]$

12           $\mathbf{D}[\text{bucket}(a_i)] \leftarrow i$;

13   **if** $\text{connect}(a_0, a_i) \leq B$ **then** $\triangleright$ initial anchor $a_0 = a_{\text{start}}$

14             $\mathbf{C}[i] \leftarrow \text{connect}(a_0, a_i)$;

15   **else**

16             $\mathbf{C}[i] \leftarrow +\infty$;

17   **for** $k' \leftarrow i - 1$ **downto** 1 **do** $\triangleright$ iterate over all endpoints q_{e}^j at distance $\leq B$

18             $(q', j) \leftarrow A[k']$;

19             $([q'_{\text{s}}..q'_{\text{e}}], [t'_{\text{s}}..t'_{\text{e}}]) \leftarrow a_j$;

20   **if** $q_s - q'_e > B$ **then** $\triangleright$ check distance

21   **break**;

22   **if** $q' = q'_e$ *and* $a_j \prec a_i$ *and* $\text{connect}(a_j, a_i) \leq B$ **then**

23               $\mathbf{C}[i] \leftarrow \min\big(\mathbf{C}[i], \mathbf{C}[j] + \text{connect}(a_j, a_i)\big)$; $\triangleright$ compute $\text{gap}_Q(i)$

24   **for** $f \in [1..d] : |\text{diag}(f) - \text{diag}(a_i)| \leq B$ **do**

25   **if** $\mathbf{D}[f] \neq \bot$ **then**

26               $\mathbf{C}[i] \leftarrow \min\big(\mathbf{C}[i], \mathbf{C}[\mathbf{D}[f]] + |\text{diag}(f) - \text{diag}(a_i)|\big)$; $\triangleright$ compute $\text{overlap}_Q(i)$

27   **if** $\text{connect}(a_i, a_{n+1}) \leq B$ **then** $\triangleright$ final anchor $a_{n+1} = a_{\text{end}}$

28             $\mathbf{C}[n+1] \leftarrow \min\big(\mathbf{C}[n+1], \mathbf{C}[i] + \text{connect}(a_i, a_{n+1})\big)$;

29   **if** $q = q_e$ **then** $\triangleright$ if endpoint, remove as active anchor

30           $\text{bucket}(a_i) \leftarrow \bot$;

31      $B_{\text{last}} \leftarrow B$;

32      $B \leftarrow B \cdot \alpha$;

33 **until** $\mathbf{C}[n+1] \leq B_{\text{last}}$;

34 **return** $\mathbf{C}[n+1]$;

---

and thus the loop 17–23 takes $O(nB)$ average time. The time complexity of the main computation (lines 6–34) is then $O\Big(B_{\text{start}} \cdot n \cdot \big(1 + \alpha + \alpha^2 + \cdots + \alpha^{\lceil \log_\alpha \text{OPT} \rceil}\big)\Big) = O(n \cdot \text{OPT})$. $\square$

Given anchor set $\mathcal{A}$, it takes $O(\text{OPT} \cdot n + n \log n)$ total time to preprocess it as per Lemma 2 and solve the chaining problem with Theorem 2. We leave the proof that chaining under strict precedence $\prec$ is equivalent to chaining under ChainX precedence $\prec_{\text{ChainX}}$, implying that the transformation of Lemma 2 maintains the optimal chain cost under $\prec_{\text{ChainX}}$, to the extended version this paper.[4]

5   Experiments

We implemented Algorithm 1 and integrated it in a fork of the C++ tool ChainX, available at https://github.com/algbio/ChainX. This provably correct version of ChainX can be invoked with flag --optimal. We replicated the original experiment of ChainX [7, Table 2] in Table 1 to compare ChainX to the --optimal version, that we denote as ChainX-opt, on the University of Helsinki cluster ukko, limiting the task to 64 GB of memory, 4 cores, using the Lustre Vakka cluster filesystem (comparable to SSD performance). Since the original parameters $B_{\text{start}} = 100$ (initial guess) and $\alpha = 4$ (ramp-up factor) were hard-coded constants, we tested the variant of ChainX-opt that we denote as ChainX-opt* using variable B_{start} equal to the maximum between 100 and the inverse coverage of query Q (number of bases that are not covered by any anchor) multiplied by 1.5. A similar optimization was previously introduced and used in chainx-block-graph [2, 15]. All costs of the output chains in the original experiments have the same exact value as reported by ChainX-opt (and ChainX-opt*), verifying the results of the work by Jain et al. The implementation of Algorithm 1 is, naturally, slightly more computationally expensive, however the optimization introduced for ChainX-opt* appears to mitigate the additional computations. We successfully replicated [7, Table 1] with analogous results, that we do not show here for the sake of space.

We additionally tested the semiglobal mode of ChainX and ChainX-opt* on the T2T-CHM13 reference [13, 14] and a sample of 100k PacBio HiFi (run m64004[5]) reads used in the assembly of the HG002 reference [14]. On this dataset, ChainX and ChainX-opt* took 1 610 and 1 631 s, respectively, 49 GB of memory, and had an average number of iterations of the main loop of 4.39 and 2.61, respectively. ChainX-opt* improved the optimal chaining cost of 2 297 long reads out of 100 000 (2.30 %). For these improved reads, the distribution of the absolute value improvement—the ChainX-opt* cost minus the ChainX

---

[4] Even though we do not prove that the optimal chains of $\mathcal{A}$ and $\mathcal{A}'$ in Lemma 2 under ChainX precedence have the same cost, the overall goal of finding the anchored edit distance is correctly maintained.

[5] Available at https://s3-us-west-2.amazonaws.com/human-pangenomics/index.html?prefix=T2T/scratch/HG002/sequencing/hifi/.

Table 1. Replication of [7, Table 2], using MUM seeds of length at least 20. Label avg. iters refers to the average number of iterations of the main loop of each algorithm. All modes output a chain with the same cost, verifying the original results.

Similarity	ChainX			ChainX-opt			ChainX-opt*		
	time (s)	space (MB)	avg. iters	time (s)	space (MB)	avg. iters	time (s)	space (MB)	avg. iters
Semiglobal sequence comparison, sequence sizes 10^4 (100 queries) and $5 \cdot 10^6$ (reference)									
90–100%	0.89	57.816	3.87	0.91	57.592	3.87	0.87	57.788	1.00
80–90%	0.98	57.672	5.00	0.98	57.824	5.00	1.02	57.604	1.00
75–80%	1.01	57.464	5.00	0.98	57.808	5.00	1.03	57.820	1.00
Global sequence comparison, sequence sizes 10^6 (100 queries and reference)									
90–100%	13.53	120.976	8.00	12.84	121.104	8.00	12.28	120.820	1.00
80–90%	27.37	120.932	8.00	37.20	120.812	8.00	23.38	121.092	1.00
75–80%	13.53	120.976	8.00	12.84	121.104	8.00	12.28	120.820	1.00

cost—presents a minimum of 11, first quartile of 835, median of 1888, third quartile of 4080, and maximum of 6394. The relative improvement—ChainX-opt* cost divided by the ChainX cost—presents statistics of 1.04 (minimum), 18.39 (first quartile), 186.00 (median), 663.86 (third quartile), and 6293.00 (maximum). These results show that cases where the ChainX solution fails occur in realistic data.

Acknowledgements. This project has received funding from the European Union's Horizon Europe research and innovation programme under grant agreement No 101060011 (TeamPerMed) and from the Helsinki Institute for Information Technology (HIIT).

References

1. ChainX. GitHub repository. https://github.com/at-cg/ChainX. Accessed 25 Mar 25
2. SRFAligner. GitHub repository. https://github.com/algbio/SRFAligner. Accessed 25 Mar 25
3. Abboud, A., Backurs, A., Williams, V.V.: Tight hardness results for LCS and other sequence similarity measures. In: FOCS 2015, pp. 59–78. IEEE Computer Society (2015)
4. Abouelhoda, M.I., Ohlebusch, E.: Chaining algorithms for multiple genome comparison. J. Discrete Algorithms 3(2), 321–341 (2005). CPM Special Issue
5. Bringmann, K., Künnemann, M.: Quadratic conditional lower bounds for string problems and dynamic time warping. In: FOCS 2015, pp. 79–97. IEEE Computer Society (2015)
6. Koerkamp, R.G., Ivanov, P.: Exact global alignment using A* with seed heuristic and match pruning. Oxford Bioinformatics (2024)
7. Jain, C., Gibney, D., Thankachan, S.V.: Algorithms for colinear chaining with overlaps and gap costs. J. Comput. Biol. **29**(11), 1237–1251 (2022)

8. Kucherov, G.: Evolution of biosequence search algorithms: a brief survey. Bioinformatics **35**(19), 3547–3552 (2019)
9. Li, H.: Minimap2: pairwise alignment for nucleotide sequences. Bioinform. **34**(18), 3094–3100 (2018)
10. Mäkinen, V., Sahlin, K.: Chaining with overlaps revisited. In: CPM 2020, vol. 161. LIPIcs, pp. 25:1–25:12. Schloss Dagstuhl - Leibniz-Zentrum für Informatik (2020)
11. Marçais, G., Delcher, A.L., Phillippy, A.M., Coston, R., Salzberg, S.L., Zimin, A.: MUMmer4: a fast and versatile genome alignment system. PLoS Comput. Biol. **14**(1), e1005944 (2018)
12. Myers, G., Miller, W.: Chaining multiple-alignment fragments in sub-quadratic time. In: SODA '95, pp. 38–47, USA (1995). Society for Industrial and Applied Mathematics
13. Nurk, S., et al.: The complete sequence of a human genome. Science **376**(6588), 44–53 (2022)
14. Rhie, A., et al.: The complete sequence of a human y chromosome. Nature **621**(7978), 344–354 (2023)
15. Rizzo, N., Cáceres, M., Mäkinen, V.: Exploiting uniqueness: seed-chain-extend alignment on elastic founder graphs. bioRxiv, pp. 2024–11 (2024)
16. Sahlin, K., Baudeau, T., Cazaux, B., Marchet, C.: A survey of mapping algorithms in the long-reads era. Genome Biol. **24**(1), 133 (2023)
17. Shibuya, T., Kurochkin, I.: Match chaining algorithms for cdna mapping. In: Algorithms in Bioinformatics, pp. 462–475. Springer, Heidelberg (2003)

EnzHier: Accurate Enzyme Function Prediction Through Multi-scale Feature Integration and Hierarchical Contrastive Learning

Hongyu Duan[1], Ziyan Li[1], Yixuan Wu[1], Bozhen Ren[1], Wen Chen[2], Fanghua Wang[2], Dongming Lan[2], Yonghua Wang[3], and Li C. Xia[1(✉)] [iD]

[1] Department of Statistics and Financial Mathematics, School of Mathematics, South China University of Technology, Guangzhou 510640, China
`lcxia@scut.edu.cn`
[2] School of Food Science and Engineering, South China University of Technology, Guangzhou 510640, Guangdong, China
[3] School of Biology and Biological Engineering, South China University of Technology, Guangzhou 510006, Guangdong, China

Abstract. Accurate enzyme function prediction is essential for enzyme design and discovery. Existing methods face challenges with understudied enzyme families and multifunctional enzymes. We present EnzHier, a machine learning model that combines multi-scale feature integration with hierarchical triplet loss to predict Enzyme Commission (EC) numbers. By leveraging the hierarchical structure of EC classifications and multi-scale sequence similarity, EnzHier captures both local motifs and global sequence patterns. EnzHier outperforms state-of-the-art methods by achieving a 23% higher F1-score on benchmark cross-validation, and exhibits superior generalizability in external validations. The model also has high performance with challenging cases, correctly classifying difficult halogenases and identifying multifunctional enzymes like farnesyl pyrophosphate synthase–areas where other models often fail. Overall, EnzHier provides a robust and interpretable tool for enzyme function prediction, particularly for solving challenging cases where previous methods have shown limitations. EnzHier is publicly available at https://github.com/labxscut/EnzHier.

Keywords: Enzyme Function Prediction · Hierarchical Triplet Loss · Contrastive Learning · Multi-Scale Feature Integration

1 Introduction

Accurate enzyme function prediction is crucial for advancing enzyme design and discovery, and has far-reaching implications in food science, drug development,

Supplementary Information The online version contains supplementary material available at https://doi.org/10.1007/978-981-95-0695-8_18.

and other areas of biotechnology [1,2]. The Enzyme Commission (EC) numbering system [3], a four-level hierarchical scheme, encapsulates current knowledge of catalytic function. By grouping enzymes according to the reactions they catalyze, the EC system clarifies functional relationships within biological systems and supports applications in biochemistry, pharmacology, and industrial biotechnology. However, predicting enzyme function as an EC number remains an enduring challenge, particularly for enzymes from understudied families or those exhibiting multifunctional activities, with a wide gap of such knowledge in databases [4–7].

Traditional sequence homologyâĂŞbased methods (e.g. Blast [8,9]) remain widely used but exhibit significant limitations. Because accurate sequence-based function prediction demands high sequence identity ($\geq$50–60%) [10], these approaches suffer three critical drawbacks: they often misclassify when sequence similarity is moderate, lack adequate reference data for understudied enzymes, and fail to capture complex relationships in multifunctional enzymes when similarity signals are ambiguous. These constraints underscore the need for methods that extend beyond simple sequence similarity metrics.

To overcome these drawbacks, supervised learning approaches leveraging embedded sequence features have emerged as effective alternatives. Recognized methods such as HDMLF [11], DeepEC [12], DeepECTransformer [13], among others [14–16], exploited deep learning architectures like transformers and graph learning. Although these methods provide greater scalability and predictive power than sequence similarity based methods, they still rely heavily on large, well-annotated datasets, which are often limited for many enzymes. Consequently, their generalizability remains constrained, particularly for enzymes from underexplored families or those exhibiting multiple catalytic activities.

More recently, self-supervised learning techniques [17–19], including autoregressive [20] and contrastive learning [21,22], have emerged as a powerful alternative. Models such as CLEAN [21] use contrastive objectives to differentiate enzyme functions via positive and negative sample pairs [23]. Although these methods show enhanced performance on imbalanced datasets and understudied enzymes, they still fail to predict fine-grained enzyme functions or multifunctional enzymes accurately, because they do not explicitly model the EC hierarchy's subtle, multi-level relationships [24]. This shortcoming has limited their generalizability, a trend especially clear on external benchmarks like New-392 and Price-149, where CLEAN's performance drops significantly.

The fundamental limitation of existing contrastive learning approaches lies in their treatment of enzyme functions as flat, independent categories within the embedding space. For instance, consider three enzymes: EC 2.5.1.1 (dimethylallyltransferase), EC 2.5.1.10 (farnesyltransferase), and EC 1.1.1.86 (ketol-acid reductoisomerase). Standard contrastive learning methods position these enzymes equidistantly in the embedding space, failing to reflect their hierarchical functional relationships. A hierarchical approach would recognize that EC 2.5.1.1 and EC 2.5.1.10 both catalyze prenyl group transfers and differ only at the fourth EC level, indicating substrate specificity, whereas EC 1.1.1.86 differs at the second level, representing a distinct reaction class. By adjusting the margin boundaries in the embedding space to account for EC-level similarities, such that enzymes sharing more EC levels are positioned closer together, the model can more accurately capture the nuanced relationships inherent in enzyme functions. This information about EC hierarchy is found to be effective in improving model performance with supervised approaches [11,14]

Following this rationale, we integrate information from the EC hierarchy into a triplet contrastive loss [25], dynamically adjusting the distance margins in the embedding space based on the hierarchical similarity of the enzyme (Fig. 1). Our approach preserves the biochemical relationships within the EC hierarchy, enabling more accurate predictions in areas where conventional methods typically fail. Based on that, we introduce EnzHier, a novel machine learning model that outperforms existing methods on benchmark datasets. EnzHier performs particularly well in challenging cases, correctly identifying all functions of GGPP synthase and achieving superior prediction accuracy for difficult halogenase families. In a related independent work, hierarchical multilabel contrastive learning was found to be effective in predicting enzyme function, alphabet with smaller datasets [26].

2 Methods

2.1 Benchmark

We used 227,362 protein sequences from the SwissProt database [27], reserving 20% (45,472 sequences) as a test set and using 80% (181,890 sequences) for training. To prevent data leakage, we require at most 40% sequence similarity between the kept-out set and the training set. Two independent datasets served for external validation: NEW-392 (14.8% multifunctional enzymes) and Price-149 (2.01% multifunctional enzymes) [28].

Enzymes were categorized into common (>100 sequences) and rare (<100 sequences) classes, and we constructed a dedicated dataset of multifunctional enzymes carrying multiple EC numbers. This stratification enabled evaluation of EnzHier's performance on both well-represented and understudied families and analysis under varying data sparsity conditions, focusing on multifunctional enzyme prediction accuracy. For comprehensive benchmarking, we compared EnzHier against state-of-the-art methods including CLEAN [21], DeepEC [12], ECPred [29], and BLAST-based approaches [9].

2.2 Hierarchical Triplet Loss

We developed a novel hierarchical triplet loss (HTL) to optimize enzyme embeddings representing the hierarchical nature of EC numbers. This function incorporates normalized similarity between EC numbers, weighted by their respective hierarchical levels (Fig. 1c). Specifically, for each anchor–positive–negative enzyme triplet, the HTL function $\mathcal{L}$ consists of the squared embedding distance between the anchor $z_a^{(i)}$ and positive $z_p^{(i)}$, the squared distance between the

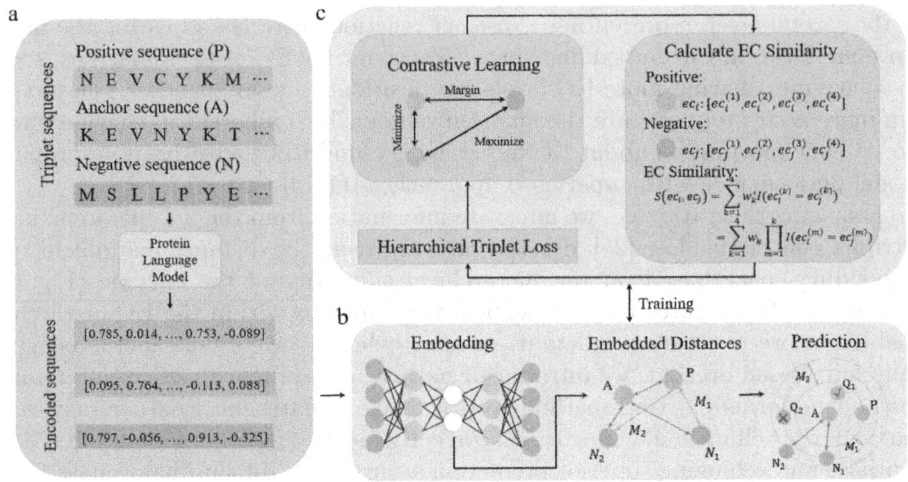

Fig. 1. EnzHier hierarchical contrastive learning framework. **(a)** Protein language models encode amino acid sequences into embedding vectors for contrastive learning. Triplets–anchor (A), positive (P) (sharing the same EC number with the anchor), and negative (N) (not sharing the same EC number with the anchor)–are marked in different colors. **(b)** Anchor-to-negative margins in the embedding space (such as M_1 and M_2) are dynamically expanded through contrastive learning, assigning hierarchical boundaries for EC levels and enabling subtle functional separation. **(c)** The final EnzHier model minimizes anchorâĂŞpositive distances while maximizing anchorâĂŞnegative distances. In the illustration, query sequences Q_1 and Q_2 are assigned to or excluded from the anchor's EC group by comparing their distances (to the anchor's EC center) against the learned margins.

anchor and negative $z_n^{(i)}$, and a dynamic margin m_{an}. $\mathcal{L}$ is minimized during training so that the model effectively separates positive from negative examples. To enforce non-negativity, we also apply a ReLU activation [30] to the HTL. In detail:

$$\mathcal{L} = \frac{1}{N} \sum_{i=1}^{N} \max\left(0,\ \|z_a^{(i)} - z_p^{(i)}\|_2^2 - \|z_a^{(i)} - z_n^{(i)}\|_2^2 + m_{an}\right) \tag{1}$$

Here, N denotes the batch size. The dynamic margin m_{an} is adjusted according to the hierarchical similarity between EC labels. It is computed as follows:

$$m_{an} = m_{\min} - (m_{\min} - m_{\max}) \exp(-\beta\, S(ec_a, ec_n)) \tag{2}$$

In this expression, $m_{\min}$ and $m_{\max}$ are the minimum and maximum margin values, and β is a hyperparameter controlling the margin's sensitivity to similarity. The similarity for the anchor–positive pair is set to $S_{ap} = S(ec_a, ec_p) = 1$, while $S_{an} = S(ec_a, ec_n)$ is the hierarchical similarity for the anchor–negative pair, as defined in Equation (3).

2.3 Hierarchical EC Similarity

To quantify hierarchical similarity between enzyme functions, we define a measure for EC numbers that honors their strict, nested relationships. Let ec_i and ec_j denote the EC numbers of enzymes i and j, each comprising four ordered levels from coarse to fine:

$$ec_i = \left[ec_i^{(1)}, ec_i^{(2)}, ec_i^{(3)}, ec_i^{(4)}\right], \quad ec_j = \left[ec_j^{(1)}, ec_j^{(2)}, ec_j^{(3)}, ec_j^{(4)}\right].$$

The similarity is defined as:

$$S(ec_i, ec_j) = \sum_{k=1}^{4} w_k \prod_{m=1}^{k} I\big(ec_i^{(m)} = ec_j^{(m)}\big) \tag{3}$$

where

$$I\big(ec_i^{(m)} = ec_j^{(m)}\big) = \begin{cases} 1, & \text{if the } m\text{th EC field of } i \text{ and } j \text{ is identical,} \\ 0, & \text{otherwise.} \end{cases} \tag{4}$$

For each enzyme pair, $\prod_{m=1}^{k} I(\cdot)$ equals 1 only when all levels $1, \dots, k$ match; it drops to 0 if any level $m \leq k$ differs. Thus, $S \in [0, \sum_{k=1}^{4} w_k]$. By normalizing $\sum_{k=1}^{4} w_k = 1$, we ensure $S \in [0, 1]$, with higher scores indicating closer functional relatedness.

To reflect biological significance, one shall set the weights to decrease with depth: $w_1 > w_2 > w_3 > w_4$. We chose $w = (0.4, 0.3, 0.2, 0.1)$, i.e. $w_k \propto \{4, 3, 2, 1\}$. This makes a discrepancy at level 1 (broad reaction class) contribute more to the overall similarity than a mismatch at level 4 (substrate specificity), aligning with the EC hierarchy's biological meaning. The values can also be fine-tuned by cross-validation.

Overall, the similarity measure remains simple, interpretable and computationally efficient; by assigning larger weights to higher (coarser) levels, it preserves the nested EC hierarchy while quantifying functional relatedness in a biologically meaningful way.

2.4 Multi-scale Feature Integration Module

To capture multi-scale information in protein sequences, we implement a modified U-Net architecture for 1D sequence processing with layer normalization. This architecture's symmetric encoderâĂŞdecoder design with skip connections effectively integrates detailed local features with broader contextual patterns.

The encoder pathway transforms input sequence features $X \in \mathbb{R}^{L \times d_{\text{in}}}$ (L: sequence length; $d_{\text{in}} = 2560$ from ESM-2 embedding) through sequential dimensionality reduction, where each layer downsamples by halfing, as follows:

$$H_1 = \text{ReLU}\big(\text{LayerNorm}(X\,W_1 + b_1)\big) \cdot M_1 \tag{5}$$

$$H_2 = \text{ReLU}\big(\text{LayerNorm}(H_1\,W_2 + b_2)\big) \cdot M_2 \tag{6}$$

$$H_3 = \text{ReLU}\big(\text{LayerNorm}(H_2\, W_3 + b_3)\big) \cdot M_3 \tag{7}$$

The decoder pathway reverses this reduction while incorporating encoder features through skip connections:

$$D_1 = \text{ReLU}\big(\text{LayerNorm}(H_3\, W_4 + b_4)\big) \cdot M_4 \tag{8}$$

$$D_1^{\text{concat}} = [\, D_1 \oplus H_2\,] \tag{9}$$

$$D_2 = \text{ReLU}\big(\text{LayerNorm}(D_1^{\text{concat}}\, W_5 + b_5)\big) \cdot M_5 \tag{10}$$

$$D_2^{\text{concat}} = [\, D_2 \oplus H_1\,] \tag{11}$$

$$\hat{Y} = D_2^{\text{concat}}\, W_{\text{out}} + b_{\text{out}} \tag{12}$$

Here $\hat{Y} \in \mathbb{R}^{L \times d_{\text{out}}}$ and $d_{out} = 2560$ is the output feature dimension. These skip connections ($D_1 \oplus H_2$ and $D_2 \oplus H_1$) preserve fine-grained local information from the encoder while incorporating global contextual features from the decoder, essential for distinguishing subtle functional differences between enzymes with similar sequences but distinct catalytic activities.

2.5   EC Number Inference Method

We employ a change-point detection inference to assign EC numbers by detecting large gaps in the sorted distances between a query and class centroids. Let E be the total number of EC classes, indexed $j = 1, 2, \ldots, E$. Denote by c_j the centroid embedding of class j and by q the query embedding. Compute

$$d_j^q = \|q - c_j\|_2, \quad j = 1, \ldots, E.$$

To focus on likely candidates, let k (default 15) be the maximum number of top classes to consider, and define the candidate index set:

$$\mathcal{C} = \{\, j : d_j^q \leq d_{(k)}^q\, \}, \quad |\mathcal{C}| = k. \tag{13}$$

Within the set $\mathcal{C}$, compute adjacent gaps:

$$\Delta_i = d_{(i+1)}^q - d_{(i)}^q, \quad i = 1, \ldots, k - 1.$$

Identify the change point i^* where Δ_{i*} is largest (and exceeds the mean plus twice the standard deviation of $\{\Delta_i\}$), indicating a natural separation between close and distant classes. Assign the query to all EC classes $j \in \mathcal{C}$ with $d_j^q \leq d_{(i^*)}^q$.

DBSCAN Fallback: Density-Based Spatial Clustering of Applications with Noise (DBSCAN) is our alternative for grouping EC centroids that are closely packed into dense regions [31]. Suppose gap-based changepoint detection fails to produce a clear separation. In that case, we apply one-dimensional DBSCAN to the distances $\{d_j^q : j \in \mathcal{C}\}$ requiring a cutoff $\epsilon = 0.5\,\sigma_d$ and a minimum one point per cluster, where σ_d is the standard deviation of these d^q's. Centroid clusters identified by DBSCAN correspond to groups of nearby centroids; the query is assigned to the EC class(es) linked to the cluster containing $d_{(1)}^q$.

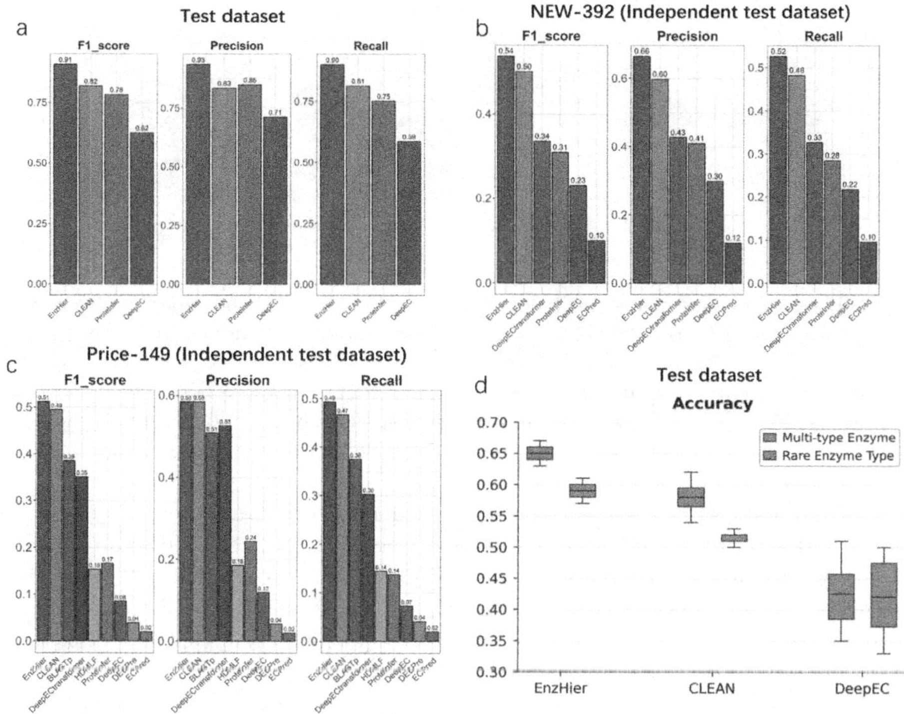

Fig. 2. The performance (including Precision, Recall, and F1-score) of EnzHier and other methods on (a) the keptaway test dataset, (b) the New-392 independent dataset, and (c) the Price-149 independent dataset. (d) compares the prediction accuracy of EnzHier, CLEAN, and DeepEC in multi-type and rare enzyme subsets.

3   Results

3.1   EnzHier Achieves State-of-the-Art Performance in Benchmarks

EnzHier demonstrates robust and consistent performance across 5-fold cross-validation (Supplementary Table S3), achieving an average precision of 0.943, recall of 0.914, F1 score of 0.919, and AUC of 0.957. On the held-out test set (20% of SwissProt), EnzHier outperforms all comparison methods–achieving an F1 of 0.91, precision of 0.93, and recall of 0.90–surpassing CLEAN, ProtInfer, and DeepEC (Fig. 2a). These results highlight EnzHier's balanced precisionâĂŞrecall trade-off in enzyme function prediction.

On the independent NEW-392 dataset, EnzHier outperforms all other methods across F1, precision, and recall (Fig. 2b). CLEAN falls behind in every metric, and ProtInfer, DeepEC, and ECpred underperform across all measures. Similarly, on Price-149, EnzHier achieves the highest F1, precision, and recall (Fig. 2c). Although CLEAN's precision is closer to EnzHier's, its recall and F1 are all lower; ProtInfer and DeepEC degrade further, and ECpred scores lowest.

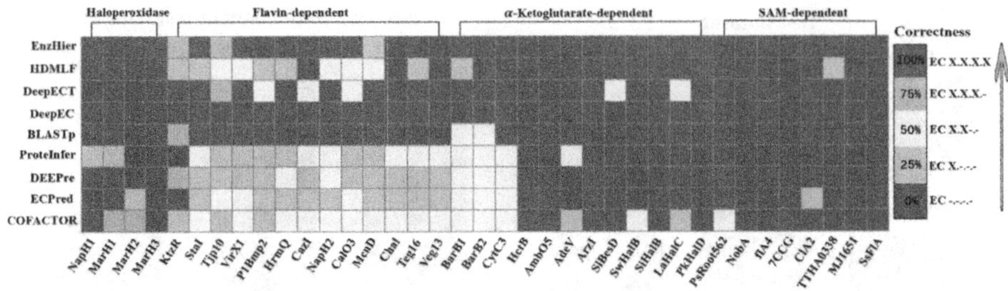

Fig. 3. Prediction correctness for halogenase classification. The heatmap shows prediction correctness (0% to 100%) for haloperoxidase, flavin-dependent, α-ketoglutarate-dependent, and SAM-dependent halogenase subtypes based on EC number matching. Red indicates complete matching (100%), followed by orange, yellow, light blue, and dark blue (75%, 50%, 25%, and 0% matching, respectively). (Color figure online)

EnzHier also works well on understudied enzyme classes. Figure 2d shows accuracy distributions for multi-type and rare enzyme test subsets. EnzHier attains median accuracies of approximately 0.65 for multi-type and 0.59 for rare classes, outperforming CLEAN (0.58 and 0.53) and DeepEC (0.43 and 0.42). All methods trend higher on multi-type enzymes than on rare types, but EnzHier's improvement is most pronounced.

3.2　EnzHier Accurately Predicts Halogenase Functions

EnzHier demonstrates exceptional accuracy in predicting complex and difficult-to-classify enzymes, such as halogenases. It has high performance in classifying all four halogenase subtypes–haloperoxidases, flavin-dependent, α-ketoglutarate-dependent, and SAM-dependent halogenases, achieving high (>90%) average correctness for all subcategories (Fig. 3). By contrast, HDMLF attains high accuracy only on a few haloperoxidases but frequently misclassifies SAM- and flavin-dependent halogenases and shows inconsistent performance on α-ketoglutarate-dependent subtypes. DeepEC and DeepECTransformer similarly misclassify large fractions of flavin- and α-ketoglutarate-dependent halogenases and fail significantly on haloperoxidases. All other methods also demonstrate significant limitations in predicting halogenase functions.

3.3　EnzHier Effectively Annotates Multifunctional Enzymes

EnzHier also excels at annotating multifunctional enzymes–a task where existing methods often struggle. A prime example is geranylgeranyl pyrophosphate synthase (GGPP synthase; UniProt ID: B1XJV9), shown in Supplementary (Fig. 3). Encoded by the *CRTE* gene, this 302-amino-acid enzyme sequentially adds three isopentenyl pyrophosphate molecules to dimethylallyl pyrophosphate, producing GGPP–a critical step in cyanobacterial terpenoid biosynthesis confirmed by crystal structure. UniProt currently assigns GGPP synthase to three EC categories:

EC 2.5.1.1, EC 2.5.1.10, and EC 2.5.1.29. EnzHier correctly recovers all three functional annotations, whereas DeepECTransformer and DeepEC capture only a subset and DEEPre fails entirely. This highlights EnzHier's superior performance in annotating multifunctional enzymes.

3.4   Ablation Studies

Table 1. Performance of Ablated Model Variants

Model Variant	Precision	Recall	F1-Score	AUC
Base (Flat T-Loss + CNN)	0.8245	0.8102	0.8173	0.8956
+ Hierarchical Triplet Loss	0.9021	0.8743	0.8880	0.9312
+ U-Net Architecture	0.9094	0.8891	0.8877	0.9287
EnzHier	**0.9132**	**0.9038**	**0.8994**	**0.9469**

To evaluate the contribution of each component of EnzHier to overall performance, we conducted comprehensive ablation studies. First, we compared various protein language models ESM-1b and ESM-2 across parameter scales from 8 million up to 3 billion. While larger models provided gains, those improvements plateaued beyond 150 million parameters, leading us to select ESM-2 (150 M) for an optimal performance-efficiency trade-off.

Next, we replaced the standard CNN architecture with our modified U-Net (Table 1). This "encoderâĂŞdecoder with skip connections" design outperformed CNN (by 2.85%), Transformer (by 1.33%), and ResNet (by 1.83%) across all metrics. U-Net's ability to capture local motifs (via convolutions) and global context (via skip links) makes it particularly effective in distinguishing subtle sequence features relevant to enzyme function.

Finally, switching from flat triplet loss (Flat T-Loss) to hierarchical triplet loss (HTL) provided the single largest boost: F1 score increased by 7.07% (from 0.8173 to 0.8880). Incorporating U-Net alone improved F1 by 7.04% (to 0.8877). Combining HTL and U-Net yielded the highest F1 (0.8994; an 8.21% jump) and the highest AUC (0.9469; a 5.13% increase). Repeating training with different random seeds produced consistent results (± 1.2% variation), confirming the robustness of these design choices.

4   Conclusion

In summary, EnzHier advances enzyme function prediction with improved accuracy, robustness, and scalability. It effectively predicts functions of understudied and multifunctional enzymes like halogenases and geranylgeranyl pyrophosphate synthase, addressing key challenges in enzyme engineering. The model combines contrastive learning with hierarchical triplet loss and U-Net architecture for optimal feature extraction. With its high performance and versatility, EnzHier could be a valuable tool added for enzyme function prediction.

Acknowledgments. This study was funded by the Guangdong Basic and Applied Basic Research Foundation (2022A1515-011426 and 2024A1515-010699) to LCX. We thank the anonymous reviewers for their constructive comments helped improve the paper.

References

1. Rehm, F., Chen, S., Rehm, B.: Enzyme engineering for In Situ immobilization. Molecules **21**(10), 1370 (2016)
2. Liu, Q., Xun, G., Feng, Y.: The state-of-the-art strategies of protein engineering for enzyme stabilization. Biotechnol. Adv. **37**(4), 530–537 (2019)
3. Li, F., Chen, Y., Anton, M., Nielsen, J.: Gotenzymes: an extensive database of enzyme parameter predictions. Nucleic Acids Res. **51**(D1), D583–D586 (2023)
4. Boger, R.S., Chithrananda, S., Angelopoulos, A.N., Yoon, P.H., Jordan, M.I., Doudna, J.A.: Functional protein mining with conformal guarantees. Nat. Commun. **16**(1), 85 (2025)
5. Zhou, N., et al.: The cafa challenge reports improved protein function prediction and new functional annotations for hundreds of genes through experimental screens. Genome Biol. **20**, 244 (2019)
6. Wilson, M., Coudrat, T., Warden, A.: Selfprot: effective and efficient multitask finetuning methods for protein parameter prediction. J. Chem. Inf. Model. **65**(7), 3226–3238 (2025)
7. The UniProt Consortium: Uniprot: the universal protein knowledgebase in 2021. Nucleic Acids Res. **49**(D1), D480–D489 (2021)
8. Altschul, S.F., Gish, W., Miller, W., Myers, E.W., Lipman, D.J.: Basic local alignment search tool. J. Mol. Biol. **215**(3), 403–410 (1990)
9. Altschul, S.F., et al.: Gapped blast and psi-blast: a new generation of protein database search programs. Nucleic Acids Res. **25**(17), 3389–3402 (1997)
10. Steinegger, M., Meier, M., Mirdita, M., Vöhringer, H., Haunsberger, S.J., Söding, J.: Hh-suite3 for fast remote homology detection and deep protein annotation. BMC Bioinform. **20**, 473 (2019)
11. Shi, Z., Deng, R., Yuan, Q., Mao, Z., Wang, R., Li, H., Liao, X., Ma, H.: Enzyme commission number prediction and benchmarking with hierarchical dual-core multitask learning framework. Research **2023**, 0153 (2023)
12. Ryu, J.Y., Kim, H.U., Lee, S.Y.: Deep learning enables high-quality and high-throughput prediction of enzyme commission numbers. Proc. Natl. Acad. Sci. U.S.A. **116**(28), 13996–14001 (2019)
13. Kim, G.B., Kim, J.Y., Lee, J.A., Norsigian, C.J., Palsson, B.O., Lee, S.Y.: Functional annotation of enzyme-encoding genes using deep learning with transformer layers. Nat. Commun. **14**(1), 7370 (2023)
14. Memon, S.A., Khan, K.A., Naveed, H.: Hecnet: a hierarchical approach to enzyme function classification using a siamese triplet network. Bioinformatics **36**(17), 4583–4589 (2020)

15. Song, Y., Yuan, Q., Chen, S., Zeng, Y., Zhao, H., Yang, Y.: Accurately predicting enzyme functions through geometric graph learning on esmfold-predicted structures. Nat. Commun. **15**(1), 8180 (2024)

16. Zhao, Y., Su, B., Chen, J., Wen, J.R.: Interpretable enzyme function prediction via residue-level detection (2025). https://arxiv.org/abs/2501.05644

17. You, Y., Chen, T., Sui, Y., Chen, T., Wang, Z., Shen, Y.: Graph contrastive learning with augmentations. Adv. Neural. Inf. Process. Syst. **33**, 5812–5823 (2020)

18. Zhao, H., Yang, X., Wang, Z., Yang, E., Deng, C.: Graph debiased contrastive learning with joint representation clustering. In: Proceedings of the Thirty-First International Joint Conference on Artificial Intelligence (IJCAI), pp. 3434–3440 (2021)

19. Kim, M., Tack, J., Hwang, S.J.: Adversarial self-supervised contrastive learning. Adv. Neural. Inf. Process. Syst. **33**, 2983–2994 (2020)

20. Rong, D., Zheng, W., Zhong, B., Lin, Z., Hong, L., Liu, N.: Autoregressive enzyme function prediction with multi-scale multi-modality fusion (2024). https://arxiv.org/abs/2408.06391

21. Yu, T., Cui, H., Li, J.C., Luo, Y., Jiang, G., Zhao, H.: Enzyme function prediction using contrastive learning. Science **379**(6639), 1358–1363 (2023)

22. Yang, Y., et al.: Improved enzyme functional annotation prediction using contrastive learning with structural inference. Commun. Biol. **7**(1), 1690 (2024)

23. Awasthi, P., Dikkala, N., Kamath, P.: Do more negative samples necessarily hurt in contrastive learning? In: Proceedings of the 39th International Conference on Machine Learning (ICML), pp. 1101–1116 (2022)

24. Roy, A., Yang, J., Zhang, Y.: Cofactor: an accurate comparative algorithm for structure-based protein function annotation. Nucleic Acids Res. **40**(W1), W471–W477 (2012)

25. Chen, W., Chen, X., Zhang, J., Huang, K.: Beyond triplet loss: a deep quadruplet network for person re-identification. In: Proceedings of the IEEE Conference on Computer Vision and Pattern Recognition, pp. 403–412 (2017)

26. Yim, S., Hwang, D., Kim, K., Han, S.: Hierarchical contrastive learning for enzyme function prediction. In: Proceedings of the ICML 2024 Workshop on Machine Learning for Life and Material Science: From Theory to Industry Applications (2024)

27. Bairoch, A., Apweiler, R.: The swiss-prot protein sequence database and its supplement trembl in 2000. Nucleic Acids Res. **28**(1), 45–48 (2000)

28. Lin, Z., et al.: Evolutionary-scale prediction of atomic-level protein structure with a language model. Science **379**(6637), 1123–1130 (2023)

29. Dalkiran, A., Rifaioglu, A.S., Martin, M.J., Cetin-Atalay, R., Atalay, V., Doğan, T.: Ecpred: a tool for the prediction of the enzymatic functions of protein sequences based on the ec nomenclature. BMC Bioinform. **19**, 334 (2018)

30. Banerjee, C., Mukherjee, T., Pasiliao, E.: An empirical study on generalizations of the relu activation function. In: Proceedings of the 2019 ACM Southeast Conference, pp. 164–167 (2019)

31. Deng, D.: Dbscan clustering algorithm based on density. In: Proceedings of the 2020 7th International Forum on Electrical Engineering and Automation (IFEEA), pp. 949–953 (2020)

Bidirectional Position-Context Feature Representation for Predicting DNA/RNA Modification Sites

Cheng Xu[1], Mingzhao Wang[1] ⓘ, Jinyan Li[2(✉)], and Juanying Xie[1(✉)] ⓘ

[1] School of Artificial Intelligence and Computer Science, Shaanxi Normal University, Xi'an 710119,
People's Republic of China
xiejuany@snnu.edu.cn

[2] Faculty of Computer Science and Control Engineering, Shenzhen University of Advanced Technology, Shenzhen 518055, People's Republic of China
jinyan.li@siat.ac.cn

Abstract. Accurate identification of DNA/RNA modification sites is imperative for the study of their biological functions. Machine learning algorithms are unable to utilize sequence data directly to construct models for predicting these sites. Consequently, the development of DNA/RNA sequence feature representation algorithms is paramount for the effective encoding of sequence data into a usable numerical format, thereby facilitating the construction of high-performance machine learning predictive models. Existing DNA/RNA sequence feature representation algorithms suffer from the problems of simple extracting information, failure to take into account the sequence position and order information, and irrelevant or redundant features brought about by multi-methods together. This leads to the inability of machine learning models to break through the bottleneck of prediction performance. To address the aforementioned issues, this paper introduces the BiPSDP (Bidirectional Position-Specific Dinucleotide Propensities) algorithm. This algorithm extracts dinucleotide position-specific propensities from both forward and backward sequence directions. The incorporation of a parameter for dinucleotide spacing is pivotal in capturing global order information, with DNA/RNA sequences being encoded as numerical features that are rich in class-distinguishing information. The validity of the BiPSDP algorithm was tested by constructing a DNA/RNA modification site prediction model using the SVM learning machines, and a comparison was made with seven existing representation algorithms across seven modification types. The experimental results demonstrate that the prediction model with BiPSDP consistently outperforms the comparison models, thus validating its value as a tool for constructing prediction models for various DNA/RNA modification sites. The code of BiPSDP is available at https://github.com/Mingzhao2017/BiPSDP.

Keywords: Feature representation · Position-specific propensities · Prediction models · Modification sites · Machine learning

---

C. Xu and M. Wang—Co-first author.

J. Tang et al. (Eds.): ISBRA 2025, LNBI 15757, pp. 228–240, 2026.
https://doi.org/10.1007/978-981-95-0695-8_19

1 Introduction

DNA/RNA modifications represent critical epigenetic mechanisms that regulate gene expression and maintain cellular stability, playing a key role in diseases like cancer [1]. The impact of DNA modifications, including N4-methylcytosine (4mC), 5-methylcytosine (5mC), and N6-methyladenine (6mA), on gene expression and chromatin structure is well documented [2, 3]. In as similar fashion, RNA modifications, including N6-methyladenine (m^6A), N1-methyladenine (m^1A), and m^5C, have been shown to regulate processes such as RNA stability, translation, and are linked to cancer development [4]. Accurate identification of DNA/RNA methylation sites is imperative for comprehending their biological functions [5]. Conventional experimental methods for methylation site identification are costly, time-consuming, and prone to false positives [6], while high-throughput technologies like WGBS (Whole-genome bisulphite sequencing) and SMRT (Single-molecule real-time) offer improved accuracy but still face issues of high cost and long duration [7].

The present study explores the application of artificial intelligence (AI) and machine learning (ML) techniques, a research direction that has garnered significant attention in the field of computer science. These techniques have been successfully implemented in various real-life applications, including the prediction of antibiotic resistance [8] and the utilization of AlphaFold3 for drug discovery [9]. In the field of bioinformatics, the modelling of large-scale sequence data using machine learning has emerged as a pivotal research area. The identification of DNA/RNA modification sites is a binary or multiclass classification task, requiring training on high-throughput sequencing data to predict methylation sites in unknown sequences. This approach enhances methylation detection and facilitates research on its role in complex diseases, drug development, and personalized treatment [10]. The construction of methylation modification site prediction models involves several interconnected processes, including data acquisition, sequence feature representation, model construction, and performance evaluation [11]. As machine learning algorithms cannot utilize the original sequence data to construct predictive models, DNA/RNA sequence feature representation methods are required to convert sequence data into a form of numerical data that retains the interpretable information of the original DNA/RNA sequences as much as possible. This step is a necessary and critical one in the process of building predictive models for methylation modification sites, and it can effectively improve the predictive and generalization performance of the models.

Classical DNA/RNA sequence feature representation methods are characterized by simplicity and are primarily implemented through the calculation of local compositional information of nucleotides [11]. Examples of such methods include the k-mer method for calculating the composition of four nucleotide components and its variants, such as RCKmer (Reverse complementary k-mer), MisKmer (Mismatches k-mer) and KSNPF (K-spaced nucleotide pair frequencies). NBE (Nucleotide binary encoding) and DBE (Dinucleotide binary encoding) methods [12].

In order to integrate the compositional and sequential information of nucleotides in DNA/RNA sequences, Chen et al. [13] proposed the sequence feature representation method PseDNC (Pseudo dinucleotide composition) based on dinucleotide materialization properties and applied it to the prediction of recombination spots and splicing sites.

Guo et al. [14] proposed the sequence feature representation method PseKNC (Pseudo k-tuple nucleotide composition) on the basis of the PseDNC method, which was used for nucleosome positioning. RNA secondary structure is the stem-loop structure formed by RNA molecules through their own refolding and base complementary pairing. In order to make the RNA secondary structure reflect the compositional and sequential information of RNA sequences, Liu et al. proposed PseSSC (Pseudo structure status composition) [15] and PseDPC (Pseudo distance-pair composition) [16] methods and used them for microRNA precursor (pre-miRNAs) prediction, and achieved good prediction performance. Furthermore, Li et al. [17] proposed PSNP (Position-specific nucleotide propensities) and PSDP (Position-specific dinucleotide propensities) methods based on nucleotide position-specific propensities. These were combined with an SVM (Support Vector Machine) learning algorithm to establish the RNA m^6A modification site prediction model TargetM6A. We also proposed BiPSTP [18], PSP-PMI (Position-specific propensities and pointwise mutual information) [19] and PSP-PJMI (Position-specific propensities and pointwise joint mutual information) [20], and the established prediction models have achieved SOTA performance on the benchmark datasets of DNA/RNA modification sites.

The existing DNA/RNA sequence feature representation methods are inadequate in their capacity to extract features from sequences that contain key class-discriminatory information, and they also fail to take into account the positional and sequential information possessed by sequence nucleotides. In order to enhance this, multiple representation methods are combined to create high-dimensional features. However, there is a paucity of clear guidance on selecting these methods, which has the effect of creating redundant features. To improve model performance, additional feature selection algorithms are required to optimize the feature space [20]. In addition, deep learning-based word embedding models such as BERT (Bidirectional encoder representations from transformers) and Word2vec have also been used for encoding DNA/RNA sequence. However, they are still challenging for the computational requirements and model interpretability [21]. Consequently, how to extract features from DNA/RNA sequences with rich category discriminative information is crucial for training high performance prediction models.

In order to address the limitations of current DNA/RNA sequence feature representation methods, the BiPSDP (bidirectional dinucleotide position-specific propensities) method is proposed. This approach extracts position-specific propensity information from both forward and backward directions of DNA/RNA sequences, while incorporating a parameter for dinucleotide spacing. The integration of features from diverse spacing dimensions enables BiPSDP to capture both global positional and sequential information, yielding high-dimensional numerical features with substantial class-distinguishing information. The experimental results demonstrate the efficacy of models based on BiPSDP in identifying modification sites, outperforming existing algorithms and enhancing the robustness and generalization of prediction models.

2   Methods

2.1   Datasets

We use the open access benchmark DNA/RNA sequence datasets [22–27] across six different modification types, including two DNA sequence datasets and five RNA sequence datasets, to validate the performance of the proposed sequence feature representation method BiPSDP. The sequence lengths in the datasets are all 41nt, with a balanced number of positive and negative class samples. Their specific information is shown in Table 1.

Table 1. Details of the benchmark datasets with different types DNA/RNA modification

Types	Species	Sites	Benchmark datasets			Length
			#Positive	#Negative	#Total	
RNA	*H. sapiens* [22]	Nm	147	147	294	41
	H. sapiens [23]	D	29	29	58	41
	S. cerevisiae [23]	D	68	68	136	41
	S. cerevisiae [24]	m^2G	67	67	134	41
	H. sapiens [25]	m^5C	120	120	240	41
DNA	*A. thaliana* [26]	4mC	1978	1978	3596	41
	R. chinensis [27]	6mA	1067	1067	2134	41

2.2   BiPSDP Method

The DNA/RNA sequence feature representation method BiPSDP proposed in this paper utilizes the position-specific propensity information of bidirectional dinucleotides in the sequence fragments to encode the sequence, the position-specific propensity frequency of dinucleotides in the sequence is calculated from the forward and backward directions of the sequence simultaneously, and the forward and backward dinucleotide position-specific propensity frequency matrices are constructed based on the positive class dataset and negative class dataset, respectively. The difference of both is used to represent the DNA/RNA sequences as numerical feature vectors.

A DNA/RNA sequence dataset with sequence length l is denoted as $D = D^+ \cup D^-$, where D^+ denotes the positive dataset, that is the true methylation modification sites dataset, D^- denotes the negative dataset, that is the non-methylation modification sites dataset. A sequence in the dataset D is $R = N_1 \cdots N_i \cdots N_l$ and the nucleotide at position $i(1 \leq i \leq l)$ of the sequence R is $N_i \in \{A, C, G, T/U\}$.

To extract bidirectional dinucleotide position-specific propensity frequency information from DNA/RNA sequences, the frequency of occurrence of dinucleotides at each position of all sequences based on the positive dataset D^+ and the negative dataset D^- was counted from the forward and backward directions of the sequences, respectively.

A parameter $\alpha(\alpha \geq 0)$ was introduced to denote the interval of the current nucleotide from its forward or backward nucleotide. When $\alpha = 0$ is used, it means two consecutive nucleotides, and when $\alpha = 1$ is used, it means that the interval between the current nucleotide and its forward or backward consecutive nucleotide is one nucleotide. To illustrate this point, the RNA sequence is shown schematically in Fig. 1. It is worth noting that as the value of the parameter α increases, the number of nucleotides satisfying the coding conditions decreases.

Fig. 1. Schematic representation of bidirectional dinucleotide position-specific propensities with intervals for α

Taking RNA sequences as an example, there are 16 types of dinucleotides $\{A, C, G, U\} \times \{A, C, G, U\}$. Based on the positive dataset D^+, the forward dinucleotide position-specific propensity frequency at position $i(1 \leq i \leq l-\alpha-1, 0 \leq \alpha \leq (l-3)/2)$ can be expressed as a 16-dimensional feature vector, which represents the frequency of occurrence of the 16 forward dinucleotides at position i among all sequences in the positive dataset D^+, respectively, as shown in Eq. (1).

$$\overrightarrow{f}_i^{\,+} = [\overrightarrow{f}_{\alpha,\text{AA},i}^{\,+}, \overrightarrow{f}_{\alpha,\text{AC},i}^{\,+}, \cdots, \overrightarrow{f}_{\alpha,\text{UU},i}^{\,+}]^{\text{T}} \tag{1}$$

where the first element $\overrightarrow{f}_{\alpha,\text{AA},i}^{\,+}$ in the feature vector $\overrightarrow{f}_i^{\,+}$ denotes the probability that the i position is nucleotide A and the $i+\alpha+1$ position is nucleotide A in all sequences of the positive dataset D^+; the second element $\overrightarrow{f}_{\alpha,\text{AC},i}^{\,+}$ represents the probability that the i position is nucleotide A and the $i+\alpha+1$ position is nucleotide C in all sequences of the positive dataset D^+, and so on. The forward dinucleotide position-specific propensity frequency matrix $\overrightarrow{M}^+ = [\overrightarrow{f}_1^{\,+}, \overrightarrow{f}_2^{\,+}, \cdots, \overrightarrow{f}_{l-\alpha-1}^{\,+}]^T$ based on the positive dataset D^+, is shown in Eq. (2).

$$\overrightarrow{M}^+ = \begin{bmatrix} \overrightarrow{f}_{\alpha,\text{AA},1}^{\,+} & \overrightarrow{f}_{\alpha,\text{AA},2}^{\,+} & \cdots & \overrightarrow{f}_{\alpha,\text{AA},i}^{\,+} & \cdots & \overrightarrow{f}_{\alpha,\text{AA},l-\alpha-1}^{\,+} \\ \overrightarrow{f}_{\alpha,\text{AC},1}^{\,+} & \overrightarrow{f}_{\alpha,\text{AC},2}^{\,+} & \cdots & \overrightarrow{f}_{\alpha,\text{AC},i}^{\,+} & \cdots & \overrightarrow{f}_{\alpha,\text{AC},l-\alpha-1}^{\,+} \\ \vdots & \vdots & \ddots & \vdots & \ddots & \vdots \\ \overrightarrow{f}_{\alpha,\text{UU},1}^{\,+} & \overrightarrow{f}_{\alpha,\text{UU},2}^{\,+} & \cdots & \overrightarrow{f}_{\alpha,\text{UU},i}^{\,+} & \cdots & \overrightarrow{f}_{\alpha,\text{UU},l-\alpha-1}^{\,+} \end{bmatrix}, \quad 0 \leq \alpha \leq \frac{l-3}{2} \tag{2}$$

Based on the positive dataset D^+, the position-specific propensity frequency of the backward dinucleotide at the position of i $(\alpha+2 \leq i \leq l, 0 \leq \alpha \leq (l-3)/2)$ is defined as shown in Eq. (3), which denotes the frequency of occurrence of the 16 backward dinucleotides $\{A, C, G, U\} \times \{A, C, G, U\}$ at the i position among all sequences in the positive dataset D^+.

$$\overleftarrow{f}_i^{\,+} = [\overleftarrow{f}_{\alpha,\text{AA},i}^{\,+}, \overleftarrow{f}_{\alpha,\text{AC},i}^{\,+}, \cdots, \overleftarrow{f}_{\alpha,\text{UU},i}^{\,+}]^{\text{T}} \tag{3}$$

where the first element $\overleftarrow{f}^{+}_{\alpha,AA,i}$ in $\overleftarrow{f}^{+}_{i}$ represents the probability that the i position and its backward $i - \alpha - 1$ position are nucleotide A in all sequences of the positive dataset $\boldsymbol{D}^{+}$; the second element $\overleftarrow{f}^{+}_{\alpha,AC,i}$ represents the probability that the i position and its backward $i - \alpha - 1$ position are nucleotide A and nucleotide C, respectively, in all sequences of the positive dataset $\boldsymbol{D}^{+}$. The backward dinucleotide position-specific propensity matrix $\overleftarrow{\boldsymbol{M}}^{+} = [\overleftarrow{f}^{+}_{1}, \overleftarrow{f}^{+}_{2}, \cdots, \overleftarrow{f}^{+}_{l-\alpha-1}]^{T}$ based on the positive dataset $\boldsymbol{D}^{+}$, is shown in Eq. (4).

$$
\overleftarrow{\boldsymbol{M}}^{+} = \begin{bmatrix}
\overleftarrow{f}^{+}_{\alpha,AA,1} & \overleftarrow{f}^{+}_{\alpha,AA,2} & \cdots & \overleftarrow{f}^{+}_{\alpha,AA,i} & \cdots & \overleftarrow{f}^{+}_{\alpha,AA,l-\alpha-2} \\
\overleftarrow{f}^{+}_{\alpha,AC,1} & \overleftarrow{f}^{+}_{\alpha,AC,2} & \cdots & \overleftarrow{f}^{+}_{\alpha,AC,i} & \cdots & \overleftarrow{f}^{+}_{\alpha,AC,l-\alpha-2} \\
\vdots & \vdots & \ddots & \vdots & \ddots & \vdots \\
\overleftarrow{f}^{+}_{\alpha,UU,1} & \overleftarrow{f}^{+}_{\alpha,UU,2} & \cdots & \overleftarrow{f}^{+}_{\alpha,UU,i} & \cdots & \overleftarrow{f}^{+}_{\alpha,UU,l-\alpha-2}
\end{bmatrix}, \quad 0 \le \alpha \le \frac{l-3}{2} \quad (4)
$$

Based on the negative dataset $\boldsymbol{D}^{-}$, the calculation of the forward dinucleotide position-specific propensity frequency matrix $\overrightarrow{\boldsymbol{M}}^{-} = [\overrightarrow{f}^{-}_{1}, \overrightarrow{f}^{-}_{2}, \cdots, \overrightarrow{f}^{-}_{l-\alpha-1}]^{T}$ and the backward dinucleotide position-specific propensity matrix $\overleftarrow{\boldsymbol{M}}^{-} = [\overleftarrow{f}^{-}_{1}, \overleftarrow{f}^{-}_{2}, \cdots, \overleftarrow{f}^{-}_{l-\alpha-2}]^{T}$ as same as that of $\overrightarrow{\boldsymbol{M}}^{+}$ and $\overleftarrow{\boldsymbol{M}}^{+}$.

From dataset $\boldsymbol{D}^{+}$, we can determine the encoding value of the nucleotide in position i in the sequence R, such as that in Fig. 1. This is calculated as the mean value of the forward dinucleotide position-specific propensity frequency and the backward dinucleotide position-specific propensity frequency of the position i, that is $y^{+}_{i} = (\overrightarrow{y}^{+}_{i} + \overleftarrow{y}^{+}_{i})/2$, where $\overrightarrow{y}^{+}_{i}$ and $\overleftarrow{y}^{+}_{i}$ are $\overrightarrow{f}^{+}_{\alpha,AC,i}$ and $\overleftarrow{f}^{+}_{\alpha,AU,i}$ in $\overrightarrow{\boldsymbol{M}}^{+}$ and $\overleftarrow{\boldsymbol{M}}^{+}$, respectively. Similarly, based on dataset $\boldsymbol{D}^{-}$, the mean value of the forward dinucleotide position-specific propensity frequency $\overrightarrow{y}^{-}_{i}$ and the backward dinucleotide position-specific propensity frequency $\overleftarrow{y}^{-}_{i}$ for the i position is the position i nucleotide encoding value of the sequence R shown in Fig. 1, that is $y^{-}_{i} = (\overrightarrow{y}^{-}_{i} + \overleftarrow{y}^{-}_{i})/2$, where $\overrightarrow{y}^{-}_{i}$ and $\overleftarrow{y}^{-}_{i}$ are the elements $\overrightarrow{f}^{-}_{\alpha,AC,i}$ and $\overleftarrow{f}^{-}_{\alpha,AU,i}$ in $\overrightarrow{\boldsymbol{M}}^{-}$ and $\overleftarrow{\boldsymbol{M}}^{-}$.

Assume that the number of nucleotides contained in the fragment R of the sequence is l. Based on the dataset $\boldsymbol{D}^{+}$, the encoding value of the position i ($\alpha+2 \le i \le l-\alpha-1, 0 \le \alpha \le (l-3)/2$) in the sequence is y^{+}_{i}. Based on the dataset $\boldsymbol{D}^{-}$, the encoding value of the position i of the sequence R is y^{-}_{i}. The encoding value Y_{i} at position i of sequence R is expressed as the difference between the two, that is $Y_{i} = y^{+}_{i} - y^{-}_{i}$. Finally, the sequence R with the length of l is encoded as a $l - 2\alpha - 2$ dimensional feature vector $Y_{\alpha} = [Y_{\alpha+2}, Y_{\alpha+3}, \cdots, Y_{l-\alpha-1}]$.

Figure 2 shows the flow diagram of the DNA/RNA sequence feature representation method BiPSDP. For a DNA/RNA sequence R, based on the dinucleotide position-specific propensity matrices $\overrightarrow{\boldsymbol{M}}^{+}$ and $\overleftarrow{\boldsymbol{M}}^{+}$, the encoding value y^{+}_{i} of the position i ($\alpha+2 \le i \le l-\alpha-1, 0 \le \alpha \le (l-3)/2$) nucleotide is expressed as the mean value of the forward and backward dinucleotide position-specific propensity frequencies. Similarly, the encoding value y^{-}_{i} of the position i ($\alpha+2 \le i \le l-\alpha-1, 0 \le \alpha \le (l-3)/2$) nucleotide is denoted as the average of the forward and backward dinucleotide position-specific propensity frequencies, based on the dinucleotide position-specific preference matrices $\overrightarrow{\boldsymbol{M}}^{-}$ and $\overleftarrow{\boldsymbol{M}}^{-}$. The nucleotide at the position i of sequence R is encoded as the

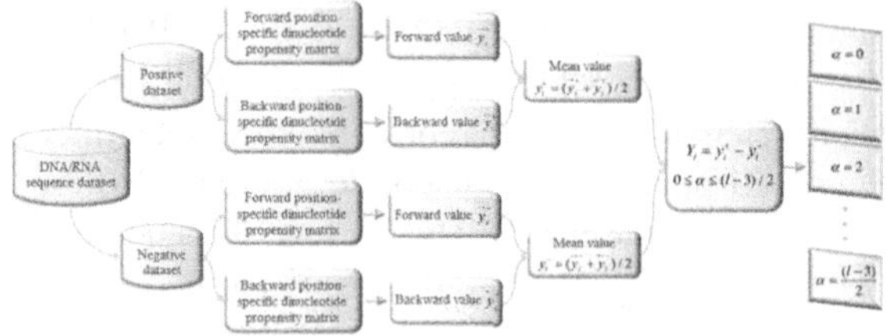

Fig. 2. The flow diagram of the DNA/RNA sequence feature representation method BiPSDP

difference between the encoding value of the nucleotide in the dataset D^+ and D^-, that is $Y_i = y_i^+ - y_i^-$, $(\alpha+2 \leq i \leq l - \alpha - 1)$. In order to extract the global dinucleotide position-specific preference information from the sequence and to reflect the sequence order information, the parameter α $(0 \leq \alpha \leq (l - 3)/2)$ is introduced to denote the spacing between the *ith* nucleotide and its forward or backward nucleotide. The feature vectors encoded by different values of the parameter α are combined to finally obtain a $(l - 3)^2/4$ dimensional feature vector $Y = \left[Y_0, Y_1, Y_2, \cdots, Y_{(l-5)/2}, Y_{(l-3)/2}\right]$.

2.3 Predictive Model and Evaluation

We constructed the methylation modification site prediction model based on SVM learning algorithm, and used the 10-fold cross-validation method to verify the robustness and generalizability of the model. For the acquired DNA/RNA methylation modification sites dataset, the bidirectional dinucleotide position-specific propensity information of the sequences was first extracted using the sequence feature representation method BiPSDP and encoded into numerical feature vectors. Then, the DNA/RNA modification sites prediction model based on the SVM learning algorithm was trained using the LibSVM toolkit developed by Lin et al. [28]. The SVM learning algorithm utilizes a radial basis kernel function. The penalty factor C and the kernel function parameters γ are set to search in the range of $[2^{-5}, 2^{15}]$ and $[2^{-15}, 2^5]$ with a search step of 1. The grid search method is used to obtain the parameter values that optimize the performance of the prediction model.

We use Acc (Accuracy), Sn (Sensitivity), Sp (Specificity) and MCC (Mathew's correlation coefficient), and two visualized composite metrics AUROC (Area under the receiver operating characteristic curve) and AUPRC (Area under the precision recall curve) as indicators for evaluating the performance of the prediction mode.

3 Results

3.1 Effects of the Parameter α

To extract global bidirectional dinucleotide position-specific propensity and nucleotide order information, we incorporated a parameter α $(0 \leq \alpha \leq (l - 3)/2)$ representing the distance between the target nucleotide and its upstream or downstream flanking nucleotide. Different values of the parameter generate distinct numerical feature vectors, which in turn affect the performance of SVM prediction models built upon these features.

To validate the impact of parameter values on the BiPSDP method's performance, this study constructed SVM prediction models based on both numerical features encoded by different parameter values and their cumulative combinations. Model performance was evaluated using the mean values of Acc, Sn, Sp, and MCC from 10-fold cross-validation experiments. Selected experimental results for two representative datasets are presented in Fig. 3, with corresponding data listed in Table 1. Specifically, bar charts illustrate the performance of models using features from different parameter values, while line charts display the performance of models incorporating cumulative combination features.

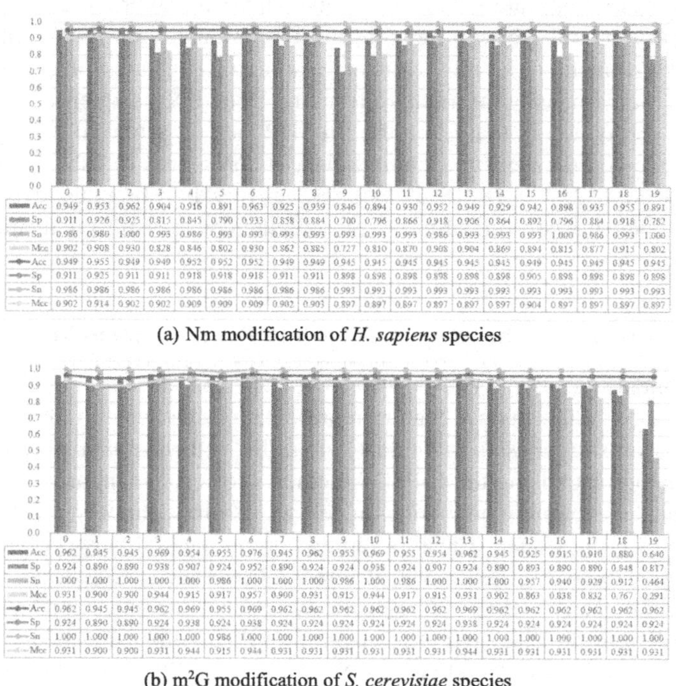

	0	1	2	3	4	5	6	7	8	9	10	11	12	13	14	15	16	17	18	19
Acc	0.949	0.953	0.962	0.904	0.916	0.891	0.963	0.925	0.939	0.846	0.894	0.930	0.952	0.949	0.929	0.942	0.898	0.935	0.955	0.891
Sp	0.911	0.926	0.925	0.815	0.845	0.790	0.933	0.858	0.884	0.700	0.796	0.866	0.918	0.906	0.864	0.892	0.796	0.884	0.918	0.782
Sn	0.986	0.980	1.000	0.993	0.986	0.993	0.993	0.993	0.993	0.993	0.993	0.993	0.986	0.993	0.993	0.993	1.000	0.986	0.993	1.000
Mcc	0.902	0.908	0.930	0.828	0.846	0.802	0.930	0.862	0.885	0.727	0.810	0.870	0.908	0.904	0.869	0.894	0.815	0.877	0.913	0.802
Acc	0.949	0.955	0.949	0.949	0.952	0.952	0.952	0.949	0.949	0.945	0.945	0.945	0.945	0.945	0.945	0.949	0.945	0.945	0.945	0.945
Sp	0.911	0.925	0.911	0.911	0.918	0.918	0.918	0.911	0.911	0.898	0.898	0.898	0.898	0.898	0.898	0.905	0.898	0.898	0.898	0.898
Sn	0.986	0.986	0.986	0.986	0.986	0.986	0.986	0.986	0.986	0.993	0.993	0.993	0.993	0.993	0.993	0.993	0.993	0.993	0.993	0.993
Mcc	0.902	0.914	0.902	0.902	0.909	0.909	0.909	0.902	0.903	0.897	0.897	0.897	0.897	0.897	0.897	0.904	0.897	0.897	0.897	0.897

(a) Nm modification of *H. sapiens* species

	0	1	2	3	4	5	6	7	8	9	10	11	12	13	14	15	16	17	18	19
Acc	0.962	0.945	0.945	0.969	0.954	0.955	0.976	0.945	0.962	0.955	0.969	0.955	0.954	0.962	0.945	0.925	0.915	0.910	0.880	0.640
Sp	0.924	0.890	0.890	0.938	0.907	0.924	0.952	0.890	0.924	0.924	0.938	0.924	0.907	0.924	0.890	0.893	0.890	0.890	0.848	0.817
Sn	1.000	1.000	1.000	1.000	1.000	0.986	1.000	1.000	1.000	0.986	1.000	0.986	1.000	1.000	1.000	0.957	0.940	0.929	0.912	0.464
Mcc	0.931	0.900	0.900	0.944	0.915	0.917	0.957	0.900	0.931	0.915	0.944	0.917	0.915	0.931	0.902	0.863	0.838	0.832	0.767	0.291
Acc	0.962	0.945	0.945	0.962	0.969	0.955	0.969	0.962	0.962	0.962	0.962	0.962	0.962	0.962	0.969	0.962	0.962	0.962	0.962	0.962
Sp	0.924	0.890	0.890	0.924	0.938	0.924	0.938	0.924	0.924	0.924	0.924	0.924	0.924	0.924	0.938	0.924	0.924	0.924	0.924	0.924
Sn	1.000	1.000	1.000	1.000	1.000	0.986	1.000	1.000	1.000	1.000	1.000	1.000	1.000	1.000	1.000	1.000	1.000	1.000	1.000	1.000
Mcc	0.931	0.900	0.900	0.931	0.944	0.915	0.944	0.931	0.931	0.931	0.931	0.931	0.931	0.931	0.944	0.931	0.931	0.931	0.931	0.931

(b) m²G modification of *S. cerevisiae* species

Fig. 3. The performance of SVM models on features by BiPSDP method via varying parameter on (a) Nm modification of *H. sapiens* species, (b) m²G modification of *S. cerevisiae* species

As can be seen from the bar charts of Fig. 3, as the value of parameter α increases, the performance of the SVM prediction model established based on the numerical features encoded by the BiPSDP method continuously declines. The reason is that when the value of parameter α increases, the interval between dinucleotides also increases accordingly, resulting in a gradual decrease in the number of bidirectional dinucleotides that meet the encoding requirements in the DNA/RNA sequence. When parameter α takes the maximum value $(l - 3)/2$, only the nucleotide at the middle position of the sequence meets the encoding conditions. At this time, the sequence can only be encoded into one numerical feature, and the performance of the SVM prediction model established based on this is the worst. It can be seen that as the value of parameter α continues to increase, the interval between the currently encoded nucleotide and its upstream/downstream nucleotides keeps getting larger, leading to a continuous decrease in the dimension of the encoded numerical features. As a result, effective classification information cannot be extracted from the DNA/RNA sequence.

The results of the line charts of Fig. 3 show that as the value of α increases, the performance of the SVM prediction model established based on the cumulative combined numerical features continuously rises until α reaches a certain value, at which point the performance of the prediction model reaches its maximum, and then remains stable or slightly declines. This indicates that the BiPSDP method can extract features containing local nucleotide position-specific propensity information from a DNA/RNA sequence with different values of α, which is helpful for improving the performance of the prediction model. This further confirms the rationality of introducing parameter α in the BiPSDP method, as this parameter can extract features of global nucleotide position-specific propensity information from the DNA/RNA sequence.

It is noteworthy noting that when the BiPSDP method achieved the highest classification accuracy on the seven benchmark datasets presented in Table 1, the values of parameter α were 1, 2, 1, 0, 18, 18, and 16, respectively. In subsequent experiments, we uniformly adopted the best prediction results obtained by the BiPSDP method under the optimal parameter α.

3.2 Comparison with Other Sequence Feature Representation Methods

In order to validate the effectiveness of BiPSDP, its performance is compared with seven existing very common sequence feature representation methods on the three methylation modification site datasets in Table 1. First, the sequence data were encoded into numerical feature data using the BiPSDP method and seven comparison methods, and then SVM machine learning prediction models were built separately, and the prediction performance of each sequence feature representation method was verified by 10-fold cross-validation method. The results of three datasets are selected and presented in Table 2. The parameter settings in comparative sequence feature representation methods are as follows: the DAC and DCC methods utilize 10 physicochemical properties of RNA dinucleotides for encoding of RNA sequences [29]; the 38 physicochemical properties of DNA dinucleotides for encoding DNA sequences; the parameter k in the k-mer method takes the value 3.

These seven counterpart sequence feature representation methods are as follows: DAC (Dinucleotide-based autocovariance), DCC (Dinucleotide-based cross-covariance), DBE (Dinucleotide binary encoding), ENAC (Dinucleotide-based cross-covariance), k-mer, KSNPF and LPDF (Local-position-specific dinucleotide frequency).

As can be seen from the experimental results in Table 2, the SVM prediction model trained based on the BiPSDP method, achieved the best classification accuracy on the three datasets. Compared with the second-ranked DCC, DBE, and DBE methods on the three datasets, the classification accuracy was improved by 12.94%, 20.69%, and 19.22% respectively. In terms of the metric of Sn, the prediction rate of our BiPSDP for positive-class samples was slightly inferior to that of some comparison methods, though it still demonstrated good prediction performance and was superior to most of the comparison methods. It can be concluded that the BiPSDP method can extract features with key class-distinguishing information from DNA/RNA sequences, and the prediction model

Table 2. Performance comparison of different sequence feature representation methods

Datasets	Methods	# feature	ACC	Sn	Sp	MCC	AUROC	AUPRC
H. sapiens m^{5}C	BiPSDP	**361**	**0.969**	0.938	**1.000**	**0.944**	**0.985**	**0.987**
	DAC	152	0.725	0.667	0.783	0.459	0.808	0.827
	DCC	160	0.858	0.817	0.900	0.722	0.928	0.943
	DBE	41	0.608	0.600	0.617	0.219	0.653	0.665
	ENAC	64	0.804	0.833	0.775	0.615	0.891	0.889
	k-mer	40	0.837	0.875	0.8000	0.683	0.901	0.900
	KSNPF	164	0.829	0.883	0.775	0.670	0.900	0.902
	LPDF	41	0.525	**0.958**	0.092	0.108	0.731	0.730
H. sapiens D	BiPSDP	**361**	**0.945**	0.850	**1.000**	**0.870**	**0.989**	**0.990**
	DAC	152	0.658	0.683	0.633	0.407	0.819	0.829
	DCC	160	0.708	0.733	0.683	0.455	0.828	0.820
	DBE	41	0.783	0.733	0.833	0.648	0.861	0.898
	ENAC	64	0.700	**0.967**	0.433	0.517	0.789	0.771
	k-mer	40	0.642	0.700	0.583	0.311	0.783	0.794
	KSNPF	164	0.733	0.717	0.750	0.490	0.794	0.761
	LPDF	41	0.492	0.433	0.550	0.019	0.778	0.641
S. cerevisiae D	BiPSDP	**361**	**0.918**	0.850	**0.986**	**0.849**	**0.977**	**0.981**
	DAC	152	0.643	0.712	0.574	0.308	0.733	0.737
	DCC	160	0.726	0.676	0.776	0.466	0.808	0.821
	DBE	41	0.770	0.762	0.779	0.555	0.852	0.862
	ENAC	64	0.727	0.781	0.674	0.469	0.831	0.838
	k-mer	40	0.610	0.824	0.395	0.243	0.811	0.855
	KSNPF	164	0.621	0.881	0.362	0.261	0.817	0.857
	LPDF	41	0.529	**1.000**	0.057	0.277	0.649	0.651

established based on this method can effectively identify methylated and non-methylated modification sites.

4 Conclusions

Accurate identification of DNA/RNA modification sites is the base to understand their functional mechanisms. To extract numerical features with critical class discriminative capabilities of DNA/RNA sequences, this paper proposed a sequence feature representation method named BiPSDP. Two contributions were proposed in BiPSDP. The first is that a bidirectional dinucleotide position-specific preference approach was proposed, which calculates the bidirectional dinucleotide position-specific preference frequencies simultaneously of DNA/RNA sequences, enabling the extraction of more nucleotide positional preference information from DNA/RNA sequences. The second is the parameterized distance mechanism is proposed by introducing parameter α to represent the distance between the target nucleotide and its upstream/downstream nucleotides in the bidirectional approach. High-dimensional features are constructed by concatenating feature vectors derived from different α values, approximating the positional and sequential information of DNA/RNA sequences. These innovations ensure that BiPSDP encodes DNA/RNA sequences into numerical features with rich class-discriminative information.

We validated the performance of the BiPSDP method on the datasets with different types of DNA/RNA modification sites by developing SVM prediction models built on the features extracted by BiPSDP method. The results of 10-fold cross-validation experiments show that the prediction model based on BiPSDP method can effectively identify multi-species and multi-type DNA/RNA modification sites. This shows that BiPSDP captures nucleotide positional and sequential information to generate high-quality discriminative features, enhancing the robustness and generalization performance of prediction models.

However, the high-dimensional feature vectors generated by BiPSDP may limit the discriminative ability of SVM models for real modification site samples. Future work will optimize the feature space through feature selection and integrate deep learning networks to further improve model performance by mining task-specific information.

Acknowledgments. The authors would like to thank those who provide public access datasets for us to use in this paper. This study is supported in part by the National Natural Science Foundation of China under Grant No. of 12031010, 62076159 and 61673251, and is also supported by the Natural Science Basic Research Plan in Shaanxi Province of China under Grant No. of 2024JC-YBQN-0662, and the China Postdoctoral Science Foundation under Grant No. 2024M761906.

References

1. Deng, X., et al.: The roles and implications of RNA m6A modification in cancer. Nat. Rev. Clin. Oncol. **20**, 507–526 (2023). https://doi.org/10.1038/s41571-023-00774-x

2. Han, K., et al.: A review of methods for predicting DNA N6-methyladenine sites. Briefings Bioinform. **24**(1), bbac514 (2022). https://doi.org/10.1093/bib/bbac514

3. Ye, P., et al.: MethSMRT: an integrative database for DNA N6-methyladenine and N4-methylcytosine generated by single-molecular real-time sequencing. Nucleic Acids Res. **45**(D1), D85–D89 (2016). https://doi.org/10.1093/nar/gkw950

4. Zhang, T., et al.: Programmable RNA 5-methylcytosine (m5C) modification of cellular RNAs by dCasRx conjugated methyltransferase and demethylase. Nucleic Acids Res. **52**(6), 2776–2791 (2024). https://doi.org/10.1093/nar/gkae110

5. Michalak, E.M., et al.: The roles of DNA, RNA and histone methylation in ageing and cancer. Nat. Rev. Mol. Cell Biol. **20**, 573–589 (2019). https://doi.org/10.1038/s41580-019-0143-1

6. Liu, R., et al.: TransAC4C—a novel interpretable architecture for multi-species identification of N4-acetylcytidine sites in RNA with single-base resolution. Briefings Bioinform. **25**(3) (2024). https://doi.org/10.1093/bib/bbae200

7. Lefin, N., et al.: Review and perspective on bioinformatics tools using machine learning and deep learning for predicting antiviral peptides. Mol. Divers. **28**, 2365–2374 (2024). https://doi.org/10.1007/s11030-023-10718-3

8. Asnicar, F., et al.: Machine learning for microbiologists. Nat. Rev. Microbiol. **22**, 191–205 (2024). https://doi.org/10.1038/s41579-023-00984-1

9. Desai, D., et al.: Review of AlphaFold 3: transformative advances in drug design and therapeutics. Cureus **16**(7), e63646 (2024). https://doi.org/10.7759/cureus.63646

10. Kong, Y., et al.: Navigating the pitfalls of mapping DNA and RNA modifications. Nat. Rev. Genet. **24**, 363–381 (2023). https://doi.org/10.1038/s41576-022-00559-5

11. Xie, J.Y., et al.: DNA/RNA sequence feature representation algorithms for predicting methylation-modified sites. Sci. Sin. Vitae **53**(6), 841–875 (2022). https://doi.org/10.1360/SSV-2022-0074

12. Yuge, C.C., et al.: RNA-ModX: a multilabel prediction and interpretation framework for RNA modifications. Briefings Bioinform. **26**(1), bbae688 (2024). https://doi.org/10.1093/bib/bbae688

13. Liu, B., et al.: BioSeq-Analysis2.0: an updated platform for analyzing DNA, RNA and protein sequences at sequence level and residue level based on machine learning approaches. Nucleic Acids Res. **47**(20), e127 (2019). https://doi.org/10.1093/nar/gkz740

14. Guo, S.H., et al.: INuc-PseKNC: a sequence-based predictor for predicting nucleosome positioning in genomes with pseudo k-tuple nucleotide composition. Bioinformatics **30**(11), 1522–1529 (2014). https://doi.org/10.1093/bioinformatics/btu083

15. Liu, B., et al.: Identification of real MicroRNA precursors with a pseudo structure status composition approach. PLoS ONE **10**(3), e0121501 (2015). https://doi.org/10.1371/journal.pone.0121501

16. Liu, B., et al.: MiRNA-dis: microRNA precursor identification based on distance structure status pairs. Mol. BioSyst. **11**, 1194–1204 (2015). https://doi.org/10.1039/C5MB00050E

17. Li, G.Q., et al.: Target M6A: identifying N6-methyladenosine sites from RNA sequences via position-specific nucleotide propensities and a support vector machine. IEEE Trans. Nanobiosci. **15**(7), 674–682 (2016). https://doi.org/10.1109/TNB.2016.2599115

18. Wang, M.Z., et al.: BiPSTP: sequence feature encoding method for identifying different RNA modifications with bidirectional position-specific trinucleotides propensities. J. Biol. Chem. **300**(4) (2024). https://doi.org/10.1016/j.jbc.2024.107140

19. Wang, M.Z., et al.: M6A-BiNP: predicting N6-methyladenosine sites based on bidirectional position-specific propensities of polynucleotides and pointwise joint mutual information. RNA Biol. **18**(12), 2498–2512 (2021). https://doi.org/10.1080/15476286.2021.1930729

20. Wang, M.Z., et al.: PSP-PJMI: An innovative feature representation algorithm for identifying DNA N4-methylcytosine sites. Inf. Sci. **606**, 968–983 (2022). https://doi.org/10.1016/j.ins.2022.05.060

21. Pham, N.T., et al.: ac4C-AFL: a high-precision identification of human mRNA N4-acetylcytidine sites based on adaptive feature representation learning. Mol. Therapy Nucleic Acids **35**(2) (2024). https://doi.org/10.1016/j.omtn.2024.102192

22. Ao, C., et al.: NmRF: identification of multispecies RNA 2'-O-methylation modification sites from RNA sequences. Briefings Bioinform. **23**(1) (2021). https://doi.org/10.1093/bib/bbab480

23. Feng, P., et al.: Identification of D modification sites by integrating heterogeneous features in Saccharomyces cerevisiae. Molecules **24**(3), 380 (2019)

24. Chen, W., et al.: IRNA-m2G: identifying N2-methylguanosine sites based on sequence-derived information. Mol. Ther. Nucleic Acids **18**, 253–258 (2019). https://doi.org/10.1016/j.omtn.2019.08.023

25. Song, J., et al.: Transcriptome-wide annotation of m5C RNA modifications using machine learning. Front. Plant Sci. **9** (2018). https://doi.org/10.3389/fpls.2018.00519

26. He, W., et al.: 4mCPred: machine learning methods for DNA N4-methylcytosine sites prediction. Bioinformatics **35**(4), 593–601 (2018). https://doi.org/10.1093/bioinformatics/bty668

27. Hasan, M.M., et al.: I6mA-Fuse: improved and robust prediction of DNA 6mA sites in the Rosaceae genome by fusing multiple feature representation. Plant Mol. Biol. **103**, 225–234 (2020). https://doi.org/10.1007/s11103-020-00988-y
28. Chang, C.-C., et al.: LIBSVM: a library for support vector machines. ACM Trans. Intell. Syst. Technol. **2**(3), Article 27 (2011). https://doi.org/10.1145/1961189.1961199
29. Liu, Z., et al.: PRNAm-PC: predicting N6-methyladenosine sites in RNA sequences via physical–chemical properties. Anal. Biochem. **497**, 60–67 (2016). https://doi.org/10.1016/j.ab.2015.12.017

Optical Flow-Augmented Dual-Stream Network for Left Ventricular Ejection Fraction Prediction

Feng Deng[1,2], Yi Tang[3,4], Qinghua Fu[3], Lin Guo[1], and Ying An[1(✉)]

[1] Big Data Institute, Central South University, Changsha 410083, China
anying@csu.edu.cn
[2] School of Computer Science and Engineering, Central South University,
Changsha 410083, China
[3] Department of Cardiology, Hunan Provincial People's Hospital/
The First Affiliated Hospital of Hunan Normal University,
Changsha 410083, China
[4] Clinical Medicine Research Center of Heart Failure of Hunan Province,
Hunan Normal University, Changsha 410083, China

Abstract. The accurate prediction of the left ventricular ejection fraction (LVEF) in echocardiograms is limited by low image resolution, artifact interference, and the complexity of cardiac motion. These challenges lead to significant deficiencies in most existing methods in terms of local spatio-temporal dependency modeling and fine-grained motion capture. To address these issues, this paper proposes an Optical Flow-Augmented Dual-Stream Network (OFDS). The innovation of this model lies in the construction of an optical flow feature enhancement branch to compensate for the limitations of the global spatio-temporal feature extraction method based on Uniformer. Specifically, the optical flow enhancement branch optimizes the local motion representation ability through the following techniques: 1) Segmentation Enhanced Feature Extraction Module: by combining semantic segmentation and optical flow calculation, it enables the extraction of targeted optical flow features of the left ventricle, effectively isolating the motion interference from non-target regions such as other chambers; 2) Optical Flow Correction Module: by introducing the irrotational condition constraint and the strain rate consistency constraint, it adaptively corrects the optical flow features in the ultrasound modality based on the reconstruction task, overcoming the adaptability limitations of traditional optical flow algorithms for low-quality ultrasound sequences; 3) Adaptive Gating Fusion Module: it dynamically integrates the global spatio-temporal features extracted by Uniformer with the corrected local optical flow features, balancing the global structure and local motion information, and improving the robustness of LVEF calculation. Our model is validated on two datasets and the experimental results demonstrate that OFDS outperforms the state-of-the-art methods.

Keywords: Echocardiogram · Optical Flow · LVEF Prediction

J. Tang et al. (Eds.): ISBRA 2025, LNBI 15757, pp. 241–252, 2026.
https://doi.org/10.1007/978-981-95-0695-8_20

1   Introduction

As global population aging intensifies and cardiovascular disease incidence rises [1], cardiac health assessment has become increasingly crucial. Echocardiography, due to its advantages such as non-invasiveness, real-time nature, and high efficiency, is widely used in the screening and diagnosis of cardiovascular diseases. In particular, the Left Ventricular Ejection Fraction (LVEF), as a core indicator for measuring the heart's pumping function, has important guiding value in the diagnosis and treatment of diseases such as heart failure, coronary heart disease, and valvular heart disease [2]. However, echocardiogram analysis and LVEF calculation are highly dependent on the professional knowledge of clinicians. According to the requirements of the guidelines [3], in order to accurately assess the left ventricular pumping function, five cardiac cycles should be continuously analyzed and their average value should be used for evaluation. This process not only has problems such as strong subjectivity, poor repeatability, large inter-observer and intra-observer errors, but is also extremely time-consuming and laborious.

Medical image analysis based on deep learning has shown great potential in many medical problems, such as the analysis of the causes of left ventricular hypertrophy [4], brain tumor classification [5], etc. Many researchers have also applied the latest achievements of deep learning to automated LVEF prediction, leading to significant breakthroughs in this field in recent years. These efforts can be roughly divided into two approaches: two-stage LVEF calculation based on echocardiogram analysis and end-to-end LVEF prediction.

The two-stage calculation method means a deep learning model is used to complete the prediction of relevant indicators in the first stage, and then the relevant calculation formulas of Simpson's method or the area-length method are used to calculate LVEF [6–10]. The drawback of these methods is the final LVEF calculation depends on the prediction accuracy of the pre-task and the calculation method based on geometrically assumed cardiac modeling. The error accumulation of the pre-task and the difficulty of the actual heart fully fitting the geometric assumptions will both lead to the accumulation of LVEF calculation errors. End-to-end LVEF prediction directly predicts LVEF using the powerful feature extraction ability of deep learning models. Ouyang et al. [11] was the first attempt at end-to-end LVEF prediction. It used R2plus1d to predict LVEF and finally achieved an accuracy comparable to that of human experts. Subsequently, a large number of researchers have applied the latest deep learning techniques to the LVEF prediction task, For example, Transformer models [12,13], CNN and Transformer hybrid architecture models [14], graph convolutional network [15], etc. However, most existing methods implicitly enhance the network's expression ability in a certain aspect from the perspective of network design to improve the accuracy of the LVEF task, without considering explicitly enhancing the network's expression ability through artificially designed features.

Optical flow is a motion vector field that describes the corresponding pixel points between video frames and is a key technology for studying the motion information of objects between adjacent frames. Compared with implicitly enhancing the model's local or global temporal feature extraction ability only by means of network module design, explicitly embedding a strong temporal feature can further enhance the network's expression ability [16].

Drawing on the successful practices in the field of action recognition [17], we introduce the two-stream network architecture to the LVEF prediction for the first time, and propose a Optical Flow-Augmented Dual-Stream Network (OFDS). OFDS consists of two streams and a fusion module. The spatio-temporal feature extraction stream (STFES) uses Uniformer [18] for spatio-temporal feature extraction, and the optical flow features augmented stream (OFFAS) is used to capture the fine-grained local motion patterns of the left ventricle. There is also an Adaptive Gated Fusion Module (AGFM) for dynamically fusion of spatio-temporal features and optical flow features. Specifically, we design two modules for optical flow feature extraction in OFFAS: (1) To avoid the optical flow information of other ventricles interfering with the learning of target ventricular motion patterns, a Segmentation Enhancement feature extraction Module (SEM) was proposed. By using a lightweight segmentation network to extract the left ventricular region and using R2plus1d [19] to feature only the optical flow in this region, SEM significantly avoids the interference of motion patterns between different structures. (2) In order to solve the inadaptability of traditional optical flow algorithm in echocardiography, an Optical Flow Correction Module (OFCM) is designed. The optical flow feature extractor corrects features during the optical flow reconstruction process with the help of kinematic constraints, ensuring that the optical flow features conform to the kinematic laws of the heart.

The remainder of the paper is structured as follows: Sect. 2 elaborates on the detailed design of OFDS. Section 3 outlines the experimental setup and presents the analysis of results, while Sect. 4 offers the paper's conclusion.

2 Methodology

2.1 Problem Definition

The objective of this paper is to predict LVEF based on two-dimensional echocardiograms of the four-chamber view. Specifically, given the echocardiogram data $X^u = [x_1^u, x_2^u, \ldots, x_T^u]$ of a patient u, where T represents the total number of frames and x_t^u represents ultrasound image of the t-th frame. Therefore, the task of OFDS can be formulated as: based on the echocardiogram data X^u of patient u, predict the LVEF y^u of the patient, that is $y^u = OFDS(X^u)$.

2.2 Overview

The architecture diagram of the OFDS model is presented in Fig. 1. This framework is composed of two branches: STFES and OFFAS. STFES utilizes Uniformer [18] to extract the spatial structure and temporal information of the heart from the original echocardiogram. In OFFAS, the optical flow of the echocardiogram was first calculated using the algorithm TV-L1 [20]. After that,

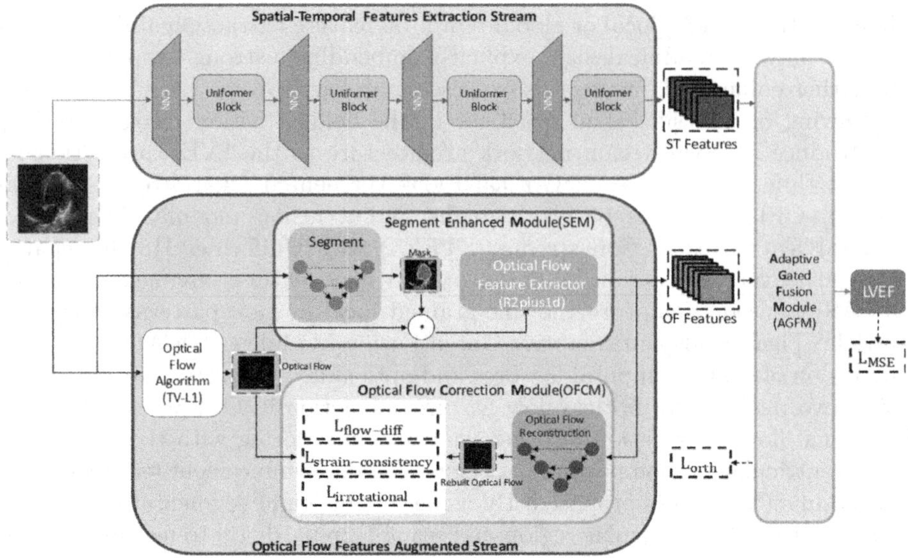

Fig. 1. The overall architecture diagram of OFDS

SEM combines the segmentation mask with the optical flow and extract the optical flow features. Then, OFCM is used to correct the optical flow representation. Finally, the framework dynamically weights and fuses the features of the two streams through AGFM to suppress redundant information. Finally, the fused features pass through a classifier to estimate LVEF.

2.3 STFES

STFES is responsible for extracting the spatio-temporal features of the heart from the original echocardiogram. As a fundamental module of the two-stream network, the design goal of STFES is to provide high-quality spatio-temporal feature representations for subsequent feature fusion. STFES uses Uniformer [18] as the feature extractor to perform spatio-temporal feature extraction on the echocardiogram input. As shown in Fig. 1, Unifromer is a hybrid CNN and transformer framework. It designs a module combining DW convolution and multi-head attention, called Uniformer Block, which realizes efficient global spatio-temporal feature extraction by stacking CNN and Uniformer Block. Specifically, for an echocardiogram X^u, the processing flow of STFES can be simply symbolized as

$$F_{st}^u = STFES(X^u) = Uniformer(X^u) \tag{1}$$

2.4 OFFAS

OFFAS aims to extract physiologically reasonable motion features from the optical flow field by introducing segmentation knowledge and kinematic constraints.

First, this branch uses an optical flow algorithm TV-L1 to calculate the optical flow features V^u of the input echocardiogram X^u. Then the segmentation enhanced optical flow representation F_{of}^u is obtained through the SEM. During this process, both the original optical flow representation V^u and the final optical flow representation F_{of}^u need to be corrected by the OFCM.

Calculation of the Optical Flow Field: The calculation of the optical flow field is the first step of OFATMS. We adopt the TV-L1 optical flow algorithm [20] to generate the initial optical flow field $V^u = [v_1^u, v_2^u, \cdots, v_{T-1}^u]$, where V_t^u represents the optical flow field between the t-th frame and the $(t+1)$-th frame. The TV-L1 algorithm is a dense optical flow algorithm based on variational optimization. This algorithm performs excellently in handling complex dynamic scenes. Especially in data such as echocardiograms with high noise and low resolution, the TV-L1 algorithm can generate a more accurate and stable optical flow field.

SEM: SEM is a two-stage optical flow feature extractor. Firstly, the left ventricle is segmented through a lightweight segmentation network and the optical flow in the left ventricular region is extracted by the segmentation mask. Then the optical flow feature is extracted through R2plus1d. SEM can significantly increase the attention of the optical flow branch to the target area and avoid the interference of different motion patterns of other ventricular cavities on the learning of the motion pattern of the target region. Due to the use of a lightweight segmentation network, there may inevitably be inaccurate segmentation boundaries. To prevent the target features from being masked, the mask is expanded by dilating the edges. That is, 5 pixels are expanded outward on the basis of the original mask M^u to obtain the final mask representation M_{final}^u, as

$$M_{final}^u(t, i, j) = \begin{cases} 1, & dist(t, i, j, M^u) <= 5 \\ 0, & dist(t, i, j, M^u) > 5 \end{cases} \tag{2}$$

where $dist(\cdot)$ computes the minimum Euclidean distance from the point (i, j) in the t-th frame to the contour of the mask region in the reference frame.

After extracting the optical flow field, SEM applies the extended segmentation mask M_{final}^u to the optical flow field V^u frame by frame, retaining only the optical flow information of the left atrial region, as shown in

$$V_{sem}^u = V^u * M_{final}^u \tag{3}$$

R2plus1d is used to perform optical flow feature extraction on the segmented enhanced optical flow V_{sem}^u which can be formulated as

$$F_{of}^u = R2plus1d(V_{sem}^u) \tag{4}$$

OFCM: OFCM reconstructs the optical flow by upsampling the multilevel optical flow feature F_{of}^u obtained by SEM, denoted as $V_{rebuilt}^u$. In this process, the representation of the reconstructed optical flow is constrained to modify the features learned by SEM. Specifically, we set a series of physical constraints to force the reconstructed optical flow to be numerically and physically similar to the original optical flow. Finally, it is ensured that the optical flow features extracted by SEM could not only accurately capture the inter-frame motion information, but also conform to the motion law of the heart.

The Jacobian matrix of the optical flow field can be used to describe the motion state of the heart. For the optical flow V is denoted as $V = (u, v)$, where u and v denote the horizontal and vertical motion vectors respectively, the Jacobian matrix J is defined as

$$J = \begin{pmatrix} \frac{\partial u}{\partial x} & \frac{\partial u}{\partial y} \\ \frac{\partial v}{\partial x} & \frac{\partial v}{\partial y} \end{pmatrix} \tag{5}$$

The Jacobian matrix can be decomposed into a symmetric part E_{sym} and an anti-symmetric part $E_{anti-sym}$. The symmetric part E_{sym} represents the strain rate tensor, which reflects the stretch and compression of the cardiac tissue. The antisymmetric part $E_{anti-sym}$ represents the rotational component.

Cardiac motion is a highly regular biomechanical process, and its motion pattern should satisfy the irrotational condition. The so-called irrotational condition means that there is no local rotation component in the cardiac tissue during motion, that is, the curl of the motion vector field is zero. The irrotational condition requires that $E_{anti-sym} = 0$. In order to make the reconstructed optical flow satisfy the irrotational condition, we propose the irrotational conditional loss which is defined as

$$L_{irrotational} = \lambda_1 \cdot ||E'_{anti-sym}||_F^2 \tag{6}$$

where λ_1 is the weight coefficient. $|| \cdot ||_F^2$ denotes the Frobenius norm.

The strain rate tensor describes the local deformation properties of the cardiac tissue, including stretching, compression, etc. In order to ensure that the strain rate tensor E'_{sym} of the reconstructed optical flow field $V^u_{rebuilt}$ is consistent with the strain rate tensor E_{sym} of the initial optical flow field V^u, the strain consistency loss is introduced which is written as

$$L_{strain-consistency} = \lambda_2 \cdot ||E'_{sym} - E_{sym}||_F^2 \tag{7}$$

where λ_2 is the weighting coefficient. Through this constraint, it is ensured that the learned optical flow field features are consistent with the cardiac kinematics.

To ensure that the reconstructed optical flow field $V^u_{rebuilt}$ is as consistent as possible with the initial optical flow field V^u, the optical flow difference constraint is introduced. The goal of this constraint is to ensure that the features generated by the optical flow feature extractor can accurately reflect the information of the original optical flow field by minimizing the difference between them. Mathematically, this constraint can be expressed as

$$L_{flow-diff} = \lambda_3 \cdot ||V^u_{rebuilt} - V^u||_F^2 \tag{8}$$

where λ_3 is the weight coefficient. This constraint ensures that the reconstructed optical flow field $V^u_{rebuilt}$ is numerically close to the initial optical flow field V^u, thus improving the accuracy of the optical flow representation.

2.5   AGFM

AGFM aims to effectively fuse the feature representation of the spatio-temporal feature extraction branch and the optical flow feature enhancement branch through a dynamic weighting mechanism.

Dynamic Weight Calculation: In order to dynamically adjust the contribution ratio of the two branches, we introduce a gated network for generating the weight matrix, which is shown as

$$g = \sigma(W_g[F_{st}, F_{of}] + b_g) \tag{9}$$

where $g \in R^d$ is the gated weight vector used to control the contribution ratio of F_{st} and F_{flow}, $W_g \in R^{d*2d}$ is the learnable weight matrix, $b_g \in R^d$ is the bias term, σ is the Sigmoid activation function, $[F_{st}, F_{flow}]$ represents the concatenation of F_{st} and F_{flow}.

Output Feature Representation: Based on the gating weight g, the fusion feature F_{fusion} can be expressed as

$$F_{fusion} = g \odot F_{st} + (1 - g) \odot F_{of} \tag{10}$$

where $\odot$ represents an element-by-element multiplication operation, which can dynamically adjust the contribution ratio of the two branches according to the task requirements, so as to suppress redundant information and improve the efficiency of feature fusion.

Feature Orthogonality Constraint: To further improve the feature complementarity, we add a regularization term to the loss function called feature orthogonality constraint. Its mathematical expression is

$$L_{orth} = \lambda||F_{st}^\top F_{of}||_F^2 \tag{11}$$

where L_{orth} is the regularization term used to constrain the orthogonality of F_{st} and F_{of}, λ is the balance factor that controls the strength of the regularization term.

3   Experiments

3.1   Data Description and Preprocessing

In this chapter, the dataset published in Echonet-Dynamic and a private dataset EchoHPPS are used to verify the effectiveness of the OFDS model.

1) Echonet-Dynamic [11]: The Echonet-Dynamic dataset was collected by Stanford University Hospital during routine clinical examinations from 2016 to 2018. It contains 10,030 Apical Four-Chamber (A4C) view echocardiography videos and corresponding cardiac function measurements. Echonet-Dynamic is the largest publicly available echocardiogram dataset, which mainly contains LVEF labels and LV segmentation labels of some frames.

2) EchoHPPS: EchoHPPS dataset contains 777 four-chamber echocardiography videos collected from clinical examinations in Hunan Provincial People's

Hospital from 2023 to 2024, and the corresponding ejection fraction measurements and left ventricular segmentation labels annotated by human experts.

The preprocessing scheme for the datasets are the same. Namely, personal information processing, downsampling to standardized video, optical flow video computation, and segmentation. Finally, the datasets will be split at 70:15:15 into training, test, and validation sets.

3.2   Implementations

We implemented all the codes based on PyTorch1.6.0, and all the experiments were done in a computing environment equipped with a single NVIDIA A30 GPU. To ensure the stability and efficiency of model training, we use the AdamW optimizer and carefully configure its key parameters. The initial learning rate was set to $1e^{-4}$, and the learning rate was dynamically adjusted using a cosine annealing strategy, which was attenuated to 0.1 times of the original after every 15 rounds of training. The total training rounds were set to 45 rounds, the weight attenuation coefficient was set to $1e^{-4}$, and the gradient clipping threshold was set to 1.0. The batch size is set to 8.

In addition, to comprehensively evaluate the performance of the model, we use the following various evaluation metrics: Mean Absolute Error (MAE), Mean Squared Error (MSE), and Coefficient of Determination (R^2).

3.3   Baselines

We consider the following baselines to compare with the proposed OFDS.

- *Echonet* [11]: Efficient 3D convolution Model based on Spatio-temporal separated convolution.
- *Echo-CoTr* [14]: A CNN and Transformer hybrid network which is good at capturing long-range temporal dependencies and local spatial features.
- *UVT* [12]: It is a model based on Transformer architecture. It uses residual autoencoder network for visual feature extraction, and then uses BERT model for time series modeling.
- *EchoGraph* [15]: It is a model based on graph neural network. Its core idea is to consider multiple points of the left ventricular wall as graph nodes, and optimize the echocardiogram representation by capturing the correlation between these points through the graph structure.
- *CNNLSTM* [21]: A CNN and LSTM hybrid network. CNN was used to extract the spatial features of a single frame, and LSTM was used to model the spatial features of consecutive frames.

Table 1. Performance Results of OFDS vs Baseline Model

Model	Echonet-Dynamic			EchoHPPS		
	MAE	MSE	R^2	MAE	MSE	R^2
EchoNet	4.22	5.62	0.789	5.28	6.88	0.456
Echo-CoTr	4.05	5.34	0.809	5.07	6.72	0.590
UVT	5.95	8.38	0.521	7.79	10.75	0.237
EchoGraph	4.12	5.53	0.791	5.64	6.99	0.534
CNNLSTM	6.11	8.47	0.492	7.57	9.89	0.254
OFDS	**3.86**	**5.29**	**0.814**	**4.75**	**6.50**	**0.677**

3.4 Comparison with Baseline Results

The detailed results are given in Table 1, where bold underlined values indicate the best values for the current column. In both datasets, OFDS obtains the best results, which strongly demonstrates the gain of local motion pattern modeling brought by the introduction of optical flow branches for the LVEF prediction task. CNN-LSTM achieves the worst performance among all compared methods due to its insufficient ability to model spatio-temporal joint features. Although the transformer-based architecture of UVT is good at modeling long-range temporal dependencies, it cannot well understand the spatial structure of the left ventricle, and there is still a lot of room for improvement in LVEF prediction. Although EchoNet uses R(2+1)D convolution operation to model the spatio-temporal relationship of multiple 2D ultrasound image sequences, its performance is moderate because it mainly focuses on local spatio-temporal characteristics and is difficult to capture long-distance dependencies. Its overall performance is limited by insufficient modeling of global dependencies. Echo-Graphs considers multiple points of the left ventricular wall as graph nodes, and captures the correlation between these points through the graph structure. However, its ability to model time series information is weak, and its overall performance is limited by the insufficient ability to model time series. With a hybrid architecture combining CNN and Transformer, Echo-CoTr can efficiently extract local features and model global spatio-temporal dependencies, so it performs the best among all baseline models. This result suggests that jointly modeling spatio-temporal features is extremely important for LVEF prediction in echocardiographic analysis. The experimental results in smaller volume EchoH-PPS reflect a similar trend, which also proves the good generalization of OFDS network.

3.5 Ablation Experiments

In order to deeply analyze the contribution of each module in OFDS to the model performance, this study will conduct several ablation experiments and observe the changes in model performance. Among them, for the removal of the

Table 2. Ablation Study of OFDS Design on Echonet-Dynamic

Group	Module			Echonet-Dynamic			EchoHPPS		
	AGFM	**S**EM	**O**FRM	MAE	MSE	R^2	MAE	MSE	R^2
OFDS	✓	✓	✓	**3.86**	**5.29**	**0.814**	**4.75**	**6.50**	**0.677**
OFDS-w/o O	✓	✓	×	4.15	5.55	0.789	5.04	6.76	0.652
OFDS-w/o S	✓	×	✓	4.10	5.48	0.795	4.99	6.69	0.658
OFDS-w/o A	×	✓	✓	4.01	5.36	0.807	4.90	6.57	0.670
OFDS-w/o AS	×	×	✓	4.12	5.30	0.793	5.01	6.51	0.656
OFDS-w/o ASO	×	×	×	4.22	5.62	0.786	5.11	6.83	0.649

AGFM module, the average will be used for feature fusion. All experiments will be evaluated on the Echonet-Dynamic dataset with the same training set and test set to ensure the fairness of experimental results. The results of ablation experiments are shown in Table 2. From the experimental results, we can see that there are some differences in the contribution of different modules to the model performance.

Observe the results found on Echonet-Dynamic, after removing OFCM, there is a significant decrease in performance. This result shows that OFCM plays a crucial role in optimizing the optical flow representation. The optical flow calculated based on echocardiography is itself coarse, and it is difficult to provide accurate and beneficial timing features for downstream tasks due to large noise and low image contrast. Therefore, the overall performance is decreased after removing OFCM. This phenomenon fully demonstrates the critical role of OFCM in improving the quality of optical flow and improving the prediction accuracy. MAE, and MSE increased by 3.27% and 3.20% respectively while R^2 decreased by 2.00% after removing SEM. This shows that SEM can effectively reduce the interference of irrelevant regions by introducing segmentation masks, that is, reduce the interference of different motion patterns of other ventricles, thereby improving the ability of the model to capture the dynamic characteristics of the left atrial region. After removing AGFM, the performance of the model drops slightly, with only 0.49% drop in R^2, indicating that the role of this module is relatively limited. After removing SEM on the basis of removing AGFM, the performance further decreases, and the decrease is larger, which shows that the effect of SEM is larger than that of AGFM. After removing OFCM on the basis of removing AGFM and SEM, all indicators have fallen sharply. This result shows that OFCM plays a key role in optimizing the optical flow representation, and precisely proves that the optical flow features corrected by this module can bring further performance improvement to the model. The experimental results in EchoHPPS reflect a similar trend.

4   Conclusion

In this paper, OFDS is proposed for the LVEF prediction task in echocardiography. By introducing the SEM and the OFCM, OFDS avoids the motion patterns of other ventricles from interfering with the learning of the motion patterns of the left ventricle, which significantly improves the attention of the model to the key regions and the physiological rationality of the optical flow field. Under the action of AGFM, OFDS realizes the complementary fusion of spatio-temporal features and optical flow features. The experimental results show that OFDS outperforms the existing methods in LVEF prediction task, and the ablation analysis of different modules further verifies the effective role of each module in improving the performance of the model.

Acknowledgement. This work is supported in part by the National Natural Science Foundation of China(62372476, 62402532), and the Natural Science Foundation of Hunan Province in China(2024JJ5446, 2024JJ6533).

References

1. Nedkoff, L., Briffa, T., Zemedikun, D., Herrington, S., Wright, F.L.: Global trends in atherosclerotic cardiovascular disease. Clin. Ther. **45**(11), 1087–1091 (2023)
2. Chow, B., et al.: Prognostic value of 64-slice cardiac computed tomography severity of coronary artery disease, coronary atherosclerosis, and left ventricular ejection fraction. J. Am. Coll. Cardiol. **55**(10), 1017–28 (2010)
3. Lang, R.M., et al.: Recommendations for cardiac chamber quantification by echocardiography in adults: an update from the American society of echocardiography and the european association of cardiovascular imaging. Europ. Heart J.-Cardiovascular Imaging **16**(3), 233–271 (2015)
4. Holste, G., Oikonomou, E.K., Mortazavi, B.J., Wang, Z., Khera, R.: Efficient deep learning-based automated diagnosis from echocardiography with contrastive self-supervised learning. Commun. Med. **4**(1), 133 (2024)
5. Liu, X., Wang, Z.: Deep learning in medical image classification from mri-based brain tumor images. In: 2024 IEEE 6th International Conference on Power, Intelligent Computing and Systems (ICPICS), pp. 840–844 (2024)
6. Zhang, J., et al.: Fully automated echocardiogram interpretation in clinical practice: feasibility and diagnostic accuracy. Circulation **138**(16), 1623–1635 (2018)
7. Smistad, E., et al.: Real-time automatic ejection fraction and foreshortening detection using deep learning. IEEE Trans. Ultrason. Ferroelectr. Freq. Control **67**(12), 2595–2604 (2020)
8. Asch, F.M., et al.: Deep learning–based automated echocardiographic quantification of left ventricular ejection fraction: a point-of-care solution. Circulation: Cardiovascular Imaging **14**(6), e012293 (2021)
9. Smistad, E., Østvik, A., Salte, I.M., Leclerc, S., Bernard, O., Lovstakken, L.: Fully automatic real-time ejection fraction and mapse measurements in 2d echocardiography using deep neural networks. In: 2018 IEEE International Ultrasonics Symposium (IUS), pp. 1–4 (2018)

10. Silva, J.F., Silva, J.M., Guerra, A., Matos, S., Costa, C.: Ejection fraction classification in transthoracic echocardiography using a deep learning approach. In: 2018 IEEE 31st International Symposium on Computer-Based Medical Systems (CBMS), pp. 123–128 (2018)

11. Ouyang, D., et al.: Video-based ai for beat-to-beat assessment of cardiac function. Nature **580**(7802), 252–256 (2020)

12. Reynaud, H., Vlontzos, A., Hou, B., Beqiri, A., Leeson, P., Kainz, B.: Ultrasound video transformers for cardiac ejection fraction estimation. In: Medical Image Computing and Computer Assisted Intervention – MICCAI 2021. LNCS, vol. 12906, pp. 495–505. Springer, Cham (2021)

13. Fazry, L., Haryono, A., Nissa, N.K., Hirzi, N.M., Rachmadi, M.F., Jatmiko, W., et al.: Hierarchical vision transformers for cardiac ejection fraction estimation. In: 2022 7th International Workshop on Big Data and Information Security (IWBIS), pp. 39–44. IEEE (2022)

14. Muhtaseb, R., Yaqub, M.: Echocotr: Estimation of the left ventricular ejection fraction from spatiotemporal echocardiography. In: Medical Image Computing and Computer Assisted Intervention – MICCAI 2022. LNCS, vol. 13434, pp. 370–379. Springer, Cham (2022)

15. Thomas, S., Gilbert, A., Ben-Yosef, G.: Light-weight spatio-temporal graphs for segmentation and ejection fraction prediction in cardiac ultrasound. In: International Conference on Medical Image Computing and Computer-Assisted Intervention, pp. 380–390. Springer (2022)

16. Mu, X., Kon, M.: Feature network methods in machine learning and applications. ArXiv abs/2401.04874 (2024)

17. Simonyan, K., Zisserman, A.: Two-stream convolutional networks for action recognition in videos. Advances in neural information processing systems **27** (2014)

18. Li, K., Wang, Y., Zhang, J., Gao, P., Song, G., Liu, Y., Li, H., Qiao, Y.: Uniformer: unifying convolution and self-attention for visual recognition. IEEE Trans. Pattern Anal. Mach. Intell. **45**(10), 12581–12600 (2023)

19. Tran, D., Wang, H., Torresani, L., Ray, J., LeCun, Y., Paluri, M.: A closer look at spatiotemporal convolutions for action recognition. In: Proceedings of the IEEE conference on Computer Vision and Pattern Recognition, pp. 6450–6459 (2018)

20. Sánchez Pérez, J., Meinhardt-Llopis, E., Facciolo, G.: Tv-l1 optical flow estimation. Image Process. Line **3**, 137–150 (2013)

21. Barros, B., Lacerda, P., Albuquerque, C., Conci, A.: Pulmonary covid-19: Learning spatiotemporal features combining cnn and lstm networks for lungultra sound video classification. Sensors **21**(16), 5486 (2021)

Joint Sparse Precision Matrix Estimation
for Cancer Diagnosis

Rwan Ahmed[1] , Kang Jiang[1] , and Fang-Xiang Wu[1,2,3(✉)]

[1] Division of Biomedical Engineering, University of Saskatchewan, Saskatoon, Canada
{dbh158,kaj014}@mail.usask.ca
[2] Department of Mechanical Engineering, University of Saskatchewan, Saskatoon,
Canada
faw341@mail.usask.ca
[3] Department of Computer Science, University of Saskatchewan, Saskatoon, Canada

Abstract. Covariance or its inverse (called precision) matrix estimation is very useful in data analyses. In principle, the empirical covariance matrix calculated with the unlimited samples is an unbiased estimation of the covariance matrix of the distribution from which samples are drawn, but there are only a very limited samples available in many real-life applications. Therefore, ℓ_1-regularized estimation methods are developed in recovering a sparse precision matrix. However, the ℓ_1-regularization has its own drawbacks. To address these drawbacks and the issue of limited samples with multi-classes in biomedical applications, we propose a joint sparse precision matrix estimation method, in which the SCAD-regularization is used for sparsity and the Frobenius norm of the between-class precision matrix difference is adopted to reinforce the similarity among classes. An alternating direction method of multipliers and an iterative weighted penalized method are developed to optimize the objective function. Fisher's linear discriminant analysis with the estimated precision matrices is applied to two gene expression datasets for lung cancer diagnosis. The diagnosis results indicate the excellent performance of our proposed method for estimating precision matrices.

Keywords: Precision matrix · Sparsity · Alternating direction method of multipliers · Iterative weighted penalized method · Fisher's linear discriminant analysis · Cancer diagnosis

1 Introduction

For a p-dimensional random vector X with a covariance matrix $\Sigma \in \mathbb{R}^{p \times p}$, the precision matrix $\Theta \in \mathbb{R}^{p \times p}$ is defined as the inverse covariance matrix, that is $\Theta = \Sigma^{-1}$. While the covariance matrix Σ describes the pairwise linear relationships between variables, the precision matrix Θ captures conditional dependencies between variables [1]. Specifically, the element $\Theta_{ij} = 0$ means that variables X_i and X_j are conditionally independent, given all other variables. This makes precision matrices useful in Gaussian graphical models (GGMs), where they

J. Tang et al. (Eds.): ISBRA 2025, LNBI 15757, pp. 253–264, 2026.
https://doi.org/10.1007/978-981-95-0695-8_21

define the structure of an undirected graph among variables [2], as well as in estimation of covariance matrices [3].

Given an observation dataset $\mathbf{X} \in \mathbb{R}^{n \times p}$ sampled from a normal distribution, where n is the number of observations and p is the number of features, the precision matrix Θ can be estimated with the maximum likelihood. Letting $\mathbf{S}$ denote the empirical covariance matrix of $\mathbf{X}$, the negative log-likelihood takes the form (up to a constant)

$$\frac{n}{2} \left[\mathrm{tr}(\mathbf{S}\Theta) - \log \det(\Theta) \right] \tag{1}$$

where $\mathrm{tr}(\cdot)$ and $\det(\cdot)$ denote the trace and determinant of a matrix, respectively.

Minimizing (1) with respect to Θ yields the maximum likelihood estimate $\mathbf{S}^{-1}$. However, two issues can arise with this maximum likelihood approach to estimate Θ. First, in case that the number of features p is larger than the number of observations n (for example, the number of genes (features) is typically much larger than the number of patients (observations)), the empirical covariance matrix $\mathbf{S}$ is singular and so cannot be inverted to yield an estimate of Θ. Second, even if the inverse of $\mathbf{S}$ exists, it is generally a dense matrix, which is not interesting in practical applications.

To address these issues, the sparsity of Θ is studied via the penalized negative log-likelihood, with an appropriately chosen penalty function. A challenge in the sparse precision matrix estimation is to optimize the penalized likelihood, subject to the positive-definiteness constraint of the precision matrix and the proper choice of penalty function. A common penalty function is the L_1 norm of Θ, which is defined as $\|\Theta\|_1 = \sum_{i=1}^{p} \sum_{j=1}^{p} |\Theta_{ij}|$. As a result, the L_1 norm penalized negative log-likelihood becomes

$$\frac{n}{2} \left[\mathrm{tr}(\mathbf{S}\Theta) - \log \det(\Theta) \right] + \lambda \|\Theta\|_1 \tag{2}$$

which is also called the L_1 regularized negative log-likelihood, where λ is called a regularization coefficient.

Although the L_1 regularized maximum likelihood estimator has strong statistical guarantees in recovering a sparse precision matrix, such an estimator is biased with the shift of the regularization coefficient λ [4]. To address this issue, a smoothly clipped absolute deviation (SCAD) penalty is proposed [4], which is a symmetric and quadratic spline on $[0, \infty)$, and whose first order derivative is given by

$$\mathrm{SCAD}'_{\lambda,a}(x) = \lambda \left\{ I(|x| \le \lambda) + \frac{a\lambda - |x|)_+}{(a-1)\lambda} I(|x| > \lambda) \right\} \tag{3}$$

where $\lambda > 0$ and $a > 2$ are two tuning parameters. When $a = \infty$, SCAD is exactly the L_1 penalty. The SCAD penalized negative log-likelihood becomes [2]

$$\frac{n}{2} \left[\mathrm{tr}(\mathbf{S}\Theta) - \log \det\Theta) \right] + \mathrm{SCAD}_{\lambda,a}(\Theta) \tag{4}$$

where $\mathrm{SCAD}_{\lambda,a}(\Theta) = \sum_{i=1}^{p} \sum_{j=1}^{p} \mathrm{SCAD}_{\lambda_{ij},a}(\theta_{ij})$.

In the formulations (1), (2) and (4) for estimating a precision matrix, it is assumed that all observations are drawn from the same distribution. However, in many data sets the observations may correspond to several distinct classes, so the assumption that all observations are drawn from the same distribution is inappropriate. For instance, many datasets in GEO database [5] are made up of gene expression measurements from one set of cancer tissue samples and another set of normal tissue samples. As both sets of samples are from the same type of tissue, the true precision matrices for the cancer and normal samples should have some similarity. On the other hand, as gene networks are often dysregulated in cancer, two precision matrices should also have some important differences. Therefore, it is inappropriate to either estimating two separate precision matrices: one for the cancer samples and another for normal samples (no similarity guarantee) or estimating a single precision matrix by combining the cancer and normal samples (no difference) together.

In this study, we propose a novel method for jointly estimating sparse precision matrices based on limited observations from two difference distributions. The SCAD penalty is adopted to reinforce the sparsity while the Frobenius norm of the difference between two precision matrices is used to guarantee both the similarity and important differences. An alternating direction method of multipliers (ADMM) and an iterative weighted penalized method are developed to optimize the objective function. To investigate its performance, our proposed methods are applied to two real datasets for cancer diagnosis with Fisher's linear discriminate analysis (FLDA) [6].

2   Methods

2.1   Formulations

Suppose that our dataset consists of $n_0 + n_1$ multivariate normal observations of dimension p from two classes C_0 and C_1. Specifically n_k observations in C_k are sampled from $\mathcal{N}(\mu_k, \Sigma_k)(k = 0, 1)$. Let $\Theta_k = \Sigma_k^{-1}$ be the precision matrix of class C_k for $k = 0, 1$, and S_k be the empirical covariance matrix calculated with samples from class C_k $(k = 0, 1)$. Our joint sparse precision matrix estimation is to solve the following optimization problem (minimizing the penalized negative log-likelihood).

$$\min_{\Theta_k \in \mathcal{S}_+} \sum_{k=0,1} \{n_k[\operatorname{tr}(S_k\Theta_k) - \log \det\Theta_k)] + \mathrm{SCAD}_{\lambda_k,a}(\Theta_k)\} + \frac{\gamma}{2}\|\Theta_0 - \Theta_1\|_F^2 \quad (5)$$

where $\mathcal{S}_+$ consists of all nonnegative definite matrices Θ_k. $\| \cdot \|_F$ represents the Frobenius norm of a matrix. $\mathrm{SCAD}_{\lambda_k,a}$ reinforces the sparsity of the precision matrices. Based on an argument of minimizing the Bayes risk, Fan and Li [4] recommended the choice $a = 3.7$, in the SCAD function, which is used in this study. γ is a positive regularization coefficient.

The last term in (5) control both the similarity and important differences of two precision matrices. Actually, a larger value of γ leads to more similar precision matrices while a smaller value of γ leads to more different precision matrices. In two extremely cases: $\gamma = 0$ corresponds to estimating two separate precision matrices (no similarity guarantee) while $\gamma = \infty$ corresponds to estimating a single precision matrix (no difference). The last term in (5) can be replaced by other penalties. For example in [7,8], the L_1 penalty is used for this purpose, which may leads to unnecessarily complicated solution procedures.

2.2 ADMM Solution

To solve problem (5) subject to the constraint that Θ_0 and Θ_1 are positive definite, using the ADMM algorithm, the problem can be reformulated as follows:

$$\min_{\Theta_k, Z_k \in \mathcal{S}_+} \sum_{k=0,1} \{n_k[\operatorname{tr}(S_k\Theta_k) - \log\det\Theta_k] + \operatorname{SCAD}_{\lambda_k,a}(Z_k)\} + \frac{\gamma}{2}\|\Theta_0 - \Theta_1\|_F^2 \quad (6)$$

subject to the positive definiteness constraint as well as the constraint that $Z_k = \Theta_k$ for $k = 0, 1$. Let $\{Z\} = \{Z_0, Z_1\}$ and $\{\Theta\} = \{\Theta_0, \Theta_1\}$. The scaled augmented Lagrangian for this problem is given by

$$L_\rho(\{\Theta\}, \{Z\}, \{U\}) = \sum_{k=0,1} \{n_k[\operatorname{tr}(S_k\Theta_k) - \log\det\Theta_k] + \operatorname{SCAD}_{\lambda_k,a}(Z_k)\}$$
$$+ \frac{\gamma}{2}\|\Theta_0 - \Theta_1\|_F^2 + \frac{\rho}{2}\sum_{k=0}^{1}\|\Theta_k - Z_k + U_k\|_F^2 - \frac{\rho}{2}\sum_{k=0}^{1}\|U_k\|_F^2 \quad (7)$$

where $\{U\} = \{U_0, U_1\}$ are dual variables and ρ serves as a 'penalty parameter'. The ADMM algorithm corresponding to Eq. (7) results from iterating three steps. At the tth iteration, ADMM performs

i) $\{\Theta^{(t)}\} \leftarrow \arg\min_{\{\Theta\}}\{L_\rho(\{\Theta\}, \{Z^{(t-1)}\}, \{U^{(t-1)}\})\}$
ii) $\{Z^{(t)}\} \leftarrow \arg\min_{\{Z\}}\{L_\rho(\{\Theta^{(t)}\}, \{Z\}, \{U^{(t-1)}\})\}$
iii) $\{U^{(t)}\} \leftarrow \{U^{(t-1)}\} + (\{\Theta^{(t)}\} - \{Z^{(t)}\})$

In the following, we present the ADMM solution for the Joint Sparse Precision Matrix Estimation (JSPME) problem in detail.

1. Initialize the variables: $\Theta_0 = \Theta_1 = I, U_0 = U_1 = 0$ and $Z_0 = Z_1 = 0$
2. Select a scalar $\rho > 0$.
3. For $t = 1, 2, \cdots$ until convergence update as follows.
   (a) Update Θ_0 as the minimizer of

$$n_0[\operatorname{tr}(S_0\Theta_0) - \log\det\Theta_0] + \frac{\gamma}{2}\|\Theta_0 - \Theta_1^{(t-1)}\|_F^2 + \frac{\rho}{2}\|\Theta_0 - Z_0^{(t-1)} + U_0^{(t-1)}\|_F^2$$

Taking the derivative with respec to Θ_0 and letting it equal to 0 yield to

$$(\rho + \gamma)\Theta_0 + [n_0 S_0 + \rho U_0^{(t-1)} - \gamma\Theta_1^{(t-1)} - \rho Z_0^{(t-1)}] - n_0\Theta_0^{-1} = 0$$

Letting $V_0 D_0 V_0^T$ denote the eigendecomposition of $[n_0 S_0 + \rho U_0^{(t-1)} - \gamma \Theta_1^{(t-1)} - \rho Z_0^{(t-1)}]$, then update Θ_0 with $\Theta_0^{(t)} = V_0 \bar{D}_0 V_0^T$, where $\bar{D}_0$ is the diagonal matrix with jth diagonal element

$$\bar{d}_{0jj} = \frac{-d_{0jj} + \sqrt{d_{0jj}^2 + 4(\rho + \gamma)n_0}}{2(\rho + \gamma)} \tag{8}$$

Similarly, letting $V_1 D_1 V_1^T$ denote the eigendecomposition of $[n_1 S_1 + \rho U_1^{(t-1)} - \gamma \Theta_0^{(t)} - \rho Z_1^{(t-1)}]$, update Θ_1 with $\Theta_1^{(t)} = V_1 \bar{D}_1 V_1^T$, where $\bar{D}_1$ is the diagonal matrix with jth diagonal element

$$\bar{d}_{1jj} = \frac{-d_{1jj} + \sqrt{d_{1jj}^2 + 4(\rho + \gamma)n_1}}{2(\rho + \gamma)} \tag{9}$$

(b) For $k = 0, 1$, update Z_k as the minimizer of

$$\frac{\rho}{2}\|Z_k - (\Theta_k^{(t)} - U_k^{(t-1)})\|_F^2 + \text{SCAD}_{\lambda_k, a}(Z_k) \tag{10}$$

which can be solved by an iterative weighted penalized method as follows: Denote the r-step solution by $\{\hat{Z}_k^{(r)}\}$. As a result, we get $\{\hat{Z}_k^{(r+1)}\}$ by optimizing, up to a constant,

$$\min_{Z_k} \frac{\rho}{2}\|Z_k - (\Theta_k^{(t)} + U_k^{(t-1)})\|_F^2 + \sum_{ij} w_{ij}|z_{kij}| \tag{11}$$

where $w_{ij} = p'_{\lambda_k}(|\hat{z}_{kij}^{(r)}|)$ and $p_{\lambda_k}(x) = \text{SCAD}_{\lambda_k, a}(x)$. The optimization problem (11) can be solved by the soft thresholding operator as follows

$$\hat{z}_{kij}^{(r+1)} = sgn(a_{ij})\max(|a_{ij}| - w_{ij}/\rho, 0), \qquad a_{ij} = (\Theta_k^{(t)} + U_k^{(t-1)})_{ij} \tag{12}$$

Similar to [2], it can be proved that the above iteration converges to the minimizer of (10). Let R be the number of iterations for convergence, then $Z_k^{(t)} = (\hat{z}_{kij}^{(R)})$ for $k = 0, 1$

(c) For $k = 0, 1$ update $U_k^{(t)} = U_k^{(t-1)} + \Theta_k^{(t)} - Z_k^{(t)}$

2.3   Fisher's Linear Discriminant Analysis

In Fisher's linear discriminant analysis (FLDA) [6], suppose two classes of observations have means μ_0, μ_1 and covariances Σ_0, Σ_1, respectively. Then the linear combination of features $\mathbf{w}^T \mathbf{x}$ will have means $\mathbf{w}^T \mu_k$ and variances $\mathbf{w}^T \Sigma_k \mathbf{w}$ for $k = 0, 1$. Fisher defined the separation between these two distributions to be the ratio of the variance between the classes to the variance within the classes:

$$S = \frac{\sigma_{between}^2}{\sigma_{within}^2} = \frac{(\mathbf{w}^T \mu_1 - \mathbf{w}^T \mu_0)^2}{\mathbf{w}^T \Sigma_1 \mathbf{w} + \mathbf{w}^T \Sigma_0 \mathbf{w}} = \frac{(\mathbf{w}^T(\mu_1 - \mu_0))^2}{\mathbf{w}^T(\Sigma_0 + \Sigma_1)\mathbf{w}} \tag{13}$$

It can be shown that the maximum separation occurs when

$$\mathbf{w} \propto (\Sigma_0 + \Sigma_1)^{-1}(\mu_1 - \mu_0) \tag{14}$$

In this study, we take

$$\mathbf{w} = \frac{(\Sigma_0 + \Sigma_1)^{-1}(\mu_1 - \mu_0)}{\|(\Sigma_0 + \Sigma_1)^{-1}(\mu_1 - \mu_0)\|} \quad \text{and} \quad c = \frac{1}{2}\mathbf{w}^T(\mu_1 + \mu_0) \tag{15}$$

and calculate the FLDA score for a sample $\mathbf{x}$ as follows

$$FLDA(\mathbf{x}) = \mathbf{w}^T\mathbf{x} - c \tag{16}$$

3   Experiments and Discussion

3.1   Data Preprocessing and Gene Selection

The datasets utilized in this study are derived from publicly available gene expression data repositories, specifically the Gene Expression Omnibus (GEO) database. We employed two distinct datasets: GSE10072 [9] and GSE19804 [10], both of which are focused on lung cancer diagnosis but target different population demographics and clinical contexts.

GSE10072 Dataset investigates the molecular signature of lung adenocarcinoma in the context of smoking. It comprises gene expression data from 107 samples, including 58 lung cancer samples and 49 normal tissue samples from different patients.

GSE19804 Dataset focuses on the molecular characterization of non-smoking female lung cancer patients. This dataset consists of 120 samples, equally divided between cancer and normal tissues (60 each). The RNAs were extracted from paired tumor and normal tissues from the same patients.

The raw Affymetrix CEL files were loaded using the `affy` package, which provides functions to read and preprocess raw microarray data. The FARMS algorithm was employed to preprocess expression values to provides robust and accurate measurements of gene expression levels [11]. The t-test and Log Fold Change (LogFC) were performed to identify significantly differentially expressed genes between the cancer and normal groups. To control for multiple testing, the Benjamini-Hochberg (BH) method was applied to calculate the adjusted p-values, which minimizes the false discovery rate (FDR) [12]. The Log Fold Change (LogFC) was computed as:

$$\text{LogFC} = \left| \log_2\left(\frac{\text{mean expression in cancer}}{\text{mean expression in normal}} \right) \right| \tag{17}$$

As the 10-fold cross validation was used to evaluate the performance of the methods, the number of selected significantly differentially genes was one plus the number of samples in the training dataset, which is about 90% of the number of total samples. This allowed us to examine the performance when $p > n$. All selected genes in GSE10072 had p-value $\leq 2.64 \times 10^{-9}$ and LogFC ≥ 0.26 while those in GSE19804 had p-value $\leq 1.7 \times 10^{-12}$ and LogFC ≥ 0.36. The statistics of final datasets are shown in Table 1.

Table 1. Statistics of Datasets

Accession Number	Cancer Samples	Normal Samples	Total Samples	Selected Genes
GSE10072	58	49	107	97
GSE19804	60	60	120	109

3.2   Evaluation

The 10-fold cross validation is used to evaluate the performance of our proposed method (JSPME) and two competing methods: SSPME [3] estimates two precision matrices via optimizing (4) based on the cancer samples and normal samples, separately, and CSPME [2] estimated a single precision matrix via optimizing (4) based on the combined the cancer and normal samples. In the 10-fold cross validation, a dataset is randomly divided into 10 folds, each having approximately 10% of total samples. In turn, one fold is used as the test dataset while other nine folds are used as the training datatset.

From each training data, we performed gene-wise normalization by first centering each gene expression value around its mean, followed by dividing the centered values by the corresponding standard deviation, both calculated from the training dataset. This normalization procedure ensures that the resulting data have a mean of zero and a unit variance for each gene, thereby eliminating differences in magnitude and scale between genes.

Then, we estimated the precision matrix and calculated the with-in class mean vectors by

$$\mu_k = \frac{1}{n_k} \sum_{i \in class-k} \mathbf{x}_i, \qquad \text{for} \quad k = 0, 1 \tag{18}$$

Finally, to compare the prediction performance, we used specificity (True Negative Rate), sensitivity (True Positive Rate) and also Matthews Correlation Coefficient (MCC). They are defined as follows:

$$Specificity = \frac{TN}{TN + FP}, \qquad Sensitivity = \frac{TP}{TP + FN},$$

$$MCC = \frac{TP \times TN - FP \times FN}{\sqrt{(TP + FP)(TP + FN)(TN + FP)(TN + FN)}}$$

where TP, TN, FP and FN are the numbers of true positives, true negatives, false positives and false negatives, respectively. MCC is widely used in machine learning as a measure of the quality of binary classifiers [13]. It takes true and false, positives and negatives, into account and is generally regarded as a balanced measure, which can be used even if the classes are of very different sizes. The larger the MCC is, the better the classification is.

Additionally, to facilitate a more intuitive understanding of the comparative performance, for each dataset, we provide both a radar plot and a bar plot (see

Figs. 1 and 2) to summarize the classification performance on multiple metrics. The bar graph offers a concise side-by-side comparison of key measures, such as accuracy, sensitivity, specificity, and MCC, while the radar graph gives a more holistic view by mapping these metrics onto separate axes in a single diagram. This radar visualization not only highlights the balance between different performance aspects but also accentuates the overall shape of the model's performance profile.

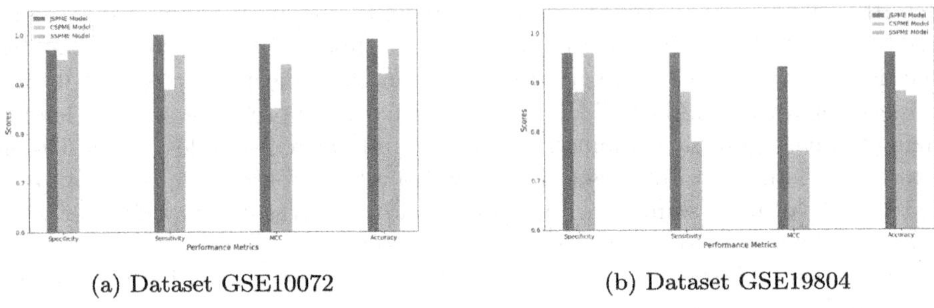

(a) Dataset GSE10072   (b) Dataset GSE19804

Fig. 1. Quantitative Comparison of Classification performance Metrics (Accuracy, Sensitivity, Specificity, and MCC) for the JSPME, CSPME, and SSPME Models.

In the results presented, our proposed method JSPME approach demonstrates superior performance across all evaluation metrics compared to both the combined and separate models as shown in Figs. 1 and 2, as well as in Tables 2 and 3, underscoring its ability to balance similarities and variations between cancer and normal samples. Specifically, for the dataset GSE10072, the separate model outperforms the combined approach, as shown Figs. 1a and 2a, as well as in Table 2, indicating that the cancer and normal classes are considerably different, which aligns with the fact that normal samples and cancer samples were from different patients. Despite this increased distinction, it is important to recognize that the two classes are not entirely unrelated, as they still share some degree of commonality. The JSPME's remarkable performance in this scenario reflects its unique ability to efficiently balance between capturing class-specific differences and identifying shared structures, making it more robust than both the combined and separate models in handling complex biomedical data. In contrast, for the dataset GSE19804, the combined model slightly outperforms the separate model, as shown in Figs. 1b and 2b, as well as in Table 3, suggesting that the two classes exhibit a high degree of similarity, possibly due to shared biological characteristics or minimal variation between diseased and normal cells. This is in agreement with the fact that a paired tumor and normal tissues were from the same patient. In this context, the JSPME method proves highly effective, as it leverages shared structures while simultaneously capturing subtle variations, thereby achieving the highest accuracy and robustness.

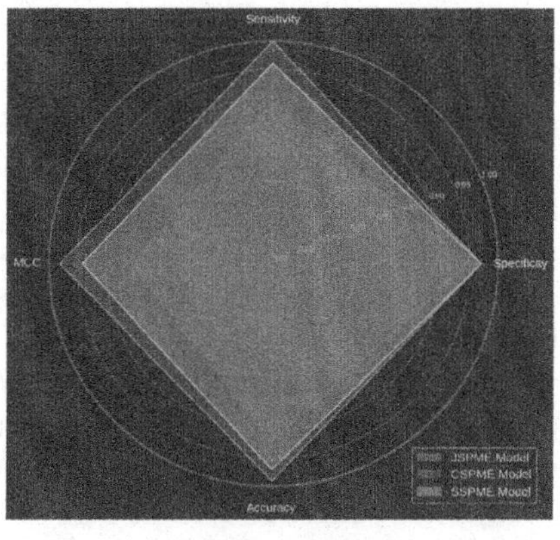

(a) Dataset GSE10072

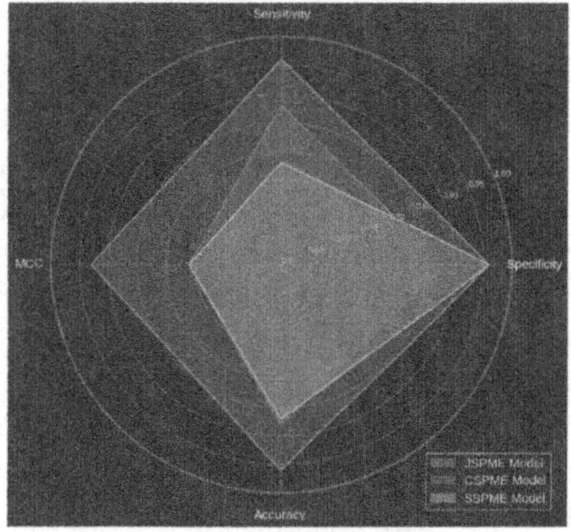

(b) Dataset GSE19804

Fig. 2. Holistic Performance Assessment of JSPME, CSPME, and SSPME Models Through a Radar Plot that Visualizes Key Metrics (Accuracy, Sensitivity, Specificity, and MCC) on Separate Axes.

Table 2. Classification Performance Metrics for Dataset GSE10072

Model	Specificity	Sensitivity	MCC	Accuracy
JSPME	0.97	1.0	0.98	0.99
CSPME	0.95	0.89	0.85	0.92
SSPME	0.97	0.96	0.94	0.97

Table 3. Classification Performance Metrics for Dataset GSE19804

Model	Specificity	Sensitivity	MCC	Accuracy
JSPME	0.96	0.96	0.93	0.96
CSPME	0.88	0.88	0.76	0.88
SSPME	0.96	0.78	0.76	0.87

3.3 Hyperparameter Selection

As in all machined learning methods, careful selection of hyperparameters in our method was crucial to achieve optimal performance and ensure robust model comparisons [14]. In this study, we performed systematic cross-validation experiments to select appropriate values for the regularization parameter λ in SCAD and the similarity-control parameter γ.

To determine the optimal value of λ, we conducted a cross-validation experiment evaluating a range of candidate values ($\lambda \in \{0.01, 0.1, 1, 10, 100\}$). Performance was evaluated using the Matthews correlation coefficient (MCC), given its robustness as a balanced metric for binary classification tasks. For an unbiased selection, we computed MCC scores separately for three competing SSPME,

CSPME, and JSPME methods and subsequently calculated the average MCC across these three methods for each candidate λ. The optimal λ value was selected to maximize this average MCC, ensuring an objective and balanced criterion that did not favor any single approach. Through this procedure, $\lambda = 0.01$ and $\lambda = 0.02$ were selected for datasets, GSE19804 and GSE10072, respectively, which provided the highest average MCC across all three evaluated methods. This chosen λ was subsequently fixed and consistently applied for all three competing methods to ensure a fair and meaningful comparison.

To determine the optimal value of γ, we conducted additional experiments exploring different γ values. Specifically, we evaluated a set of candidate values $\gamma \in \{10^{-3}, 10^{-2}, \ldots, 10^4\}$ and tracked the accuracy of the resulting model for the JSPME method.

Analysis of these results revealed a clear performance trend: as the value of γ increased, the performance of the JSPME method converged towards that of the Combined model, reflecting stronger enforcement of similarity between the precision matrices of different classes. Conversely, lower values of γ resulted in JSPME performance resembling that of the Separate model, reflecting weaker similarity constraints.

A performance plot illustrating this relationship highlighted a clear peak, identifying an optimal γ value that balanced the similarity constraint with individual class differentiation, ultimately maximizing model performance in terms of accuracy.

Consequently, $\gamma = 10.0$ and $\gamma = 200.0$ were selected for the datasets, GSE19804 and GSE10072 respectively, as they achieved optimal balance, providing superior accuracy by effectively capturing both the similarity and important differences between the two class-specific precision matrices Figs. 3a and b.

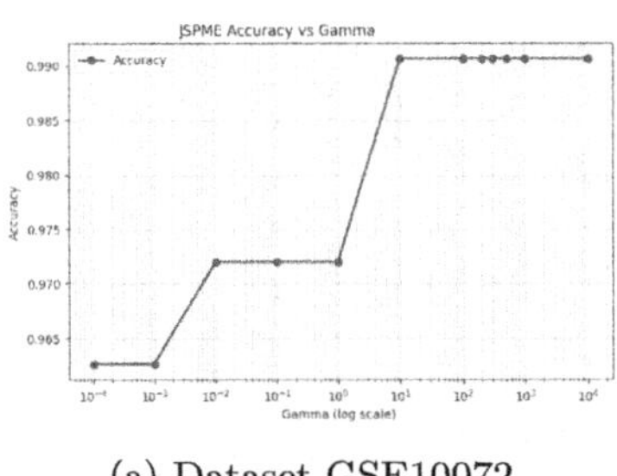

(a) Dataset GSE10072

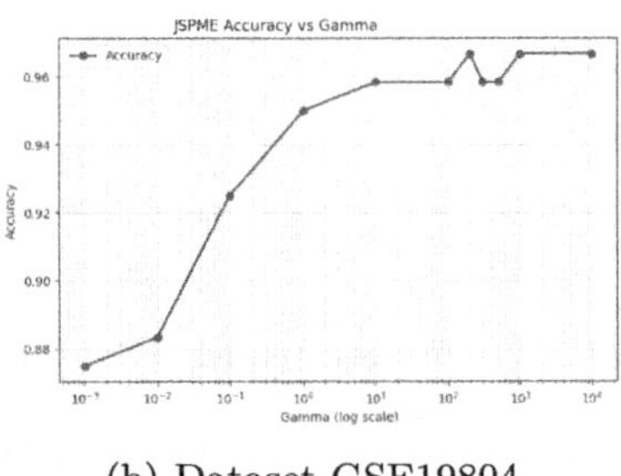

(b) Dataset GSE19804

Fig. 3. Effect of Varying the Regularization Parameter γ on the Accuracy of the JSPME Model.

The parameter ρ serves as the penalty parameter in the ADMM optimization algorithm. It primarily influences convergence speed and stability but has minimal effect on the final precision matrix estimation once convergence is achieved. To ensure stable and efficient convergence, ρ was chosen to be exactly equal to

γ to maintain consistency and balance between the penalty terms in the optimization framework.

Through this rigorous and systematic selection process, we ensured that our hyperparameter choices (λ, γ, ρ) maximized model performance and facilitated fair, comprehensive comparisons among the evaluated methods.

4   Conclusion

In this study, we have presented the Joint Sparse Precision Matrix Estimation (JSPME) model, which demonstrates remarkable accuracy and robustness in estimating precision matrices from high-dimensional biomedical data. By combining SCAD regularization and the Frobenius norm, the method effectively balances shared and distinct features between cancer and normal samples. By rigorously selecting significant genes through statistical testing and controlling false discovery rates, JSPME ensures that the retained features are both informative and biologically meaningful. The model balances the trade-off between shared similarities across classes and class-specific variations, integrating these patterns into a positive definite precision matrix that is optimally tailored for robust classification. This innovative integration allows JSPME to diagnose lung cancer with high accuracy. The experimental evaluation demonstrated that JSPME outperforms both Separate and Combined approaches across diverse scenarios. In the GSE19804 dataset, where cancer and normal samples exhibit a high degree of similarity, the CSPME approach demonstrated relatively strong performance, reflecting the intrinsic biological resemblance between the two classes. However, JSPME clearly outperformed the CSPME approach by effectively capturing the subtle differences within this shared biological landscape, balancing the inherent similarities and the distinctive features associated with the diseased state. This result underscores the model's capability to integrate shared patterns while accentuating variations crucial for accurate classification. In contrast, the GSE10072 dataset presented a markedly different scenario, where the cancer and normal classes were substantially distinct, leading to the SSPME surpassing the CSPME. Nevertheless, JSPME still exhibited superior performance by capturing the significant divergence between classes while retaining a nuanced understanding of any overlapping gene expression characteristics. This robust performance in diverse conditions highlights JSPME's potential as a cutting-edge solution for precision matrix estimation in complex and heterogeneous biomedical data, making it an invaluable tool for identifying disease-specific biomarkers and advancing precision medicine.

Acknowledgments. This study is supported by the Natural Sciences and Engineering Research Council of Canada (NSERC).

References

1. Baba, K., Shibata, R., Sibuya, M.: Partial correlation and conditional correlation as measures of conditional independence. Aust. N. Z. J. Stat. **46**(4), 657–664 (2004)
2. Fan, J., Feng, Y., Wu, Y.: Network exploration via the adaptive lasso and SCAD penalties. Ann. Appl. Stat. **3**(2), 521–541 (2009)
3. Huang, J.Z., Liu, N., Pourahmadi, M., Liu, L.: Covariance matrix selection and estimation via penalised normal likelihood. Biometrika **93**(1), 85–98 (2006)
4. Fan, J., Li, R.: Variable selection via nonconcave penalized likelihood and its oracle properties. J. Am. Stat. Assoc. **96**(456), 1348–1360 (2001)
5. Clough, E., Barrett, T.: The gene expression omnibus database. Methods Mol. Biol. **1418**, 93–110 (2016)
6. Fisher, R.A.: The use of multiple measurements in taxonomic problems. Ann. Eugen. **7**(2), 179–188 (1936)
7. Guo, J., Levina, E., Michailidis, G., Zhu, J.: Joint estimation of multiple graphical models. Biometrika **98**(1), 1–15 (2011)
8. Danaher, P., Wang, P., Witten, D.M.: The joint graphical lasso for inverse covariance estimation across multiple classes. J. Roy. Stat. Soc. Ser. B (Stat. Methodol.) **76**(2), 373–397 (2014)
9. Landi, M., et al.: Gene expression signature of cigarette smoking and its role in lung adenocarcinoma development and survival (GSE10072) [data set]. Gene Expression Omnibus (2008)
10. Lu, T., Lai, L., Chuang, E.Y.: Genome-wide screening of transcriptional modulation in non-smoking female lung cancer in Taiwan (GSE19804) [data set]. Gene Expression Omnibus (2011). Accessed https://www.ncbi.nlm.nih.gov/geo/query/acc.cgi?acc=GSE19804
11. Hochreiter, S., Clevert, D.A., Obermayer, K.: A new summarization method for Affymetrix probe level data. Bioinformatics **22**(8), 943–949 (2006)
12. Benjamini, Y., Hochberg, Y.: Multiple hypotheses testing with weights. Scand. J. Stat. **24**(3), 407–418 (1997)
13. Chicco, D., Jurman, G.: The advantages of the Matthews correlation coefficient (MCC) over F1 score and accuracy in binary classification evaluation. BMC Genomics **21**, 1–13 (2020)
14. Fu, M., Wu, F.X.: QLABGrad: a hyperparameter-free and convergence-guaranteed scheme for deep learning. In: Proceedings of the AAAI Conference on Artificial Intelligence, vol. 38, pp. 12072–12081. AAAI (2024)

An Efficient Parallel List Ranking Algorithm for Graph Concatenation on BSP Graph System

Maocheng Cao[1], Zhelang Deng[2,3], Qiucheng Miao[3], Jintao Meng[3(✉)], Yanjie Wei[3], and Jiefeng Cheng[4]

[1] Shenzhen FuYong People's Hospital, Shenzhen, People's Republic of China
[2] Faculty of Health Sciences, University of Macau, Macau, People's Republic of China
[3] Shenzhen Institutes of Advanced Technology, CAS, Shenzhen, People's Republic of China
`jt.meng@siat.ac.cn`
[4] Hong Kong Productivity Council, Hongkong, People's Republic of China

Abstract. We proposed a practical non-recursive parallel list ranking algorithm, NR-Ranking. NR-Ranking adopts an independent set to avoid potential operation contention between neighbor nodes. In each communication round, every node in an independent set bridges its left neighbor and right neighbor by adding edges with new distance; then all nodes in this independent set are excluded from previous linked lists. The probability of one node being selected into the independent set is about 1/3. According to the stop criterion of selecting an independent set, the number of communication rounds of NR-Ranking is different. It is bounded by $log(p)$ if the selection step stops when the number of nodes in the reminder lists is less than $\frac{n}{p}$, where n is the number of nodes in the linked lists and p is the number of processors, or $O(logw)$ if all nodes in the remaining lists are end nodes, where w is the length of the longest linked list. The complexity of computation and communication on both stop criteria is bounded by $O(n)$. Experimental results confirm the above complexity analysis, and the implementation of NR-Ranking in GPS has achieved a speed increase of $4X$ when the number of workers increases from 8 to 48.

Keywords: list ranking · independent set · non-recursive · parallel algorithm

1 Introduction

List ranking is a very popular subroutine for obtaining numerous parallel tree and graph algorithms [1–4]. The list ranking algorithm can be generalized to compute prefix or suffix sums [3,5] for associative operators by replacing the addition operation for node distances with a respective associative operator.

List ranking also plays a central role in graph concatenation in the genome assembly problem [6,7]. Each linked list in the De Bruijn graph constructed from the sequencing reads needs to be concatenated into one edge. Most De Bruijn graphs constructed for large genomes are enormous; for example, the sequencing data from humans can generate twenty billion nodes. These De Bruijn graphs are generally stored by distributed file systems in clusters or the cloud. On these parallel systems with distributed memory,

J. Tang et al. (Eds.): ISBRA 2025, LNBI 15757, pp. 265–278, 2026.
https://doi.org/10.1007/978-981-95-0695-8_22

ranking the lists brings locality to this problem and greatly minimizes the complexity of communication on the post-processing task.

Improvement of list ranking algorithms generally follows the evolution of computational models, which has a roadmap from Von Neumann's RAM model, PRAM to BSP [8]. The basic approach for list ranking in RAM is "pointer jumping" [1,9,10], and this is the simplest solution which has a computation workload of $O(nlogn)$. Several PRAM list ranking algorithms have been proposed [11–14], and according to the contention resolving strategy they can be divided into deterministic algorithms and randomized algorithms. For deterministic algorithms, pioneer works are "k-ruling set" technology [11,12]. With $\frac{n}{log(n)}$ processors, Anderson and Miller's work has a complexity of $O(log(n))$ for each processor, and the total computation workload can be reduced to $O(n)$ [12]. For randomized algorithms, the "independent set" technology is used to improve the list ranking algorithm [13]. During each round a subset of nodes is selected as the independent set, and excluded after bridging their neighbors. With this strategy the size of nodes in the remaining lists can be reduced by a constant factor in every round. Reid-Miller's randomized algorithm, which uses the "sparse-ruling-set" algorithm [14] can achieve a complexity of $O(\frac{n}{p} + log_2 n)$ for each processor and a total workload of $O(n + plog_2 n)$.

As the h-relation in each superstep in BSP [8,15] is time consuming, minimizing the number of communication rounds is the main concern in the design algorithms on the BSP model. Profound contributions on this issue in the list ranking include [1,10,16,17]. In 1997, Frank Dehne proposed a randomized parallel list ranking algorithm using "k-ruling set" method [16], the communication round of his work is limited by $log(p)$, and its computational complexity is $O(n)$. Two years later, Sibeyn developed a new algorithm using the sparse ruling set approach [1,17], which requires only $6 + 2d\lceil log(log(n)) \rceil$ communication rounds and has a total communication size of $6 + \frac{3ln(d)+6ln(p)}{d+1}$, here d is the number of recursion steps. This algorithm can handle the length of the list up to 200 million in practice. In 2002, Isabelle Guerin Lassous presented a portable list ranking solution using independent set methods [10], which has a limited communication round by $O(log(p))$ and the complexity of computation and communication by $O(n)$.

With the widely usage of cloud [18,19] on storing and processing large volume of data, Pregel [20] as an example provides a portable framework for programming the graph algorithm on the cloud. As a vertex centric approach, Pregel and its implementations [21–25] are flexible enough for a broad set of algorithms, and these implementations automatically inherit Pregel's advantages on efficiency, scalability and fault-tolerance. However, some graph algorithms need to modify two adjacent vertexes at the same time; this is difficult to implement on Pregel. To design a contention-avoiding mechanism for Pregel is one of the key issues [9,25]. List ranking, is a representative example of this type of algorithms, and here we aim at addressing this challenge.

In this paper, we propose a practical non-recursive parallel list ranking algorithm, NR-Ranking. NR-Ranking can avoid the potential operation contention between neighbor nodes by selecting a subset of nodes in each communication round in which no two nodes are neighbors. This subset is called an independent set. In each communication round, every node in the independent set has to bridge its left neighbor and right neighbor by adding edges with new distance; then all nodes in the independent set are excluded from previous linked lists. In each communication round, a proportion of nodes in the linked lists are selected into the independent set and then removed, and the proportion in this paper is proved to be about $1/3$. According to the stop criterion of selecting the independent set, the number of communication rounds of NR-Ranking is different. It is limited by $log(p)$ if the number of nodes in the remaining lists is less than n/p, or $O(log(w))$ if all nodes in the remaining lists are end nodes, where w is the length of the longest list. The complexity of computation and communication on both stop criteria is bounded by $O(n)$.

A practical Pregel framework, GPS, is selected to develop our NR-Ranking. As a non-recursive algorithm, NR-Ranking can be easily implemented on GPS. Experimental results show that our implementation has the following three properties:

- If the stop criterion is that all nodes in the remaining lists are end nodes, the number of communication round of NR-Ranking is linearly related to the length of longest list in the set of linked lists.
- When the length of longest list is fixed, the number of communication round on processing the linked list is nearly the same. The total running time grows slowly with the increasing time usage of each communication round, which is caused by the gradually increasing workload in each superstep.
- Given a set of linked list with 50 million nodes, the time usage decreases when the number of workers increases from 8 to 48. A speedup of 4X is achieved by our implementation on GPS.

This paper is organized as follows: the list ranking problem is introduced in Sect. 2, then we present the algorithm of NR-Ranking in Sect. 3. Section 4 illustrates the implementation of NR-Ranking on the Pregel system. The performance and scalability results of NR-Ranking are given in Sect. 5. Section 6 concludes this paper.

2 List Ranking Problem

List and list ranking: List consists of nodes which are linked together, such that every node has one left neighbor and one right neighbor, except for the left end node and the right end node. List ranking determines the rank of every node, which is a node's distance to its left and right end node of the list [1,9,10]. The assumption is listed below:

- A set of linked lists L contains n listed nodes. In all these lists, the longest linked list is denoted as W, and its length is w.
- Each node v in L has a left neighbor $l[v]$ and a right neighbor $r[v]$, except for the left end node and the right end node.
- p processors or workers in a cloud are used to solving the list ranking problem. Each processor or worker i holds a subset of list-nodes. For a given node v, it will be stored in processor $v\%p$.

Following the above three assumptions, one example of the list ranking problem and its solution is given in Fig. 1. The description of the list ranking problem can be summarized as below:

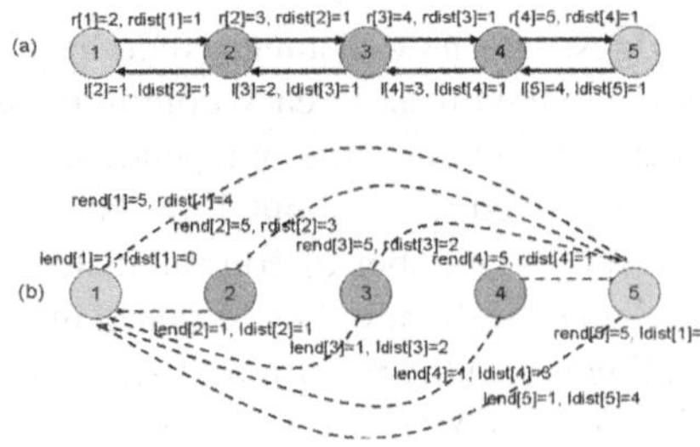

Fig. 1. A linked list with five nodes are given in Fig. 1(a), three internal nodes are colored yellow and two end nodes are colored blue. The initial value $(l[v], r[v], ldist[v], rdist[v])$ is given for each node v. The final rank value $(lend[v], rend[v], ldist[v], rdist[v])$ is given in Fig. 1(b).

Definition 1. For a set of linked lists L, list ranking includes two operations: (1) label each node v in L with its left and right end node $(lend[v], rend[v])$, (2) compute the rank of each node, that is the distance to its left and right end node $(ldist[v], rdist[v])$.

3   List Ranking Algorithm

In this section, we first describe NR-Ranking, and then present the detailed analysis on the communication round, and complexity of computation, communication, and memory usage. Unlike most previously published recursive algorithms, NR-Ranking is suitable to be implemented on Pregel, and this will be discussed in Sect. 4.

3.1   Description of NR-Ranking Algorithm

Independent set is first introduced by Jaja in 1992 [13], NR-Ranking uses this technology to avoid the contention between neighbor nodes. Given a set of nodes in linked lists L, an independent set is a subset I of L such that no two items in I are neighbors in the linked lists. In fact, such a set I only contains internal nodes, i.e. nodes that are not the terminal nodes of the sublists. These nodes in I are 'shortcut' in the algorithm: they can help exchange information between their left and right neighbors in order to connect the two neighbors directly. There are three advantages on using an independent set in NR-Ranking:

1. Independent set can be constructed in one communication round.
2. Independent set can help exchange data between its two neighbors, which is the key to shrink the length of the list.
3. In each communication round, independent set gives an order on shrinking the original list, which avoid the contention of shrinking two neighbors at the same time.

The main NR-Ranking schedule is described in Algorithm 2 in the Appendix. Explanations of this algorithm are given below.

Line 1: Each round of the while loop corresponds to one communication round. NR-Ranking has two stop criterions:

1. The number of nodes in the remaining lists is less than n/p,
2. All nodes in the remaining lists are end nodes.

Two stop criteria have direct effects on the number of communication rounds. Users can select a stop criterion according to their requirements.

<u>Line 1</u>: The independent set is used to select a subset I from the nodes in linked list L. The remaining nodes in L are denoted as D. Here, the probability that one node is selected in the independent set is denoted as ϵ, here $\epsilon = \frac{|I|}{|L|}$. Where $|I|$ and $|L|$ are the number of nodes in the independent set I and the set of linked lists L. This independent set subroutine and the value of proportion ϵ will be discussed in the next subsection.

<u>Line 4,5</u>: Each node v in the independent set I exchanges messages $(r[v], rdist[v])$ and $(l[v], ldist[v])$ with its left neighbor $l[v]$ and right neighbor $r[v]$.

<u>Line 6 to 14</u>: For a node v in an independent set I, its two neighbors $l[v]$ and $r[v]$ will keep the old values of $r[l[v]]$ and $l[r[v]]$ in $or[l[v]]$ and $ol[r[v]]$ respectively, then $l[v]$ and $r[v]$ will be updated to be interconnected accordingly.

<u>Line 15</u>: If the stop criterion on line 1 has been satisfied, all remaining nodes will be sent to one processor. The problem will be solved sequentially using the pointer jumping algorithm introduced in [1, 3].

<u>Line 16</u>: Each round of the while loop corresponds to one communication round.

<u>Line 17 to 22</u>: Each node v in the current set L sends its left end node $lend[v]$ and right end node $rend[v]$, and the corresponding distances $ldist[v]$ and $rdist[v]$ to $ol[v]$ and $or[v]$.

<u>Line 23 to 132</u>: After receiving the rank value $(lend, rend, ldist, rdist)$ from its neighbors, each node v calculates its rank value $(lend[v], rend[v], ldist[v], rdist[v])$.

Note that each while loop in line 1 and line 16 invokes one communication round. In Algorithm 1, we can divide the pseudo-code into two parts; the first part from line 1 to line 15 is the top-down part, which continuously shrinks the set of nodes using independent set, and the second part from line 16 to line 32 is the bottom-up part, which reversely restores the linked list and computes the rank value for each internal node. An example of the top-down and bottom-up part of Algorithm 1 with the second stop criterion is illustrated in Fig. 2-(a) and Fig. 2-(b). In Fig. 2-(a) an example illustrates the bottom-up part of Algorithm 1. In communication round 4, node 1 and node 5 send messages of their rank value (lend, rend, ldist, rdist) (1, 5, 0,4) and (1, 5, 4, 0) to node 3. Then in round 5, after receiving these messages, node 3 can compute its rank value (1, 5, 2, 2) using its previous value of ldist [3] and rdist [3]. Then node 3 sends messages of this rank value to node 2 and node 4. Finally, node 2 and node 4 will calculate their rank value with the messages received from node 3. In Fig. 2-(b), an example of the top-down part of Algorithm 1 is presented. In communication round 1, node 2 and node 3 are selected into the independent set; here we color them red. After receiving messages from round 1, node 1 and node 3, node 3 and node 5 are connected; at the same time, node 2 and node 3 are excluded from the original list. In order to restore the original list, ol[v] and or[v] are used to store each node's previous value of l[v] and r[v]. The same situation happens in round 3, and node 3 is selected and excluded from the list. Finally, after round 3, only two end nodes are left, and the top-down part stops.

The number of communication rounds of NR-ranking with these two stop criterions is given by Lemma 1 and Lemma 3 respectively.

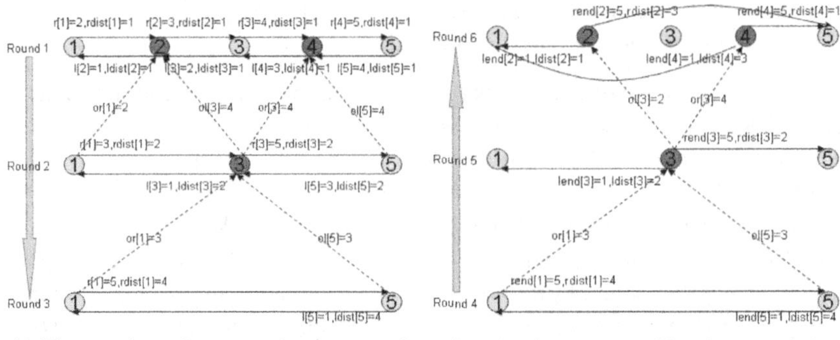

(a) The number of communication round.   (b) The time usage of implementation.

Fig. 2. Two example illustrates the bottom-up part and top-down part of Algorithm 1 respectively.

Lemma 1. Given a set of linked lists with n nodes, in each round of communication, one node has a probability of ϵ being selected in the independent set and excluded from the original linked lists, and this process stops when the number of nodes in the current linked lists is less than n/p. The total number of communication rounds is $O(log_{\frac{1}{1-\epsilon}} p)$.

Proof: we can denote the number of communication rounds as t, then the number of remaining nodes after the communication round t is $n \times (1 - \epsilon)^t = \frac{n}{p}$, and we get

$$t = log_{\frac{1}{1-\epsilon}} p \tag{1}$$

Lemma 2. Given a set of linked lists with n nodes, in each communication round, one node has the probability of ϵ being selected in the independent set and excluded from the original linked lists, and this process stops when all nodes in the remaining list are end nodes. The total number of communication rounds is $O(log_{\frac{1}{1-\epsilon}} m)$.

Proof: The number of communication rounds is written as t, then the number of remaining nodes after the t communication round is $n \times (1 - \epsilon)^t = 2$, and we can get

$$t = log_{\frac{1}{1-\epsilon}} n - log_{\frac{1}{1-\epsilon}} 2 \approx log_{\frac{1}{1-\epsilon}} n \tag{2}$$

Lemma 3. Given a set of linked lists L with n nodes, the set of lists is written as $l_1, l_2, l_3, \ldots, l_k$, and the length of these lists is $w_1, w_2, w_3, \ldots, w_k$, here the length of the longest linked list is w. If the stop criterion on selecting the independent set is that all nodes in the remaining list are end nodes. The total number of communication rounds is $O(log_{\frac{1}{1-\epsilon}} w)$.

Proof: According to Lemma 2, the number of communication rounds t is:

$$t = max_{i=1}^{k}(log_{\frac{1}{1-\epsilon}} w_i) = log_{\frac{1}{1-\epsilon}} w \tag{3}$$

According to Lemma 3, the number of communication rounds has no direct relation with the total number of nodes in linked lists, it increases linearly with the logarithm of the length of longest linked list.

In the top-down part of Algorithm 1, each node in the independent set communicates (sending packets) only a constant number of times (at most two times) during every communication round; in the bottom-up part, each node in the previous independent set communicates (receiving packets) at most two times. As each node can be selected into the independent set only once, the communication complexity of NR-Ranking is $O(n)$. Only two extra arrays ol and or are introduced into Algorithm 1, and the memory usage is bounded by $O(n)$.

In Algorithm 1, each loop while on line 0 and line 6 will invoke one communication round. In the top-down part, each node in the independent set communicates (sending packets) only a constant number of times (at most two times) within every communication round; in the bottom-up part, each node in previous independent set communicates (receiving packets) at most two times. As each node can be selected into an independent set only once, the communication complexity of NR-Ranking is $O(n)$. Only two extra arrays ol and or are introduced in Algorithm 1, then the memory is bounded by $O(n)$.

Algorithm 1: IndependentSet (L, K)

Input   : A node set L of linked lists (linked via $l[v]$ and $r[v]$) with n nodes, and an integer number K.

Output: The independent Set I, which is a subset of nodes of L, Every two nodes in I must not be neighbors in L.

1 Foreach node v in L
2   Generate three random vote keys $A[v]$, $A[l[v]]$ and $A[r[v]]$ in the interval $[1, K]$ for node v, $l[v]$ and $r[v]$.
3   If $A[v] \geq A[l[v]]$ and $A[v] > A[r[v]]$
4   Then v is selected into I. ;
5 Return I;

3.2   Description of Independent Set Subroutine

The independent set subroutine is the key part of the NR-Ranking algorithm. In order for the NR-Ranking algorithm to have the computational complexity within $O(n)$, the independent set subroutine has to keep its computational complexity bounded by $O(n)$, The independent set subroutine is presented in Algorithm 2, and we will prove that Algorithm 2 meets the above requirements.

According to Algorithm 2, each node v in a given set L generates a random number $A[v]$ in the interval $[1, K]$. For any node v, v can be included in the independent set I, if and only if its random number $A[v]$ is greater than or equal to its left neighbor $l[v]$, $A[v]A[l[v]]$, and strictly larger than its right neighbor $r[v]$, $A[v] > A[r]$. The following lemma is given to calculate the probability that one node will be selected as an independent set.

Lemma 4. Given three random numbers x, y, z in the interval $[1, K]$, the probability of $x \geq y$ and $x > z$ is:

$$\epsilon_1 = \frac{1}{3}(1 - \frac{1}{K^2}) \tag{4}$$

Proof. The observed probability of x larger or equal to y will be $\frac{x}{K}$ and the probability of x larger than z is $\frac{x-1}{K}$. Finally the total probability over all values of x for $x \geq y$ and $x > z$ is:

$$\epsilon_1 = \frac{1}{K}\sum_{i=1}^{K}\left(\frac{i^2}{K^2} - \frac{i}{K^2}\right) = \frac{1}{3}\left(1 - \frac{1}{K^2}\right) \tag{5}$$

According to Lemma 4, the expected size of the independent set I is:

$$E(|I|) = \frac{1}{3}\left(1 - \frac{1}{K^2}\right)|L| \tag{6}$$

Here $|I|$ denotes the number of nodes in I, and $|L|$ denotes the number of nodes in L.

When K is a large number, then the expected probability of one node v in L being selected into the independent set I is:

$$\epsilon_2 = \lim_{K \to \infty} \epsilon_1 = \lim_{K \to \infty} \frac{1}{3}\left(1 - \frac{1}{K^2}\right) = \frac{1}{3} \tag{7}$$

Then the expected size of independent set I is:

$$E(|I|) = \epsilon_2|L| = \frac{1}{3}|L|, when K \to \infty \tag{8}$$

From Eqs. (8) and (9), the number of nodes in linked lists will shrink $\frac{1}{3}$ at each communication round. It is clear that the computation complexity of Algorithm 2 is $O(n)$, here n is the number of nodes in all input linked lists. The computation complexity of Algorithm 1 on selecting the independent set is:

$$C_1 = \sum_{i=1}^{t}(1 - \epsilon_1)^{i-1} \leq \frac{n}{1 - \epsilon_1} \tag{9}$$

When $K \to \infty$, we have

$$C_2 = \frac{3n}{2} \tag{10}$$

From Eqs. (10) and (11), the computational complexity of selecting the independent set in Algorithm 1 is $O(n)$ regardless of the value of K. As two communications on sending and receiving messages will recall one computation operation, the actual computation work in the other part of Algorithm 2 is proportional to the number of communications. These computations can also be bounded by $O(n)$. Overall, the computation complexity of Algorithm 1 is $O(n)$.

In this section, we have presented a non-recursive algorithm on list ranking, NR-Ranking. More importantly, we have shown NR-Ranking has its computation, communication, and memory usage complexity limited by $O(n)$. Compared with previous work, this has the lowest complexity limit. The communication round of NR-Ranking is $O(log(p))$ if NR-Ranking adopts the first stop criterion, and $O(log(w))$ if NR-Ranking adopts the second one.

```
class TopDown: public Vertex<Vetex vetex, Edge edge, Message msg>{
public: virtual void Computing(MessageIterator* msgs) {
    for(;!msgs->Done();msgs->next()) {
        if(edge.left == msgs->source()) {
            vetex.oldLeft = edge.left;
            edge.left = msgs->value().first;
            edge.leftDist= msgs->value().second;
        }
        if(edge.right == msgs->source()) {
            vetex.oldRight = edge.right;
            edge.right = msgs->value().first;
            edge.rightDist= msgs->value().second;
        }
        //Two end nodes have been connected
        if(vetex.oldLeft == edge.left && vetex.key == edge.right ||
            vetex.oldRight == edge.right && vetex.key == edge.left)
            vetex.independentFlag=true;
    }

    //The independentFlag for each node is initialized as false
    if(vetex.independentFlag==false) {
        //This node is an internal node
        if(edge.right!=vetex.key && edge.right!=vetex.key)
            vetex.independentFlag = IndependentSet(
            vetex.key, edge.left, edge.right);
        if(vetex.independentFlag==true) {
            SendMessageTo(edge.right, (edge.left, edge.leftDist));
            SendMessageTo(edge.left, (edge.right, edge.rightDist));
        }
    }
    else    VoteToHalt();
}
}
```

(a) Top-down class.

```
class TopDown: public Vertex<Vetex vetex, Edge edge, Message msg>{
public: virtual void BottomUp(MessageIterator* msgs) {
    for(;!msgs->Done();msgs->next()) {
        (lend, rend, ldist, rdist) = msgs->value();
        //Calculate the rank of internal nodes in the independentset
        if(edge.left == msgs->source())
            vetex.rank(lend,rend,edge.leftDist+ldist,edge.rightDist-ldist);
        if(edgeValue.right == msgs->source())
            vetex.rank(lend,rend,edge.leftDist+ldist,edge.rightDist-ldist);
    }
    if(vetex.independentFlag==true)
    {
        //Init rank value for the end node
        if(edge.left==Vertex.key || edge.right==vetexValue.key)
            vetex.rank(edgeValue.left,
                edge.right, edge.leftDist, edge.rightDist);

        SendMessageTo(vetex.oldLeft, vetex.rank);
        SendMessageTo(vetex,oldRight, vetex.rank);
        vetex.independetFlag = false;
    }
    else  VoteToHalt();
}
}
```

(b) Bottom-up class.

Fig. 3. (a) Top-down class of NR-Ranking implemented in Pregel. (b) Bottom-up class of NR-Ranking implemented in Pregel.

4 Implementation on Pregel

This non-recursive version of the list ranking solution will be much easier to implement on Pregel. We will first discuss some important features of the Pregel system and then explain how to use these features to implement the non-recursive list ranking algorithm.

4.1 Features of Pregel System

Pregel is a system for large-scale graph processing. At the beginning of the computation, the vertices of the graph are distributed across compute nodes. Computation and communication are embedded into iterations of superstep, and each vertex is parallel processed in each superstep. At the end of each superstep, all compute nodes will synchronize before starting the next superstep. The iterations stop when all vertices are inactive and no further messages are sent to the next superstep. There are two key features of Pregel that are

1. **Vertex-centric.** Each vertex is processed parallel using the same user-defined function. Every vertex has two states: active and inactive. When the vertex is in an inactive state, it will not be processed in the next superstep until it received a message and became active. The vertex deactivates itself by explicitly voting to halt. When the states of all vertices are inactive and no more messages are sent to the next superstep, the iterations of superstep will be stopped.
2. **Message-driven.** The behavior of the vertex depends on the message it received. In each superstep, the vertex will receive the messages sent from the previous superstep, and the messages sent from this superstep can only be received by the next superstep. The separate stage on sending and receiving messages gives the opportunity to aggregate messages sent to the same destination node.

Table 1. The runtime and communication round statistics on NR-Ranking algorithm processing 500 linked lists with a length of 100k.

Number of processors	Number of supersteps	Total Time usage	Time usage per superstep
8	134	1688.7	12.6
16	147	989.1	6.73
24	152	714.2	4.7
32	138	570.4	4.13
40	131	468.9	3.58
48	129	426.7	3.31

4.2 Implemetation Details

The non-recursive list ranking algorithm NR-Ranking can be directly mapped to the Pregel implementation and some problems still need to be solved. When a node is selected into the independent set, it will stop joining the rest of superstep in the top-down part by setting its status to inactive. Pregel maintains the information about how many vertices are active in each superstep, and this can be used to identify whether the first stop criterion is satisfied. For the second criterion, it needs to know when a list contains only two end nodes. This can be solved by checking every end node whether their previous edge $ol[v]$ or $or[v]$ and the updated edge $l[v]$ or $r[v]$ have the same value; if so, it means that this list contains only two end nodes now, and this end node will be set to inactive. Figure 3-(a) illustrates the procedure of the top-down class of NR-Ranking implementation following the second stop criterion.

The bottom-up part is implemented as the algorithm described. The end node sends the message to the nodes that were previously selected in the independent set, updates its rank, and restores them to the list. Then the end node votes to halt and become inactive. This procedure is repeated until all the nodes are restored, and after all nodes have voted to halt, the process of the bottom-up part in Pregel is also finished. The bottom-up class of the NR-Ranking implementation in Pregel is shown in Fig. 3-(b):

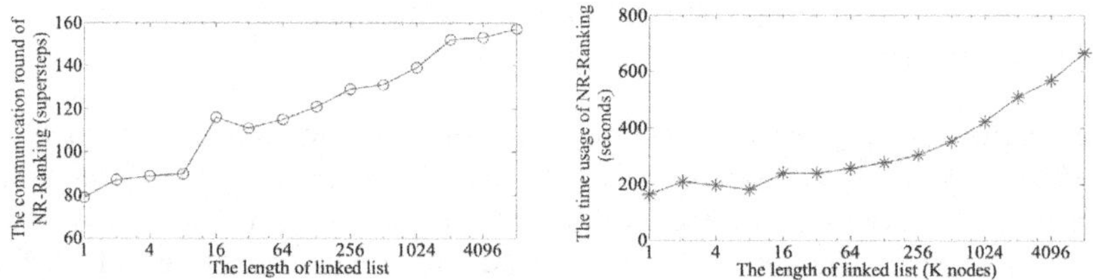

(a) The number of communication round. (b) The time usage of NR-Ranking implementation.

Fig. 4. (a) The number of communication round of NR-Ranking on processing linked list with its length from 1K to 8192K. (b) The time usage of NR-Ranking on processing linked list with its length varying from 10K to 100M.

5   Experiments

NR-Ranking has been implemented on GPS [20], a practical implementation of Pregel. In the experiment, we use a high performance cluster with 6 servers; each server has 8 cores, 24 GB memory, and 2.4T storage. All these servers are interconnected with 1 Gbit twisted-pair cables. The following parts of this section will evaluate and analyze the performance of the NR-Ranking algorithm on GPS.

5.1   Compelexity Evaluation

Firstly, we evaluate how the length of longest list affects the running time of NR-Ranking. Seventeen data sets were generated with each having 10 linked lists. The maximum length of the linked list in these datasets is 1K to 8192K. Experimental results on the number of communication round and time usage are demonstrated in Fig. 4-(a) and Fig. 4-(b), respectively.

In Fig. 5, the number of communication rounds increases linearly as the maximum length of the linked list grows exponentially. The same trend can also be seen in Fig. 5, where the time usage of NR-Ranking also increases linearly. The experimental results confirm that the number of communication round and running time is linearly related to the logarithm of the length of longest linked list, which is consistent with our complexity analysis in Sect. 3.

Next, we have fixed the length of linked list to 100K, and generated another series of datasets by increasing the number of linked lists from 10 to 100. The experimental results on the number of communication rounds, the time usage, and the average time usage in each communication round are illustrated in Figs. 4-(a), 4-(b), and 5.

According to Fig. 5-(a), the number of communication rounds retains its value around 125 supersteps and varies between 120 and 140 supersteps. However, the time usage of NR-Ranking in Fig. 5-(b) is growing steadily when the number of linked lists increases from 10 to 100. More detail can be found in Fig. 5-(c), where the average time usage in one communication round sharing the same trend with the total time usage of NR-Ranking. As the communication and computation workload of one processor has a complexity of $O(n/p)$, here n is the number of nodes in the linked lists, the workload and the use of time in one communication round will increase along with the amount of problems thrown out n.

5.2   Scalability Evaluation

In order to evaluate the scalability of NR-Ranking, we have randomly created a dataset including 500 linked lists with a length of 100k in average, and this dataset has 107 nodes in total. The simulation results are illustrated in Table 1.

In Table 1, the number of communication rounds (supersteps) in processing this dataset is almost constant when the number of workers increases from 8 to 48. However, the overall running time of NR-Ranking is decreasing following a trend of decreasing time usage on each superstep, and more than 4 times speedup has been achieved when the number of workers scales from 8 to 48. Finally, we conclude that, given a fixed dataset of linked list, the running time per superstep will decrease when the number of jobs increases and the number of communication rounds remains constant.

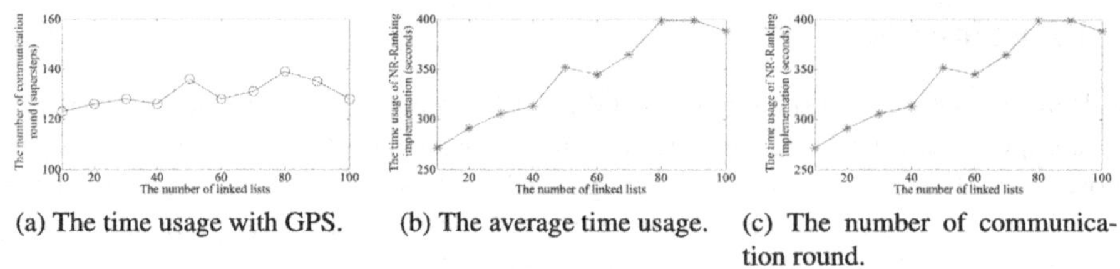

(a) The time usage with GPS.   (b) The average time usage.   (c) The number of communication round.

Fig. 5. (a) The time usage with GPS when the number of linked lists with fixed length increases from 5 to 100. (b) The average time usage in one communication rounds when the number of linked lists increases from 10 to 100. (c) The number of communication round of NR-Ranking implementation on processing linked list with its length from 1K to 8192K.

6 Conclustion

List ranking is the kernel in genome assembly; however, a parallel practical solution for enormous large volumes of data is still a hard problem for many years. This situation blocks many genome assembly projects on the cloud, such as SOAP-Hecate and Contrail.

In order to radically change this situation, we have proposed a NR-Ranking algorithm for the list ranking problem. NR-Ranking has its communication, computation, and memory usage complexity bounded by $O(n)$, it has hit the bottom line among its previous solutions. According to the stop criterion of selecting an independent set, the number of communication rounds of NR-Ranking is different. It is limited by $\log(p)$ if the number of nodes in the reminder lists is less than (n/p), or $O(logw)$ if all the nodes in the remaining lists are end nodes, where p is the number of processors, n is the number of nodes in the linked lists, w is the length of the longest list. As a non-recursive solution, NR-Ranking can be directly implemented on the Pregel system. In the experiment, we have developed the NR-Ranking algorithm on GPS, which is a practical implementation of Pregel on the Hadoop MapReduce platform. Statistical results confirm the above complexity analysis, and the NR-Ranking implementation on GPS has achieved a speedup of 4X when the number of workers increases from 8 to 48.

Acknowledgment. This work is supported by the Shenzhen-HongKong Joint Funding Project (Category A) under Grant No. SGDX20230116092056010, National Key Research and Development Program of China under Grant No. 2023YFF1206103, National Science Foundation of China under grant no. 62272449(iPS NSFC), Shenzhen Basic Research Fund under Grant No. 20220527112947006, KQTD20200820113106007, ZDSYS20220422103800001. We would also like to thank the funding support by the Key Laboratory of Quantitative Synthetic Biology, Chinese Academy of Sciences under grant no. CKL075.

A   Appendix

Algorithm 2: NR-Ranking(L)

Input   : A family of double linked lists L (linked via $l[v]$ and $r[v]$) with n nodes and for each node v has a distance value $ldist[v]$ to its left neighbor $l[v]$ and a distance value $rdist[v]$ to its right neighbor $r[v]$. Each node v has $ol[v]$ and $or[v]$ to store its previous left and right neighbors.

Output: For each node v, compute the distance $ldist[v]$ between v and the left end node $lend[v]$, the distance $rdist[v]$ between v and the right end node $rend[v]$.

6 While (stop criterion is not satisfied)

7   I = IndependentSet(L);

8   D = L - I;

9   For each i in I do send (l[v], ldist[v]) to r[v];

10   For each i in I do send (r[v], rdist[v]) to l[v];

11   For each v in D with l[v] in I do ;

12   Let (nl[v], nldist) be the value received from l[v]; ;

13   Set ol[v] = l[v]; ;

14   Set l[v] = nl[v] and ldist[v] += nldist[v]; ;

15   For each v in D with r[v] in I do

16   Let (nr[v], nrdist) be the value received from r[v]; ;

17   Set or[v] = r[v]; ;

18   Set r[v] = nr[v] and rdist[v] += nrdist[v]; ;

19   L = D;

20 Send L to processor 0 and solve the problem sequentially

21 While(L is smaller than n)

22   Foreach v in L with ol[v] != NULL do

23   Send rank value (lend, rend, ldist[v], rdist[v]) to ol[v]; ;

24   Set ol[v] = NULL; ;

25   Foreach v in L with or[v] != NULL do

26   Send rank value (lend, rend, ldist[v], rdist[v]) to or[v]; ;

27   Set or[v] = NULL; ;

28   Foreach v not in L with l[v] in L do

29   (lend, rend, ldist, rdist) is the value received from l[v]; ;

30   Set lend[v] = lend and rend[v] = rend; ;

31   Set rdist[v] = rdist-ldist[v], ldist[v]=ldist[v]+ldist; ;

32   L = L + v; ;

33   Foreach v not in L with r[v] in L do

34   (lend, rend, ldist, rdist) is the value received from r[v]; ;

35   Set lend[v] = lend and rend[v] = rend; ;

36   Set ldist[v] = ldist-rdist[v] and rdist[v]=rdist[v]+rdist; ;

37   L = L + v; ;

References

1. Sibeyn, J.F., Guillaume, F., Seidel, T.: Practical parallel list ranking. J. Parallel Distrib. Comput. **56**(2), 156–180 (1999). https://doi.org/10.1006/jpdc.1998.1508
2. Reid-Miller, M.: List ranking and list scan on the Crayc-C90. In: Proceedings of the Sixth Annual ACM Symposium on Parallel Algorithms and Architectures, SPAA '94, pp. 104–113. Association for Computing Machinery, New York, NY, USA (1994). https://doi.org/10.1145/181014.181049
3. Atallah, M.J., Hambrusch, S.E.: Solving tree problems on a mesh-connected processor array. Inf. Control **69**(1–3), 168–187 (1986). https://doi.org/10.1016/S0019-9958(86)80046-8
4. Cong, G., Bader, D.A.: The Euler tour technique and parallel rooted spanning tree. In: Proceedings of the 2004 International Conference on Parallel Processing, ICPP '04, pp. 448–457. IEEE Computer Society, USA (2004)
5. Cole, R., Vishkin, U.: Faster optimal parallel prefix sums and list ranking. Inf. Comput. **81**(3), 334–352 (1989). https://doi.org/10.1016/0890-5401(89)90036-9. https://www.sciencedirect.com/science/article/pii/0890540189900369
6. Jackson, B.G., Schnable, P.S., Aluru, S.: Parallel short sequence assembly of transcriptomes. BMC Bioinf. **10**, 1–12 (2009)
7. Jackson, B.G., Regennitter, M., Yang, X., Schnable, P.S., Aluru, S.: Parallel de novo assembly of large genomes from high-throughput short reads. In: IEEE International Symposium on Parallel & Distributed Processing (IPDPS), vol. 2010, pp. 1–10. IEEE (2010)
8. Valiant, L.G.: A bridging model for parallel computation. Commun. ACM **33**(8), 103–111 (1990)
9. Anderson, R.J., Miller, G.L.: Deterministic parallel listranking. Algorithmica **6**(1–6), 859–868 (1991). https://doi.org/10.1007/BF01759076
10. Lassous, I.G., Gustedt, J.: Portable list ranking: an experimental study. ACM J. Exp. Algorithmics **7**, 7 (2003). https://doi.org/10.1145/944618.944625
11. Cole, R., Vishkin, U.: Deterministic coin tossing with applications to optimal parallel list ranking. Inf. Control **70**(1), 32–53 (1986)
12. Anderson, R.J., Miller, G.L.: Deterministic parallel list ranking. Algorithmica **6**(1), 859–868 (1991)
13. Joseph, J., et al.: An Introduction to Parallel Algorithms. Addison, USA (1992)
14. Reid-Miller, M., Miller, G.L., Modugno, F.: List ranking and parallel tree contraction. In: Synthesis of Parallel Algorithms, pp. 115–194 (1993)
15. Skillicorn, D.B., Hill, J.M., McColl, W.F.: Questions and answers about BSP. Sci. Program. **6**(3), 249–274 (1997)
16. Dehne, F., Song, S.W.: Randomized parallel list ranking for distributed memory multiprocessors. Int. J. Parallel Prog. **25**(1), 1–16 (1997)
17. Sibeyn, J.F.: Better trade-offs for parallel list ranking. In: Proceedings of the Ninth Annual ACM Symposium on Parallel Algorithms and Architectures, pp. 221–230 (1997)
18. Schatz, M.C., Langmead, B., Salzberg, S.L.: Cloud computing and the DNA data race. Nat. Biotechnol. **28**(7), 691–693 (2010)
19. Malewicz, G., et al.: Pregel: a system for large-scale graph processing. In: Proceedings of the 2010 ACM SIGMOD International Conference on Management of Data, pp. 135–146 (2010)
20. Salihoglu, S., Widom, J.: GPS: a graph processing system. In: Proceedings of the 25th International Conference on Scientific and Statistical Database Management, pp. 1–12 (2013)
21. Xavier, C., Iyengar, S.S.: Introduction to Parallel Algorithms, vol. 1. Wiley (1998)
22. Apache: Apache incubator giraph. http://incubator.apache.org/giraph/
23. raveldata, goldenorb. http://www.raveldata.com/goldenorb/
24. Apache: Apache Hama. http://incubator.apache.org/hama/
25. Phoebus: github phoebus. http://github.com/xslogic/phoebus

scCMA: A Contrastive Masked Autoencoder for Single-Cell RNA-Seq Embedding

Xiang Chen[1]([✉]), Wenfeng He[1], Junnan Yu[1], and Zhaoyu Fang[2]

[1] Hunan University of Science and Technology, Xiangtan, Hunan, China
chenxofhit@gmail.com
[2] Central South University, Changsha, Hunan, China

Abstract. Single-cell RNA sequencing (scRNA-seq) data analysis faces significant challenges due to high dimensionality, sparsity, noise, and batch effects, all of which complicate accurate cell clustering and downstream tasks. To address these issues, we introduce scCMA, a novel method that integrates contrastive learning with a masked autoencoder framework to generate robust, high-quality cell embeddings. Through contrastive learning, scCMA enhances the discriminative power of feature representations by maximizing similarity within cell types and minimizing it across types, implicitly reducing batch effects without prior dataset knowledge. Simultaneously, the masked autoencoder randomly masks and reconstructs gene expression data, enabling the model to capture global dependencies and rare features while mitigating the impact of noise and sparsity. Evaluations across diverse datasets demonstrate that scCMA achieves superior accuracy in cell clustering, effectively mitigates batch effects without compromising biological heterogeneity, and sensitively identifies rare cell populations. Furthermore, the learned embeddings preserve developmental dynamics, enabling precise reconstruction of differentiation trajectories. The implementation code for scCMA is available at the following link: https://github.com/chenxofhit/scCMA.

Keywords: Single-cell RNA sequencing · Masked autoencoders · Contrastive learning · Cell clustering · Batch effect correction

1 Introduction

scRNA-seq technology has revolutionized our understanding of cellular heterogeneity by enabling high-resolution exploration of gene expression profiles. This technology has been instrumental in identifying novel cell types, elucidating developmental trajectories, and uncovering molecular mechanisms underlying complex diseases [1]. However, the inherent characteristics of scRNA-seq data—high dimensionality, sparsity, and noise—pose substantial challenges for accurate cell clustering [2], a critical step in downstream analyses including cell type annotation, trajectory inference, and differential expression analysis. Traditional clustering algorithms, including K-means, hierarchical clustering, and community

J. Tang et al. (Eds.): ISBRA 2025, LNBI 15757, pp. 279–294, 2026.
https://doi.org/10.1007/978-981-95-0695-8_23

detection methods such as Louvain and Leiden, have been extensively applied to scRNA-seq data analysis [3,4]. Although these methods have shown effectiveness, they often struggle to resolve fine-grained differences between cell populations, especially in identifying rare cell types and analyzing continuous cell state transitions. Moreover, technical artifacts, batch effects, and dropout events in gene expression measurements substantially impair the clustering accuracy, resulting in suboptimal performance [5,6].

Recent advancements in single-cell clustering have introduced several effective methods, each with its strengths and limitations. For example, scVI [7] and scANVI [8] use variational autoencoders to integrate batch effect correction and clustering, improving performance but struggling with high sparsity or noise. SIMLR [9] employs multi-kernel optimization for robust clustering but faces scalability issues. SCLC [10] leverages contrastive learning for rare cell type detection, yet its reliance on pairwise similarity computation can be computationally challenging. scMAE [11] uses masked self-encoders to generate low-dimensional representations, but complex nonlinear relationships in data remain a hurdle. Methods like scGNN [12] and scDeepCluster [13] utilize neural networks to capture complex relationships, but they are computationally intensive and prone to overfitting in large datasets. scGCNClustering [14] and other graph-based methods face challenges with sparse, high-dimensional data and graph structure design. Other approaches, such as scDCC [15] and DCA+K-means [16], show promise but struggle with small sample sizes or sensitivity to initialization. scNAME [17] simplifies preprocessing but faces scalability issues with large datasets. In summary, while these methods advance single-cell clustering, challenges with scalability, data sparsity, and computational efficiency remain.

Therefore, we propose a novel computational method, scCMA, which integrates contrastive learning with the masked autoencoder architecture. Contrastive learning enhances the discriminative power of feature representations by maximizing the similarity between cells of the same type and minimizing the similarity between cells of different types; furthermore, the discriminative property of contrastive learning could implicitly alleviate the batch effect together without knowing the prior knowledge of the dataset [18], thereby learning robust feature representations that are less sensitive to noise. On the other hand, the masked autoencoder learns latent relationships and dependency structures between samples from high-dimensional sparse data by randomly masking and reconstructing gene expression data, while also enhancing the ability to capture key rare features. Inspired by these two techniques, scCMA innovatively integrates the contrastive learning mechanism into the masked autoencoder architecture, effectively reducing the model's sensitivity to input data types. By continuously optimizing the discrepancy between the predicted masked data and the original masked data, the model progressively improves its learning capability. Ultimately, scCMA reconstructs the input data, reducing the impact of noise and high-dimensional interference, alleviating batch effects, while enhancing the robustness of feature representations and preserving rare feature signals, thereby improving the accuracy of downstream analyses. We conducted extensive evaluations of scCMA on multiple publicly available scRNA-seq datasets and compared its performance with several state-of-the-art methods. Experimental results demonstrate that scCMA exhibits favorable advantages in scRNA-seq data clustering tasks, particularly in its strong sensitivity to rare cell type identification. Further analysis also reveals that the robust embedded representations obtained through scCMA not only effectively alleviate batch effects in the data but also show distinguished performance in tasks such as trajectory inference.

2 The Proposed scCMA

The overall structure of the proposed scCMA method is illustrated in Fig. 1. Initially, the raw data is processed through two different paths to it: one is used to generate View1, and the other is used to perform a reorganization operation of the expression matrix of the raw data to obtain a masked matrix and further create View2, the view corresponding to the masked matrix. The two views are fed into an encoder that captures the correlations between genes and further learns through contrastive learning. This process maximizes the similarity of embedded data from the same cell across different views, while minimizing the similarity of embedded data from different cells. As a result, similar samples are placed closer together in the embedding space, while dissimilar samples are positioned further apart, ultimately generating an effective low-dimensional cellular embedding. These embeddings are then fed into the mask predictor to determine whether the mask is applied to the gene expression matrix in the first step and integrated to obtain high-quality low-dimensional cellular embeddings, which are used to perform a number of different downstream tasks. Ultimately, the integrated features are then fed into the decoder in order to reconstruct the original gene expression matrix and obtain the final predicted data.

2.1 Generation of Masked Gene Expression Matrix

To introduce variability and perturbation into the gene expression matrix, a three-step approach is implemented. First, the expression values for each gene in the matrix X are randomly rearranged. This involves shuffling the order of expression values within each gene while preserving the associations for that gene. The resulting shuffled matrix is denoted as X_0.

Next, a mask matrix M is created using the Bernoulli distribution. This matrix determines which elements in the gene expression matrix will be altered. The mask is generated based on a list of probabilities $\{p_1, p_2, \ldots, p_G\}$, where each p_j represents the likelihood of modifying the expression values of the corresponding gene. The generation process is defined as follows:

$$M_{ij} \sim \text{Bernoulli}(p_j), \tag{1}$$

where M_{ij} indicates the element in the i-th row and j-th column of the mask matrix, and p_j controls the proportion of modifications applied to the expression values for the j-th gene.

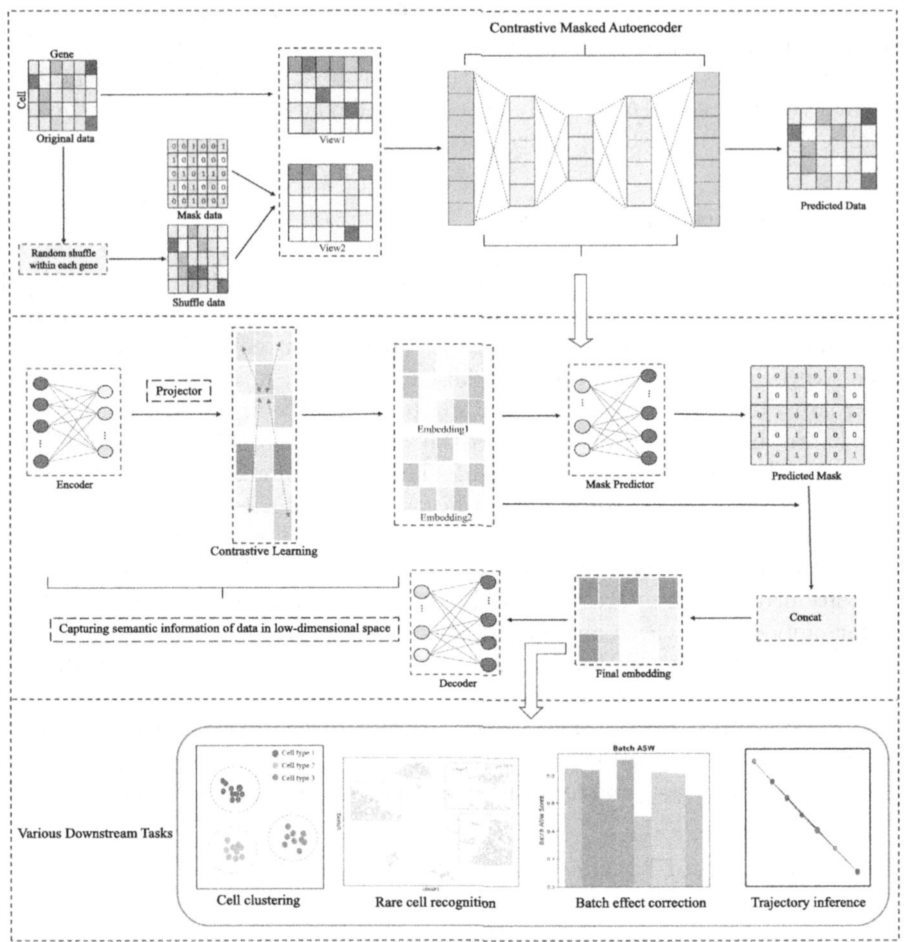

Fig. 1. Overview of scCMA method. Firstly, the raw data is processed through two different paths to it: one is used to generate View1, and the other is used to perform a reorganization operation of the expression matrix of the raw data to obtain a masked matrix and further create View2, the view corresponding to the masked matrix. The two Views are then fed into an encoder which captures the correlation between the genes and further learns by comparison to maximize the similarity of the embedded data from the same cell in the different Views and minimize the similarity of the embedded data from different cells to produce low-dimensional cell embedding. These embeddings are then fed into the mask predictors to determine whether the mask was applied to the gene expression matrix in the first step and integrated to obtain high-quality low-dimensional cellular embeddings. Finally, these high-quality low-dimensional cellular embeddings were used to perform a number of different downstream tasks.

Finally, the masked gene expression matrix X_M is computed through element-wise operations, following existing studies [17]. The calculation is represented as:

$$X_{Mij} = X_{ij} \cdot (1 - M_{ij}) + X'_{ij} \cdot M_{ij},\tag{2}$$

where X_{ij} represents the element in the i-th row and j-th column of the original gene expression matrix X, X'_{ij} corresponds to the element in the i-th row and j-th column of the shuffled matrix X_0, and X_{Mij} denotes the element in the masked gene expression matrix X_M. This formulation guarantees that each element X_{ij} is substituted with its shuffled counterpart X'_{ij} with a probability p_j, as determined by the mask matrix M. The resulting matrix X_M, which incorporates both the original and shuffled values according to the mask, is subsequently employed as the input for downstream model training.

Through this procedure, the gene expression matrix X undergoes a transformation where the expression values within each gene are randomly rearranged to introduce controlled perturbations. Additionally, the matrix is modified by applying a mask matrix that selectively obscures certain values. This combined process results in the altered gene expression matrix X_M, which retains the overall structure of the original data while incorporating variability designed to challenge the model's predictive capabilities and enhance its robustness.

2.2 Masked Autoencoder

The Masked Autoencoder module is a crucial component of scCMA, designed to learn robust and informative latent representations from scRNA-seq data. The MAE module operates by reconstructing the original input data from a partially masked version, thereby forcing the model to capture the underlying structure and dependencies within the data. This approach is particularly effective in handling the high-dimensional and sparse nature of scRNA-seq data.

The MAE module consists of three main components: an encoder, a mask predictor, and a decoder. Given an input gene expression vector $\mathbf{x} \in \mathbb{R}^d$, where d is the number of genes. A subset of the input features is randomly masked (set to zero) with a probability p. Let $\mathbf{m} \in \{0,1\}^d$ denote the binary mask vector, where $m_i = 1$ indicates that the i-th gene is masked. The corrupted input $\tilde{\mathbf{x}}$ is then given by:

$$\tilde{\mathbf{x}} = \mathbf{x} \odot \mathbf{m},\tag{3}$$

where $\odot$ denotes element-wise multiplication. The corrupted input $\tilde{\mathbf{x}}$ is passed through the encoder f_{enc}, which maps it to a lower-dimensional latent representation $\mathbf{z} \in \mathbb{R}^h$:

$$\mathbf{z} = f_{\text{enc}}(\tilde{\mathbf{x}}),\tag{4}$$

The encoder is implemented as a multi-layer neural network with non-linear activation functions (e.g., Mish) to capture complex patterns in the data. The latent representation $\mathbf{z}$ is fed into the mask predictor f_{mask}, which predicts the original mask $\mathbf{m}$:

$$\hat{\mathbf{m}} = f_{\text{mask}}(\mathbf{z}),\tag{5}$$

The mask predictor is a linear layer followed by a sigmoid activation function to produce probabilities for each gene being masked. The latent representation $\mathbf{z}$ and the predicted mask $\hat{\mathbf{m}}$ are concatenated and passed through the decoder f_{dec}, which reconstructs the original input $\mathbf{x}$:

$$\hat{\mathbf{x}} = f_{\text{dec}}(\mathbf{z} \oplus \hat{\mathbf{m}}), \tag{6}$$

where $\oplus$ denotes concatenation. The decoder is also implemented as a multi-layer neural network.

2.3 Contrastive Learning

The Contrastive Learning (CL) module is a critical component of scCMA, specifically designed to enhance the discriminative capability of latent representations derived from scRNA-seq data. By leveraging the principles of contrastive learning, the CL module enables the model to learn representations that are robust to noise and variations while preserving the intrinsic structure of the data. It achieves this by maximizing the similarity between samples belonging to the same class and minimizing the similarity between samples from different classes. This approach is particularly well-suited for scRNA-seq data, which is inherently high-dimensional and sparse.

The foundational concept of contrastive learning is to distinguish between positive pairs (samples sharing the same class) and negative pairs (samples from different classes). In scCMA, the CL module operates on latent representations $\mathbf{z} \in \mathbb{R}^h$ produced by the encoder. For a batch of N samples, multiple augmented views of each sample are created using data augmentation techniques such as random masking, noise injection, or feature dropout. These augmentations are used to generate positive pairs while treating the rest of the samples in the batch as negative examples.

To enhance the discriminative power of the learned representations, the CL module employs a projection head f_{proj}, which maps the latent representations $\mathbf{z}_i \in \mathbb{R}^h$ to a lower-dimensional space $\mathbf{p}_i \in \mathbb{R}^p$, where $p < h$. The projection head is implemented as a multi-layer perceptron (MLP) with non-linear activation functions such as ReLU. The projection step can be expressed as:

$$\mathbf{p}_i = f_{\text{proj}}(\mathbf{z}_i). \tag{7}$$

The lower-dimensional projected features $\mathbf{p}_i$ are used to compute the contrastive loss, which allows the model to learn more abstract, class-discriminative features. The effectiveness of this approach lies in decoupling the representation learning from the projection step, as the encoder focuses on learning generalizable features while the projection head adapts these features for contrastive optimization.

Additionally, to stabilize training and further improve representation quality, the cosine similarity between two embeddings $\mathbf{z}_i$ and $\mathbf{z}_j$ is often normalized:

$$\text{sim}(\mathbf{z}_i, \mathbf{z}_j) = \frac{\mathbf{z}_i \cdot \mathbf{z}_j}{\|\mathbf{z}_i\| \|\mathbf{z}_j\|}, \tag{8}$$

where $\| \cdot \|$ denotes the Euclidean norm. This normalization ensures that the model focuses solely on the angular relationship between vectors, which is crucial for contrastive learning.

2.4   Loss Function

The total loss function consists of three components: reconstruction loss, mask loss, and contrastive loss. Each component serves a distinct purpose in optimizing the model.

Reconstruction Loss: The reconstruction loss ensures that the model can accurately reconstruct the original input data from its masked version. This loss is critical for learning a faithful representation of the data, as it forces the model to capture the underlying structure and dependencies among genes. Given an input gene expression vector $\mathbf{x} \in \mathbb{R}^d$ and its reconstructed counterpart $\hat{\mathbf{x}}$, the reconstruction loss is defined as the mean squared error (MSE) between the two vectors:

$$\mathcal{L}_{\text{recon}} = \frac{1}{d} \sum_{i=1}^{d} (x_i - \hat{x}_i)^2, \tag{9}$$

where d is the number of genes, x_i is the expression value of the i-th gene in the original input, and $\hat{x}_i$ is the corresponding reconstructed value.

Mask Loss: The mask loss is designed to improve the model's ability to predict which genes were masked during the input corruption process. This loss encourages the model to learn features that are informative for recovering the original data distribution. Let $\mathbf{m} \in \{0,1\}^d$ denote the binary mask vector, where $m_i = 1$ indicates that the i-th gene was masked, and $\hat{\mathbf{m}} \in [0,1]^d$ denote the predicted mask probabilities. The mask loss is computed using the binary cross-entropy (BCE) loss:

$$\mathcal{L}_{\text{mask}} = -\frac{1}{d} \sum_{i=1}^{d} \left[m_i \log(\hat{m}_i) + (1 - m_i) \log(1 - \hat{m}_i) \right], \tag{10}$$

Contrastive Loss: The contrastive loss is a supervised learning objective designed to enhance the discriminative power of latent representations by explicitly leveraging class label information. It aims to ensure that samples belonging to the same class have representations that are closer in the latent space, while simultaneously pushing apart the representations of samples belonging to different classes. This behavior fosters better class separation and improves the model's ability to generalize to unseen data. Given a batch of N samples, let $\mathbf{z}_i$ and $\mathbf{z}_j$ denote the latent representations of two samples, and let y_i and y_j denote their corresponding class labels. The supervised contrastive loss is defined as:

$$\mathcal{L}_{\text{contrast}} = -\frac{1}{N} \sum_{i=1}^{N} \frac{1}{|P(i)|} \sum_{j \in P(i)} \log \left(\frac{\exp(\mathbf{z}_i \cdot \mathbf{z}_j / \tau)}{\sum_{k=1}^{N} \mathbb{1}_{k \neq i} \exp(\mathbf{z}_i \cdot \mathbf{z}_k / \tau)} \right), \tag{11}$$

where $P(i)$ is the set of indices of all samples in the batch that belong to the same class as sample i (i.e., $y_j = y_i$), τ is a temperature parameter that controls the sharpness of the distribution, $\mathbb{1}_{k \neq i}$ is an indicator function that equals 1 if $k \neq i$ and 0 otherwise.

The total loss $\mathcal{L}_{\text{total}}$ is a weighted sum of the three losses:

$$\mathcal{L}_{\text{total}} = \alpha \mathcal{L}_{\text{recon}} + \beta \mathcal{L}_{\text{mask}} + \gamma \mathcal{L}_{\text{contrast}}, \tag{12}$$

where $0 \leqslant \alpha, \beta, \gamma \leqslant 1$ and $\alpha + \beta + \gamma = 1$, they are hyperparameters that control the relative importance of each loss term.

3   Experiments

We utilized 14 real scRNA-seq datasets collected from public platforms to validate the performance of our proposed scCMA method, with the first 13 datasets employed for cell clustering experiments and the remaining one dataset used for other experiments. The number of cells in these datasets ranges from thousands to tens of thousands. Some datasets exhibit pronounced batch effects, while others represent large-scale datasets. Table 1 provides detailed information on these real scRNA-seq datasets. Throughout the experimental process, we used evaluation metrics such as ARI, NMI, Cell-type ASW score, and Batch ASW score. The experimental parameters in scCMA were also carefully designed.

Table 1. Description of scRNA-seq datasets

No.	Dataset	Cell number	Gene number	Cell type	Source
1	10X_PBMC	4340	33694	8	[2]
2	Worm_neuron_cell	4186	13488	10	[19]
3	CITE_CBMC	8617	2000	15	[20]
4	Human_kidney	5685	25215	11	[21]
5	Human1	1937	20125	14	[22]
6	Human2	1724	20125	14	[22]
7	Human3	3605	20125	14	[22]
8	Human4	1303	20125	14	[22]
9	HumanLiver	8444	5000	11	[23]
10	Mouse1	822	14878	13	[24]
11	Mouse2	1064	14878	13	[24]
12	Zeisel	3005	19972	9	[25]
13	Mouse_bladder_cell	2746	20670	16	[26]
14	Romanov	2881	24341	7	[27]
15	CellLine	9531	16602	2	[28]

4   Results

4.1   scCMA Achieves Excellent Clustering Performance

We performed 10 independent runs for scCMA and each of the seven methods including scGNN, scDeepCluster, scGCNClustering, scDCC, DCA+K-means, scNAME, and scMAE to ensure the stability and reliability of the results. After each run, we recorded the performance of each method on NMI and ARI, and we also recorded the Cell-type ASW of scCMA and 7 competitive methods for subsequent comparative analyses. In order to eliminate the bias introduced by randomness, we calculated the average value of each method on these different metrics and used it as the basis for the final performance evaluation.

scCMA achieved high NMI scores and ARI scores in 10X_PBMC, CITE_CBMC, Human_kidney, Human1, Human2, Human3, Human4, Human-Liver, Mouse1, Mouse2, the 10 datasets, achieved the highest NMI scores and ARI scores (Fig. 2(a)). Not only that, scCMA outperforms the second method with NMI scores and ARI score margins greater than 0.01 for all eight datasets. Notably, scCMA has an ARI score of 0.904 on the HumanLiver dataset, leading the other methods, followed by scMAE, which also achieved a good ARI score.

scCMA achieved the highest mean score ranking across the 13 datasets, followed closely by scNAME and scMAE (Fig. 2(b)). It is worth noting that the two better performing methods, scNAME and scMAE, both use the same enhancement method as scCMAE, which involves generating masked gene expression matrices, which force the model to capture the intrinsic structure and covariance patterns of the data by masking part of the input data and training the model to reconstruct the complete data. This demonstrates the effectiveness of this augmentation method for deep learning models of scRNA-seq data. Building upon the use of the generative masking enhancement method, scCMA further integrates contrastive learning. Contrastive learning enhances the clustering process by learning the similarities between samples, making the embedded data more conducive to clustering, while also resulting in clearer boundaries for the identified cell populations. The excellent performance of scCMA on a large number of datasets also suggests that the features extracted by the method are universal and applicable to different types and sizes of single-cell data. Overall, scCMA achieved substantially higher average ARI and NMI scores across all datasets, demonstrating superior performance compared to other methods.

4.2   scCMA Implements Batch Effect Correction

The batch effect is a pervasive and challenging problem in scRNA-seq data analysis. Batch effects usually originate from non-biological factors such as experimental conditions, sequencing platforms, sample processing time, or operator differences, which can introduce systematic biases and mask real biological differences, thus affecting the reliability and interpretability of data. Especially when integrating multiple batches of data, batch effects may lead to incorrect cell type identification, distorted gene expression patterns, and biased results

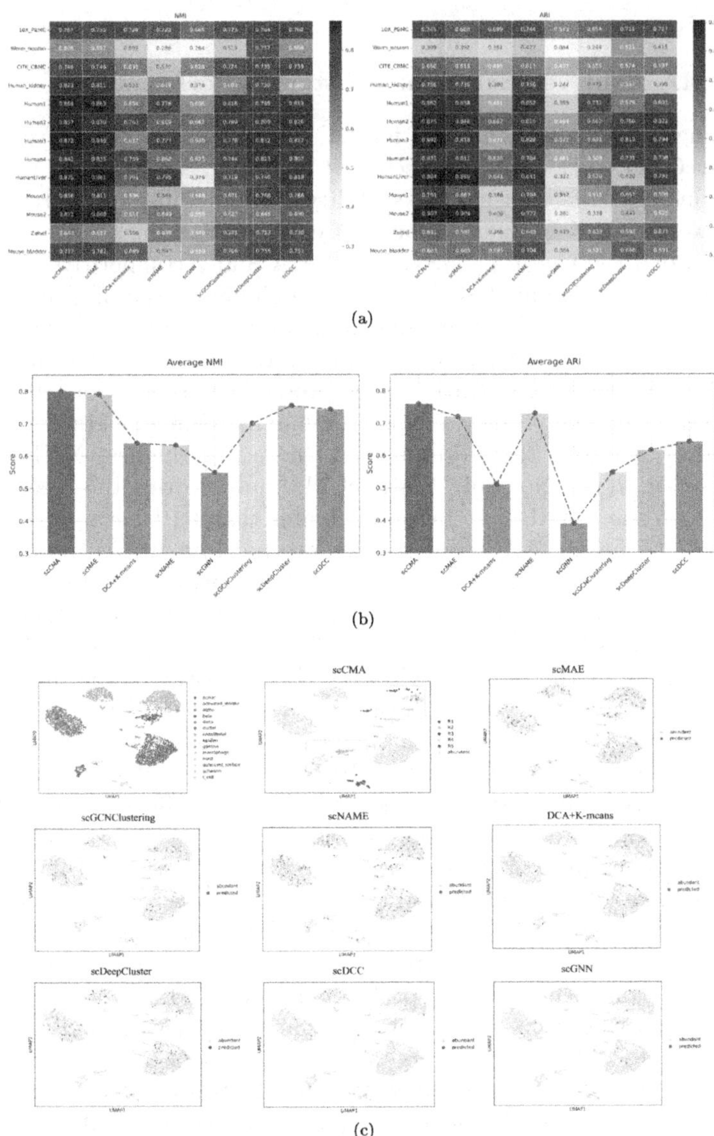

Fig. 2. Results of clustering experiments. (a) Heat maps of NMI and ARI for scCMA and 7 competitive methods on 13 datasets. (b) Mean NMI and ARI scores for scCMA and 7 competitive methods on 13 datasets. (c) Results of rare cell types identification for scCMA and seven comparison methods in terms of recall, precision, and F1 score on the Human3 dataset.

in downstream analysis. Therefore, the development of computational methods that can effectively correct for batch effects and maintain the biological characterization of the data is essential for improving the accuracy and reproducibility of single-cell data analysis. The scCMA method demonstrates its unique advantages in this context, not only efficiently handling large-scale single-cell data, but also excelling in the scalability and robustness of batch effects.

In our experiments, we utilized the Mouse1 dataset [29], which includes inherent batch effects. scCMA achieved high scores on both the clustering metrics ARI and NMI (Fig. 2(a)). As demonstrated in Fig. 3, scCMA also achieved the highest Cell-type ASW score and Batch ASW score. Notably, scCMA attained a high score of 0.998 in the metric of Batch ASW, ahead of the other seven methods. These results indicate that contrastive learning enhances scCMA's sensitivity to fine data structures, improving its ability to extract biologically meaningful features and effectively handle batch effects.

4.3   scCMA Achieves High Sensitivity in Rare Cell Types Detection

The human pancreas includes a variety of rare cell types, such as Epsilon cells, t-cells, etc. [30]. The four datasets Human1, Human2, Human3, and Human4 all belong to human pancreatic cells, with the Human3 dataset containing a higher number of cells. We applied scCMA to the Human3 dataset with seven other comparative methods and used UMAP to visualize the identification results of each method used to predict rare cell types. Human3 dataset contains 14 cell types annotated in the original study, of which 5 are considered rare cell types [31], ranging from 0.027% to 1.497%. A total of five rare cell clusters were identified by scCMA, denoted as R1 (0.19%), R2 (0.06%), R3 (0.38%), R4 (0.06%), and R5 (0.49%). Cluster R1 consists mainly of epsilon cells, R2 consists mainly of schwann cells, R3 consists mainly of mast cells, R4 consists mainly of macrophage cells, and R5 consists mainly of t_cells. The results of scCMA and 7 competitive methods are indicated in Fig. 2(c), where cell types belonging to rare

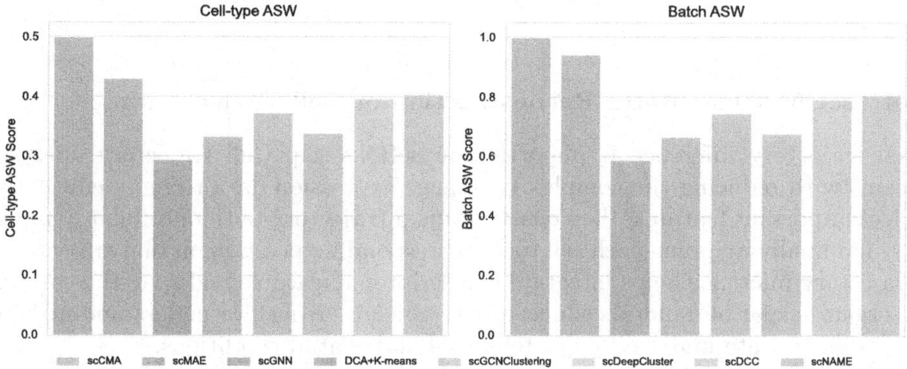

Fig. 3. Results of batch effect correction in terms of Cell-type ASW and Batch ASW on the Mouse1 dataset.

cell subtypes are marked with different colors to indicate their identities. Rare cell clusters identified by scCMA are visually distinguished using five different colors, while rare cells identified by the other methods are identified using red.

Combined with the annotated cell type information, we observe that scDCC and scGNN identify very few cells belonging to the major cell types, and DCA+K-means identifies only a small number of alpha and delta cells. For scGC-NClustering and scDeepCluster, both are more sensitive to acinar and alpha cells. scNAME and scMAE, while recognizing more cell types, are mostly other major cell types (e.g., alpha and delta cells). Although scNAME and scMAE identified more epsilon cells, these two methods were not sensitive to t-cells and the identification was not accurate enough. The results demonstrated that only scCMA accurately identified rare cell clusters corresponding to t-cells. We also used three widely used metrics, recall, precision, and F1 score, to further evaluate the ability of each method to identify rare cell types. scCMA has outstanding performance in terms of accuracy and F1 score (Fig. 4). The experimental results indicate that scCMA has obvious advantages in accuracy and overall performance, and can effectively suppress technical noise while retaining rare cell signals.

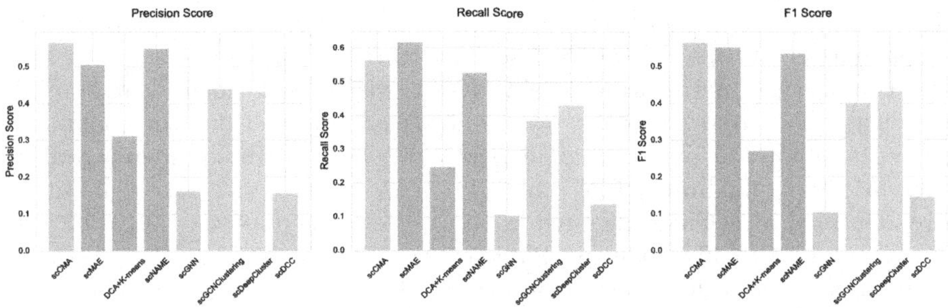

Fig. 4. Results of rare cell types identification for scCMA and seven comparison methods in terms of recall, precision, and F1 score on the Human3 dataset.

4.4 scCMA Facilitates Reconstruction of Cell Trajectories

Cell trajectory inference is important in scRNA-seq. Cell trajectory analysis begins with reducing the complexity of gene expression data to more efficiently select important features, then constructing a trajectory path of cellular dynamics, and finally mapping each cell to its corresponding position on that trajectory. Trajectory inference helps integrate transcriptome features and spatial locations to organize spatiotemporal cellular order, which is critical for understanding how cells differentiate under different temporal and spatial conditions.

To assess the effectiveness of scCMA to reduce the dimensionality of the data, we used PAGA [32], a commonly used method, to perform a single-cell trajectory inference analysis on the Romanov dataset to reveal the dynamics of the cell state over time. PAGA is a trajectory inference method for scRNA-seq data that is particularly well suited for studying cellular developmental processes and state transitions. It reveals the transition paths between cell states by translating their relationships in gene expression space into a graph structure. In our experiments, we input the low-dimensional cell features obtained by scCMA into PAGA to obtain cell trajectories. As depicted in Fig. 5, which illustrates the dynamics of cellular differentiation in the Romanov dataset, this process captures transitional states between cellular identities and uncovers the continuum of cellular differentiation. The results indicate that scCMA can effectively reduce the data dimensionality and facilitate the reconstruction of cell trajectories, clearly separating discrete cell types while preserving the smooth transition of developmental trajectories.

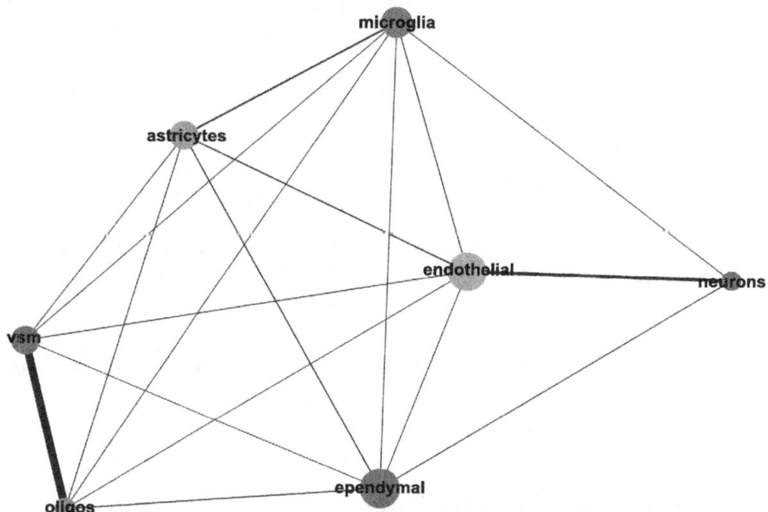

Fig. 5. Cell trajectory inference results. The result of cell trajectory inference, which reveals the dynamic process of cell differentiation. The seven different colored dots correspond to seven different cell types, while the size of the dots reflects the number of cells.

4.5   Ablation Analysis

To rigorously evaluate the contribution of each core component in scCMA, we performed ablation studies by systematically removing key functional modules: (1) scCMA-R: Removing the autoencoder module responsible for reconstruction loss; (2) scCMA-M: Disabling the masking mechanism that generates the masking loss; (3) scCMA-C: Excluding the contrastive learning head associated with contrastive loss. This design isolates the impact of each module while maintaining the integrity of the remaining architecture.

The experimental results reveal that deleting the reconstruction partial module leads to a substantial decrease in the final clustering results, especially for the Human2, Mouse1, and Mouse2 datasets, and the decrease is the most obvious; secondly, deleting the contrastive module also affects the final clustering results of the vast majority of datasets in a somewhat negative way, and only a small improvement is observed on the three datasets CITE_CBMC, Human3, and Zeisel datasets a small boost was observed in Fig. 6. The results also suggest that the Cell-type ASW scores of the Human4 dataset show a pronounced decrease when the autoencoder module is deleted, and the Cell-type ASW score for the Worm_neuron dataset showed a more substantial decrease when the masking module was removed. In summary, all components in scCMA play an important role in improving the overall performance of the model.

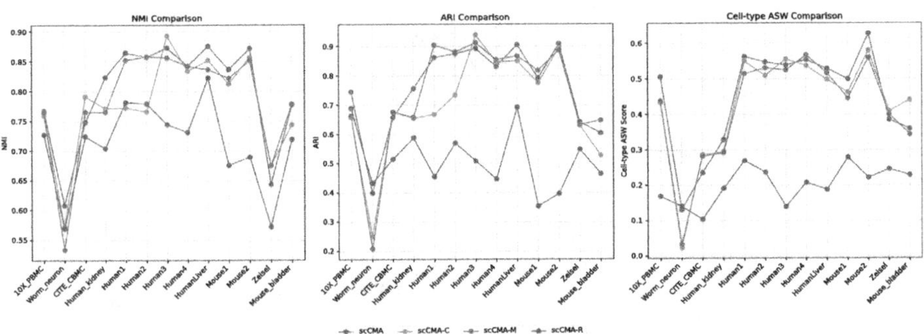

Fig. 6. NMI, ARI, and Cell-type ASW scores for scCMA, scCMA-R, scCMA-M, and scCMA-C on 13 datasets.

5   Discussion and Conclusion

In this study, we propose scCMA, a novel method that integrates masked autoencoders and contrastive learning to address key challenges in single-cell RNA sequencing (scRNA-seq) data analysis. By leveraging the contrastive learning component, scCMA enhances the discriminative power of feature representations, while the masked autoencoder effectively captures inter-sample dependencies, mitigating the impact of data sparsity and technical noise. Extensive experiments on 14 scRNA-seq datasets demonstrate that scCMA outperforms state-of-the-art methods in clustering accuracy, batch correction, rare cell type detection, and trajectory inference following dimensionality reduction. The modular design of scCMA ensures scalability and adaptability to diverse datasets and experimental conditions. Our results highlight the potential of scCMA as a powerful tool for uncovering cellular heterogeneity and advancing single-cell genomics research. In future work, we aim to extend scCMA to multi-omics data and explore automated hyperparameter optimization to further enhance its applicability.

Acknowledgements. This work is supported by the National Natural Science Foundation of China under Grants (No. 62202162).

Competing Interests. The authors declare no competing interests.

References

1. Stegle, O., Teichmann, S.A., Marioni, J.C.: Computational and analytical challenges in single-cell transcriptomics. Nat. Rev. Genet. **16**(3), 133–145 (2015)
2. Zheng, G.X.Y., et al.: Massively parallel digital transcriptional profiling of single cells. Nat. Commun. **8**(1), 14049 (2017)
3. Kiselev, V.Y., et al.: SC3: consensus clustering of single-cell RNA-SEQ data. Nat. Methods **14**(5), 483–486 (2017)
4. Traag, V.A., Waltman, L., Van Eck, N.J.: From Louvain to Leiden: guaranteeing well-connected communities. Sci. Rep. **9**(1), 5233 (2019)
5. Haghverdi, L., Lun, A.T.L., Morgan, M.D., Marioni, J.C.: Batch effects in single-cell RNA-sequencing data are corrected by matching mutual nearest neighbors. Nat. Biotechnol. **36**(5), 421–427 (2018)
6. Kharchenko, P.V., Silberstein, L., Scadden, D.T.: Bayesian approach to single-cell differential expression analysis. Nat. Methods **11**(7), 740–742 (2014)
7. Xu, B., Braun, R.: Variational inference of single cell time series. bioRxiv (2024)
8. Lopez, R., Regier, J., Cole, M.B., Jordan, M.I., Yosef, N.: Single-cell transcriptome integration reveals characteristics of cell state metabolism. Nat. Methods **19**(2), 165–176 (2022)
9. Ramazzotti, D., Wang, B., De Sano, L.: SIMLR: single-cell interpretation via multi-kernel learning. R Package Version 1.8.0 (2018)
10. Wang, J., et al.: Single-cell latent contrastive clustering for cell-type discovery and annotation. Nat. Commun. **13**(1):1–12 (2022)
11. Fang, Z., Zheng, R., Li, M.: scMAE: a masked autoencoder for single-cell RNA-seq clustering. Bioinformatics **40**(1), btae020 (2024)
12. Wang, J., et al.: scGNN is a novel graph neural network framework for single-cell RNA-seq analyses. Nat. Commun. **12**(1), 1882 (2021)
13. Tian, T., Wan, J., Song, Q., Wei, Z.: Clustering single-cell RNA-seq data with a model-based deep learning approach. Nat. Mach. Intell. **1**(4), 191–198 (2019)
14. Chen, X., Yu, J., Peng, L., Li, M.: A deep graph convolution network with attention for clustering scRNA-seq data. In: 2023 IEEE International Conference on Bioinformatics and Biomedicine (BIBM), pp. 320–323. IEEE (2023)
15. Wang, J., et al.: scDCC: single-cell deep constrained clustering for cell-type identification and characterization. Nat. Commun. **12**(1), 1–13 (2021)
16. Eraslan, G., Simon, L.M., Mircea, M., Mueller, N.S., Theis, F.J.: Single-cell RNA-seq denoising using a deep count autoencoder. Nat. Commun. **10**(1), 390 (2019)
17. Wan, H., Chen, L., Deng, M.: scNAME: neighborhood contrastive clustering with ancillary mask estimation for scRNA-seq data. Bioinformatics **38**(6), 1575–1583 (2022)
18. Li, W., et al.: A versatile deep graph contrastive learning framework for single-cell proteomics embedding. bioRxiv (2022). 2022–12
19. Cao, J., et al.: Comprehensive single-cell transcriptional profiling of a multicellular organism. Science **357**(6352), 661–667 (2017)

20. Stoeckius, M., et al.: Simultaneous epitope and transcriptome measurement in single cells. Nat. Methods **14**(9), 865–868 (2017)
21. Stewart, B.J., et al.: Spatiotemporal immune zonation of the human kidney. Science **365**(6460), 1461–1466 (2020)
22. Ding, J., et al.: Systematic comparison of single-cell and single-nucleus RNA-sequencing methods. Nat. Biotechnol. **38**(6), 737–746 (2020)
23. MacParland, S.A., et al.: Single cell RNA sequencing of human liver reveals distinct intrahepatic macrophage populations. Nat. Commun. **9**(1), 1–21 (2018)
24. Consortium, T.M., et al.: Single-cell transcriptomics of 20 mouse organs creates a Tabula Muris. Nature **562**(7727), 367–372 (2018)
25. Zeisel, A., et al.: Molecular architecture of the mouse nervous system. Cell **174**(4), 999–1014 (2018)
26. Chen, X., et al.: Single-cell RNA sequencing identifies distinct mouse bladder cell types. Sci. Rep. **10**(1), 1–12 (2020)
27. Romanov, R.A., et al.: A novel organizing principle of the hypothalamus reveals molecularly segregated periventricular dopamine neurons. Nat. Neurosci. **20**(2), 176 (2016)
28. Tran, H.T.N., et al.: A benchmark of batch-effect correction methods for single-cell RNA sequencing data. Genome Biol. **21**, 1–32 (2020)
29. Baron, M., et al.: A single-cell transcriptomic map of the human and mouse pancreas reveals inter-and intra-cell population structure. Cell Syst. **3**(4), 346–360 (2016)
30. Dominguez, G., et al.: Gene signature of the human pancreatic ε cell. Endocrinology **159**(12), 4023–4032 (2018)
31. Yunpei, X., et al.: scCAD: cluster decomposition-based anomaly detection for rare cell identification in single-cell expression data. Nat. Commun. **15**(1), 7561 (2024)
32. Alexander Wolf, F., et al.: PAGA: graph abstraction reconciles clustering with trajectory inference through a topology preserving map of single cells. Genome Biol. **20**, 1–9 (2019)

Drug-Target Interaction Prediction via Substructure Similarity-Guided Denoising and Hierarchical Feature Fusion

Minzhu Xie$^{(\boxtimes)}$, Dongze Deng , and Yabin Kuang

College of Information Science and Engineering, Hunan Normal University, Changsha, China
xieminzhu@hunnu.edu.cn

Abstract. The Drug-Target interaction (DTI) prediction is a crucial step in drug discovery and repositioning. Although traditional biochemical experiments yield highly reliable results, their high cost and low efficiency limit large-scale screening. Most existing computational methods rely on multi-dimensional features to achieve good predictive performance but overlook in-depth exploration of the intrinsic features of drugs and targets. This study introduces SSTDTI, a novel approach that computes similarity coefficients by analyzing substructure features of drugs and the functional annotations of targets. These coefficients are utilized to construct directed, weighted adjacency graphs for both drugs and targets. The model employs convolutional operations to efficiently extract features from the resulting graph structures. Additionally, our newly designed attention mechanism facilitates mutual layer-wise fusion encoding between drugs and targets, enabling the extraction of deeper interaction features. By integrating multi-scale features, SSTDTI outperforms existing methods across multiple benchmark datasets, with ablation studies further validating the efficacy of its constituent modules.

Keywords: Drug Repositioning · Substructure Similarity Coefficients · Attention-based Layer Fusion

1 Introduction

The drug development pipeline is highly complex and cost-intensive, encompassing multiple stages including molecular design, preclinical research, and clinical trials [10]. Statistical evidence indicates that the average clinical development timeline for novel molecular entities reaches 13.9 years, with a success rate of merely 2.01% [10,21]. DTI prediction models demonstrate remarkable efficacy in identifying potential drug-target associations through systematic analysis of existing interaction data. These methodologies not only accelerate drug repurposing but also substantially reduce development costs, establishing themselves as a focal research direction in bioinformatics [4,10].

© The Author(s), under exclusive license to Springer Nature Singapore Pte Ltd. 2026
J. Tang et al. (Eds.): ISBRA 2025, LNBI 15757, pp. 295–306, 2026.
https://doi.org/10.1007/978-981-95-0695-8_24

The DTI prediction methodologies can be broadly classified into three categories: structure-based, ligand-based, and machine learning-based approaches [17]. Structure-based methods depend on the availability of three-dimensional target structures but face limitations due to the scarcity of membrane protein [16,17] and other challenging structural data. Ligand-based methods employ known active small molecules to develop quantitative structure-activity relationship (QSAR) models, where predictive performance is directly proportional to the volume of available ligand data [18]. In comparison, machine learning-based methods demonstrate superior adaptability by integrating multidimensional features including drug chemical structures and target genomic sequences, thereby effectively addressing the constraints posed by incomplete structural or ligand information while achieving enhanced predictive capabilities [4,17].

Current machine learning-based approaches for DTI prediction primarily enhance performance through multidimensional data integration, yet often fail to adequately explore the intrinsic structural features of drugs and targets themselves. Recent studies demonstrate that systematic multiscale feature extraction - spanning from macroscopic molecular properties to microscopic substructure characteristics - not only reduces dependence on auxiliary data and alleviates cold-start problems, but also uncovers fundamental molecular interaction mechanisms [10,21,22].

Based on the feature extraction strategies, these prediction methods can be categorized into three distinct paradigms: independent feature extraction, as exemplified by DeepDTA [14] which employs dual Convolutional Neural Networks (CNNs) to separately extract local features from drugs and targets before concatenating the pooled feature vectors; interactive feature extraction, implemented in MolTrans [11] through substructure encoding followed by cross-attention mechanisms to simulate biochemical interactions; and hybrid approaches such as IIFDTI [4] and FMCA-DTI [22] that integrate both macroscopic and microscopic features. However, these methods exhibit several critical limitations: (1) deep neural networks either insufficiently capture interaction features or lose essential structural information during processing; (2) substructure-based simulation of drug-target interactions introduces substantial noise-contaminated data; and (3) current investigations into substructure similarity remain superficial.

To address the aforementioned limitations including noise interference and insufficient feature extraction, we propose SSTDTI—a novel DTI prediction method inspired by substructure similarity and deep attention mechanisms. SST-DTI calculates similarity coefficients between nodes and uses these coefficients to construct weighted directed adjacency graphs. Through Graph Convolutional Networks (GCNs), it learns and updates features of similar nodes to achieve denoising effects, then integrates the features learned by the GCNs with embeddings obtained from original features to acquire independent features of drugs and targets. Using our designed deep layer-wise attention network, we perform deep extraction of interaction features by encoding drug and target features while preserving original features at each layer, ensuring both depth of feature extraction and preservation of feature originality. Finally, we integrate the independent and interaction features for prediction. Our main contributions are summarized as follows:

- A substructure similarity-based denoising strategy that significantly enhances DTI prediction accuracy.
- An innovative deep layer-wise interactive attention network architecture.
- Comprehensive experimental validation demonstrating method effectiveness.

2   Materials

This study utilizes three DTI datasets for experimental analysis: (1) the original Davis [8] dataset comprising 30,056 interaction pairs between 68 compounds and 442 proteins; (2) the Biosnap [23] dataset containing 27,464 interaction pairs involving 4,510 drugs and 2,181 proteins - both providing complete SMILES molecular representations and protein sequence information; and (3) the filtered Davis dataset from MdeePred [15], which includes 9,125 experimentally validated binding affinity entries after removal of default affinity values. Table 1 presents the summary.

To comprehensively characterize target proteins, we annotated all protein sequences with Gene Ontology (GO) [5] terms obtained from UniProt, including molecular function, biological process, and cellular component classifications.

Table 1. Summary of the benchmark datasets.

Datasets	Compounds	Proteins	Interactions
Davis	68	442	30056
BioSNAP	4510	2181	27464
Filtered Davis	68	379	9125

3   Method

Figure 1 illustrates the network architecture of SSTDTI, which integrates target features extracted by both the independent feature extraction module and interactive feature extraction module, then feeds them into the prediction module. During training, SSTDTI employs cross-entropy loss as the objective function, optimizing model parameters by minimizing the loss L:

$$L = -\frac{1}{N} \sum_{i=1}^{N} (y_i \log(\hat{y}_i) + (1 - y_i) \log(1 - \hat{y}_i)) \tag{1}$$

where $y_i \in \{0, 1\}$ represents the ground truth label, $\hat{y}_i$ is the predicted label, and N is the number of training samples.

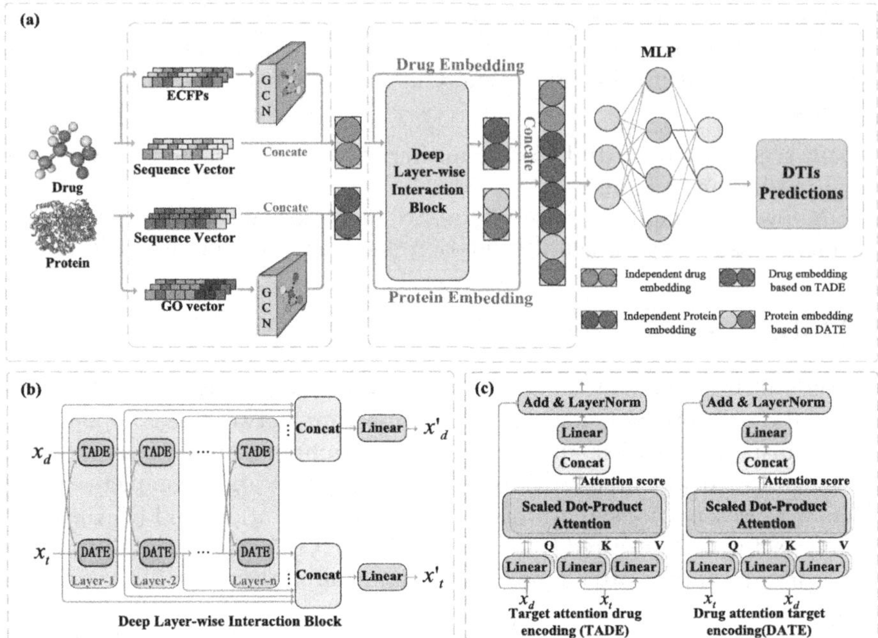

Fig. 1. Framework of SSTDTI. (a) The overall architecture of SSTDTI, which consists of three main modules: an independent feature processing module, an interaction feature extraction module, and a final prediction module. (b) Deep layer-wise interaction attention mechanism. (c) The TADE and DATE mechanisms within the interaction feature extraction module.

3.1   Independent Features of Drugs and Targets

Drug and Protein Feature Representation. Extended Connectivity Fingerprints (ECFP) is a widely used molecular representation for drug structures. Unlike variable-length SMILES strings, ECFP provides a fixed-length one-hot encoding, capturing the presence of specific substructures regardless of the molecule's size. Although the datasets provide SMILES notations for the drugs, lacks explicit substructure information, making it unsuitable for direct structural similarity calculations. To address this, we use RDKit [2] to convert drug SMILES into ECFP vectors (radius = 4, length = 1024). For a dataset containing m drugs $\{d_1, d_2, \ldots, d_m\}$, this yields a binary ECFP matrix $D_{ef} \in \mathbb{Z}^{m \times 1024}$, where each row x_i represents the ECFP vector of drug i.

We compute drug-drug similarities based on these ECFP vectors and construct a weighted graph. A GCN is applied to extract drug substructure features from the graph, using a substructure similarity denoising strategy (detailed in the next subsection). Additionally, we employ Mol2Vec [12] to generate 300-dimensional drug embeddings from SMILES, producing a matrix $D_{mf} \in \mathbb{R}^{m \times 300}$. These embeddings are combined with the substructure features to enhance drug representation.

Following drug feature extraction, we apply analogous processing to protein sequences. Unlike fixed-length molecular representations, protein sequences exhibit significant length variation. While conventional CNN-based approaches typically require length normalization through truncation, this risks losing critical functional domains and biologically significant motifs. To overcome this limitation, we employ ProtTrans [9], a protein-specific adaptation of the BERT model that preserves complete sequence context.

For our dataset of n proteins $\{p_1, p_2, \ldots, p_n\}$, ProtTrans generates 1024-dimensional embeddings, producing a feature matrix $P_{pf} \in \mathbb{R}^{n \times 1024}$. Building on the substructure similarity principle established for drugs, we extend our graph-based framework to proteins. Using the GO data, we construct protein adjacency graphs that capture functional relationships at multiple biological levels, from molecular function to cellular localization.

Substructure Similarity Denoising Strategy. Biochemical evidence shows structural similarity correlates with shared pharmacological properties. While conventional GCNs rely on binary interaction data and symmetric weight matrices, these approaches often introduce noise through: (1) non-specific feature aggregation and (2) spurious topological connections. To address these limitations, we developed a substructure similarity-based denoising strategy (Fig. 2) that selectively propagates features between nodes exhibiting structural (drugs) or related functional (protein) patterns.

For two drugs i and j, our approach calculates a substructure similarity coefficient (SSC) from i to j based on their ECFP vectors x_i and x_j as Eq. (2).

$$\mathrm{SSC}_{i,j} = \frac{|x_i \cap x_j|}{|x_j|}, \tag{2}$$

where $|x_i \cap x_j|$ represent the number of shared substructures of the drug pair i and j, and $|x_j|$ is the total number of substructures that drug i contains. Taking $SSC_{i,j}$ as the weight of the edge from node i to j, we generates a directed graph representation where: edge weights are asymmetric, weight magnitudes directly reflect structural similarity, and the adjacency matrix captures nuanced substructure relationships.

Based on the directed graph, we use GCN to selectively aggregate features from nodes with similar substructures during feature propagation, thereby significantly mitigating noise interference. The GCN update formula is as follows:

$$X' = \hat{D}^{-1/2} \hat{A} \hat{D}^{-1/2} X \Theta \tag{3}$$

Each GCN layer takes as input a set of samples $\mathbf{X} \in \mathbb{R}^{N \times d}$ $(N = |V|)$ and produces the corresponding convolutional output $X' \in \mathbb{R}^{N \times k}$ for that layer. Unlike traditional binary adjacency matrices, $\hat{A}$ implemented through SSC scoring offers three key advantages: (1) asymmetric information propagation with edge weights reflecting substructure similarity, (2) directional feature updating, and (3) adaptive noise reduction. This design significantly enhances feature

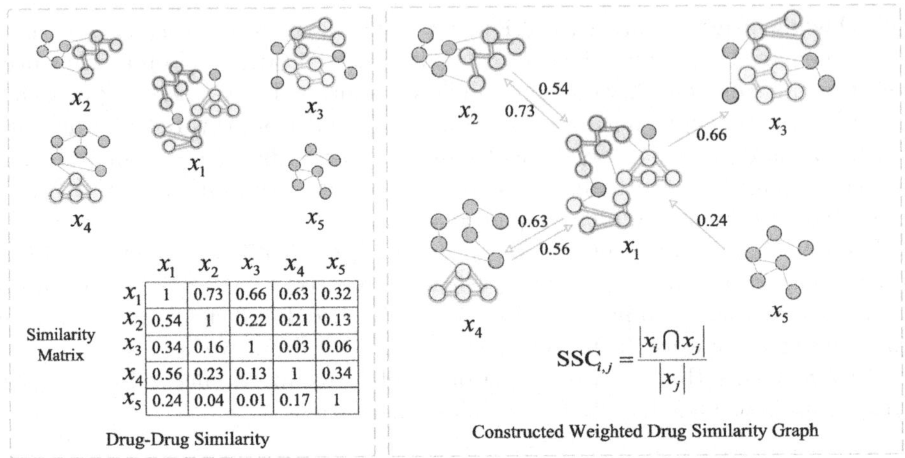

Fig. 2. Taking drugs as an example, the process simulates how drugs with five different substructures construct a directed weighted graph under the substructure similarity denoising strategy by calculating similarity coefficients. The differently colored regions in the drugs represent distinct substructures.

selection and information propagation efficiency while maintaining the benefits of the GCN framework. Here, $\hat{D}_{ii} = \sum_{j=0} \hat{A}_{ij}$ constitutes the pairwise degree matrix, and $\Theta \in \mathbb{R}^{d \times k}$ represents a learnable matrix parameter, where d indicates the feature dimension from the previous layer and k denotes the output feature dimension of the current layer.

3.2   Interactive Features of Drug-Target Pairs

Feature Embedding Learning Based on DATE and TADE Mechanisms. With attention mechanism, Target Attention Drug Encoding (TADE) focuses on learning the contribution of different parts of the target to the drug's effect, while Drug Attention Target Encoding (DATE) focuses on learning the contribution of different parts of the drug to the target's effect, as shown in Fig. 1. The scaled dot-product attention input is composed of three matrices: query, key, and value, and the calculation formula is:

$$Q = Linear_Q(X_{de}) \tag{4}$$

$$K = Linear_K(X_{te}) \tag{5}$$

$$V = Linear_V(X_{te}) \tag{6}$$

Based on the calculations of these three matrices, the attention score can be computed as follows:

$$\text{Attention}(Q, K, V) = \text{softmax}\left(\frac{QK^T}{\sqrt{d}}\right) V \tag{7}$$

Here, $\sqrt{d}$ serves to scale the result, ensuring the attention matrix conforms to a standard normal distribution.

To further enhance the expressiveness of the SSTDTI model, we incorporate a Multi-Head Attention (MHA) mechanism in both the TADE and DATE mechanisms. The embedding of x_d obtained with the MHA mechanism is represented as $x_{(d,mh)}$, which would be fed into the feed-forward layer and dropout layer. To improve the model's robustness, we also introduce residual connections and layer normalization. The final output embedding results of the TADE and DATE mechanisms are computed as follows:

$$X_d = \text{Layernorm}(x_{(d,mh)} + Dropout(\text{FL}(x_{(d,mh)}))) \tag{8}$$

Here, $\text{FL}(\cdot)$ represents the feedforward layer, $\text{Layernorm}(\cdot)$ represents layer normalization, and $\text{Dropout}(\cdot)$ denotes the dropout layer.

Deep Layer-Wise Interactive Attention Mechanism. We propose a deep layer-wise interactive attention mechanism that achieves hierarchical fusion of drug-target features through alternating TADE and DATE modules. This architecture integrates both modules at each layer: the TADE module updates drug features conditioned on target embeddings, while the DATE module conversely updates target features based on drug embeddings. The modules operate through an iterative workflow, where TADE's updated drug embeddings serve as input to DATE at the subsequent layer, and vice versa. This bidirectional interaction mechanism progressively refines feature representations across layers, enabling deep modeling of drug-target interactions. The final interaction features at each layer can be expressed as:

$$\mathbf{x'}_d^{(n+1)} = \text{TADE}\left(\text{TADE}\left(\mathbf{x'}_d^{(n)}\right), \text{DATE}\left(\mathbf{x'}_t^{(n)}\right)\right) \tag{9}$$

$$\mathbf{x'}_t^{(n+1)} = \text{DATE}\left(\text{DATE}\left(\mathbf{x'}_t^{(n)}\right), \text{TADE}\left(\mathbf{x'}_d^{(n)}\right)\right) \tag{10}$$

where $\mathbf{x'}_d^{(n)}$ and $\mathbf{x'}_t^{(n)}$ represent the feature representations of the drug and target, respectively, after the nth layer's interaction.

Extensive studies have demonstrated that increasing model complexity does not necessarily lead to performance improvement, as higher-level features extracted by deep networks may lose essential original characteristics due to excessive abstraction. Inspired by residual connections, we therefore incorporate a feature preservation strategy into our deep interactive attention mechanism. This approach is implemented through hierarchical feature concatenation:

$$x'_d = \text{concat}\left(x_d'^{(0)}, x_d'^{(1)}, x_d'^{(2)}, \ldots, x_d'^{(n)}\right) \tag{11}$$

$$x'_t = \text{concat}\left(x_t'^{(0)}, x_t'^{(1)}, x_t'^{(2)}, \ldots, x_t'^{(n)}\right) \tag{12}$$

After this concatenation, we perform an averaging operation on the concatenated results to obtain the final representations of the drug and target: $\hat{\mathbf{x}'_d}$ and $\hat{\mathbf{x}'_t}$.

4   Experiments and Results

4.1   Experimental Setup

In this study, We compared ten competitive methods with SSTDTI, covering a variety of strategies including traditional machine learning, deep learning, and graph neural networks. To comprehensively evaluate the performance of the models, we employed four commonly used metrics: AUC (Area Under the Curve), AUPR (Area Under the Precision-Recall Curve), Precision, and Recall. All methods were evaluated using five-fold cross-validation to minimize the bias introduced by data partitioning and ensure the fairness and reliability of the experimental results.

4.2   Baseline Methods

This study selected representative benchmark models in DTI prediction that have made significant methodological and performance contributions. The models fall into three categories: traditional machine learning methods including SVM [6], RF [3] and LR [7] that pioneered combining ECFP4 molecular fingerprints with protein sequence features; deep learning approaches comprising CNN-based DeepDTA [14] and DeepConv-DTI [13], GNN-based GNN-CPI [19] and 3DProtDTA [20], and Transformer-based MolTrans [11]; and advanced attention-based models DrugBAN [1] and FMCA-DTI [22]. These benchmarks demonstrate progressive technical developments in feature extraction from sequence motif recognition to 3D structural processing, and in interaction modeling from simple feature concatenation to sophisticated attention mechanisms, thereby establishing a multidimensional reference framework for comprehensively evaluating SSTDTI's performance advantages.

4.3   Performance Analysis

The best results are highlighted in bold, and the experimental results on the Davis and Biosnap datasets are shown in Table 2 and Table 3.

Experimental results demonstrate that the SSTDTI model achieves significant performance advantages across both benchmark datasets. On the Davis dataset, it shows enhancements of 1.08% in AUC and 2.01% in AUPR respectively. For the Biosnap dataset, SSTDTI improves the AUC metric by 1.91% over the suboptimal method while maintaining comparable AUPR performance. To highlight the comparative effectiveness, Fig. 3 presents cross-dataset performance comparisons between SSTDTI and four representative methods, visually demonstrating the superior performance of our approach.

4.4   Ablation Experiments

To systematically validate the effectiveness of SSTDTI, we conducted ablation studies on the Filtered Davis dataset, focusing on evaluating the contributions

Table 2. Comparative Results on the Davis Dataset **(Best)**.

Methods	AUC	AUPR	Precision	Recall
LR (1958)	0.821	0.792	0.731	0.664
SVM (1995)	0.827	0.801	0.745	0.673
RF (2011)	0.838	0.797	0.766	0.711
DeepDTA (2018)	0.828	0.811	0.745	0.688
GNN-CPI (2019)	0.880	0.873	0.762	0.786
DeepConv-DTI (2019)	0.884	0.867	0.863	0.804
MolTrans (2020)	0.907	0.887	0.901	0.822
DrugBAN (2023)	0.904	0.878	0.886	0.794
3DProt-DTA (2023)	0.914	0.923	0.907	0.896
FMCA-DTI (2024)	0.927	0.944	0.899	0.874
SSTDTI	**0.937**	**0.963**	**0.913**	**0.895**

Table 3. Comparative Results on the BioSNAP Dataset **(Best)**.

Methods	AUC	AUPR	Precision	Recall
LR (1958)	0.832	0.822	0.725	0.713
SVM (1995)	0.837	0.844	0.737	0.711
RF (2011)	0.845	0.863	0.714	0.802
DeepDTA (2018)	0.853	0.867	0.733	0.780
GNN-CPI (2019)	0.857	0.879	0.779	0.773
DeepConv-DTI (2019)	0.864	0.872	0.791	0.770
MolTrans (2020)	0.870	0.883	0.811	0.775
DrugBAN (2023)	0.885	0.887	0.800	0.803
3DProt-DTA (2023)	0.880	**0.893**	0.813	0.806
FMCA-DTI (2024)	0.887	0.864	0.828	0.727
SSTDTI	**0.904**	0.892	**0.830**	**0.813**

of two core modules. The experimental configurations included: (1) using only sequence features ("only-sequence"); (2) separately removing the interaction feature module ("no-inter") and independent feature module ("no-independent"); and (3) employing either TADE or DATE mechanism alone to examine the attention mechanism's efficacy. The results demonstrate that both the substructure similarity-based denoising strategy and the deep layer-wise interactive attention mechanism play decisive roles in model performance. Detailed experimental results are presented in Table 4.

As demonstrated in Table 4, SSTDTI consistently outperforms all variant models across all evaluation metrics. Specifically: (1) Compared to the sequence-only model, SSTDTI achieves improvements of 2.36% in AUC, 0.36% in AUPR,

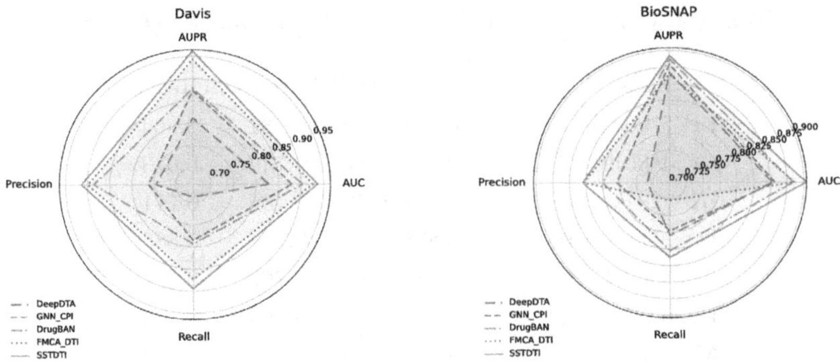

Fig. 3. The figures above respectively visualize the cross-dataset comparison of five methods across four metrics on the Davis and BioSNAP datasets.

Table 4. Ablation Study of the Proposed Model Components (**Best**).

Methods	AUC	AUPR	Precision	Recall
SSTDTI	**0.823**	**0.802**	0.701	**0.786**
only sequence feature	0.804	0.799	0.698	0.741
no-inter feature	0.794	0.780	**0.703**	0.720
no-independent feature	0.778	0.753	0.683	0.753
only TADE	0.768	0.750	0.680	0.713
only DATE	0.773	0.744	0.663	0.705

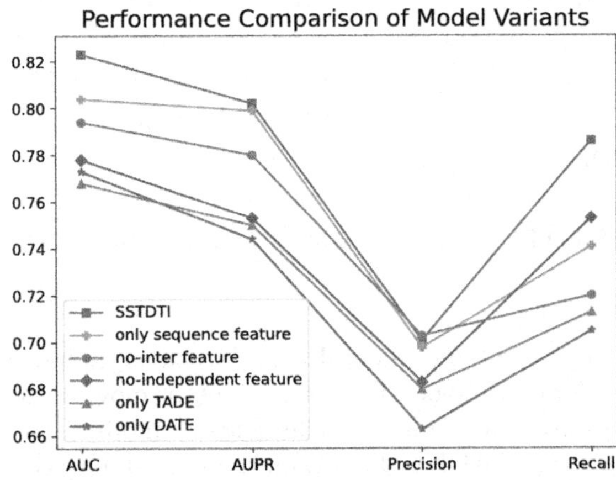

Fig. 4. Performance of different model variants in cross-comparison.

0.43% in precision, and 6.07% in recall, validating the efficacy of our denoising strategy; (2) In feature module ablation studies, the maximum enhancements reach 5.78% for AUC and 6.51% for AUPR, confirming the critical importance of integrating macro- and micro-scale features; (3) Attention mechanism experiments reveal that the complete model attains maximum gains of 7.16% in AUC and 11.49% in recall, highlighting the pivotal role of the deep interactive attention mechanism (Fig. 4).

5 Conclusion

This study presents SSTDTI, an innovative end-to-end deep learning framework that integrates multi-scale feature learning for DTI prediction. The framework makes two major contributions: First, it introduces a novel asymmetric weighted directed graph representation based on substructure similarity coefficients, where edge weights directly reflect structural similarity and the adjacency matrix captures nuanced substructure relationships. This graph architecture effectively addresses the limitations of conventional GCN iterative update strategies in handling non-specific aggregation and spurious topological connections, thereby significantly improving the model's noise reduction capability. Second, the proposed multi-level deep feature fusion encoding mechanism that effectively preserves the integrity of molecular features while ensuring the depth of interaction feature extraction, thereby providing a novel solution for DTI prediction. Future research will focus on optimizing the similarity measurement algorithms to further improve model performance.

References

1. Bai, P., Miljković, F., John, B., Lu, H.: Interpretable bilinear attention network with domain adaptation improves drug-target prediction. Nat. Mach. Intell. **5**(2), 126–136 (2023)
2. Bento, A.P., et al.: An open source chemical structure curation pipeline using RDKit. J. Cheminformatics **12**, 1–16 (2020)
3. Breiman, L.: Random forests. Mach. Learn. **45**, 5–32 (2001)
4. Cheng, Z., Zhao, Q., Li, Y., Wang, J.: IIFDTI: predicting drug-target interactions through interactive and independent features based on attention mechanism. Bioinformatics **38**(17), 4153–4161 (2022)
5. Gene Ontology Consortium: The gene ontology project in 2008. Nucleic Acids Res. **36**(suppl_1), D440–D444 (2008)
6. Cortes, C., Vapnik, V.: Support-vector networks. Mach. Learn. **20**, 273–297 (1995)
7. Cox, D.R.: The regression analysis of binary sequences. J. R. Stat. Soc. Ser. B Stat Methodol. **20**(2), 215–232 (1958)
8. Davis, M.I., et al.: Comprehensive analysis of kinase inhibitor selectivity. Nat. Biotechnol. **29**(11), 1046–1051 (2011)
9. Elnaggar, A., et al.: ProtTrans: toward understanding the language of life through self-supervised learning. IEEE Trans. Pattern Anal. Mach. Intell. **44**(10), 7112–7127 (2021)
10. Ezzat, A., Wu, M., Li, X.L., Kwoh, C.K.: Computational prediction of drug-target interactions using chemogenomic approaches: an empirical survey. Brief. Bioinform. **20**(4), 1337–1357 (2019)

11. Huang, K., Xiao, C., Glass, L.M., Sun, J.: MolTrans: molecular interaction transformer for drug-target interaction prediction. Bioinformatics **37**(6), 830–836 (2021)
12. Jaeger, S., Fulle, S., Turk, S.: Mol2vec: unsupervised machine learning approach with chemical intuition. J. Chem. Inf. Model. **58**(1), 27–35 (2018)
13. Lee, I., Keum, J., Nam, H.: DeepConv-DTI: prediction of drug-target interactions via deep learning with convolution on protein sequences. PLoS Comput. Biol. **15**(6), e1007129 (2019)
14. Öztürk, H., Özgür, A., Ozkirimli, E.: DeepDTA: deep drug-target binding affinity prediction. Bioinformatics **34**(17), i821–i829 (2018)
15. Rifaioglu, A.S., Cetin Atalay, R., Cansen Kahraman, D., Doğan, T., Martin, M., Atalay, V.: MDeePred: novel multi-channel protein featurization for deep learning-based binding affinity prediction in drug discovery. Bioinformatics **37**(5), 693–704 (2021)
16. Shaikh, N., Sharma, M., Garg, P.: An improved approach for predicting drug-target interaction: proteochemometrics to molecular docking. Mol. BioSyst. **12**(3), 1006–1014 (2016)
17. Song, W., Xu, L., Han, C., Tian, Z., Zou, Q.: Drug–target interaction predictions with multi-view similarity network fusion strategy and deep interactive attention mechanism. Bioinformatics **40**(6), btae346 (2024)
18. Tian, Z., Peng, X., Fang, H., Zhang, W., Dai, Q., Ye, Y.: MHADTI: predicting drug–target interactions via multiview heterogeneous information network embedding with hierarchical attention mechanisms. Briefings Bioinf. **23**(6), bbac434 (2022)
19. Tsubaki, M., Tomii, K., Sese, J.: Compound-protein interaction prediction with end-to-end learning of neural networks for graphs and sequences. Bioinformatics **35**(2), 309–318 (2019)
20. Voitsitskyi, T., et al.: 3DProtDTA: a deep learning model for drug-target affinity prediction based on residue-level protein graphs. RSC Adv. **13**(15), 10261–10272 (2023)
21. Yeu, Y., Yoon, Y., Park, S.: Protein localization vector propagation: a method for improving the accuracy of drug repositioning. Mol. BioSyst. **11**(7), 2096–2102 (2015)
22. Zhang, Q., et al.: FMCA-DTI: a fragment-oriented method based on a multihead cross attention mechanism to improve drug–target interaction prediction. Bioinformatics **40**(6), btae347 (2024)
23. Zitnik, M., Agrawal, M., Leskovec, J.: Modeling polypharmacy side effects with graph convolutional networks. Bioinformatics **34**(13), i457–i466 (2018)

Bioinformatics Course Reform Through Projects Integrating History, Theory, and Practice

Jianxin Wang[1], Hongdong Li[1(✉)], Guihua Duan[1], Jin Liu[1,2], and Min Li[1]

[1] School of Computer Science and Engineering, Central South University, Changsha 410083, Hunan, China
`hongdong@mail.csu.edu.cn`
[2] Xinjiang Engineering Research Center of Big Data and Intelligent Software, School of Software, Xinjiang University, Urumqi, China

Abstract. Bioinformatics is an interdisciplinary field that has been playing key roles in understanding biology and medicine. Currently, bioinformatics education faces several challenges, including incomplete understanding of the overall knowledge system of the discipline, lack of in-depth understanding of theory, limited hands-on practice opportunities. These issues make it difficult for students to integrate theoretical knowledge with practical applications, thereby weakening their innovative capabilities and ability to solve real-world bioinformatics problems. To address these challenges, we propose an approach that integrates history, theory, and practice, and applies it to the reform of bioinformatics teaching. Taking the analysis of expression quantitative trait loci (eQTL) as an example, we show how to incorporate historical context, theoretical knowledge, and actionable projects into course teaching. This reform aims to promote the interest, practical skills, and innovative abilities of students, providing a reference for training high-quality bioinformatics talent.

Keywords: Bioinformatics · Teaching Reform · History · Theory · Practice

1 Introduction

Bioinformatics, as an interdisciplinary field integrating biology, computer science, statistics, and information technology, faces multiple challenges in education, including incomplete understanding of the overall knowledge system of the discipline, lack of in-depth understanding of theory, limited hands-on practice opportunities. With the rapid development of high-throughput sequencing technologies and the explosive growth of biological big data, the traditional lecture-based teaching model is no longer efficient in meeting the needs for the education of bioinformatics courses [1].

© The Author(s), under exclusive license to Springer Nature Singapore Pte Ltd. 2026
J. Tang et al. (Eds.): ISBRA 2025, LNBI 15757, pp. 307–319, 2026.
https://doi.org/10.1007/978-981-95-0695-8_25

Recent years have witnessed substantial advances in reforming bioinformatics education. John et al. [2] developed an innovative pedagogical model integrating evolutionary computation principles into instructional design. Tambi et al. [3] established a structured framework that significantly enhances medical students' comprehension and application of bioinformatics knowledge. Achappa et al. [4] created a comprehensive "data-to-discovery" project pipeline to cultivate students' collaborative skills and research ability. Yang et al. [5] implemented a blended learning approach incorporating the ARCS motivational model in curriculum design. Jennifer et al. [6] systematically analyzed implementation barriers in bioinformatics education while proposing possible solutions. Nevertheless, current research in the field of bioinformatics education often neglects a systematic review of the evolution of methods that are taught. This lack of historical perspective leaves educational innovation without a background understanding. Traditional teaching models tend to overemphasize the mastering of theoretical knowledge, while failing to adequately integrate hands-on practice into course design. As a result, students face significant gaps in the development of practical application skills. Furthermore, many studies still rely on decade-old technical approaches and evaluation systems, lacking timely updates to keep pace with advancements. Teaching frameworks designed for specific institutions or specialized programs often prove difficult to generalize to broader educational contexts. Although existing research offers valuable insights for bioinformatics education innovation, substantial challenges remain in their practical implementation.

To address these limitations, we propose a bioinformatics education reform approach that integrates historical context, theoretical knowledge, and practical operations. By incorporating historical context into curriculum design, strengthening the systematic learning of theoretical knowledge, and designing highly actionable practical components, this approach aims to promote the understanding of theoretical knowledge and problem-solving abilities. Taking expression quantitative trait loci (eQTL) analysis as an example, we elaborate on how to combine historical context, theoretical knowledge, and project-based learning concepts, and systematically integrate them into course teaching. The educational reform approach not only provides an operational model for bioinformatics course teaching but also offers valuable references and insights for the reform of other courses.

2   The Approach of Reform

Our approach emphasizes the integration of the three elements of "history, theory, and practice" into the teaching framework. By guiding students to understand the development trajectory of the discipline (history), master core knowledge and methodologies (theory), and apply them to solve practical problems (practice), it aims to comprehensively enhance students' overall competencies. Figure 1 illustrates the schematic diagram of the overall implementation plan for this course. The following sections will provide a detailed explanation of the course design and implementation.

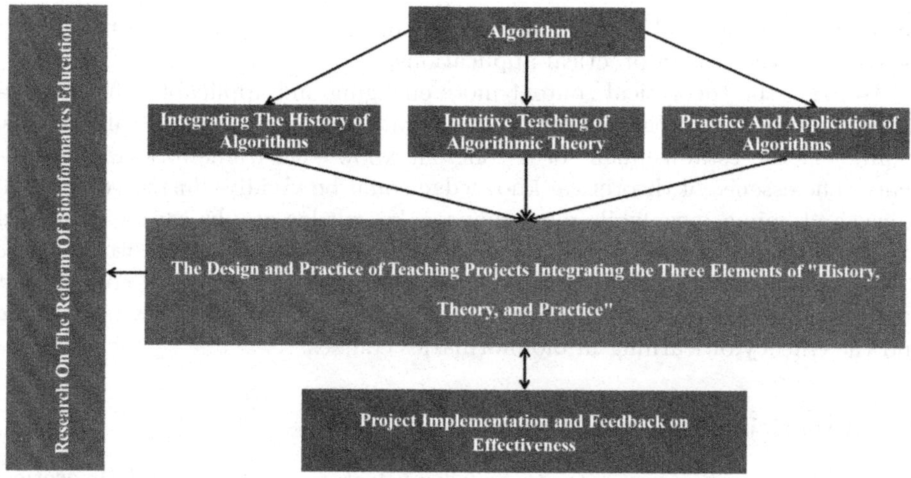

Fig. 1. Schematic of designing projects by integrating history, theory, and practice.

2.1   Understanding the History

In bioinformatics courses, the inclusion of historical content is not only a highlight of curriculum design but also a crucial component for achieving teaching objectives. As an interdisciplinary field, the development of bioinformatics is driven by historical events, scientific ideas, and technological evolution. By systematically introducing significant events, key figures, and milestone achievements in the history of bioinformatics, students can gain a comprehensive understanding of the discipline's origins, developmental trajectory, and their critical roles in scientific research. The invention and succession of various computational tools throughout the history of bioinformatics reflect trends in technological evolution. The rapidly evolving technologies in the field of bioinformatics often lead students to focus on fragmented learning of specific tools and methods, neglecting the holistic profiles of the knowledge system. The incorporation of historical content in the curriculum not only helps students build an overall understanding of the discipline and avoid the pitfall of "tool-centric" learning but also stimulates their interest in learning and desire for exploration, enabling them to grasp the inheritance and improvement of key technologies.

2.2   Mastering the Theory

In the context of learning within bioinformatics courses, the theoretical component is key for students to grasp the core knowledge and methodologies of the discipline. Bioinformatics encompasses a vast array of mathematical models and computational methods. Without a solid theoretical foundation, students may limit themselves to very shallow understanding of a method, and do not really know what he could do with it. Therefore, it is imperative that students comprehend the strengths, weaknesses, and applicable scenarios of various methods during their theoretical studies, allowing them to select appropriate techniques for specific problems in practical applications.

To make the theoretical content more engaging and applicable, the instruction is structured to progress from fundamental concepts to advanced algorithms, facilitating the establishment of a coherent knowledge framework among students. The essence of theoretical knowledge could be vividly illustrated through videos and animations, while mind maps or knowledge graphs can be employed to assist students in constructing the bioinformatics knowledge framework. These strategies not only enhance students' comprehension of theoretical content but also stimulate their interest in learning, thereby elevating the quality of teaching and the efficacy of learning in bioinformatics courses.

2.3 Practicing Through Actionable Projects

Actionable project design aims to transform historical context and theoretical knowledge into practical skills through real or simulated research projects, fostering the students' ability to solve complex biological problems. The objectives of project design include enhancing students' programming capabilities and cultivating teamwork spirit [7], making the selection of highly operational projects particularly crucial. Students need to be familiar with basic skills, such as downloading and processing data from public datasets, utilizing various tools for analysis, employing visualization tools to present analytical results, and providing biological interpretations of the results through functional enrichment analysis and literature research. The writing of project reports and team collaboration are also integral components of the practice design. Students are required to compose well-structured, scientific project reports and ensure the smooth progression of the project through team task division and regular discussions. Through highly operational project-based practice design, students not only convert theoretical knowledge into practical skills but also deepen their understanding of the knowledge while tackling complex problems [8].

3 Case Study

eQTL analysis is a pivotal method for investigating gene regulatory mechanisms and is widely applied in the fields of genetics, genomics, and precision medicine. eQTL computation encompasses biological context, statistical models, and computational methods, making it an essential interdisciplinary problem and an ideal case for the reform of bioinformatics curriculum. Through an integrated instructional design that combines "history, theory, and practice", students can gain a profound understanding of the developmental trajectory and core theoretical foundations of eQTL computation. Moreover, by engaging in actual data analysis, they can master key technologies and enhance their comprehensive capabilities.

3.1   History of eQTL

To accurately delineate the historical trajectory of eQTL research and its significant roles within the realms of genetics and bioinformatics, the following will systematically elucidate its development from three perspectives: the origins of eQTL research, pivotal breakthroughs, and the evolution of analytical techniques.

Firstly, we embark on the origins of eQTL research, intertwining with the progression of genetics to aid students in comprehending the background and significance of this concept. The genesis of eQTL research can be traced back to the nascent stages of genetics. At the dawn of the 20th century, Mendel's laws of inheritance unveiled the principles of segregation and combination of genetic factors, while Morgan's Drosophila experiments further substantiated the linear arrangement of genes on chromosomes, laying the theoretical groundwork for modern genetics. Building upon this foundation, the concept of Quantitative Trait Loci (QTL) was introduced to describe genetic variants influencing complex traits. QTL mapping studies, by analyzing the association between genetic markers and phenotypes, shed light on the genetic underpinnings of complex traits. With advancements in molecular biology, scientists gradually recognized that gene expression levels could also serve as quantitative traits influenced by genetic variations, thus giving rise to the concept of eQTL. The advent of eQTL marked a shift in genetic research from phenotypic to gene expression levels, offering a new research direction for unraveling the genetic regulatory mechanisms of gene expression.

Next, we focus on the pivotal breakthroughs in eQTL research, elucidating how innovations in research methodologies and technological means have propelled the field forward. Early eQTL studies primarily relied on microarray technology to obtain gene expression data, coupled with simple statistical models for analysis. Although these methods provided preliminary tools for eQTL research, their resolution and accuracies were limited. The rapid development of high-throughput sequencing technologies heralded a revolutionary breakthrough in eQTL research. RNA-seq technology, with its high throughput and coverage in measuring gene expression levels, enabled scientists to conduct genome-wide eQTL analysis. In addition, a series of significant scientific discoveries have greatly advanced the development of eQTL research. These breakthroughs have not only deepened our understanding of gene regulatory mechanisms but also laid a solid theoretical foundation for precision medicine.

Lastly, we delve into the evolution of eQTL analysis techniques, aiding students in understanding how advancements in statistical methods and computational tools have driven the field's progress. The evolution of eQTL analysis techniques mirrors the continuous progress in statistical methods and computational tools. In terms of statistical methods, eQTL analysis has evolved from early simple linear models to mixed models and machine learning approaches. Mixed models better handle confounding factors such as population structure and batch effects, while machine learning methods offer new tools for analyzing complex gene regulatory networks. In the realm of computational tools, the tools and platforms for eQTL analysis have also undergone significant evolution. Early eQTL analysis mainly depend on basic statistical software for data processing and model fitting, which, while flexible, were inefficient in handling large-scale data. With the deepening of eQTL research and the exponential growth of data volume, specialized tools and platforms like Matrix eQTL and FastQTL emerged, optimizing algorithms and parallel computing to significantly enhance analysis efficiency. Additionally, integrated analysis platforms such as QTLtools and eQTL Catalogue provide comprehensive support from data preprocessing to result visualization, greatly simplifying the analysis process and lowering technical barriers. Furthermore, with the ever-expanding data scale, cloud computing platforms have been gradually introduced into eQTL analysis, offering robust computational support for processing massive datasets.

Through a systematic review of the origins, pivotal breakthroughs, and the evolution of analytical techniques in eQTL research, students can gain a comprehensive understanding of the developmental trajectory and scientific logic of eQTL research, thereby establishing an overarching cognitive framework for the fields of genetics and bioinformatics. The technological innovations and methodological evolution in eQTL research provide students with vivid case studies, helping them appreciate the importance of technology-driven approaches in scientific research and stimulating their interest in exploring new technologies and methods.

3.2   eQTL Theories

After introducing the historical background of eQTL research, we systematically elaborate on the related theories of eQTL to help students comprehensively understand its scientific logic and application value. First, we introduce the necessity of studying eQTL and discuss the relationship between genes and phenotypes. Traditional genetics primarily focuses on how genetic variations directly influence traits, while gene expression, as an intermediate phenotype, serves as a crucial bridge connecting genotypes and final phenotypes. eQTL research focuses on how genetic variations regulate gene expression levels, thereby indirectly affecting phenotypes. The importance of eQTL lies in its ability to link genotypes to gene expression, revealing how genetic variations influence physiological and pathological processes in organisms by regulating gene expression. This connection provides a theoretical foundation for precision medicine and personalized treatment, making eQTL research a significant direction in modern genetics and bioinformatics.

Following this introduction, we present the basic concepts of eQTL. eQTL refers to specific regions or loci in the genome that can influence gene expression levels. These loci indirectly affect an individual's phenotypic traits by regulating gene transcription or translation processes. Next, we provide a detailed introduction to the research methods of eQTL, including the acquisition of experimental data and the workflow of data analysis, to help students master the core techniques of eQTL analysis. The core of eQTL analysis lies in detecting the association between genetic variations and gene expression levels through statistical methods. First, the acquisition of experimental data is the foundation of eQTL research. RNA-seq technology, due to its high accuracies and coverage, has become the mainstream method for eQTL studies. In terms of data analysis, eQTL analysis typically includes the following steps: data preprocessing, association analysis, multiple testing correction, and result interpretation. Data preprocessing involves quality control of genotype data, normalization of gene expression data, and correction of batch effects.

Association analysis is the core step of eQTL research, with commonly used statistical methods including linear regression models and mixed-effects models. Linear regression models are the most commonly used statistical method in eQTL analysis, detecting the linear relationship between single nucleotide polymorphisms and gene expression levels. To account for confounding factors such as population structure and batch effects, mixed models are introduced to improve the accuracy of the analysis. Since eQTL analysis typically involves a large number of statistical tests, multiple testing correction is an essential step, with commonly used correction methods including Bonferroni correction and false discovery rate (FDR) correction. Notably, FDR is a core quality control metric, defined as the expected proportion of incorrectly rejected null hypotheses among all rejected hypotheses. For example, an FDR of 5% means that for every 100 significant eQTLs identified, approximately 5 are expected to be false positives. Using PCA-based visualization, we help students intuitively understand population stratification effects. We also guide students to understand confounding factor control strategies and the effects of confounding factors. Finally, findings should be validated using independent genomic data to ensure reliability. When research findings contradict existing knowledge, we will guide students to conduct systematic analyses. This includes evaluating potential experimental noise, accounting for demographic confounders such as sex and age. We may also perform in-depth functional characterization of SNPs, e.g. investigating whether they are located in functional genomic elements and whether they affect transcription factor binding motifs.

Furthermore, the tools and platforms for eQTL analysis are continuously evolving. Initially, eQTL analysis primarily relied on simple statistical software. However, with the ever-expanding scale of data, many efficient tools and platforms have emerged, such as MatrixEQTL [9], FastQTL [10], and QTLtools [11], which can effectively meet the demands of large-scale data analysis. Meanwhile, cloud computing platforms have gradually been introduced into eQTL analysis, providing robust computational support for processing massive datasets. By briefly introducing these tools and platforms, we lay the groundwork for students' hands-on practice in subsequent sessions.

3.3 Practical Operations

Building on the theoretical foundation, the course incorporates practical exercises to help students translate theoretical knowledge into practical skills. To assist students in better understanding and mastering cutting-edge technologies, this course has specially designed hands-on sessions following the theoretical explanations. These sessions guide students from conceptual understanding to tool usage and result interpretation, enabling them to progressively acquire core skills.

eQTL analysis is a crucial method for studying the relationship between single nucleotide polymorphisms and gene expression data [12]. By exploring how genetic variations at specific genomic locations influence gene expression levels, eQTL analysis reveals the association between genetic variations and gene expression regulation. Through eQTL analysis, students can intuitively grasp how genetic variations affect gene expression, thereby better understanding core concepts in genomics. Below, we will provide a detailed guide on how to guide students through eQTL analysis, covering the explanation of SNP concepts, gene expression and preprocessing, as well as the entire process of eQTL computation.

SNP and Its Numeric Expression. We utilize images and visualization tools to start from the most basic DNA structure, providing a detailed explanation of the concept of single nucleotide polymorphisms, to help students gain a deep understanding of the fundamental definition of SNPs and their significant role in genetic variation.

SNPs refer to variations at a single nucleotide position in the genome. As one of the most common forms of genetic variation, SNPs typically manifest as the substitution of one nucleotide for another at a specific location. These variations can differ significantly among individuals and are closely associated with various genetic traits and diseases [13]. Understanding the concept of SNPs and their role in genetic variation is foundational for learning eQTL analysis.

In human somatic cells, chromosomes appear in pairs, and the DNA in each chromosome is structured as a double helix. DNA is composed of four bases (A, T, C, G), following the principle of complementary base pairing (A-T, C-G). As shown in Fig. 2a, the basic composition of human chromosomes and DNA structure is illustrated.

To help students better understand SNPs, we use Fig. 2b for explanation. In SNP analysis, the information scientists typically obtain from DNA sequence reads pertains to one of the two strands. Because of complementary base pairing, the alleles on both strands can be inferred by reading the sequence of one strand. Therefore, in the SNP analysis process, it is sufficient to read the sequence from one strand. Figure 2b shows the sequences of multiple individuals at the same locus. It can be observed that different individuals may have different bases at this position, such as C or T.

We can represent the SNP information of these individuals using the SNP genotype matrix. To facilitate modeling and statistical analysis, SNP data is typically converted into numerical form. In the matrix, the number in each cell represents the base encoding of the corresponding SNP for that sample. Common encoding methods are as follows: 0: Both alleles are the reference allele. 1: One reference allele and one alternative allele. 2: Both are alternative alleles.

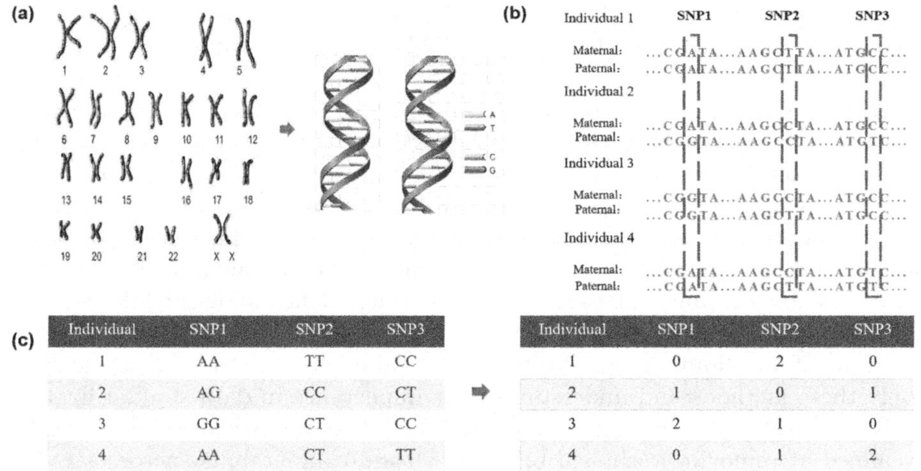

Fig. 2. SNP. (a) Human chromosome and DNA structure diagram. (b) SNP illustration at multiple individual loci. (c) Convert the SNP genotype matrix into a numerical matrix.

For example, when base A is treated as the reference allele for SNP1 and base C is selected as the reference allele for SNP2 and SNP3, the transformation process is shown in Fig. 2c. Through this digital representation, students can more intuitively understand the structure of SNP data and lay the groundwork for subsequent eQTL analysis.

Gene Expression and Preprocessing. In eQTL research, gene expression data is a core component, reflecting the expression levels of genes across different individuals or conditions. The quality and preprocessing of gene expression data directly impact the accuracy and reliability of eQTL analysis. Therefore, we need to focus on introducing gene expression data.

In eQTL analysis, gene expression data is typically obtained through high-throughput technologies, primarily RNA sequencing (RNA-seq) and gene expression microarrays. Among these, RNA-seq data has become the preferred method for eQTL studies due to its significant advantages. RNA-seq technologies not only offers high precision and coverage but also enables genome-wide detection of gene expression. Additionally, RNA-seq data provides flexibility in quantitative analysis, allowing for the detection of low-expression genes and rare transcripts, as well as supporting the integration of multi-omics data. These advantages make RNA-seq data highly valuable in uncovering the genetic regulatory mechanisms of gene expression. Given these characteristics of RNA-seq data, we choose it as the core content of our teaching, guiding students to master the basic workflow of eQTL analysis through hands-on practice.

Raw gene expression data may contain technical noise, batch effects, and low-quality samples, which can significantly affect the accuracy of subsequent analyses [14]. Therefore, data preprocessing is a critical step in eQTL analysis. Rigorous preprocessing can help provide high-quality input data for subsequent eQTL analysis [15].

After obtaining gene expression data, the first step is to perform strict quality control. Sample quality control is the initial step in preprocessing, aimed at checking whether the expression data of samples exhibit anomalies. To improve the effectiveness of model training, we need to filter out low-expression genes and apply a logarithmic transformation to the filtered gene expression data. Additionally, if gene expression data comes from different experimental batches, batch effects may be introduced. Batch effects can obscure true biological differences, so correction is necessary. Commonly used batch effect correction methods include ComBat [2] and limma [16]. Through practical exercises, students can learn to apply these methods and understand their importance in data standardization.

Normalization of gene expression data is a key step in preprocessing, primarily aimed at removing technical biases to ensure comparability across samples. We provide students with a detailed introduction to normalization methods for different data types and their application scenarios, helping them understand the importance of normalization and master specific operations. In RNA-seq data analysis, normalization is a critical step, with commonly used methods including RPKM (Reads Per Kilobase per Million mapped reads), FPKM (Fragments Per Kilobase per Million mapped reads), and TPM (Transcripts Per Million) [17].

We will briefly introduce the formulas for data normalization calculations, and use practical examples to help students understand and apply these methods.

Processed data are typically stored in matrix form, with rows representing genes and columns representing samples. Through practical teaching, students can learn the basic standards for data storage and understand its importance in data management and analysis, as well as its advantages and disadvantages in different research contexts.

eQTL Calculation. To assist students in better completing practical exercises, the course has introduced commonly used eQTL analysis tools and platforms. Among the many tools available, MatrixEQTL is an efficient and widely used R package specifically designed for detecting associations between SNPs and gene expression levels. MatrixEQTL not only handles large-scale datasets but also features fast computation and user-friendly operation, making it highly suitable for both teaching and practical research applications. Therefore, we choose MatrixEQTL as the core tool for student practice, helping them master the basic workflow and methods of eQTL analysis through hands-on experience. Previously, students have learned the fundamental concepts of SNPs, their digital representation, and preprocessing methods for gene expression data. Building on these foundation, we further guide students through the following six steps to help them grasp the complete eQTL analysis process.

1. Data Preparation: Students need to prepare gene expression data, SNP genotype data, and covariate data. Gene expression data and SNP genotype data are obtained from public databases and, after processing as described above,

are stored in matrices. Covariate data can be directly retrieved from public databases, and students need to simply format it into rows representing covariates and columns representing samples. This study utilizes publicly available data, which were generated with ethics approval, for subsequent analyses. Should alternative data be generated, researchers must obtain ethics approval for any studies involving humans and animals.

2. Loading Data: Use functions provided by MatrixEQTL to load the data, ensuring the correct data format.
3. Setting Model Parameters: Students need to select the model type and set thresholds for p-values and false discovery rates.
4. Running eQTL Analysis: Students use MatrixEQTL to perform eQTL analysis, generating results that show associations between SNPs and gene expression.
5. Interpreting Results: Students learn how to interpret key metrics in the output files, such as regression coefficients, t-statistics, p-values, and false discovery rates, to identify significant SNP-gene associations.
6. Presenting and Evaluating Results: After completing the eQTL analysis, students need to visualize the results and write an analysis report. The report should include data preparation, analysis methods, result interpretation, and conclusions. Students are expected to discuss significant SNP-gene associations and their biological significance, supported by visualization results. Instructors evaluate the reports and visualizations, providing feedback and suggestions for improvement. Through group discussions and presentations, students share their analysis experiences and insights.

Through the eQTL analysis teaching based on MatrixEQTL, students are expected to master the complete workflow from data preparation to result interpretation and enhance their ability to solve practical problems. Teaching feedback indicates that students highly appreciate the simplicity and powerful functionality of MatrixEQTL. They believe that the learning and practice process deepens their understanding of bioinformatics-related knowledge and theories. In addition, we encourage students to independently design exploratory topics based on the existing experimental data to enhance their innovative and practical abilities.

4 Conclusion

We propose a project design approach that integrates history, theory, and practice, using eQTL computation as an example to elaborate on this framework in detail. Through the combination of historical context, theoretical explanations, and hands-on practice, students can comprehensively grasp the knowledge system, technical logic, and application scenarios of eQTL analysis. This teaching model not only helps students understand the scientific basis of eQTL analysis but also cultivates their practical skills and innovative thinking, laying a solid foundation for their future research careers and professional development.

Part of this course is in the demand of biotechnology industry. For example, sequencing data analysis is intensively used and required in biotechnology companies involved in genome or transcriptome sequencing. It is also required in the area of disease risk evaluation, a common service in biotechnology companies with healthcare management.

Furthermore, during the teaching process, we observed significant improvements in students' computational thinking and data analysis abilities, particularly in areas such as data preprocessing, model selection, and result interpretation. They demonstrated stronger self-directed learning and problem-solving skills. This indicates that by introducing highly operational projects, students can engage in exploratory learning within real-world research contexts, fostering core competencies essential for future bioinformatics research. We conducted a questionnaire survey to collect students' feedback on the curriculum design. The questionnaire was designed to include two questions each on history, theory, and practice, respectively. We received feedbacks from 56 students. The survey data indicate that the vast majority of participating students (92.9%) found the historical contextualization enhanced their understanding of core biological concepts or methods. In terms of theoretical instruction, 85.9% of respondents reported the course content was clearly structured with a coherent knowledge framework. 92.9% of students thought that the bioinformatics experiment sessions effectively improved their data processing and analytical skills. These results demonstrate the efficacy of our curriculum design in facilitating both professional knowledge acquisition and practical competency development.

In the future, we will further refine the bioinformatics education model by exploring more diverse teaching methods and evaluation mechanisms. For example, we plan to introduce automated data analysis platforms, develop interactive visualization tools, and expand teaching content using online learning resources. Additionally, we aim to collaborate with research institutions and biopharmaceutical companies to integrate project-based learning with actual research needs. This will enable students to gain more practical experience during their studies, contributing to the cultivation of outstanding bioinformatics talent.

Acknowledgements. This work is supported by Hunan Provincial Graduate Education Teaching Reform Research Project (2023JGZD009), Central South University Graduate Education Teaching Reform Research Project (2023JGA005, 2023JGB137), Xinjiang Autonomous Region Graduate Education Innovation Program (XJ2024GY01), Central South University Graduate Practical Training Reform Project (2023sjyr036). The computational resource at the High Performance Computing Center of Central South University is also gratefully acknowledged.

References

1. Attwood, T.K., Blackford, S., Brazas, M.D., Davies, A., Schneider, M.V.: A global perspective on evolving bioinformatics and data science training needs. Brief. Bioinform. **20**, 398–404 (2019)

2. Johnson, W.E., Li, C., Rabinovic, A.: Adjusting batch effects in microarray expression data using empirical Bayes methods. Biostatistics **8**(1), 118–127 (2007)
3. Tambi, R., Bayoumi, R., Lansberg, P., Banerjee, Y.: Blending Gagne's instructional model with Peyton's approach to design an introductory bioinformatics lesson plan for medical students: proof-of-concept study. JMIR Med. Educ. **4**(2), e11122 (2018)
4. Achappa, S., Patil, L., Hombalimath, V., Shet, A.: Implementation of project-based-learning (PBL) approach for bioinformatics laboratory course. J. Eng. Educ. Transformations **33**, 247–252 (2020)
5. Yang, Y., Ouyang, T., Zhang, L., Wang, J.: Study on blended teaching mode and its application based on the arcs motivational model: taking bioinformatics course as an example. Medicine **101**(40), e30801 (2022)
6. Drew, J., et al.: Revisiting barriers to implementation of bioinformatics into life sciences education. Front. Educ. **8** (2023). Article 1317191
7. Emery, L.R., Morgan, S.L.: The application of project-based learning in bioinformatics training. PLoS Comput. Biol. **13**(8), e1005620 (2017)
8. Poličar, P.G., Špendl, M., Curk, T., Zupan, B.: Teaching bioinformatics through the analysis of SARS-CoV-2: project-based training for computer science students. Bioinformatics **40**(Suppl 1), i20–i29 (2024)
9. Shabalin, A.A.: Matrix eQTL: ultra fast eQTL analysis via large matrix operations. Bioinformatics **28**(10), 1353–1358 (2012)
10. Ongen, H., Buil, A., Brown, A.A., Dermitzakis, E.T., Delaneau, O.: Fast and efficient QTL mapper for thousands of molecular phenotypes. Bioinformatics **32**(10), 1479–1485 (2016)
11. Delaneau, O., Ongen, H., Brown, A.A., Dermitzakis, E.T.: QTLtools: a complete tool set for molecular QTL discovery and analysis. Nat. Commun. **8**, 15452 (2017)
12. Lappalainen, T., Sammeth, M., Friedländer, M.R., et al.: Transcriptome and genome sequencing uncovers functional variation in humans. Nature **501**(7467), 506–511 (2013)
13. Lander, E.S., Botstein, D., Brown, P.O., et al.: Genomewide genetic variation in a population sample of the human genome. N. Engl. J. Med. **334**(11), 774–781 (1996)
14. Conesa, A., et al.: A survey of best practices for RNA-Seq data analysis. Genome Biol. **17**(1), 13 (2016)
15. Hitzemann, R., et al.: Genes, behavior and next-generation RNA sequencing. Genes Brain Behav. **12**(1), 1–12 (2013)
16. Ritchie, M.E., et al.: LIMMA powers differential expression analyses for RNA-sequencing and microarray studies. Nucleic Acids Res. **43**(7), e47 (2015)
17. Mortazavi, A., Williams, B.A., McCue, K., Schaeffer, L., Wold, B.: Mapping and quantifying mammalian transcriptomes by RNA-Seq. Nat. Methods **5**(7), 621–628 (2008)

BiGDC-BrainAgeNet: Enhancing EEG-Based Brain Age Prediction with Bidirectional Graph Diffusion Convolutions

Jian Wang[1,2]([✉]) [iD], Yiding Zhang[1,2] [iD], Zhengyang Song[1,2] [iD], and Ting Cheng[1,2] [iD]

[1] Faculty of Information Engineering and Automation, Kunming University of Science and Technology, Kunming 650500, Yunnan, China
`jianwang@kust.edu.cn`
[2] Yunnan Key Lab of Artificial Intelligence, Kunming 650500, Yunnan, China

Abstract. Brain age has emerged as a crucial biomarker in neuroscience research, where MRI-based methods currently dominate due to their established predictive accuracy. However, MRI's prohibitive cost and technical constraints severely limit its clinical scalability. While EEG offers a cost-effective alternative, existing EEG-driven approaches have consistently underperformed in brain age estimation, with reported MAE values typically exceeding 6 years in prior studies. To overcome these limitations, we present BiGDC-BrainAgeNet – the first graph neural architecture specifically designed for EEG-based brain age estimation. Our model synergistically integrates a bidirectional graph diffusion convolutional gated recurrent unit with self-attention mechanisms, enabling simultaneous capture of spatiotemporal dynamics and global feature interdependencies within EEG signals. This innovative framework achieves state-of-the-art performance with unprecedented accuracy, delivering $MAEs$ of 4.026 years ($R^2 = 0.83$) and 1.756 years ($R^2 = 0.885$) on the TUAB and CHBMP datasets respectively. Spatial analysis further reveals that central sulcus and occipital electrodes contribute most significantly to age prediction, providing novel neurophysiological insights. As the first successful application of graph neural networks in EEG-based brain aging research, our work establishes a new framework for affordable, large-scale brain health monitoring.

Keywords: Brain age · Electroencephalogram (EEG) · Graph diffusion convolutional · Graph neural networks

1 Introduction

Electroencephalogram (EEG) has long been used in clinical research and practice as a non-invasive tool for measuring brain activity. In recent decades, its application has expanded in neurology, psychiatry, and drug development [1]. EEG

J. Tang et al. (Eds.): ISBRA 2025, LNBI 15757, pp. 320–332, 2026.
https://doi.org/10.1007/978-981-95-0695-8_26

captures synchronized cortical potentials across multiple scalp electrodes, generating multidimensional time-series data rich in information on spectral power, spatial patterns, and waveform morphology. This makes EEG a valuable resource for identifying biomarkers of cognitive function, central nervous system (CNS) pathology, and pharmacological effects [2].

Research shows that neuropsychiatric disorders, such as traumatic brain injury [3], schizophrenia [4,5], bipolar disorder [5], epilepsy [6], and Alzheimer's [7], often involve structural and functional brain changes. These conditions accelerate brain aging, creating a significant gap between estimated brain age and chronological age [8]. Accurate brain age prediction offers valuable insights into the risks of cognitive decline, neurological diseases, psychiatric disorders, and even mortality.

Current non-invasive brain age estimation predominantly relies on structural magnetic resonance imaging (MRI) coupled with machine learning. Conventional approaches employ feature-based regression models that extract MRI-derived biomarkers such as cortical thickness and gray/white matter volume [9], leveraging prior anatomical knowledge to enhance interpretability. The development of MRI-driven deep learning, particularly convolutional neural networks (CNNs), has demonstrated improved predictive accuracy through automated feature extraction from volumetric scans [10]. This MRI-CNN approach nevertheless faces dual constraints—its inherent sensitivity to gradual structural changes limits detection of subtle functional aging patterns, while the prohibitive costs of MRI acquisition restrict longitudinal monitoring applications. Emerging research now explores electroencephalogram (EEG) as a transformative alternative, motivated by these limitations. Although some progress has been achieved in leveraging EEG data, substantial challenges still remain [11], primarily due to its inherent complexity, individual variability, and the time-series nature of the signals. Unlike structural neuroimaging data, EEG captures transient, millisecond-scale brain activity that is influenced by both internal cognitive states and external environmental factors, making it highly variable across time and individuals. This inter-individual variability in EEG patterns, coupled with the complexity of extracting meaningful features from high-dimensional time-series data, poses significant barriers to model generalization. Additionally, EEG reflects functional rather than anatomical processes, which may evolve with age in subtler and more context-dependent ways, further obscuring predictive signals. These issues often lead to suboptimal accuracy and generalizability in brain age estimation models, as they fail to account for the complex interplay between various brain regions and their temporal dynamics. Therefore, addressing these challenges is crucial for improving the robustness and accuracy of brain age predictions.

In recent years, graph neural network (GNN) have made significant progress in EEG signal analysis, becoming a focal point of interest for researchers. GNN model EEG signals as graph structures, enabling better capture of the complex connectivity and dynamic interactions between brain regions, offering new solutions for EEG data that traditional methods cannot handle effectively. In EEG signal analysis, GNN have been applied to various tasks such as emotion recognition [12], seizure detection [13], and cognitive state classification [14]. Unlike traditional CNN or recurrent neural network (RNN), GNN can process irregular graph-structured data, more accurately reflecting the spatiotemporal dependencies between different brain regions in EEG signals. This characteristic allows GNN to extract more representative features from EEG data, improving the classification and regression performance of models. Moreover, recent studies suggest that incorporating techniques such as the Graph Attention Mechanism has further enhanced the performance of GNN in EEG signal processing [15]. These methods not only improve the model's robustness but also enhance its feature extraction ability, achieving results that surpass traditional methods in complex tasks.

In this study, we have developed innovative extensions to the diffusion convolutional gated recurrent unit (DCGRU) framework by designing a bidirectional structure that captures both forward and backward information flows, optimizing its ability to handle the temporal dynamics of EEG signals. This design directly addresses the non-linear and dynamic nature of EEG by enabling richer temporal context modeling. Additionally, the model integrates a self-attention mechanism that dynamically focuses on key features, enhancing its ability to represent the complex characteristics of EEG data, extract relevant patterns despite inter-individual variability, and identify subtle, age-related functional signals that might otherwise be obscured. Building on these improvements, we introduce Bidirectional Graph Diffusion Convolutional Brain Age Prediction Network (BiGDC-BrainAgeNet), which excels in EEG age estimation, achieving an MAE of 4.026 years and R^2 of 0.83 on TUAB normal subject data, and an MAE of 1.756 years with R^2 of 0.885 on CHBMP data. To our knowledge, this significantly outperforms existing methods. Specifically, the best previously reported MAE for the TUAB normal subjects dataset was 6.5 years [16], while for the CHBMP dataset, the best previously reported MAE was 6.48 years [17]. Furthermore, the overall best reported MAE using EEG data stood at 5.96 years with an R^2 score of 0.81 [18]. To our best knowledge this study is the first to apply a Graph Neural Network (GNN) that effectively integrates both spatial and temporal relationships in EEG data for brain age estimation. Consequently, our BiGDC-BrainAgeNet represents a meaningful advancement in EEG-based brain age estimation.

2   Methods

2.1   Graph-Based Modeling for EEG

The graph structure is constructed to capture functional connectivity across brain regions using the EEG electrode layout based on the international 10–20 system. We represent functional connectivity by measuring the similarity between signals from different sensors through normalized cross-correlation. Given preprocessed signals x_i and x_j from sensors i and j, the cross-correlation is defined as

$$W_{ij} = \frac{\sum_{t=1}^{T \times D} (x_i[t] \cdot x_j[t])}{\sqrt{\sum_{t=1}^{T \times D} x_i[t]^2 \cdot \sum_{t=1}^{T \times D} x_j[t]^2}} \qquad (1)$$

Here, W_{ij} represents the weight of the edge between sensors i and j, indicating the similarity of their signals. The index t runs over individual time samples, where each unit represents $1\,\text{s}$ of EEG data. T is the window length, and D is the sampling rate, so $T \times D$ gives the total number of samples used for cross-correlation. This process is applied to all sensor pairs, resulting in a symmetric correlation matrix of size $N \times N$, where N is the number of sensors. To reduce computational complexity and emphasize the most significant connections, we sparsify the correlation matrix by retaining only the top k most correlated neighbors for each node, setting all other edge weights to zero. This yields a sparse matrix W, which represents the final graph structure.

2.2 Graph Diffusion Convolution in EEG Signals

We referred to DCGRU, a variant of the gated recurrent unit (GRU) that replaces the standard matrix multiplication with diffusion convolution. Originally developed for traffic prediction, DCGRU models the dynamics of traffic flow as a diffusion process [19]. Similarly, the spatial dependencies in EEG signals can be modeled as a diffusion process, where an electrode is influenced by neighboring electrodes that are functionally close, as measured by correlation. Specifically, the diffusion process is characterized by bidirectional random walks on a directed graph G, and its diffusion convolution is as follows

$$X_{:,m} *_G f_\theta = \sum_{k=0}^{K-1} \left(\theta_{k,1} \left(D_O^{-1} W \right)^k + \theta_{k,2} \left(D_I^{-1} W^T \right)^k \right) X_{:,m} \qquad (2)$$

Here, $X \in R^{N \times M}$ represents the preprocessed EEG data segment at time step $t \in \{1, \ldots, T\}$, where N denotes the number of nodes and M represents the number of features, corresponding to different EEG channels or time points. The index m denotes the feature index, indicating that for each $m \in \{1, \ldots, M\}$, the corresponding m-th feature of the EEG signal is processed. f_θ is the convolution filter with parameters $\theta \in R^{K \times 2}$; D_O and D_I are the diagonal degree matrices associated with the out-degrees and in-degrees of the graph, respectively; $D_O^{-1} W$ and $D_I^{-1} W^T$ represent the state transition matrices for the outward and inward diffusion processes, respectively; and K is the maximum number of diffusion steps.

2.3 Bidirectional Diffusion Convolutional Gated Recurrent Unit for EEG Signals

To better capture temporal and spatiotemporal dependencies in EEG signals, we extended DCGRU into a bidirectional structure, resulting in the Bidirectional Diffusion Convolutional Gated Recurrent Unit (BiDCGRU) (See Fig. 1).

324   J. Wang et al.

BiDCGRU can simultaneously model information from both the past and the future along the time dimension. For each time step t, the forward computation in BiDCGRU is as follows

$$\overrightarrow{H}(t) \; = \; \overrightarrow{u}(t) \odot \overrightarrow{H}(t-1) \; + \; (1 \; - \; \overrightarrow{u}(t)) \odot \overrightarrow{C}(t) \tag{3}$$

$$\overrightarrow{r}(t) \; = \; \sigma\left(\overrightarrow{\Theta_r} *_G \left[X(t), \overrightarrow{H}(t-1)\right] + b_{\overrightarrow{r}}\right) \tag{4}$$

$$\overrightarrow{u}(t) \; = \; \sigma\left(\overrightarrow{\Theta_u} *_G \left[X(t), \overrightarrow{H}(t-1)\right] + b_{\overrightarrow{u}}\right) \tag{5}$$

$$\overrightarrow{C}(t) \; = \; \tanh\left(\overrightarrow{\Theta_C} *_G \left[X(t), \overrightarrow{r}(t) \odot \overrightarrow{H}(t-1)\right] + b_{\overrightarrow{C}}\right) \tag{6}$$

For each time step t, the backward computation in BiDCGRU is as follows

$$\overleftarrow{H}(t) \; = \; \overleftarrow{u}(t) \odot \overleftarrow{H}(t+1) \; + \; (1 \; - \; \overleftarrow{u}(t)) \odot \overleftarrow{C}(t) \tag{7}$$

$$\overleftarrow{r}(t) \; = \; \sigma\left(\overleftarrow{\Theta_r} *_G \left[X(t), \overleftarrow{H}(t+1)\right] + b_{\overleftarrow{r}}\right) \tag{8}$$

$$\overleftarrow{u}(t) \; = \; \sigma\left(\overleftarrow{\Theta_u} *_G \left[X(t), \overleftarrow{H}(t+1)\right] + b_{\overleftarrow{u}}\right) \tag{9}$$

$$\overleftarrow{C}(t) \; = \; \tanh\left(\overleftarrow{\Theta_C} *_G \left[X(t), \overleftarrow{r}(t) \odot \overleftarrow{H}(t+1)\right] + b_{\overleftarrow{C}}\right) \tag{10}$$

Let $X(t)$ and $H(t)$ denote the input and output at time step t, respectively. The function σ represents the Sigmoid function, and $\odot$ denotes the Hadamard product. $r(t)$, $u(t)$ and $C(t)$ correspond to the reset gate, update gate, and candidate value, respectively. $*_G$ denotes the diffusion convolution, and Θ_r, b_r, Θ_u, b_u, Θ_C and b_C are the weights and biases of the corresponding convolutional filters.

The forward hidden state $\overrightarrow{H}(t)$ and backward hidden state $\overleftarrow{H}(t)$ are concatenated to form the joint output $H(t) = [\overrightarrow{H}(t); \overleftarrow{H}(t)]$, enabling the model to integrate information from both the past and future at each time step, thus improving the capture of global spatiotemporal features in EEG signals.

2.4 Self-attention Enhancement

While BiDCGRU capture bidirectional dependencies by incorporating both forward and backward temporal information, there may be an imbalance in contributions across time steps. The self-attention mechanism addresses this by adaptively focusing on the most relevant time-step features for brain age prediction [20]. It applies weighted processing to the output of BiDCGRU as follows

$$z = \sum_{t=1}^{12} \mathrm{Softmax}\left(W_q \cdot H + M \times (-\infty)\right) t \cdot H(t) \tag{11}$$

Here, $H(t)$ is the joint output of BiDCGRU at each time step, W_q computes query weights, and $\alpha = \mathrm{Softmax}\left(W_q \cdot H + M \times (-\infty)\right)$ represents the normalized importance weights of each time step. M is a mask matrix used to exclude irrelevant time steps, and the context vector z is a weighted sum of the most important features within the 12-s window.

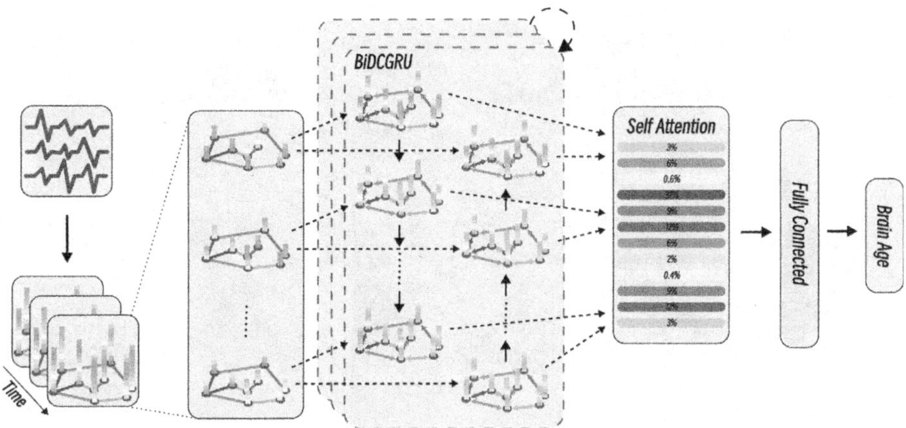

Fig. 1. The overall architecture of BiGDC-BrainAgeNet. After the EEG data is transformed into a graph, it is processed through multiple layers of BiDCGRU, followed by a self-attention mechanism and fully connected layers to ultimately generate the brain age estimate.

3   Experiment

3.1   Datasets

We focus on datasets sampled from healthy volunteers within the general population or clinically labeled EEG data subsets marked as non-pathological by medical experts. In our study, we selected the non-pathological subject subsample from the Temple University Hospital Abnormal EEG Corpus (TUAB) [21] and the EEG data sample set from the Cuban Human Brain Mapping Project (CHBMP) dataset [22].

3.2   Experiment Setup

Data Preprocessing. The datasets contain EEG recordings from various devices with different sampling rates and channel configurations. To ensure consistency, we selected 19 common channels, normalized the values using the mean and standard deviation for each channel, and resampled all data 200 Hz. Signals were segmented using a non-overlapping 12-second window, with shorter segments discarded. Log-amplitude spectrum features were extracted via Fast Fourier Transform (FFT) to incorporate frequency domain information into model training.

Dataset Partition. The dataset was partitioned into training, validation, and test sets in a 6:2:2 ratio to ensure non-overlapping data sources for model training, validation, and testing.

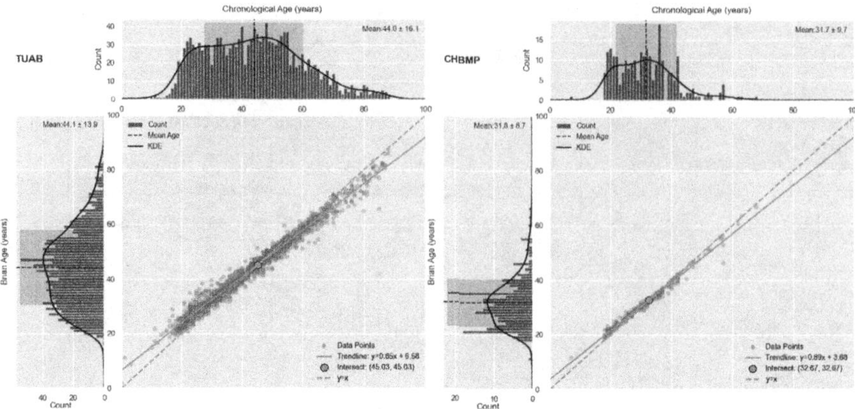

Fig. 2. 2D scatter plots of brain age versus chronological age for TUAB and CHBMP. The blue dots represent the sample points, and the cyan dots mark the intersections between the trend line (solid cyan line) and the diagonal (dashed cyan line). The model tends to overestimate brain age in younger subjects and underestimate it in older subjects. (Color figure online) (Color figure online)

Hyper-Parameter Setting. In training the BiGDC-BrainAgeNet model, the number of BIDCGRU layers was set to 2, with 64 units per layer. The maximum diffusion step in the graph neural network was set to 3. During graph construction, only the top 3 strongest connections were retained for each node.

Evaluation Metrics. In this study, two primary evaluation metrics were employed to comprehensively assess the performance of the proposed model in regression tasks: Mean Absolute Error (MAE) and R-squared (R^2).

Table 1. Specific performance scores of different models on the TUAB and CHBMP datasets.

No.	Models	TUAB(R^2)	TUAB(MAE)	CHBMP(R^2)	CHBMP(MAE)
1	LSTM	0.46	9.193	0.566	4.992
2	BiLSTM	0.377	9.93	0.585	4.638
3	GRU	0.449	9.283	0.523	5.081
4	BiGRU	0.347	10.186	0.588	4.578
5	GCN	0.295	10.605	0.407	6.421
6	GAT	0.295	10.62	0.46	5.893
7	DCRNN [19]	0.407	9.578	0.61	4.668
8	DCNN [18]	0.44	9.385	0.687	3.925
9	SincNet [23]	0.567	8.038	0.698	3.747
10	**BiGDC-BrainAgeNet**	**0.83**	**4.026**	**0.885**	**1.756**

Comparison with Other Methods. We evaluated the performance of BiGDC-BrainAgeNet against recent EEG-based age prediction methods and widely used deep learning models for brain age estimation. To ensure fairness, all models were trained using the same EEG channel configurations and input lengths. The comparative models included LSTM, BiLSTM, GRU, BiGRU, GCN, GAT, and DCRNN [19], a spatiotemporal model originally developed for traffic forecasting using DCGRU. We also included DCNN [18] and SincNet [23], both of which are convolutional neural networks specifically applied to EEG-based brain age prediction in their respective studies. Training was conducted separately on the TUAB and CHBMP datasets for model optimization, validation, and evaluation, providing a comprehensive assessment of the model's generalization and predictive performance across different age groups. Figure 2 presents the 2D scatter plots of predicted brain age versus chronological age for both the TUAB and CHBMP datasets. Experimental results show that BiGDC-BrainAgeNet outperforms all other models on both datasets. Detailed performance comparisons are provided in Table 1.

We conducted a comprehensive comparison between our approach and several established MRI-based brain age prediction methodologies across three critical metrics: parameter quantity, train time, and test time. The proposed method demonstrates notable advantages in all three dimensions, particularly achieving superior inference efficiency compared to other approaches. The comparative results are explicitly presented in Table 2.

Table 2. A comparative analysis of computational cost and performance between BiGDC-BrainAgeNet and established MRI-based brain age prediction methodologies.

No.	Models	Data type	Parameter quantity	Train time	Test time
1	3D-CNN [26]	T1MRI	889,960	83 h	290–940 ms
2	VGG Net [27]	T1MRI	11,890,305	12 h	20 ms
3	SFCN [28]	T1MRI	3,000,000	>50 h	5 ms
4	3D-CNN [29]	T1MRI	720,481	6.75 h	320 ms
5	DCNN [18]	EEG	373,137	3.5 h	8.6 ms
6	SincNet [23]	EEG	1,157,313	25 h	9.7 ms
7	BiGDC-BrainAgeNet	EEG	790,529	31 h	4.6 ms

3.3 Analysis of Brain Age and Chronological Age

Figure 3 illustrates the two-dimensional plot of the deviation between predicted brain age and chronological age for the TUAB and CHBMP datasets. We observed a strong positive correlation between the predicted brain age and chronological age, although the slope was slightly lower than the ideal 45° line, indicating a minor discrepancy from perfect prediction. A more detailed analysis of the differences between the predicted and chronological ages showed a slight overestimation for younger subjects and a slight underestimation for older subjects. On the TUAB dataset, the predicted brain age was, on average, overestimated by 0.152 years, whereas on the CHBMP dataset, the overestimation was 0.114 years on average.

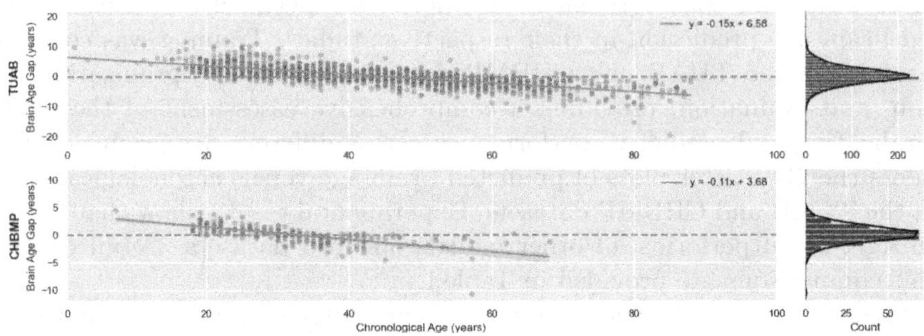

Fig. 3. 2D plot showing the brain age prediction bias for TUAB and CHBMP. The cyan solid line represents the univariate fit to chronological age. The brain age bias appears to roughly follow a normal distribution.

3.4   Brain Age Prediction for TUAB Pathological Subjects

We used a model trained on non-pathological subjects from TUAB to predict the brain age of pathological subjects from TUAB. As shown in Fig. 4, we again observe an overestimation for younger subjects and an underestimation for older subjects. Overall, the predicted brain age was underestimated by an average of 7.829 years, and our BiGDC-BrainAgeNet achieved an MAE of 16.406 years. When comparing the results of pathological and non-pathological subjects, several notable differences become apparent: (a) The performance of non-pathological subjects was significantly superior to that of pathological subjects (MAE of 4.026 years vs. 16.406 years). (b) The prediction errors for pathological subjects were much larger than those for non-pathological subjects (compare the cyan and orange trendlines in Fig. 2 and Fig. 4, as well as the distribution of the blue and orange sample points). (c) The bias in brain age predictions for pathological subjects was much greater compared to non-pathological subjects (compare the cyan and orange circular markers in Fig. 2 and Fig. 4).

3.5   Model Interpretation

Although BiGDC-BrainAgeNet shows strong performance in brain age prediction, interpreting its predictions remains challenging. One approach is to assign an attribution value to each input feature, representing its contribution to the

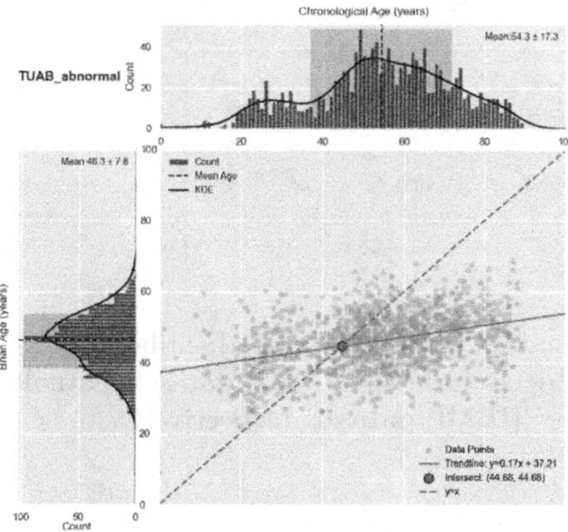

Fig. 4. 2D scatter plot of brain age against chronological age for pathological subjects in TUAB. Similar to Fig. 2, the orange dots represent the sample points, with the orange circles indicating the intersection of the trend line (solid orange line) and the diagonal (dashed orange line). (Color figure online)

output. For a specific target neuron c, the attribution method aims to determine the contribution of each input feature x_i to the output S_c, represented as $R_c = [R_{c1}, R_{c2}, \ldots, R_{cN}] \in R^N$ [24]. We computed gradients for the TUAB and CHBMP datasets and visualized the influential brain regions for prediction using heatmaps [25]. Larger gradient values indicate greater sensitivity to input changes.

Figure 5 shows the electrode gradient sensitivity distribution, generally symmetric with some differences in the CHBMP dataset. These variations may result from differences in dataset sources, subject age, recording conditions, or equipment. Positive gradients were observed at the P3 and P4 electrodes and central sulcus region, suggesting that increased signal strength in these areas correlates with higher predicted age. Strong negative gradients were found in the occipital regions, indicating that stronger signals there lower predicted age. The brain longitudinal fissure region exhibited lower sensitivity.

While the gradient heatmaps highlight the spatial importance of signals, their interpretation is limited. Higher power in the central sulcus correlates with older predicted brain age, and higher power in the occipital region with younger predicted age, but we cannot definitively claim these effects cause faster or slower brain aging. These patterns represent the most crucial information the model uses for distinguishing the data.

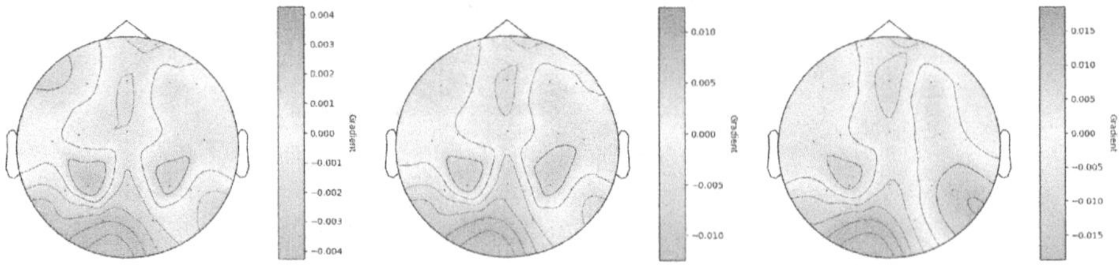

Fig. 5. Panels (a), (b), and (c) illustrate the gradient heatmaps of BiGDC-BrainAgeNet for non-pathological subjects from the TUAB dataset, pathological subjects from the TUAB dataset, and the CHBMP dataset, respectively.

4   Conclusion

In conclusion, our research demonstrates that BiGDC-BrainAgeNet, by integrating graph structures and GRU units across both past and future temporal scales, achieves superior accuracy in predicting brain age from resting EEG signals compared to existing methods. Although a performance gap remains relative to MRI-based approaches, EEG's advantages as a low-cost, efficient, and accessible physiological measurement highlight its substantial predictive potential. Further analysis of the relationship between brain age and chronological age, combined with exploration of brain age prediction gradients, reveals that brain age tends to be overestimated in younger individuals and underestimated in older adults. Moreover, the observed bilateral symmetry in brain sensitivity to age predictions indicates nearly equivalent contributions from both hemispheres in determining brain age. These findings enrich our understanding of brain aging dynamics and highlight essential considerations for enhancing the accuracy and reliability of EEG-based brain age prediction models.

Acknowledgments. This work was supported by the Major Science and Technology Program of Yunnan Province (Grant No. 202102AA100021).

References

1. Gaubert, S., et al.: A machine learning approach to screen for preclinical Alzheimer's disease. Neurobiol. Aging **105**, 205–216 (2021)
2. Zijlmans, M., Jiruska, P., Zelmann, R., Leijten, F.S., Jefferys, J.G., Gotman, J.: High-frequency oscillations as a new biomarker in epilepsy. Ann. Neurol. **71**(2), 169–178 (2012)
3. Cole, J.H., Leech, R., Sharp, D.J., Initiative, A.: Prediction of brain age suggests accelerated atrophy after traumatic brain injury. Ann. Neurol. **77**(4), 571–581 (2015)
4. Shahab, S., et al.: Brain structure, cognition, and brain age in schizophrenia, bipolar disorder, and healthy controls. Neuropsychopharmacology **44**(5), 898–906 (2019)

5. Tønnesen, S., et al.: Brain age prediction reveals aberrant brain white matter in schizophrenia and bipolar disorder: a multisample diffusion tensor imaging study. Biol. Psychiatry Cogn. Neurosci. Neuroimag. 5(12), 1095–1103 (2020)
6. Pardoe, H.R., et al.: Structural brain changes in medically refractory focal epilepsy resemble premature brain aging. Epilepsy Res. 133, 28–32 (2017)
7. Vanni, S., Colini Baldeschi, A., Zattoni, M., Legname, G.: Brain aging: a Ianus-faced player between health and neurodegeneration. J. Neurosci. Res. 98(2), 299–311 (2020)
8. Cole, J.H., Franke, K.: Predicting age using neuroimaging: innovative brain ageing biomarkers. Trends Neurosci. 40(12), 681–690 (2017)
9. Kondo, C., et al.: An age estimation method using brain local features for t1-weighted images. In: 2015 37th Annual International Conference of the IEEE Engineering in Medicine and Biology Society (EMBC), pp. 666–669. IEEE (2015)
10. Jónsson, B.A., et al.: Brain age prediction using deep learning uncovers associated sequence variants. Nat. Commun. 10(1), 5409 (2019)
11. Al Zoubi, O., et al.: Predicting age from brain EEG signals—a machine learning approach. Front. Aging Neurosci. 10, 184 (2018)
12. Pan, J., Liang, R., He, Z., Li, J., Liang, Y., Zhou, X., He, Y., Li, Y.: St-SCGNN: a spatio-temporal self-constructing graph neural network for cross-subject EEG-based emotion recognition and consciousness detection. IEEE J. Biomed. Health Inform. 28(2), 777–788 (2023)
13. Wang, J., et al.: EEG signal epilepsy detection with a weighted neighbor graph representation and two-stream graph based framework. IEEE Trans. Neural Syst. Rehabil. Eng. 31, 3176–3187 (2023)
14. Sun, J., et al.: Adaptive spatiotemporal encoding network for cognitive assessment using resting state EEG. NPJ Dig. Med. 7(1), 375 (2024)
15. Cisotto, G., Zanga, A., Chlebus, J., Zoppis, I., Manzoni, S., Markowska-Kaczmar, U.: Comparison of attention-based deep learning models for EEG classification. arXiv preprint arXiv:2012.01074 (2020)
16. Jusseaume, K., Valova, I.: Brain age prediction/classification through recurrent deep learning with electroencephalogram recordings of seizure subjects. Sensors 22(21), 8112 (2022)
17. Engemann, D.A., et al.: A reusable benchmark of brain-age prediction from M/EEG resting-state signals. Neuroimage 262, 119521 (2022)
18. Khayretdinova, M., Shovkun, A., Degtyarev, V., Kiryasov, A., Pshonkovskaya, P., Zakharov, I.: Predicting age from resting-state scalp EEG signals with deep convolutional neural networks on td-brain dataset. Front. Aging Neurosci. 14, 1019869 (2022)
19. Li, Y., Yu, R., Shahabi, C., Liu, Y.: Diffusion convolutional recurrent neural network: data-driven traffic forecasting. arXiv preprint arXiv:1707.01926 (2017)
20. Vaswani, A., et al.: Attention is all you need. In: Advances in Neural Information Processing Systems, vol. 30 (2017)
21. Obeid, I., Picone, J.: The temple university hospital EEG data corpus. Front. Neurosci. 10, 196 (2016)
22. Valdes-Sosa, P.A., et al.: The Cuban human brain mapping project, a young and middle age population-based EEG, MRI, and cognition dataset. Sci. Data 8(1), 45 (2021)
23. Ansari, A., et al.: Resting state electroencephalographic brain activity in neonates can predict age and is indicative of neurodevelopmental outcome. Clin. Neurophysiol. 163, 226–235 (2024)

24. Zintgraf, L.M., Cohen, T.S., Adel, T., Welling, M.: Visualizing deep neural network decisions: prediction difference analysis. arXiv preprint arXiv:1702.04595 (2017)
25. Adebayo, J., Gilmer, J., Muelly, M., Goodfellow, I., Hardt, M., Kim, B.: Sanity checks for saliency maps. In: Advances in Neural Information Processing Systems, vol. 31 (2018)
26. Cole, J.H., et al.: Predicting brain age with deep learning from raw imaging data results in a reliable and heritable biomarker. Neuroimage **163**, 115–124 (2017)
27. Huang, T.W., et al.: Age estimation from brain MRI images using deep learning. In: 2017 IEEE 14th International Symposium on Biomedical Imaging (ISBI 2017), pp. 849–852. IEEE (2017)
28. Peng, H., Gong, W., Beckmann, C.F., Vedaldi, A., Smith, S.M.: Accurate brain age prediction with lightweight deep neural networks. Med. Image Anal. **68**, 101871 (2021)
29. Rao, G., Li, A., Liu, Y., Liu, B.: A high-powered brain age prediction model based on convolutional neural network. In: 2020 IEEE 17th International Symposium on Biomedical Imaging (ISBI), pp. 1915–1919. IEEE (2020)

CT-Semi-net: Segmentation of Infected Areas in Lung CT Images Based on Attention Mechanism and Semi-supervised Learning

Haoze Du[1]([envelope]) [iD], Shumei Hou[2,3] [iD], Xiaolei Wang[2,3] [iD], Bin Sun[2,3] [iD], Dongfang Zhang[2,3] [iD], Junliang Du[2,3] [iD], Qingkai Hu[2,3] [iD], Weifeng Guo[4] [iD], and Xianfang Wang[2,3]([envelope]) [iD]

[1] Department of Computer Science, North Carolina State University, Raleigh, NC 27606, USA
hdu5@ncsu.edu

[2] School of Computer Science and Technology, Henan Institute of Technology, Xinxiang 453003, People's Republic of China
2wangfang@163.com

[3] Manufacturing IoT Big Data Engineering Technology Research Center of Henan Province, Xinxiang 453003, People's Republic of China

[4] School of Electrical and Information Engineering, Zhengzhou University, Zhengzhou 450001, People's Republic of China

Abstract. CT image is the primary basis for doctors to judge whether the lung is infected with lung disease based on experience, and it is of great significance for the screening of pneumonia patients. In this paper, deep convolutional neural networks were used to segment the infected area of COVID-19 lung CT images. After collecting network data and consulting relevant literature, a total of 2,338 CT images were selected as the dataset for model training and testing, comprising 100 labeled CT images and 2,238 unlabeled CT images. Using the newly proposed Res2Net algorithm as the backbone algorithm of model design, CT images are input into the first two convolutional layers to extract high-resolution and semantically weak features. The attention mechanism was employed to enhance the boundary's expression ability within the target region. Finally, the obtained low-level features were fed to the last three convolutional layers and aggregated with the high-level features. Finally, a Basic-Net segmentation model comprising five convolutional layers and three attention modules was designed to obtain preliminary segmentation results for the pulmonary infection region. Based on this, the self-training method is employed to develop a semi-supervised segmentation model (CT-Semi-Net) for COVID-19 CT images. Through practical experiments, it has been demonstrated that the design model exhibits good performance and can effectively address the issues of positioning, fine segmentation, and label data scarcity, with significant practical implications.

Keywords: CT image · Res2Net algorithm · Attention mechanism · Semi-supervised learning

J. Tang et al. (Eds.): ISBRA 2025, LNBI 15757, pp. 333–346, 2026.
https://doi.org/10.1007/978-981-95-0695-8_27

1   Introduction

A CT image is a routine examination for lung disease, providing an important basis for doctors to diagnose whether patients have lung disease. However, the task of artificially mapping areas of lung infection is tedious and time-consuming, and it is highly subjective, often influenced by personal biases and clinical experience. Using computed tomography (CT) technology, the typical signs of lung infection can be clearly observed in CT sections [4]. Image segmentation is a crucial step in the qualitative assessment of transverse and longitudinal changes in infected areas using CT sections, which directly impacts the quality of pulmonary disease diagnosis. Therefore, it is of great significance to use artificial intelligence to segment CT lung images.

Shi et al. [15] studied how injecting cellular features from pathological images into CT images can improve the quality of subsequent analysis. Ezhilraja et al. [3] proposed a multilevel modified binary subimage histogram equalization method (ML-DSIHE) to segment the CT image histogram into two parts using the midpoint of the gray scale. Zhu et al. [23] proposed the concept of pixel intensity skewness and proposed an image decomposition model based on adaptive symbiotic filters to improve the quality of fused images.

Based on the concept of stream network, Zhang et al. [21] introduced multihead stream attention mechanism to mine the deep features of the sequence and improve the efficiency of the model. Messay et al. [13] used the shape, position, brightness and gradient characteristics of candidate nodules to conduct segmented detection of lung nodules. However, due to the small size and low contrast of lung nodules, the image of lung nodules segmented by this algorithm had blurred edges. In view of the problems in the above algorithms, another method has been proposed, which uses a deep learning algorithm to enhance the feature performance of images [10,11,16]. Compared with the traditional method, the algorithm can learn the training data iteratively and extract the effective features of the sample. Meanwhile, the algorithm can reduce the recognition error and improve the segmentation accuracy. For example, He et al. [8] first proposed an algorithm based on residual learning, which solves the degradation problem of deep networks well and greatly reduces the phenomenon of network overfitting. Keles et al. [12] proposed to transfer the pre-trained model of ResNet algorithm to the diagnostic inference engine, which could be used for the early detection of COVID-19. In August 2019, researchers from Nankai University, the University of Oxford and the University of California Merced [7] jointly proposed the Res2Net algorithm based on hierarchical residual connection, which not only has stronger multi-scale expression ability, but also can expand the receptive field range of each network layer. Since the multi-scale representation of the algorithm is independent of the hierarchical feature aggregation model of convolutional neural networks, the algorithm can be integrated into other excellent algorithms as a module to improve the overall performance of the algorithm.

The urgency of developing accurate and efficient lung CT image segmentation methods has been underscored by the COVID-19 pandemic, which has led to a significant increase in the demand for rapid and reliable diagnostic tools. Manual segmentation of lung infections in CT images is not only time-consuming but also subject to inter-observer variability, which can impede timely diagnosis and treatment planning. Recent studies have highlighted that existing segmentation techniques often struggle with challenges such as intensity inhomogeneity, noise, and complex anatomical structures, leading to suboptimal performance in clinical settings. Moreover, the variability in CT imaging protocols and the presence of overlapping pathological features further complicate the segmentation process, necessitating the development of more robust and generalizable algorithms. These limitations highlight the critical need for advanced deep learning approaches that can effectively address the complexities inherent in lung CT image segmentation, thereby improving diagnostic accuracy and patient outcomes [9,22].

In this paper, deep convolutional neural networks were used to segment the infected area of COVID-19 lung CT images. After collecting network data and consulting relevant literature, a total of 2,338 CT images were sorted out as the data set for model training and testing (including 100 labeled CT images and 2,238 unlabeled CT images). Using the newly proposed Res2Net algorithm as the backbone algorithm of model design, CT images are input into the first two convolutional layers to extract high-resolution and semantically weak features. The attention mechanism was used to improve the expression ability of the boundary of the target region. Finally, the obtained low-level features were fed to the last three convolutional layers and aggregated with the high-level features. Finally, a Basic-Net segmentation model consisting of five convolutional layers and three attention modules was designed to obtain the preliminary segmentation results of the pulmonary infection region. Building upon this, a semi-supervised segmentation model, known as Semi-Net, was developed for COVID-19 CT images using a self-training approach. Experimental results demonstrate that the proposed model achieves strong performance, effectively addressing challenges such as lesion localization, fine-grained segmentation, and limited labeled data. By enhancing the model's ability to delineate infection boundaries and reducing classification errors, the system contributes to improved diagnostic accuracy for clinicians.

2 Segmentation Principle of Lung Infection in CT Images Based on Semi-Net

2.1 Basic-Net Model Design

The Basic-Net model is primarily based on the backbone network Res2Net, which incorporates an attention mechanism and a loss function to achieve fine segmentation of the edge contour of the target infected area. The Basic-Net model architecture is shown in Fig. 1

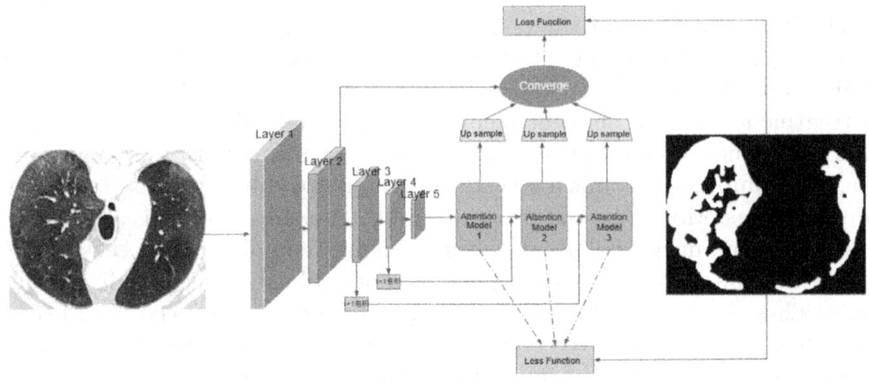

Fig. 1. Architecture of Basic-Net Model

CT images first pass through two convolutional layers to extract low-level features, followed by an attention mechanism to enhance boundary representation. A loss function measures the error between predicted and true segmentation maps, which is minimized through training to construct the Basic-Net model.

2.2 Attention Mechanism

The attention mechanism is a progressive framework strategy to distinguish the infected area by erasing [1,18]. This module mainly adaptively learns the output features from three parallel high-level features, then deletes the infected area with predicted errors from the high-level feature output, and gradually improves and accurately locates the infected area by sampling upward from a deeper level.

First, the advanced output feature $\{f_i, i = 3, 4, 5\}$ is fused with the edge attention feature $e_{\mathrm{att}} = f_2$, and then multiplied with the attention module weight to obtain the weight A_i of the output feature, as shown in Eq. (1):

$$R_i = \left(f_i, \mathrm{Dow}(e_{\mathrm{att}})\right)eA_i \tag{1}$$

where $\mathrm{Dow}(e_{\mathrm{att}})$ represents a downsampling operation, and $(f_i, \mathrm{Dow}(e_{\mathrm{att}}))$ represents a subsequent two-dimensional convolution layer that operates in series with 64 filters.

The weight A_i of the attention module is a weight used in the computer vision community [1] for the detection of prominent objects, which is defined as shown in the following.

$$A_i = \varepsilon\left(\Theta\left(\sigma\left(P\left(S_{i+1}\right)\right)\right)\right) \tag{2}$$

And, the $P(S_{i+1})$ means the sampling operation, $\sigma(\cdot)$ is the sigmoid function, $\Theta(\cdot)$ is the inverse operation of minus the input from the matrix E, in which all values are 1. This symbol ε represents the extension of the single-channel feature to 64 repeated tensors, which is related to each channel that inverts the candidate tensor in Eq. (1).

2.3   Loss Function Design

Through the attention mechanism mentioned above, the edge contour information retained by low-level features can be fed to high-level features at medium resolution to enhance the model's learning of edge contour features. For example, the feature map within the second convolution layer is first fed to a filter to generate the edge map. Then the difference between the generated edge map and the real map is measured, thus enhancing the feature extraction of the image edge contour, which can be calculated by the standard binary cross-entropy (BCE) loss function, as shown below.

$$L_{\text{edge}} = -\sum_{x=1}^{w}\sum_{y=1}^{h}\big(G_e \log(S_e) + (1 - G_e \log(1 - S_e))\big) \tag{3}$$

Here, (x, y) is the coordinate of each pixel in the predicted edge graph S_e and the edge true graph G_e. Additionally, G_e is calculated using the gradient of the real graph G_s. To clarify, w and h represent the width and the height of the related graph, respectively.

Then, the loss function L_{edge} is used to supervise the edge features. The segmentation loss L_{seg} is defined as a combination of the weighted Intersection over Union loss L_{IoU}^{w}, and the weighted binary cross-entropy loss L_{BCE}^{w}, applied to guide each segmentation. This is formally expressed in Eq. (4):

$$L_{\text{seg}} = L_{\text{IoU}}^{w} + \lambda L_{\text{BCE}}^{w} \tag{4}$$

Here, λ denotes the linear weight, which is set to 1 in this experiment. The two components of L_{seg} provide complementary supervision: global supervision through L_{IoU}^{w} and local supervision through L_{BCE}^{w}, enabling more precise segmentation. The weighted loss L_{IoU}^{w} emphasizes difficult pixels by assigning them higher weights, thereby highlighting their importance. The loss function L_{seg} is defined the same as [14, 17], and its validity has been verified.

Finally, the three feature outputs and the global graph are thoroughly supervised. Each layer is upsampled to the same size as the object-level segmentation truth graph G_s. Therefore, the total loss in Eq (4) is generalized as

$$L_{\text{total}} = L_{\text{seg}}(G_s, S_g^{\text{up}}) + L_{\text{edge}} + \sum_{i=3}^{5} L_{\text{seg}}(G_s, S_g^{\text{up}}) \tag{5}$$

where L_{seg} represents the segmentation loss computed between the predicted segmentation map G_s and the upsampled ground truth mask S_g^{up}. This loss integrates a weighted Intersection over Union (IoU) loss and a weighted binary cross-entropy (BCE) loss to provide both global and local supervision, enhancing segmentation precision. The term L_{edge} is used to supervise edge features and improve the model's ability to delineate infection boundaries accurately. Additionally, segmentation losses are applied to intermediate feature layers 3–5 (illustrated in Fig. 1) through deep supervision, as represented by the summation term. This multi-level guidance facilitates more robust feature learning and improves overall segmentation performance.

2.4 CT-Semi-net Model

Because it is difficult and time-consuming to segment the infected area of the lung manually, the number of CT images with segmentation annotations is minimal. To address this problem, this paper employs a semi-supervised strategy based on the self-training method to enhance the Basic-Net model. This strategy primarily utilizes a large number of unlabeled CT images to effectively enhance the training dataset by constructing pseudo-tags, thereby improving the model's performance. The primary process is divided into the following five steps:

1. The data samples are divided into two categories, namely the train set and the test set. The Basic-Net model is then used to train the labeled training set.
2. Prediction classification of unlabeled sample data is carried out through the model of trained data, and all predicted labels are used as "false labels" at the same time.
3. Combine these "pseudo-labeled" data to form a new data set to retrain the Basic-Net model, and generate the pseudo-labeled weight model after training.
4. Using the real data set to train the pseudo-label weight model, the CT-Semi-Net model can be generated.
5. The CT-Semi-Net model was used to test the test set and evaluate the performance.

It can be seen from the steps that constructing a pseudo-label dataset is crucial to the training of the semi-supervised model. The pseudo-label data set built in this paper is mainly based on a random sampling strategy, so as to expand the training data set gradually. Specifically, the steps described in Algorithm 1 are used to generate false labels for unlabeled CT images, and then the model is trained using the CT images with false labels through the associated method (which will be covered in Sect. 3.2).

3 Test Design and Process

3.1 Data Sources

The following three published data sets are used in this paper: the COVID-19 CT segmentation dataset, containing 100 labeled CT slices [20]; the COVID-19 CT ensemble dataset, containing 1,600 unlabeled CT slices [2]; and the COVID-19 CT test dataset, containing 638 images [20]. The types of data sets and data sources are shown in Table 1:

Table 1. COVID-19 CT data sets and their sources

Data Set	Source
COVID-19 CT segmentation data set [20]	https://medicalsegmentation.com/covid19/
COVID-19 CT ensemble data set [2]	https://github.com/ieee8023/covid-chestxray-dataset
COVID-19 CT test data set [20]	https://paperswithcode.com/dataset/covid-ct

The data of CT images in this table contains only one segmentation dataset, that is, the COVID-19 CT segmentation dataset [20], which includes 100 CT images marked with the pulmonary infection area of COVID-19 patients, all of which are collected by the Italian Society of Medical and Interventional Radiology. However, due to its small sample size, which consists of only 100 labeled images, this work on building the model creates a segmentation dataset based on semi-supervised COVID-19 infection. The COVID-19 CT segmentation dataset was constructed from a semi-supervised dataset [20] and the COVID-19 CT ensemble dataset [2]. Large-scale, unlabeled CT images were used to train the dataset, aiming to maximize the model's efficiency. In this paper, the COVID-19 CT segmentation dataset [20] was used as the labeled dataset. First, two low-resolution CT images with black backgrounds were removed from the dataset. Then, 45 CT images were randomly selected as training samples, 5 CT images were used for model validation, and the remaining 48 images were used for model testing. The unlabeled CT images were extracted from the COVID-19 CT ensemble dataset [2]. The COVID-19 CT test dataset [20] was used for the final evaluation of model performance, comprising 638 CT images (285 non-infected maps and 353 infected maps).

3.2   Model Training

The implementation details of the model designed in this paper are as follows:

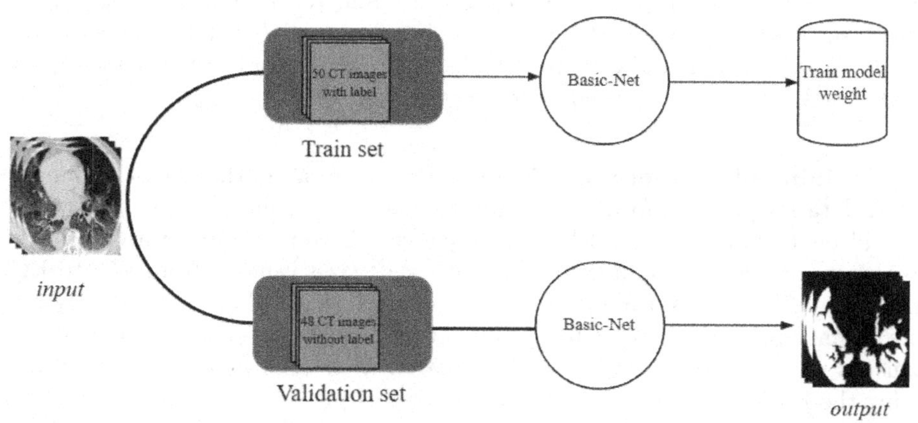

Fig. 2. Training and verification process of Basic-Net model

(1) Basic-Net Model Training. Figure 2 shows the training and verification process of the Basic-Net model on CT images. Both the training set and verification set of this model are from the COVID-19 CT segmentation data set [20], and the data set distribution method is described in Sect. 3.1.

(2) Pseudo-label Generation Process. The steps for generating pseudo-labels using the Basic-Net model are outlined in Algorithm 1, and pseudo-labels can be generated for unlabeled CT images through the process described in Algorithm 1. In this process, the number of CT images selected by random sampling is set to 5, i.e., $K = 5$. At the same time, the batch size is set to 16, and since the unlabeled data set contains 1,600 CT images, the process requires 320 iterations to generate the pseudo-labeled data set.

Algorithm 1. The pseudo-label training of the COVID-19 infection segmentation network model

---

Require: D_{Labeled} and $D_{\text{Unlabeled}}$
Ensure: Output result M
1: Build D_{Training} with D_{Labeled}
2: Train $M_{\text{Basic-Net}}$ using D_{Training}
3: Train K with trained $M_{\text{Basic-Net}}$ to build $D_{\text{Net-Labeled}}$
4: Expand training datasets with $D_{\text{Net-Labeled}}$, which is $D_{\text{Training}} = D_{\text{Training}} \cup D_{\text{Net-Labeled}}$
5: Remove K test images from $D_{\text{Unlabeled}}$
6: **repeat**
7:      Steps 3 to 5
8: **until** $D_{\text{Unlabeled}} = \varnothing$
9: **return** training model M

In Algorithm 1, D_{Labeled} means data sets with labels, $D_{\text{Unlabeled}}$ means data sets without labels, D_{Training} represents training data sets, and $D_{\text{Net-Labeled}}$ means data sets with network labels. The data included K CT images with false labels, $M_{\text{Basic-Net}}$ denoted COVID-19 infection segmentation network model, and K denoted K CT images randomly selected from the $D_{\text{Unlabeled}}$.

(3) Training of CT-Semi-net Model. Before training, the size of CT images in all data sets was uniformly adjusted to 352×352. A multi-scale strategy [19] is utilized to train the model. In this paper, different scaling ratios are first used to resample the training images, with scale sizes ranging from 0.75 to 1.25. Then, the CT-Basic-Net model is trained on the resampled images. Additionally, the Adam optimizer is used to optimize the parameters. The training process consists of two steps: first, 1,600 CT images with false labels are pre-trained using the Basic-net model (the batch size of this process is set to 24), and then 50 CT images with real image labels are trained (the batch size in this work is set to 16). Finally, the training of the CT-Semi-Net model is completed.

4   Result Analysis

4.1   Qualitative Analysis

For the evaluation of the Basic-Net and Semi-Net segmentation network models of COVID-19, to compare the effect of infection segmentation, the two latest models (U-Net and U-NET++) were used for comparative tests in this experiment. The visualization of the segmentation results of the pulmonary infection region is shown in Fig. 3.

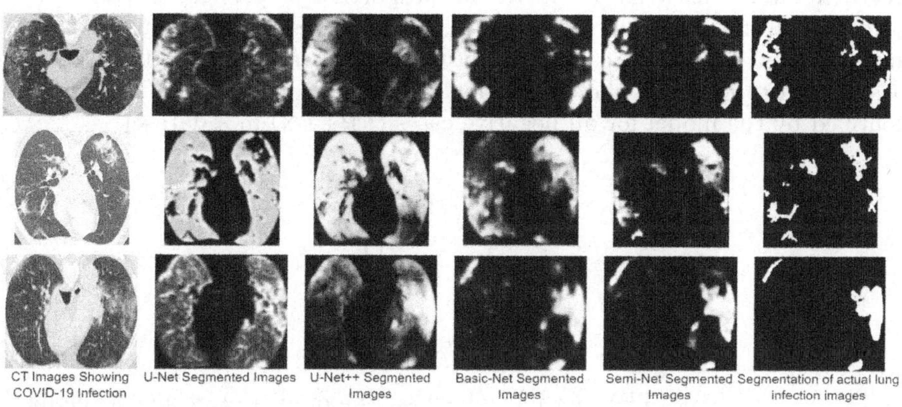

Fig. 3. Visual comparison of segmentation results of COVID-19 lung infection region

It can be clearly and intuitively reflected that the visualized images of the Basic-Net and CT-Semi-Net models designed in this paper are closest to the real ones, and the organization of wrong segmentation is tiny. On the contrary, the U-Net model yields numerous incorrect results in the organization's division. Although the U-NET++ model can improve the result, the performance is still not ideal, and there are still many partition errors in the organization. The excellent results of the Basic-Net model are attributed to the attention mechanism. Under this mechanism, the Basic-Net model can segment the edge contour of the infected area, thereby achieving a more effective segmentation.

Additionally, Fig. 3 confirms the advantages of semi-supervised learning strategies. It can be seen from the visualization that CT-Semi-Net has more accurate boundary segmentation results than Basic-Net, while Basic-Net gives relatively fuzzy boundaries.

4.2   Quantitative Analysis

To evaluate the effectiveness of the designed CT-Semi-Net segmentation model, this section employs commonly used evaluation indicators and methods in machine learning to assess the model's performance. The evaluation indicators selected for this model are Precision, Sensitivity, Specificity, and the Dice coefficient. These evaluation indices are the most commonly used in segmentation networks, measuring the similarity between two sets. In addition, this paper introduces three gold measures from the field of target region detection as additional evaluation indicators, namely, the Structure Measure [5], Enhanced Alignment Measures [6], and Mean Absolute Error (MAE).

The principles of Precision, Sensitivity, and Specificity are shown in Eq. (6), (7), (8). Precision is the proportion of actual cases (TP) to all positive cases (TP+FP) identified by the model. The accuracy rate is also referred to as the precision rate. Sensitivity refers to the proportion of positive instances (TP) correctly determined by the model for all positive cases (TP+FN) in the data set, and the sensitivity is also called the actual positive rate. Specificity, as opposed to sensitivity, describes the proportion of negative cases (FP+TN) correctly identified by the model for all negative cases (FP+TN) in a dataset.

$$\text{Precision} = \frac{\text{TP}}{\text{TP} + \text{FP}} \tag{6}$$

$$\text{Sensitivity} = \frac{\text{TP}}{\text{TP} + \text{FN}} \tag{7}$$

$$\text{Specificity} = \frac{\text{TP}}{\text{FP} + \text{TN}} \tag{8}$$

The true positive (TP) rate indicates that the prediction result of the model is true, and in fact the CT image is also true. The true negative (TN) rate indicates that the prediction result of the model is false, in fact, the CT image is also false. The false positive (FP) rate indicates that the prediction result of the model is true, but the CT image is false. Here the false negative (FN) rate indicates that the model prediction is false, and the CT image is in fact true.

Dice coefficient is a measure of the degree of similarity between sets, ranging from 0 to 1. As shown in Eq. (9), A represents the correct region of segmentation of COVID-19 CT images, and B represents the region obtained after segmentation by the Basic-net model of COVID-19. The calculated Dice coefficient represents the ratio between twice the overlap of the two regions and the sum of the two regions.

$$\text{Dice} = \frac{2\,A \cap B|}{|A| + |B|} \tag{9}$$

The Structure Measure is designed to measure the structural similarity between the target predicted region and the real region. This evaluation method is the same as that of the human visual system, as shown in Eq. (10):

$$S_\alpha = (1 - \alpha) \cdot S_o(S_p, G) + \alpha \cdot S_r(S_p, G) \tag{10}$$

S_α is the structure measure, where α is the balance factor between the object perceived similarity S_o and the region perceived similarity S_r. In this paper, the default setting ($\alpha = 0.5$) suggested in [5] is adopted for S_α.

The enhanced alignment measure is a metric proposed in recent years to evaluate the local and global similarity between two binary graphs, as shown in Eq. (11),

$$E_\varphi = \frac{1}{w \times h} \sum_x^w \sum_y^h \varphi\big(S_p(x,y) - G(x,y)\big) \tag{11}$$

where w and h are the width and height of the real CT map G of the target region, while (x,y) represents the coordinates of each pixel in the real map G of the region. The symbol φ is the enhanced alignment matrix related to the coordinates in the given graph. In this paper, the S_3 in the convolutional layer 3 with the Sigmoid function is taken as the final prediction S_p, and the prediction S_p is converted into a binary mask with a threshold from 0 to 255 to obtain the E_φ index value.

The MAE is used to measure the pixel orientation error between S_p and the real picture G of the target area, and its calculation is shown in Eq. (12).

$$\text{MAE} = \frac{1}{w \times h} \sum_x^w \sum_y^h \big|S_p(x,y) - G(x,y)\big| \tag{12}$$

The quantitative results of infected areas on the COVID-19 CT test data set are shown in Table 2.

Table 2. Quantitative results of infected areas on the COVID-19 CT test dataset

Network segmentation model	Dice	Sen.	Spec.	S_α	E_φ^{mean}	MAE
U–Net	0.439	0.534	0.858	0.622	0.625	0.186
U–Net++	0.581	0.672	0.902	0.722	0.720	0.120
Basic–Net	**0.682**	**0.692**	**0.943**	**0.781**	**0.838**	**0.082**
CT–Semi–Net	**0.739**	**0.725**	**0.960**	**0.800**	**0.894**	**0.064**

As shown in Table 2, the Basic-Net and Semi-Net models outperform the baseline U-Net and U-Net++ models across multiple evaluation metrics, including Dice, S_α, E_φ^{mean}, and MAE. Among them, the CT-Semi-Net model achieves the highest overall performance, followed by the Basic-Net model. These results suggest that the superior performance of Basic-Net and Semi-Net can be attributed to the choice of backbone network and the integration of attention mechanisms, which enhance the models' ability to capture discriminative features. Furthermore, by incorporating a semi-supervised strategy based on the self-training method into the Basic-Net architecture, the Dice coefficient improves by 6%, indicating better model fitting and further enhanced segmentation performance.

5   Conclusion

In this paper, CT-Semi-NET, a deep convolutional neural network-based segmentation method for identifying the infected area in COVID-19 lung CT images, was designed. The model was embedded in the Res2Net backbone network, and the attention mechanism enhanced the recognition of the infected area contour. In addition, a semi-supervised segmentation network model, CT-Semi-Net, based on a self-training method, is designed and developed to address the issue of low model efficiency resulting from the scarcity of high-quality labeled data. After conducting a large number of experiments and analyzing the research, the Basic-Net and CT-Semi-Net models proposed in this paper demonstrate exemplary performance. They can significantly enhance the screening efficiency of medical staff for patients infected with COVID-19. For example, quantifying areas of infection, monitoring longitudinal changes in disease, and mass screening for treatments. The model can also be applied to other related layer segmentation tasks, such as polyp segmentation and camouflage animal detection.

Although the model has achieved good results in segmenting infected areas, it has some limitations. On the one hand, because this design can only provide the work of infection segmentation area, in clinical practice, doctors often need to classify COVID-19 patients and then subdivide the infected area for further treatment. Therefore, an AI automatic diagnosis system that can integrate COVID-19 detection, lung infection segmentation, and quantification of infected regions into a unified framework is needed to utilize the model's characteristics more effectively and complete the screening of patients infected with COVID-19 more quickly and efficiently. On the other hand, the network model designed in this paper can only segment the infected area of 2D CT images, and cannot segment 3D CT images. Therefore, a general segmentation model can be designed in the future, which can segment both 2D CT and 3D CT images.

Acknowledgments. This work was supported by the National Natural Science Foundation of China (No. 62072157, 62476253), Key Industrial Projects in Henan Province (245101610001), the Natural Science Foundation of Henan province (202300410102, 242300421401), the Doctoral program of Henan Institute of Technology (KQ2002).

References

1. Chen, S., Tan, X., Wang, B., Hu, X.: Reverse attention for salient object detection. In: Proceedings of the European Conference on Computer Vision (ECCV), pp. 234–250 (2018)
2. Cohen, J.P., Morrison, P., Dao, L., Roth, K., Duong, T.Q., Ghassemi, M.: Covid-19 image data collection: prospective predictions are the future. arXiv preprint arXiv:2006.11988 (2020)
3. Ezhilraja, K., Shanmugavadivu, P.: Contrast enhancement of lung CT scan images using multi-level modified dualistic sub-image histogram equalization. In: 2022 International Conference on Automation, Computing and Renewable Systems (ICACRS), pp. 1009–1014 (2022). https://doi.org/10.1109/ICACRS55517.2022.10029217

4. Ezhilraja, K., Shanmugavadivu, P.: Performance evaluation of histogram equalization based enhancement on lung CT scan images. In: 2022 International Conference on Augmented Intelligence and Sustainable Systems (ICAISS), pp. 682–688 (2022). https://doi.org/10.1109/ICAISS55157.2022.10010831

5. Fan, D.P., Cheng, M.M., Liu, Y., Li, T., Borji, A.: Structure-measure: a new way to evaluate foreground maps. In: Proceedings of the IEEE International Conference on Computer Vision, pp. 4548–4557 (2017)

6. Fan, D.P., Gong, C., Cao, Y., Ren, B., Cheng, M.M., Borji, A.: Enhanced-alignment measure for binary foreground map evaluation. arXiv preprint arXiv:1805.10421 (2018)

7. Gao, S.H., Cheng, M.M., Zhao, K., Zhang, X.Y., Yang, M.H., Torr, P.: Res2net: a new multi-scale backbone architecture. IEEE Trans. Pattern Anal. Mach. Intell. **43**(2), 652–662 (2019)

8. He, K., Zhang, X., Ren, S., Sun, J.: Deep residual learning for image recognition. In: Proceedings of the IEEE Conference on Computer Vision and Pattern Recognition, pp. 770–778 (2016)

9. Hiraman, A., Viriri, S., Gwetu, M.: Lung tumor segmentation: a review of the state of the art. Front. Comput. Sci. **6**, 1423693 (2024)

10. Jiang, J., et al.: Multiple resolution residually connected feature streams for automatic lung tumor segmentation from CT images. IEEE Trans. Med. Imaging **38**(1), 134–144 (2018)

11. Jin, D., Xu, Z., Tang, Y., Harrison, A.P., Mollura, D.J.: CT-realistic lung nodule simulation from 3D conditional generative adversarial networks for robust lung segmentation. In: Frangi, A.F., Schnabel, J.A., Davatzikos, C., Alberola-López, C., Fichtinger, G. (eds.) MICCAI 2018. LNCS, vol. 11071, pp. 732–740. Springer, Cham (2018). https://doi.org/10.1007/978-3-030-00934-2_81

12. Keles, A., Keles, M.B., Keles, A.: Cov19-CNNet and cov19-resnet: diagnostic inference engines for early detection of covid-19. Cogn. Comput. **16**(4), 1612–1622 (2024)

13. Messay, T., Hardie, R.C., Tuinstra, T.R.: Segmentation of pulmonary nodules in computed tomography using a regression neural network approach and its application to the lung image database consortium and image database resource initiative dataset. Med. Image Anal. **22**(1), 48–62 (2015)

14. Qin, X., Zhang, Z., Huang, C., Gao, C., Dehghan, M., Jagersand, M.: Basnet: Boundary-aware salient object detection. In: Proceedings of the IEEE/CVF Conference on Computer Vision and Pattern Recognition, pp. 7479–7489 (2019)

15. Shi, Y., Gottipati, A., Yan, Y.: Path-CT image registration with self-supervised vision transformer for lung cancer. In: 2024 IEEE International Symposium on Biomedical Imaging (ISBI), pp. 1–5 (2024).https://doi.org/10.1109/ISBI56570.2024.10635584

16. Wang, S., et al.: Central focused convolutional neural networks: developing a data-driven model for lung nodule segmentation. Med. Image Anal. **40**, 172–183 (2017)

17. Wei, J., Wang, S., Huang, Q.: F^3net: fusion, feedback and focus for salient object detection. In: Proceedings of the AAAI Conference on Artificial Intelligence, vol. 34, pp. 12321–12328 (2020)

18. Wei, Y., Feng, J., Liang, X., Cheng, M.M., Zhao, Y., Yan, S.: Object region mining with adversarial erasing: a simple classification to semantic segmentation approach. In: Proceedings of the IEEE Conference on Computer Vision and Pattern Recognition, pp. 1568–1576 (2017)

19. Wu, Z., Su, L., Huang, Q.: Stacked cross refinement network for edge-aware salient object detection. In: Proceedings of the IEEE/CVF International Conference on Computer Vision, pp. 7264–7273 (2019)
20. Yang, X., He, X., Zhao, J., Zhang, Y., Zhang, S., Xie, P.: Covid-CT-dataset: a CT scan dataset about covid-19. arXiv preprint arXiv:2003.13865 (2020)
21. Zhang, S., Zhao, Y., Liang, Y.: Aacflow: an end-to-end model based on attention augmented convolutional neural network and flow-attention mechanism for identification of anticancer peptides. Bioinformatics **40**(3), btae142 (2024)
22. Zheng, J., Wang, L., Gui, J., Yussuf, A.H.: Study on lung CT image segmentation algorithm based on threshold-gradient combination and improved convex hull method. Sci. Rep. **14**(1), 17731 (2024)
23. Zhu, R., Li, X., Huang, S., Zhang, X.: Multimodal medical image fusion using adaptive co-occurrence filter-based decomposition optimization model. Bioinformatics **38**(3), 818–826 (2021). https://doi.org/10.1093/bioinformatics/btab721

Dynamic Knowledge-Aware LLM for Adverse Drug Reaction Entity Recognition

Yunzhi Qiu[1], Bo Zhang[1], Haohao Zhu[1], Changrong Min[2], Haifeng Liu[3], Tongxuan Zhang[4], Liang Yang[1], and Hongfei Lin[1(✉)]

[1] School of Computer Science and Technology, Dalian University of Technology, Dalian, Liaoning, China
`yzqiu@mail.dlut.edu.cn`, `hflin@dlut.edu.cn`
[2] Criminal Investigation Police University of China, Shenyang, Liaoning, China
[3] Nanjing Normal University, Nanjing, Jiangsu, China
[4] Tianjin Normal University, Tianjin, China

Abstract. Adverse drug reaction (ADR) entity recognition is crucial for ensuring patient medication safety and remains a focus of sustained attention in biomedical research. However, distinct from general-domain entity recognition, ADR entity recognition from social media faces two key challenges: **informal linguistic expressions** and **concept representation diversity**. The existing methods mainly focus on introducing domain knowledge into traditional small language models. However, how to incorporate external knowledge into large language models remains a blank. To address these challenges, we propose DKLLM, a **D**ynamic **K**nowledge-aware **L**arge **L**anguage **M**odel specifically designed for ADR entity extraction. Our approach introduces the Unified Medical Language System (UMLS) as a biomedical knowledge base, where conceptual definitions enhance model understanding of informal social media expressions, while unique Concept Unique Identifiers (CUIs) help mitigate conceptual expression variability. Furthermore, we design a plug-and-play Dynamic Adapter module (D-Adapter) that incorporates gating mechanisms to filter noise from external knowledge. Finally, we explore two integration methods: D-Adapter-aware Attention Network(DAN) and D-Adapter-aware Feedforward Network(DFN). Experimental results demonstrate that DKLLM outperforms all baseline methods while updating fewer than 4% of parameters. The model achieves an average F1-score improvement of 3.27% across two public datasets.

Keywords: Adverse drug reaction · Large Language Model · Named Entity Recognition · Adapter · External Knowledge

1 Introduction

Adverse drug reactions (ADRs) are harmful and unintended responses that occur when using a qualified drug at normal doses. In the United States alone, over

Y. Qiu and B. Zhang contributed equally to this work.

1 million people visit emergency departments annually because of ADRs [1]. Therefore, research on ADRs is critical for ensuring patient safety and optimizing pharmacotherapy. Among these efforts, ADR entity recognition serves as a key task in drug safety monitoring, where the core objective is to automatically identify ADR entities from textual data to support pharmacovigilance and clinical decision making. This task can be viewed as a specialized form of named entity recognition (NER).

The early detection of ADRs primarily relies on reporting during clinical trials. However, owing to limited sample sizes and strict participant selection criteria, many ADRs may not be detected until after drug approval. In recent years, researchers have made significant efforts to advance the study of ADR entity recognition from social media. In terms of resource development, Karimi et al. released a series of datasets, including CADEC V1 and V2 versions [2,3]. Regarding workshops and shared tasks, the continuous organization of the Social Media Mining for Health Applications (SMM4H) task has effectively promoted research in this field [4]. Despite these efforts, the extraction of ADRs from social media still faces major challenges.

- **informal linguistic expressions**: The colloquial nature of social media expressions leads to insufficient conceptual understanding by models. Unlike conventional biomedical texts, social media data typically exhibit informal expressions that contain substantial noise. For instance, the concept "*#headache*" is composed of the special character "*#*" and "headache", which undoubtedly presents a challenge to the model's understanding.
- **concept representation diversity**: The diversity of concept expressions tends to cause entity name sparsity, making it difficult to achieve comprehensive learning from limited annotated corpora. For example, the ADR entity "*headache*" has multiple expression forms, such as "*Cephalodynia*" and "*Head Pain*".

To address the aforementioned two challenges, researchers have conducted extensive explorations, primarily focusing on incorporating external knowledge into models. For instance, Stanovsky et al. proposed embedding DBpedia knowledge graphs into models [5], while Li et al. alleviated the issue by introducing an ADR lexicon [6]. Zhang et al. integrated knowledge from the PubMed database into social media-based ADR entity recognition models [7]. Although these methods have effectively addressed the issues, they have primarily focused on incorporating domain knowledge into traditional small language models. How to introduce external knowledge into large language models remains an unexplored area. In particular, under the supervised learning paradigm, the effective integration of external knowledge into large language models is still an urgent problem to be solved.

Based on this analysis, we propose a novel adverse drug reaction entity recognition method called the DKLLM. First, to mitigate the inherent lack of domain knowledge in LLMs when handling domain-specific problems, we incorporate two types of domain knowledge from the UMLS: CUIs and definition information. The retrieved knowledge undergoes filtering to form contextual knowledge, thereby compensating for the domain knowledge gap in the general models. Furthermore, to ensure relevance of incorporated knowledge, we design a plug-and-play D-Adapter. This adapter not only integrates domain knowledge, but also employs a gating mechanism to filter out noise from external knowledge and selectively retain contextually relevant information. Finally, we develop two distinct approaches for inserting the D-Adapter into LLMs: DAN and DFN.

The contributions of this study are summarized as follows.

- We propose the first end-to-end framework that integrates domain knowledge into LLMs for ADR entity recognition, effectively addressing the lack of domain-specific knowledge in LLMs.
- We design a plug-and-play D-Adapter module that successfully incorporates domain knowledge while effectively preventing noise introduction from external knowledge sources.
- We explore two D-Adapter injection methods for knowledge integration.
- Experimental results demonstrate that our approach achieves state-of-the-art performance across two datasets while requiring updates to less than 4% of model parameters.

2   Related Work

Early approaches for ADR entity recognition primarily relied on machine learning [8]. With the advent of attention mechanisms [7,9], pre-trained language models have been introduced to this task, including encoder-only architectures such as BERT [10] and encoder-decoder models such as T5 [11]. For instance, to handle various entity extraction types (flat entities, overlapping entities, and discontinuous entities), [12] reformulated the task as a sequence-to-sequence generation problem and achieved performance improvements under a multitask learning framework. Recently, researchers have begun to explore the application of LLMs technology in ADR entity recognition. To the best of our knowledge, the current approaches mainly adopt two paradigms: one directly utilizes LLMs api for zero-shot or few-shot learning [13,14]. For example, [13] investigated the potential of LLMs in ADR NER tasks through prompt engineering to enhance performance while reducing reliance on large annotated datasets. The other paradigm involves instruction fine-tuning to adapt LLMs to specific domain tasks, as demonstrated by [15] who fine-tuned various LLMs (e.g., GPT-2, GPT-3.5, and LLaMA-2). In contrast to these approaches, we propose an end-to-end framework that injects domain knowledge into LLMs to provide more effective ADR entity recognition.

3   Methodology

The proposed DKLLM framework is shown in Fig. 1. The LLMs in this work utilize the open-source LLaMA model[1]. Compared with the standard LLaMA,

---

[1] https://huggingface.co/meta-llama/Meta-Llama-3-8B-Instruct.

DKLLM exhibits two primary distinctions. First, DKLLM takes both text and knowledge features as input, enabling end-to-end fine-tuning that incorporates external knowledge into the LLaMA. Second, a D-Adapter is inserted into each Transformer layer to effectively integrate external knowledge with LLaMA.

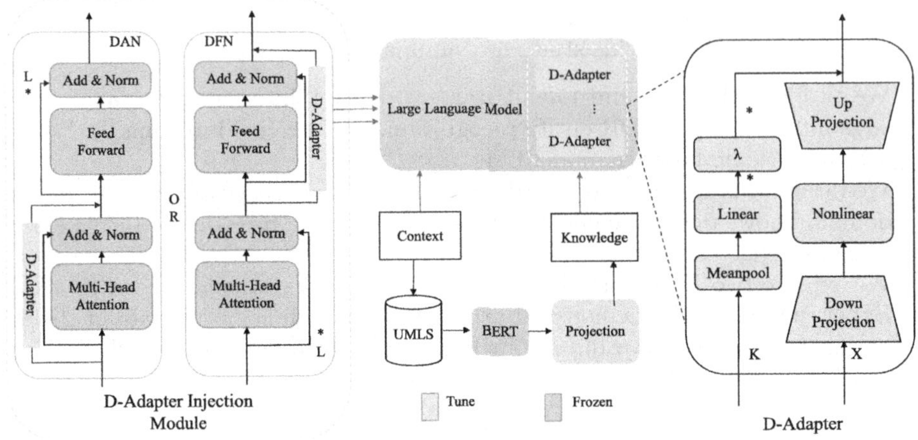

Fig. 1. The overall architecture of the DKLLM.

3.1   Knowledge Acquisition Module

This section details the methodology for extracting ADR domain knowledge from the UMLS. UMLS comprises three primary knowledge sources: Metathesaurus, Semantic Network, and Specialist Lexicon. The Metathesaurus serves as the core component of UMLS, aggregating terms from various controlled vocabularies (including MeSH, SNOMED CT, and ICD) and clustering synonyms into unified concepts through Concept Unique Identifiers (CUIs), enabling terminology mapping and conversion. We aim to obtain both the CUI and the corresponding definition knowledge from the UMLS knowledge base for input text sequences. Fortunately, MetaMap[2] provides a convenient UMLS concept mapping tool for acquiring knowledge. Note that we only consider the mappings with the highest MetaMap Index (MMI) scores. During the mapping process, each word in the sequence may have zero or one corresponding CUI and definition. Taking the sentence "*#headache & stomach ache. i'm never forgetting my effexor again.*" as an example, the MetaMap tool can identify biomedical concepts such as "*headache*", "*stomach ache*", and "*effexor*". CUI information helps address concept expression variability, while definition knowledge assists model comprehension of concepts, mitigating the challenges posed by colloquial social media expressions. We represent the tokens identified from the MetaMap tool as K_t, CUI information as K_c, and definition knowledge as K_d. To ensure consistency between the two types of knowledge, we introduce three prompt texts: $P_1 = $ "*For*

---

[2] https://lhncbc.nlm.nih.gov/ii/tools/MetaMap.html.

the token span", $P_2 =$"*the corresponding UMLS CUI is*", and $P_3 = $ "*the corresponding definition is*". Using the concatenation operator $\oplus$, the final knowledge representation can be expressed as shown in Eq. 1:

$$K = P_1 \oplus K_t \oplus P_2 \oplus K_c \oplus P_3 \oplus K_d \tag{1}$$

3.2 Dynamic Adapter

Through the knowledge acquisition module described above, we obtain the domain knowledge K corresponding to text T. Our objective is to integrate domain knowledge into the LLaMA model. Inspired by recent work on adapters [16,17], we propose a novel dynamic adapter, as shown in Fig. 1, that injects domain knowledge into LLaMA while reducing interference from noise in the knowledge. Before feeding text and knowledge into the adapter, dimension-matching operations are required, consisting of two main steps: The first step is encoding text and knowledge as vector representations. For text, we set the LLaMA input "*instruction*" as "*You are a knowledge-based information extraction system. Given a sentence, your task is to extract all adverse reaction entities based on the corresponding knowledge.*". Using LLaMA's word-embedding mapping function, we transform the input text T and instruction into the corresponding vector representations, denoted as $\mathbf{X} = \{\mathbf{x}_1, \mathbf{x}_2, \cdots, \mathbf{x}_m\}$, where m represents the number of words in the text and $\mathbf{X} \in \mathbb{R}^{m*4096}$. For knowledge, we employ the pretrained BERT model[3] to map knowledge K into vector representations $\mathbf{K} = \{\mathbf{k}_1, \mathbf{k}_2, \cdots, \mathbf{k}_n\}$, where n denotes knowledge length and $\mathbf{K} \in \mathbb{R}^{n*768}$. The second step is to transform the dimensionality of the knowledge vectors $\mathbf{K}$ to match the text vectors $\mathbf{X}$'s dimension, as formalized in Eq. 2:

$$\mathbf{K} \leftarrow \text{Projection}(\mathbf{K}) \tag{2}$$

where Projection() represents the dimension transformation operation, $\mathbf{K} \in \mathbb{R}^{n*4096}$.

The key difference between our proposed dynamic adapter and the traditional adapter lies in the incorporation of a dynamic gating mechanism to filter noise from knowledge. Specifically, for text vectors, we first apply a standard bottleneck operation: downsampling text $\mathbf{X}$, passing the output through an activation function, and then performing upsampling, as shown in Eq. 3:

$$\overline{\mathbf{X}} = \text{Linear}_{Up}(\text{SiLU}((\text{Linear}_{Down}(\mathbf{X}))) \tag{3}$$

where $\overline{\mathbf{X}} \in R^{m*4096}$, Linear_{Up} denotes upsampling, SiLU denotes the activation function, and Linear_{Down} denotes downsampling. For knowledge vectors, we first apply average pooling and linear scaling and then add a learnable scaling weight to the knowledge vectors, as shown in Eq. 4:

$$\overline{\mathbf{K}} = \lambda \cdot \text{SiLU}(\text{Linear}(\text{Meanpool}(\mathbf{K}))) \tag{4}$$

---

[3] https://huggingface.co/google-bert/bert-base-uncased.

where λ is a dynamically learnable parameter that functions similarly to a gating mechanism, regulating the influence of knowledge vectors on text. Finally, we multiply knowledge $\overline{\mathbf{K}}$ and text $\overline{\mathbf{X}}$ as shown in Eq. 5:

$$\mathbf{X}_K = \overline{\mathbf{K}}.\overline{\mathbf{X}} \tag{5}$$

3.3 D-Adapter Injection Network

Taking LLaMA as an example, the DKLLM combines D-Adapter with LLaMA, where the adapter is integrated into each transformer layer of LLaMA to inject external knowledge. As previously described, given text $\mathbf{X} = \{\mathbf{x}_1, \mathbf{x}_2, \cdots, \mathbf{x}_m\}$ and knowledge $\mathbf{K} = \{\mathbf{k}_1, \mathbf{k}_2, \cdots, \mathbf{k}_n\}$, we fed both text and knowledge into the transformer decoder. Assuming that the LLaMA model contains L Transformer layers, we consider the ℓ-th transformer layer $(\ell < L)$ as an example. The input text and knowledge representations for the ℓth transformer decoder layer can be denoted as $\mathbf{E}^{\ell-1}$ and $\mathbf{K}$ respectively.

Note that based on the insertion position of D-Adapter within the Transformer architecture, we design two integration modes: D-Adapter-aware Attention Network and D-Adapter-aware Feedforward Network. Taking the D-Adapter-aware Attention Network as an example, we present the injection process of the D-Adapter-aware Attention Network.

$$
\begin{aligned}
\mathbf{H} &= \mathbf{E}^{\ell-1} + \mathrm{MHAtt}(\mathrm{LN}(\mathbf{E}^{\ell-1})), \\
\mathbf{G} &= \text{D-Adapter}(\mathbf{E}^{\ell-1}, \mathbf{K}), \\
\mathbf{H}' &= \mathbf{H} + \mathbf{G}, \\
\mathbf{E}^{\ell} &= \mathbf{H}' + \mathrm{FFN}(\mathrm{LN}(\mathbf{H}'))
\end{aligned}
\tag{6}
$$

where $\mathbf{E}^{\ell}$ represents the output of the ℓ-th transformer layer and $\mathbf{E}^0 = \mathbf{X}$. LN denotes layer normalization, MHAtt denotes the multi-head attention mechanism, and FFN refers to a two-layer feedforward network with a SiLU activation function. This yields the output of the ℓ-th transformer layer enriched with external knowledge.

3.4 Training Objective

During DKLLM training, only the D-Adapter and dimension transformation parameters underwent updates, whereas both the LLaMA and BERT parameters remained frozen. The cross-entropy loss objective minimizes the discrepancy between the predicted probability distributions and the true distributions, thereby improving the predictive accuracy of the model. By minimizing this loss function, the model learns to generate more accurate and contextually relevant tokens given the input text and corresponding knowledge. By fine-tuning the dynamic adapter and dimension transformation matrix parameters, the model achieves a better integration of knowledge, resulting in more precise and informative outputs. The optimization process is formally defined as follows:

$$Loss = - \sum_i \log p_\theta(Y_i | Y_{<i}, T, K) \tag{7}$$

where $Loss$ represents the generation loss of the model and Y_i denotes the i-th token in the generated entity sequence. The term $p_\theta(Y_i | Y_{<i}, C, K)$ formally describes the entity generation process that combines text T and knowledge K through the D-Adapter.

Table 1. An Illustration of the prompt framework.

Prompt types	Examples
Task Description	Identify the adverse reaction entities in the given text. Please refer to the examples below:
Few-shot Demonstration	Input: The patient experienced nausea and dizziness after taking the medication.
	Output: nausea;dizziness
	Input: The patient felt fine after taking the medication.
	Output: no adverse reaction entities found.

4   Experimental Setup

4.1   Datasets

We evaluate our method on two public ADR entity recognition datasets: CADEC [2] and SMM4H2020[4]. The CADEC dataset includes both discontinuous and flat entities. We adopt the same methodology for dataset splitting as [18] to maintain consistency with previous studies. The number of samples in the training, validation, and test sets is 5340, 1097, and 1160, respectively. The SMM4H2020 dataset contains only flat entities. Because the original dataset provides only training and test sets, we randomly split the training set into training and validation sets in an 8:2 ratio, and the numbers of samples in the training, validation, and test sets are 687, 172, and 216, respectively.

4.2   Implementation Details

The experiments are implemented using PyTorch and trained on an RTX 3090 GPU (24GB). We employ the AdamW optimizer with dataset-specific learning rates of 5e-4 for CADEC and 5e-5 for the SMM4H2020 dataset. Our training configuration uses a 0.1 warmup ratio, 0.05 weight decay, 0.05 dropout rate, and

---

[4] https://huggingface.co/datasets/KevinSpaghetti/smm4h20.

a batch size of 1. Each model undergoes two training epochs. For knowledge representation, we set the vector length $n = 16$ to maintain an optimal balance between representation capacity and computational efficiency.

We employ exact-match evaluation criteria where predicted entity text must exactly match gold-standard entities to be considered correct. To comprehensively assess DKLLM's performance, we report three standard metrics: precision (P), recall (R), and micro-averaged F1 score (F1).

4.3   Baseline Models

To comprehensively evaluate the effectiveness of DKLLM, we compare it with two categories of baseline models. The first group comprises Small Language Model(SLM) approaches, such as **CRF** [19], **LSTM-CRF** [20], **Transition-basedNER** [18], **Maximal Clique** [21], **Pointer-Network** [22], **Bart-NER** [23], **DebiasNER** [24], **W2NER** [25], **MMT** [26], **MC-DRE** [27]. For all small model approaches, we directly report the experimental results from the original papers. It is worth noting that owing to differences in experimental data processing, no directly comparable small model results are available for the SMM4H2020 dataset.

The second category consists of methods that employ LLMs for ADR entity recognition. These include two types: LLMs fine-tuned with LoRA (**LLM-lora**) and LLM-based API approaches (**LLM-api**). Since existing large model methods have not been tested on two datasets, we implement both types of LLM approaches across all datasets. For the first type, due to computational constraints in fine-tuning LLMs, we use LoRA [28], an efficient parameter fine-tuning method, to evaluate three open-source LLMs on two datasets. The prompt used is: *"Your task is to generate all adverse reaction entities in the following text."* The three open-source models tested are: **Mistral-7B**[5], **Qwen2-7B**[6], and **LLaMA3-8B**[7]. For the second type, given the high cost of API-based LLMs calls, we evaluate only three LLMs on the two datasets. To enhance performance, we adopt a few-shot setup. The prompt design is detailed in the Table 1. By including two representative demonstrations, the prompt not only guides the model to follow a specified output format but also provides direct task evidence and reference for predictions. The three LLMs tested are: **LLaMA3-70B**[8], **GPT3.5**[9], and **GPT4o**[10].

5   Results and Analysis

Table 2 presents the entity recognition performance of the DKLLM model and baseline methods on the CADEC and SMM4H2020 datasets. Our proposed

---

[5] https://huggingface.co/mistralai/Mistral-7B-Instruct-v0.3.

[6] https://huggingface.co/Qwen/Qwen2-7B-Instruct.

[7] https://huggingface.co/meta-llama/Meta-Llama-3-8B-Instruct.

[8] https://huggingface.co/meta-llama/Meta-Llama-3-70B.

[9] https://openai.com/index/chatgpt/.

[10] https://openai.com/index/hello-gpt-4o/.

DKLLM model includes two variants: **DAN**, **DFN**, which represent the injection of D-Adapter into the attention mechanism, and feedforward neural network, respectively. **w/o knowledge** and **w/o gate** represent the versions of the DKLLM model where the external knowledge module and the gating module are removed, respectively. Notably, the bold font in the tables indicates the best results among all models. PTT is the proportion of trainable parameters to total parameters. The following conclusions can be drawn from Table 2:

1) Compared with the baseline methods, the DKLLM approach achieves the best performance across two datasets. Particularly, on the SMM4H2020 dataset, DKLLM(DAN) improves the F1 score by 4.13% over the best baseline results. These results demonstrate that DKLLM exhibits strong performance advantages in handling different types of NER tasks (both flat and discontinuous entities), thereby enabling more accurate entity identification and classification. This improvement likely stems from DKLLM's ability to fully leverage the powerful capabilities of LLMs in text understanding, generation, and generalization while effectively mitigating hallucination issues through integration with external knowledge bases, thereby enhancing performance on ADR entity recognition tasks.

Table 2. The overall performance for the CADEC and SMM4H2020 datasets.

	Models	CADEC			SMM4H2020			PTT(%)
		P(%)	R(%)	F1(%)	P(%)	R(%)	F1(%)	
SLM	CRF	64.40	56.50	60.20	–	–	–	100
	LSTM-CRF	67.80	64.99	66.36	–	–	–	100
	Transition-based	68.90	69.00	69.00	–	–	–	100
	Maximal Clique	70.50	72.50	71.50	–	–	–	100
	Pointer-Network	75.50	71.80	72.40	–	–	–	100
	BartNER	70.08	71.21	70.64	–	–	–	100
	DebiasNER	71.35	71.86	71.60	–	–	–	100
	W2NER	74.09	72.35	73.21	–	–	–	100
	MMT	73.40	74.14	73.77	–	–	-	100
	MC-DRE	–	–	76.50	–	–	–	100
LLM-lora	Qwen2-7B	59.86	72.96	65.76	53.66	57.68	55.60	2.08
	Mistral-7B	64.50	69.24	66.77	63.76	69.85	66.67	2.26
	LLaMA3-8B	65.61	76.63	70.69	70.03	65.05	67.45	2.05
LLM-api	LLaMA3-70B	50.04	37.56	42.91	28.51	21.95	24.80	0
	GPT3.5	55.34	39.20	45.89	24.32	18.82	21.22	0
	GPT4o	57.85	39.79	47.15	38.43	28.92	33.00	0
DKLLM	DAN	**78.87**	75.59	77.20	**73.98**	69.34	**71.58**	3.34
	w/o knowledge	77.50	75.41	76.44	59.86	61.32	60.59	3.34
	w/o gate	77.98	74.41	76.16	72.26	68.99	70.59	3.34
	DFN	78.50	**76.29**	**77.38**	72.30	**70.03**	71.15	3.34
	w/o knowledge	78.11	73.30	75.63	63.10	59.58	61.29	3.34
	w/o gate	77.76	74.36	76.02	72.45	66.90	69.57	3.34

2) The performances of models with different parameter scales for this task are compared. By analyzing the relationship between model performance and

the proportion of trained parameters (PTT), the following conclusions can be drawn. Lower PPT values can significantly reduce training costs but may limit the model's adaptability to specific tasks. Higher PPT values can enhance model adaptability but increase training costs. Although the DKLLM model has a higher number of trained parameters than the models using LoRA fine-tuning, it generally achieves more efficient performance improvements than LoRA-based methods.

3) Removing external knowledge from DKLLM leads to performance declines for both DKLLM(DAN) and DKLLM(DFN) across all datasets. The F1 scores decrease by {0.76%, 10.99%} and {1.75%, 9.86%} for the CADEC and SMM4H2020 datasets respectively. We observe notably smaller impacts on CADEC compared to the SMM4H2020 dataset, potentially because SMM4H2020 contains expressions such as "#headache" absent in CADEC. Our external knowledge concept definitions effectively mitigate such cases by reducing special symbol interference.

4) Removing the gating mechanism from the DKLLM model results in performance degradation for both DKLLM (DAN) and DKLLM (DFN) across the CADEC and SMM4H2020 datasets. In terms of the F1 score, the decreases are {1.04%, 0.99%} and {1.36%, 1.58%}, respectively. These results indicate that the incorporated external knowledge contains some noise, the proposed gating mechanism effectively mitigates its impact, thereby enhancing model performance. For example, in the SMM4H2020 dataset, the MetaMap system incorrectly identified the concept *"my"* in the sample *"between the fucking redbull and vyvanse i popped to energize my triple yesterday... couldn't fall asleep for the life of me."* as CUI: C0024552, mistakenly interpreting *"my"* as a Southeast Asian country, Malaysia.

6   Conclusion

In this study, we present DKLLM, a novel framework for adverse drug reaction entity recognition that dynamically integrates domain knowledge to enhance large language model performance. Specifically, we incorporate two types of domain knowledge from the UMLS biomedical repository: CUI and concept definitions, which are systematically combined with the LLMs through a D-Adapter module. This adapter not only facilitates effective knowledge integration but also employs gating mechanisms to select contextually relevant knowledge while filtering noise. The experimental results demonstrate state-of-the-art performance across two benchmark datasets while updating fewer than 4% of the model parameters, confirming both efficiency and effectiveness. Future work will explore applications in related medical domains such as drug interaction monitoring, while investigating multisource knowledge integration to address potential knowledge gaps and further improve model generalization and practical utility.

Acknowledgement. This work is supported by grant from the Natural Science Foundation of China (No. 62306213, No. 62302076).

References

1. Sarkar, U., López, A., Maselli, J.H., Gonzales, R.: Adverse drug events in us adult ambulatory medical care. Health Serv. Res. **46**(5), 1517–1533 (2011)
2. Karimi, S., Metke-Jimenez, A., Kemp, M., Wang, C.: Cadec: a corpus of adverse drug event annotations. J. Biomed. Inform. **55**, 73–81 (2015)
3. Dai, X., Karimi, S., Sarker, A., Hachey, B., Paris, C.: Multiade: a multi-domain benchmark for adverse drug event extraction. J. Biomed. Inform. **160**, 104744 (2024)
4. Weissenbacher, D., et al.: Overview of the seventh social media mining for health applications (# smm4h) shared tasks at coling 2022. In: Proceedings of the Seventh Workshop on Social Media Mining for Health Applications, Workshop & Shared Task, pp. 221–241 (2022)
5. Stanovsky, G., Gruhl, D., Mendes, P.: Recognizing mentions of adverse drug reaction in social media using knowledge-infused recurrent models. In: Proceedings of the 15th Conference of the European Chapter of the Association for Computational Linguistics: Volume 1, Long Papers. pp. 142–151 (2017)
6. Li, Z., Yang, Z., Wang, L., Zhang, Y., Lin, H., Wang, J.: Lexicon knowledge boosted interaction graph network for adverse drug reaction recognition from social media. IEEE J. Biomed. Health Inform. **25**(7), 2777–2786 (2020)
7. Zhang, T., et al.: Adversarial transfer network with bilinear attention for the detection of adverse drug reactions from social media. Appl. Soft Comput. **106**, 107358 (2021)
8. Yates, A., Goharian, N., Frieder, O.: Extracting adverse drug reactions from social media. In: Proceedings of the AAAI Conference on Artificial Intelligence, vol. 29 (2015)
9. Kayesh, H., Islam, M.S., Wang, J., Ohira, R., Wang, Z.: Scan: a shared causal attention network for adverse drug reactions detection in tweets. Neurocomputing **479**, 60–74 (2022)
10. Devlin, J., Chang, M.W., Lee, K., Toutanova, K.: Bert: pre-training of deep bidirectional transformers for language understanding. In: Proceedings of the 2019 Conference of the North American Chapter of the Association for Computational Linguistics: Human Language Technologies, Volume 1 (long and short papers), pp. 4171–4186 (2019)
11. Raffel, C., et al.: Exploring the limits of transfer learning with a unified text-to-text transformer. J. Mach. Learn. Res. **21**(140), 1–67 (2020)
12. Raval, S., Sedghamiz, H., Santus, E., Alhanai, T., Ghassemi, M., Chersoni, E.: Exploring a unified sequence-to-sequence transformer for medical product safety monitoring in social media. In: 2021 Findings of the Association for Computational Linguistics, Findings of ACL: EMNLP 2021. pp. 3534–3546. Association for Computational Linguistics (ACL) (2021)
13. Hu, Y., et al.: Improving large language models for clinical named entity recognition via prompt engineering. J. Am. Med. Inform. Assoc. **31**(9), 1812–1820 (2024)
14. Gu, Y., et al.: Distilling large language models for biomedical knowledge extraction: a case study on adverse drug events. arXiv preprint arXiv:2307.06439 (2023)
15. Li, Y., et al.: Improving entity recognition using ensembles of deep learning and fine-tuned large language models: A case study on adverse event extraction from vaers and social media. J. Biomed. Inform. 104789 (2025)
16. Houlsby, N., et al.: Parameter-efficient transfer learning for NLP. In: International Conference on Machine Learning, pp. 2790–2799. PMLR (2019)

17. Zhang, R., et al.: Llama-adapter: Efficient fine-tuning of large language models with zero-initialized attention. In: The Twelfth International Conference on Learning Representations (2024)
18. Dai, X., Karimi, S., Hachey, B., Paris, C.: An effective transition-based model for discontinuous ner. In: Proceedings of the 58th Annual Meeting of the Association for Computational Linguistics. pp. 5860–5870 (2020)
19. Metke-Jimenez, A., Karimi, S.: Concept identification and normalisation for adverse drug event discovery in medical forums. In: BMDID@ ISWC (2016)
20. Tang, B., Hu, J., Wang, X., Chen, Q.: Recognizing continuous and discontinuous adverse drug reaction mentions from social media using LSTM-CRF. Wirel. Commun. Mob. Comput. **2018**(1), 2379208 (2018)
21. Wang, Y., Yu, B., Zhu, H., Liu, T., Yu, N., Sun, L.: Discontinuous named entity recognition as maximal clique discovery. In: Proceedings of the 59th Annual Meeting of the Association for Computational Linguistics and the 11th International Joint Conference on Natural Language Processing (Volume 1: Long Papers), pp. 764–774 (2021)
22. Fei, H., Ji, D., Li, B., Liu, Y., Ren, Y., Li, F.: Rethinking boundaries: end-to-end recognition of discontinuous mentions with pointer networks. In: Proceedings of the AAAI Conference on Artificial Intelligence, vol. 35, pp. 12785–12793 (2021)
23. Yan, H., Gui, T., Dai, J., Guo, Q., Zhang, Z., Qiu, X.: A unified generative framework for various NER subtasks. In: Proceedings of the 59th Annual Meeting of the Association for Computational Linguistics and the 11th International Joint Conference on Natural Language Processing (Volume 1: Long Papers), pp. 5808–5822 (2021)
24. Zhang, S., Shen, Y., Tan, Z., Wu, Y., Lu, W.: De-bias for generative extraction in unified NER task. In: Proceedings of the 60th Annual Meeting of the Association for Computational Linguistics (Volume 1: Long Papers), pp. 808–818 (2022)
25. Li, J., Fei, H., Liu, J., Wu, S., Zhang, M., Teng, C., Ji, D., Li, F.: Unified named entity recognition as word-word relation classification. In: Proceedings of the AAAI Conference on Artificial Intelligence, vol. 36, pp. 10965–10973 (2022)
26. Mo, Y., Liu, J., Tang, H., Wang, Q., Xu, Z., Wang, J., Quan, X., Wu, W., Li, Z.: Multi-task multi-attention transformer for generative named entity recognition. In: IEEE/ACM Transactions on Audio, Speech, and Language Processing (2024)
27. Yang, J., Han, S.C., Long, S., Poon, J., Nenadic, G.: MC-DRE: multi-aspect cross integration for drug event/entity extraction. In: Proceedings of the 32nd ACM International Conference on Information and Knowledge Management, pp. 4385–4389 (2023)
28. Hu, E.J., et al.: Lora: low-rank adaptation of large language models. ICLR **1**(2), 3 (2022)

LiteSCTransNet: Lightweight CNN-Transformer for 3D Medical Image Segmentation

Yu Sheng, Yiyi Hong, Yongchang Jia, and Guihua Duan[✉]

School of Computer Science, Central South University, Changsha, China
`duangh@csu.edu.cn`

Abstract. Although the medical image segmentation model SCTrans-Net based on convolutional neural network and Transformer performs well, SCTransNet has the problems of large number of parameters and computation. When SCTransNet processes the 3D shadow data, the 3D convolution operation in the CNN encoder and the decoder, and the Transformer model needs a large number of parameters to learn when operating on the 3D feature image, leading to the increase in the number of model parameters and the rising computational cost. Considering the problem of large number of parameters and calculation, this paper proposed the lightweight model LiteSCTransNet to effectively reduce the parameters and computation of the model while ensuring the segmentation accuracy. The encoder module in the Transformer model is refined using the channel separation idea, replacing the conventional convolution operation using deeply separable convolution. Experiments show that the calculated lightweight method reduced the number of parameters and calculations by 74.43% and 75.21%, respectively. Moreover, the Dice coefficient of liver and liver tumor segmentation in the LiTS-2017 dataset are 96.91% and 70.13%, respectively. The lightweight model has high operation efficiency and segmentation accuracy.

Keywords: Liver and Liver Tumors · Image segmentation · Depth-separable convolution · Channel separation

1 Introduction

3D medical image segmentation plays a crucial role in modern medicine by assisting doctors in diagnosing and delineating lesion areas. In recent years, with the rapid advancement of deep learning, significant progress has been made in this field. Convolutional neural networks (CNNs) [1] have demonstrated remarkable success in image segmentation, particularly through encoder-decoder architectures like U-Net [2], which have been widely adopted in medical image analysis. Building upon U-Net's success, numerous CNN-based models such as V-Net [3], RFCN [4], UNet++ [5], Unet3+ [6], 3D DenseNet [7], and Attention-UNet [8] have emerged. However, CNNs primarily focus on extracting local features from

J. Tang et al. (Eds.): ISBRA 2025, LNBI 15757, pp. 359–370, 2026.
https://doi.org/10.1007/978-981-95-0695-8_29

3D medical images. In contrast, The self-attention based Transformer architecture can capture long-range dependencies in sequences. Following the introduction of the Vision Transformer (ViT [9]), Transformer-based models such as TransBTS [10], Swin-UNet [11], and MedT [12] have gained traction in medical image segmentation. These models outperform traditional CNNs in various segmentation tasks due to their ability to model global contextual information [13].

However, despite their advantages, Transformer-based models suffer from high data requirements and increased computational complexity [14]. Moreover, they are less effective than CNNs in capturing local and channel-wise contextual information [15]. To address these limitations, researchers have proposed hybrid architectures that integrate CNNs and Transformers, leveraging the strengths of both paradigms, such as Trans-UNeter [16]. SCTransNet [17] employs CNNs for feature extraction while incorporating spatial and channel attention mechanisms within the Transformer framework. This design allows SCTransNet to effectively capture both global dependencies via the Transformer and local dependencies via CNNs, leading to improved segmentation performance.

In addition, Meta has introduced a pre-trained Model for 2D image segmentation called Segment Anything Model (SAM) [18]. Researchers have proposed a number of SAM-based methods, such as 3D-U-SAM [19], 3DSAM-Adapter [20], and DEAP-3DSAM [21]. However, the methods based on SAM have spatial feature loss and practical limitations.

In deep learning models, the number of model parameters and computational cost are often the key factors affecting model performance and application scenarios. In medical image segmentation tasks, due to the need to process a large amount of three-dimensional data, the number of model parameters and computational cost become extremely large, which will affect the performance and application scenarios of the model [22]. On longer input sequences, the number of parameters of Transformer is often large [23]. Taking the BERT model [24] as an example, the number of model parameters can reach 110 million, while the number of parameters of the GPT-3 model [25] is as high as 1.75 trillion. The number of parameters and computational cost of the SCTransNet model are much higher than other mainstream methods. This is mainly because the Transformer model requires a large number of parameters to learn when operating on three-dimensional feature images. The three-dimensional convolution operation in the CNN encoder and decoder also inevitably increases the number of parameters and computational cost.

In order to reduce the number of parameters while maintaining the respective advantages of Transformer and convolutional neural networks in the field of medical imaging. This paper proposed a lightweight optimization method for the model. It mainly includes: (1) using depthwise separable convolution to replace the traditional convolution operation; (2) using the channel separation idea to lightweight the encoder module in the Transformer model. We named the lightweight model LiteSCTransNet. The experimental results show that while maintaining a high segmentation accuracy, the model parameters and calculation amount are significantly reduced, thereby improving the practicality and efficiency of the model.

2 Methodology

The LiteSCTransNet model proposed in this paper is a lightweight network model based on the SCTransNet model. As shown in Fig. 1, the overall architecture of the model is replaced by the deep separable three-dimensional convolution SeparableConv3D in the encoder and decoder, and the Transformer encoder module in the spatial attention module is improved using the channel separation method. In order to distinguish it from the Trans-SA in SCTransNet, this module named it Trans-SA2. The following will mainly introduce the deep separable convolution in the model and the Trans-SA2 module improved based on the channel separation idea.

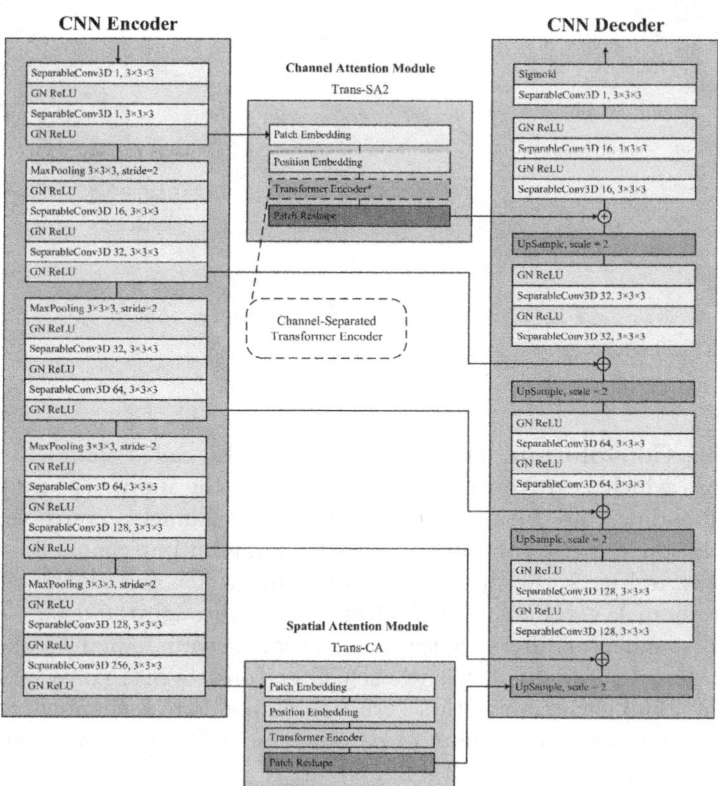

Fig. 1. LiteSCTransNet Model Architecture.

2.1   Depth-Separable Convolution

Conventional convolution is to convolve the input feature map with the convolution kernel to obtain the output feature map, where the filter is a small matrix containing weight parameters, which acts on each position of the input feature map. As shown in Fig. 2, the three-dimensional image $X \in \mathbb{R}^{3 \times 16 \times 256 \times 256}$ outputs the feature map $Y \in \mathbb{R}^{4 \times 16 \times 256 \times 256}$ after passing through the deep convolution layer. There are 4 filters in the convolution layer, each of which is composed of 3 convolution kernels $K \in \mathbb{R}^{3 \times 3 \times 3}$, and each filter acts on a channel of the input feature map. The number of parameters that need to be learned in the convolution layer is $4 \times 3 \times 3 \times 3 \times 3 = 324$.

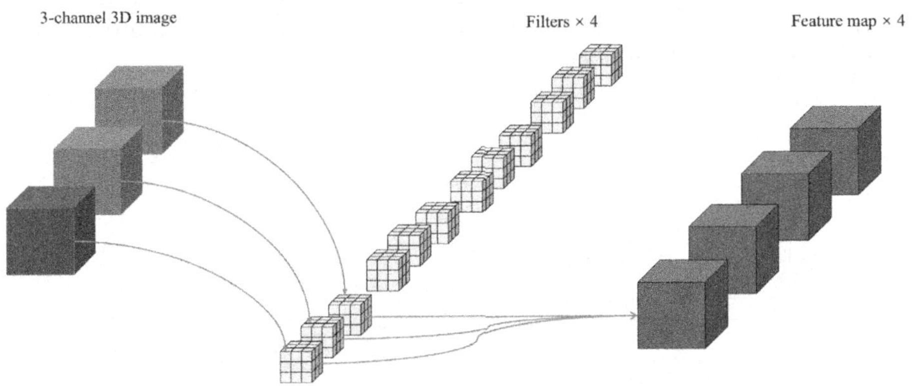

Fig. 2. Standard Convolution Operation.

Depthwise Convolution. Deep convolution is also called channel-by-channel convolution, which is to convolve each channel in the input feature map with the corresponding convolution kernel, that is, one channel is convolved by only one convolution kernel to obtain the corresponding output channel.

As shown in Fig. 2, the three-dimensional image $X \in \mathbb{R}^{3 \times 16 \times 256 \times 256}$ outputs the feature map $Y \in \mathbb{R}^{3 \times 16 \times 256 \times 256}$ after passing through the deep convolution layer. The number of filters in the convolution layer is equal to the number of input channels, that is, 3, where each filter consists of a convolution kernel $K \in \mathbb{R}^{3 \times 3 \times 3}$, and each convolution kernel corresponds to a channel of the input image X one by one. The number of parameters that need to be learned in the deep convolutional layer is $3 \times 3 \times 3 \times 3 = 81$.

Pointwise Convolution. Point-wise convolution refers to the convolution operation of the result of the depth convolution with a convolution kernel of size $1 \times 1 \times 1$, with the purpose of combining the output of each channel to obtain the final output feature map. As shown in Fig. 3b, the output of the depth convolution kernel $Y \in \mathbb{R}^{3 \times 16 \times 256 \times 256}$ outputs the feature map $Z \in \mathbb{R}^{4 \times 16 \times 256 \times 256}$ after the point-wise convolution operation. There are 4 filters in total, each of which is composed of three convolution kernels $K \in \mathbb{R}^{1 \times 1 \times 1}$.

The purpose of the point-by-point convolution operation is to improve the expressiveness of the model while ensuring that the amount of calculation is relatively small, so that the model can better capture the characteristics of the input image. Point-wise convolution is a way of performing convolution operations using a convolution kernel of $1 \times 1 \times 1$. It can be used to adjust the number of channels of feature maps to achieve features fusion, feature map transformation, etc. The number of parameters that need to be learned in the gradual convolution layer is $4 \times 3 \times 1 \times 1 \times 1 = 12$.

Under the same input, the number of parameters of traditional convolution is 324, and the number of parameters of depthwise separable convolution is $81 + 12 = 93$. It can be seen that depthwise separable convolution can well reduce the number of parameters of convolution operations. Therefore, in the LiteSCTransNet model, the convolution operations in the encoder and decoder are replaced by depthwise separable convolution. Figure 1 shows the model structure after the encoder and decoder apply depthwise separable convolution, from

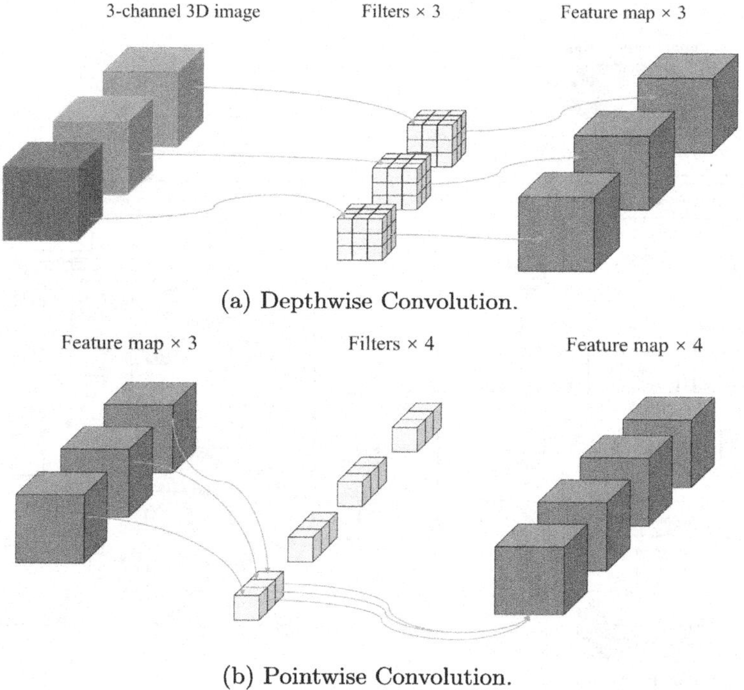

Fig. 3. LiteSCTransNet Model Architecture.

which it can be seen that the conventional convolution operations in the encoder and decoder are replaced by the depthwise separable three-dimensional volume SeparableConv3D.

2.2   Transformer Model Based on Channel Separation

The Trans-SA module of SCTransNe flattens the input feature map into a vector and then uses a multi-layer Transformer encoder for feature extraction. The multiple attention heads of the multi-head attention mechanism need to perform linear transformations of queries, keysand values. Each attention head has its own weight matrixSecondly, the MLP module contains multiple fully connected layers. Each neuron in the fully connected layer needs to be connected to all neurons in the previous layer, resulting in an exponential increase in the number of pa- rameters as the number of neurons increases. It can be seen that when the input feature map of Trans-SA is too large, the number of parameters in the Trans- former encoder layer will show an exponential increase. In order to effectively reduce the input size of the Transformer encoder layer in the Trans-SA module while ensuring that the detailed information of the in- put feature map is not lost. This paper improves the Trans-SA module based on the idea of channel separation [26]. The structure is shown in the Fig. 4.

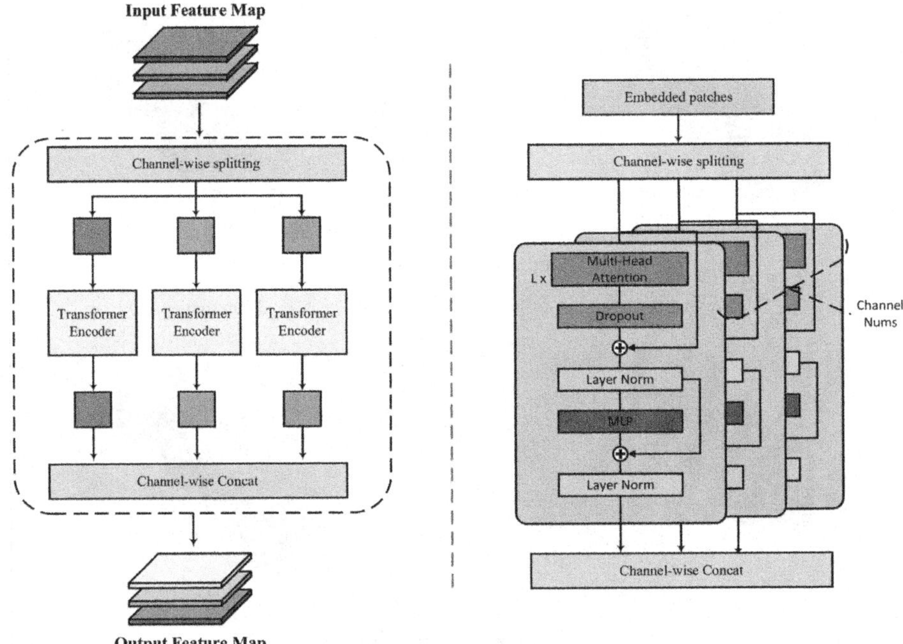

Fig. 4. Transformer Encoder based on channel separation.

The two-dimensional tensor output by the embedding layer and the position encoding layer is split according to the channel dimension, and then the data of the multiple slices obtained after the splitting are input into the corresponding Transformer encoder module. After the multi-head attention mechanism and the MLP layer, the output of all encoder layers is spliced together according to the channel dimension as the output of the Trans-SA module. In order to distinguish it from the module of SCTransNet, it is named Trans-SA2 in this paper.

Assume that the input feature map is $X \in \mathbb{R}^{16 \times 16 \times 256 \times 256}$, the patch size is $4 \times 8 \times 8$, there are $L = 6$ layers of encoders in the Transformer encoder layer, and the number of subspaces of the multi-head attention module in each Transformer encoder is $h = 4$.

Trans-SA2 uses the channel separation method after the embedding layer and the position encoding layer to convert the input X into a three-dimensional tensor $X \in \mathbb{R}^{16 \times 4097 \times 256}$ according to the channel dimension, and divides it into $x_i \in \mathbb{R}^{4097 \times 256}$ according to the first dimension, where $i \in [1, 16]$. The Trans-SA2 module has a total of 16 Transformer encoder modules, and $x_1 \cdots x_{16}$ is input into the corresponding encoder module respectively.

In the multi-head attention mechanism module of each layer of the encoder, a linear mapping XW_{qkv} is used to map the input x to the query Q, key K and value V respectively, where $W_{qkv} \in \mathbb{R}^{256 \times 768}$. The concatenated result is linearly mapped XW_O in the output layer, where $W_O \in \mathbb{R}^{256 \times 256}$. In this process, the parameter quantity comes from the weight matrices W_{qkv} and W_O of the linear mapping, and the parameter quantity is calculated as $256 \times 768 + 256 \times 256 = 262144$.

In the MLP layer of each encoder, the weight matrices of the two linear mappings are $W_1 \in \mathbb{R}^{256 \times 2048}$ and $W_2 \in \mathbb{R}^{2048 \times 256}$. The parameter quantity is calculated as $256 \times 2048 + 2048 \times 256 = 1048576$.

The input of the Transformer encoder layer is 16 channels, each channel corresponds to 6 layers of Transformer encoders, and the total number of parameters is $16 \times 6 \times (262144 + 1048576) = 103.173120M$.

In contrast, the input of the Transformer encoder layer in the Trans-SA module is $X \in \mathbb{R}^{4097 \times 4096}$, where the weight matrices of the two linear mappings of the multi-head attention mechanism are $W_{qkv} \in \mathbb{R}^{4096 \times 12288}$ and $XW_O \in \mathbb{R}^{4096 \times 4096}$. The number of parameters is calculated as $4096 \times 12288 + 4096 \times 4096 = 67.108864M$. The two linear mapping weight matrices of MLP are $W_1 \in \mathbb{R}^{4096 \times 2048}$ and $W_2 \in \mathbb{R}^{2048 \times 4096}$. The number of parameters is calculated as $4096 \times 2048 + 2048 \times 4096 = 16.777216M$. The total number of parameters of the 6-layer Transformer encoder is $6 \times (67.108864 + 16.777216) = 503.316480M$. It can be seen intuitively that the channel separation method can significantly reduce the number of parameters in the Trans-SA module.

3 Experiments and Results

3.1 Dataset and Preprocessing

In order to verify that the deep separable convolution and channel separation methods in the LiteSCTransNet model can effectively reduce the number of model parameters, the amount of calculation and the segmentation performance. The dataset used is the liver tumor LiTS (Liver Tumor Segmentation Challenge)-2017 dataset. And in view of some characteristics of the lightweight model, some methods in the data preprocessing stage are improved to improve the segmentation accuracy of the model.

In the data screening stage, this experiment divides the $n \times 512 \times 512$-sized image into multiple $32 \times 512 \times 512$-sized images according to the axial direction. This is because the model occupies less GPU video memory after lightweighting, so the axial size can be increased, so that the model can use more spatial context information, thereby improving the segmentation accuracy. After screening, a total of 269 nii image files containing liver and liver tumor data are obtained, of which the number of files in the training set, validation set and test set are 161, 54 and 54 respectively. In the data augmentation stage, the 161 training sets are horizontally flipped and randomly rotated $[-30, 30]$, so that the model samples are expanded to 483.

3.2   Experimental Setup

The model was trained on a 32GB NVIDIA Tesla V100 GPU. The learning rate of the model was set to 0.0001. The Adam optimizer was used during training, and the training cycle was set to 200 epochs.

3.3   Experimental Results and Analysis

In order to verify that the depthwise separable convolution and channel separation methods in the LiteSCTransNet model can effectively reduce the number of parameters, the amount of computation, and the segmentation performance of the model. This section will conduct comparative experiments and hyperparameter experiments.

Comparison Experiment. This experiment compares the number of parameters, the amount of computation, and the storage space occupied by the model. It can be seen from Table 1 that the number of parameters and the amount of computation of the LiteSCTransNet model are reduced by 74.43% and 75.21% respectively compared with SCTransNet. Compared with 3D U-Net, 3D DenseNet and V-net models, LiteSCTransNet still has a large number of parameters and low operating efficiency.

As can be seen in Table 2, the Unet-3D module using deep separable convolution has a 58.41% and 68.49% decrease in parameters and calculations compared to the Unet-3D module using traditional convolution, and compared to 3D U-Net, the parameters and calculations have decreased by 83.00% and 87.05% respectively. The Trans-SA2 module using the channel separation method has a 75.74% and 75.58% decrease in parameters and calculations compared to the Trans-SA module. However, the Trans-SA2 module is still the main reason for the surge in model parameters and calculations. From the above data, it can

Table 1. Comparison of computing efficiency of each model.

Model	Trainable parameters (M)	Computation (GFLOPs)	Storage space occupied (MB)
3D U-net	12.94	440.00	51.76
V-Net	12.26	86.71	47.12
3D-DenseNet	45.59	751.18	192.68
SCTransNet	533.47	4448.34	2099.43
LiteSCTransNet	136.37	1102.36	429.23

be concluded that the use of deep separable convolution and channel separation methods can effectively reduce the number of parameters and calculations of the model, improve the efficiency of model operation, and achieve the goal of lightweight.

Table 2. Comparison of computational efficiency of modules in LiteSCTransNet.

Model	Module	Trainable parameters (M)	Computation (GFLOPs)
SCTransNet	Baseline	5.29	181.03
	Trans-SA	520.23	4263.23
	Trans-CA	7.95	4.08
LiteSCTransNet	Depthwise-Baseline	2.20	57.04
	Trans-SA2	126.21	1041.24
	Trans-CA	7.95	4.08

After comparing the computational efficiency of the models, this experiment used the LiteSCTransNet model to conduct segmentation experiments on the dataset LiTS-2017, and compared it with several other models to verify that the model can still maintain high segmentation accuracy after lightweighting. Table 3 and Table 4 show the segmentation results of the liver and liver tumors by each model. The indicators of the segmentation results of the liver and liver tumors by LiteSCTransNet still exceed those of the 3D U-net, 3D DenseNet and V-Net models, which shows that the lightweight model still has good feature extraction and expression capabilities, and to a certain extent verifies the effectiveness of the combination of convolutional neural networks and Transformers. However, compared with the SCTransNet model, the indicators of the LiteSC-TransNet model have decreased significantly. After analysis, it can be seen that the decrease in the number of parameters will inevitably lead to a decrease in the expression ability of the model, resulting in a decrease in accuracy. However, in terms of the balance between operating efficiency and segmentation accuracy, the use of lightweight methods for the model is still successful.

Table 3. Indicators of liver segmentation of each model.

Model	DICE (%)	VOE (%)	RVD (%)	ASSD (mm)	MSSD (mm)
3D U-Net	95.46	8.67	1.82	0.46	27.64
3D DenseNet	95.79	8.11	1.86	0.34	27.96
V-Net	96.40	6.94	3.16	0.28	30.01
SCTransNet	97.75	6.26	1.16	0.22	27.61
LiteSCTransNet	96.91	6.82	1.84	0.77	36.49

Table 4. Indicators of liver tumor segmentation of each model.

Model	DICE (%)	VOE (%)	RVD (%)	ASSD (mm)	MSSD (mm)
3D U-Net	65.44	51.36	4.84	14.55	36.60
3D DenseNet	67.78	48.73	15.6	11.54	40.75
V-Net	69.39	46.86	-10.6	3.51	43.73
SCTransNet	73.45	40.68	-2.60	3.36	32.71
LiteSCTransNet	70.13	3.65	56.15	4.88	34.03

Hyper-parameter Related Experiments.

Batch size hyperparameter experiment. Batch size is an important hyperparameter in deep learning. In this paper, the LiteSCTransNet model is used to select multiple different batches for training and testing on the LiST-2017 dataset. The results are shown in Table 5, which records the time spent by the model in each Epoch during training, as well as the Dice value of the segmentation accuracy of the liver and liver tumors on the test set.

The experimental results show that when the batch size gradually increases from 1 to 4, the segmentation accuracy of the liver and liver tumors tends to gradually improve. However, when the batch size increases to 8, due to the limitation of GPU video memory, a CUDA out of memory error occurs and the model cannot be trained further. Therefore, in this experiment, a batch size of 4 was finally selected for training

Table 5. Batch size hyperparameter experiment results.

No.	Batch size	Time spent (s/epoch)	Liver Dice (%)	Liver tumor DICE (%)
1	1	221	96.14	69.21
2	2	201	96.51	69.45
3	4	192	96.91	70.13
4	8	–	–	–

4   Conclusion

This paper mainly improves the problem of the surge in the number of parameters and the amount of calculation in the SCTransNet model. First, the original convolution operation is replaced by a deep separable convolution, thereby reducing the number of parameters and the amount of calculation; secondly, the spatial attention module is improved using the channel separation idea, reducing the number of model parameters and improving the performance of the model. The experimental results show that while maintaining a high segmentation accuracy, the number of model parameters and the amount of calculation have been significantly reduced, thereby improving the practicality and efficiency of the model.

Acknowledgments. This work is supported in part by the National Natural Science Foundation of China (No. 61877059).

References

1. Patil, A., Rane, M.: Convolutional neural networks: an overview and its applications in pattern recognition. In: Information and Communication Technology for Intelligent Systems: Proceedings of ICTIS 2020, vol. 1, pp. 21–30 (2021)
2. Ronneberger, O., Fischer, P., Brox, T.: U-net: convolutional networks for biomedical image segmentation. In: Medical Image Computing and Computer- Assisted Intervention–MICCAI 2015: 18th International Conference Munich Germany October 5–9 2015 Proceedings Part III, volume 18, pp. 234–241 (2015)
3. Milletari, F., Navab, N., Ahmadi, S.-A.: V-net: fully convolutional neural networks for volumetric medical image segmentation. In: Proceedings of the 4th International Conference on 3D Vision, pp. 565–571 (2016)
4. Poudel, R.P., Lamata, P., Montana, G.: Recurrent fully convolutional neural networks for multi-slice MRI cardiac segmentation. In: Proceedings of the 1st International Workshops Reconstruction Segmentation Analysis Medical Images, pp. 83–94 (2017)
5. Zhou, Z., Rahman Siddiquee, M.M., Tajbakhsh, N., Liang, J.: Unet++: a nested u-net architecture for medical image segmentation. In: Deep Learning in Medical Image Analysis and Multimodal Learning for Clinical Decision Support: 4th International Workshop DLMIA 2018 and 8th International Workshop ML-CDS 2018 Held in Conjunction with MICCAI 2018 Granada Spain September 20 2018 Proceedings, vol. 4, pp. 3–11 (2018)
6. Huang, H., Lin, L., Tong, R., et al.: UNet 3+: a full-scale connected UNet for medical image segmentation. In: ICASSP 2020-2020 IEEE International Conference on Acoustics, Speech and Signal Processing (ICASSP), pp. 1055–1059 (2020)
7. Zhang, J., Zheng, B., Gao, A., et al.: A 3D densely connected convolution neural network with connection-wise attention mechanism for Alzheimer's disease classification. Magn. Reson. Imaging **78**, 119–126 (2021)
8. Oktay, O., Schlemper, J., Folgoc, L.L., et al.: Attention U-Net: learning where to look for the pancreas. arXiv (2018)

9. Dosovitskiy, A., et al.: An image is worth 16x16 words: transformers for image recognition at scale. In: Proceedings of the International Conference on Learning Representations (2021)
10. Wang, W., Chen, C., Ding, M., Yu, H., Zha, S., Li, J.: Transbts: multimodal brain tumor segmentation using transformer. In: Proceedings of the 24th International Conference on Medical Image Computing and Computing Assisted Intervention, pp. 109–119 (2021)
11. Cao, H., et al.: Swin-UNet: Unet-like pure transformer for medical image segmentation. In: Proceedings of the European Conference on Computer Vision, pp. 205–218 (2022)
12. Valanarasu, J.M.J., Oza, P., Hacihaliloglu, I., Patel, V.M. :. Medical transformer: gated axial-attention for medical image segmentation. In: Proceedings of the 24th International Conference on Medical Image Computing and Computing Assisted Intervention, pp. 36–46 (2021)
13. Shamshad, F., et al.: Transformers in medical imaging: a survey. Med. Image Anal. 88 (2023)
14. Wu, H., et al.: CVT: introducing convolutions to vision transformers. In: Proceedings of the IEEE/CVF International Conference on Computing Vision, pp. 22–31 (2021)
15. Guo, J., Zhou, H.-Y., Wang, L., Yu, Y.: UNet-2022: exploring dynamics in non-isomorphic architecture. In: Proceedings of the International Conference on Medical Imaging Computing-Aided Diagnosis, pp. 465–476 (2022)
16. Yu, J., He, X., Qin, J., Zhang, W., Xiang, J., Zhao, W.: Trans-uneter: a new decoder of transunet for medical image segmentation. In: 2023 IEEE International Conference on Bioinformatics and Biomedicine (BIBM), pp. 2338–2341 (2023)
17. Jia, Y., Duan, G., Sheng, Y.: Sctransnet: 3D medical image segmentation model based on the fusion of CNN and transformer. In: 2023 IEEE International Conference on Bioinformatics and Biomedicine (BIBM), pp. 1158–1165 (2023)
18. Kirillov, A., et al.: Segment anything. In: Proceedings of the IEEE/CVF International Conference on Computer Vision, pp. 4015–4026 (2023)
19. Zhang, Y., Liu, Z.-Q., Feng, Y., Xu, R.: 3D-U-SAM network for few-shot tooth segmentation in CBCT images. ArXiv, abs/2309.11015 (2023)
20. Gong, S., et al.: 3dsam-adapter: holistic adaptation of SAM from 2D to 3D for promptable tumor segmentation. Med. Image Anal. **98**, 103324 (2023)
21. Chen, F., Tang, J., Wang, P., Wang, T., Li, S., Deng, T.: Deap-3dsam: decoder enhanced and auto prompt SAM for 3D medical image segmentation. In: 2024 IEEE International Conference on Bioinformatics and Biomedicine (BIBM), pp. 1852–1859 (2024)
22. Jing, J., Wang, Z., Rätsch, M., et al.: Mobile-UNet: an efficient convolutional neural network for fabric defect detection. Text. Res. J. **92**(1–2), 30–42 (2022)
23. Zafrir, O., Boudoukh, G., Izsak, P., et al.: Q8bert: quantized 8bit Bert. CoRR, abs/1910.06188 (2019)
24. Devlin, J., Chang, M., Lee, K., et al.: Bert: pre-training of deep bidirectional transformers for language understanding. CoRR, abs/1810.04805 (2018)
25. Brown, T., Mann, B., Ryder, N., et al.: Language models are few-shot learners. Adv. Neural. Inf. Process. Syst. **33**, 1877–1901 (2020)
26. Chollet, F.: Xception: deep learning with depthwise separable convolutions. CoRR, abs/1610.02357 (2016)

ACMSI: An Innovative Automated Analysis Application Utilizing Computer Vision for Accurate Microsatellite Instability Classification

Jiale Wen[1,2], Xiao Lan[2], Yaru Chen[2], Kamen Ivanov[4], Jia Gu[3(✉)], and Shifu Chen[1,2,3(✉)]

[1] LifeX Institute, School of Medical Technology, Gannan Medical University, Ganzhou, Jiangxi, China
chen@haplox.com
[2] HaploX Biotechnology, Shenzhen, China
[3] Faculty of Data Science, City University of Macau, Macau, China
[4] "Acad. E. Djakov" Institute of Electronics, Bulgarian Academy of Sciences, Sofia, Bulgaria

Abstract. Microsatellite instability (MSI) results from deficient mismatch repair (dMMR) and plays a crucial role in tumorigenesis and treatment, particularly in colon cancer. The gold standard for MSI classification relies on multiplex fluorescent PCR with capillary electrophoresis (CE); however, manual interpretation is time-consuming and subjective due to panel variability. No dedicated tools currently exist for MSI classification from CE profiles.

We developed *Automated Classification of Microsatellite Instability* (ACMSI) to streamline fragment analysis and automate MSI classification. ACMSI includes size calling, manual calibration, and automated classification (Fig. 1). Evaluated on 322 electrophoresis profiles (129 tumor-normal pairs, 774 markers) using the 2B3D NCI Panel (BAT25, BAT26, D2S123, D5S346, D17S250), ACMSI achieved a 99.07% automated alignment success rate. Compared to manual classification, it demonstrated 96.3% sensitivity and 99.64% specificity per marker and 100% accuracy per patient. ACMSI provides a robust, objective solution for MSI classification and is available on GitHub: https://github.com/OpenGene/ACMSI.

Keywords: Microsatellite Instability · Capillary Electrophoresis · Computer Vision · Diagnostic Automation

1 Introduction

Microsatellites (MS) are tandemly repetitive DNA sequences characterized by motifs repeating from one to six or more base pairs [1]. Errors in microsatellites occur when DNA mismatch repair (MMR) genes such as MLH1, MSH2, MSH6, and PMS2 malfunction, leading to the accumulation of replication errors and resultant microsatellite instability (MSI) [1]. This is a molecular hall marker frequently associated with the development of malignancies such as colorectal, stomach, and sebaceous carcinomas [2,

© The Author(s), under exclusive license to Springer Nature Singapore Pte Ltd. 2026
J. Tang et al. (Eds.): ISBRA 2025, LNBI 15757, pp. 371–382, 2026.
https://doi.org/10.1007/978-981-95-0695-8_30

3]. Standard techniques for detecting MSI typically involve multiplex fluorescent polymerase chain reaction (PCR) coupled with capillary electrophoresis (CE), facilitating comprehensive analysis of microsatellite markers and difference comparison between tumor and normal tissues samples [4].

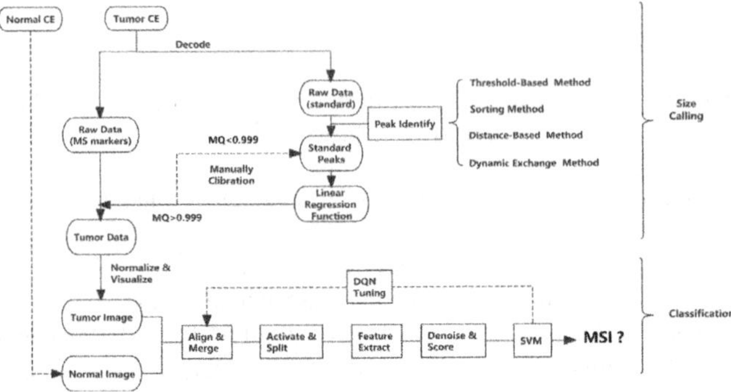

Fig. 1. The Workflow of ACMSI. It illustrates the overall workflow of the size calling, automated classification and DQN hyperparameter tuning.

Categorizing individuals based on their MSI status- classifying them as MSI-High (MSI-H), MSI-Low (MSI-L), or MSI stable (MSS) - is crucial for guiding diagnose and treatment decision in oncology. However, different panels, such as those with mononucleotide repeat markers (MONO-27, NR-21) and long mononucleotide markers (BAT-52, BAT-60), have varying criteria for instability assessment [5–7]. Interpreting the result from fluorescent capillary electrophoresis can be subject to variability, potentially affecting diagnostic accuracy.

Despite the growing application of deep learning models on image processing, such as Convolutional Neural Networks (CNNs), Transformers, and Diffusion models, there remains a notable lack of effective tools for MSI classification. While these models often yield satisfactory classification results when applied to CE profiles, they suffer from a critical limitation: their "black-box" nature. This lack of interpretability presents a significant challenge, particularly given the clinical need for transparent and explainable decision-making in MSI classification. Traditionally, computer vision (CV) solutions for MSI classification are divided into two main stages: feature extraction and scoring [8]. However, existing feature extraction techniques, such as local extrema or edge detection methods, are often insufficiently customizable, limiting their effectiveness in achieving optimal results (Fig. 2). Furthermore, standard scoring strategies like Mean Squared Error (MSE) and Structural Similarity Index (SSIM) [9, 10], which are commonly used in image processing, fail to adequately capture the peak shifts and amplitude differences that are central to MSI classification (Fig. 5d).

To overcome interpretative challenges and enhance the objectivity of MSI classification, this study introduces the ACMSI. By integrating techniques from CV and machine learning, the ACMSI aims to automate the MSI classification and streamline tasks such as peak extraction, size calling, manual calibration, images alignment, images refinement, feature extraction and scoring. Through these advancements, the ACMSI seeks to improve the efficiency, accuracy, and reliability of MSI status determination, offering a promising solution for enhancing molecular diagnostics in cancer research and clinical settings.

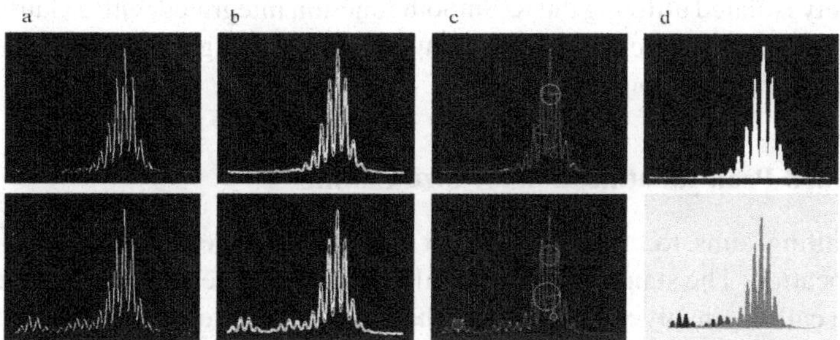

Fig. 2. Comparison of Feature Extraction Models. a) **Sobel** is a discrete differentiation operator used for edge detection, employing a two-dimensional convolution operation for signal processing [11]. b) **Canny** edge detector is a multi-stage algorithm that first applies a Gaussian filter to smooth the image before detecting edges [12]. c) **Scale-Invariant Feature Transform (SIFT)** is a computer vision algorithm designed to detect and describe local extrema in images by utilizing Euclidean distance and the Hough transformation [13]· d) **ACMSI** uses an innovative feature extraction strategy specifically tailored for CE profiles. The red portion represents peaks shared between tumor and normal tissues, the purple portion represents elevated peaks in tumor tissue compared to normal tissue, and the black portion represents new peaks in tumor tissue.

2 Method

2.1 Sample Collection and MSI Marker Detection

A cohort comprising 129 tumor samples was collected, encompassing 258 specimens with corresponding normal tissue samples for comparative analysis. In addition, 64 unpaired specimens were included in the study. The MSI markers of the 2B3D NCI Panel (BAT25, BAT26, D2S123, D5S346, D17S250) and the control marker Penta C are detected by fluorescence PCR capillary electrophoresis. NED, VIC, 6'-FAM are fluorescent labels and LIZ600 is selected as the standard substance. The experimental procedures were carried out by four different operators, resulting in the generation of four batches of data.

2.2 Data Preprocessing

The initial phase of data processing involves the conversion of raw data obtained from fluorescence PCR capillary electrophoresis, stored in FSA files in ABIF format, into discernible one-dimensional peak data across distinct fluorescence channels. This transformation is conducted using the *FSAtools* (Mareschal S, 2015). At the meanwhile, peak detection and the removal of potential spurious peaks are accomplished through crosstalk analysis, where signal leakage is identified by a 10-fold amplitude difference between standard channels and alternative channels at equivalent electrophoretic positions.

Following data preprocessing, the subsequent task includes extrema extraction from the processed dataset. All extrema points, including authentic peaks and noise elements, are effectively isolated utilizing the K-Smooth function integrated with a Gaussian kernel algorithm [14]. This extraction method, implemented through the *ksmooth* package in the R programming environment.

2.3 Standard Peak Identification for Size Calling

The size calling aims to establish a linear regression correlation between molecular mass and location. The standard peak identification, which serves as the cornerstone for precise size calling, involves an algorithm that incorporates four fundamental strategies:

a) **Threshold-Based Method:** Initial peak discrimination is performed by setting pre-determined thresholds for peak amplitude to differentiate true peak from initial peak attributed to sample introduction and background noise.
b) **Sorting Method:** The sorting procedure is initiated by detecting the initial peak as reference peak and then arranging subsequent peaks in a descending order relative to this reference peak for reliable standard peak extraction.
c) **Distance-Based Method:** Commencing with identifying the initial peak and noise, this method systematically aggregates potential spurious peaks and eliminates adjacent peaks until the desired number of true peaks remains, typically 36 peaks for LIZ600 standards.
d) **Dynamic Exchange Method:** This innovation approach starts with the final two confirmed peaks and utilizes a dynamic exchange rate to identify peaks in reverse order. Through iterative adjustment to the exchange rate based on newly discovered peaks, this method explores expected regions accordingly.

These peak identifications methodologies are conducted sequentially to enable the establishment of a linear regression model that yields a correlation coefficient exceeding the predefined threshold of 0.999 [15].

In cases where automatic identification of standard peaks fails, ACMSI provides a user-friendly manual calibration module. It allows users to manually drag and align peaks to expected locations, accompanied by a real-time display of the correlation coefficient, also called mapping quality (MQ) (Fig. 6B). Moreover, the module also supports simultaneous operation on multiple samples, enhancing user flexibility and efficiency.

2.4 Feature Recognition Depending on Computer Vision

The correlation established between molecular mass and location is applied to transform one-dimensional data. Subsequently, the derived values are projected onto a two-dimensional grayscale peak image. The area under curve of peak is filled with black pixel. Before image generation, the normalization process involves adjusting the peak width within the image by the segment length obtained from the expected size range of MSI marker. Also, the peak height is scaled relative to the highest peak value in the data.

Following the production of paired normal-tumor images from a sample, an alignment strategy aiming to minimize Mean Squared Error (MSE) is applied, such as:

$$MSE = \frac{1}{n}[\begin{bmatrix} T_{11} & \cdots & T_{1j} \\ \cdots & \cdots \cdots & \cdots \\ T_{i1} & \cdots & T_{ij} \end{bmatrix} - \begin{bmatrix} N_{11} & \cdots & N_{1j} \\ \cdots & \cdots \cdots & \cdots \\ N_{i1} & \cdots & N_{ij} \end{bmatrix}]^2 = \frac{1}{n}\sum\left(T_{1j} - N_{ij}\right)^2$$

where T refers to the tumor image, N refers to normal image and n is the total number of images [16]. This alignment process and subsequent subtraction result in a unified differential image revealing exclusive differences between tumor and normal tissues. Refinement of the differential image implement the following steps. Initially, the differential image, generated by subtracting tumor from aligned normal images, contains negative values for normal-specific peaks and positive values for tumor-specific peaks. An activation function, such as ReLU is used to convert negative values to 0, emphasizing tumor-specific peaks [17]. Additionally, a noise threshold (YM) is introduced to eliminate noise, while a threshold of new peak (NPR) allows for the recognition of new peaks specific to tumor tissue within predefined limits. To correct alignment errors within the differential image, a morphological opening operation is applied using minimum element structures tailored for new peaks (NPM) and elevated peaks (EPM) separately [18], ensuring the accurate refinement and optimization of the differential image for subsequent analysis and feature extraction:

$$\text{Opening}\,(A, B) = (A \ominus B) \oplus B$$
$$Erosion : A \ominus B = \{z|(B)_z \subseteq A\}$$
$$Dilation : A \oplus B = \left\{z\middle|(B)_z \bigcap A \neq \varnothing\right\}$$

where A refers to the differential image, B refers to a minimal element structure and z refers to every pixel of the differential image.

In feature extraction phase, the horizontal displacement in image alignment, representing the fragment size difference (SD) of a marker, is normalized by using the repeat unit of MSI markers to ensure consistent comparability across different markers. Subsequently, the negative values within the differential image are segmented into two categories: new peaks (NP) and elevated peaks (EP), which both are tumor-specific peaks. These categories values are then separately summed to derive the New Peak Score (NPS) and Elevated Peak Score (EPS) with distinct scoring weights allocated to the upper and lower regions, specifically 0.8 for the upper part and 0.2 for the lower part, as shown by:

$$NPS = 0.2 * \sum\left[NP_{upper}\right] + 0,8 * \sum[NP_{lower}]$$

$$EPS = 0.2 * \sum\left[EP_{upper}\right] + 0.8 * \sum[NP_{lower}]$$

This systematic extraction process culminates in the generation of essential parameters for inclusion into the further machine learning input, comprising SD, NPS and EPS.

2.5 Machine Learning and Parameters Tuning

Data from all markers of a sample containing both positive and negative samples are constructed to create a training set (54 samples, 324 markers) and a test set (129 samples, 774 markers) using the differential feature extraction algorithm. K-fold cross-validation was implemented to calculate the average F1 score of the Support Vector Machine (SVM), serving as the reward signal for the Deep Q-Network (DQN) algorithm. The DQN algorithm is applied for hyperparameter tuning, focusing on crucial parameters within the differential feature extraction algorithm: YM (noise threshold), NPR (new peak threshold), NPM (minimum element structure for new peaks), and EPM (minimum element structure for elevated peaks).

To fine-tune these parameters effectively, a suitable Q-learning rate and memory size are specified to navigate the parameter space and determine optimal configuration that maximizes the F1 score, thereby enhancing the performance of the automatic classification model. The DQN tuning algorithm is systematically deployed across various samples batches to identify a globally optimal parameter set conductive to superior model performance (Fig. 4).

2.6 Previous fragment analysis tools for comparison

GeneMapper 6.0 Software (Applied Biosystems) [20], Coffalyser.NET (Version: 24.0.1) [21], GeneMarker (Version: 2.6.3) [22] and PeakScanner (Thermo Fisher Cloud) [23] are used to process raw data with default parameter settings. The failure of size calling of Coffalyser.NET is defined as a score 0 or 1 out of 4 and the failure of PeakScanner is defined as a score less than 95, where standard peaks are misidentified. The classification of failure of GeneMapper and GeneMarker keep consistent with their corresponding built-in system (Fig. 3).

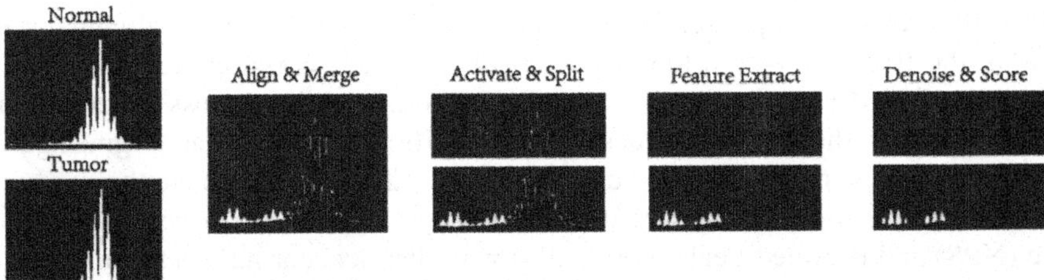

Fig. 3. Image Processing with CV. It illustrates the main steps involved in image processing using CV within the ACMSI framework.

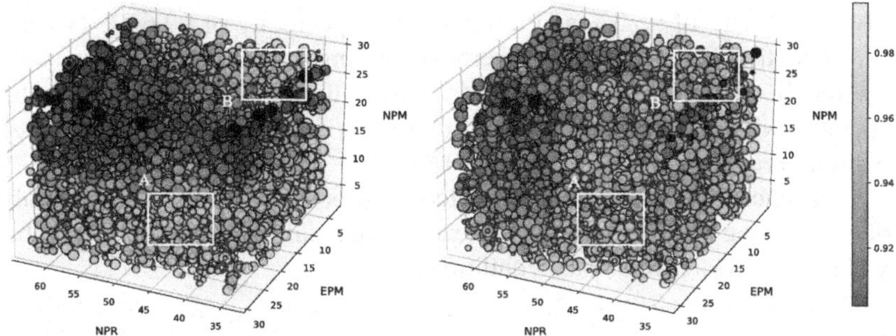

Fig. 4. Parameters Tuning with DQN. It shows the parameter spaces obtained from the DQN reinforcement learning algorithm for two different sample batches. In the parameter space, each point's 3D coordinate and size represent the NPM, NPR, EPM, and YM parameters of the differential feature extraction algorithm. Each point corresponds to the SVM classification result for a specific sample batch under a particular parameter combination, with the brightness of the point indicating the F1 score. This local optimum, region B, achieves superior performance in a specific batch by selecting a higher noise threshold and larger element structures. Conversely, region A is identified as the global optimal parameter combination, performing consistently across different batches.

3   Result

3.1   Robustness Assessment of ACMSI

The robustness of the ACMSI was evaluated using fluorescence PCR capillary electrophoresis data from 322 cases derived from paired and non-paired samples collected at different times and by different operators. The MSI markers detected are from 2B3D NCI Panel, including BAT25, BAT26, D2S123, D5S346, D17S250, with the control marker Penta C. The raw FSA files from these specimens were collectively input into the ACMSI. Initially, 2 cases failed in size calling but were successfully calibrated to achieve a mapping quality (MQ) exceeding 0.999 after manual adjustment. In contrast, GeneMapper required manual adjustments for 13 cases due to size calling failures, whereas GeneMarker faced automatic size calling challenge in 8 cases. PeakScanner failed in 8 cases and issued size calling warnings in 3 cases. Meanwhile, Coffalyser.net failed in 173 cases, likely due to strict amplitude (RFU) requirements for peak values in MLPA analysis (Fig. 5c).

Following the size calling of the ACMSI, 774 MSI markers from 129 paired samples (tumor and normal tissue), underwent quality control and MSI classification. Among these markers, 49 failed to meet quality control standards and 3 samples failed who did not contain any qualified markers. Then, 22.34% markers of the 725 qualified markers were manually classified as positive, either MSI-L (low) or MSI-H (high). To be more specific, details regarding the proportion and positivity rate of each marker can be found on Fig. 5a. At the sample level, 56 samples (44.44% out of 126 samples) exhibited at least one MSI-L or MSI-H marker.

Subsequently, the automatic classification results generated by ACMSI were compared against the manual classifications. Across 725 markers, ACMSI demonstrated an impressive sensitivity of 96.3% and a remarkable specificity of 99.64%. Notably, the performance metrics for individual markers—including sensitivity, specificity, accuracy, precision, recall, and F1 score—exceeded 95% in all cases, except for two specific metrics associated with D2S123 (Fig. 5b). Furthermore, for 126 samples, both sensitivity and specificity reached a perfect score of 100%.

The comprehensive evaluation highlighted the robustness of ACMSI, particularly in terms of size calling precision, minimal need for manual adjustment, and its ability to reliably classify across diverse data conditions.

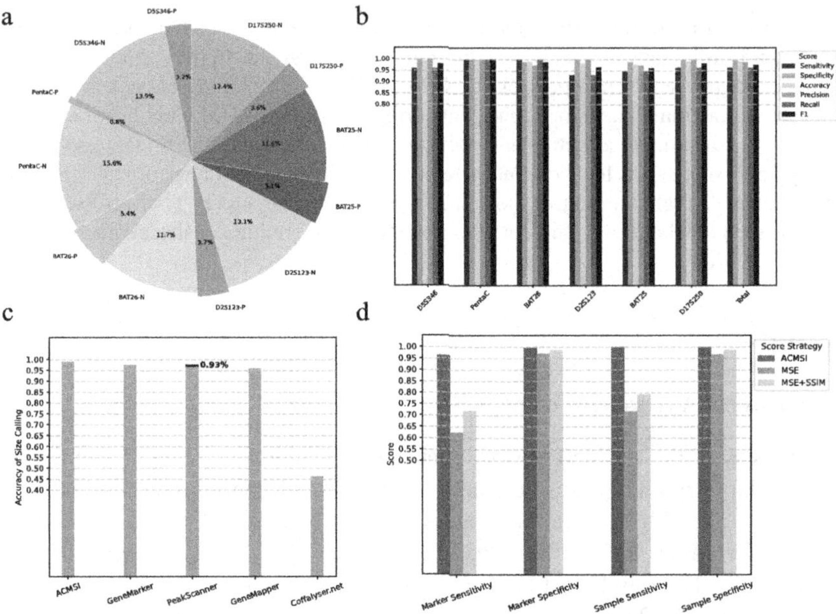

Fig. 5. The **Result of MSI Classification. a)** Details regarding six markers are presented, including their corresponding proportions and positive rates, where N refers to negative and P refers to positive. **b)** It shows the automated MSI classification scores of ACMSI across 6 distinct makers. **c)** The accuracy scores for size calling are compared among five different software tools. **d)** It displays a comparison of 3 different scoring strategies with the same features extracted by ACMSI.

3.2 User-Friendly Operation System

The ACMSI distinguishes itself with a user-friendly operation system tailored to simplify MSI classification for users with diverse technical backgrounds. This system encompasses an intuitive interface, a manual calibration model, real-time feedback mechanisms, batch processing functionality, comparative sample analysis, and the ability to zoom in on specific markers.

First, the intuitive interface of ACMSI offers users a straightforward and user-friendly experience. It facilitates the seamless navigation of the software and allows for easy loading of data with visual cues and step-by-step guidance.

Importantly, batch processing capabilities in ACMSI allow for efficient analysis of multiple samples simultaneously, reducing overall analysis time and increasing throughput. This functionality is particularly beneficial for users working with high volumes of data (Fig. 6A).

Moreover, the manual calibration module in ACMSI provides users with precision and control over peak alignment. This feature enables users to manually drag peaks, ensuring accurate localization. Importantly, ACMSI also provides real-time feedback for quality assurance, ensuring the generation of high-quality results (Fig. 6B).

Furthermore, ACMSI enables comparative sample analysis, allowing users to assess similarities and differences between samples. The application also offers flexibility to zoom in on specific markers, enhancing the detailed analysis of individual data points (Fig. 6C).

4 Discussion

As shown in Fig. 5b, ACMSI performs well across all markers, with nearly all scores exceeding 95%. However, for the D2S123 marker, ACMSI's sensitivity and recall are slightly lower, both at 94.74%. This relatively weaker performance may stem from the unique peak patterns of D2S123 during electrophoresis, which often exhibit broader, 5-fingers-like peaks. Since the training was not tailored for individual markers, ACMSI appears less sensitive to the positive peaks of the larger D2S123 patterns. Addressing this limitation will be an important consideration in future updates.

Meanwhile, the aligning algorithm of ACMSI has a stringent requirement for all theoretical standard peaks of the standard channel to be present. In scenarios where there is a limited electrophoresis time or low electrophoresis voltage, resulting in only partial success in the standard bands' run, ACMSI may reject the electrophoresis profiles even if the available successful peaks are adequate to construct a fine linear regression function for size calling. This differs from software like GeneMapper and PeakScanner which can accept incomplete electrophoresis results and successfully align standard peaks in some instances. This situation highlights a trade-off between robustness and accuracy, with a blurred boundary.

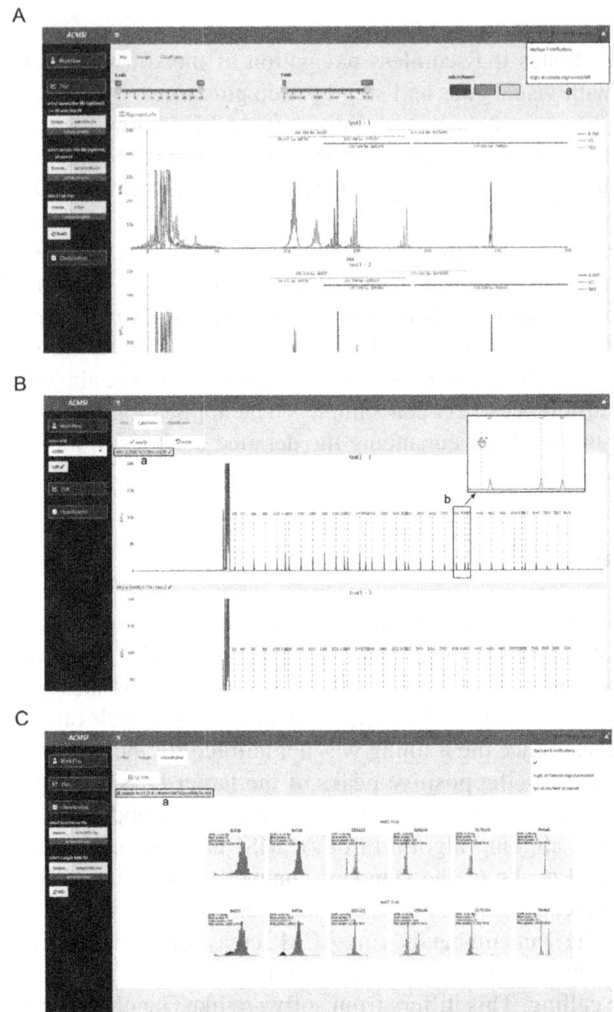

Fig. 6. User Interface of ACMSI. A) It displays the peak profiles of different channels from the original FSA files after alignment. The x-axis represents relative molecular weight, while the y-axis represents peak intensity (RFU). The window displays notifications about QC and MQ. **B)** It illustrates the manual adjustment module of the ACMSI, allowing users to manually adjust peaks by directly dragging the expected peak location (dashed line) to match the actual peak (blue), which shows as region b. Meanwhile the latest MQ of size calling is updated at region a. **C)** It shows the results of the automatic classification. The top left corner, region a, indicates samples that may be MSI positive. Each subplot is a differential feature plot synthesized from a pair of subplots (tumor tissue + normal tissue). The text in each subplot includes the fragment size difference (bp) and the highest peak amplitude.

5 Conclusion

ACMSI comprises three main modules: the size calling, the manual calibration, and the automatic classification. In the size calling module, the application employs four peak identification algorithms to effectively eliminate noise generated during upstream experimental processes, resulting in a lower error rate compared with similar software. In cases of size calling failure, the convenient and intuitive manual calibration feature allows operators to perform adjustment tasks with ease. Moreover, in the automatic classification module, by normalizing peak data and utilizing a differential feature extraction algorithm based on CV, the application achieves excellent consistency with manual classification results for both the markers and samples.

Overall, ACMSI undoubtedly reduces the time and human consumption associated with CE-based fragment analysis, especially MSI analysis. Also, it eliminates subjective errors in MSI classification. However, ACMSI currently does not support combined analysis across different experimental workflows. Additionally, automatic classification algorithms for other CE-based fragment analyses, such as MLPA analysis, are still under development. Future research will focus on enhancing and expanding these functionalities to cater to a broader spectrum of fragment analysis needs.

References

1. Ionov, Y., Peinado, M.A., Malkhosyan, S., Shibata, D., Perucho, M.: Ubiquitous somatic mutations in simple repeated sequences reveal a new mechanism for colonic carcinogenesis. Nature **363**, 558e561 (1993)
2. Maoz, A., Dennis, M., Greenson, J.K.: The Crohn's-like lymphoid reaction to colorectal cancer-tertiary lymphoid structures with immunologic and potentially therapeutic relevance in colorectal cancer. Front. Immunol. **10**, 1884 (2019). https://doi.org/10.3389/fimmu.2019.01884. PMC6714555.PMID31507584
3. Duldulao, M.P., et al.: Gene expression variations in microsatellite stable and unstable colon cancer cells. J. Surg. Res. **174**(1), 1–6 (2012). https://doi.org/10.1016/j.jss.2011.06.016. PMC3210903.PMID21816436
4. Buecher, B., Cacheux, W., Rouleau, E., Dieumegard, B., Mitry, E., Lièvre, A.: Role of microsatellite instability in the management of colorectal cancers. Dig. Liver Dis. **45**(6), 441–449 (2013). https://doi.org/10.1016/j.dld.2012.10.006. PMID23195666
5. Thibodeau, S.N., et al.: Microsatellite instability in cancer of the proximal colon. Science **260**, 816–819 (1993). https://doi.org/10.1126/science.8484122
6. Bacher, J.W., et al.: A highly sensitive pan-cancer test for microsatellite instability. J. Mol. Diagn. **25**(11), 806–826 (2023)
7. Dominguez-Valentin, M., et al.: Cancer risks by gene, age, and gender in 6350 carriers of pathogenic mismatch repair variants: findings from the Prospective Lynch Syndrome Database. Genet. Med. **22**, 15–25 (2020)
8. Lin, J.H., et al.: Validation of long mononucleotide repeat markers for detection of microsatellite instability. J. Mol. Diagn. **24**, 144–157 (2022)
9. Chitradevi, B., Srimathi, P.: An overview on image processing techniques. Inter. J. Innovative Res. Comput. Commun. Eng. **2**(11), 6466–6472 (2014)
10. Wang, Z., Bovik, A.C., Sheikh, H.R., Simoncelli, E.P.: Image quality assessment: from error visibility to structural similarity. IEEE Trans. Image Process. **13**(4), 600–612 (2004)

11. Sara, U., Akter, M., Uddin, M.S.: Image quality assessment through FSIM, SSIM, MSE and PSNR—a comparative study. J. Comput. Commun. **7**(3), 8–18 (2019)

12. Kanopoulos, N., Vasanthavada, N., Baker, R.L.: Design of an image edge detection filter using the Sobel operator. IEEE J. Solid-State Circuits **23**(2), 358–367 (1988)

13. Bao, P., Zhang, L., Wu, X.: Canny edge detection enhancement by scale multiplica-tion. IEEE Trans. Pattern Anal. Mach. Intell. **27**(9), 1485–1490 (2005)

14. Lowe, D.G.: Object recognition from local scale-invariant features. In: Proceedings of the Seventh IEEE International Conference on Computer Vision, vol. 2, pp. 1150–1157. IEEE (September 1999)

15. Khare, S.P., Anderson, J.L., Hoar, T.J., Nychka, D.: An investigation into the appli-cation of an ensemble Kalman smoother to high-dimensional geophysical systems. Tellus A: Dynamic Meteorol. Oceanography **60**(1), 97–112 (2008)

16. Covarrubias-Pazaran, G., Diaz-Garcia, L., Schlautman, B., Salazar, W., Zalapa, J.: Fragman: an R package for fragment analysis. BMC Genet. **17**, 1–8 (2016)

17. Schmidt, D. ., Shi, C., Berry, R.A., Honig, M.L., Utschick, W.: Minimum mean squared error interference alignment. In: 2009 Conference Record of the Forty-Third Asilomar Conference on Signals, Systems and Computers, pp. 1106–1110. IEEE (November 2009)

18. Dureja, A., Pahwa, P.: Analysis of non-linear activation functions for classification tasks using convolutional neural networks. Recent Patents Comput. Sci. **12**(3), 156–161 (2019)

19. Said, K.A.M., Jambek, A.B., Sulaiman, N.: A study of image processing using morphological opening and closing processes. Inter. J. Control Theory Appli. **9**(31), 15–21 (2016)

20. Hulce, D., Li, X., Snyder-Leiby, T., Johathan Liu, C.S.: (n.d.). GeneMarker® genotyping software: Tools to increase the statistical power of DNA fragment analysis. computer software, Association of Biomolecular Resource Facilities

21. Coffa, J., Van Den Berg, J.: Analysis of MLPA data using novel software coffalyser .NET by MRC-Holland. Modern approaches to quality control, pp. 125–150 (2011)

22. Haiguo, H., Hulce, D., Snyder-Leiby, T., Liu, J. C.: GeneMarker® (2009)

23. Genetic analysis tools for genome editing workflows [White paper]. Thermo Fisher Scientific Inc. https://assets.thermofisher.cn/TFS-Assets/GSD/Reference-Materials/geneticanalysistools-genomeediting-whitepaper.pdf

AlloPED: Leveraging Protein Language Models and Structure Features for Allosteric Site Prediction

Xiaochuan Chen[1]([✉]), Jianqiang Zheng[2]([✉]), Zhenni Huang[1], Ziqi Xu[1], Junye Huang[1], Yueyi Tan[1], Yanjie Wei[3]([✉]), and Huiling Zhang[1]([✉])

[1] College of Mathematics and Information & College of Software Engineering, South China Agricultural University, Guangzhou 510642, China
hl.zhang@scau.edu.cn
[2] College of Materials and Energy, South China Agricultural University, Guangzhou 510642, China
[3] Shenzhen Institute of Advanced Technology, Chinese Academy of Sciences, Shenzhen 518055, China
yj.wei@siat.ac.cn

Abstract. Allosteric regulation plays a pivotal role in modulating protein function and allosteric sites represent a promising target for drug discovery. However, identifying allosteric sites remains challenging due to their structural and evolutionary diversity. Here, we present AlloPED, a novel framework that combines protein language models and machine learning to predict allosteric sites with high accuracy. AlloPED consists of two modules: AlloPED-pocket, an ensemble model leveraging physicochemical features to predict allosteric pockets; and AlloPED-site, a dilated convolutional neural network (DCNN) augmented with a comprehensive attention mechanism for residue-level prediction. AlloPED-pocket achieves state-of-the-art performance on benchmark datasets, yielding an MCC of 0.544 and an AUC of 0.920, outperforming existing methods such as AllositePro and PARS. AlloPED-site further refines predictions using high-dimensional sequence embeddings from the ProtT5 protein language model, achieving a precision of 0.601, a recall of 0.422, and a specificity of 0.661. These results highlight the effectiveness of integrating ensemble learning and deep learning for allosteric site prediction. AlloPED also identifies critical determinants of allosteric sites, including residue clustering coefficients, van der Waals volume, and hydrophobic microenvironments. In summary, this framework provides a robust tool for advancing our understanding of allosteric regulation and facilitating structure-based drug design.

Keywords: Allosteric site prediction · allosteric pocket prediction · protein language model; ensemble learning; dilated convolutional neural network

J. Tang et al. (Eds.): ISBRA 2025, LNBI 15757, pp. 383–397, 2026.
https://doi.org/10.1007/978-981-95-0695-8_31

1 Introduction

Allosteric regulation is a fundamental biological mechanism in which an effector molecule binds to an allosteric site, inducing conformational and dynamic changes that modulate protein function. This process plays a crucial role in cellular signaling and has been described as "the second greatest secret of life" [1]. Despite its significance, the molecular basis of allosteric regulation remains incompletely understood, and no universal model applies to all proteins[2, 3].

In drug development, allosteric targeting offers advantages over orthosteric approaches. Unlike orthosteric regulators that compete with endogenous ligands, allosteric modulators fine-tune protein activity by enhancing or inhibiting ligand binding at the orthosteric site. They often exhibit greater specificity and fewer side effects [4] since their pharmacological impact plateaus once the allosteric site is saturated. Additionally, allosteric sites experience lower evolutionary pressure than orthosteric sites, making them promising targets for selective drug design with minimal off-target effects. These benefits have fueled growing interest in allosteric drug discovery.

However, identifying allosteric sites remains a major challenge. Most experimentally confirmed sites have been discovered serendipitously, and systematic, efficient prediction methods are still lacking [5]. Computational approaches, including evolutionary analysis, molecular dynamics (MD) simulations, network-based methods, and machine learning, have been explored to address this. Evolutionary analysis identifies conserved residues linked to allosteric regulation [6, 7], while MD simulations assess protein flexibility and conformational shifts under perturbations [8–10]. Network-based approaches analyze residue interaction networks within protein structures [11, 12]. Recently, machine learning has shown promise in allosteric pocket prediction [13–20], though accuracy remains a concern, as current models primarily rely on structural and dynamic features, leaving room for additional predictive factors. Despite its significance, machine learning-based allosteric site prediction remains more challenging than pocket prediction and is still in its infancy, necessitating innovative approaches to improve accuracy and expand predictive capabilities.

Protein language models (PLMs) have gained traction in bioinformatics, particularly in functional site prediction. Inspired by natural language processing (NLP), PLMs treat protein sequences as a "biological language," learning evolutionary relationships, functional patterns, and structural features from large-scale sequence data. This enables powerful functional site prediction. For instance, CLAPE-SMB integrates the ESM2 pretrained language model with contrastive learning for efficient protein-small molecule binding site prediction [21]. GraphEC employs geometric graph learning with ESMFold for high-accuracy enzyme active site prediction [22], while DPFunc combines sequence data with domain-guided structural features for precise protein function prediction [23]. These studies highlight how PLMs extend beyond sequence analysis, integrating multimodal data and multi-task learning to enhance predictions [24–26].

To develop an efficient and accurate data-driven approach for allosteric site prediction, we propose AlloPED, a novel sequence-based method. AlloPED comprises two components: (1) AlloPED-pocket, an ensemble learning model that predicts allosteric pockets by incorporating structural features; and (2) AlloPED-site, a deep neural network leveraging the ProtT5 [27] model with 3 billion parameters to generate high-dimensional embeddings. By integrating expanded convolution and attention mechanisms, AlloPED-site captures potential interactions between allosteric sites and other protein regions, enabling precise prediction. Through the combination of ensemble learning and large language model-based deep learning, AlloPED aims to advance allosteric site identification, ultimately benefiting biological research and drug discovery. AlloPED is available at https://github.com/mjcoo/AlloPED.

2   Materials and Methods

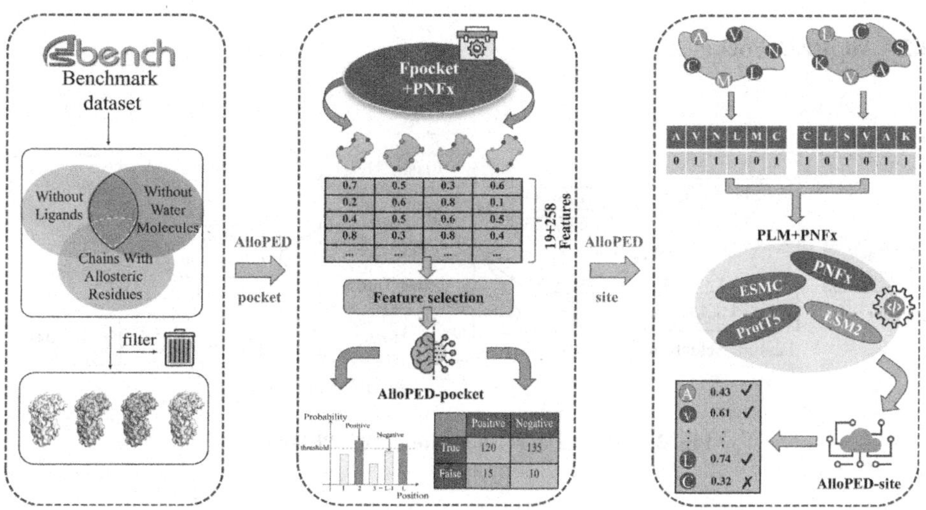

Fig. 1. Flowchart of AlloPED for identifying protein allosteric sites

The workflow of AlloPED is systematically outlined in Fig. 1. Initially, the ASBench dataset is employed as the training corpus, and protein pockets are identified using the Fpocket algorithm. AlloPED comprises two core modules: AlloPED-pocket, which employs an ensemble learning architecture to predict allosteric pockets by integrating physicochemical features and residue contact network properties; and AlloPED-site, which refines predictions at the residue level using a dilated convolutional neural network augmented with comprehensive attention mechanisms. The final model is validated using an independent test set, ensuring robust generalization performance.

2.1   Data Collection and Preprocessing

The training dataset was derived from ASBench [28], a benchmark collection of allosteric proteins curated from the Allosteric Database (ASD), comprising 146 proteins with X-ray resolution ≤ 3.0 Å, sequence identity $< 30\%$, and experimentally validated allosteric sites. An independent test set of 24 proteins from AllositePro was used for model evaluation. Structural data from PDB files underwent two preprocessing protocols: (1) removal of non-amino acid residues and non-allosteric chains for AlloPED-pocket training, and (2) exclusion of non-amino acid data only for AlloPED-site training. In this study, Fpocket [29] is used to identify binding pockets on allosteric proteins with default settings. A pocket was labeled positive if ≥ 25% of its residues overlapped with the true allosteric site; otherwise, it was negative. In the training set (146 proteins), 4,756 pockets were detected (185 positive, 4,571 negative). The test set (24 proteins) contained 53 positive and 745 negative samples. The training dataset included 22776 experiment-validated allosteric sites across 185 positive pockets, while the test set contained 555 sites within 53 positive pockets, which provided sufficient data for comprehensively assessing the model's performance in allosteric site prediction.

2.2 AlloPED-Pocket

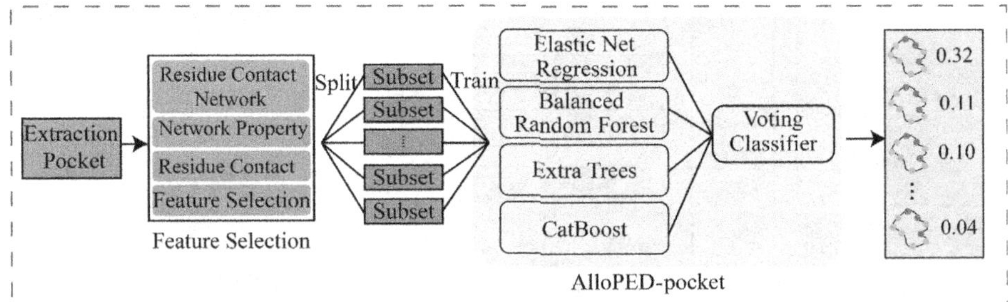

Fig. 2. The model architecture of AlloPED-pocket

The workflow of AlloPED-pocket is shown in Fig. 2.

Structure-Based Features

For allosteric pocket prediction of AlloPED, we use mainly structural features extracted by Fpocket and PNFx. Fpocket provides 19 physicochemical features as shown in **Table S1**. PNFx is a feature extraction toolbox developed by our group (https://github.com/mjcoo/PNFx). As shown in **Table S2**, PNFx provides 258 features such as solvent accessibility, contact density [30], clustering coefficient, betweenness centrality, secondary structure and microenvironment properties (**Table S2**). The detailed description of PNFx can be found at https://github.com/mjcoo/PNFx/feat_list.csv. The Fpocket and PNFx features collectively describe residue and local structural properties of the pocket, thereby enabling systematic analysis of pocket-level functional determinants.

Feature Selection

We implemented a two-stage feature optimization strategy to balance dimensionality and model performance. In the first stage, the Minimum Redundancy Maximum Relevance (mRMR) algorithm filters the 258-dimensional structural feature space, using a correlation threshold of 15 to maximize relevance while minimizing redundancy, enhancing computational efficiency and interpretability. Next, pocket-level feature descriptors are constructed by aggregating mean, minimum, and maximum values of amino acid features within each binding pocket. In the second stage, Recursive Feature Elimination with Cross-Validation (RFECV) with a random forest model refines feature selection through iterative backward elimination, dynamically assessing each feature's contribution to model performance.

Allosteric Pocket Prediction Model

AlloPED-pocket utilizes a Soft Voting Ensemble Learning model, combining CatBoost, Elastic Net Regression, Balanced Random Forest, and Extra Trees to improve prediction accuracy. CatBoost refines weak learners within a Boosting framework, excelling in handling high-dimensional data. Elastic Net integrates L1 and L2 regularization, making it suitable for correlated features. Balanced Random Forest mitigates class imbalance through resampling, while Extra Trees enhances generalization via randomized node splitting.

For training, the dataset was divided into 10 balanced groups, ensuring each positive sample was paired with a randomly selected negative sample sharing the same PDB ID. GroupKFold with 5-fold cross-validation trained the ensemble model and generated prediction probabilities for each base learner. A dynamic thresholding approach was applied, with Youden's index optimizing the decision threshold via ROC curve analysis:

$$J - Sensitivity + Specificity - 1 \tag{1}$$

Instead of using a fixed 0.5 threshold, this method ensured a better balance between recall and specificity.

2.3 AlloPED-Site

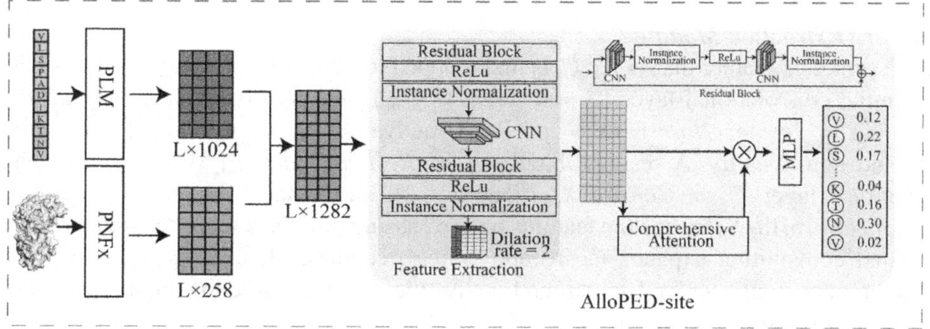

Fig. 3. The model architecture of AlloPED-site

The workflow of AlloPED-site is shown in Fig. 3.

Sequence and Structural Features

AlloPED-site integrates sequence embeddings from PLM and structural features from

PNFx to capture evolutionary and functional patterns. In this study, we conducted a comprehensive comparison of several PLMs, including ESM2 [31], ESMC (600M) [32], ProteinBERT [33], and ProtT5 (3B) [27], to evaluate their effectiveness in encoding allosteric protein sequences. Our goal was to identify the most suitable model for capturing the intricate patterns and structural information inherent in these sequences, which are crucial for understanding allosteric regulation mechanisms Structural features from PNFx, identical to those used in AlloPED-pocket, include 258 physicochemical and topological descriptors. These multimodal features are concatenated into a high-dimensional vector and processed using a sliding window approach. Unlike AlloPED-pocket's two-stage mRMR-RFECV feature selection, AlloPED-site employs end-to-end neural architecture to automatically select discriminative features, enabling adaptive learning of sequence-structure relationships for allosteric site prediction.

Allosteric Site Prediction Model

Before training AlloPED-site, protein structural data underwent preprocessing, including feature vector extraction, normalization, and window-based sampling to enhance local feature capture. The model, based on a Dilated Convolutional Neural Network (DCNN), incorporates dilated convolution, residual connections, mixed attention mechanisms, and focal loss functions to improve allosteric site prediction. Dilated convolution expands the receptive field to capture long-range dependencies, while residual connections mitigate gradient vanishing and enhance feature propagation. Mixed attention mechanisms prioritize critical feature regions, and the focal loss function emphasizes hard-to-classify samples to address class imbalance.

Training employed Kaiming normal initialization for convolutional weights and the Adam optimizer with a cyclical learning rate, following 5-fold cross-validation. Data was split into five subsets, with four for training and one for validation per fold, allowing hyperparameter tuning and refinement. The final model's performance was evaluated across all folds, ensuring reliability in allosteric site prediction.

Feature Extraction Module

Each protein's feature matrix X_{input} is first mapped to a 512-dimensional space through an initial convolutional layer $X_1 = Conv1d(X_{input})$, followed by instance normalization $X_2 = InstanceNorm1d(X_1)$ and ReLU activation $X_3 = ReLU(X_2)$ for stability and non-linearity. A residual block $X_4 = ResidualBlock(X_3, 512)$, another convolutional layer $X_5 = Conv1d(X_4; dilation = 2)$, and instance normalization $X_5 = InstanceNorm1d(X_5)$ refine the features before passing through a second residual block. Dilated convolution expands the receptive field, capturing long-range dependencies and broader contextual information. Finally, the feature extraction module outputs $X_6 = ResidualBlock(X_5, 512)$.

Residual Block

The residual block consists of two convolutional layers with instance normalization and ReLU activation $X_{res} = ReLU(InstanceNorm1d(Conv1d(X_{input})))$. The shortcut connection mitigates gradient vanishing, promoting feature reuse. To enhance representation, channel attention is applied, where X_{input} undergoes global average pooling and instance normalization to generate attention weights $X'_{res} =$

InstanceNorm1d(Conv1d(X$_{res}$)). These weights recalibrate the output $X_{output} = ReLU\left(X_{input} + ChannelAttention(X'_{res})\right)$, emphasizing key feature channels.

Channel Attension

Channel attention highlights important feature channels by reducing dimensions to 16. By learning inter-channel relationships, the model selects the most valuable features for each position.

$$y = ReLU\left(Linear\left(AdaptiveAvgPool1d\left(X_{input}\right), C, C//r\right)\right) \tag{2}$$

$$y' = Sigmoid(Linear(y, C//r, C)) \tag{3}$$

$$X_{output} = X_{input} \odot y' \tag{4}$$

Comprehensive Attention Module

This module enhances feature representation by integrating spatial and channel attention. The input matrix X_6 undergoes convolution $A_{spatial} = Conv1d(X_6)$ and Sigmoid activation to generate spatial attention weights $A'_{spatial} = Sigmoid\left(A_{spatial}\right)$, highlighting key regions for allosteric site prediction. Simultaneously, channel attention produces $y_{attn} = ChannelAttention(X_6)$. The final attention weight $A_{total} = A'_{spatial} \odot y_{attn}$, obtained by multiplying both, is applied to X_6, resulting in $X_{attn} = X_6 \odot A_{total}$, which enhances focus on crucial regions and channels, improving prediction accuracy.

Classification Module

This module maps weighted feature vectors to allosteric site labels through binary classification. The weighted feature map X_{attn} is transposed for fully connected layer operations, followed by dimensionality reduction and feature extraction via fully connected layers and layer normalization. ReLU activation enhances non-linearity, while Dropout prevents overfitting. The final classification layer applies a Sigmoid function to map output values to [0,1].

$$h_1 = ReLU\left(LayerNorm\left(Linear\left(X_{attn}^T, 256, 128\right)\right)\right) \tag{5}$$

$$p = Sigmoid(Linear(Dropout(h_1; rate = 0.75), 128, 1)) \tag{6}$$

where p represents the probability of an allosteric site.

Loss Function

The model uses the Focal Loss function as its optimization objective to effectively address class imbalance issues and increase the model's attention to hard-to-classify samples.

$$FL(p_t) = -\alpha_t(1 - p_t)^\gamma log(p_t) \tag{7}$$

where p_t represents the predicted probability of belonging to the positive class. The class imbalance coefficient α_t is set to 0.85, and the hard sample focusing parameter γ is set to 4.0, to increase the attention paid to positive examples with smaller quantities.

2.4 Performance Evaluation Metrics

To assess the performance of AlloPED, we conducted a thorough evaluation using an independent test dataset. The test dataset underwent the same feature extraction and pre-processing pipeline as the training data to ensure consistency in evaluation. To quantify the model's predictive performance, we used several standard classification metrics: Precision (PRE), Specificity (SPE), Recall, and Matthews Correlation Coefficient (MCC). These metrics are defined as follows:

$$Accuarcy = \frac{TP + TN}{TP + TN + FP + FN} \tag{8}$$

$$Precision = \frac{TP}{TP+FP} \tag{9}$$

$$Sensitivity = \frac{TP}{TP+FN} \tag{10}$$

$$Specificity = \frac{TN}{TN+FP} \tag{11}$$

$$MCC = \frac{TP \times TN - FP \times FN}{\sqrt{(TP+FP)(TP+FN)(TN+FP)(TN+FN)}} \tag{12}$$

where TP, TN, FP, and FN represent the number of true positives, true negatives, false positives, and false negatives, respectively. These metrics collectively provide a comprehensive evaluation of the model's performance. We also utilized the Area Under the Receiver Operating Characteristic Curve (AUC) to assess the model's ability to distinguish between positive and negative classes, offering an additional measure of classification accuracy.

3 Results

3.1 Characteristic Analysis of Allosteric Sites

Allosteric sites exhibit distinct evolutionary and structural characteristics compared to functional sites. Evolutionarily, they experience reduced selective pressure, enabling adaptive mutations (e.g., asparagine-related features in RNR and Asp mutations in KRAS), while maintaining functional conservation through conformational plasticity. Structurally, allosteric sites are smaller, more dynamic, and enriched in hydrophobic residues, with shallow binding pockets and network connectivity critical for signal propagation. These properties, including high clustering coefficients and β-sheet structures in hinge regions, align with previous findings highlighting their roles in regulatory flexibility and pathological processes.

In this study, (Figs. 4 and 5) we analyzed the physicochemical properties strongly associated with allosteric sites. In the first stage of feature selection, we applied mRMR analysis to systematically screen allosteric site features and compare them with other functional sites. The allosteric score and orthosteric score are relevance values calculated through mRMR that indicate how strongly each feature correlates with allosteric or orthosteric sites, respectively. Higher scores indicate that the feature is more important

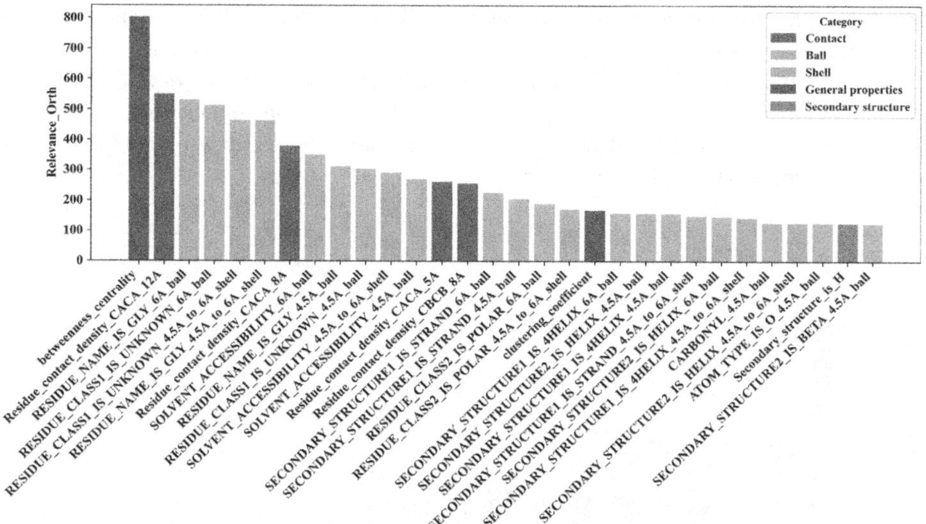

Fig. 4. Top 30 features ranked by orthosteric score using mRMR analysis

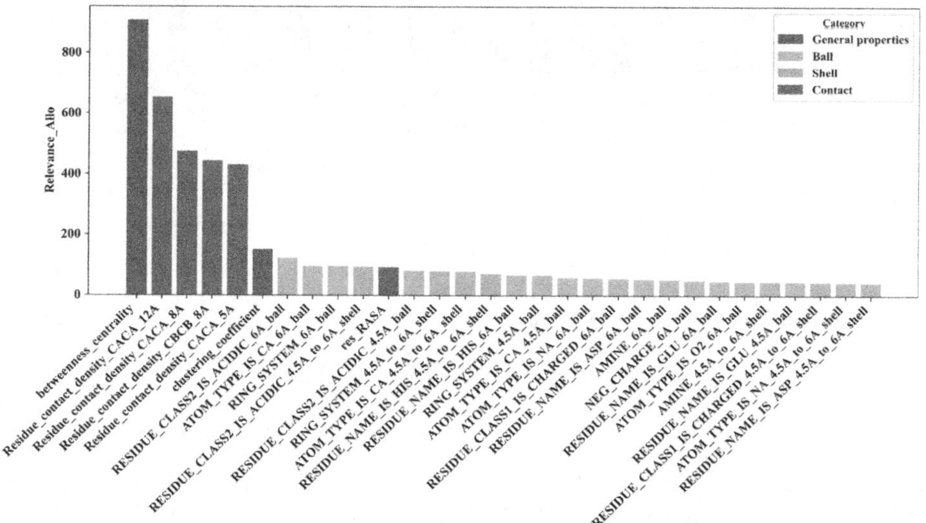

Fig. 5. Top 30 features ranked by allosteric score using mRMR analysis

in predicting that specific type of site. The results indicated that allosteric sites exhibit low sequence specificity, as seen in their conservation scores and hydrophobic microenvironment. Large-scale sequence alignment revealed an average conservation score of 0.63 for allosteric sites, significantly lower than orthosteric (active) sites (0.83, $P = 1.26 \times 10^{-23}$) [34], suggesting greater sequence plasticity during evolution. Additionally, allosteric sites are enriched in hydrophobic residues such as isoleucine (Ile), whereas active sites favor rigid residues like tryptophan (Trp) and phenylalanine (Phe) [34, 35]. Statistical analysis of 2,937 proteins (69401 allosteric sites in ASD database) further supported this trend (Fig. 6), with isoleucine appearing 4,317 times in allosteric sites (6.22%). Moreover, differences in negative charge distribution suggest that the electrostatic microenvironment of allosteric sites may dynamically regulate ligand binding, as observed in the HisH-HisF system [36].

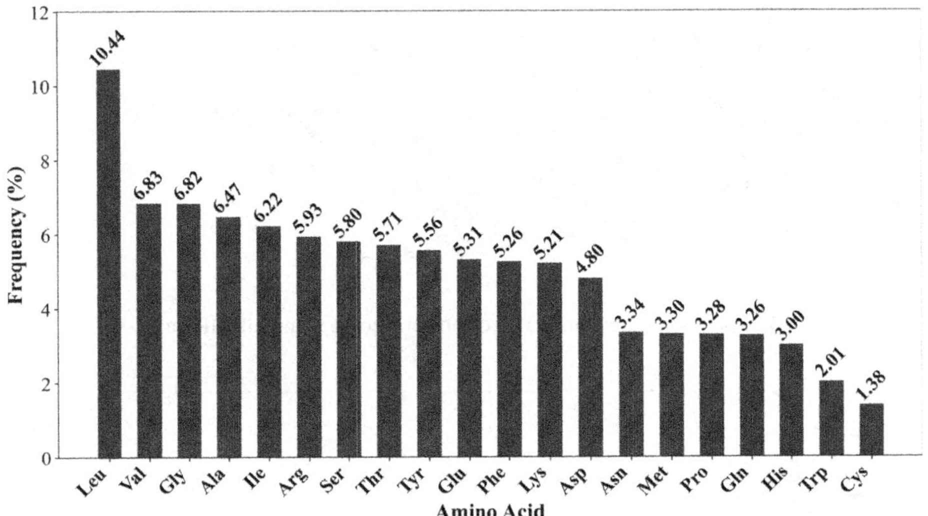

Fig. 6. Frequency distribution of amino acids at allosteric sites according to 2,937 allosteric proteins

3.2 Performance of AlloPED-Pocket

Table 1. Performance comparison of AlloPED with other methods on the test set

Methods	ACC	SPE	PRE	Recall	MCC	AUC
PARS	0.708	0.756	0.180	0.375	0.099	-
Allosite	0.828	0.858	0.245	0.500	0.264	-
AllositePro	0.863	0.885	0.333	0.625	0.388	-
AlloPED-pocket	0.952	0.965	0.471	0.686	0.544	0.920

Feature selection plays a crucial role in improving AlloPED-pocket's predictive performance. Using mRMR analysis, we identified the most informative features, enhancing accuracy and generalization. Clustering coefficient and van der Waals volume emerged as key predictors, as they are not only statistically linked to allosteric sites but also biologically relevant—clustering coefficient reflects their role in regulatory networks, while van der Waals volume captures their compact structural properties. Additionally, mRMR eliminated redundant features, ensuring the model focuses on the most relevant data. To refine feature selection, we computed aggregated statistics (e.g., mean, minimum, and maximum values) for amino acid properties to construct pocket-level descriptors. Finally, RFECV identified variables that best characterize allosteric pockets, optimizing AlloPED-pocket's predictive performance.

Table 1 presents the comparison results of AlloPED-pocket with AllositePro, Allosite, PARS, and other methods. As shown in Table 1, our model achieved a Matthews correlation coefficient (MCC) of 0.544, significantly outperforming other methods, with a 40.2% improvement over AllositePro. This indicates that our model has certain advantages in addressing the issue of class imbalance. Additionally, our model's precision was 47.1%, which represents a significant improvement over AllositePro (33.3%), Allosite (24.5%), and PARS (18.0%). Notably, our model achieved the best performance in terms of specificity and AUC, demonstrating its superior ability to avoid false positives among negative samples and indicating stronger generalization capabilities compared to other methods.

3.3 Performance of AlloPED-Site

During model training, we concatenated the features generated by ProtT5 with 258 structural features. This approach, leveraging the structural characteristics of AlloPED-site's deep learning model, helps avoid missing certain potential features that could determine allosteric sites in previous feature selection processes. By training and evaluating the AlloPED-site model using different window sizes (ranging from 5 to 45 with an interval of 4), we systematically calculated the model's performance across various window sizes (Fig. 7). The experimental results showed a significant trend in the performance metrics as the window size increased. The model achieved optimal AUC (0.72) and AUPRC (0.67) when the window size was 5, with precision and recall values of 0.63 and 0.56, respectively, indicating a good balance. As the window size increased, we observed a noticeable decline in the AUPRC metric, while the AUC showed only a slight decrease. Particularly in terms of precision and recall, both metrics exhibited a downward trend, with recall experiencing a significant drop. The F1 score also reached its highest value (0.59) at a window size of 5, while the MCC metric remained relatively stable across different window sizes but performed better at smaller windows.

After determining the optimal window size, we further compared the performance of features extracted from different protein language models in the task of predicting allosteric sites. The results in Fig. 8 indicated that the ProtT5 model performed the best, achieving an AUC of 0.671 and an AUPRC of 0.645, while also obtaining the highest MCC value of 0.205. Compared to other models, ProtT5 demonstrated a good balance in precision (0.580) and recall (0.507). The overall performance of the ProteinBERT model was a close second to ProtT5, with an AUC of 0.670 and an AUPRC of 0.634; its precision reached 0.577, but its recall was relatively low at 0.490. Although the ESM series models performed well in terms of specificity, with ESM2 reaching 0.709, their performance on other evaluation metrics was relatively weaker. The MCC metric was 0.162 for ESM2, which has 650 million parameters, and 0.169 for ESM Cambrian (ESM C), which contains 600 million parameters. Despite their large scale, these models showed suboptimal

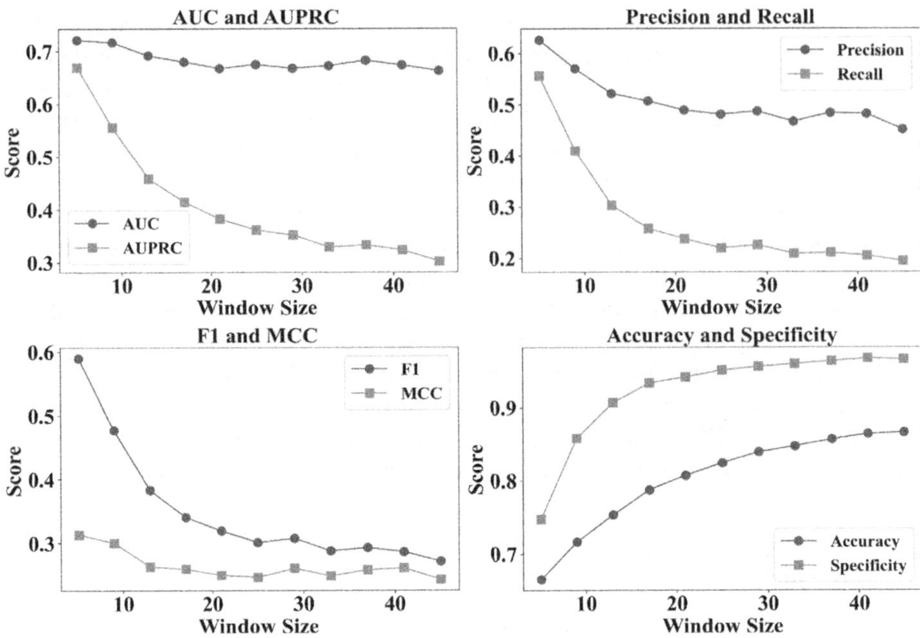

Fig. 7. Performance of AlloPED-site across different window sizes

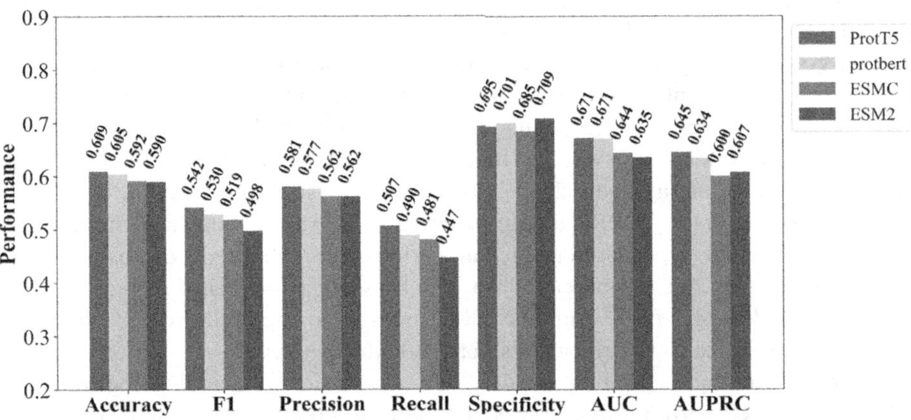

Fig. 8. Performance comparison of AlloPED-site using features from different protein language models

predictive performance for allosteric sites. These results suggest that the ProtT5 model is more effective at capturing feature information related to allosteric sites within protein sequences, providing a more reliable feature representation for subsequent prediction tasks.

To validate the reliability of our model, we evaluated it using a test set of 24 allosteric proteins developed for the AllositePro method and compared the results with those of other widely used allosteric site identification methods on the same test set. By combining the pockets predicted by AlloPED-pocket, AlloPED-site further predicted allosteric sites, achieving a precision of 0.601, a recall of 0.4218, and a specificity of 0.661. Furthermore, to assess the impact of PLM-derived features, we incorporated sequence-based representations generated by ESM2, ESM C, ProteinBERT, and ProtT5, then combined them with structural features for model evaluation (Table 2). The results indicate that the choice of PLM significantly influences predictive performance. Notably, ProtT5-based features yielded the best results, achieving a precision of 0.601, a recall of 0.422, and an AUC of 0.563, outperforming other PLM-derived feature combinations. In contrast, features derived from ESM2 and ESMC exhibited lower recall values (0.360 and 0.378, respectively), indicating potential limitations in capturing relevant allosteric site information. These findings emphasize the effectiveness of ProtT5 in enhancing allosteric site prediction when integrated with structural descriptors, further demonstrating the advantage of combining sequence-based deep learning with structural insights.

4 Conclusions

This study introduces AlloPED, a novel framework integrating ensemble learning and deep neural networks to address the challenge of predicting allosteric sites in proteins. By combining AlloPED-pocket—an ensemble model optimized for pocket-level prediction using residue contact networks and physicochemical features—and AlloPED-site—a dilated convolutional neural network augmented with ProtT5 protein language model embeddings and attention mechanisms—our approach achieves state-of-the-art performance on benchmark datasets. AlloPED-pocket yields an MCC of 0.544 and AUC of 0.920, surpassing existing methods such as AllositePro (MCC = 0.388) and PARS (MCC = 0.099). AlloPED-site further refines predictions at the residue level, achieving a precision of 0.601 and recall of 0.422, demonstrating the value of multimodal feature integration.

The success of AlloPED underscores the importance of combining evolutionary and structural insights with advanced machine learning techniques. Key features such as residue clustering coefficients and van der Waals volume highlight the role of network connectivity and compact structural properties in allosteric regulation. This framework not only advances computational prediction of allosteric sites but also provides mechanistic insights into their functional roles, with implications for drug discovery targeting proteins like GPCRs and kinases. Future work will focus on integrating dynamic features from molecular dynamics simulations and validating predictions through experimental mutagenesis, further enhancing the framework's utility in precision medicine and structural biology.

Acknowledgements. This work was partly supported by the Guangdong Natural Science Foundation (No. 2024A1515010133), the National Key Research and Development Program of China (No. 2024YFA0919702), the National Science Foundation of China (No. 12426303) and the Shenzhen Basic Research Fund (No. KQTD20200820113106007).

References

1. Liu, J., Nussinov, R.: Allostery: an overview of its history, concepts, methods, and applications. PLoS Comput. Biol. **12**(6), e1004966 (2016)
2. Xiao, S., Verkhivker, G.M., Tao, P.: Machine learning and protein allostery. Trends Biochem. Sci. **48**(4), 375–390 (2023)
3. Zhang, H., et al.: Exploring pathogenic mutation in allosteric proteins: the prediction and beyond. Tsinghua Sci. Technol. **30**(5), 2284–2299 (2025)
4. Wenthur, C.J., Gentry, P.R., Mathews, T.P., Lindsley, C.W.: Drugs for allosteric sites on receptors. Annu. Rev. Pharmacol. Toxicol. **54**(1), 165–184 (2014)
5. Hardy, J.A., Wells, J.A.: Searching for new allosteric sites in enzymes. Curr. Opin. Struct. Biol. **14**(6), 706–715 (2004)
6. Süel, G.M., Lockless, S.W., Wall, M.A., Ranganathan, R.: Evolutionarily conserved networks of residues mediate allosteric communication in proteins. Nat. Struct. Biol. **10**(1), 59–69 (2003)
7. Reynolds, K.A., McLaughlin, R.N., Ranganathan, R.: Hot spots for allosteric regulation on protein surfaces. Cell **147**(7), 1564–1575 (2011)
8. Qi, Y., Wang, Q., Tang, B., Lai, L.: Identifying allosteric binding sites in proteins with a two-state Go model for novel allosteric effector discovery. J. Chem. Theory Comput. **8**(8), 2962–2971 (2012)
9. Panjkovich, A., Daura, X.: PARS: a web server for the prediction of protein allosteric and regulatory sites. Bioinformatics **30**(9), 1314–1315 (2014)
10. Ma, X., Meng, H., Lai, L.: Motions of allosteric and orthosteric ligand-binding sites in proteins are highly correlated. J. Chem. Inf. Model. **56**(9), 1725–1733 (2016)
11. Amor, B.R., Schaub, M.T., Yaliraki, S.N., Barahona, M.: Prediction of allosteric sites and mediating interactions through bond-to-bond propensities. Nat. Commun. **7**(1), 12477 (2016)
12. Wang, J., Jain, A., McDonald, L.R., Gambogi, C., Lee, A.L., Dokholyan, N.V.: Mapping allosteric communications within individual proteins. Nat. Commun. **11**(1), 3862 (2020)
13. Huang, W., et al.: Allosite: a method for predicting allosteric sites. Bioinformatics **29**(18), 2357–2359 (2013)
14. Greener, J.G., Sternberg, M.J.: AlloPred: prediction of allosteric pockets on proteins using normal mode perturbation analysis. BMC Bioinform. **16**, 1–7 (2015)
15. Chen, A.S.Y., Westwood, N.J., Brear, P., Rogers, G.W., Mavridis, L., Mitchell, J.B.: A random forest model for predicting allosteric and functional sites on proteins. Mol. Inf. **35**(3–4), 125–135 (2016)
16. Song, K., et al.: Improved method for the identification and validation of allosteric sites. J. Chem. Inf. Model. **57**(9), 2358–2363 (2017)
17. Tian, H., Jiang, X., Tao, P.: PASSer: Prediction of allosteric sites server. Mach. Learn. Sci. Technol. **2**(3), 035015 (2021)
18. Tian, H., Xiao, S., Jiang, X., Tao, P.: PASSerRank: Prediction of allosteric sites with learning to rank. J. Comput. Chem. **44**(28), 2223–2229 (2023)
19. Xiao, S., Tian, H., Tao, P.: PASSer2. 0: accurate prediction of protein allosteric sites through automated machine learning. Front. Mol. Biosci. **9**, 879251 (2022)
20. Hu, F., et al.: Prediction of Protein Allosteric Sites with Transfer Entropy and Spatial Neighbor-Based Evolutionary Information Learned by an Ensemble Model. J. Chem. Inf. Model. **64**(15), 6197–6204 (2024)
21. Liu, Y., Tian, B.: Protein–DNA binding sites prediction based on pre-trained protein language model and contrastive learning. Brief. Bioinform. **25**(1), bbad488 (2024)
22. Song, Y., Yuan, Q., Chen, S., Zeng, Y., Zhao, H., Yang, Y.: Accurately predicting enzyme functions through geometric graph learning on ESMFold-predicted structures. Nat. Commun. **15**(1), 8180 (2024)

23. Wang, W., Shuai, Y., Zeng, M., Fan, W., Li, M.: DPFunc: accurately predicting protein function via deep learning with domain-guided structure information. Nat. Commun. **16**(1), 70 (2025)
24. Xie, J., Dong, R., Zhu, J., Lin, H., Wang, S., Lai, L.: MMFuncPhos: a multi-modal learning framework for identifying functional phosphorylation sites and their regulatory types. Adv. Sci. **12**, 2410981 (2025)
25. Kulmanov, M., Hoehndorf, R.: DeepGOPlus: improved protein function prediction from sequence. Bioinformatics **36**(2), 422–429 (2020)
26. Yuan, Q., Chen, S., Wang, Y., Zhao, H., Yang, Y.: Alignment-free metal ion-binding site prediction from protein sequence through pretrained language model and multi-task learning. Brief. Bioinform. **23**(6), bbac444 (2022)
27. Elnaggar, A., et al.: Prottrans: Toward understanding the language of life through self-supervised learning. IEEE Trans. Pattern Anal. Mach. Intell. **44**(10), 7112–7127 (2021)
28. Huang, W., et al.: ASBench: benchmarking sets for allosteric discovery. Bioinformatics **31**(15), 2598–2600 (2015)
29. Le Guilloux, V., Schmidtke, P., Tuffery, P.: Fpocket: an open source platform for ligand pocket detection. BMC Bioinformatics **10**, 1–11 (2009)
30. Zhang, H., et al.: Evaluation of residue-residue contact prediction methods: From retrospective to prospective. PLoS Comput. Biol. **17**(5), e1009027 (2021)
31. Lin, Z., et al.: Language models of protein sequences at the scale of evolution enable accurate structure prediction. BioRxiv, 2022, p. 500902 (2022)
32. Hayes, T., et al.: Simulating 500 million years of evolution with a language model. Science **387**, eads0018 (2025)
33. Brandes, N., Ofer, D., Peleg, Y., Rappoport, N., Linial, M.: ProteinBERT: a universal deep-learning model of protein sequence and function. Bioinformatics **38**(8), 2102–2110 (2022)
34. Li, X., et al.: Toward an understanding of the sequence and structural basis of allosteric proteins. J. Mol. Graph. Model. **40**, 30–39 (2013)
35. Namboodiri, S., Giuliani, A., Nair, A.S., Dhar, P.K.: Looking for a sequence based allostery definition: a statistical journey at different resolution scales. J. Theor. Biol. **304**, 211–218 (2012)
36. Van Wart, A.T., Durrant, J., Votapka, L., Amaro, R.E.: Weighted implementation of suboptimal paths (WISP): an optimized algorithm and tool for dynamical network analysis. J. Chem. Theory Comput. **10**(2), 511–517 (2014)

Parameterized Algorithms for the Tree Containment Problem on Multifurcating Phylogenetic Network

Feng Shi[✉], Zhanglian Lin, Xin Zeng, and Jingyi Liu

School of Computer Science and Engineering, Central South University,
Changsha 410083, China
`fengshi@csu.edu.cn`

Abstract. Recent studies have shown that phylogenetic trees fail to capture certain evolutionary processes, such as reticulation events. To address this, phylogenetic networks were introduced as a more expressive model. This led to the fundamental *Tree Containment Problem*, which is NP-hard even in the binary case and has been extensively studied, primarily through exponential-time algorithms for binary networks and biologically relevant subclasses. Prior to this work, the best-known fixed-parameter algorithm for binary networks ran in $O(1.618^k n^2)$, where k is the reticulation number and n is the number of vertices. In this paper, we study the Tree Containment Problem on rooted multifurcating phylogenetic networks, proposing a parameterized algorithm with a runtime of $O(1.618^k m^3)$, where m is the number of arcs. We then adapt this algorithm for parameterization by the level number l, achieving a runtime of $O(1.618^l m^3)$. Since $l \leq k$, this provides a more efficient solution when l is significantly smaller.

Keywords: Phylogenetic tree · Phylogenetic network · Tree containment problem · Fixed-parameter algorithm

1 Introduction

Since the acceptance of evolutionary theory, scientists have sought to map the tree of life. While DNA has provided key insights into species relationships, analyzing vast genetic data remains challenging. Phylogenetic trees have long been used to model species evolution, where each leaf (in-degree = 1, out-degree = 0) represents a taxon, internal vertices (in-degree = 1, out-degree ≥ 2) denote evolutionary events, and the root (in-degree = 0, out-degree > 0) represents the common ancestor. However, phylogenetic trees struggle to capture complex evolutionary processes like hybridization, recombination [20], and horizontal gene

This work is supported in part by the National Natural Science Foundation of China under Grants 62472449 and 62332020, and the Hunan Provincial Natural Science Foundation of China under Grant 2025JJ50395.

transfer [4, 27]. These reticulation events, where species inherit genetic material from multiple ancestors, necessitate the use of phylogenetic networks [17]. In such networks, reticulation vertices (in-degree ≥ 2, out-degree ≥ 1) model gene flow, while tree vertices (in-degree $= 1$, out-degree ≥ 2) represent speciation.

Despite the rise of phylogenetic networks, phylogenetic trees remain essential for tracing the evolution of individual genes [14, 15]. Genes evolve in tree-like patterns, often embedded within phylogenetic networks. Due to events like gene duplication, loss, transfer, and hybridization, different genes may yield distinct trees [3, 22]. This interplay between phylogenetic trees and networks gives rise to the *Tree Containment Problem*—determining whether a given phylogenetic network *contains* a given phylogenetic tree. This problem is fundamental in evolutionary analysis and crucial for constructing phylogenetic networks [18, 26].

The Tree Containment problem has been shown to be NP-hard by Kanj et al. [19], even in the binary case—where all internal vertices, except for the root, have a degree of 3. This underscores the computational complexity of reconciling phylogenetic trees with networks. Prior research on Tree Containment has predominantly addressed scenarios where both the phylogenetic network N and tree T are binary, with efforts concentrated on developing efficient algorithms for specialized network structures. Key complexity results include: For binary galled trees, the problem is solvable in polynomial time [19]. Binary normal networks and binary tree-child networks similarly admit polynomial time solutions [31]. In the case of binary nearly-stable networks, time complexities improve progressively from $O(n^2)$ [9] to $O(n \log n)$ [7] and ultimately $O(n)$ [10]. For binary reticulation-visible networks, algorithmic advancements have reduced complexity from $O(n^3)$ [2] through $O(n^2)$ [12] to an optimal $O(n)$ [11], where n denotes the number of vertices in the network.

The Tree Containment problem remains NP-hard for certain subclasses of binary networks, such as binary tree-sibling, binary regular, and binary time-consistent networks [31]. For general binary phylogenetic networks N, several fixed-parameter algorithms (FPT algorithms) have been proposed based on different parameters. Van Iersel et al. [31] showed that the problem is fixed-parameter tractable with respect to the level number l of N, providing an algorithm with a runtime of $O^*(2^l)$. Gunawan et al. [13] proposed an FPT algorithm parameterized by the reticulation number k, with a runtime of $O(1.618^k n^2)$. Van Iersel et al. [28] introduced an FPT algorithm parameterized by the treewidth t, with a runtime of $O(2^{O(t^2)} n)$. Weller [32] proposed an algorithm based on the maximum number t^* of "tree components with unstable roots", with a runtime of $O(3^{t^*} n^2)$. Additionally, Van Iersel et al. [30] studied the problem on unrooted binary phylogenetic networks, proposing an algorithm with a runtime of $O(4^k n^2)$ for the reticulation number k, later improved by Shi et al. [24] to $O(2.594^k n^2)$. The algorithm by Shi et al. can also solve the problem for unrooted binary phylogenetic networks when parameterized by the level number.

However, the Tree Containment problem for multifurcating networks remains unexplored. This is an important gap, as multifurcating phylogenetic trees and networks are biologically realistic, with studies such as [8, 21] highlighting their relevance. Moreover, multifurcating phylogenetic networks are frequently studied in problems like the Maximum Agreement Forest problem [5,23,25,33] and the Hybridization Number problem [1,16,29]. Therefore, addressing the Tree Containment problem in multifurcating phylogenetic networks is of great significance.

In this paper, we study the Tree Containment problem for multifurcating phylogenetic networks, parameterized by the reticulation number k and the level number l. For the reticulation number k, our approach proceeds as follows: First, we introduce two operations to simplify the multifurcating structure of the phylogenetic network N. Next, we develop reduction rules to handle trivial cases during simplification. We define *vertex depth* in N and analyze the local structures around the leaf with the largest depth. Using a branch-and-bound framework, we propose a fixed-parameter algorithm with a runtime of $O(1.618^k m^3)$, where m is the number of arcs in N. We extend this approach for parameterization by the level number l, adapting the algorithm to a divide-and-conquer strategy to achieve a runtime of $O(1.618^l m^3)$. Finally, we implement both algorithms and evaluate their performance on simulated and biological datasets.

2 Preliminary

Consider a directed acyclic graph (DAG) $G = (V, A)$, where V is the set of vertices and A is the set of arcs. Each arc $\langle u, v \rangle \in A$ represents a directed edge from u (a parent of v) to v (a child of u). The graph may contain parallel arcs. A *directed path* from v_1 to v_t is a sequence $\langle v_1, v_2, \ldots, v_t \rangle$ such that each pair $\langle v_i, v_{i+1} \rangle \in A$. Each vertex $v \in V$ has a set of parents $P_N(v)$ and a set of children $C_N(v)$. The *in-degree* $d^+(v)$ and *out-degree* $d^-(v)$ are the numbers of in-arcs and out-arcs to v, respectively. The *degree* of v is $d(v) = d^+(v) + d^-(v)$. The vertices of G are classified into four types: (1). *Root* $(d^+(v) = 0, d^-(v) > 0)$; (2). *Leaf* $(d^+(v) = 1, d^-(v) = 0)$; (3). *Tree vertex* $(d^+(v) = 1, d^-(v) \geq 2)$; (4). *Reticulation vertex* $(d^+(v) \geq 2, d^-(v) \geq 1)$, with a *mixed vertex* being a reticulation vertex where $d^-(v) \geq 2$. An arc $\langle v, v' \rangle$ is a *cut-arc* if v' is not a leaf and removing it disconnects the graph, and if there are no cut-arcs, the graph is *biconnected*. A *biconnected component* is a biconnected subgraph of G with no proper subgraph that is biconnected. A *single-rooted DAG N* has a unique root with out-degree 1, and if every vertex in N is one of the four predefined types, then N is a *reduced single-rooted DAG*. A *phylogenetic network* with label-set X is a reduced single-rooted DAG where the root and leaves are bijectively labeled by elements of X, with the root labeled by $\rho \in X$ (note that for ease of subsequent analysis we define the root as a leaf). If N is a tree, it is a *phylogenetic tree* (or X-tree). In an X-network, leaves that share a common parent form a *sibling-set*, which is *maximal* if its common parent has exactly as many out-arcs as the size of the set. A *sibling-pair* is a maximal sibling-set of size 2. The *depth* of a vertex v, denoted by $\text{dep}(v)$, is the length of the longest directed path from the root ρ to v, and the set $L_N(v)$ contains all labels reachable from v. The *reticulation number* $r(N)$ of N is given by $r(N) = |A| - |V| + 1$, and the *level number* $l(N)$ is the maximum reticulation number of any biconnected component.

The *forced contraction operation* modifies X-networks in two steps: (1). *Vertex-removal*: Remove unlabeled vertices with in-degree 1 and out-degree 0, and non-root vertices with in-degree 0, along with their incident arcs. (2). *Arc-contraction*: Replace a vertex with in-degree 1 and out-degree 1 by a new arc from its predecessor to its successor. After applying forced contraction, the graph is denoted as $(N')_{fc}$, and individual operations are denoted as $(N')_{vr}$ and $(N')_{ac}$.

Two X-trees T_1 and T_2 are *isomorphic* (denoted $T_1 = T_2$) if there exists a bijection Φ between their vertices such that the arc relationships and leaf labels are preserved. Given an X-network N and an X-tree T, if N contains T, then there exists an arc-subset $A^* \subseteq A$ such that $(N \setminus A^*)_{fc} = T$. A *reduced X-subtree* of N is a subgraph where all labels in X are connected, and removing any vertex would destroy connectivity. If N contains T, then N has a reduced X-subtree T_X with $(T_X)_{ac} = T$. Finally, we define the *Tree Containment Problem* parameterized by the reticulation number k and the level number l of X-networks, which we study in this paper.

Reticulation-Parameterized Tree Containment Problem (abbr. r-PTCP)

INPUT: An X-network N, an X-tree T, and a parameter $k = r(N)$;
OUTPUT: Return YES if N contains T; otherwise, NO.

Level-Parameterized Tree Containment Problem (abbr. l-PTCP)

INPUT: An X-network N, an X-tree T, and a parameter $l = l(N)$;
OUTPUT: Return YES if N contains T; otherwise, NO.

3   Modification Operations on X-Network

Due to space limit, the correctness analysis for the operations used in our algorithms are omitted, but will be given in a full journal version. Consider an instance $(N, T; k)$ of the r-PTCP. In the following, we introduce two modification operations to mitigate the negative impact of multifurcating structures in X-network on the analysis. For a mixed vertex v in N, we decompose it into a reticulation vertex v' with $d^-(v') = 1$ and a tree vertex v''. Formally, this Degree Decomposition operation is defined as follows.

Degree Decomposition operation (abbr. DD-operation): For each mixed vertex v in the X-network N, replace v by an arc $\langle v', v'' \rangle$ such that all in-arcs $\langle *, v \rangle$ of v are redirected to v', and all out-arcs $\langle v, * \rangle$ of v are redirected from v''. See Fig. 1(a) for an illustration.

For each reticulation vertex with in-degree at least 3, it can be replaced by a sequence of reticulation vertices with in-degree 2, by the following operation.

In-degree Binarization operation (abbr. IDB-operation): For each reticulation vertex v with parent set $P(v) = \{v_1, v_2, \cdots, v_{d^+(v)}\}$ and child u, where $|P(v)| \geq 3$, replace v with a directed path $\langle v_1', v_2', \ldots, v_{d^+(v)-1}' \rangle$, and add an arc leading from v_i to v_{i-1}' for each $3 \leq i \leq |P(v)|$, and two arcs leading from v_1 and v_2 to v_1', and an arc leading from $v_{d^+(v)-1}'$ to u. See Fig. 1(b) for an illustration.

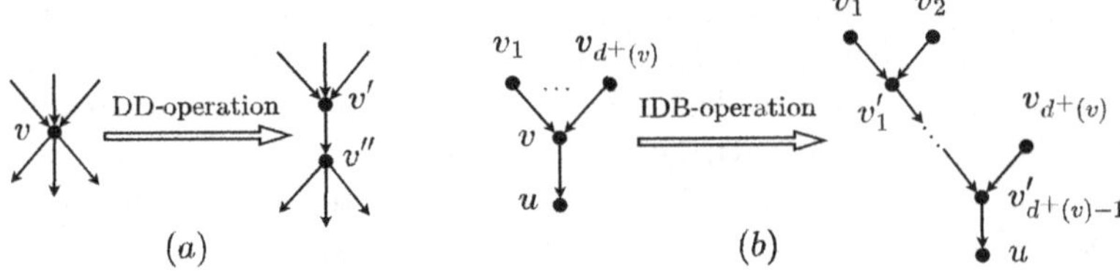

Fig. 1. (a) DD-operation; (b) IDB-operation.

An application of the IDB-operation on the vertex v in N, introduces $d^+(v) - 2$ new vertices and $d^+(v) - 2$ new arcs. Thus N and the resulting X-network have the same reticulation number. The key advantage of the IDB-operation is that it can eliminate the reticulation vertices with in-degree of at least 3. In the remaining text, we assume that both the DD-operation and IDB-operation are not applicable on the X-network N. Thus each vertex in N has either in-degree 1 or out-degree 1, and if its out-degree is 1 then its in-degree is 2.

4   Reduction Rules for Instances of the R-PTCP

In the section we propose eight reduction rules for the instance $(N, T; k)$ of the r-PTCP. Remark that all reticulation rules are applied in order; specifically, for any $1 \le j < i \le 8$, by the time Reduction Rule i is applied on $(N, T; k)$, Reduction Rule j is not applicable on $(N, T; k)$.

Reduction Rule 1. If the common label-set X of N and T has a size of at most 2, then the considered instance $(N, T; k)$ is YES.

Recall that by definition, N has neither vertex v with $d^+(v) \ge 2$ and $d^-(v) = 0$ nor parallel arc, but such vertices and arcs may be generated by some arc-removal operation during the execution of our algorithm. Thus we introduce the following two reduction rules.

Reduction Rule 2. If N has a vertex v with $d^+(v) \ge 2$ and $d^-(v) = 0$, then arbitrarily remove an in-arc of v (say e_1), $k \leftarrow k - 1$, and apply the forced contraction operation on the resulting network.

Reduction Rule 3. If N has $t \ge 2$ many parallel arcs leading from u to v, then arbitrarily remove $t - 1$ ones of them, $k \leftarrow k - (t - 1)$, and apply the forced contraction operation on the resulting network.

Because of Reduction Rule 1 we can assume that the label-set X has a size of at least 3. Under the case, sibling sets may emerge in N, with every reduced X-subtree of N inherently maintaining them.

Reduction Rule 4. If there are several labels that are siblings in N but not in T, then return NO.

Reduction Rule 5. Given a maximal sibling-set $S \subset X$ of N, if S is a non-maximal sibling-set of T, then return NO; otherwise (i.e., it is a maximal sibling-set of T), choose a label $l \in S$, remove the labels in $S \setminus \{l\}$ from N and T, and apply the forced contraction operation on the two resulting networks N' and T'.

Reduction Rule 6. Given a sibling-set $S = \{l_1, \ldots, l_t\}$ of N ($t \geq 2$), if S is a maximal sibling-set of T, then remove the out-arcs of $p = P_N(l_1)$ leading to the vertices in $C_N(p) \setminus S$, $k \leftarrow k - (r(N) - r((N')_{fc}))$, and apply the forced contraction on the resulting network N'.

Reduction Rule 7. Given a subset $S \subset X$ with $|S| \geq 3$, if S is a non-maximal sibling-set in N and T, then arbitrarily choose two labels $l, l' \in S$ and remove the labels in $S \setminus \{l, l'\}$ and their incident arcs from N and T, $X \leftarrow X \setminus (S \setminus \{l, l'\})$, and apply the forced contraction operation on the resulting networks N' and T'.

Reduction Rule 8. Given a leaf l in N, whose parent $P_N(l)$ is a reticulation vertex, then for each parent g_i ($1 \leq i \leq 2$) of $P_N(l)$, Case (I). if g_i has a leaf child l' with $P_T(l') \neq P_T(l)$, then remove the arc $\langle g_i, P_N(l) \rangle$ from N; Case (II). if g_i has a leaf child l' with $P_T(l') = P_T(l)$ but $L_T(P_T(l)) \not\subseteq L_N(g_i)$, then remove the arc $\langle g_i, P_N(l) \rangle$ from N; Case (III). if g_i has a leaf child l' such that (l', l) is a sibling-pair in T, then remove $\langle g_j, P_N(l) \rangle$ ($1 \leq j \leq 2$ and $j \neq i$) from N; Case (IV). if g_i has two leaf child l' and l'' such that $\{l, l', l''\}$ is a sibling-set of T, then remove the arc $\langle g_j, P_N(l) \rangle$ ($1 \leq j \leq 2$ and $j \neq i$) from N. Additionally, $k \leftarrow k - 1$, and apply the forced contraction operation on the resulting network.

5   Analysis on the Leaf with the Largest Depth

Assume that Reduction Rules 1–8 are not applicable to the instance $(N, T; k)$. Let l be the leaf of N with the greatest depth, and let p be its parent. Since l is the deepest leaf, it follows that all children of p, except l, must also be leaves. However, this contradicts the assumption that Reduction Rules 4 and 5 are not applicable. Hence, p must be a reticulation vertex. Let g_1 and g_2 denote the two parents of p in N, and let $e_\alpha = \langle g_1, p \rangle$ and $e'_\alpha = \langle g_2, p \rangle$ be the two in-arcs of p. If $(N, T; k)$ is a YES-instance, meaning that N contains a reduced X-subtree T_X with $(T_X)_{ac} = T$, then T_X must contain exactly one of the two arcs e_α and e'_α. By branching on these two arcs, we can iteratively analyze the leaf with the largest depth in the resulting X-network (up to the forced contraction operation). This would give an algorithm with time complexity $O^*(2^k)$. However, this runtime can be improved by exploiting the finite local structure of the leaf with the greatest depth. Specifically, we analyze the types of the vertices g_1 and g_2 as follows.

Case 1. Both g_1 and g_2 are reticulation vertices.

Under the case, denote by e_β and e'_β the two in-arcs of g_1, and by e_γ and e'_γ the two ones of g_2. See Fig. 2(a) for an illustration.

Step 1. Apply the following branching steps: (branch-1) remove the arcs e_β, e'_β from N; $k \leftarrow k - 2$; and apply the forced contraction operation on $N \setminus \{e_\beta, e'_\beta\}$; (branch-2) remove the arcs e_γ, e'_γ from N; $k \leftarrow k - 2$; and apply the forced contraction operation on $N \setminus \{e_\gamma, e'_\gamma\}$.

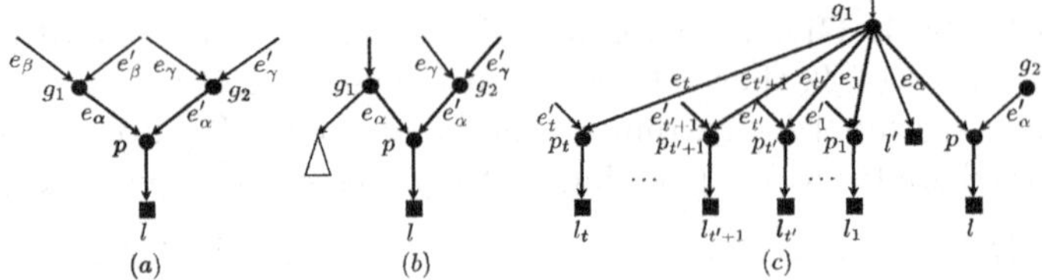

Fig. 2. Illustration of the possible local structures containing the leaf l with the largest depth (circles represent internal vertices, boxes represent leaves, and triangles represent possible graph structures). (a) Case 1; (b) Case 2; (c) Case 3.

Case 2. One of g_1 and g_2 is a reticulation vertex, and the other is a tree vertex.

Under Case 2, we assume that g_2 is a reticulation vertex. Denote by e_γ and e'_γ the two in-arcs of g_2. See Fig. 2(b) for an illustration.

Step 2. Apply the following branching steps: (branch-1) remove the arc e_α from N; $k \leftarrow k-1$; and apply the forced contraction operation on $N \setminus \{e_\alpha\}$; (branch-2) remove the arcs e_γ and e'_γ from N; $k \leftarrow k-2$; and apply the forced contraction operation on $N \setminus \{e_\gamma, e'_\gamma\}$.

Case 3. Both g_1 and g_2 are tree vertices.

W.l.o.g., assume that $\mathrm{dep}(p) = \mathrm{dep}(g_1) + 1$. As the given reduction rules are not applicable on N, g_1 satisfies the four properties given in the following lemma.

Lemma 1. *Under Case 3, g_1 satisfies the following four properties: (1). g_1 has at most one leaf as its child; (2). g_1 has no tree vertex as its child; (3). except for p, g_1 has at least one other reticulation vertex as its child; (4). for each child of g_1 that is a reticulation vertex, it has a leaf as its child.*

Denote by l' the leaf child of g_1 if it exists. If g_1 has other children that are reticulation vertices except for p, then we assume that there are $t \geq 1$ such children and have the following notations: for each $1 \leq i \leq t$, denote by p_i the i-th child of g_1 that is a reticulation vertex; denote by l_i the leaf child of p_i (i.e., $P_N(l_i) = p_i$); let $e_i = \langle g_1, p_i \rangle$; and denote by e'_i the other in-arc of p_i except for e_i. W.l.o.g., assume that the leaves $l_1, l_2, \ldots, l_{t'}$ ($0 \leq t' \leq t$) are siblings with l in T, and $l_{t'+1}, \ldots, l_t$ are not siblings with l in T. See Fig. 2(c) for an illustration.

Case 3.1. g_1 has the leaf child l'.

Under the subcase, $P_T(l) = P_T(l')$ and $L_T(P_T(l)) \subseteq L_N(g_1)$, and the common parent of l and l' in T has out-degree at least 3; otherwise, Reduction Rule 8 is applicable. Thus $|L_T(P_T(l))| \geq 3$, and g_1 has other children that are reticulation vertices except for p. Remark that under Case 3.1, g_1 may be mapped to the common parent of l and l' in T w.r.t. some isomorphism between $(T_X)_{ac}$ and T (if such an isomorphism exists). If we have extra information such as $P_T(l)$ has a child that is not a leaf, then we can conclude that g_1 cannot be mapped to the common parent of l and l' in T w.r.t. any isomorphism between $(T_X)_{ac}$ and T, as for any reduced X-subtree T_X of N, if $(T_X)_{ac}$ contains g_1 then the children of g_1 in $(T_X)_{ac}$ are all leaves. Thus we have following step for Case 3.1.

Step 3.1. If $P_T(l)$ has a child that is not a leaf, then remove the arc e_α from N, $k = k - 1$, and apply the forced contraction operation on $N \setminus \{e_\alpha\}$. Otherwise, apply the following branching steps: (branch-1) remove the arc e_α from N, $k \leftarrow k - 1$, and apply the forced contraction operation on $N \setminus \{e_\alpha\}$; (branch-2) remove the arcs $e'_\alpha, e'_1, \cdots, e'_{t'}, e_{t'+1}, \cdots, e_t$ from N, $k \leftarrow k - t - 1$, and apply the forced contraction operation on $N \setminus \{e'_\alpha, e'_1, \cdots, e'_{t'}, e_{t'+1}, \cdots, e_t\}$.

Case 3.2. g_1 has no leaf child.

As the out-degree of the reticulation vertex g_1 is at least 2, $t \geq 1$. The following discussion is divided into two subcases based on whether the two conditions are satisfied: $L_T(P_T(l)) \subseteq L_N(g_1)$ and all children of $P_T(l)$ are leaves.

Case 3.2.1. $L_T(P_T(l)) \subseteq L_N(g_1)$ and the children of $P_T(l)$ are all leaves.

Step 3.2.1. Apply the following branching steps: (branch-1) remove the arc e_α from N, $k \leftarrow k - 1$, and apply the forced contraction operation on $N \setminus \{e_\alpha\}$; (branch-2) remove the arcs $e'_\alpha, e'_1, \cdots, e'_{t'}, e_{t'+1}, \cdots, e_t$ from N, $k \leftarrow k - t - 1$, and apply the forced contraction operation on $N \setminus \{e'_\alpha, e'_1, \cdots, e'_{t'}, e_{t'+1}, \cdots, e_t\}$.

Case 3.2.2. $L_T(P_T(l)) \nsubseteq L_N(g_1)$ or some child of $P_T(l)$ is not a leaf.

Step 3.2.2. Apply the following branching steps: (branch-1) remove the arc e_α from N, $k \leftarrow k - 1$, and apply the forced contraction operation on $N \setminus \{e_\alpha\}$; (branch-2) remove the arcs $e'_\alpha, e_1, e_2, \cdots, e_t$ from N, $k \leftarrow k - t - 1$, and apply the forced contraction operation on $N \setminus \{e'_\alpha, e_1, e_2, \cdots, e_t\}$.

6 Algorithm for the R-PTCP

Now we propose the algorithm Alg-r-PTCP for the r-PTCP, given in Fig. 3.

Theorem 1. *Given an instance $(N, T; k)$ of the r-PTCP, algorithm Alg-r-PTCP can correctly solve it within time complexity $O(1.618^k m^3)$, where $k = r(N)$, and m is the number of arcs in N.*

Algorithm Alg-r-PTCP$(N, T; k)$
Input: An X-network N, an X-tree T, and a parameter $k = r(N)$;
Output: Return YES if N contains T; otherwise, return NO.

1. **if** there are labels that are disconnected in N or $k < 0$ **then** return NO;
2. **if** $k = 0$ **then if** $N = T$ **then** return YES **else** return NO;
3. apply the DD-operation and IDB-operation on N until they are not applicable;
4. **if** $|X| \leq 2$ then return YES; // Reduction Rule 1
5. **if** N has a sibling set that is not a sibling set in T **then**
5.1   return NO; // Reduction Rule 4
6. **if** N has a maximal sibling-set that is not a maximal sibling-set in T **then**
6.1   return NO; // Reduction Rule 5
7. **if** one of Reduction Rules 2-3 and 5-8 is applicable on N **then**
7.1.   apply the corresponding reduction rule, obtaining instance $(N', T'; k')$,
         and return Alg-r-PTCP$(N', T'; k')$;
8. **if** one of Case 1 – Case 3.2.2 holds **then**
8.1.   apply the given branches and call Alg-r-PTCP on the obtained sub-instances.

Fig. 3. The algorithm for the r-PTCP.

7   Algorithm Adapted for the L-PTCP

Given an instance $(N, T; l)$ of the l-PTCP, we use the concept of reticulation and level numbers. Each biconnected component of N has its reticulation number bounded by l. The core idea of the algorithm Alg-l-PTCP is to decompose the X-network N into its biconnected components by the following *Divide operation*, then apply Alg-r-PTCP to solve the resulting sub-instances.

Divide operation. Give a cut-arc $\langle v, v' \rangle$ of N (if any), if T has no arc $\langle v_T, v'_T \rangle$ such that $L_T(v'_T) = L_N(v')$ then return NO; otherwise (i.e., T has such an arc), do the following modification operations on N and T:
(1). remove $\langle v, v' \rangle$ from N; introduce a vertex with label $l \notin X$ to N and add an arc $\langle v, l \rangle$ with v as the parent of l; denote by N_1 the subgraph containing l, and by N_2 the remaining subgraph after applying the forced contraction operation;
(2). remove $\langle v_T, v'_T \rangle$ from T; introduce a vertex with label $l \notin X$ to T and add an arc $\langle v_T, l \rangle$ with v_T as the parent of l; denote by T_1 the subtree containing l, and by T_2 the other subtree after applying the forced contraction operation. Then construct two sub-instances $(N_1, T_1; l)$ and $(N_2, T_2; l)$ of the l-PTCP.

Due to space limit, the details of the algorithm Alg-l-PTCP is omitted.

Theorem 2. *Given an instance $(N, T; l)$ of the l-PTCP, the algorithm Alg-l-PTCP can correctly solve it within time complexity $O(1.618^l m^3)$, where $l = l(N)$, and m is the number of arcs in N.*

8   Experiment

We implement the algorithms Alg-r-PTCP and Alg-l-PTCP in C++, and develop the programs P-r-PTCP and P-l-PTCP, respectively. We evaluate their performance using simulated data on a system equipped with 16GB RAM, a 12-core processor, and Windows 11 operating system.

Synthetic Data Generation. Due to space limit, we defer the details of the instance construction method that can generate YES-instances to a full journal version. To introduce NO-instances, we define an additional operation called the **Disturbance Operation**, which generates possible NO-instances through a label-swap operation: two leaves in N are selected arbitrarily, their labels are swapped, and this process is repeated 1 or 2 times. Note that applying the label-swap operation multiple times allows Reduction Rule 4 to efficiently determine whether the instance is a NO-instance, leading to a short runtime. Additionally, when $|X|$ is small and k is large, random swaps rarely result in NO-instances. Thus, while the label-swap operation can generate NO-instances, it does so with a probability less than 100%.

Benchmark Evaluation. We perform comparative experiments using the dataset from [6], which contains 289,409 instances with a 19:6 ratio of randomly generated to biological data. The parameter ranges are as follows: level number $[1, 63]$, with 99% of instances in $[1, 40]$; reticulation number $[1, 64]$, with 99% of instances in $[1, 40]$. The similar ranges for the level and reticulation numbers indicate that the X-networks are biconnected. Our program P-l-PTCP achieves an average runtime of < 1 ms (worst-case 0.087s), while P-r-PTCP achieves an average runtime of approximately 1 ms (worst-case 0.089s). These results show significant speed improvements over prior work, maintaining accuracy even for complex instances, such as those with a level number $l = 60$ (Figs. 4, 5, 6, 7 and 8).

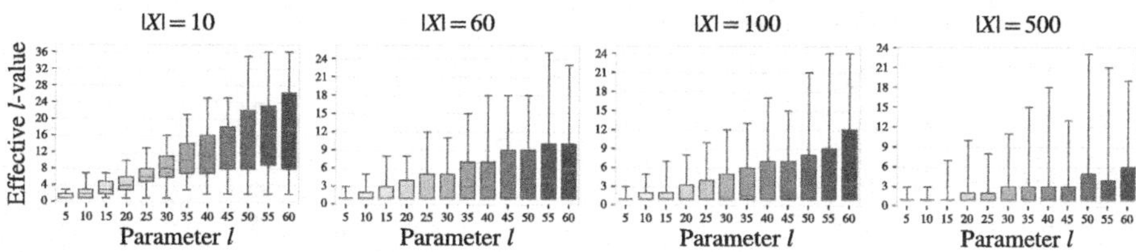

Fig. 4. Distribution of the effective l-values (fixed $|X|$).

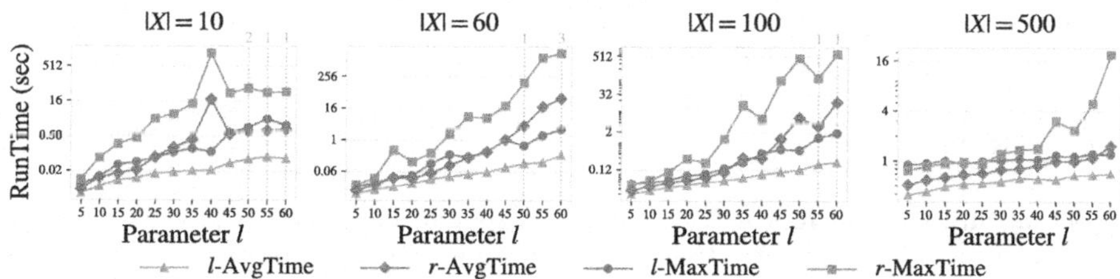

Fig. 5. Performance on instances without the Disturbance Operation (fixed $|X|$). The numbers atop the figure indicate the count of unresolved instances (out of 100 per parameter setting) due to stack overflow.

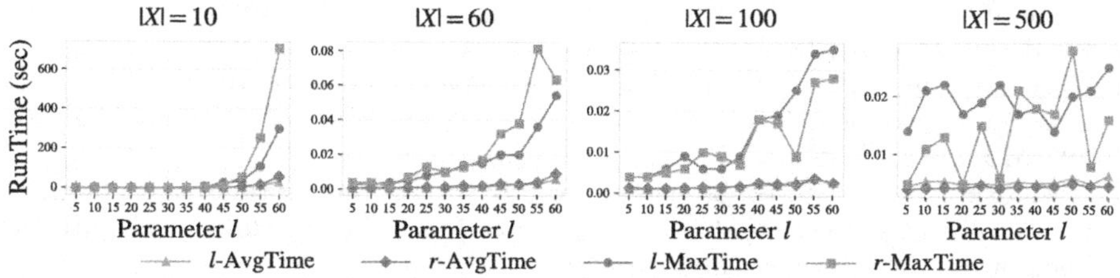

Fig. 6. Performance on instances with the Disturbance Operation (fixed $|X|$).

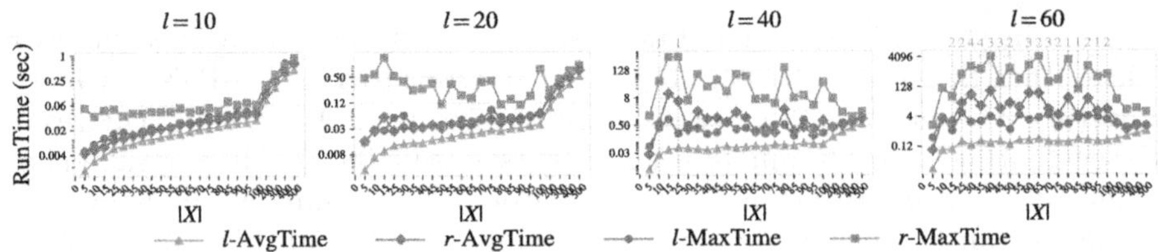

Fig. 7. Performance on instances without the Disturbance Operation (fixed l). The numbers atop the figure indicate the count of unresolved instances (out of 100 per parameter setting) due to stack overflow.

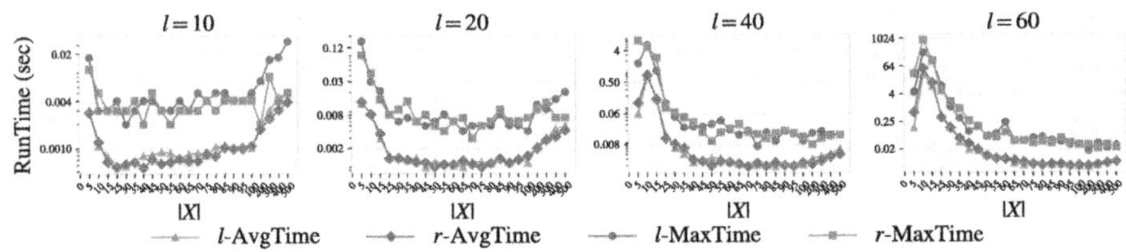

Fig. 8. Performance on instances with the Disturbance Operation (fixed l).

References

1. Bernardini, G., van Iersel, L., Julien, E., Stougie, L.: Inferring phylogenetic networks from multifurcating trees via cherry picking and machine learning. Mol. Phylogenet. Evol. **199**, 108137 (2024)
2. Bordewich, M., Semple, C.: Reticulation-visible networks. Adv. Appl. Math. **78**, 114–141 (2016)
3. Boussau, B., Scornavacca, C.: Reconciling gene trees with species trees. Phylogenetics in the genomic era pp. 3–2 (2020)
4. Chan, J.M., Carlsson, G., Rabadan, R.: Topology of viral evolution. Proc. Natl. Acad. Sci. **110**(46), 18566–18571 (2013)
5. Chen, J., Fan, J.H., Sze, S.H.: Parameterized and approximation algorithms for maximum agreement forest in multifurcating trees. Theoret. Comput. Sci. **562**, 496–512 (2015)
6. Dushatskiy, A., Julien, E., Stougie, L., van Iersel, L.: Solving the tree containment problem using graph neural networks. Trans. Mach. Learn. Res. (2024). https://openreview.net/forum?id=nK5MazeIpn
7. Fakcharoenphol, J., Kumpijit, T., Putwattana, A.: A faster algorithm for the tree containment problem for binary nearly stable phylogenetic networks. In: the 12th International Joint Conference on Computer Science and Software Engineering, pp. 337–342. IEEE (2015)
8. Fehrer, J., Gemeinholzer, B., Chrtek, J., Jr., Bräutigam, S.: Incongruent plastid and nuclear DNA phylogenies reveal ancient intergeneric hybridization in Pilosella hawkweeds (hieracium, cichorieae, asteraceae). Mol. Phylogenet. Evol. **42**(2), 347–361 (2007)
9. Gambette, P., Gunawan, A., Labarre, A., Vialette, S., Zhang, L.: Locating a tree in a phylogenetic network in quadratic time. In: Przytycka, T.M. (ed.) RECOMB

2015. LNCS, vol. 9029, pp. 96–107. Springer, Cham (2015). https://doi.org/10.1007/978-3-319-16706-0_12

10. Gambette, P., Gunawan, A.D., Labarre, A., Vialette, S., Zhang, L.: Solving the tree containment problem in linear time for nearly stable phylogenetic networks. Discret. Appl. Math. **246**, 62–79 (2018)

11. Gunawan, A.: Solving the tree containment problem for reticulation-visible networks in linear time. In: Jansson, J., Martín-Vide, C., Vega-Rodríguez, M.A. (eds.) AlCoB 2018. LNCS, vol. 10849, pp. 24–36. Springer, Cham (2018). https://doi.org/10.1007/978-3-319-91938-6_3

12. Gunawan, A.D., DasGupta, B., Zhang, L.: A decomposition theorem and two algorithms for reticulation-visible networks. Inf. Comput. **252**, 161–175 (2017)

13. Gunawan, A.D., Lu, B., Zhang, L.: A program for verification of phylogenetic network models. Bioinformatics **32**(17), i503–i510 (2016)

14. Hein, J.: Reconstructing evolution of sequences subject to recombination using parsimony. Math. Biosci. **98**(2), 185–200 (1990)

15. Hein, J.: A heuristic method to reconstruct the history of sequences subject to recombination. J. Mol. Evol. **36**, 396–405 (1993)

16. Huson, D.H., Linz, S.: Autumn algorithm—computation of hybridization networks for realistic phylogenetic trees. IEEE/ACM Trans. Comput. Biol. Bioinf. **15**(2), 398–410 (2016)

17. Huson, D.H., Rupp, R., Scornavacca, C.: Phylogenetic Networks: Concepts, Algorithms and Applications. Cambridge University Press, Cambridge (2010)

18. Jin, G., Nakhleh, L., Snir, S., Tuller, T.: Maximum likelihood of phylogenetic networks. Bioinformatics **22**(21), 2604–2611 (2006)

19. Kanj, I.A., Nakhleh, L., Than, C., Xia, G.: Seeing the trees and their branches in the network is hard. Theoret. Comput. Sci. **401**(1–3), 153–164 (2008)

20. Nakhleh, L.: Recombinatorics: The algorithmics of ancestral recombination graphs and explicit phylogenetic networks (2015)

21. Paun, O., Lehnebach, C., Johansson, J.T., Lockhart, P., Hörandl, E.: Phylogenetic relationships and biogeography of ranunculus and allied genera (ranunculaceae) in the Mediterranean region and in the European alpine system. Taxon **54**(4), 911–932 (2005)

22. Ruths, L.N.D., Innan, H.: Gene trees, species trees, and species networks

23. Shi, F., Chen, J., Feng, Q., Wang, J.: A parameterized algorithm for the maximum agreement forest problem on multiple rooted multifurcating trees. J. Comput. Syst. Sci. **97**, 28–44 (2018)

24. Shi, F., Li, H., Rong, G., Zhang, Z., Wang, J.: Improved fixed-parameter algorithm for the tree containment problem on unrooted phylogenetic network. IEEE/ACM Trans. Comput. Biol. Bioinf. **19**(6), 3539–3552 (2021)

25. Shi, F., Wang, J., Yang, Y., Feng, Q., Li, W., Chen, J.: A fixed-parameter algorithm for the maximum agreement forest problem on multifurcating trees. Science China Inf. Sci. **59**(1), 1–14 (2016). https://doi.org/10.1007/s11432-015-5355-1

26. Sridhar, S., Lam, F., Blelloch, G.E., Ravi, R., Schwartz, R.: Mixed integer linear programming for maximum-parsimony phylogeny inference. IEEE/ACM Trans. Comput. Biol. Bioinf. **5**(3), 323–331 (2008)

27. Treangen, T.J., Rocha, E.P.: Horizontal transfer, not duplication, drives the expansion of protein families in prokaryotes. PLoS Genet. **7**(1), e1001284 (2011)

28. Van Iersel, L., Jones, M., Weller, M.: Embedding phylogenetic trees in networks of low treewidth. Discrete Math. Theoret. Comput. Sci. **25**, 10 (2023)

29. Van Iersel, L., Kelk, S., Scornavacca, C.: Kernelizations for the hybridization number problem on multiple nonbinary trees. J. Comput. Syst. Sci. **82**(6), 1075–1089 (2016)
30. Van Iersel, L., Kelk, S., Stamoulis, G., Stougie, L., Boes, O.: On unrooted and root-uncertain variants of several well-known phylogenetic network problems. Algorithmica **80**, 2993–3022 (2018)
31. Van Iersel, L., Semple, C., Steel, M.: Locating a tree in a phylogenetic network. Inf. Process. Lett. **110**(23), 1037–1043 (2010)
32. Weller, M.: Linear-time tree containment in phylogenetic networks. In: Blanchette, M., Ouangraoua, A. (eds.) RECOMB-CG 2018. LNCS, vol. 11183, pp. 309–323. Springer, Cham (2018). https://doi.org/10.1007/978-3-030-00834-5_18
33. Whidden, C., Beiko, R.G., Zeh, N.: Fixed-parameter and approximation algorithms for maximum agreement forests of multifurcating trees. Algorithmica **74**(3), 1019–1054 (2016)

Automated Prediction of Protein Pair Distances Based on Deep Learning: A Novel Approach to Protein Structure Prediction in SCOP

Duo Feng[1], Shuaicheng Li[2], and Yue Zhang[1]($\boxtimes$)

[1] Thompson Rivers University, Kamloops BC V2C1T3, CA, USA
`fengd21@mytru.ca, yuezhang@tru.ca`
[2] City University of Hong Kong, Kowloon, Hong Kong
`shuaicli@cityu.edu.hk`

Abstract. This study introduces the innovative Protein Distance Model (PDM) for predicting structural distances between protein pairs in the Structural Classification of Proteins (SCOP) database. SCOP's hierarchical classification presents challenges for direct prediction, so PDM predicts distances between unknown proteins and those with known classifications to infer structural categories. Incorporating NLP's Attention mechanism and a dual-tower network, PDM extracts high-level features from two protein sequences to predict their distance. Transitioning from regression to a multiclass task improved performance, achieving over 90% AUC and Accuracy in binary classification and over 80% F1-Score and Accuracy in multiclass scenarios. PDM shows strong generalization, laying a foundation for future research in protein structural classification. The code is publicly available on GitHub.

Keywords: Protein Structure · SCOP · Deep Learning · Attention mechanism (NLP) · Dual-tower network · Hierarchical classification

1   Introduction

Proteins, essential to biological processes, have hierarchical structures crucial for understanding their functions, from the primary structure up to the quaternary structure [1]. Protein chains, also known as polypeptides, are sequences of amino acids that may have specific functions within a protein. Structural biology often focuses on individual protein chains to study their unique properties and functions [2]. Analyzing these chains is vital for understanding protein behavior and has broad biological implications. The SCOP database [3] has significantly impacted molecular biology by organizing 356,132 proteins into a hierarchical structure of Representatives, Families, Superfamilies, Folds, and Classes [4,5]. Despite its success, SCOP's manual process faces scalability challenges due to the rapid increase in discovered protein structures. This has led to the development of automated classification models, including Structural Classification of Proteins—extended (SCOPe), which integrates automated methodologies with manual curation to enhance coverage and accuracy [6]. While traditional sequence alignment algorithms form the basis of these methods, there is significant room for improvement. Our work leverages deep learning to develop a neural network-based structural classification model using SCOP as a benchmark.

Table 1. Relationship between proA & proB and Corresponding Distances or Category

Relationship between proA & proB	Distance	Distance Class
Same Representative	0	0
Same Family	1	1
Same Superfamily	2	2
Same Fold/IUPR	4	3
Same Class/protein type	8	4
Otherwise	16	5

This research aims to innovate in bioinformatics by developing a deep learning model, PDM, for automatic protein classification, leveraging the SCOP database. The complexity of directly classifying proteins into one of the 6000 SCOP families is a significant challenge due to the vast number of categories. To address this, we propose predicting distances between protein pairs, such as Protein A (proA) and Protein B (proB), as shown in Table 1, to infer the most probable category for unclassified proteins. We set the distance of two proteins to increase exponentially due to the hierarchical category system of SCOP. This method helps to classify unknown proteins within SCOP more effectively by treating distance prediction as a regression problem. However, due to confusion in the model for certain distances, we transitioned to treating the task as a classification problem, categorizing the distances into six classes, and improving PDM's performance. This approach, rooted in the SCOP hierarchical structure, facilitates a nuanced understanding of protein structural and evolutionary relationships while bypassing the challenges of direct multiclass classification. Meanwhile, it is so far new that we know. By integrating deep learning, we aim to advance protein structure classification and contribute a novel perspective to bioinformatics.

2   Literature Review

SCOP, introduced by Murzin et al. in 1995, classifies protein structures based on structural and evolutionary relationships. It organizes proteins hierarchically into classes (CL) or protein types (TP), folds, superfamilies, and families, facilitating protein function prediction and structural genomics [2,4]. SCOP has undergone significant updates, including SCOP 1.75 and SCOP 2.0, which introduced automated classification methods. The SCOPe extension now provides more frequent updates and improved accuracy through automation [5,6]. The classification relies on the manual curation of structural similarity, evolutionary relationships, and functional similarity, which has been enhanced by automated methods in SCOPe [5]. The SCOP database's hierarchical organization helps understand protein structures and their relationships [5,6]. Despite its strengths, SCOP faces challenges like the scalability of manual curation and the need for frequent updates. Future improvements may involve integrating AI and machine learning to address these limitations [2,4].

The Protein Data Bank (PDB) is a crucial repository for three-dimensional structural data of biological macromolecules, established in the 1970s. It archives structural data from techniques such as X-ray crystallography, NMR spectroscopy, and cryo-electron microscopy [2,7,8]. Initially a tiny collection at Brookhaven National Laboratory, PDB has expanded significantly, facilitated by the transition to digital platforms, which enabled global access and contributions [8]. In 2003, the creation of the worldwide Protein Data Bank (wwPDB) consortium was a milestone in ensuring the sustainability and reliability of PDB as a global resource [7]. The consortium has standardized data formats, ensured data quality, and expanded accessibility while integrating advanced computational tools for data analysis and visualization. PDB's commitment to open access has supported advancements in computational biology, drug discovery, and molecular modeling [9]. PDB has significantly impacted research in structural genomics, protein function, and drug design [2,7]. It provides detailed structural information critical for understanding protein folding and function and has enabled structure-based drug design (SBDD), leading to novel drug targets and therapeutic developments [10]. PDB also serves as an educational resource and has driven the development of computational tools for structural prediction and analysis [11]. Data retrieval from PDB is facilitated through the RCSB PDB website, tools like PyMOL and BioPython, and automated scripts utilizing PDB's RESTful API [2,12–14].

Deep Neural Networks (DNN) have transformed artificial intelligence, significantly advancing machine learning, natural language processing, and computer vision. Originating from early multi-layer network training methods [15,16], DNNs have evolved to include sophisticated techniques like Attention Mechanisms and Dual Tower Networks. Attention Mechanisms, introduced by [17], enable models to focus on relevant parts of input data dynamically, greatly enhancing performance in sequence-based tasks. Dual Tower Networks, on the other hand, process and compare two distinct data sets efficiently, making them valuable for recommendation systems and similarity matching [18–20]. The foundations of DNNs, established by the development of backpropagation [21], have paved the way for complex network architectures that learn intricate data patterns [22]. Modern DNNs balance depth and computational efficiency, incorporating mechanisms such as dual-tower and attention features to improve performance. These advancements enable more accurate predictions and efficient model operation. Attention Mechanisms have revolutionized how models handle sequential data by focusing computational resources on the most relevant parts of the input [17,23]. This has led to breakthroughs in NLP tasks and computer vision [24–26]. Similarly, Dual Tower Networks facilitate effective comparison and relationship understanding between data sets, benefiting recommendation systems and similarity detection [27,28]. Innovations in these areas continue to drive improvements in AI applications.

3   Methodology

3.1   Dataset

Table 4 in the Appendix showcases schematic diagrams of protein structures from the SCOP database derived from the Protein Data Bank (PDB). Each protein name in the diagrams is formatted as "pdb_id_chain_id," where "pdb_id" is a four-character identifier from the PDB and "chain_id" represents the specific chain of the protein. These diagrams are available on the PDB website [29]. The first row of Table 4 features three proteins with diverse structural details: 4PXJ_B represents a dimeric LZII fragment from *Homo sapiens*, 6QM3_B is a calcium- and sodium-bound dimer from *Mus musculus*, and 7A9A_B depicts rubredoxin B from *Mycobacterium tuberculosis*. The subsequent rows display proteins from the same Representative and Family, illustrating the decreasing similarity and increasing evolutionary distance from the initial proteins. This hierarchical arrangement highlights the SCOP database's organization of protein structures and their evolutionary relationships, emphasizing the PDB's utility in providing detailed structural information.

Table 2. Different datasets.

Dataset No.	Condition	Proteins Count	Size of Training Set
I	(1)Selected Representatives	302	4,649
II	(1) & TP = 3	4,433	706,764
III	(1) & CL = 1000001	64,274	882,396
IV	(1) & CL = 1000000	68,971	1,231,206
V	(1) & CL = 1000002	70,454	1,251,885
VI	(1) & CL = 1000003	86,164	2,314,977
VII	(1) & CL = 1000004	11,639	538,719

On the macro-level, we summarized the hierarchical classification method of SCOP. Figure 10 in the Appendix illustrates the origin of manually compiled statistics. Through meticulous deduplication, we distilled 115,605 unique Protein Data Bank identifiers (PDB_IDs), identifying 356,132 non-redundant {pdb_id, chain_id} pairs. This step highlighted the SCOP database's nuanced structure representation. Our analysis identified 301,502 proteins for subsequent statistical analysis after excluding complex many-to-many relationships. These efforts provided crucial insights into protein structure diversity and classification within the SCOP database.

The dataset is based on 301,502 proteins from the SCOP database, but due to network transmission limitations, sequences for only 284,821 proteins were successfully retrieved. Table 2 presents detailed information on the datasets used. Here CL=1000001, for example, means we selected proteins under Class 1000001 in SCOP. We constructed pairs of proteins to create training datasets from these proteins and employed a targeted sampling strategy. This strategy ensures a sufficient number of protein pairs with various distances corresponding to different hierarchical levels of protein classification (Representative, Family, Superfamily, etc.). Additionally, to maintain dataset balance, proteins within Representatives were downsampled if they exceeded a certain threshold (typically 3 or 5).

Validation Set. To evaluate the effectiveness of PDM, we constructed a validation set that reflects the model's capabilities across different protein pair scenarios. These scenarios include: (I) bothin: both proteins in the training set, (II) onlyone: one protein in the training set and the other unseen, and (III) neither: neither protein present in the training set. The model is expected to perform best in scenario I, with decreasing accuracy in scenarios II and III. We aim for robust generalization across all scenarios. Additionally, to address the impact of validation set size, we created sets ranging from 200 to 3,000 samples, using ten separate test sets for each size to average various performance metrics, thereby minimizing randomness in our evaluations.

3.2   Model Architecture

To construct our model, we addressed the challenge of classifying nearly 6,000 categories at the SCOP Family level by adopting the dual tower network architecture commonly used in recommendation systems. Protein pairs are input into identical neural networks with shared weights, and their outputs are merged to compute protein similarity or distance. This approach effectively doubles the dataset size during training, improving model efficiency. Since protein sequences resemble natural language data, we integrated the Attention mechanism, which has been highly influential in NLP tasks [17]. Our resulting PDM model estimates structural distances between SCOP protein pairs by leveraging the dual tower architecture and Attention mechanisms for sequence processing [19,20].

Figure 1 outlines the architecture of PDM. Two amino acid sequences from proteins are input into the same neural network, which includes embedding and attention layers. First, the sequences are transformed into dense vectors via the embedding layer, capturing semantic relationships between amino acids. The attention mechanism then enables the model to focus on the most relevant parts of the sequences. The output vectors from the attention layer are concatenated and passed through fully connected layers, activated by ReLU, with dropout for regularization. Finally, a softmax layer classifies the interaction between the protein sequences. This model effectively captures individual sequence features and their interactions, enabling accurate predictions.

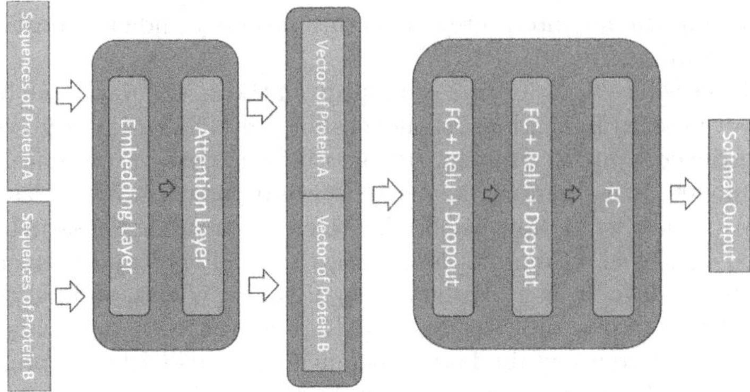

Fig. 1. Model Architecture of PDM

Initially, PDM used regression models with the Mean Square Error (MSE) to predict distances, but struggled with subtle distinctions in target values. The model shifted to a classification framework to improve accuracy, mapping target distances into five categories. The cross-entropy loss function replaced MSE, significantly improving performance by reducing confusion in closely spaced values. This transition illustrates the importance of adapting model objectives to the nature of the data, leading to more effective predictions of protein interactions.

3.3 Deployment

During the development and testing of our neural network models, particularly for datasets II and III, we faced significant computational challenges due to the massive data volume. Initially, we explored Google Colab [30] for its access to GPUs, which is essential for accelerating neural network training. However, the scale of our data required a Colab Pro subscription, which exceeded our project's budget. To address this, we turned to Sharcnet [31], a free GPU cluster provided by the Digital Research Alliance of Canada [32], offering the computational power we needed without financial constraints. Deploying our model on Sharcnet involved configuring the `device` parameter for GPU usage and utilizing SBATCH scripts to customize the computing environment, with detailed instructions on our GitHub page [33].

4   Evaluation

4.1   Metric

In developing and assessing machine learning models, a rigorous evaluation process is essential for understanding the model's accuracy, predictive performance, and operational efficiency. This evaluation covers a broad range of metrics, including traditional ones like accuracy, precision, recall, and F1 score, and execution time to assess computational demands. Accuracy provides a general view of performance, precision, and recall, offering insights into handling imbalanced classes, and the F1 score balances these aspects [34,35]. Execution time, though secondary, is crucial for understanding practical feasibility. By analyzing performance across different datasets and conditions, we aim to validate the model's effectiveness, uncover areas for improvement, and explore implications for future research and development.

4.2 Benchmark

Finding suitable benchmarks for our model, which predicts protein distances and categorizes them into five classes, was challenging due to the specificity of our approach. We identified three benchmarks—Needleman-Wunsch, Smith-Waterman, and BLAST—that, while primarily for sequence similarity, can be adapted for our comparison. Using these tools to classify protein pairs into binary categories and normalize their scores against the validation set, we facilitate partial comparison despite the lack of granularity in our five categories. Needleman-Wunsch, designed for global sequence alignment [36], and Smith-Waterman, for local alignment [37], both utilize dynamic programming but differ in their alignment scope. BLAST [38], a heuristic-based tool, offers rapid sequence comparison with adjustable parameters to balance speed and accuracy. Each benchmark contributes to understanding our model's performance, with detailed comparisons provided in subsequent sections.

4.3 Result

As previously mentioned, due to the exponential increase in protein pairs, we confined our training and testing datasets within protein pairs constituted by proteins in SCOP Class CL=1000001. This approach has proven effective in achieving accurate Distance Classification of protein pairs within the CL=1000001 range, and this section will elaborate on these findings in detail. To ensure that our results were not a fluke, we constructed datasets for four additional classes: CL=1000000, 1000002, 1000003, and 1000004.

Furthermore, as outlined earlier, we compared the Protein Distance Model (PDM) against three benchmark models. Given the computational bottleneck of the Blast interface and in pursuit of a comprehensive assessment, we included validation sets for CL=1000001 and CL=1000000 in our evaluation of the benchmark models' performance. The initial objective of developing the PDM was to predict the structural classification of unknown proteins in the SCOP database. The ideal scenario occurs when an unknown protein shares the same Family or even Representative protein within SCOP. If only the same Superfamily proteins are present, it is still desirable for the PDM to identify the Superfamily of the unknown protein. Even recognizing the same Class contributes to our understanding, showcasing a significant advantage of PDM over benchmark models.

In summary, the evaluation of the PDM encompasses the binary classification performance comparison between PDM and benchmark models and the demonstration of PDM's quintuple classification performance within various

Class scopes. These dimensions collectively illustrate the comprehensive capability of PDM in accurately classifying protein distances and predicting structural categories for unknown proteins within the SCOP database.

Execution Time. In terms of execution time, PDM demonstrates a processing capability nearly on par with the Smith-Waterman (SW) and Needleman-Wunsch (NW) algorithms, efficiently predicting 3,000 records in just 3 s. In contrast, BLAST shows a substantial delay, taking approximately 1800 seconds (30 min) for the same number of records. This considerable time discrepancy positions BLAST as a significant bottleneck in the overall computational process, underscoring the efficiency and speed advantages of PDM, SW, and NW for handling large datasets.

Binary Classification. To evaluate the effectiveness of PDM in binary classification tasks, we converted PDM's five-category outcomes into binary results. Specifically, categories $\{0, 1\}$ were remapped into a single category $\{0\}$, while categories $\{2, 3, 4\}$ were consolidated into $\{1\}$. This transformation allows for a straightforward comparison of model performance across various metrics. Figures 2 through 5 present the binary classification results for the PDM and benchmark models across different validation sets and scenarios.

Figure 2 illustrates the performance metrics for CL=1000001 when binary classification is applied with the $\{0, 1\}$ vs. $\{2, 3, 4\}$ mapping. The PDM model demonstrates high AUC values, indicating excellent discriminative power between the two classes. Notably, PDM's performance in terms of precision and F1 score is consistently strong, outpacing BLAST significantly, which shows a pronounced trade-off between precision and recall. Figure 3 showcases the results for CL=1000001 with the binary classification mapping $\{0, 1, 2\}$ vs. $\{3, 4\}$. Here, PDM again shows superior AUC, accuracy, and F1 score compared to other models. The precision of the PDM remains high, illustrating its capability to identify relevant protein pairs while minimizing false positives accurately. In Fig. 4, the metrics are analyzed for CL=1000000 using the binary classification of $\{0, 1\}$ vs. $\{2, 3, 4\}$. PDM's AUC is comparable to or surpasses that of SW, reflecting its robustness in classifying protein pairs into Families. The precision and F1 score metrics underscore PDM's strong performance, with SW showing high precision but slightly lower F1 scores due to its recall limitations. Finally, Fig. 5 presents the binary classification results for CL=1000000 with $\{0, 1, 2\}$ vs. $\{3, 4\}$. PDM continues to excel in AUC and F1 scores, confirming its capability to effectively predict Superfamilies, with SW maintaining higher precision but poorer recall.

The binary classification results highlight the PDM model's exceptional performance across various scenarios. The consistently high AUC values, balanced precision and recall, and strong F1 scores across different classes underscore PDM's effectiveness in accurately predicting protein distances and structural classifications.

Multiple Classification. Next, we focus on the multiclass classification performance of PDM. Given the vast scale of the SCOP database and our computa-

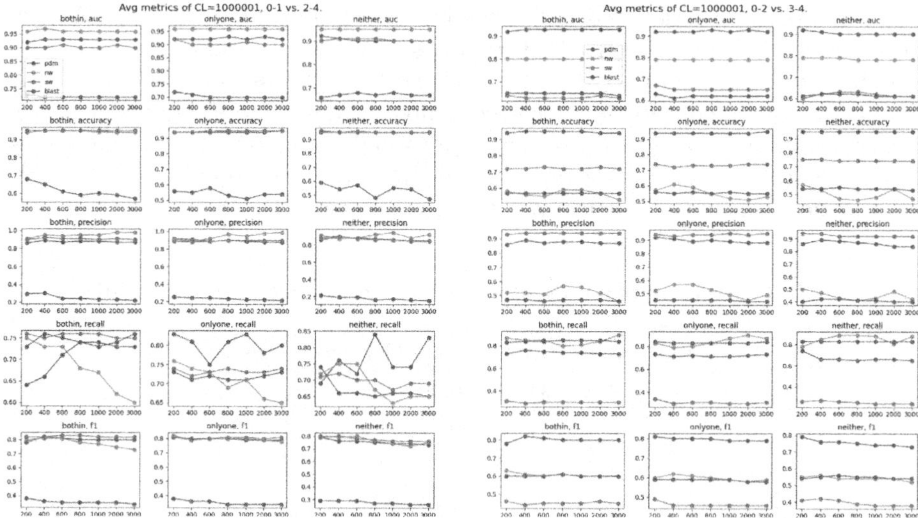

Fig. 2. Binary classification (CL = 1000001, 0–1 vs. 2–4).

Fig. 3. Binary classification (CL = 1000001, 0–2 vs. 3–4).

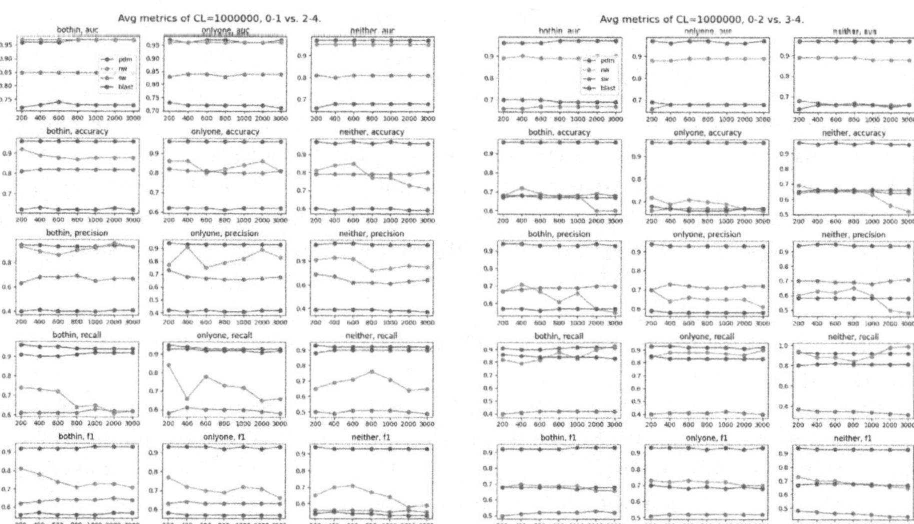

Fig. 4. Binary classification (CL = 1000000, 0–1 vs. 2–4).

Fig. 5. Binary classification (CL = 1000000, 0–2 vs. 3–4).

tional constraints, we initially focused on protein pairs within the Class 1000001 range. The promising results from this range prompted us to extend our analysis to additional SCOP Class ranges to evaluate PDM's performance across multiple classification scenarios.

Table 3 presents a detailed PDM classification Report applied to a validation set of size 1000 within the CL=1000001 range. This report includes vital metrics and the size of the support case for each Distance Class. The 'accuracy' row provides the overall proportion of correctly predicted instances, while 'macro avg' and 'weighted avg' rows offer averaged and weighted metrics across categories. The weighted average, in particular, provides a more nuanced view of the model's performance, accounting for the varying sizes of each Class.

Table 3. An Example of PDM's Classification Report (CL = 1000001)

Distance Class	Precision	Recall	F1-Score	Support
0	0.00	0.00	0.00	3
1	0.88	0.72	0.79	151
2	0.82	0.70	0.75	225
3	0.74	0.78	0.76	298
4	0.71	0.82	0.76	323
Accuracy			0.76	1000
Macro Avg	0.63	0.60	0.61	1000
Weighted Avg	0.77	0.76	0.76	1000

As the classification hierarchy progresses from Representative to Family, Superfamily, Fold, and Class, the number of protein pairs increases exponentially. Despite our efforts to mitigate data imbalances through downsampling, the scarcity of Distance Class 0 records remains challenging. Also, the limited presence results in lower discriminative ability for protein pairs in the same Representative. However, PDM demonstrates commendable performance for Distance Classes 1 and 2, with a weighted average precision nearing 85% and recall reaching 70%. This indicates PDM's effectiveness in distinguishing Families and Superfamilies.

The performance of PDM across various SCOP classes is further illustrated through Figs. 6, 7, 8, and 9 in the Appendix. Figure 6 depicts the average precision of PDM for different SCOP classes. The precision results for Distance Class 1 are presented across multiple scenarios, showing how PDM performs across various validation set sizes and SCOP classes. The colored lines in this figure reflect precision values for different classes, with a notable focus on CL=1000001.

Similarly, Figs. 7, 8, and 9 provide insights into recall, F1-score, and overall accuracy, respectively. The consistency of PDM's performance across the SCOP classes, except CL=1000004, highlights the model's robustness and generalization capability. Specifically, PDM achieves over 72% accuracy for validation sets larger than 2000, with CL=1000000, 1000003, and 1000004 exceeding 80%. This demonstrates PDM's strong performance in multiclass classification tasks.

In particular, Figs. 6 and 7 reveal that PDM maintains high precision for Distance Class 1, reaching above 85% in most scenarios except CL=1000002

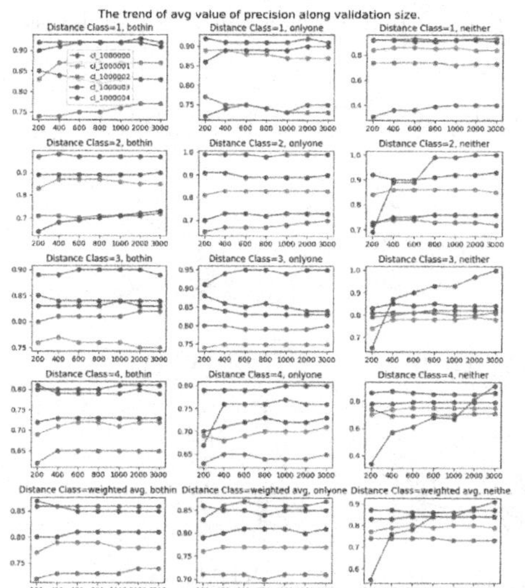

Fig. 6. Average Precision of PDM across various SCOP Classes.

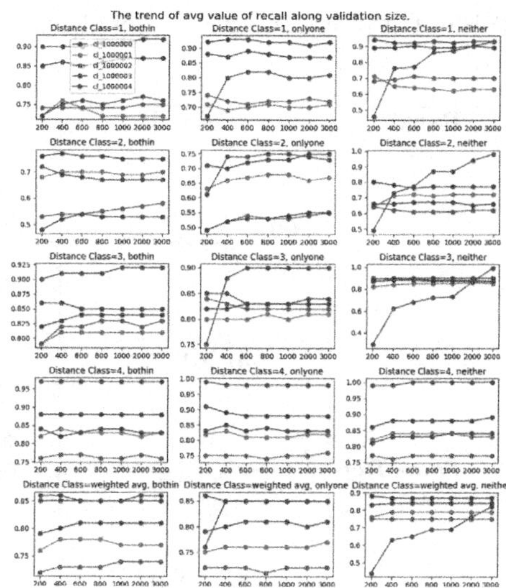

Fig. 7. Average Recall of PDM across various SCOP Classes.

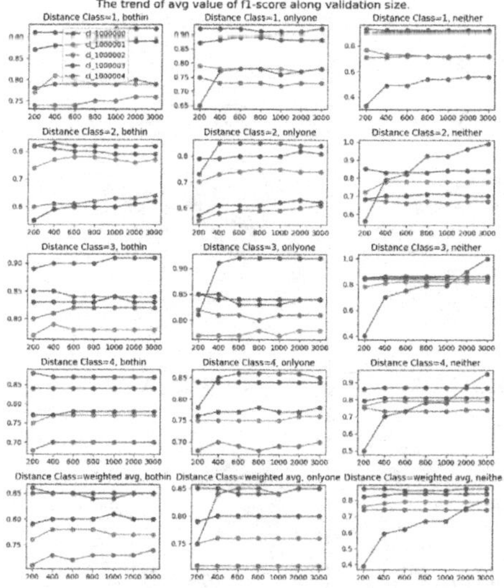

Fig. 8. Average F1-Score of PDM across various SCOP Classes.

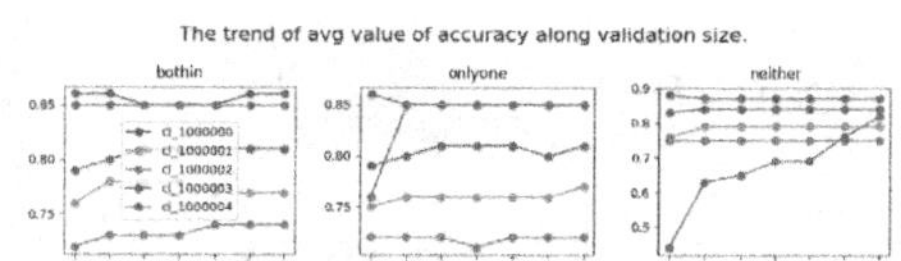

Fig. 9. Average Accuracy of PDM across various SCOP Classes.

and CL=1000004. For Distance Class 2, CL=1000000 and CL=1000001 achieve accuracies above 80%, while CL=1000004 approaches near 100% accuracy for Distance Class 2, despite a trade-off in accuracy for Distance Class 1. This pattern underscores PDM's ability to deliver excellent performance across multiple Distance Classes within each SCOP Class range.

Table 4. Protein structure examples in SCOP and their relatives in different levels. [29]

Range	4PXJ_B 	6QM3_B 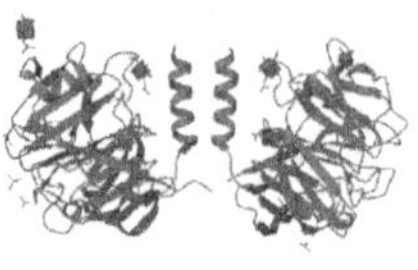	7A9A_B 
Same Rep	4PXJ_C 	5AMO_B 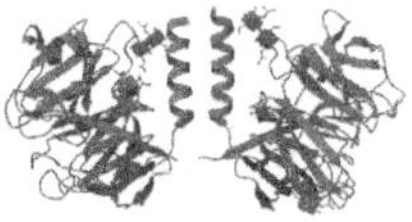	7A9A_D 
Same Family	2W83_D 	5CMN_F 	1DX8_A 
Same Super-Family	1NWQ_C 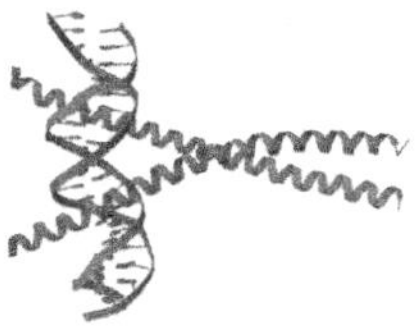	2FAW_A 	1DHG_A 
Same Fold	1HGV_A 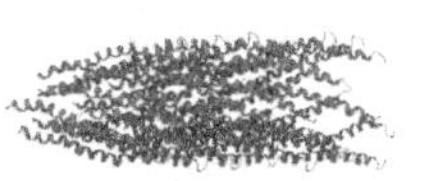	2H2U_A 	3P8B_A 
Same Class / Protein Type	1XAW_A 	6XB9_C 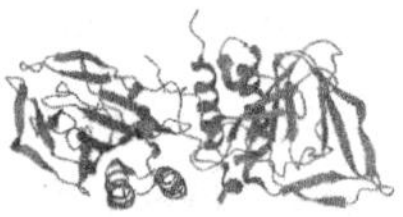	7JZV_B 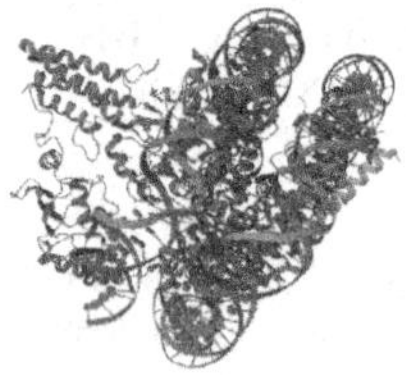

The analysis of PDM's multiclass classification results demonstrates its effectiveness in predicting protein pair distances within various SCOP classes. The consistent performance across different classes and scenarios suggests that PDM is a viable tool for large-scale protein classification tasks. With expanded computational resources, extending PDM's capabilities to a global scale for protein pair distance prediction appears promising.

5   Conclusion

PDM leverages the SCOP database, categorizing protein structures into a detailed hierarchical system. SCOP's classification spans approximately 6,000 Families, presenting challenges for direct classification. To address this, PDM uses a distance metric to represent differences between protein pairs, with distances ranging from 0 (same SCOP Representative) to 16 (different SCOP Classes). This model was initially designed as a regression model but was adapted to a six-class classification problem due to the exponential growth pattern of distance data. By integrating modern deep learning techniques, such as the Attention mechanism from NLP and the Deep and Cross framework, PDM employs a dual-tower neural network to manage this hierarchical complexity effectively.

To handle the dataset's immense size, we performed intelligent sampling, focusing on specific SCOP Classes and Representatives to reduce the dataset to a manageable size while maintaining comprehensive coverage. Evaluations in binary classification scenarios showed that PDM outperforms Needleman-Wunsch (NW), Smith-Waterman (SW), and BLAST, achieving an AUC exceeding 90% and handling predictions without the batch limitations found in NW and SW. Furthermore, PDM demonstrated remarkable performance across up to six distinct categories, with accuracy nearing 80% and recall around 70%, particularly excelling in predicting distances of 1. The model's ability to generalize across multiple categories and its strong performance in diverse scenarios underscore its potential as a significant advancement in protein structure prediction.

6   Future Work

PDM has achieved notable results but has potential for further refinement. Future improvements could involve incorporating three-dimensional structural information from PDB or predictions from Alphafold, which may enhance prediction accuracy. Additionally, overcoming computational constraints to handle larger datasets could improve efficiency and accuracy. Achieving high accuracy and recall across all Distance Classes would also enable the automated classification of unknown proteins into SCOP categories, advancing the model's capability in protein structure prediction.

Appendix

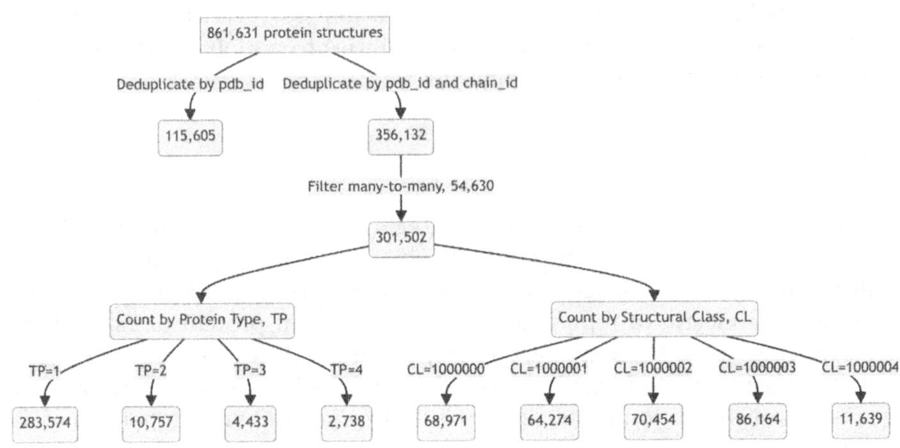

Fig. 10. Procedures of Manual Global Statistics

References

1. Wikipedia contributors. Protein structure — Wikipedia, The Free Encyclopedia (2024). https://en.wikipedia.org/wiki/Protein_structure. Accessed 2 Sept 2024
2. Berman, H.M., et al.: The protein data bank. Nucl. Acids Res. **28**(1), 235–242 (2000)
3. SCOP: Structural Classification of Proteins. https://scop.mrc-lmb.cam.ac.uk. Accessed 2 May 2024
4. Murzin, A.G., et al.: SCOP: a structural classification of proteins database for the investigation of sequences and structures. J. Mol. Biol. **247**(4), 536–540 (1995)
5. Andreeva, A., et al.: SCOP database in 2020: expanded classification of representative family and superfamily domains of known protein structures. Nucl. Acids Res. **48**(D1), D376–D382 (2020)
6. Fox, N.K., Brenner, S.E., Chandonia, J.-M.: SCOPe: structural classification of proteins–extended, integrating SCOP and ASTRAL data and classification of new structures. Nucl. Acids Res. **42**(D1), D304–D309 (2014)
7. wwPDB consortium: Protein data bank: the single global archive for 3D macromolecular structure data. Nucl. Acids Res. **47**(D1), D520–D528 (2019)
8. Westbrook, J., et al.: The Protein Data Bank and structural genomics. Nucl. Acids Res. **31**(1), 489–491 (2003)
9. Burley, S.K., et al.: RCSB Protein Data Bank: powerful new tools for exploring 3D structures of biological macromolecules for basic and applied research and education in fundamental biology, biomedicine, biotechnology, bioengineering and energy sciences. Nucl. Acids Res. **49**(D1), D437–D451 (2021)
10. Congreve, M., Murray, C.W., Blundell, T.L.: Keynote review: structural biology and drug discovery. Drug Disc. Today **10**(13), 895–907 (2005)

11. Sussman, J.L., et al.: The protein data bank: bridging the gap between the sequence and 3D structure world. Struct. Biol. Funct. Genom. 251–264 (1999)
12. DeLano, W.L., et al.: Pymol: an open-source molecular graphics tool. CCP4 Newsl. Protein Crystallogr. **40**(1), 82–92 (2002)
13. Cock, P.J.A., et al.: Biopython: freely available Python tools for computational molecular biology and bioinformatics. Bioinformatics **25**(11), 1422–1423 (2009)
14. RCSB Protein Data Bank Web Services Overview. https://www.rcsb.org/docs/ programmatic-access/web-servicesoverview#data-api
15. Goodfellow, I., Bengio, Y., Courville, A.: Deep Learning. MIT Press, Cambridge (2016)
16. LeCun, Y., et al.: Backpropagation applied to handwritten zip code recognition. Neural Comput. **1**(4), 541–551 (1989)
17. Bahdanau, D., Cho, K., Bengio, Y.: Neural machine translation by jointly learning to align and translate. arXiv preprint arXiv:1409.0473 (2014)
18. Bromley, J., et al.: Signature verification using a "Siamese" time delay neural network. In: Advances in Neural Information Processing Systems, vol. 6 (1993)
19. Cheng, H.-T., et al.: Wide and deep learning for recommender systems. In: Proceedings of the 1st Workshop on Deep Learning for Recommender Systems, pp. 7–10. ACM (2016)
20. Wang, R., et al.: Deep and cross network for ad click predictions. In: Proceedings of the ADKDD 2017, p. 12. ACM (2017)
21. Rumelhart, D.E., Hinton, G.E., Williams, R.J.: Learning representations by back-propagating errors. Nature **323**(6088), 533–536 (1986)
22. LeCun, Y., Bengio, Y., Hinton, G.: Deep learning. Nature **521**(7553), 436–444 (2015)
23. Vaswani, A., et al.: Attention is all you need. In: Advances in Neural Information Processing Systems, pp. 5998–6008 (2017)
24. Devlin, J., et al.: BERT: Pre-training of deep bidirectional transformers for language understanding. arXiv preprint arXiv:1810.04805 (2018)
25. Brown, T., et al.: Language models are few-shot learners. Adv. Neural. Inf. Process. Syst. **33**, 1877–1901 (2020)
26. Xu, K., et al.: Show, attend and tell: neural image caption generation with visual attention. In: International Conference on Machine Learning, pp. 2048–2057. PMLR (2015)
27. Covington, P., Adams, J., Sargin, E.: Deep neural networks for YouTube recommendations. In: Proceedings of the 10th ACM Conference on Recommender Systems, pp. 191–198 (2016)
28. Schroff, F., Kalenichenko, D., Philbin, J.: Facenet: a unified embedding for face recognition and clustering. In: Proceedings of the IEEE Conference on Computer Vision and Pattern Recognition, pp. 815–823 (2015)
29. Research Collaboratory for Structural Bioinformatics Protein Data Bank. RCSB PDB: Homepage (2023). https://www.rcsb.org/. Accessed 06 Feb 2024
30. Google Colaboratory. https://colab.research.google.com/. Accessed 11 Feb 2024
31. SHARCNET: Shared Hierarchical Academic Research Computing Network. https://www.sharcnet.ca. Accessed 10 Feb 2024
32. Digital Research Alliance of Canada. https://ccdb.alliancecan.ca/. Accessed 11 Feb 2024
33. Duo Feng. Protein Distance Model. https://github.com/duoduoduofeng/ MultiClassPSC. Accessed 11 Feb 2024
34. Mood, A.M., Graybill, F.A., Boes, D.C.: Introduction to the Theory of Statistics, 3rd edn. McGraw-Hill, New York (1974)

35. Christopher, M.: Bishop, Pattern Recognition and Machine Learning. Springer, New York (2006). https://link.springer.com/book/9780387310732
36. Needleman, S.B., Wunsch, C.D.: A general method applicable to the search for similarities in the amino acid sequence of two proteins. J. Mol. Biol. **48**(3), 443–453 (1970)
37. Smith, T.F., Waterman, M.S.: Identification of common molecular subsequences. J. Mol. Biol. **147**(1), 195–197 (1981)
38. Altschul, S.F., et al.: Basic local alignment search tool. J. Mol. Biol. **215**(3), 403–410 (1990)

Author Index

Made in the USA
Monee, IL
07 July 2026